2/27

D1616961

How to Engineer Software

About IEEE Computer Society

IEEE Computer Society is the world's leading computing membership organization and the trusted information and career-development source for a global workforce of technology leaders including: professors, researchers, software engineers, IT professionals, employers, and students. The unmatched source for technology information, inspiration, and collaboration, the IEEE Computer Society is the source that computing professionals trust to provide high-quality, state-of-the-art information on an on-demand basis. The Computer Society provides a wide range of forums for top minds to come together, including technical conferences, publications, and a comprehensive digital library, unique training webinars, professional training, and the TechLeader Training Partner Program to help organizations increase their staff's technical knowledge and expertise, as well as the personalized information tool myComputer. To find out more about the community for technology leaders, visit http://www.computer.org.

IEEE/Wiley Partnership

The IEEE Computer Society and Wiley partnership allows the CS Press authored book program to produce a number of exciting new titles in areas of computer science, computing, and networking with a special focus on software engineering. IEEE Computer Society members receive a 35% discount on Wiley titles by using their member discount code. Please contact IEEE Press for details.

To submit questions about the program or send proposals, please contact Mary Hatcher, Editor, Wiley-IEEE Press: Email: mhatcher@wiley.com, Telephone: 201-748-6903, John Wiley & Sons, Inc., 111 River Street, Hoboken, NJ 07030-5774.

How to Engineer Software

A Model-Based Approach

Steve Tockey

WILEY

Published by John Wiley & Sons, Inc., Hoboken, New Jersey.
Published simultaneously in Canada.

For general information on our other products and services or for technical support, please contact our Customer Care Department within the United States at (800) 762-2974, outside the United States at (317) 572-3993 or fax (317) 572-4002.

Wiley also publishes its books in a variety of electronic formats. Some content that appears in print may not be available in electronic formats. For more information about Wiley products, visit our web site at www.wiley.com.

Library of Congress Cataloging-in-Publication Data is available.

hardback: 9781119546627

Set in 10/12pt Warnock by SPi Global, Pondicherry, India

Printed in the United States of America.

For Deanne

Contents

Foreword

Meilir Page-Jones

People often ask me:

> *"Would you say that software development is more an art or a science?"*

I reply,

> *"Neither. It's a branch of the fashion industry."*

Every couple of years the software industry is gripped by one hot fad or another. We've had "structured stuff," "relational stuff," "agile stuff," "RAD stuff," "Kanban stuff," "DevOps stuff," "cloud stuff," and so on. Each fad attracts its fanatical adherents, as well as its outraged opponents. Then, after a few years of heated passion, the fires die down on that particular fad. It becomes "old hat" and the fad's remaining adherents are called dinosaurs. (How's that for a mixed metaphor?) Then it's time to move on to the next craze.

I'm not saying that these fads are bad or useless. Most are effective in the right contexts. The problem is sociological. Software can never become a true engineering discipline if techniques are hailed as game changing at one time and decried as antiquated the next—for no reason other than that the fashion changed.

So it is with modeling. For the most part, software modeling arrived during the 1970s. It included (loosely speaking) approaches such as data flow diagrams, control flow diagrams, entity-relationship diagrams, state-transition diagrams, and code-structure diagrams. These diagrams were made more robust by standardized textual definitions of their components. Some were aimed at the elicitation of software requirements, and others more at the sound construction of code.

This was a healthy trend for a field that was supposedly seeking to become an engineering discipline. After all, other engineering disciplines (such as civil, mechanical, industrial, and electrical engineering) depend on diagrams of components with their relationships and specifications.

When software modeling arrived, three things happened. The first was that people found it intellectually more difficult than the code-and-fix approach. The second (stemming from the first) was that many people gave up before they mastered it. The third was that—in shops that persevered with modeling—software productivity, quality, and manageability all increased markedly—in other words, a mixed landscape where some made great advances through modeling ... and unfortunately others did not.

It didn't help that in the 1970s software modeling was an experimental craft, which only a few dedicated early adopters could take to its full potential. It was immature and lacked solid standards and support tools. But the situation gradually improved so that by the mid-1980s software modeling was mature enough to be called mainstream.

Well, sort of. There was indeed a deeper understanding of modeling techniques, more conferences and seminars about it, further standardization, and some tool support. But there were still enough gaps to keep modeling from being universal in the software industry. Nevertheless, I naively thought that the progress would continue: modeling would remain mainstream and become more widely adopted, more sophisticated, and better supported by automated tools. The trend was certainly in that direction.

But I'd reckoned without the Forces of Fashion. By the 1990s, and definitely into the 2000s, software modeling had been dubbed "antiquated and only for the Triassic reptiles of the 1980s." More than once I heard comments such as:

> *"That modeling crap is just for structured stuff. We're an object-oriented shop."*

It was into this world of the 1990s that the Unified Modeling Language (UML) entered. UML synthesized some of the modeling approaches of the 1970s and 1980s, along with object-oriented constructs and a couple of techniques from electrical engineering. UML both standardized modeling notation and embraced object-oriented concepts. Though not perfect, UML was a major step forward and also ushered in a new generation of robust and sophisticated modeling tools.

It was ironic timing. The fashion pendulum was already swinging against modeling. In the 2000s the agile movement pushed the pendulum further against modeling by—perhaps deliberately, perhaps inadvertently—decrying documentation, which apparently included models. (I have more to say about that below.)

Currently, we're in the bizarre situation where, in what should be a golden age for software modeling with stable notation and mature tools, fewer software engineers by proportion are practicing modeling than in the 1980s. Software modeling is in danger of becoming lost knowledge.

The previous paragraph makes a mockery of the term "software engineering." Do you know any serious branch of real engineering that does not use rigorous "talking" models of whatever they plan to build? ("Talking model" is my term for a predictive model—one that can answer within acceptable tolerance qualitative or quantitative questions about the subject to be built and maintained. For example, "What overall load and local pressure can this new bridge support?")

At this point, enters Steve Tockey. Because software modeling is probably now at its most retrograde phase, it's poised to swing back into favor. So Steve's book on software engineering comes at just the right time to give modeling a hefty shove in the right direction.

Steve, whom I've known for over 30 years, is also just the right person to write this book. He's an adept programmer and a remarkable teacher. More germanely, he's about the best modeler of the business world and of software systems that I know. And, to top it all, he's a fan of Bert Weedon.[1]

This book represents the confluence of all Steve's talents. He brings to bear his teaching ability, as well as his vast experience on all kinds of systems: large and small, embedded and business, noncritical and safety-critical. Some of that experience was as a programmer. Some was as an analyst. Most of it was as a modeler.

I have voluntarily and happily flown in planes whose test software was developed from models that Steve produced. I can't think of anyone better placed than Steve to write a comprehensive book on software modeling.

But why should *you* bother to read this book? Didn't I just say that software modeling is out of fashion? Maybe so, but from your perspective, that's not the point. If you're a true engineer, fashion doesn't matter. When I first learned modeling as a developer, the quality and quantity of my code took an immediate jump for the better. That's a very typical experience, by the way. I adopted this motto:

> *"I'm a software engineer. I don't need anyone else's permission to do modeling. I don't even care whether it's fashionable or not. It works."*

This is even more true today: half a day's salary can buy you your own state-of-the-art (not a toy) software modeling tool. You really don't need anyone else's

---

1 Bert Weedon was a guitar legend of the 1950s, who inspired many people to take up the instrument, including Eric Clapton, Brian May, Jimmy Page, John Lennon, and Pete Townshend.

permission. So I expect that software modeling will swing back into fashion before long. Quietly, some of the top companies are already doing it—for several good reasons.

Modeling promotes better communication among teams well before code is written. *After the code has been written* is a bit late! Software modeling also embodies true engineering tenets. You'll find a lot of them in this book, but let me just call out one in particular, which is probably the best-kept secret in software engineering: domain separation (Chapter 6). Here's an illustration of what it means.

On the desk in front of me is a lamp with domain separation. Without that separation, in order to change the bulb, I'd need to unsolder the wires from the old bulb and resolder them on to the new bulb. But the domain of *transporting electricity to my desk* (including wires) is cleanly separated from the domain that *turns electricity into light* (the bulb). The screw-in socket is the well-defined bridge between the two domains.

That's just a small illustration; Steve will take you more deeply into how it applies to software. Without domain separation in software, code gets "soldered together" in ugly ways that degrade portability, optimization, debugging, and even team organization. In fact, modeling itself becomes difficult.

OK, domain separation is not very useful for tiny systems. But it's vital for the medium and large systems that most of us encounter now in commerce, industry, science, and the military. I know of several large-system efforts that produced unmaintainable code or collapsed altogether because they'd failed to appreciate domain separation.

I won't take any more space in this foreword to promote arguments for modeling—or the arguments against not modeling—because Steve himself makes those arguments so well in this book. But I'd better mention the "A" word again or you'll think I'm not agile enough for prime time. (*You think I'm not Agile? Oh, the shame of it!*)

A powerful myth has arisen that if you do any modeling at all then you're not agile. But it is just a myth. In fact, modeling is highly compatible with Agile. I've been on four significant agile projects. One was very successful, two turned out reasonably well, and one was a disaster.

The most successful one made heavy use of both requirements and design modeling. It was very productive, kept up a good agile rhythm, and delivered high quality, very usable, and useful software. In that project, the business analysts, database designers, developers, user interface (UI) designers, and testers all used portions of the same models, which enhanced both team communication and consistency. User stories were treated as brief commands to go forth and refine, enhance, or augment some portion of the requirements model (or other model, as the case may be). I won't get into the details of the models that we used, because you'll be reading all about them in this very book. But I will remark that all our modeling was done with a robust modeling tool and stored within its repository.

(Incidentally, the disaster project was a management circus. It started agile and well organized enough, but it rapidly descended into such chaos that it became agile in name only. It used no modeling—but frankly, modeling probably wouldn't have saved this project anyway.)

Steve has packed a lot of software modeling into this book. But don't let that intimidate you. Don't think that you have to learn all of modeling in a single waterfall, big-bang, death-march weekend. Approach it incrementally. Start with just one kind of model—whichever model will best clarify the project you're working on now.

Perhaps you're a business analyst, trying to capture the states of a customer-order-item. In that case, learn about state modeling first (Chapter 10). Or maybe you're a developer trying to design a robust handshaking protocol between two machines. In that case, knowing interaction diagrams would be very helpful (Chapter 9).

But my personal favorite is the class model (Chapter 8). So much within the other models depends on the focus and understanding that the class model gives you. It's also versatile. As a business analyst, you can capture the heart and soul of a company with a class diagram, which can be as sketchy or as detailed as you choose. If you're a developer, with a class diagram, you can literally illustrate the classes in your code and how they interrelate.

If you're a student who's studying software modeling in an academic course, such as a bachelor's degree in software engineering, the sequence of models you need to work on will be outlined in your course curriculum. Actually, the organization of chapters in this book is about right for a good sequence of course topics. (In reality, the complete contents of this book will probably need several courses to navigate through.)

Whatever your situation, I wish you all the best in mastering the software engineering that Steve's book explains. Modeling and reasoning about software before you build it might seem alien and difficult at first. But then suddenly you'll get it. Just like Eric Clapton did. And then you'll wonder how you ever managed without modeling.

Preface

Software *can* be engineered. Software *should* be engineered. But true engineering—in the sense of civil engineering, chemical engineering, mechanical engineering, aeronautical engineering, industrial engineering, etc.—of software requires more than just claiming "software engineer" as a job title:

- *Engineering requires application of scientific and mathematical knowledge*— Some software professionals have computer science or mathematics backgrounds, while many do not. Set manipulation and finite automata are recurring themes in software. Proper reasoning about code behavior requires application of propositional calculus. How can reliable software be built without understanding these basic topics?
- *Engineering requires application of a body of practice*—Many software professionals don't even know, let alone know how to apply, key practices like abstraction, encapsulation, Design by Contract™, cohesion, coupling, design to invariants, design for change, programming by intent, software proof of correctness, design patterns, test coverage criteria, and so on.
- *Engineering requires economic decision-making*—The vast majority of software professionals have no idea how to factor economic analysis into technical decision-making. Important decisions are usually based on "What would look good on my resume?" rather than what makes the most financial sense for the organization. This has been facetiously referred to as "Resume Driven Development."

In many jurisdictions it is illegal to call yourself an engineer if you are not licensed or chartered by a government body. Licensing usually also carries personal liability for damage caused by errors in an engineer's work. If you are a practicing software professional, would you be willing to take on personal liability for the software you develop and maintain? Read any typical Software End User License Agreement to see how much liability today's developers are willing to take on.

This book brings true engineering discipline to software development and maintenance, resulting in software for which you should be willing to take on personal liability.

Why This Book?

Said another way, "Why should software be engineered?" This is explained fully in Chapters 1–3, and 27. In brief

- Mainstream software projects are chronically late and over budget, the code is riddled with defects, and long-term maintenance is costly and labor intensive.
- There are clear reasons why: poor requirements, overdependence on testing, and code not being self-documenting. Woven into this is an essentially complete disregard of software semantics along with unmanaged complexity.
- The model-based software engineering approach in this book has been used on many projects across a wide variety of industry verticals and has shown consistent success. These projects are on time or early, are on budget or under budget, deliver all intended scope or more, and amaze users with high quality.
- This approach is different from others, and these differences are critical in solving the software industry's problems. These differences are presented in Chapter 1 and explain why this approach to model-based software engineering *is* true engineering and also why projects using it are so successful.

Who Is This Book for?

This book is aimed at the software development and maintenance technical community such as developers, development leads, architects, and so on *with intent to prepare them to be true software engineers.* In some organizations, business analysts will do semantic modeling. User experience professionals can base UI design on semantic models. Software testers/QA professionals can derive verification test cases from semantic models. Project managers need a high-level understanding of work being done on the project but tend to be most interested in estimation and software process.

Table P.1 defines a set of comprehension levels used in Table P.2. Table P.2 recommends comprehension levels for each chapter based on software project role.

History of the Author and of This Approach

I first learned programming in the fall of 1975: my senior year of high school.[1] I started my first paid programming job in June 1977 when I developed software for radiation monitoring at nuclear power plants around the world. Concurrently,

---

1 Thanks, Ken, I owe you big time for getting me started down this lifelong path.

Table P.1 Comprehension levels used in Table P.2.

Level	Meaning
H	This reader should read this chapter very carefully to get complete, detailed understanding and be able to fully apply it on projects
M	This reader should understand most of the chapter, but it's not necessary to be able to apply everything on projects
L	This reader should gain a broad understanding of chapter content, but it's not necessary to go beyond
—	The reader does not need anything from this chapter, it is to safe skip

Table P.2 Recommended comprehension levels, by project role.

Chapter	Developer	Business analyst	User experience	Tester	Project manager
1	H	H	H	H	H
2	H	M or L	M or L	M or L	M or L
3	H	M	M or L	L or –	L or –
4	H	H	M	M or L	L or –
5	M	M or L	L or –	L or –	L or –
6	H	H	M or L	M	M or L
7	H	H	M	M or L	L or –
8	H	H	M or L	M or L	L or –
9	H	H	M or L	M or L	L or –
10	H	H	M	M or L	L or –
11	H	H	M or L	M or L	L or –
12	H	H	M or L	M or L	L or –
13	H	L	M or L	L or -	L or –
14	H or M	H or M	H or M	M or L	L or –
15	H	L or –	—	L or –	L or –
16	H	L or –	—	L or –	L or –
17	H	L or –	—	L or –	L or –
18	H	L or –	—	L or –	L or –
19	H	L or –	—	L or –	L or –

(Continued)

Table P.2 (Continued)

Chapter	Developer	Business analyst	User experience	Tester	Project manager
20	H	L or –	—	L or –	L or –
21	H or M	L or –	—	L or –	L or –
22	H	L or –	—	L or –	L or –
23	H or M	M or L	L or –	L or –	H
24	H or M	M or L	L or –	L or –	H
25	H	H or M	H or M	L or –	L or –
26	M or L	M or L	M or L	M or L	M or L
27	H	H	H	H	H

I spent two years in the aeronautical engineering degree program at San Jose State University before transferring to University of California, Berkeley. I finished a Letters & Science Computer Science degree in 1981 and was two classes short of a minor in economics.

In August 1984 I joined Lawrence Livermore National Laboratory (LLNL) to work in the Laser Isotope Separation[2] program. This is where I was introduced to model-based software development using Ward and Mellor Real-Time Structured Analysis and Design.[3] Two model-based projects at LLNL were:

- Vapor rate monitor—By measuring absorption of a frequency-scanned laser beam shone through a vapor stream, compute vapor density.
- Engineering demonstration system—Production-scale software and hardware to demonstrate Laser Isotope Separation technology at factory production rates. Steve Mellor was a consultant on this project.

My next career move was to Boeing Computer Services in the Seattle area in October 1987 where the goal was to unify real-time structured analysis approaches[4] with logical data modeling.[5] This was where, on 13 November 1987, Mark K. Smith and I created the core of the object-oriented approach in this book.[6] While at Boeing I completed a Masters of Software Engineering degree at Seattle University. From 1994 to 1997 I taught as an adjunct professor in that same master's degree program, presenting requirements, design, programming methods, Smalltalk programming, and engineering economics.

---

2 See, for example, [Zare77].
3 See [Ward86a], [Ward86b], and [Ward86c].
4 Specifically, [Ward86a], [Ward86b], [Ward86c], and [Hatley88].
5 For example, [Flavin81].
6 First published as [Smith88].

I was Boeing's representative to the Object Management Group[7] (OMG) from 1993 to 1997.

Model-based software engineering was used on several Boeing projects:

- Airport traffic capacity simulator—Discrete event simulation model of air traffic into and out of civilian airports. This is used to study the effects of reconfiguring airport facilities, changing air traffic load, or modifying Federal Aviation Administration (FAA)/European Union Aviation Safety Agency (EASA) "Separation rules."
- Data center trouble tracking—Track problems reported by users at the Boeing Wichita data center and manage those problems to closure.
- Advanced Graphics Production System—Allow aeronautical engineers to visualize input to, and output from, computational fluid dynamics code.
- Airplane Flight Manual/Digital Pilot's Interface—A nontrivial proof of concept for putting an electronic flight manual into a cockpit, replacing traditional paper. The code is a mathematical simulation that uses flight test data and physics first principles[8] to calculate the V1 speed[9] for a commercial airplane.
- Integrated Network Management System—A voice and data network management system covering network engineering (installation, configuration, performance monitoring, troubleshooting, etc.) and network operations (billing, trouble ticketing, service ordering, etc.)
- 767 Engine Simulator Automated Test Equipment (ATE)—Prior to 767 Engine Sim ATE, all automated airplane tests were C implementations from English language specifications written by airplane test engineers. This project developed a Simplified English Test Language (SETL) that is interpreted and executed, allowing airplane test engineers to write executable tests directly.
- 777 Automated Test Equipment—An interpreter that supports the full system functional test suite for the entire 777 airplane, from AC/DC power on through avionics and flight controls.
- COMBASE—Re-implementation of the corporate employee records system.
- DCAC/MRM[10] Application Integration—A large-scale business process reengineering effort to revamp how Boeing designs, builds, sells, and supports commercial airplanes. The Application Integration layer allows the more than 800 separate computing systems in DCAC/MRM to talk to each other.

---

7 See www.omg.org
8 For example, F = MA.
9 The speed at which the airplane can no longer stop safely in the remaining runway; they are committed to fly.
10 See, for example, http://www.boeing.com/news/frontiers/archive/2003/december/i_ca2.html

- Flight Effects Test System—Make an airplane think it is flying while it is still on the ground: read cockpit commands from airplane communication buses, compute the airplane's reaction based on flight test data, and then inject simulated responses back onto airplane communication buses.

Concurrent with Boeing, model-based software engineering was applied to the probe placement subsystem for an automated silicon wafer tester at KLA. This subsystem loads new, untested etched wafers into the tester and sequentially locates chip-level test probes onto each etched chip. Another subsystem tests the chip. This subsystem then marks that chip with color-coded paint to signify pass/fail. After testing all chips on a wafer, the next wafer is loaded and the process repeats until no more wafers are in the tester.

My next career move was to Rockwell-Collins Avionics in Cedar Rapids, Iowa, in July 1996. I brought Rockwell-Collins Avionics into the OMG and was the corporate representative. Two Rockwell-Collins Avionics projects used model-based software engineering:

- Distributed Rodentia—Allow users to access adjacent monitor screens from multiple mice all at the same time.
- TCP/IP in Java—Rockwell-Collins Avionics built the first hardware Java virtual machine (the hardware directly executes JVM byte codes; there is no software virtual machine interpreter as in most Java environments) and wanted to demonstrate OMG's CORBA on this hardware. All existing TCP/IP implementations were either in C or C++, which the hardware JVM can't execute. This project developed a Java implementation of TCP/IP.

UML was released to the public in 1997. The model-based software engineering approach was converted to UML notation shortly after that. The original modeling notation was unique.

I began working for Construx Software back in the Seattle area in November 1998. Model-based software engineering projects that I have been directly or indirectly involved in since then include:

- Peopleware at Peopleware, Inc.—A conference planning and management tool.
- Altair and Oso at Los Alamos National Laboratory—Front-end and back-end visualization of input to, and output from, computational fluid dynamics code.
- 777 ATE ARINC-629 Driver replacement at Boeing—The FAA prohibits testing a commercial airplane using equipment that has been obsoleted by its manufacturer. The original ARINC-629 interface hardware used in 777 ATE was about to be obsoleted. The new hardware is different enough that it required a new driver. Based on the size of the original driver code, the most credible estimate was that replacement would take four people about one

year. By evolving from the original models of the driver, code was successfully replaced in under six weeks.

- Facilities management at Nordstroms—Allow the corporate facilities department to plan and manage facilities and facilities changes.
- 787 Automated Test Equipment at Boeing—An interpreter that supports the full system functional test suite for the entire 787 airplane, from AC/DC power on through avionics and flight controls.
- P-8[11] Mission Systems at Boeing—The fly-the-airplane avionics are essentially stock 737 equipment. This project developed the back-end "in-the-tube" software that manages coastal defense mission planning and execution, identify-friend-or-foe, secure communication, weapons stores management and deployment, etc.
- Pelican Well Placement Engineering upgrade at Schlumberger—Oil wells are rarely drilled entirely vertically. Most often, the optimum path has significant horizontal components. Thus, the drill bit that is boring the well has to be steered. Pelican allows the drill operator to know the location of the drill bit in 3D space and steer it to follow a preplanned optimum path. This project added critical functionality.
- Comprehensive cost estimation—A complex and highly proprietary tool for estimating the cost of building very large chemical plants for a multinational corporation. Two previous attempts used mainstream development and had both failed miserably.

Model-based software engineering was successful in all cases:

- Not one of these projects was late; some were early.
- Not one of these projects was over budget; most were under budget.
- Every project delivered at least the agreed-on functionality; some delivered more.
- Users were consistently amazed how few defects were delivered, despite having far fewer testers than on equivalent mainstream software projects.

Most of this book explains *how* model-based software engineering works—how to apply it on real-world software development and maintenance projects under both waterfall and agile development lifecycles. Chapters 1, 2, 12, 22, and 27 explain *why* it works. There is a direct correlation between the problems facing the software industry and critical elements of model-based software engineering that address those problems.

Steve Tockey

---

11 See, for example, https://en.wikipedia.org/wiki/Boeing_P-8_Poseidon

Acknowledgments

First, this approach builds on contributions of many,[1] in particular:

- Mark K. Smith
- Steve McMenamin and John Palmer
- Sally Shlaer and Steve Mellor
- Meilir Page-Jones
- OMG's Analysis and Design Task Force
- ModelDriven.org
- Dr. Sid Dijkstra

Second, thanks to all who reviewed and commented on manuscript drafts. I have tried hard to ensure everything in the book is correct. Nevertheless, many errors inevitably remain. Errors that remain are entirely my fault. Manuscript comments were provided by (in alphabetical order):

- Fumihiro Besso
- J. David Blaine
- Les Chambers
- Kristof Claeskens
- Brian Cohen
- Melina Costa
- Joachim Cruetz
- Marisette Edwards
- Ben Erickson
- C. Ross Eskridge
- Rik Essenius
- Dan George
- Regis George
- David Harold
- A. Lathif Masood

---

1 Stand, as they say, on the shoulders of giants.

- Alberto Melacini
- Eric Rimbey
- Ken Rose
- Hugo Sanchez
- Jeff Schroeder
- Arthur Sehn
- Michael Tempest
- Brian Wren
- Wu YongWei
- Zhang JianYang
- Theo Zimmerman

Warmest and sincerest thanks to Rik Essenius, Wu Yongwei, Eric Rimbey, Michael Tempest, and Zhang JianYang for their extensive and invaluable feedback.

Online Resources

Online resources related to this book are available on a companion website:

http://www.construx.com/howtoengrsw/

This includes a free demonstration semantic model editor and open model compiler.

Part I

Introduction and Foundations

Part I sets the foundation for this book through the following chapters:

- *Introduction*—Overviews how to truly engineer software and explains why it is a superior approach over mainstream software development and maintenance.
- *The Nature of Code*—Explains the role that precise, concise models can and must play in software development and maintenance.
- *Fundamental Principles*—This entire book explains how to develop and maintain software, this chapter explains how to do it *well*.
- *Functional and Non functional Requirements*—Identifies the different kinds of software requirements and shows how those kinds need to be specified, designed, and implemented in different ways.
- *UML Overview*—Provides an introduction to the Unified Modeling Language (UML): the language used for model-based requirements and design.
- *Partitioning Large Systems into Domains*—Explains how to scale up to very large systems involving hundreds of developers and millions of lines of code.

How to Engineer Software: A Model-Based Approach, First Edition. Steve Tockey.
© 2019 the IEEE Computer Society, Inc. Published 2019 by John Wiley & Sons, Inc.

1

Introduction

Almost everyone has heard of failed and troubled software projects costing many millions of dollars that returned little or no value.[1] Media and industry literature paint a picture of software development as being in the Stone Age: it is hard to figure out what needs to be built, not enough attention is paid to design, and countless defects are found after developers thought the code was ready to ship. Schedules slip to fix as many of those defects as practical. Projects are cancelled because the software couldn't be made reliable enough or their business cases went away during the slips.

The software industry can do much better. This book describes how software that reliably does what users want can be delivered at low cost, at short schedule, and with minimal long-term maintenance. Using this approach, projects typically finish in half the time at half the cost and require no more than one quarter of the long-term maintenance of their mainstream counterparts. Total cost of ownership (TCO) for software can be less than one third of what it is today.

Recognized engineering disciplines—civil engineering, chemical engineering, mechanical engineering, aeronautical engineering, industrial engineering, etc.—realized long ago that natural languages are inadequate. In the same way that electrical engineers use circuit schematics to drive construction and maintenance of electronic circuits, aeronautical engineers use engineering drawings to drive construction and maintenance of aircraft, and structural engineers use blueprints to drive construction and maintenance of buildings, and the software industry can use drawings for the same reasons and to get the same benefits. This book is about "model-based software engineering": using precise, concise models—blueprints—to drive development and maintenance of code.

---

1 See, for example, [Rosenberg08] or [Zachary94]. Using search terms "worst software project failures" and "worst software products" in your favorite search engine also gives many examples.

How to Engineer Software: A Model-Based Approach, First Edition. Steve Tockey.
© 2019 the IEEE Computer Society, Inc. Published 2019 by John Wiley & Sons, Inc.

1.1 Mainstream Software Projects Perform Poorly

The "software crisis" is common knowledge in the industry: software projects are chronically late, over budget, and under-featured, and the code is full of defects. But instead of just repeating what everyone already knows, this chapter quantifies the extent of that crisis and analyzes root causes.

The Standish Group has been publishing "Chaos Reports" for over 25 years. Results reported in the 2013 edition[2] are as follows:

- *Only 39% of software projects are successful*—The Standish Group defines success as finishing within 10% of agreed schedule, budget, and scope.
- *43% of software projects are challenged*—A challenged project deviates more than 10% in at least one of schedule, budget, or scope but still delivers software of value.
- *18% of software projects fail*—A failed project is cancelled before delivering software of any value.

Of software projects that do deliver, the successful and challenged projects combined, the Chaos report shows the average:

- *42% late*—A planned 10-month project is more reasonably expected to take about 14 months.
- *35% over budget*—A planned $10 million project is more reasonably expected to cost about $13.5 million.
- *25% under scope*—In spite of overrunning both schedule and budget, software projects do not deliver all agreed-on functionality. A project that expects to satisfy 100 requirements should be more reasonably expected to satisfy only 75.

To be fair, Chaos reports have been showing modest improvement in software project performance over the last 20 years. The 1999 Chaos report stated that 26% of projects were successful, 45% challenged, and 29% failed. At least the industry is moving in the right direction. Despite improvement, however, these are still not enviable results, particularly considering the size of the industry worldwide. An enormous amount of *someone else's* money is invested in software projects every year. The term "someone else's" is emphasized because if it were *your* money, you would almost certainly want to be a lot more careful about how it was being spent. A lot of people are paying a lot of money for software and many of them are not seeing much, if any, return on that investment.

---

2 See [Standish13].

Examination of mainstream software projects reveals common reasons why they get into trouble. In my experience the three most significant reasons,[3] in decreasing order of importance, are:

1) Vague, ambiguous, incomplete requirements.
2) Overdependence on testing.
3) "Self-documenting code" is a myth.

Each will be discussed, together with explaining how model-based software engineering fixes it. This chapter then presents what "software engineering" is and shows how model-based software engineering is consistent with that definition. It is well within the software industry's grasp to do a far better job on projects, and this book explains how.

1.2 Problem #1: Vague, Ambiguous, Incomplete Requirements

It might be difficult to find an experienced professional software developer who doesn't agree that vague, ambiguous, incomplete requirements are a problem. Over the last 20 years, I have surveyed thousands of software practitioners: developers, technical leads, architects, testers, test leads, test managers, project managers, product managers, business analysts, and so on. Respondents were asked to identify and rank the challenges they face on their software projects. Forty-six percent of the time, "vague, ambiguous, incomplete requirements" is ranked as the number one challenge. This same survey showed "lack of business domain knowledge" and "requirements keep changing" are common challenges that capture this same problem in a slightly different way. Only 5% did not identify requirements as a challenge.

James Martin[4] reports that 56% of defects in mainstream software are the direct result of poor requirements: roughly half are due to vague, ambiguous, or incorrect requirements, and the other half are due to missing (incomplete) requirements. Capers Jones[5] states that for plan-based (i.e., "waterfall" and its variants) projects, about 30% of the requirements are found after the requirements specification has been signed off. Jones also reports that the rate of "requirements creep" averages between 1 and 4% per month. Susan Brilliant et al.[6] report that about 80% of defects in the software they studied were

---

3 As relevant to this book, another significant reason (#2 overall) is inadequate project management but that is outside the scope of this book.
4 See [Mogyorodi03].
5 Personal communication.
6 See [Brilliant90].

"boundary value" defects: the direct result of unspecified, poorly specified, or misunderstood requirements.

The root cause is overdependence on natural languages, like English, to specify requirements. There are two aspects: ambiguity and verboseness.

1.2.1 Requirements Ambiguity

Ambiguity is built into natural languages. The same word often has different meanings and different words can have the same meaning. In everyday conversation, ambiguity usually isn't a problem and can even be entertaining, as shown by these unintentionally humorous newspaper headlines[7]:

> *"Youths steal funds for charity"*
> (Reporter Dispatch, White Plains, NY, February 17, 1982)

> *"Sisters reunited after 18 years in checkout line at supermarket"*
> (Arkansas Democrat, September 29, 1983)

> *"Large church plans collapse"*
> (Spectator, Hamilton, Ont, June 8, 1985)

> *"Police discover crack in Australia"*
> (International Herald Tribune, September 10, 1986)

> *"Air force considers dropping some new weapons"*
> (New Orleans Times-Picayune, May 22, 1983)

Consider how poetry works: varying shades of meaning lead to different and interestingly contrasting interpretations, for example, the classic poem "Fog" by Carl Sandburg:

> *"The fog comes*
> *on little cat feet.*
>
> *It sits looking*
> *over harbor and city*
> *on silent haunches*
> *and then moves on."*

---

7 See [Cooper87].

Fog and cat feet have nothing to do with each other in reality. Sandburg's creative use of ambiguity leads to mental images of quiet, autonomous, curiosity-driven movement although fog is clearly incapable of any such of self-direction.

Advertising slogans often play off these same shades of meaning. The public transport system in Oxford, England, has the slogan "We're all about Oxford." This could mean the transport company covers the region, as in "We are all about (around) the area." The slogan could also mean the company is dedicated to the welfare of the people in the region, as in "We are all about (for) you." Clever.

When it comes to engineering, ambiguity is problematic. A very real example is a natural language requirement for an embedded system to remotely inspect pipes in chemical plants:

> *"The system shall detect a 1/4 inch defect in a pipe section."*

Start with the word "detect"; what could it mean?

- *Measure?* The software only needs to sense a pipe defect and the requirement has been met? Nobody ever has to be told about it?
- *Record?* The software only has to make a note somewhere about the defect and the requirement has been satisfied?
- *Report?* The software has to be sure that someone is aware of the defect?
- *Locate?* The software only has to say, "Yes, there's a defect"; it's up to someone else to find where it is.
- ...
- *Some combination of the above?*

Move on to "a"; what could it mean?

- *One?* Can the system stop after having detected the first defect?
- *Some?* Is it ok to detect more than one, but also ok to not detect all?
- *All?* Do all defects have to be detected?

Move on to "1/4 inch"; what could that mean?

- *As small as?* It's ok not to detect defects smaller than that?
- *As big as?* It's ok not to detect defects bigger than that?
- *Exactly as big as?* Defects that are smaller or larger must not be detected?

Next, consider "defect." What could it mean?

- *Hole?*
- *Dent or crease?*
- *Bulge?*
- *Corrosion?*
- ...
- *Some combination of the above?*

And this says nothing about the meaning of "pipe section."

- *Isolated volumes when all valves are closed?*
- *Straight-line segments in the piping network?*
- *Any volume that would be defined by considering the raw pieces of pipe before they were joined?*
- *A fixed distance, say, 5 or 10 m?*
- *...*

Considering the different interpretations for each word, there are at least 9,216 valid interpretations[8] of that one requirement. The organization was forced into a very time-consuming and expensive rewrite when they discovered the stakeholders' interpretation was completely different than the developers'. The chances of the developers getting that one right interpretation were extremely remote, to say the least.

Simply,

> *"Any language sufficiently ambiguous to be used for poetry or clever advertising slogans fails as a specification language."*

1.2.2 Requirements Incompleteness

Natural languages are verbose. It takes many words to precisely communicate even relatively simple ideas. People are reluctant to say things in a precise way because of the effort. This is also why the recognized engineering disciplines abandoned natural language and developed their own. Circuit schematics in electronics design, blueprints for airplanes, and construction drawings for buildings are all examples.

Several years ago I had a new house custom-designed and built. The house I wanted was specified in nine pages of drawings. Figure 1.1 shows standard house design notation for doors.

Something as simple as a line and arc on a house drawing stands for an entire paragraph of natural language:

> *"The main floor guest bathroom shall have a door. That door shall be a left-hand door. That left-hand door shall be oriented so the hinges are on the South side of the door frame."*

If someone were silly enough to translate the information on those nine pages of drawings into natural language, the resulting "house requirements

---

8 2^4 interpretations of "detect" × 3 interpretations of "a" × 3 interpretations of "1/4 inch" × 2^4 interpretations of "defect" × 4 interpretations of "pipe section" = 9,216.

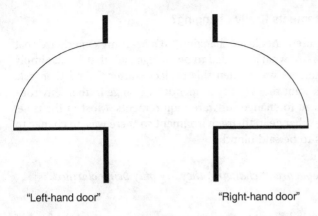

"Left-hand door"   "Right-hand door"

Figure 1.1 House design notation for doors.

specification"[9] would be hundreds if not thousands of pages.[10] There would be a high risk of missing critical details. It would be nearly impossible to check that no natural language statement contradicted any other: something said on the bottom of page 47 could easily contradict something said in the middle of page 692. Nobody might notice until well after it was too late. Also, the same content could be stated more than once (redundancy), and the natural language version may include content not in the drawings.

Consider the complexity of a typical house: how difficult is it to understand? Compared to software, houses are mere child's play. This leads to the very serious question:

> *"The people who design and build houses gave up trying to describe them in natural language over one hundred years ago. What makes you think you can successfully describe something that's orders of magnitude more complex using natural language?"*

---

9 An argument can be made that house drawings are designs, not requirements—they are a response to requirements, a design, rather than requirements themselves. The same can be said for electronic circuit schematics, airplane engineering drawings, and building blueprints. In practice, house requirements (and for other engineering disciplines) aren't very complex. Only designs tend to be complex. Software is unique in that it often has significant requirements complexity, not just design complexity. As will be shown in this book, software benefits greatly from blueprinting not only design, but requirements as well.

10 Translation of software functional requirements models into natural language is discussed in Chapter 12.

1.2.3 Are the Requirements Really Changing?

Many claim, "Our requirements keep changing." It's been my experience that most—as much as 80%—of what's claimed to be change isn't that at all. Simply ask, "What did stakeholders want when this project started?" And then ask, "What do stakeholders want today?" Try to identify a change in their environment that led to the need to change software requirements. Most of the time, you can't. There was no change in their environment so there was no change to requirements. It needs to be said bluntly:

"Most requirements aren't changing, they are only being clarified."

Natural languages make it difficult to communicate requirements at the level of precision needed. Requirements writers are not forced down to necessary levels of detail, and at the same time it's so much work to do so. So they don't. As a result, developers are forced—consciously or unconsciously—to guess: what do "detect," "a," "1/4 inch," "defect," and "pipe section" mean?

If developers guess, there is a chance they guess wrong. All other things being equal, when there are N valid interpretations of some statement, the probability that any two people have the same interpretation is 1/N. The probability of differing interpretations is (N – 1)/N. Even when N is small, the odds are against you. When the developers guess wrong, code will be written incorrectly: it will have defects—defects that are now just waiting to be discovered. Those defects might be discovered in testing, but that is unlikely because testers will be testing against the same incomplete and imprecise requirements. More likely, defects won't be found until the software is in use: when the damage done and the effort and cost to repair are highest.

This is illustrated in the "Dreaded Phone Call Syndrome." Imagine a developer is quietly coding away when their phone rings. They have caller ID so they know immediately it's one of those pesky users. They think, "Should I answer? Or, should I just let it go to voice mail?" Reluctantly, they answer. But—as usual—they quickly regret it. The first thing they hear is that pesky user yelling, "Your stupid software just (fill in the blank)!" In their defense, and in a valiant attempt to defend the software they work so hard on, the developer replies, "It's your fault, you never told us that's what you meant!" That pesky—and, unfortunately, correct—user simply replies, "No. It's your fault because you never asked. Had you asked, I certainly would have told you! But you didn't ask, so I thought you already knew."

One of my former supervisors once said,

"Requirements aren't created, they surface."

(Joe Brandt, Lawrence Livermore National Laboratory)

The real requirements have been there all along, so how good a job is done surfacing them before software is written? Most software organizations are bad at eliciting, specifying, and validating requirements because they depend on natural languages. The problem isn't that requirements are changing; the problem is a faulty requirements process.

To be sure, some software projects are in dynamic stakeholder environments. Sometimes there really is a lot of legitimate requirements change. "Research-oriented" projects—where even stakeholders don't know what they want until after they've seen it—are an example. But in my experience these projects are far less prevalent than most people think. Agile development is an excellent choice for these highly dynamic projects, and model-based software engineering works just as well with agile development as it does with waterfall development and every other software development lifecycle in between. This is discussed in detail in Chapter 24.

1.2.4 How Model-Based Software Engineering Helps

Model-based software engineering improves requirements in several ways. First and foremost, the requirements modeling language has precisely defined meanings for all of its elements.[11] A requirements model can only mean one thing. Two people reading the same model must come to the same conclusion about the requirements; there can be no room for different interpretations. Precision also makes communicating requirements easier for non-native English speakers. As many software projects are now executed around the globe, knowledge transfer of requirements is safeguarded. It's the same on house drawings, airplane blueprints, and circuit schematics: they mean exactly one thing—intentionally. Model-based software engineering is simply incorporating a lesson learned long ago in the recognized engineering disciplines: you need a precise specification language.

Second, the modeling language is very concise. Just like the paragraph of text about the guest bathroom door versus a line and arc on a drawing, more information is packed into a smaller space with less effort. It's easy to specify requirements at the level of precision needed, so we are less reluctant to do so.

Third, a model of requirements needs to be precise and detailed before it can be considered done. Requirements writers are forced to ask very specific questions of stakeholders because the model would otherwise be incomplete. This forces hidden requirements to be surfaced. Specific examples will be discussed in Part II including kinds of use cases, attribute ranges, association multiplicities, all events in all states, etc. This level of precision is highly unlikely to appear in natural language requirements and is the source of many software defects.

---

11 See Appendix L.

Large numbers of requirements defects are avoided. Defect prevention is much more cost effective than defect detection and repair.

Fourth, a requirements model intentionally organizes related detail together so contradiction, conflict, and incompleteness are more obvious. There is never any guarantee that requirements models are 100% complete, but incompleteness tends to stand out much more in models than in natural language requirements.

Fifth, it is much quicker and easier to review a model than natural language. Chapter 12 explains how a requirements model is interpretable. We can set up demonstration scenarios with stakeholders to show them how the model behaves. They only need to determine if modeled behavior is what they want automated. We can illustrate the consequences of different requirements decisions without ever writing code. Chapter 20 explains how a requirements model can be compiled and executed.

Last, and certainly not least, it is much quicker and easier to build a model than to build code. And it is much quicker and easier to change a model if it is incorrect. It has been said many times, "build one to throw away."[12] Unfortunately, we already know that it is very expensive to write code, particularly if the intent is to then just throw it away. It's much less expensive to build a model and throw that model away if it is incorrect. Iterating on models is much cheaper and faster than iterating on code, and Chapter 2 explains why.

1.3   Problem #2: Overdependence on Testing

One well-researched aspect of software development and maintenance is the "defect cost increase effect." Simply, as more time passes between when a defect is injected and when it is found and fixed, it becomes exponentially more expensive to fix. Waiting twice as long means it's more than twice as expensive. Citations in Table 1.1 confirm this effect.

This effect doesn't only apply to code defects; it applies to all software defects. A defective requirement – one that is vague, ambiguous, incorrect (i.e., doesn't represent stakeholder need), missing, etc. – is as much a defect as an improper assignment statement or misplaced semicolon in code. As more time passes between when a requirements mistake is injected and when it is found and fixed, exponentially more effort is needed to fix it.

The defect cost increase effect isn't unique to software. Consider designing and building a house. If all you have is a general sketch of the house and you decide to make a certain window bigger, it is not expensive to make the change. Simply erase a few lines on a drawing, draw in a few new lines, and you are done. What

---

12 See, for example, [Brooks75].

Table 1.1 Credible, published reports confirming the defect cost increase effect.

Publication
Michael E. Fagan, "Design and Code Inspections to Reduce Errors in Program Development", *IBM Systems Journal*, Vol. 15, No. 3, pp. 182–211, 1976
Watts Humphrey, Terry R. Snyder, and Ronald R. Willis, "Software Process Improvement at Hughes Aircraft." *IEEE Software*, Vol. 8, No. 4 (July), pp. 11–23, 1991
Dean Leffingwell, "Calculating the Return on Investment from More Effective Requirements Management," *American Programmer*, Vol. 10, No. 4, pp. 13–16, 1997
Ron R. Willis, *Hughes Aircraft's Widespread Deployment of a Continuously Improving Software Process*, Software Engineering Institute/Carnegie Mellon University, CMU/SEI-98-TR-006, May 1998
Robert Grady, "An Economic Release Decision Model: Insights into Software Project Management," *Proceedings of the Applications of Software Measurement Conference*, Software Quality Engineering, 1999
Shull F., et al., "What We Have Learned About Fighting Defects," *Proceedings 8th IEEE Symposium on Software Metrics 2002*, IEEE, pp. 249–258, 2002
Barry Boehm and Richard Turner, *Balancing Agility and Discipline: A Guide for the Perplexed*, Addison Wesley, 2000

if the blueprints—the engineering drawings—have been approved when you decide to change the window? It will be more expensive than before, but not as expensive as after the walls have been framed. What about after exterior siding has been installed? What about after that window has been installed? What about after interior drywall has been installed? What about after interior walls have been textured and painted? What if curtains have already been hung? At each subsequent stage, the cost of making the same change increases substantially.

1.3.1 Sources of Software Defects

As stated earlier, James Martin reports that 56% of software defects are the result of faulty requirements. Martin also says that 27% of defects are due to faulty design. Only 7% of defects are due to code itself. The remaining 10% is for organizations that, for example, log defects against test cases and/or defects found in reviews of nontechnical documents like project plans and test plans. If 56% of defects are faulty requirements and 27% are faulty design, then

> *"83% of software defects exist before the corresponding code is ever written!"*

If the majority of defects exist before that code is written, why are most software organizations waiting until after that code is written to even start looking for them?

Making matters worse, a typical software test team is only 60–70% effective at finding defects.[13] For every 100 defects in software given to the test organization, testers are able to find 60–70. This leaves 30–40 defects for users to find. But we are not done yet. Robert Grady at HP reports that software testing is more effective at finding code defects than finding requirements and design defects.[14] This further extends the time between injection and repair for requirements and design defects because it's normally users that find them.

1.3.2 Rework Percentage: R%

Table 1.2 shows an effort breakdown for what most people think happens on software projects.

As per Section 1.2 on requirements, a developer is never given 100% of the requirements. Developers are forced into doing some requirements work on their own. The same is true for design; it is extremely rare that a developer is given 100% of the design, so they are forced into doing some design work on their own. Of course, developers are supposed to write code. And we should hope the developers are testing their code before passing it to others. We might disagree on appropriate values for a%, b%, c%, and d%, but that isn't relevant for now.[15] What is relevant is that most people believe this is everything a developer does. It's the developer's job. So regardless of proportions, they must add up to 100%.

In my experience, the single most important indicator of the health of a software organization today is "rework percentage" ("R%"). At the end of a software project, that project's R% can be calculated by first adding up the total effort to repair all defects resolved during that project. A defect

Table 1.2 Software project effort: what most people think happens.

Requirements	a%
Design	b%
Coding	c%
Testing	d%
Total	100%

---

13 See, for example, [Fagan96], [Jones99], [O'Neill97], [Russell91], or [Wagner06].
14 See [Grady92].
15 Values derived from many past model-based projects are presented in Chapter 23.

is defined as incorrectness in work that was found after the worker(s) claimed it was complete and correct, that is, corrective maintenance. Adaptive and perfective maintenance are not considered rework. Simply, "How many labor hours were spent isolating, fixing, and verifying defect repairs during this project?" The second step is finding the total development labor hours spent on the project. The project manager should know this or at least be able to find it. R% is calculated by dividing defect rework effort by total development effort:

$$R\% = \frac{LaborHoursSpentOnDefects}{LaborHoursSpentOverall}$$

If you are a developer, ask yourself:

> "Over the last year or so, how much of my time has been spent adding new functionality vs. how much has been spent fixing code that someone had earlier claimed to be correct?"

Michael Fagan[16] reports that R% is between 30% and 80% for typical software projects. My own polling of thousands of professional developers gives responses consistent with Fagan's. Most mainstream developers estimate their rework percentage is around 50%. R% has been measured in five organizations:

- 350-developer organization measured 57%.
- 60-developer organization measured 59%.
- 125-developer organization measured 63%.
- 100-developer organization measured 65%.
- 150-developer organization measured 67%.

I now ask those same developers if assuming a value of 51% is unreasonable. It's very close to the 50% they estimated. It's also less than all five measured organizations. Virtually everyone considers 51% rework to be a reasonable estimate. Unfortunately, if R% really is 51% or greater, then it completely changes the way software projects need to be seen. Table 1.3 shows the more realistic view.

Yes, developers are spending time on requirements, design, coding, and testing, but that's for new development—adding functionality that wasn't there before. Rework also needs to be included and the total still needs to add up to 100%. Since rework has been agreed to be 51%, then clearly requirements,

---

16 See [Wheeler96].

Table 1.3 Software project effort: what really happens.

Requirements	a%
Design	b%
Coding	c%
Testing	d%
Rework (R%)	51%
Total	100%

design, coding, and testing effort cannot add up to any more than 49%. We are forced into the striking conclusion:

> *"Rework is not only the single largest driver of cost and schedule on a typical software project; it is bigger than all other drivers <u>combined</u>!"*

Most software organizations are spending more on rework than on all other activities put together. Consider the words "motion" and "progress." Development of new code is progress: adding functionality to the code that wasn't there before. Rework is motion, not progress. Rework is waste. If an organization's R% is 51% or greater, and it usually is, more than half of their capacity to deliver value is wasted. Less than half of work being done is progress toward the goal of delivering useful software.

1.3.3 Testing as a Crutch

Mainstream developers use testing as a crutch. They fully expect testers to find defects and would be surprised if none were found. Martyn Thomas[17] captures the contradiction succinctly:

> *"An engineer wants their system to be fit for purpose and chooses methods, tools and components that are expected to achieve fitness for purpose. It's poor engineering to have a system fail in testing, partly because that puts the budget and schedule at risk but mainly because it reveals that the chosen methods, tools or components have not delivered a system of the required quality, and that raises questions about the quality of the development processes."*

> (Martyn Thomas)

---

17 Personal communication.

Similarly, C. A. R (Tony) Hoare said[18] (paraphrased):

"The real value of tests is not that they detect [defects] in the code, but that they detect inadequacies in the methods, concentration, and skills of those who design and produce the code."

1.3.4 How Model-Based Software Engineering Helps

Model-based software engineering helps address this problem in several ways. First, precision and conciseness of models means they are easier to review objectively—instead of depending on subjective review. Second, models should be available before code. Third, model-based software engineering includes specific quality criteria (e.g., a "Definition of done") as a further aid in building, maintaining, and reviewing models. These quality criteria can be found in every chapter that describes work on model-based software engineering projects. Combining early model availability with objective review criteria minimizes the delay between defect injection and repair, resulting in massive reduction in rework. On properly run model-based software engineering, project's R% is under 10%.

Assume that two projects have the same amount of functionality (scope) to deliver. If one project's R% is around 60% and the other is less than 10%, the second project will finish in about half the time and cost of the first. We see this on model-based software engineering projects: they finish quicker and cheaper than would be expected for mainstream projects of equivalent scope.

It's not that defects aren't being injected on model-based software engineering projects. Mistakes *are* being made. The difference is that fewer defects are injected due to requirements conciseness and precision. Real requirements are surfaced long before there could ever be a problem. And what few defects remain tends to be found sooner—through review—so they are cheaper and quicker to fix.

A claim heard repeatedly in mainstream software organizations is:

"We need to be better at testing!"

Nothing could be further from the truth. You need to be better at avoiding defects. And you need to be better at finding and fixing requirements and design defects, well before writing code. Model-based software engineering is an effective way to do that.

1.4 Problem #3: "Self-Documenting Code" Is a Myth

Every developer knows the frustration of struggling with code written by someone else. Experienced developers also know the frustration of struggling with

---

18 See [Hoare96].

their own code—but code written so long ago it might as well have been written by someone else. When looking at unfamiliar code, a maintainer needs to answer two simple but critical questions:

- *What is this code intended to do?*
- *Why does this code look the way it does?*

And yet these two questions are essentially impossible to answer when all you have is code.

Reading code comments is usually an exercise in futility and far more trouble than it's worth:

- More often than not, comments don't even exist.
- When comments do exist, they can be woefully out of date. Figuring out which comments are still valid can take longer than just trying to reason through the code.
- Comments often say completely inane, useless things like " a++; // incre- ment a ."

1.4.1 Code Can Never Be Self-Documenting

There are two reasons why code can never be self-documenting: code describes a solution not the problem, and it's impossible to distinguish has-to-be from happens-to-be. A professional acquaintance says:

> *"Code overspecifies."*
>
> (H.S. Lahman)

Code expresses how a particular problem is being solved, not what the original problem is. Code will only allow you to figure out what it does, which is not necessarily what it is *intended* to do.

And even when you are able to figure out what code does, whether or not that's what it is intended to do, you still have the question of "Why?" Why does this code look the way it does? Does the code *have* to look this way? Or, does the code just *happen* to look this way? Most critically, you need an answer to:

> *"What will happen if I change it?"*

If some change is made to this code, can it, or will it, break something?

1.4.2 How Model-Based Software Engineering Helps

Model-based software engineering helps address this problem in two ways. First,

"Model-based software engineering is literally 'self-coding documentation.'"

You may think it a bizarre statement the first time you read it. But bear with me; the claim is substantiated in Chapters 15–19 on manual derivation of design and code and Chapter 20 on model compilation. The primary focus of model-based software engineering is on a complete, consistent, clear, correct, concise, and precise model of a "business" to be automated. This model completely defines policies that stakeholders want software to enforce and processes that stakeholders want software to carry out. This model defines precisely "What this code is intended to do."

Second, most organizations' design documentation—if it even exists, let alone whether it's up to date—is useless. It says things that are already better said in code. You don't need to tell a C++ developer what C++ code looks like. If the developer wants to know, they can just read that code. It's by far the most complete and accurate description of what that code looks like. So instead of merely repeating what's already in code,

"Design documentation should be more about why that code looks the way it does than how that code looks."

Mainstream software organizations spend about 80% of their capacity maintaining existing code. This is easy to verify in your own organization. Take a poll: how many developers are working on brand-new development projects? About one in five—20%—is typical. So for every dollar spent on development, four dollars is spent on maintenance. Considering the TCO of software, cutting new development cost in half only leads to a 10% net reduction in TCO. On the other hand, cutting maintenance cost in half—through useful software documentation—leads to a 40% reduction in TCO. Experience with model-based software engineering has shown maintenance cost drops by at least 75% on average. We should be a lot more concerned with improving software maintainability than developability, and model-based software engineering has improving maintainability as one of its primary goals. The emphasis on documenting "Why?" is discussed more thoroughly in Chapter 19.

1.5 Why Agile Development Doesn't Solve These Problems

Many believe that agile development solves all software project ills. Simply, it does not. It cannot. This section explains why.

Agile development means different things to different people. There is no consensus on "agile development" other than, simply, "not waterfall development." So I need to define what I mean when I say agile development. According to a survey by VersionOne,[19] 72% of projects reporting use of agile development use Scrum or a close variant of Scrum. Since Scrum is the most widely used, I'll define agile development as Scrum. And for a definition of Scrum, I refer to its creators: Ken Schwaber and Jeff Sutherland. They define Scrum as[20]:

- *Three team roles*—product owner, development team, and scrum master
- *Five events*—sprint, sprint planning, daily scrum, sprint review, and sprint retrospective
- *Three artifacts*—product backlog, sprint backlog, and increment

Scrum is said to provide:

> "... *a framework within which people can address complex adaptive problems, while productively and creatively delivering products of the highest possible value.*"
>
> ...*a process framework that has been used to manage complex product development since the early 1990s. Scrum is not a process or a technique for building products; rather, it is a framework within which you can employ various processes and techniques. Scrum makes clear the relative efficacy of your product management and development practices so that you can improve.*"

The top two challenges on software projects are vague, ambiguous, incomplete requirements and overdependence on testing to find defects. The Schwaber–Sutherland definition says nothing about how either requirements or testing are done on a Scrum project. The Scrum team is free to take any approach they want for requirements and testing.

1.5.1 Scrum and Requirements

It needs to be stated clearly that a product backlog item (i.e., a user story) is *not* a requirement. Waterfall projects need a work breakdown structure (WBS): a hierarchical decomposition of work to be done to call that project done. Scrum's product backlog is nothing more and nothing less than a WBS. Product backlog items are nothing more and nothing less than WBS elements. Nobody would ever call a WBS element a requirement,[21] so why call a product backlog item a requirement? Instead,

---

19 See [VersionOne15].
20 See [Schwaber13].
21 Requirements are explained in detail in Chapter 4.

"A user story is a promise for a future conversation."

(Alistair Cockburn)

Requirements work on Scrum projects happens during conversations between developers and product owners when a user story is being worked on—either within a sprint or in pre-sprint "backlog grooming." That communication typically uses natural language, so requirements on Scrum projects is subject to the same issues of ambiguity and incompleteness as any other software project.

1.5.2 Scrum and Testing

Some Scrum projects use test-driven development[22] (TDD). The philosophy of TDD is[23]:

"We only write new code when we have a test that doesn't work."

The full TDD process is shown in Figure 1.2.

Full TDD operates at two levels. The higher level, on the left side of Figure 1.2, is acceptance testing for product backlog items. This higher level is sometimes called acceptance test-driven development (ATDD) and answers the question "How will we know the developer's code meets the intent of a user story?" The lower level, on the right, is unit test-driven development (UTDD) for each method and answers the question "How will the developer know this method has been implemented properly?" Many teams seem to think that TDD operates only at the lower UTDD level and ignore story acceptance testing. This means that the code will do what developer thinks the code should do, but that is not necessarily what stakeholders want it to do. To be effective, TDD *must* operate at the user story acceptance level, ATDD.

Some Scrum projects use behavior-driven development[24] (BDD). BDD is a structured approach to ATDD and operates entirely at the user story acceptance level. Each user story is defined using a prescribed template:

Title: [user story name]
   As a [role]
   I want [feature]
   So that [benefit]

---

22 See, for example, [Freeman09].
23 See [Jeffries01].
24 See, for example, [Chelimsky10].

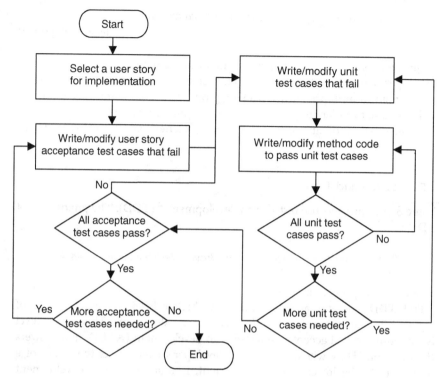

Figure 1.2 The full test-driven development process.

For example,

Title: Account Holder withdraws cash
   As an Account Holder
   I want to withdraw cash from an ATM
   So that I can get money when the bank is closed

Acceptance criteria drive user story acceptance test cases and follow a prescribed template:

Scenario x: [Title]
   Given [context]
   and [some more context...]
   When [event]
   Then [outcome]
   and [another outcome...]

As in

Scenario 1: Account has sufficient funds
Given the account balance is $100
and the card is valid
and the machine contains at least $20
When the Account Holder requests $20
Then the ATM should dispense $20
and the account balance should be $80
and the card should be returned

Other scenarios would be specified for:

- Account has insufficient funds
- Card has been disabled
- ATM has insufficient funds
- ...

Acceptance test cases for each scenario should be obvious.

When using ATDD or BDD, each acceptance test case is a proxy for one or more requirements: it is simply requirements being expressed in test case language. The test case for scenario 1 in the BDD example is:

- *Initial configuration*—A bank account has $100, the account holder has a valid ATM card, and the ATM has enough money in it.
- *Stimulus*—The account holder requests $20.
- *Expected result*—The account holder has $20 cash, the ATM card has been returned, and the account balance is $80.

This test case is a proxy for the natural language requirement:

> "If an account has sufficient funds, the account holder has a valid ATM card, and the ATM has enough money, when the account holder requests money the ATM shall give it to them, return their ATM card, and reduce the account balance by the amount withdrawn."

Abstractly, a test case is expressed in the form

> "When given input that looks like X, <u>we expect to see</u> output that looks like Y"

This is a minor change from a requirement expressed in natural language:

> "When given input that looks like X, <u>the software shall produce</u> output that looks like Y"

The critical difference is that test case language is inherently less ambiguous. This helps solve the ambiguity problem of natural language requirements. This still leaves the issue of completeness. To be effective, ATTD/BDD must be combined with appropriate test coverage criteria like input domain coverage, boundary value coverage, etc.

Even if an agile project is not using ATDD or BDD, one might expect the short sprints in Scrum to reduce the time between making a requirements mistake and repairing it. In theory, R% on Scrum projects should be lower than on waterfall projects. In practice, however, there is no significant difference in R% of Scrum projects and waterfall projects. In fact, four of the five organizations where measured R% was cited above claim to follow Scrum. The theory that Scrum reduces R% is just that—a theory—and not borne out in practice.

In truth, the earlier stated relationship of time to defect cost increase, time is only a proxy. Cost is driven by downstream decisions made based on an earlier, upstream decision. More time generally—but not necessarily—means more downstream decisions. The analogy of making the window bigger is appropriate: it doesn't matter if the house is being built in traditional design–build sequence (i.e., waterfall) or incrementally (i.e., one room at a time). What matters is how much work has been done on that one wall when the decision to change the window is made. Regardless of how much of the rest of the house has been built, the farther along that one wall is, the more expensive it is to change.

The cost of any requirements correction, change, or clarification depends on the number of subsequent architecture, design, construction, and testing decisions based on it—not on time alone. Agile development's push to executable code forces architecture, design, construction, and testing decisions to be made before a requirement is truly verified with stakeholders. Subsequent decisions have been made in either case, Scrum or waterfall, so the cost of making the change is the same regardless of how much clock time passed between requirement decision and validation.

In the end, Scrum does not make a perceivable difference in how well requirements and testing are done on most software projects. Requirements and testing are still done essentially the same way as on non-Scrum projects—the only difference is when that work is being done: more continuously in Scrum versus concentrated in phases on waterfall projects. Scrum, ATDD, and BDD—by their very nature—tend to put even more emphasis on testing to find defects. The emphasis should not be on more testing; the emphasis needs to be on better requirements and design. If, as Schwaber and Sutherland say,

> "Scrum makes clear the relative efficacy of your product management and development practices so that you can improve"

then it appears Scrum has a major blind spot regarding rework (R%).

1.5.3 Scrum and Self-Documenting Code

The number three challenge on software projects is assuming that code can be self-documenting. The Schwaber–Sutherland definition says nothing about software documentation on a Scrum project. A Scrum team is free to take any approach to documentation.

Whether it is appropriate or not is another matter, but many project teams use agility as the excuse for not doing any documentation at all— or at least for doing very minimal documentation. Considering how bad most mainstream software documentation is, not doing it at all may not be such a bad idea. But that means the only artifact at the end of the project is code itself. Thus, Scrum falls into the same trap as non-Scrum projects, depending entirely on code as the only persistent software documentation.

Software documentation per se is not inherently bad. The problem is in how most teams approach documentation—specifically in ways that are non-value adding:

- Dependence on natural language requirements leads to predictable problems of ambiguity and incompleteness.
- Design documentation at best only describes the structure of code, not why it looks the way it does. Mainstream design documentation is also completely disconnected from code, so it's difficult to keep it synchronized. This will be expanded in the discussion of literate programming in Chapter 22.

Model-based software engineering, as demonstrated in Part III, is literally "self-coding documentation." Requirements and design documentation are intentionally focused precisely on adding value over the entire software product lifetime.

This section presented how agile development is most often practiced today. Do not get the impression that model-based software engineering and agile are in any way incompatible. They are perfectly compatible.[25]

1.6   Truth in Advertising

Previous sections explained how model-based software engineering addresses very serious and pervasive software problems. However, it is not a silver bullet. Model-based software engineering cannot and does not solve all problems. Even

---

25 See, for example, [Mellor11] and Chapter 24.

after fully adopting model-based software engineering, other serious problems may remain:

- Not connecting to real users.[26]
- Stakeholders constantly change priorities: shifting resources on and off projects.
- Unrealistic, externally imposed schedule, budget, and scope constraints.
- Excessive personnel turnover.
- Developers spread across too many projects at the same time.
- Failure to account for and manage project risk.
- Inadequate project planning.
- Insufficient project tracking.
- A one-size-fits-all development process mentality.
- Too much time wasted in ineffective meetings.
- Organizational politics.
- "Quick and dirty" mentality leading to excessive technical debt.[27]
- "No bad news" cultures.
- ...

1.7 Software Engineering

Any book titled *How to Engineer Software* should define what it means by "software engineering" and show how it measures up to that definition. For a definition of "engineering," we should look to recognized professional engineers. The Accreditation Board of Engineering and Technology (ABET) is the authority for accrediting engineering and technology degree programs at colleges and universities in the United States. ABET defines engineering as[28]:

> *"... the profession in which a knowledge of the mathematical and natural sciences gained by study, experience, and practice is applied with judgment to develop ways to utilize, economically, the materials and forces of nature for the benefit of mankind."*

or, simply,

Engineering = scientific theory + practice + engineering economy

---

26 As Karl Wiegers says, "The voice of customer needs to be very close to the ear of the developer."
27 Always remember, "The dirty remains long after the quick has been forgotten." At one company, the saying among developers was "The management wanted it badly, and that's just how they got it."
28 See [ABET00].

It should follow that software engineering can be defined as[29]:

> *"... the profession in which a knowledge of the mathematical and comput-ing sciences gained by study, experience, and practice is applied with judg-ment to develop ways to utilize, economically, computing systems for the benefit of mankind."*

So, from the equation above, we can derive

Software engineering = computer science + practice + engineering economy

Relevant computer science (and discrete mathematics) is cataloged in Chapters 13 and 14 of the "Guide to the Software Engineering Body of Knowledge"[30] ("SWEBOK Guide"). The following is intended only to overview the science and math of software engineering:

- Programming fundamentals
- Programming language basics
- Data structure and representation
- Algorithms and complexity
- Database basics and data management
- Basic user human factors
- Set, relations, and functions
- Basic logic
- Finite state machines
- Numerical precision, accuracy, and error
- Measurement theory
- ...

Jeannette Wing[31] explains how most developers would understandably cringe at having to use the "upside down A's and backwards E's" (referring to "for all" and "there exists") notation commonly associated with formal methods. Just the same, a building architect would probably cringe at the underlying mathematics of structural analysis of their designs. Wing's insight is to allow work in comfortable, everyday, surface notations while being certain of an anchoring in underlying formalisms. A model can be mechanically translated into equivalent "upside down A's and backwards E's" at a moment's notice.

The mathematics—the underlying formalisms—gives a model its single, pre-cise, unambiguous interpretation. But everyday developers don't have to work in that ultra-formal world. They can work in the comfortable world of class

---

29 See [Tockey05].
30 See [IEEE14].
31 See [Wing90].

diagrams (based on set theory, relational algebra, measurement theory, etc.) and state charts (based on finite automata theory, functions, etc.) knowing that someone has already provided the linkage to the underlying formalisms. Formalisms for model-based software engineering are presented in Appendix L.

Some of the critical elements of software engineering practice are detailed in Chapter 3. There is more to software engineering practice than just that, for example, several chapters in SWEBOK Guide discuss critical practice-based elements that are entirely consistent with model-based software engineering:

- Software requirements
- Software design
- Software construction
- Software testing
- Software maintenance
- Software configuration management
- Software engineering management
- Software engineering process
- Software engineering models and methods
- Software quality
- Software engineering professional practice

Software engineering economy is explicitly identified as a required knowledge area in SWEBOK Guide and is covered extensively in [Tockey05]: how to apply science, math, and practice in an economic context to cost effectively solve real-world computing problems.

It should now be apparent, but will be shown throughout the remainder of this book, that model-based software engineering *is* entirely consistent with this definition of software engineering.

1.8 Overview of Model-Based Software Engineering

Figure 1.3 shows the primary deliverables from a model-based software engineering project.

1.8.1 Background

The deliverable labeled Background refers to the product requirements document (PRD)/marketing requirements document (MRD)/product vision/scope statement/overview or whatever project teams typically get from stakeholders. This provides a high-level description of what developers are supposed to build in software. This is normally given to the development team; it is not something they should produce. An example Background for a case study used in this book, WebBooks 2.0, is shown in Appendix B.

Some organizations find it useful to include minimum conditions of acceptance, either as a section in the Background or as a separate deliverable. The minimum conditions of acceptance identify the most vital requirements against which the development organization will be held accountable. This would typically include critical functional and nonfunctional requirements (these terms are more clearly defined in Chapter 4). This may be considered a contractual (i.e., legal) document on some projects and can serve as the basis for acceptance testing and requirements traceability, if appropriate.

1.8.2 Semantic Model

The semantic model is the specification of policies and processes to be automated: the complete, consistent, clear, concise, precise, unambiguous, and validated functional requirements. The structure and content of this model is introduced in Chapter 2 and described in detail in Part II. Example semantic models are shown in Appendices D, F, H, and J.

1.8.3 Interface Specification

The interface specification defines how real-world external entities (actors in the semantic model) will interact with the software. This can include either or both human–computer (i.e., user) interfaces and application program(mer) interfaces (APIs). This content is critical for developing View and Controller software (assuming a Model–View–Controller style of software architecture[32]). The deliverable is described in Chapter 14. Partial examples of interface specifications are shown in Appendices E, G, I, and K.

1.8.4 Software Design Specification

The software design specification is, for example, classic object-oriented design as you would find on a typical software project that uses UML, except that this specification has much more emphasis on explaining why the design and code look the way they do. The structure and content is described in detail in Part III. Partial examples of design specifications are also shown in Appendices E, G, I, and K.

---

32 See, for example, http://en.wikipedia.org/wiki/Model–view–controller

1.8.5 Source Code

The last technical deliverable is the source code itself. This includes compileable source code along with necessary make files, build files, and, as needed, run-time configuration data.

1.8.6 Traceability

Crosshatched shapes between deliverables in Figure 1.3 identify opportunities for traceability between pairs of deliverables. More specifically, they call out necessary consistency. A semantic model might say, abstractly, that customers can place orders for books so the user interface for customers needs to give a way to place book orders. The core of the software design and code (Model region in Model–View–Controller) needs to automate placing orders, while View-controller region needs to implement the interface defined in the interface specification. Full traceability is possible, if needed—it's only a question of granularity.

1.8.7 Implications on Software Testing

Not shown in Figure 1.3 are implications of these deliverables on software testing. For each deliverable, tests of one kind or another can be derived:

- Unit tests from code itself
- Integration and component tests from the software design specification

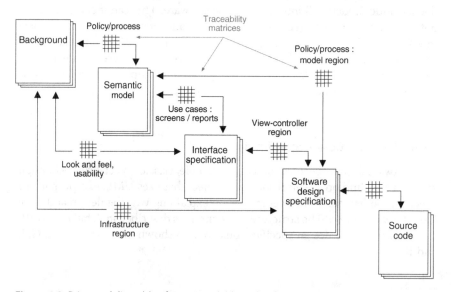

Figure 1.3 Primary deliverables from a model-based software engineering project.

- Usability and interface tests from the interface specification
- Functional tests from the semantic model
- Acceptance tests from the minimum conditions of acceptance in the Background

1.8.8 Deliverables Versus Lifecycles

A final comment on Figure 1.3 is that you shouldn't be blamed if "Waterfall process!" leapt into your mind. However, it needs to be said very clearly:

> *"Model-based software engineering does not require Waterfall development processes. Model-based software engineering is perfectly compatible with highly iterative (e.g., Agile) development processes as well."*

Applying model-based software engineering in an agile process is explained in Chapter 24.

1.9 Relation to Other Similar Approaches

Model-based software development in general has existed for many years. There are several other model-based approaches, for example, Rational Unified Process (RUP) and Executable UML.[33] What separates this approach from those others is the follows:

- *The primary goal of this approach is to bring true engineering discipline to software development and maintenance*—There is a deliberate emphasis on grounding in underlying theory and formalisms, a deliberate emphasis on elements of professional practice (in particular, the fundamental principles in Chapter 3), and a deliberate emphasis on engineering economy as a key driver in technical decision-making.
- *There is a strong emphasis on surfacing as many precise requirements as possible, as early as appropriate*—The semantic model is driven down to a very precise level of detail (e.g., attribute ranges and association multiplicities in class modeling in Chapter 8), and tactics are provided (e.g., event types in use case modeling in Chapter 7 and considering all state–event pairs in state models in Chapter 10) to surface functional requirements before corresponding code is written. Tactics for being more complete and precise in nonfunctional requirements are also explained in Chapter 4.

---

33 See, for example, [Kruchten03] and [Mellor02], respectively.

- *No other approach separates business complexities from technology complexities as completely*—Per the definitions and techniques in Chapter 4, every other approach incorporates some degree of technology and design into all models, thus potentially railroading downstream development into specific implementations that could easily be suboptimal. A semantic model, as defined in this approach, must be completely independent of computing technology. This gives developers the most freedom in finding optimal designs and code.
- *There is an emphasis on scalability through domain partitioning (Chapter 6) and subdomain partitioning (Chapter 11)*—This approach has been used on software projects involving as many as 350 developers over 7 years, delivering several million lines of high-quality, mission-critical, and safety-critical code.[34]
- *There is an emphasis on semantics, not just syntax, in both code and in modeling the business to be automated*—This is introduced in Chapter 2 and continues throughout the book.
- *There is a focus on software documentation that specifically and intentionally adds value for development and maintenance*—Chapter 20 shows how semantic models can be mechanically translated into executable code, although that is not required. Time and money needed to take advantage of a model compiler may not be affordable to some organizations. That a semantic model *is* compilable should be clear demonstration of its value. Chapters 15–19 present manual derivation of design and code from a semantic model.
- *This approach provides very specific quality criteria (i.e., "definition of done") for all work*—Work products of all kinds can be reviewed against these quality criteria to identify and remove defects as quickly as possible, greatly reducing rework (R%).

This approach has evolved over more than 30 years, with the explicit goal of solving the three most significant problems in software development and maintenance:

1) Vague, ambiguous, incomplete requirements
2) Overdependence on testing
3) Assuming that code can be self-documenting

Other model-based approaches may address some of these, but this is the only approach that completely addresses all three. Results of using this approach on real software projects are consistent:

- Development projects finish in about half of the usual time and budget.
- User-reported defects are about one tenth of typical.
- Maintenance costs drop by at least a factor of four.

---

34 Such scalability is not unique to this approach. Domain partitioning was pioneered by Sally Shlaer and Steve Mellor—they clearly deserve credit.

1.10 An Overview of This Book

This book is divided into six parts:

- **Part I: Introduction and Foundations**. This part establishes the foundation on which model-based software engineering is built. This part includes chapters on the nature of code, fundamental principles, functional and nonfunctional requirements, an overview of the UML, and partitioning large systems into domains.
- **Part II: Model-Based Requirements**. In this part, the four primary elements of technology-independent requirements modeling are explained: use case diagrams, class models, interaction diagrams, and state models. Partitioning domains into subdomains, simulating models, and deriving verification test cases from models are also presented.
- **Part III: Model-Based Design and Code**. This part explains how to translate technology-independent requirements models into technology-dependent design models and executable code. This part includes discussions of how requirements and design modeling differ, designing interfaces, high-level design, detailed design, code, optimization, formal disciplines of code including software proofs of correctness, and the nature of design itself. This part also demonstrates model compilation, mechanically generating code from requirements models.
- **Part IV: Related Topics**. This part provides an estimation model, discusses model-based software engineering in the context of alternative software development processes, explains how to approach error handling from an economic perspective, and rebuts common arguments against this approach.
- **Part V: Summary**. This part summarizes the book.
- **Part VI: Appendices**. Additional resources such as references, documentation principles, example semantic models and designs, a semantic model of semantic modeling, example semantic model translation rules for Java, and a discussion of software structural complexity metrics.

1.11 Summary

In the past, users were willing to tolerate defects because the software was not performing a critical service. Maybe a user was editing a photo prior to posting on social media when the photo editing software crashed. No big deal, just restart and try again. But, as Bob Dylan said,

"The times they are a-changin'"

More and more, software *is* being used for critical purposes, like:

- Emergency services[35]
- Transportation[36,37,38,39,40]
- Medical care[41,42]

---

35 "The outage was caused by a software coding error in the Colorado facility, and resulted in a loss of 911 service for more than 11 million people for up to six hours. ... Although, fortunately, it appears that no one died as a result, the incident – and the flaws it revealed – is simply unacceptable." See http://transition.fcc.gov/Daily_Releases/Daily_Business/2014/db1017/DOC-330012A1.pdf.

36 "An American Airlines spokesperson confirmed the issue, ... 'Some flights are experiencing an issue with a software application on pilot iPads ....'" See http://www.theguardian.com/technology/2015/apr/29/apple-ipad-fail-grounds-few-dozen-american-airline-flights.

37 "Federal regulators will order operators of Boeing 787 Dreamliners to shut down the plane's electrical power periodically after Boeing discovered a software error that could result in a total loss of power." See http://www.nytimes.com/2015/05/01/business/faa-orders-fix-for-possible-power-loss-in-boeing-787.html?_r=0.

38 "The causes of the National Air Traffic Services (NATS) flight control centre system failure in December 2014 that affected 65,000 passengers directly and up to 230,000 indirectly have been revealed in a recently published report ... How could an error not tolerated in undergraduate-level programming homework enter software developed by professionals over a decade at a cost approaching a billion pounds?" See https://theconversation.com/air-traffic-control-failure-shows-we-need-a-better-approach-to-programming-42496.

39 "... give the attacker wireless control, via the Internet, to any of thousands of vehicles. Their code is an automaker's nightmare: software that lets hackers send commands through the Jeep's entertainment system to its dashboard functions, steering, brakes, and transmission, all from a laptop that may be across the country." See http://www.wired.com/2015/07/hackers-remotely-kill-jeep-highway/.

40 "The US car company General Motors is recalling more than four million vehicles worldwide due to a software defect linked to at least one death ... the defect concerns the sensing and diagnostic module. In rare cases it can go into test mode, meaning airbags will not inflate in a crash." See http://www.bbc.com/news/world-us-canada-37321361.

41 "A flaw found in a calculator tool used by doctors at GP surgeries has potentially led to a number of patients being erroneously prescribed or denied statins across England. ... Due to the unidentified error in the code, it's possible that the risk of CVD was overstated ... This could—in turn—have led to mistakes in prescriptions for statins." See http://arstechnica.co.uk/security/2016/05/bug-in-gp-heart-risk-calculator-tool-tpp/.

42 "... vulnerability in Hospira's Symbiq Infusion System ... could allow an attacker to remotely control the operation of the device, potentially impacting prescribed therapy and patient safety." See https://ics-cert.us-cert.gov/advisories/ICSA-15-174-01.

- Banking and finance[43,44,45]
- Networks, communication, and telecommunication[46,47,48]
- Criminal justice[49]

---

43 "... Apple Pay users with Bank of America accounts have reported that Apple's new tap-to-pay solution has become a huge headache by charging their accounts twice for a single purchase. Bank of America has confirmed ... that it is issuing refunds for duplicate Apple Pay charges." See http://www.cultofmac.com/300574/apple-pay-customers-getting-charged-twice-purchases/.

44 "... a currency exchange-rate error in 3rd party software supplied to United (Airlines) affected several thousand bookings on United's Denmark-facing website. Specifically, this error temporarily caused flights originating in the United Kingdom and denominated in Danish Kroners (DKK) to be presented at only a fraction of their intended prices. While United filed fares correctly, this software error caused amounts charged to be significantly lower than prices offered through all other distribution channels or available in any other currency." See http://www.united.com/web/en-US/content/travel/exchange-rate-error.aspx?v_ctrk=HHLN$0-202-7697-1-5798.

45 "A programming blunder in its reporting software has led to Citigroup being fined $7m (£5m) ... When the system was introduced in the mid-1990s, the program code filtered out any transactions that were given three-digit branch codes from 089 to 100 and used those prefixes for testing purposes. But in 1998, the company started using alphanumeric branch codes as it expanded its business. Among them were the codes 10B, 10C and so on, which the system treated as being within the excluded range, and so their transactions were removed from any reports sent to the SEC." See http://www.theregister.co.uk/2016/07/13/coding_error_costs_citigroup_7m/.

46 "The embedded Web server in the Cisco Cable Modem with Digital Voice ... contains a buffer overflow vulnerability that can be exploited remotely without authentication. The flaw could result in arbitrary code execution." See http://www.itnews.com/article/3042664/cisco-patches-serious-flaws-in-cable-modems-and-home-gateways.html?token=%23tk.ITN_nlt_ITnews_Daily_2016-03-10&idg_eid=3223a51d2577b180c5ff5baf4855a77a&utm_source=Sailthru&utm_medium=email&utm_campaign=ITnews%20Daily%202016-03-10&utm_term=ITnews_Daily.

47 "Juniper Networks is warning customers to patch their NetScreen enterprise firewalls against bad code that enables attackers to take over the machines and decrypt VPN traffic among corporate sites and with mobile employees. ... attackers could exploit the code 'to gain administrative access to NetScreen devices and to decrypt VPN connections,' ... It would enable smart attackers to exploit the vulnerability and wipe out log files, making compromises untraceable." See http://www.itnews.com/article/3016992/security/juniper-firewalls-compromised-by-spy-code-what-you-need-to-know.html.

48 "Google has released one of the largest Android monthly security updates, fixing a total of 39 vulnerabilities — 15 rated critical, including four that can lead to a complete device compromise." See http://www.itnews.com/article/3052203/google-fixes-39-android-flaws-some-allow-hackers-to-take-over-your-phone.html?token=%23tk.ITN_nlt_ITnews_Daily_2016-04-06&idg_eid=3223a51d2577b180c5ff5baf4855a77a&utm_source=Sailthru&utm_medium=email&utm_campaign=ITnews%20Daily%202016-04-06&utm_term=ITnews_Daily.

49 "More than 3,000 inmates in Washington state prisons were released early because of a software bug. The glitch caused the computer system to miscalculate the sentence reduction inmates received for good behavior, according to a press statement from the state governor's office." See http://www.techinsider.io/washington-prisons-software-glitch-2015-12.

- Tax administration, licensing, and other government services[50,51]
- Manufacturing automation
- ...

My own car has been recalled twice *because of a software defect in the engine control code that could shut down the car while it is being driven.*[52,53] The Goto Fail[54] and Heartbleed[55] defects in low-level security software did expose, and Freak[56] had the potential to expose, banking, credit card, and other personally identifying information of thousands of individuals.[57] We may never know how many people's identities were stolen. We may never know how much money was lost. But without a doubt, identities were stolen and money was lost due to these defects. How tolerant are *those* people of defective software now? How tolerant would *you* be if *your* identity was stolen and *your* money was lost?

---

50 For example, "... a Department of Revenue (DOR) contractor underestimated the complexity of adapting the sales and use tax software component of DOR's Integrated Tax System. Doing so contributed to significant programming errors, ... and compromised the accuracy of sales and use tax distributions to counties and professional sports districts." See http://legis.wisconsin.gov/lab/reports/07-5full.pdf.

51 "US tax authorities (IRS) said ... that the personal information of a further 390,000 individuals may have been accessed by cyber criminals. ... the IRS said it discovered the data of 114,000 US taxpayers had been illegally accessed through the" Get Transcript "page ... A review conducted by the agency has revealed over 700,000 people affected. ... The IRS said it found a further 295,000 taxpayer accounts were targeted, but not accessed by cyber criminals." See http://www.bbc.com/news/business-35673999.

52 "the current software could result in high temperatures on certain transistors and possibly damage them. When it fails, the error forces the car into failsafe mode. Toyota says that in rare circumstances, it could even shut the hybrid system down while the car is being driven." See http://www.autoblog.com/2014/02/12/toyota-recalling-1-9m-prius-models-globally/.

53 "This recall provides a remedy to address a new condition in the vehicles involved in the previous recalls ... dealers will update the software for all involved vehicles." See https://pressroom.toyota.com/releases/toyota+is+conducting+a+safety+recall+involving+certain+prius+vehicles+october+5+2018.htm.

54 "The result is that the code leaps over the vital call to sslRawVerify(), and exits the function. This causes an immediate 'exit and report success', and the TLS connection succeeds, even though the verification process hasn't actually taken place." See http://nakedsecurity.sophos.com/2014/02/24/anatomy-of-a-goto-fail-apples-ssl-bug-explained-plus-an-unofficial-patch/.

55 "... results from improper input validation (due to a missing bounds check) in the implementation of the TLS heartbeat extension ... The vulnerability is classified as a buffer over-read, a situation where more data can be read than should be allowed." See http://en.wikipedia.org/wiki/Heartbleed.

56 "Microsoft has issued a security warning about a bug that could let attackers spy on supposedly secure communications ... attackers force data travelling between a vulnerable site and a visitor to use weak encryption. This makes it easier to crack open the data and steal sensitive information." See http://www.bbc.com/news/technology-31765672.

57 Many security threat vectors (see, e.g., "WASC Threat Classification" available from the Web Application Security Consortium at http://www.webappsec.org) are the direct result of poor requirements, design, and programming practices.

I dare say you would be a lot less tolerant of defective software than you probably are today.

Even social media, which is not generally seen as critical, can suffer significant consequences from software defects.[58]

1.11.1 Stop Calling Them "Bugs"!

For that matter, we shouldn't even call them "bugs" anymore. That term is too cute, as in (said in a lilting voice)

> *"Oh... Imagine that... The software has a bug"*

The term "bug" completely fails to acknowledge the magnitude of consequential damage. Whether you realize it or not, so-called bugs have killed people. See, for example, descriptions of Therac-25, which is known to have killed six people and is strongly suspected of having killed as many as 25.[59] Even if nobody is hurt or killed, how much valuable data gets lost, and how much valuable user time gets wasted from these so-called bugs? The word processing program used to write this book has had major defects for years. On average, several times per hour a cut and paste sends the word processor into an infinite loop. I have to go to the operating system control panel to manually terminate the editor and then restart, losing all changes since the last save. My survival tactic is to always save before every cut/paste to minimize lost work.

It's well beyond the time when being cute is appropriate. We need to be blunt:

> *"Stop calling them bugs. We need to call them what they really are: developer malpractice."*

1.11.2 You Want It When?

Quality issues aside, consider cost and schedule. The mantra across the software industry is:

> *"We need it quicker than that."*
> *"We need it NOW!"*
> *"We need it YESTERDAY!"*

---

58 "An unusual bug on Facebook briefly labelled many people as dead... The error on Friday caused the social network to show a memorial banner on user profiles for people who were still alive." See http://www.bbc.com/news/technology-37957593
59 See also, for example, [Selwood12].

The irony is exquisite when you realize that more than half of a typical software organizations' capacity is wasted: R%. If by using model-based software engineering, cost and schedule can be cut in half, why the reluctance to adopt? Look how many development resources could be freed by reducing maintenance. You want it quicker and cheaper? You *can* have quicker and cheaper. You just can't develop and maintain it the same way it's always been done. Can you afford *not* to adopt model-based software engineering?

1.11.3 The Ultimate Goal of Model-Based Software Engineering

I have been unable to find the source of the following quote, but it perfectly summarizes the ultimate goal of model-based software engineering:

> *"... change the nature of programming from a private, puzzle solving activity to a public, mathematics based activity of translating specifications into programs ... that can be expected to both run and do the right thing with little or no debugging."*

This book not only shows that software *can* be developed and maintained under a true engineering discipline; it shows precisely how to make that happen.

> *"We <u>can</u> engineer high quality software quickly and easily."*

It *is* well within our industry's grasp to build high-quality software, quickly and cheaply, much quicker and cheaper than we are doing it now, to be sure. This book explains how.

2

The Nature of Code

This chapter explains the nature of software: lines of code that developers write. This chapter starts by defining the terms syntax and semantics and explains why they are important to software development and maintenance. The nature of code is derived from these definitions. The role of semantic models in software development and maintenance is also described, and important implications of the nature of code are presented.

2.1 Syntax and Semantics in Natural Languages

Understanding the nature of code requires understanding the terms "syntax" and "semantics" and how they relate to software. Start with natural languages, like English. Table 2.1 shows sentences in three languages.

Sentence S1 should be obvious. S2 is probably not obvious to most readers because it's Chinese. The first two characters, "天空" (pronounced "tiānkōng" in Mandarin[1]), mean "sky." The third character, "是" ("shì"), is the verb "is." The next character, "蓝" ("lán"), means "blue." The last two characters, "色的" ("sè de"), mean "colored." The meaning of sentence S2 is "天空 (sky) 是 (is) 蓝 (blue) 色的 (colored)" or "The sky is blue."

S3 is probably even less obvious because it's Korean. The first two symbols, "하늘" ("ha nul"), mean "sky." The third symbol, "은" ("un"), marks the preceding noun as the subject of the sentence. The next two symbols, "파란" ("pa ran"), mean "blue." The next symbol, "색" ("saek"), mean "color." The final two symbols, "이다" ("i da"), are the verb "is."

Semantics is meaning. Sentences S1, S2, and S3 have the same semantics: they have the same meaning. Syntax, on the other hand, is structure: how words are assembled into sentences. To an English speaker learning Chinese, and to a Chinese speaker learning English, the syntax of English is close to the syntax of

---

1 All dialects of Chinese—Mandarin, Jin, Wu, Min, Xiang, Hakka, etc.—use essentially the same character set (ignoring simplified vs. traditional), but pronunciation varies.

How to Engineer Software: A Model-Based Approach, First Edition. Steve Tockey.
© 2019 the IEEE Computer Society, Inc. Published 2019 by John Wiley & Sons, Inc.

Table 2.1 Sentences in three languages.

No.	Sentence
S1	"The sky is blue"
S2	"天空是蓝色的"
S3	"하늘은 파란색이다"

Table 2.2 Three more sentences.

No.	Sentence
S4	"I give you this book"
S5	"我给你这本书"
S6	"나는 당신에게 책을 줍니다"

Chinese. Words usually appear in the same order in both languages. There are variations, of course. English tends to express subject first, and Chinese tends to express time and place first. In Korean, word order is very different: the verb is always at the end of the sentence. Table 2.2 shows another example.

S4 is again obvious. In S5 (Chinese) the first character, "我" ("wǒ"), is "I." The next character, "给" ("gěi"), is the verb "give." The next character, "你" ("nǐ"), is "you." The next two characters, "这本" ("zhè běn"), are "this." The last character, "书" ("shū"), is "book." To construct an equivalent Chinese sentence, the English speaker usually only has to start with the English sentence and substitute words: "我 (I) 给 (give) 你 (you) 这本 (this) 书 (book)."

English speakers learning Korean—and, conversely, Korean speakers learning English—aren't so lucky because word substitution doesn't work. Korean sentences are structured very different from English and Chinese. In S6 the first symbol, "나" ("na"), is "I." The second symbol, "는" ("nun"), marks the preceding noun as the subject of this sentence.[2] The next two symbols, "당신" ("dang shin"), are "you." The next two symbols, "에게" ("eh geh"), are the indirect object marker, in this case combining with the preceding "당신" ("you") to mean "to you, as indirect object." The next symbol, "책" ("chaek"), is book. The next symbol, "을" ("ul"), is the direct object marker, in this case combining with the preceding "책" ("book") to mean "book, as direct object." The final three symbols, "줍니다" ("jum ni da"), are the verb "give." To construct the equivalent

2 Note that "은" ("un") and "는" ("nun") are both sentence-subject markers, nouns that end in a consonant use "은" ("un") and nouns that ends in a vowel use "는" ("nun").

Table 2.3 One more sentence.

No.	Sentence
S7	"Colorless green dreams sleep furiously"

Korean sentence, a different word order is needed: "나는 (I, as subject) 당신에게 (to you, as indirect object) 책을 (book, as direct object) 줍니다 (give)."

The verb is always at the end of the sentence in Korean. If the verb were anywhere else, someone fluent in Korean would be confused. "나는 (I, as subject) 줍니다 (give) 책을 (book, as direct object) 당신에게 (to you, as indirect object)" would be as odd to someone fluent in Korean as "I to you book give" is in English.

Table 2.3 shows a sentence attributed to linguist Noam Chomsky.

S7 satisfies all rules of English syntax; it has a subject, a verb, and a predicate—all in proper order. It is a correctly structured sentence. But what does it mean? It is syntactically correct, but semantically meaningless.

2.2 Syntax and Semantics in Programming Languages

Just like natural languages, programming languages—and the code written by developers—have both syntax and semantics. Traditionally there has been an overemphasis on programming language syntax and an underemphasis on semantics. Consider Code Sample 2.1, an operation in real-world code. The Unified Modeling Language (UML) uses the term "operation" to represent functionality visible on the interface of a class. "Method" refers to lines of executable code that implement an operation. This terminology was deliberately chosen to emphasize abstraction and encapsulation. This book adopts the same view and uses the same vocabulary.

Code Sample 2.1 An Example Operation from Production Code

```
public static boolean isLanguageInstalled (LanguageCode l, boolean b) {

  // some method implementation goes here

}
```

This code runs in a particular vendor's internationalized office automation equipment. As shown earlier, English and Chinese are largely syntactically the same. But creating output text for, say, an error message requires a different sentence structure when the device has been localized to Korean. This operation exists in generic framework code to allow device-specific code to query if a particular localization—there can be more than one installed at a time—is present in this office automation device.

An operation's "signature" is the operation's name, return type(s), and ordered list of parameters and types—as shown in Code Sample 2.1. An operation's signature is just a syntactic declaration of the interface. The compiler/linker[3] is perfectly happy to accept any call that matches this syntax. The behavior (semantics) of the operation should at least be implied by the operation and parameter names, but precise behavior is not specified. The problem is when a caller's expectation of semantics (behavior) differs from the actual semantics.

For the sake of argument, assume that type LanguageCode is equivalent to type int, meaning that there are (in Java) about 4.3 billion possible values for the l parameter. But there clearly aren't 4.3 billion written languages on Earth; only about 220 languages are used by more than 1 million people. The vast majority of values in type LanguageCode do not correspond to any existing written language. As long as client code gives an l value corresponding to an actual written language, then the operation probably behaves properly. But what if client code provides an l value that doesn't correspond to any known language? Would the operation return "false?" Or would it do something else—possibly completely unexpected—like crashing because of an unhandled "array index out of bounds" exception?

In the vast majority of mainstream software organizations, the only way for a client developer to be sure of the semantics of a called operation is to read the called operation's method code. While that may seem reasonable on the surface, at a minimum it destroys encapsulation (explained in Chapter 3). Client code is now written with knowledge of server code; client code is almost certainly more tightly coupled to server code than it should be.

2.2.1 Effect of Maintenance

Even if the original client developer is careful to not tightly couple, what will happen under long-term maintenance. It is certainly possible—and highly likely in my experience—that a maintainer will unknowingly make a change to either client code or server code that introduces semantic inconsistency.

---

3 Or interpreter. Since compiled languages are far more common, I will refer to them but imply interpreters as well.

The compiler/linker—and any static or dynamic code analysis tool, for that matter—only enforces syntactic consistency and is of essentially no help in recognizing semantic inconsistency.

Based on my more than 40 years of experience in the software industry, I am willing to claim:

- A significant fraction of software defects are rooted in semantic inconsistencies between client code and server code.
- These semantic inconsistencies are amazingly difficult to isolate and correct.

The remedy for this underemphasis on code semantics is "design by contract."

2.3 Design by Contract™ and Software Semantics

Bertrand Meyer first published Design by Contract[4] in the early 1990s.[5] Under design by contract, an operation provides a "contract," which has two parts[6]:

- A *"requires" or "preconditions" clause*—Conditions that are the responsibility of the client program(mer) to assure before calling this operation
- A *"guarantees" or "postconditions" clause*—Conditions that are the responsibility of the server program(mer) to make true by the time this operation completes

The term "contract" is intentional; a software contract is like a legal contract. A legal contract has two parts:

- *What one of the parties must do*—A legal contract might assert that a building contractor will remodel a homeowner's kitchen using appropriate materials and workmanship within a specified time.
- *What the other party must do in exchange*—That homeowner will pay an agreed sum of money to the contractor on completion.

If the contractor remodels the kitchen as agreed, then the homeowner is legally bound to pay the agreed amount. However, just as important, if the contractor uses substandard materials or workmanship, or does not complete on time, the homeowner is not necessarily obliged to pay.

---

4 ™ Trademark Eiffel Software. All further references to design by contract assume the reader is aware of trademark status.

5 See, for example, [Meyer92].

6 Design by contract also includes "class invariants," but they are not relevant here. Class invariants are discussed in Chapter 16. See, for example, https://www.eiffel.com/values/design-by-contract/introduction

In software, conditions in the requires clause of an operation typically specify:

- *Constraints on input parameters*—for example, "the amount to deposit must be in US dollars, between $0.01 and $100,000.00"
- *Constraints on state*—for example, "the log file must be opened for write" or "the buffer cannot be full"

Conditions in the guarantees clause typically specify:

- *Constraints on output parameters, including meaning*—for example, "returns true only when successful, otherwise ..."
- *Constraints on state*—for example, "the log file has been closed for write"
- *Errors/exceptions*—for example, "throws AccountNotOpen when ..." or "returns -1 when ..."
- *Possibly, performance limits*—for example, "uses no more than 200 bytes per instance" or "returns in 25mSec or less"

The contract for isLanguageInstalled() can be specified as in-line comments in the operation header, as shown in Code Sample 2.2. To be more precise, the set of valid language codes needs to be either listed or referenced.

The client program(mer) is now aware of what needs to be true before isLanguageInstalled() can be called. They also know what will be true when the operation returns. The signature declares the syntax of the interface; the contract completes that by declaring semantics. By exporting a signature and contract (through code documentation generation tools like JavaDoc, Doxygen, or any equivalent), the client program(mer) knows precisely the syntax and semantics of that operation without having to read method implementation or—worse yet—guess.

Code Sample 2.2 An Example Operation with Its Contract

```
public static boolean isLanguageInstalled (LanguageCode l, boolean b) {
// requires
//    l refers to a valid, recognized written language
// guarantees
//    if the language package identified by l is present
//       then TRUE will be returned
//       otherwise FALSE will be returned

  // some method implementation goes here
}
```

If any "requires" condition is not satisfied, the client program(mer) knows nothing. Execution is now in a logically indeterminate state. The server method can do whatever it wants—up to and including crashing the system—and it is not the fault of the server code. Just as when the building contractor didn't remodel the kitchen as agreed, the other party is free of obligations. The homeowner may be unlikely to pay nothing, but they are certainly in a position to negotiate paying far less. The calling program(mer) was told explicitly what they needed to do and failed to do it. It's the same with a bridge that has a maximum weight limit; we don't blame the bridge designer or bridge builder if a bridge collapses under the load of too heavy a truck. We blame the truck driver for not obeying explicitly stated constraints. The relationship between design by contract and defensive programming is discussed in Chapter 3 and in Chapter 16.

2.4   Liskov Substitutability and Software Semantics

Barbara Liskov and Jeannette Wing published "Liskov substitutability" in the mid-1990s.[7] Remember the compiler/linker only cares about syntactic compatibility and design by contract shows how semantic compatibility matters too. "Liskov substitutability" formalizes semantic compatibility. Figure 2.1 shows an example of three inheritance-related classes.

Formally, Liskov substitutability says,

> *"If T is superclass of S, then objects of class T in a program may be replaced with objects of class S without altering any desirable properties of that program (e.g., correctness)."*

Figure 2.1 Three superclass–subclass-related classes.

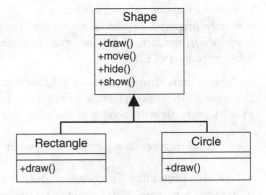

---

7 See, for example, [Liskov94].

Said more plainly,

> *"Client code that is written to the interface (both syntax and semantics) of class Shape must behave correctly when it encounters any object of class Rectangle or Circle."*

For Rectangle and Circle to guarantee correctness with respect to Shape, three conditions must hold:

- *Requires (preconditions) clauses for operations on a subclass may be as strict or less strict than those on the superclass, but they cannot be more strict*—If Shape.draw() requires "an open graphics palette exists," then Circle.draw() probably also requires the same. Circle.draw() could be written so that if no graphics palette were open, then it would just open one and draw there. Shape.draw()'s client code will still work. If such functionality exists in Circle.draw(), it would simply be unusable by clients of Shape.draw(). Circle.draw() cannot require any more than the open graphics palette because client code for Shape may not satisfy that extra requirement.

- *Guarantees (postconditions) clauses for operations on a subclass may be as strict or more strict than those on the superclass, but they cannot be less strict*—If Shape.draw() guarantees "the visible portion of the shape appears in the open graphics palette," then Circle.draw() must also guarantee at least that. In fact, Circle.draw() guarantees that "the visible portion of the circle appears in the open graphics palette," which is more restrictive because "circle" is more specific than "shape." Circle.draw() cannot guarantee any less than the "the visible portion of the shape appears" because client code for Shape may not be prepared to handle that.

- *No new exceptions are introduced in the subclass*—If the client program(mer) is only prepared to handle exceptions thrown by operations of Shape, it would—by definition—be unprepared to handle any new exceptions thrown by operations of Circle.

As long as these three conditions hold for every operation on a subclass, then client code that works correctly with objects of the superclass is also guaranteed to work correctly with objects of the subclass. Meyer summarized,

> *"A subclass must require no more and promise no less than its superclass."*

Liskov substitutability is normally described and applied only in terms of inheritance (superclass–subclass) relationships, but is not limited to only that case. It can also be applied to any interface, as will be shown in Part III.

2.4.1 An Example of Non-substitutability

An intentionally extreme counterexample illustrates the importance of Liskov substitutability. Imagine a developer writes code for a class, "WildWestGunfighter." Clint Eastwood's characters in the classic Western movies *The Good, the Bad and the Ugly, A Fistful of Dollars*, and *For a Few Dollars More* could be example objects of this class. WildWestGunfighters can move(), hide(), and show(). They can also draw(). The syntax of the interface of Shape is identical to the syntax of the interface of WildWestGunfighter. The compiler/linker would have no complaints about making WildWestGunfighter a subclass of Shape.

But consider operation WildWestGunfighter.draw(). It requires a pistol in the holster on the gunfighter's hip, and it guarantees the pistol is out of the holster aimed at a target (presumably another WildWestGunfighter), with this gunfighter ready to pull the trigger. Imagine client code that has been written to the interface (again, both syntax and semantics) of Shape. What happens when it encounters an object of class WildWestGunfighter? The client code is almost certainly not prepared to make sure there is a pistol in the holster on the gunfighter's hip. Nor is it likely prepared to deal with a gun being aimed rather than a shape being rendered in an open graphics palette. Syntactically, shapes and gunfighters are indistinguishable. The compiler/linker can't tell them apart, but semantically they are very different. This situation has been called "accidental polymorphism." The compiler/linker only cares about syntactic compatibility; semantic compatibility is the developer's responsibility.

2.5 The Importance of Semantics in Programming

Developers are forced by the compiler to pay attention to syntax: violate a syntax rule and the code won't compile. Syntax can't be ignored; the compiler guarantees it. But if developers focus too much on syntax, for example, operation interface syntax, they leave the door wide open to semantic inconsistencies.

The compiler is of little to no help with semantics. In fact, code defects ("bugs") are simply semantic inconsistencies between how stakeholders want code to behave and how it actually behaves. Recall the statement "Colorless green dreams sleep furiously." It is syntactically correct but semantically meaningless. It is analogous to defective software: the code is syntactically correct (or it wouldn't compile), but it is semantically meaningless in light of behavior the stakeholders want. Debugging means trying to root out all those pesky semantic inconsistencies.

> *"Semantic inconsistencies are code defects. Code defects are semantic inconsistencies. They are one and the same thing."*

It should now start to become clear why mainstream software is as defective as it is, given how little attention is paid to code semantics. It's no wonder our industry has to depend so much on testing to give even a faint glimmer of hope that code will work. It's no wonder that faint glimmer of hope is crushed when the harsh realities of production are encountered. Software semantics is not only as important as software syntax, but also it is more important. Software correctness depends on semantics. The compiler/linker forces developers to pay attention to syntax; otherwise code won't compile. Developers can choose to pay attention to semantics or they can choose not to. If they underemphasize semantics, they do so at their own risk and, unfortunately, at the risk of users who have to deal with defective software.

2.6   Software Automates "Business"

All nontrivial software exists to automate some kind of business: that software is intended to enforce some set of policies and/or carry out some set of processes. The term "business" is used loosely here. Operating systems and user interface (UI) toolkits both enforce certain policies and carry out certain processes, so they too automate a "business"—however abstract that business might be.

Banking software would involve policies like the following:

- *Each savings account must have a balance.*
- *Each savings account must have an overdraft limit.*
- *The status of each savings account can only be normal or overdrawn.*
- *Each savings account must be owned by at least one customer.*
- *A customer must own at least one bank account, but may own many.*
- *A customer's date of birth cannot be later than today.*
- *...*

Banking software would involve processes like the following:

- *Create a customer.*
- *Open a savings account.*
- *Deposit money into a savings account.*
- *See how much money is in a savings account.*
- *Withdraw money from a savings account.*
- *Transfer money from one savings account to another.*
- *Close a savings account.*
- *Etc.*

The business being automated might be obscure, but there is definitely still a "business." Take Transmission Control Protocol[8] (TCP) as another example. Business policies in TCP include:

---

8 See, for example, [IETF98].

- *A TCP connection connects exactly one TCP user to exactly one TCP port.*
- *Every TCP connection has exactly one state.*
- *Allowable values for connection state are "listen," "syn sent," "established," "closing," etc.*
- *A segment must either be incoming or outgoing.*
- *Etc.*

TCP's business processes involve things like the following:

- *Open a connection (session).*
- *Send a segment.*
- *If a segment time-to-live expires, delete that segment.*
- *Receive a segment.*
- *Close a connection.*
- *Etc.*

Even the game Angry Birds™ has policies and processes:

- *Birds can be launched into pigs, not into other birds.*
- *A player has only one high score.*
- *A player's high score cannot be negative.*
- *Launch a bird (with consequences based on what the bird hit when it lands).*
- *Reset a player's high score.*
- *Etc.*

Separating policies and processes to be automated from automation technology is covered in Chapter 4.

Given that nontrivial software exists to automate some business, it follows that:

> *"For software developers to be successful automating someone's business, those developers need to understand that business at least as well as—if not better than—the business experts understand it.[9]"*

Policies and processes automated in software can be very complex, and we tend to be bad at communicating with the necessary level of precision and completeness. So it should be no surprise that the biggest problem in mainstream software development is vague, ambiguous, and incomplete requirements.

---

9 To the extent that business is being automated, a developer doesn't need a PhD in Aeronautical Engineering to develop software for computational fluid dynamics (CFD) simulation of flight; however they do need to know everything about the CFD that is being automated. The developer needs to know what CFD means and how it is to be done (e.g., Eulerian vs. Lagrangian); they don't need to know why it is being done that specific way and not some other way as the PhD would.

2.7 Model-Based Software Requirements

"Model-based software requirements"—specifying software functional requirements in models rather than natural language—have existed since the 1970s; the idea itself is not at all new. The difference is in how those requirements are modeled. While there are many approaches, this book will focus on four primary components:

- Use case diagram
- Class model
- Interaction diagrams
- State models

Each is introduced here; full details are presented in Part II.

Start with a very simple mythical example, Silly Bank, to introduce modern model-based requirements and the four primary components. In the business of Silly Bank, three kinds of things are important:

- *Customers*—Persons or businesses that own savings accounts. Customers can deposit money into, see the balance of, and withdraw money from savings accounts they own.
- *Tellers*—Bank employees who can deposit money into, see the balance of, and withdraw money from savings accounts on behalf of the owning customer. Tellers can also open and close savings accounts, but customers cannot open or close savings accounts themselves.
- *Silly Savings Accounts*—Money that customers have on deposit at Silly Bank. Savings accounts have a balance and an overdraft limit. The balance is established when the account is opened. Depositing increases the balance by the amount deposited. Withdrawing decreases the balance by the amount withdrawn. There are three additional constraints. One constraint is that if the balance falls below $0, then that account is considered overdrawn and no more money can be withdrawn. Money can only be deposited into an overdrawn account until the balance rises back over $0. Another constraint is that the balance is never allowed to fall below an overdraft limit specified for that account. The last constraint is that overdrawn accounts cannot be closed. When a non-overdrawn account is closed, the account's balance is refunded to the owning customer.

Of course, no real bank would operate this way; this is only intended to illustrate policies, processes, and software requirements models.

2.7.1 Model-Based Requirements: Use Case Diagram

The first component is the "use case diagram." This diagram communicates scope and context. Scope is described by a set of use cases; context is described by a set of actors. Figure 2.2 shows a use case diagram for Silly Bank.

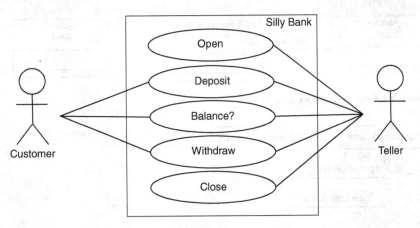

Figure 2.2 Use case diagram for Silly Bank.

The context of Silly Bank's business is defined in terms of two actors: customers and tellers. The scope of Silly Bank's business is described in terms of five use cases: opening, depositing, seeing a balance, withdrawing, and closing accounts. One can presume that use cases define the scope of functionality software is to deliver and the context is the real-world entities that will interact with the delivered software. For various technical and economic reasons, the software does not always implement all scope and context in the use case diagram, but it is usually a safe assumption. Use case diagrams are explained in Chapter 7.

2.7.2 Model-Based Requirements: Class Model

The second is the "class model." The class model defines significant elements of the structure of the business together with important relationships between those elements. The class model is a precise specification of policies to be enforced. Each of the Silly Bank policy statements earlier would appear as elements in this model. Figure 2.3 shows a class diagram for Silly Bank.

The class diagram in Figure 2.3 shows the three main elements of business structure: Customers, Tellers, and Silly Savings Accounts. The diagram shows an important relationship between Customers and Silly Savings Accounts, namely, Customers' own savings accounts (or savings accounts are owned by customers). Example policies expressed in this diagram include the following:

- A Customer must own at least one Silly Savings Account; otherwise they are not a customer.
- A Customer may own many savings accounts at the same time.
- A Silly Savings Account must be owned by exactly one customer, never more and never less.

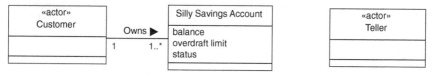

Figure 2.3 Class diagram for Silly Bank.

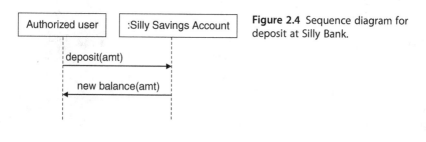

Figure 2.4 Sequence diagram for deposit at Silly Bank.

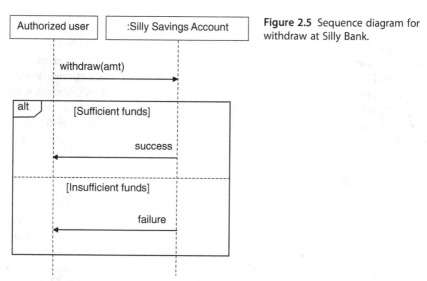

Figure 2.5 Sequence diagram for withdraw at Silly Bank.

- Every savings account has a balance, an overdraft limit, and a status.
- Etc.

Class models are covered in Chapter 8.

2.7.3 Model-Based Requirements: Interaction Diagrams

The third is the "interaction diagram." "Interaction diagram" is a general term that includes both sequence diagrams and communication diagrams. These diagrams describe business processes at an intermediate level. Figures 2.4 and 2.5

show example interaction diagrams, in this case sequence diagrams, for Silly Bank.

Figure 2.5 shows that when an authorized user (either a teller or the owner of that account) wants to withdraw some amount of money, two alternate outcomes are possible. When there are sufficient funds in the account, the withdraw will be successful, and the customer will get their money. If there are not sufficient funds, the customer will not get any money. Interaction diagrams are covered in Chapter 9.

2.7.4 Model-Based Requirements: State Models

The fourth and final component is the "state model." The state model is a precise specification of details of (a fragment) business process. The state model fills in detail underneath the process(es) identified in interaction models. As a specific example, the sequence diagram for the withdraw process of Silly Bank (Figure 2.5) only identifies two possible outcomes following a request to withdraw: success and failure. How to determine success or failure is only implied in the sequence diagram. Defining process at the fine-grained level is the role of the state model. Figure 2.6 shows the state diagram for Silly Savings Accounts.

The three transitions on the right-hand side of the state diagram—labeled (5), (6), and (7) in the annotated state diagram in Figure 2.9—precisely define three possibilities. One is that the account is in the normal state (its balance is positive) and the withdraw request is for an amount less than that balance (labeled

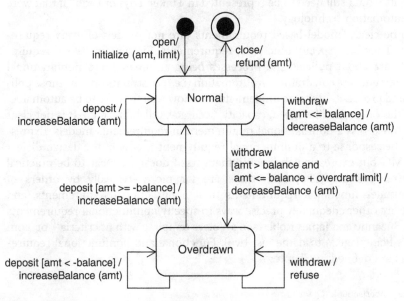

Figure 2.6 State diagram for Silly Savings Accounts.

(7) in Figure 2.9). The balance will be reduced, the requester will be given money, and the account will remain in the normal state. The second is that the account has a positive balance but the requester is asking for more than the balance (labeled (6) in Figure 2.9). Silly Bank will allow such withdraws as long as the amount being withdrawn won't cause the balance to be more negative than the overdraft limit. In this case, the balance will be reduced, and the requester will be given money, but now the account is in the overdrawn state. If the account is already in the overdrawn state, the request will be refused (labeled (5) in Figure 2.9). A different way of running the bank would, of course, lead to a different state model. State models are explained in Chapter 10.

2.7.5 No Automation Technology

These four components intentionally describe only policy and process, not automation technology. These components intentionally avoid bits, bytes, database tables, stored procedures, memory-resident C++ classes, data files, threads, network packets, cloud, and so on. Class Silly Savings Account in the requirements model does not represent a memory-resident Java or C++ class, a database table with stored procedures, etc. It simply defines a business concept that must be present in any correct automation of Silly Bank. Chapter 4 on functional and nonfunctional requirements gives an example of one particular business that is automated both as a smart phone app and in the children's construction toy, Tinker Toys™. The policy and process elements in these components would still need to be represented in Tinker Toys or Lego™ if that were the automation technology.

To be clear, "model-based requirements" are not models of every requirement. They only specify functional requirements. Simply, functional requirements are about policies and processes being automated and nonfunctional requirements are constraints on automation (i.e., constraints on how those policies and processes are to be implemented or how well they are to be automated: qualities of service like speed, capacity, accuracy, reliability, etc.). It is not clear how to express a nonfunctional requirement in requirements models. Expressing the response to a nonfunctional requirement is easy in the design dialect of UML, but expressing the requirement itself doesn't appear to be practical or even possible. That said, there are far more—typically by orders of magnitude—functional requirements than nonfunctional requirements, and there are other adequately precise ways to specify nonfunctional requirements (e.g., Suzanne and James Robertson's Volere template with fit criteria[10] or Tom Gilb's Planguage,[11] to name just two). Functional and nonfunctional requirements are defined in Chapter 4.

---

10 See [Robertson06].
11 See [Gilb05].

The four components form a semantic model of a business to automate, for example, Silly Bank. They precisely defined the following:

- *What it means to be a Silly Savings Account*
- *What it means to deposit money into a Silly Savings Account*
- *What it means to withdraw money from a Silly Savings Account*
- *Etc.*

The class model is a semantic model of policies to enforce. The use case diagram, interaction diagrams, and state models are semantic models—at differing levels of detail—of processes to carry out. The use case diagram is the most coarse grained, the interaction diagrams are at an intermediate level, and state models are the most fine grained.

2.8 Semantic Models of Automation Technology

Not only can we model the semantics of a business, but we can also model the semantics of an automation technology: a programming language. Consider a semantic model of Java. The syntax of Java is precisely defined in the Java Language Specification.[12] A complete semantic model would be too large and complex for this book; however Figure 2.7 shows a partial use case diagram.

Figure 2.8 shows a class diagram covering a small portion of Java policy semantics.

Policies of Java expressed in Figure 2.8 include the following:

- *An entity type is either a primitive type or a class.*
- *A (sub)class may extend at most one (super)class.[13]*
- *A (super)class may be extended by zero to many (sub)classes.*
- *A class may be final or not.*
- *A class is implemented by one to many members.*
- *A member may not exist outside of a class.*
- *A member is either a variable or an operation.*
- *A member has a name.*
- *A member has an accessibility (public, protected, or private).*
- *A member may be static or not.*
- *An operation is implemented by zero to many statements.*
- *Every statement is in the implementation of exactly one operation.*
- *Every member has exactly one declared entity type.*

---

12 http://docs.oracle.com/javase/specs/
13 That is, single inheritance. A semantic model of C++ would allow a class to extend more than one class.

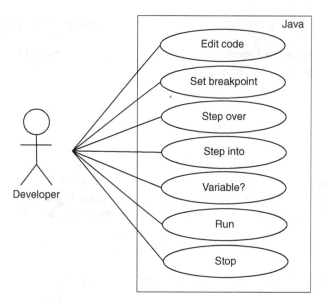

Figure 2.7 Partial use case diagram for Java development and maintenance.

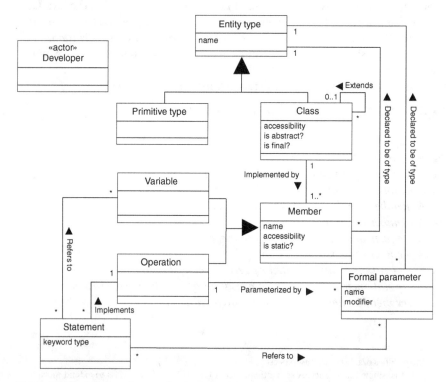

Figure 2.8 Partial class diagram for Java development and maintenance.

Not shown in Figure 2.8 are many additional policies—semantics—for Java:

- *A statement is either: assignment, if, for, while, switch/case, try, ... return, or a block.*
- *A block contains zero to many statements.*
- *An "if" statement must have a "then" clause but does not need to have an "else" clause.*
- *Etc.*

The semantic model of Java would also need to express process semantics such as the following:

- *The result of an assignment statement is to ....*
- *The order of operations in evaluating an expression is ....*
- *An expression using divide when the denominator is 0 results in NaN.*
- *Accessing a reference (a pointer) when its value is null results in throwing "NullPointerException."*
- *When executing a statement that includes "super.", the most immediate super-class' definition is used.*
- *The "then" clause on an "if" statement will only be executed when the logical expression evaluates to "true."*
- *Etc.*

A sequence diagram for the Run use case could start with, say, Jane (a developer) wanting to run her program, so main:Operation would see a Run message. main:Operation would find its first line of code, say, 1:Statement and signal for it to execute if it exists. Line of code 1:Statement might involve executing other operations on other classes if it included any invocations (message sends). On completion of 1:Statement, main:Operation would see if there was another line of code, say, 2:Statement, and signal for it to execute it if it exists. The cycle of sequential execution of statements continues until there are no more statements to execute, a breakpoint is hit, the developer signals "Stop," or an unhandled exception is encountered.

Today, developers build an implicit mental model of programming language semantics as they learn to program in that language. On the other hand, if language designers published an explicit semantic model, it could help avoid common misinterpretations of language elements as well as ensure that all compilers for that language behave in exactly the same way.

2.9 We're Finally Ready to Write Code

Silly Bank will be the business to automate and Java will be the automation technology. Start with a developer writing:

```
public class SillySavingsAccount {
}
```

This code maps—in the set theory sense—the business concept Silly Savings Account onto the Java technology concept Class and names that Java class SillySavingsAccount.[14]

When the developer writes

```
private double balance;
```

they are mapping the business concept Balance onto the Java technology concept instance variable, naming that instance variable balance, and further giving it the Java built-in data type double.

When the developer writes

```
private double overdraftLimit;
```

they are mapping the business concept Overdraft Limit onto the Java technology concept instance variable, giving that Java variable the name overdraftLimit, and further giving it the Java built-in data type double, too.

When the developer writes

```
private SillyStatus status;
```

they are mapping the business concept Status onto the Java technology concept instance variable, giving that Java variable the name status, and further giving it a custom type called SillyStatus. SillyStatus is presumably an enumerated type with values NORMAL and OVERDRAWN.

When the developer writes

```
public double withdraw ( double amt ) {
}
```

they are mapping the business process Withdraw onto the Java technology concept operation, giving that Java operation the name withdraw, and further declaring its return type to be double. The lines of code inside the withdraw () method would almost certainly include at least

```
if ( status == SillyStatus.NORMAL && amt <= balance ) {
    balance = balance - amount;
}
```

This code maps a transition in Silly Savings Account's state model that goes out of state Normal on event Withdraw onto Java's if decision construct. The

---

14 Credit for the insight of code being a mapping is due to Sally Shlaer and Steve Mellor.

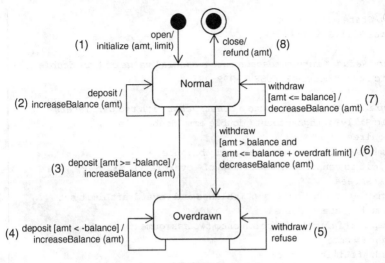

Figure 2.9 Annotated state diagram for Silly Savings Accounts.

assignment statement in the then clause maps the decrease in the balance (a transition action) onto Java's arithmetic subtraction.

Figure 2.9 is an annotated state model for Silly Savings Accounts to reference the state model elements as they are mapped onto Java.

Code Sample 2.3 is a complete mapping of Silly Savings Account onto Java. Each line of code is commented (above it, *in italics*) explaining the mapping.

Code Sample 2.3 Mapping Silly Savings Account to Java

```java
// map Silly Savings Account onto a Java class
public class SillySavingsAccount {

  // map the states of a Silly Savings Account onto an enum
  public enum SillyStatus { NORMAL, OVERDRAWN };

  // map Balance onto an instance variable of type double
  private double balance;

  //map Overdraft Limit onto an instance variable of type double
  private double overdraftLimit;
```

```
// map State onto the enum
private SillyStatus state;

// map "Refuse" return message onto a special value of type double
public static double REFUSE = -999.99;

// map initial state (1) onto a constructor with two parameters
public SillySavingsAccount ( double amt, double limit ) {
// requires
//   amt is consistent with range of .balance
//   limit is consistent with range of .overdraftLimit
// guarantees
//   one new account exists w/ .balance and .overdraftLimit set
//     and .state == Normal
  // map initialization action onto two assignments
  balance = amt;
  overdraftLimit = limit;
  // map resulting state onto enum value assignment
  state = SillyStatus.NORMAL;
}

// map deposit message onto a public operation with one parameter
public double deposit ( double amt ) {
// requires
//   amt is consistent with range of .balance
// guarantees
//   .balance has been increased by amt
//   when .state was Overdrawn and new balance is positive ➔
//       .state == Normal
//   .balance is returned
  // map transition actions 2,3,4 onto addition
  balance = balance + amt;
  // map transitions 2,3,4 onto enum value change as needed
  if ( balance >= 0.0 ) {
    // map transitions 2,3 onto change in enum value
    state = SillyStatus.NORMAL;
  } else {
    // map transition 4 onto change in enum value
    state = SillyStatus.OVERDRAWN;
  }
  // map reply message onto a return with value
  return balance;
}
```

```
//map withdraw message onto a public operation with 1 parameter
public double withdraw ( double amt ) {
// requires
//   amt is consistent with range of .balance
// guarantees
//   when .state was Normal and amt <= .balance →
//       .balance has been decreased by amt, .balance is returned
//   when .state was Normal and amt won't violate overdraft limit →
//       .balance have been decreased by amt, .state == Overdrawn,
//       .balance is returned
//   when .state was Overdrawn → "Refuse" is returned
  // map check for transition 7 onto an if statement
  if ( state == SillyStatus.NORMAL && amt <= balance ) {
   // map transition 7 action onto subtraction
   balance = balance - amt;
   // map transition 7 onto a change in enum value
   state = SillyStatus.NORMAL;
   // map reply message onto a return with value
   return balance;
  } else {
   // map check for transition 6 onto else & if
   if ( state == SillyStatus.NORMAL && amt <=
                            balance + overdraftLimit ) {
    // map transition 6 action onto subtraction
    balance = balance - amt;
    // map transition 6 onto change in enum value
    state = SillyStatus.OVERDRAWN;
    // map reply message onto a return with value
    return balance;
   } else {
    // map transition 5 onto remaining else clause
    // map reply message onto a return with unique value
    return REFUSE;
   }
  }
}

//map close message onto public operation
public double close () {
// requires
//   none
// guarantees
//   when .state was Normal → .balance is returned
//   when .state was Overdrawn → "Refuse" is returned
```

```
// map check for transition 8 onto if statement
if ( state == SillyStatus.NORMAL ) {
 // map reply message onto a return with value
 return balance;
} else {
 // map refusal to close onto a return with unique value
 return REFUSE;
 }
 }
}
```

2.9.1   Some Comments About the Sample Code

Some comments on the mapping in Code Sample 2.3 are needed:

- Invalid withdraw (transition (5) in Figure 2.9) could have been mapped onto an exception instead of returning an error code. This illustrates the kinds of choices developers need to make and is discussed further in Chapters 16 and 25.
- The final transition (transition (8)) is actually not correctly mapped because a run-time Java object doesn't go out of existence—get deleted—until its reference count is zero and the garbage collector reclaims the memory. A safer, more semantically correct mapping would add an additional enum state value, say, "DELETED," to signify that the business object has been marked for delete but the Java run-time object has not been deleted yet. This is an example of clashes between business semantics and not-exactly-equivalent automation technology semantics that can be a source of defects: as long as any other code still has a reference to this object, that code could potentially treat this object as a still opened Silly Bank Account because method code implementing the close() operation leaves the object state set to NORMAL.
- This Java code is not as efficient as it could be. This example tries to maintain as straightforward a mapping as possible from business onto automation technology. A more efficient implementation would obscure the mapping, making it harder to understand.

2.10   Code Is a Mapping

Lines of code are a mapping—in the set theory sense—from elements of the semantic model of business policies and processes onto elements of the semantic model of the technology. Chapters 15 and 16 on high-level design, Chapter 17 on detailed design and code, Chapter 19 on optimization, and

Chapter 20 on model compilation give additional insight into code as a mapping, along with many, and more comprehensive, examples.

2.10.1 Many Mappings Are Possible

For a given semantic model of a business and a given semantic model of a technology, many mappings are possible: there are many ways to code some business in some programming language. That said, three critical properties must be present in any correct mapping:

- *Sufficiently complete*—Every element in the semantic model of the business that stakeholders want automated needs to be mapped to at least one element of the semantic model of the technology. Nothing stakeholders want automated can be unmapped.
- *Preserve semantics*—All business policy and process semantics must be faithfully represented in technology semantics. As an example, Withdraw in the semantic model of Silly Bank is (partially) mapped onto arithmetic subtraction in Java. Mapping withdraw onto addition, multiplication, or division would be incorrect because they don't preserve Silly Bank's process semantics. Mapping amounts and account balances onto Java's type double is risky because floating point suffers from loss of precision when values are large: a real bank's business semantics would not be preserved. A real bank would use a special fixed point Money or Currency type to preserve business semantics.
- *Satisfy all nonfunctional requirements*—All nonfunctional requirements such as technology, performance, reliability, portability, scalability, accuracy, security, etc. are met.

Any mapping satisfying those three properties will—by definition—be a well-behaved computer program that automates that (semantic model of) business in terms of (the semantics of) that automation technology: the programming language.

Semantic models are not restricted to being expressed only in UML. Other semantic modeling languages are also possible, say, for example, a fast Fourier transform (FFT) algorithm, Kalman filtering, or any other computationally intensive numerical analysis technique could be expressed as mathematical formula. Also, I have only shown what happens to functional requirements. Assuming you are familiar with the Model-View-Controller architectural style, this shows what lines of code in Model region mean. View and Controller regions are also a mapping, but they map from a definition of an interface: wire frames, UI specs, low- or high-fidelity UI prototypes, etc. onto automation technology (e.g. a windowing toolkit such as Swing, Abstract Windowing Toolkit [AWT], etc.). View-controller region as a mapping from an interface specification is discussed in Chapters 15–17.

2.11   The Most Important Implication
of "Code Is a Mapping"

Once you accept that lines of code in Model region are a mapping from the semantic model of business policies and processes onto the semantic model of the technology that must satisfy the three properties, then a critical implication necessarily follows.

> *"How can software developers successfully automate complex business policies and processes without a complete, consistent, clear, concise, precise, unambiguous, and validated semantic model of those policies and processes?"*

Real-world policies and processes are far too complex for developers to keep straight in their head. Without a complete, consistent, clear, concise, precise, unambiguous, and validated semantic model of a complex business (or external interface, for View-controller region code) as an anchor point, the mapping—the code—will be equally incomplete, inconsistent, and incorrect. The code will have semantic inconsistencies (defects, bugs) because policy and process semantics have not been clearly defined, communicated, or validated. The root of most software defects is simply incomplete, inconsistent, ambiguous, misunderstood, or incorrect business policy and process semantics. Most remaining defects are incorrect mappings of policy and process semantics onto technology semantics—the business semantic was not preserved. The remaining defects are in not satisfying one or more nonfunctional requirements. Part II explains how to build semantic models, and Part III explains how to map semantic models onto automation technology while preserving business policy and process semantics.

2.12   Summary

Syntax is about structure—how things are arranged. Semantics is about what those things mean. Programming languages, as well as code written by developers, have both syntax and semantics. Compilers are ruthless enforcers of syntax but offer little to no help with semantics.

An operation's signature is a syntactic declaration of its interface; a contract is needed to define semantics. Liskov substitutability principle (LSP) is an example of the importance of code semantics. Accidental polymorphism happens when there is syntactic consistency but semantic inconsistency. Compilers don't prevent, or even identify, semantic inconsistency; it's entirely up to developers to manage semantics.

Nontrivial software exists to automate a business: it needs to enforce policies and carry out processes. If software developers hope to successfully automate a business, they have to understand it at least as well—if not better—than the business experts understand it. We can build semantic models of businesses to capture, communicate, and validate a complete and consistent understanding of policies and processes the stakeholders want automated. We can also build a semantic model of the automation technology: the programming language.

The code that developers write must map—in the set theory sense—elements of the semantic model of the business onto elements of the semantic model of the technology. That mapping must be:

- Sufficiently complete
- Preserve semantics
- Satisfy all nonfunctional requirements

Any mapping that satisfies these properties is, by definition, a well-behaved computer program that automates the specified business semantics in terms of the technology semantics.

Semantic inconsistencies in code are defects. Defects are semantic inconsistencies. They are one and the same. If you want to avoid defects in code, then you need to pay close attention to policy and process semantics and to properly mapping those onto technology semantics.

3

Fundamental Principles

This book explains how to develop and maintain software using model-based software engineering. This chapter explains how to do it *well*. Remember from Chapter 1:

Engineering = scientific theory + practice + engineering economy

This chapter is about software engineering practice. Fundamental principles described in this chapter include:

- Focus on semantics
- Control complexity
- Use appropriate abstractions
- Encapsulate accidental complexity
- Maximize cohesion and minimize coupling
- Design to invariants and design for change
- Avoid premature design and optimization
- Name things carefully

The chapter closes with a discussion of how these fundamental principles relate to the SOLID principles created by Robert ("Uncle Bob") Martin.

3.1 Focus on Semantics

This first fundamental principle was covered in Chapter 2. Specifically, the semantic model is intended to be exactly a complete, consistent, clear, concise, precise, unambiguous, and validated specification of policy and process semantics. Design by contract and Liskov substitutability are two of several ways to focus on semantics in design and code. Programming by intent, assertions, and proof of correctness are other ways that are described in Chapter 18. It is also important to understand that code is a mapping from those policy and process semantics onto automation technology (i.e., programming

How to Engineer Software: A Model-Based Approach, First Edition. Steve Tockey.
© 2019 the IEEE Computer Society, Inc. Published 2019 by John Wiley & Sons, Inc.

language) semantics. As long as you do all of these, then you have an adequate focus on semantics.

3.2 Control Complexity

Software complexity comes at a cost:

- More complex things cost more and take longer to understand, design, and build.
- More complex things cost more and take longer to maintain.
- More complex things tend to have more defects, further increasing cost and time to maintain.

An increase in defects leads to a decrease in user perception of quality. More defects also mean higher maintenance cost and effort to fix those defects. The decrease in user perception of quality and the increase in maintenance both have economic implications. And this says nothing about damage caused: how much valuable user time, effort, data, etc. were lost due to a defect while the software was used in production?

3.2.1 Essential Versus Accidental Complexity

Software complexity comes in two forms: essential and accidental.[1] Essential complexity is in the problem space: it is in the policies and processes being automated. Consider TurboTax™[2] by Intuit.[3] This software automates personal income tax preparation in a wide variety of jurisdictions; one is for the US Internal Revenue Service. Personal income tax law at the US federal level is quite complex.[4] Despite that complexity, TurboTax has to automate as much as possible. Nothing anyone at Intuit can do would ever reduce the complexity of US federal income tax law. That is entirely the responsibility of the US government. The same can be said for versions of TurboTax for each of the states that levy personal income tax. Also, there are versions of TurboTax for Revenue Canada and for each Canadian province that levies personal income tax. At best, essential complexity can only be managed.

---

1 The terms "essential" and "accidental" come out of Greek philosophy. See, for example, https://plato.stanford.edu/entries/essential-accidental/.
2 http://www.turbotax.com/
3 http://www.intuit.com/
4 See, for example, http://www.irs.gov/Tax-Professionals/Tax-Code,-Regulations-and-Official-Guidance.

The other kind of complexity is accidental: in the solution space. Threaded code is more complex than non-threaded code. Caching, data compression, data de-normalization, and making software scalable are other examples of solution space complexities. Structural complexity, as described in Appendix N, is also in the solution space. These have nothing to do with the policies and processes being automated and everything to do with how the developers are doing that automation.

3.2.2 Necessary Versus Unnecessary Accidental Complexity

Accidental complexity itself comes in two forms: necessary and unnecessary. Necessary accidental complexity is unavoidable due to nontrivial performance requirements. Without that solution space complexity, the software would not satisfy stakeholder requirements.

Unnecessary accidental complexity, on the other hand, is solution space complexity that is not helping to meet any performance requirement. Imagine a developer is taking evening classes in a computer science or software engineering degree program at a local university. Assume that last night's lecture was on how to write threaded code. What is the most likely thing that developer will do at work the next day? They will add threading to their code, even though it is completely unnecessary. The only one benefiting is that developer because now they can claim on their resume,[5] "Writes threaded production code." Everyone else is left to deal with code that doesn't need to be as complex as it is. Remember that it took more time (thus costing more) to put threading in. It will take longer (thus costing more) for other developers to figure out why the code is threaded when it really doesn't need to be. Also, threaded code is more defect prone because of increased complexity—increasing long-term cost and schedule by having the team tied up fixing more defects. Technical debt can be considered unnecessary accidental complexity.

Refactoring[6] is generally intended to reduce unnecessary accidental complexity. Developers should strive to eliminate unnecessary accidental complexity at every reasonable opportunity. In fact, developers should strive to keep it out in the first place. As for essential complexity and necessary accidental complexity, the best that can be done is to manage it.

> *"You can never eliminate complexity. The best you can do is to eliminate unnecessary accidental complexity, and manage as much of the remaining complexity as you can: by reducing the amount you have to deal with at any one time."*

---

5 Or curriculum vitae (CV), outside of North America.
6 See, for example, [Fowler99].

3.2.3 Economic Implications of Complexity

Complexity—in all forms—has clear economic implications, some positive and some negative. Adding loan processing functionality to Silly Bank's software clearly adds essential (and, almost certainly, accidental) complexity. On the other hand, it should be safe to assume the added value far outweighs its cost. The same can be said for necessary accidental complexity: its presence comes at a cost but that cost is outweighed by the value of meeting performance requirements.

The same cannot be said for unnecessary accidental complexity. That complexity is also coming at a cost: the cost to put it there in the first place. Not only is there no business benefit, but also there is a business *dis*benefit. Additional maintenance cost and schedule comes from needing to fix additional defects. And again, this is not considering damage caused by those defects in terms of time and value lost when a user encounters the defect.

It has been said many times:

> "*Do the simplest possible thing that would work.*"

This view, while inviting, is unfortunately too simplistic. Rather,

> "*Do the most cost-effective thing stakeholders can afford, considering the expected service life of the software.*"

Unless the value of added complexity sufficiently outweighs the cost of it being there, that complexity should not be added—and should be removed if already present—assuming, of course, that the cost of removing it is sufficiently less than the cost of leaving it in. Economic analysis of technical alternatives, like adding functionality to a project, is explained in any good engineering economy textbook.[7]

The remaining principles are subordinate to controlling complexity, as they are all ways to:

- Manage essential complexity
- Manage necessary accidental complexity
- Eliminate unnecessary accidental complexity

3.3 Use Appropriate Abstractions

Abstraction can be defined as[8]:

> "*The principle of ignoring those aspects of a subject that are not relevant to the current purpose in order to concentrate solely on those that are.*"

---

7 For example, [Tockey05].
8 See, for example, [Oxford97].

Literally, abstraction is "permission to ignore." Consider the following line of code in a generic programming language:

```
putc('f');
```

As most developers can assume, executing this line of code would cause the letter "f" to appear on the console terminal. Easy. But how many lines of run-time library and operating system code are between the `putc('f');` and the letter "f" actually appearing on the console? Easily hundreds if not thousands of lines are involved in a typical input/output (I/O) subsystem. This is due to complexities of output queuing, character rendering, hardware synchronization, and so on. Does the developer who wrote this one line care? No. This is abstraction in action: all that other complexity can be ignored and the developer can focus on what they want—outputting the letter "f." This is abstracting the solution (operating system and I/O subsystem complexity, in this case) away from the problem at hand.

3.3.1 Abstracting Away Implementation Technology

Model-based software engineering intentionally abstracts automation technology away from the semantic model. Abstracting away solution complexities allows focus solely on understanding the policies and processes to be automated completely, consistently, clearly, concisely, and correctly and not be distracted by (at that time) irrelevant technical details. This is discussed in the next chapter.

3.3.2 Abstracting Away Business Details

Another is abstraction in the problem (policy and process) space. I have a bank account, in fact several. Most adults have one or more bank accounts. It would be impractical to specify each individual account separately—thus the concept of a class in object-oriented software[9]:

> *"A class is an abstraction of a set of existing or potential business-relevant things that are subject to the same policies, processes, and constraints."*

The class Silly Savings Account in the previous chapter is based on abstracting away account-specific details like a particular balance, a particular overdraft limit, and a particular status. That class is a cookie cutter-like template representing all possible savings accounts at Silly Bank. As long as any new savings account is subject to the same policies, processes, and constraints of Silly Savings Account, the bank can use that template to create a new savings account whenever they need.

---

9 This definition is from [Shlaer88].

Abstraction is, in my opinion, the single most powerful complexity management tool software professionals have. It is so important that it is part of how I interview candidates for a software development job. This part of the interview is loosely based on the US children's television show *Sesame Street*.[10] Their game "One of these things is not like the others" involves showing four pictures and having the viewer identify which of the pictures is different. It's an exercise in abstraction. A similar exercise can be used in an interview of a candidate developer: show the candidate four pictures, such as in Figure 3.1, and ask them to find ways of eliminating one of the four. Figure 3.1 is an introductory example to be sure they understand the exercise. Everyone quickly gets the idea that "banana is different because it's not a transportation device."

The next step is to show the four pictures in Figure 3.2 and ask them how many different ways they can eliminate any one of those pictures.

Figure 3.1 A simple test for abstraction skills.

---

10 See, for example, http://www.sesamestreet.org/.

Figure 3.2 A harder test for abstraction skills.

Acceptable responses include but are not limited to:

- Pizza because the others are not edible
- Seashells because they are the only one in a natural, unprocessed form
- Pizza because it has not been recognized as a form of payment
- Paper money because it's flat
- A slice of pizza because the others are collections while it is a single thing
- Gold bars because they are the only one in pure element form and the rest are compounds
- Pizza because it is a drawing and the others are photographs
- ...

The more abstractions a candidate can identify, the better. Developers who are good at abstracting—those who can cover a problem space with the fewest, cleanest, simplest abstractions—write the smallest, cleanest, simplest, most understandable, and easiest-to-maintain code. Developers who have difficulty abstracting tend to write a lot of ugly, complex, defect-ridden, and hard-to-maintain code.[11]

---

11 To fully appreciate the implications, see [Schulmeyer92].

3.4 Encapsulate Accidental Complexity

Abstraction and encapsulation are related concepts, but are different in a very important way. As stated, abstraction is "permission to ignore." Encapsulation takes that one step further by actively preventing you from knowing. Under abstraction you could probably find out if you looked hard enough. Under encapsulation, there is a deliberate attempt to make it as hard as possible—if not impossible—for you to find out. Encapsulation doesn't help manage essential complexity because that can't be hidden. Encapsulation helps manage accidental complexity: we want to hide as much accidental complexity—implementation detail—as possible.

Without encapsulation, the developer who wants to use operation isLanguageInstalled() needs to read the method implementation to understand its semantics. But this exposes that developer to its underlying implementation. Either consciously or unconsciously, that developer is likely to use knowledge of how isLanguageInstalled() is implemented when they write their code. Knowing it is implemented as a linked list, the caller's code might be written in a way that now depends on it being a linked list. The problem is when someone later changes the implementation of isLanguageInstalled(). Maybe system performance is suffering because the operation is called far more often than originally anticipated and a linked list is simply too slow. Knowing that there are only about 220 written languages, a maintainer may rewrite isLanguageInstalled() to use a BitArray. That change breaks all client code that depends on a linked list implementation. Encapsulation means we don't ever want client developers to know how a called operation is implemented.

"Develop to an interface, not through an interface."

Client developers clearly need to know the syntax of the server operation's interface: they see that in the signature. But operation semantics can't be hidden either. The semantics need to be exposed—that's the role of the contract. Using only the signature (syntax) and contract (semantics), client developers can code *to* an interface, not *through* it. Implementation details are accidental complexity because they relate to how the function is designed and built. Design by contract is critical to encapsulation.

"Without design by contract, there can be no encapsulation!"

A few more comments on design by contract are in order.

First, anything enforced by the compiler, linker, or run-time system should not be specified in a contract. The contract for isLanguageInstalled() should not require the caller's first parameter to be type compatible with Language-Code and the second to be type compatible with Boolean because the compiler/linker already enforces that. In fact, appropriate use of strong typing can reduce (but not necessarily eliminate) contract preconditions (requires clauses). Instead of having LanguageCode to be equivalent to int, the developer can declare LanguageCode to be an enumeration that only allows the 220 or so known written languages. The contract precondition goes away because the parameter can't refer to anything other than a known language. There's no need for a range check inside the method because the run-time system does that automatically (and probably more efficiently). Just be careful about cases where the type needs to include a special case value for, say, "we don't know yet" or "none of the above." The implementation of isLanguageInstalled() would still need to treat that special case appropriately.

Second, a maintainer is free to make any change to method code as long as they don't violate its contract. All callers are guaranteed to not break. If the contract must, for some reason, be changed, then it is the responsibility of both client and server developers to negotiate a new contract. All client code needs to be prepared to deal with that contract change.[12] Failure to do so can inject subtle, difficult-to-find, and difficult-to-fix defects.

3.4.1 Contracts and "Defensive Programming"

Finally, the term "defensive programming" can be interpreted as meaning that an operation requires nothing; it is capable of handling any and all situations it is given. Unfortunately, defensive programming has unavoidable consequences in terms of complexity, run-time performance, and development and maintenance cost and schedule that are not always affordable (this is explained in more detail in Chapter 16). Why aren't all bridges designed to hold the weight of the heaviest truck? Why aren't all tunnels tall enough to hold the tallest trailer? Simply, it would be too expensive. Economic constraints can force less-than-perfect implementations. When a bridge collapses under the load of an overweight truck or the top of a trailer is torn off because it is too tall for a tunnel, nobody should ever blame the designer or builder. The best that could have been done within the economic constraints was done. The blame needs to be placed on the driver: the one who didn't pay attention to published constraints.

The same has to be true in software: the economics of design and code place constraints on client program(mer)s. In practice, being defensive on input parameters to an operation is usually relatively cheap. Being defensive on state can be much more difficult. In any case, whatever constraints do apply need to be

---

12 Per Liskov substitutability, some changes to an operation's contract are safe and do not require negotiation. As long as the change only relaxes preconditions (requires) and/or tightens postconditions (guarantees), then no client code could ever be adversely affected by that change.

communicated, and that's the role of the contract requires (precondition) clause.

A common question is if it's acceptable to have a contract precondition like "the l value is in the set of known languages" but still implement a range check inside the method. The answer is the same as for someone who designed a bridge that could safely hold 30 ton trucks but published a weight limit of 10 tons. If the bridge can safely handle 30 tons, then say so. If isLanguageInstalled() can handle all possible l values, then say so. The contract and the method implementation should be consistent.

3.5 Maximize Cohesion and Minimize Coupling

We build software by first decomposing the problem into pieces that are small enough to solve. We then solve those pieces. Finally, we compose those small solutions into something that solves the original problem. It's a process of decomposition, solution, and then recomposition. For any problem, there are virtually an infinite number of ways to decompose it. It should be clear that not all possible decompositions are as good as all others. Some decompositions will be better and some will be worse. This leads to important questions:

- "How can I tell a good decomposition from a bad decomposition?"
- "Is there a better decomposition than this one?"
- "If so, what would that better decomposition look like?"

Cohesion and coupling are a means to assess a candidate decomposition to see if it is good or if it could be improved.

3.5.1 Cohesion

Cohesion considers the extent to which elements in a decomposition solve single subproblems. Do the elements each solve exactly one subproblem? Do they solve more than one subproblem? Do they solve less than one subproblem? Things that belong together should be close together and things that don't belong together should be separated. Code Sample 3.1 shows the actual contract that was reverse engineered from the production implementation of isLanguageInstalled(). This contract represents the actual behavior of the implementation.

Clearly, isLanguageInstalled() is solving two very different subproblems: querying for a language package and deleting one. The remedy is to split the code into two distinct operations, one to only query and the other to only delete.

Code Sample 3.1 The Actual Semantics of Operation isLanguageInstalled()

```
public static boolean isLanguageInstalled (LanguageCode l, boolean b) {

// requires
//   l refers to a valid, recognized written language
// guarantees
//   when b is TRUE
//        then returns true when language package l is present
//        otherwise returns FALSE
//   when b is not TRUE
//        then deletes language package l and returns FALSE

  // some method implementation goes here

}
```

After the split, the two operations will each do one single thing; they will now each be highly cohesive.

The isLanguageInstalled() example is another argument for design by contract. The contract makes operation-level cohesion problems obvious. When you first saw the operation signature, you may have wondered about the b parameter. It wasn't clear what it was for, but it also wasn't obvious that it wasn't needed either. It probably wasn't enough of an issue to convince anyone that something was wrong. On the other hand, when you look at the contract in Code Sample 3.1, it's obvious there's a problem that needs to be fixed.

3.5.2 Coupling

Coupling is about connections between elements. Elements that don't need to be connected shouldn't be connected. If class A is in direct need of an operation on class C, then class A should not have to go through class B to get there. Class A should communicate only with classes that it directly needs services of. Further, when two things do need to be connected, that connection should be as loose as possible. In the isLanguageInstalled() example, a client developer may have depended on it being implemented as a linked list. If the implementation changed to a BitArray, that client would break. That's an example of coupling too tightly. Programming to an interface, instead of programming through an interface, is one way to reduce coupling.

The Law of Demeter[13] addresses one manifestation of coupling. Another way to think about coupling is that it's the cause of the so-called ripple effect: where a change in one place leads to a cascade of changes through the code. When a system is loosely coupled, changes are localized and don't ripple.

It should be clear that high cohesion and loose coupling apply at the operation level. Every operation should be highly cohesive and loosely coupled with all operations around it. When a set of operations are gathered into a class, that class should be highly cohesive and loosely coupled with the classes around it. When a set of classes are gathered into a package, that package should be highly cohesive and loosely coupled with the packages around it. When a set of packages are gathered into a system, that system should be highly cohesive and loosely coupled with the systems around it. Chapter 18 also discusses how cohesion and coupling can also be applied at the line of code level. Cohesion and coupling are pervasive properties that apply at all levels of decomposition, not just to operations.[14]

3.6 Design to Invariants and Design for Change

In most software organizations, a software product is born when some stakeholder, call them Entity A, says, "We'll give you lots of money if you solve our problem." Developers like solving problems and getting money, so they are happy to build a solution. Later, Entity B comes along and says, "We really like what you did for Entity A. We will give you lots of money if you solve our problem, too." The trouble starts when Entity B says, "Our problem is just like Entity A's problem *except* ...." Again, developers like solving problems and getting money, so they attack Entity B's problem. With some amount of folding, spindling, and mutilating of the code, they now have something that solves Entity B's problem too.

Some time later, along comes Entity C saying, "We like what you did for Entity A and Entity B. We will also give you lots of money if you solve our problem too. Our problem is just like Entity A's and Entity B's problem *except* ...." Again, developers like solving problems and getting money, so they attack Entity C's problem. With more folding, spindling, and mutilating, they finally have something that solves Entity C's problem too. Later, along comes Entity D and the cycle repeats. Unfortunately, with each cycle, the folding, spindling, and mutilating become exponentially harder. After even just a few cycles, the code has been folded, spindled, and mutilated so much that any new entity—regardless of how much money they have—will be impossible to satisfy.

---

13 See, for example, https://en.wikipedia.org/wiki/Law_of_Demeter.
14 See www.phonebloks.org for an example of high cohesion and loose coupling in smart phone hardware.

3.6.1 Product Families: Being Proactive Instead of Reactive

Those developers have been entirely reactive. They reacted to Entity A with a solution that solved that one problem. They reacted to Entity B with another solution that tried to solve both A's and B's problem together. Reactionary cycles repeated until they couldn't make solutions anymore: the code simply couldn't support it.

The "product family" approach, on the other hand, is intentionally proactive. Before anyone starts solving Entity A's problem, they ask, "What other entities would be interested in solutions similar to this?" They identify Entities B through Z up front. Knowing this range of potential customers, they now ask, "What needs do all of those customers have in common?" These are the "invariant requirements." The other question is, "What are the ranges of varying needs across these same entities?" These are the "variant requirements": support differing needs across ranges of options. Cars are good example of product families. The earlier example of TurboTax™ is a software product family, so are operating systems in their ability to deal with widely varying hardware.

3.6.2 Design to Invariants and Design for Change

"Product family development" bases the core product on the common needs—the invariant requirements. This is "design to invariants." They do this because the design has to be based on something; it makes the most sense to base it on things that are least likely to change. An invariant need across a customer base is the most likely to be stable. They also use "design for change": adding configuration zones. Design-for-change strategies include:

- *Separate common from variable functionality*—Using conditional compilation (e.g., #define and #ifdef: everything outside #ifdef blocks is invariant, and variants are coded into the #ifdef blocks). Inheritance: The superclasses represent invariants, subclasses represent variants. Aspect-oriented programming[15]: Variation is hidden inside aspects.
- *Hide variation behind an abstract interface*—Architectural layering, for example, domain separation as described in Chapter 6. Several design patterns[16] including Adapter, Bridge, Strategy, Factory Method, Template Method, Iterator, Decorator, Proxy, etc. also use this strategy.
- *Use delayed binding*—Using #define-ed constants instead of magic numbers, dependency injection,[17] self-configuration,[18] data-driven design,[19] etc.

---

15 See, for example, https://en.wikipedia.org/wiki/Aspect-oriented_programming.
16 See, for example, [Gamma95].
17 See, for example, https://en.wikipedia.org/wiki/Dependency_injection.
18 The software senses the execution environment and adapts itself as necessary: operating systems typically use this approach during boot up.
19 Sometimes called "interpreter" architectural style: TurboTax™ makes extensive use of this approach.

When Entity B says, "Can you solve our problem too?," it can be done without much effort. Developers may only need to redefine a constant or two over here, make a new subclass over there, provide a small implementation behind some PQR interface, etc. The response to Entity B is, in essence, "Yes, we've just been waiting for you to ask." The same is true for Entity C, Entity D, and all the way to Entity Z.

The critical difference is in being proactive rather than reactive. The ability for the code to support different customers is built in because the developers recognized those needs from the start. There are no point solutions to point problems, instead developers build families of related solutions to sets of customers' related problems.

Of course, this depends on good predictive skills. Something that was originally thought to be invariant could later turn out to be a variant. "Stuff happens," as they say. And it could be just as disruptive as in the reactive case. But the product family approach at least minimizes the probability of this happening. Also, appropriate application of all the other fundamental principles will tend to make it easier to manage when it does happen.

3.6.3 Another Way to Deal with Changing Requirements

This principle also helps deal with changing (i.e., unstable) requirements. My first software development job was developing radiation monitoring software for nuclear power plants. We had to be familiar with "half-lives" of radioactive isotopes. The half-life is the time it takes for half of some given quantity to decay[20]. The half-life of uranium-238 (U-238) is about 4.5 billion years. If you get 100 g of U-238 and wait 4.5 billion years, you will then have 50 g of U-238 and 50 g of other isotopes as a result of radioactive decay. If you get 100 g of iodine-134 (I-134), you only have to wait 53 minutes for it to decay into 50 g of I-134 and 50 g of other isotopes.

A coworker at that radiation monitoring company offered an insightful observation:

> *"Requirements have half-lives."*
>
> (Ken Rose)

Some requirements have very long half-lives; they are unlikely to change over the life of the software product. We can count on these being stable, that is, invariant. At the same time, some requirements have short half-lives, possibly as short as days or weeks: these need to be treated as variants. The question becomes, "How

---

20 See, for example, https://en.wikipedia.org/wiki/Half-life.

much can this variant requirement be expected to change over the service life of the software?" Software can be structured around the invariants and configuration zones put in for the requirements that are likely to change.

Adding scope to a system necessarily introduces complexity, even if it is invariant. Adding the ability to handle variation is even more complex. Be sure any complexity added to handle variation is adequately compensated by increased value.

3.7 Avoid Premature Design and Optimization

Premature design and optimization run rampant in the software industry. It will probably continue for a long, long time—possibly forever. This may even be due to the psychology of developers: one doesn't choose a career in software unless one likes solving problems. Unfortunately, in the desire to solve problems quickly (sometimes just so we can start to work on another, possibly even more interesting problem), we tend to rush to a solution before really understanding the problem that needs solved.

The following excerpt was originally published by Michael Jackson[21] and has been copied with only slight modification.

3.7.1 An Example of Premature Design and Optimization

Consider a boat owner who offers her boat for rental on a scenic lake. A renter comes to the boathouse and asks a hired attendant if the boat can be rented. If so, the attendant readies the boat, helps the renter into the boat, and then logs the start of the rental on a paper form: a rental session identifier, the name of the renter, and the time the renter departed the dock. When the boat is returned, the attendant completes the rental record by entering the time of return. The attendant then calculates the cost of rental and takes the renter's payment, and the rental is complete.

The boat owner wants some management information to help her better manage her business. At the end of the day, she wants an automated report on the day's activity:

- Number of rental sessions
- Average rental session duration

The owner, being nontechnical, decides to buy a simple data entry terminal and a low-cost computer that can connect with the terminal. As Jackson says,

---

21 See [Jackson83].

"We may note that the management of the company has already chosen and purchased the ... hardware, although the system specification is not yet written. This conforms to a practice widely established among some organizations."

From a technical perspective, when the boat is rented, the data entry terminal allows the attendant to key in a session identifier and a code (S) to indicate that a rental session is starting. The terminal sends that in a data packet along with a timestamp to the computer. On return of the boat, the attendant keys in the same session ID and a code (E) to indicate that the rental has ended. The terminal sends another data packet to the connected computer along with a timestamp. The terminal sends an end-of-file (EOF) marker when it is turned off at the end of the day.

The boat owner desperately wants this business problem solved and advertises in local media about her need for software. A developer responds, the owner explains her problem, they agree on an hourly rate, and the developer sets to programming a solution.

The developer, being the rather clever sort that developers usually are, sees immediately that the required function has two parts: compute the information from the input messages, and print the results when done. Computing the information consists of counting the sessions, totaling the time, and calculating the average. Counting sessions is easy: the number of sessions is the same as the number of S messages. Totaling the time is not that much harder:

$$\text{totaltime} = (\text{end time of session 1} - \text{start time of session 1})$$

$$+ (\text{end time of session 2} - \text{start time of session 2})$$

$$+ (\text{end time of session 3} - \text{start time of session 3})$$

$$+ \cdots$$

or, more cleverly and conveniently,

$$\text{totaltime} = \text{end time of session 1} + \text{end time of session 2}$$

$$+ \text{end time of session 3} + \cdots$$

$$- \text{start time of session 1} - \text{start time of session 2}$$

$$- \text{start time of session 3} - \cdots$$

The developer codes a solution that follows the pseudo-code in Code Sample 3.2.

The system goes into production, the developer is paid, and everyone is happy.

Code Sample 3.2 Pseudo-code That Solves the Boat Owner's Business Problem

```
{
    // at the start of the day
    rentalCount = 0
    totalTime = 0
    connect to the terminal

    // during the rental day
    while ( the next message is not an end-of-file )
        if message code == 'S'
            then rentalCount++
                totalTime = totalTime - startTime
            else totalTime = totalTime + endTime
    end while

    // at the end of day (on receiving the EOF)
    output ( "Number of rental sessions = ", rentalCount )
    output ("Average session time = ", totalTime / rentalCount )
    disconnect from the terminal
}
```

Before long, the boat owner comes to the developer with a request for enhancement. She wants the report to contain a third line: the duration of the longest rental session of the day.

Careful examination of the existing code convinces the developer that the requested enhancement cannot be made without throwing away what has already been developed and building a completely new system. The developer is able to persuade the boat owner that there are technical reasons, having to do with the computer's operating system, why the requested change cannot be made. The owner is dazzled by the technical brilliance of the developer's explanation and agrees that the change was not that important anyway. As Jackson says,

> "Notice that no costs are debited to the system maintenance account: calculations of maintenance costs often omit the cost of not doing maintenance."

Later, the owner is back with another request. This time she is sure the change will be easy. All she wants is two simple reports, each one exactly like the report she is already receiving. One report should address sessions starting before noon, and the other the remaining sessions of the day. Once again the developer (and, hopefully, the reader!) sees that the change cannot be made to the existing system without a major rewrite. This time the developer devises an excuse based on the recent introduction of a new compiler; the owner is somewhat less dazzled by the developer's technical brilliance and is definitely dissatisfied with the service she is getting.

After a while, she returns with yet another request. This time the change is vitally important: the communication link is unreliable and has been dropping messages. As a result, there are some sessions for which only one message, either the S or the E, is received. The system must be changed to exclude these sessions from the report. Unfortunately, this change is no easier than the first two: it simply cannot be made without abandoning code and creating an entirely new program. Neither time nor budget is available, and there is no way out. The developer's explanations (something to do with communication protocols) fall on deaf ears, and the developer is soon updating his resume, seeking another job.

The original solution was clever but limiting; there was no room for growth. Had the developer built the code around business problem elements, namely, boat rental, start of a rental, end of a rental, etc., the changes desired by the boat owner would have been simple.

3.7.2 Another Example of Premature Design and Optimization

The sad but true story of a large development project for the US military is also relevant. This particular project featured communication between various "platforms": tanks, unmanned aerial vehicles (UAVs), fighter airplanes, bomber airplanes, gun batteries, infantry forward observers, and so on. The subject of one particular meeting was to decide the bandwidth for the satellite link that would be used for inter-platform communication. The two options being considered were 1 and 10 Mbps. The implications of deciding wrong were enormous. If they chose 1 Mbps and really needed 10 Mbps, then it would require a very expensive redesign. If they chose 10 Mbps and only needed 1 Mbps, it would have meant lots of taxpayer money were wasted—money that could have been better spent on other important things. Baseless arguments and unfounded assertions for choosing one bandwidth over the other had already dragged on for hours. Getting entirely fed up with the complete lack of progress, an astute consultant asked these simple questions:

> "*Does anybody know <u>what kind of information</u> needs to be sent between platforms?*
> *<u>How much</u> data needs to be communicated?*
> *<u>How often</u> does that data need to be communicated?*
> *Shouldn't <u>that</u> be the key driver of bandwidth on the communication link?*"

The consultant was told—in no uncertain terms—"You clearly don't understand the problem here!" and debate immediately fell back into baseless arguments and unfounded assertions. The consultant realized the futility of the situation and ducked out of the meeting as quickly as he could. As far as anyone knows, that meeting would probably still be going on today had that project not been cancelled.

Premature design in a semantic model is dangerous because it railroads designers and developers into seeing only the solution that was modeled. Other possibly more optimal designs are difficult to see. Part II details several ways premature design can sneak into a semantic model:

- Modeling control flow instead of data flow
- Assigning data types to attributes instead of ranges
- Using keys and foreign keys
- Specifying actions using algorithms
- ...

3.7.3 Fudd's First Law of Creativity

Fudd's First Law of Creativity says,

> *"To come up with a really good idea, start by coming up with as many ideas as you can, then throw away the bad ones."*

The semantic model isn't a solution to a problem. In fact, it's only a precise statement of what that problem is. Chapter 2 shows how code (the solution) is a mapping from this semantic "statement of the problem" model onto the semantics of the automation technology and that many such mappings are possible. This plays right into Fudd's First Law of Creativity. Cost, schedule, and complexity implications of any number of proposed mappings can be considered, before committing to any one. Developers will be more likely to arrive at an optimal solution. There's never any guarantee the developers will find that one single most optimal solution. However, at a minimum, avoiding premature design and optimization—as manifested in model-based software engineering—reduces the risk of getting trapped in a suboptimal solution because ill-informed choices were made too early.

3.7.4 How to Avoid Premature Design and Optimization

Tactics for avoiding premature design in the semantic model are as follows:

- *Convince yourself of the value of Fudd's First Law of Creativity*—Overcome the instinctive urge to solve problems too early by telling yourself, "If I can just wait until I really understand the problem, then (and only then) will I be able to come up with a killer solution."

- *Be careful to model only the true nature of the policies and processes*—Follow the rules and guidelines presented along with each semantic model element.
- *Review models with others*—We are naturally blind to our own mistakes; it's part of being human. Our coworkers can help point out premature design. The quality criteria include explicitly looking for premature design in semantic models.

The following three quotes discuss the dangers of premature optimization in design:

> *"More computing sins are committed in the name of efficiency (without necessarily achieving it) than for any other single reason including blind stupidity."*
>
> (W. A. Wulf)

> *"We should forget about small efficiencies, say about 97% of the time: premature optimization is the root of all evil."*
>
> (Donald Knuth)

> *"Jackson's Rules of Optimization:*
>
> *Rule 1: Don't do it.*
> *Rule 2 (for experts only): Don't do it yet—that is, not until you have a perfectly clear and un-optimized solution."*
>
> (– M. A. Jackson)

Premature optimization in design also risks suboptimal solutions, and there can be significant cost, schedule, and (unnecessary) accidental complexity implications as well. Always:

- *Start with the simplest possible design*—Develop initial design and code, emphasizing simplicity, readability, maintainability, modularity, etc. This is covered in Chapters 15–17.
- *Only optimize when and where there is sufficient value*—Use the engineering process in Chapter 19 or use an open model compiler as discussed in Chapters 20 and 21.

3.8 Name Things Carefully

A former coworker once said,

> *"Assigning good names is 90% of programming."*
>
> (Dan Jinguji, Boeing)

His saying may go too far, but not by much. Naming is vitally important, particularly in how it affects abstraction and encapsulation. The following are general naming guidelines appropriate across semantic modeling, software design, and code. Names should:

- Be in the problem space (policy and process) vocabulary.[22]
- Fully and accurately describe the meaning of the named thing.
- Be unique and have exactly one meaning within its context.
- Be clear, obvious, readable, and pronounceable to a typical reader.
- Not be contractions (e.g., getWindow() rather than getWin()).
- Abbreviate only when necessary and then always consistently.
- Be similar for similar things (e.g., don't use dependent.GetId(), supervisor(), employee.Id.Get(), or candidate.Id() for operations that all return entity identifiers).
- Be contrasting for contrasting things (e.g., open/close, start/finish, ... not open/finish).
- Be identical for the same thing. Sometimes the same concept appears in different places—that one concept needs to have the same name in all places to emphasize that it is the same thing.

> *"A good name is like a walking comment."*
>
> (Meilir Page-Jones)

3.9 Quality Criteria

Model-based software engineering provides very specific quality criteria (e.g., "definition of done" or checklists). Work products of all kinds can be reviewed against these quality criteria to identify and remove defects as quickly as possible, greatly reducing rework percentage (R%). In addition to the documentation principles in Appendix A, Table 3.1 shows quality criteria that apply to all model-based software engineering work. Criteria specific to design, like encapsulation and design by contract, are in checklists in Part III.

Table 3.2 shows quality criteria that can be applied to naming in various models and in code.

---

22 In design and code, the "problem" is mapping policy and process to automation technology; some technology-based names are acceptable.

Table 3.1 Overall quality criteria for work products.

Item	Criterion
OV-1	Given the expected service life of the software and constraints and priorities of the project (schedule, cost, scope), the work represents the most cost-effective solution to the stakeholder's problem
OV-2	The work product is complete: all necessary content is present
OV-3	The work product is concise: only necessary content is present
OV-4	The work product is internally consistent: it does not contradict itself
OV-5	The work product is externally consistent: it does not contradict any other relevant related work product
OV-6	The work product is clear
OV-7	The work product is correct: it represents or satisfies stakeholder need
OV-8	The value of all complexity sufficiently outweighs its cost: there isn't any unnecessary complexity
OV-9	As appropriate, the work product covers the problem space and/or solution space with the fewest, cleanest, simplest abstractions
OV-10	The work product is highly cohesive: each element serves exactly one purpose, never more and never less
OV-11	The work product is loosely coupled: things that don't need to be connected aren't connected, and things that need to be connected are connected as loosely as possible
OV-12	Cohesion and coupling have been applied at all levels: lines of code, methods, operations, classes, packages, subsystems, subdomains, domains, systems, etc.
OV-13	The work product is appropriately structured around invariants
OV-14	The work product appropriately accounts for anticipated variation
OV-15	Premature design and optimization have been avoided

3.10 Relationship to the SOLID Principles

The SOLID principles[23] were introduced by Robert ("Uncle Bob") Martin in 1995. SOLID is an acronym:

- *S ("Single responsibility")*—A class should have a single responsibility[24]: this expresses part of "Maximize cohesion." "Maximize cohesion says, "Do exactly one thing, no more and no less," while "Single responsibility" says, "Do no

---

23 See, for example, [Martin02]. See also [Suryanarayana15]; it is in terms of the SOLID principles and contains many practical examples of fundamental principles being violated in design and code.
24 See, for example, https://en.wikipedia.org/wiki/Single_responsibility_principle.

Table 3.2 Quality criteria for naming.

Item	Criterion
NM-1	Each name is in the relevant policy and process vocabulary
NM-2	Each name accurately describes the meaning of the named thing
NM-3	Each name is unique and has exactly one meaning in its context
NM-4	Each name is clear, obvious, readable, and pronounceable
NM-5	Each name avoids contractions (e.g., getWindow() not getWin())
NM-6	Abbreviations are used only when necessary and always consistently
NM-7	Similar things are similarly named
NM-8	Contrasting things are named to highlight that contrast
NM-9	When the same concept exists in multiple places, it has the same name

more than one thing." A class could have a single responsibility and yet not provide a complete implementation; necessary elements could be missing. Further, as published, single responsibility is stated to apply to classes; however high cohesion clearly applies at all levels: lines of code, methods, operations, classes, collections of classes (e.g., packages), systems in a systems of systems environment, etc.

- *O ("Open/closed")*—Software entities (classes, operations, methods, etc.) should be open for extension and closed for modification[25]: literally by definition, every class is already open for extension.[26] Being closed for modification is most commonly interpreted as meaning encapsulate design decisions, but SOLID never mentions use of design by contract to enforce it.
- *L ("Liskov substitution")*—This is the same as described in Chapter 2 and is covered more broadly under Sections 3.1 and 3.4. The only difference is that the common interpretation is thought to apply only to inheritance, but this principle is much more broadly applicable.
- *I ("Interface segregation")*—Many client-specific interfaces are better than one general-purpose one[27]: this is simply a manifestation of single responsibility and thus already covered under the more general principle of "Maximize cohesion, minimize coupling."
- *D ("Dependency inversion")*—This means you should depend on abstract things, not concrete things[28]: this is one specific dimension of minimizing coupling.

---

25 See, for example, https://en.wikipedia.org/wiki/Open/closed_principle.
26 Unless it is declared "final" as in Java.
27 See, for example, https://en.wikipedia.org/wiki/Interface_segregation_principle.
28 See, for example, https://en.wikipedia.org/wiki/Dependency_inversion_principle.

I don't have any issues with the SOLID principles per se; the concern is that they don't go far enough:

- Where is any explicit focus on semantics?
- Where is any emphasis on controlling complexity?
- Where is any economic basis for making engineering decisions?
- There are many other ways to design to invariants and design for change beyond just open/closed and dependency inversion.
- Where is any warning against premature design and optimization?
- There is no guidance on naming.

Adopting the fundamental principles described in this chapter, even if they don't have as memorable an acronym, will better serve the software industry in the long run.

3.11 Summary

Complexity costs in terms of time and money—both in initial development and in long-term maintenance. Sometimes complexity costs less than the value it brings; sometimes it costs more. Either way, we need to be smart about complexity: find ways to eliminate it when it has negative value and manage it when it has positive value. The fundamental principles in this chapter are part of software engineering practice: ways of approaching problem solving that help manage the complexity that needs to be managed, because it's complexity with net economic benefit, and avoiding or eliminating unnecessary complexity, because it's complexity that doesn't bring enough economic benefit to justify its presence.

4

Functional and Nonfunctional Requirements

This chapter defines the term "requirement," both formally and informally. The critical properties of requirements are discussed. Two kinds of requirements, functional and nonfunctional, are defined and described. An approach for separating these kinds of requirements is given, along with a justification for why they should be separated. This chapter closes with additional detail about specifying nonfunctional requirements.

4.1 What Is a Requirement?

A formal definition of "requirement" comes from the IEEE Computer Society[1]:

1) *A condition or capability needed by a user to solve a problem or achieve an objective*
2) *A condition or capability that must be met or possessed by a system or system component to satisfy a contract, standard, specification, or other formally imposed document*
3) *A documented representation or capability as in (1) or (2)*

This definition is technically correct, but it doesn't seem particularly useful. Approaching it from a different angle can help.

It has been said, "you cannot cook without breaking eggs." In a similar sense, "you cannot build software without making decisions." At its core, software development is a decision-making activity. Thousands of decisions are needed for even relatively small amounts of code. The Silly Bank code in Chapter 2 was the result of many decisions, such as:

- What's in scope, what's not in scope?
- What will a particular operation interface be?
- What does Silly Bank want a customer to be?

---

1 See [IEEE].

How to Engineer Software: A Model-Based Approach, First Edition. Steve Tockey.
© 2019 the IEEE Computer Society, Inc. Published 2019 by John Wiley & Sons, Inc.

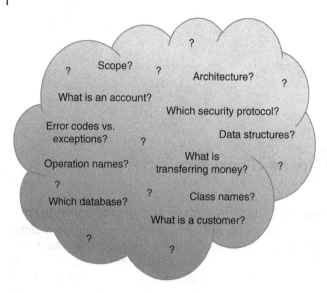

Figure 4.1 A set of decisions about software.

- Should operations return error codes or throw exceptions?
- What does Silly Bank want a savings account to be?
- How should the data be organized?
- What does it mean to transfer money from one account to another?
- What should some variable in the code be named?
- ...

Figure 4.1 represents the set of decisions needed to create, for example, some banking software. There would be thousands, if not tens of thousands or even millions, of such decisions in nontrivial software.

4.2 Who Made the Decision?

The decisions in Figure 4.1 can be partitioned based on who made them. The developers make some decisions: nobody tells developers what to name a particular variable. Nobody tells developers to throw exceptions and not return error codes. Nobody tells them how to structure data.

On the other hand, developers do not get to decide what is in scope and what is not. Developers do not get to decide what it means to be a customer or a savings account. It isn't up to the developers to define what transferring money between accounts means. These are decisions that external stakeholders—the bank—make. Figure 4.2 shows those same decisions partitioned into subsets based on who made them.

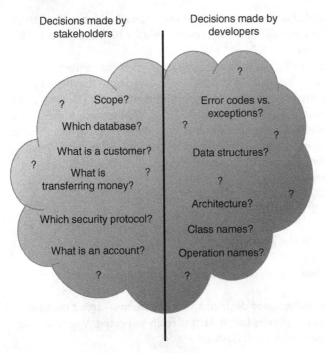

Figure 4.2 The decisions partitioned by who made them.

Informally, a requirement is simply a decision made by somebody other than the developers—the subset on the left of Figure 4.2. Whenever somebody outside a development team makes a decision and imposes that decision on the developers, that decision is a requirement. This is a more straightforward and useful definition. I can't tell how many times in reviewing a project's so-called requirements specification, it clearly includes decisions made by developers themselves (e.g., a database schema), not stakeholders. If a document purports to be a "requirements specification," then it should contain all—*and only*—decisions made by external stakeholders. Decisions made within that development team should be strictly out of bounds.

4.2.1 "Derived Requirements"

In practice, "Which decisions are requirements?" is context sensitive. It depends on who "the development team" is. An external stakeholder will usually make a decision about scope. That decision would be a requirement for the entire project, even if the project involves hundreds of developers. A chief architect's decision to use a pipes-and-filters architecture style would not be a requirement from the perspective of the overall project—the architect's choice is a design decision to the external stakeholders. But that same decision, when seen from the perspective of a four-person sub-team responsible for building the third filter, would be a requirement.

The aerospace community has long used the term "derived requirement" to mean a decision that was not made by a stakeholder external to the overall project: that decision was made inside the larger development team. The architect's pipes-and-filters decision would fit this definition. That choice would be a design decision to external stakeholders; but that same decision is imposed on one or more sub-teams responsible for developing each filter. That decision is most definitely a requirement to those sub-teams.

4.3   Is It Really a Requirement?

There is a lot of truth in the statement

> *"There are no bad requirements, just badly stated requirements"*

Most, if not all, externally imposed decisions—requirements—aren't communicated in a way that lets developers know what is really expected. Vague, ambiguous statements abound, like the following:

- "The system shall be fast."
- "The system shall be user friendly."
- "The system shall detect a ¼ inch defect in a pipe section."
- ...

Developers can't know what they are accountable for unless they truly understand what decision has been made. The term "requirement" needs to include only decisions that are:

- *Unambiguous*—That decision can only be interpreted in exactly one way; no interpretations other than what was intended by the decision maker are possible.
- *Testable*—It is possible to demonstrate compliance or noncompliance.
- *Binding*—That decision maker is willing to pay for it, and is unwilling not to have it.

Statements like "The system shall be fast" and "The system shall be user friendly" fail because they are grossly ambiguous. Many very different interpretations of "fast" and "user friendly" are possible. Similarly, user friendliness isn't testable per se. How user friendly is enough? Finally, many statements could be made about software that are unambiguous and testable, just not binding. Maybe the statement is that the background color on user screens be a particular shade of blue. If external decision makers don't care about screen

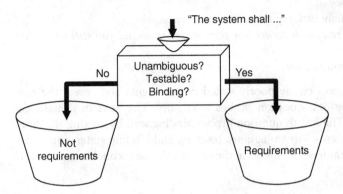

Figure 4.3 Separating requirements from non-requirements.

background color—they would be just as happy with almost any color, then that decision fails the binding criterion.

This leads to a recommendation to begin development with a filter as shown in Figure 4.3. Somehow or another, someone comes up with a statement of the form "the software shall ..." (i.e., a candidate requirement) and runs that statement through the filter.

Of course, this begs the question "How does one come up with those statements in the first place?" This is "requirements elicitation." Effective requirements elicitation is critical in software development and maintenance but is not covered in this book. It is adequately covered elsewhere.[2]

Remember my former boss said,

> "Requirements aren't created, they surface"

He meant that the real requirements have been there all along. The question is, "how good a job was done of finding what those real requirements were?" Said another way, many statements might fail the ambiguity or testability criteria and thus not qualify as requirements. But that same former boss would also say,

> "The mere fact that they said anything at all on that topic almost certainly means there is at least one real requirement lurking in there somewhere, your challenge is to find it"

Ask probing questions like the following:

- *What did you mean when you said ____?*
- *How could I measure ____?*

---

2 See, for example, [Robertson06], [Wiegers03], [Gause89], and [IIBA09].

- *How much (or how little) of that measure is enough?*
- *If developers weren't able to achieve that measure, would you still be willing to pay?*
- *Why is this a requirement?*[3]

This helps refine and clarify poorly stated requirements and reveal the real requirements. The first question probes ambiguity. The next two questions probe testability. The fourth question probes bindingness. By seeking clarification, real requirements—unambiguous, testable, and binding statements—can be surfaced. Leave as few statements in the not-requirements bucket as practical.

4.4 An Example: Tic Tac Toe Smart Phone App

Assume that someone wants to build a smart phone app that plays the game "Tic Tac Toe" ("Naughts and crosses" to UK English speakers).[4] This app pits the human against the computer in their smart phone. Of course, as long as requirements are being written in a natural language, it will be impossible to remove all ambiguity, but we can try to get as close as we can. The following are candidate requirements for that smart phone app:

- The game board shall look like:

- There shall be two players, one human and one machine.
- The only valid symbols allowed on the game board shall be X, O, and blank.
- One player shall be assigned X, and the other assigned O.
- The human shall choose to play X or O for the first game.
- In each subsequent game, the most recent winner shall choose to play X or O.
- When a new game starts, all cells on the game board shall be blank.
- The player assigned X shall make the first move.
- After the first move, the players shall alternate turns.
- On one player's turn, that player shall place their symbol into a blank square.

---

3 Often, developers are given solutions to implement as if they were requirements. The "Five Whys" technique presented in chapter 4 of [Tockey05] and elsewhere can be effective at exposing the true requirements.

4 See, for example, http://en.wikipedia.org/wiki/Tic-tac-toe.

- Once played, that X or O shall remain in that cell until the end of game.
- The first player to place three of their symbols in a row, column, or diagonal shall be the winner.
- When no blank squares remain and neither player has won, the game is a draw.
- The app shall run on the latest smart phone operating systems.
- The app shall be written in Objective-C.
- The app shall fit in less than 1 megabyte of run-time memory.
- The app shall respond to each human move in less than one second.

Some example "not requirements" could be:

- The app shall be fast.
- The app shall be user friendly.
- The app shall be fun to play.

4.5 A Tinker Toy™ Computer That Plays Tic Tac Toe

A. K. Dewdney wrote a fascinating article in Scientific American about a "computer" that plays Tic Tac Toe.[5] The computer was built using the children's construction toy, Tinker Toy™,[6] and is shown in Figure 4.4.

The design is based on the realization that, after accounting for mirror images and rotation, there are only 48 valid, unique configurations of the game board (e.g., any configuration in which there are more O's than X's is invalid because X always moves first. The number of X's can only be equal to or one greater than the number of O's). The designers developed a way to encode each valid configuration into a "memory spindle." They also have one movable "core piece" that encodes the current game board. Figure 4.5 shows the coding schemes for memory spindles and the core piece.

Memory spindles and the core piece are divided into nine zones, one for each cell on the game board. On memory spindles,

- O is encoded by putting two Tinker Toy spools on the left side of the zone, leaving a gap on the right.
- Blank is encoded by putting two Tinker Toy spools on either side of the zone, leaving a gap in the middle.
- X is encoded by putting two Tinker Toy spools on the right side of the zone, leaving a gap on the left.

---

5 See [Dewdney89].
6 See, for example, http://en.wikipedia.org/wiki/Tinkertoy.

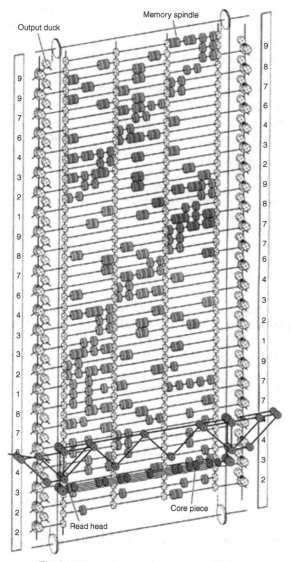

The tinkertoy computer: ready for a game of tic-tac-toe

Figure 4.4 A Tinker Toy Tic Tac Toe computer.

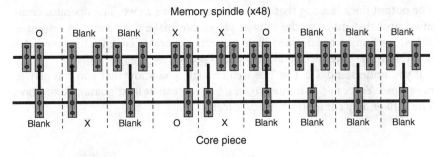

Figure 4.5 Encodings for the Tinker Toy Tic Tac Toe computer.

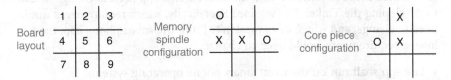

Figure 4.6 Configurations for the memory spindle and core piece in Figure 4.5.

The core piece uses a complementary coding scheme:

- O is encoded by sliding the Tinker Toy spool to the right side of the zone.
- Blank is encoded by putting the Tinker Toy spool in the middle of the zone.
- X is encoded by sliding the Tinker Toy spool to the left side of the zone.

Figure 4.6 illustrates the encodings on the memory spindle and the core piece in Figure 4.5.

Each spool on the core piece includes a 5cm (2″) dowel that is blocked by a spool on the memory spindle whenever cell encodings don't match. The first cell on the left of Figure 4.5 shows a mismatch because there is an O in the memory spindle cell and a blank in the same cell on the core piece. There is a match on the last cell on the right; both are blank.

An operator is needed to play against the Tinker Toy computer. Assuming the human player chooses to play X and move first, the human gives their move to the operator. The operator accounts for rotation and mirror imaging as appropriate then encodes that configuration into the core piece. The operator then pulls strings to lift the core piece to the top of the memory spindles. When the operator lets go of the strings, the core piece rattles down the stack of memory spindles. When the core piece reaches the memory spindle matching the current game board configuration, none of the core piece's dowels are blocked so the core piece rotates. Not shown well in Figure 4.4 are "output ducks": when the core piece rotates, it kicks the output duck for that memory spindle.

The output duck is a flag that shows the computer's move. The operator communicates that move so the human player can make their move in response. When the human has decided their move, the operator encodes the new game board into the core piece and the cycle repeats.

If you understand Tic Tac Toe well enough, you know that you can play to never lose. You can't guarantee to win, but you can at least guarantee to draw. The Tinker Toy computer has never lost.

4.6   Kinds of Requirements

How would the requirements from the smart phone app need to change to lead to developing the Tinker Toy version? Specifically, which requirements would need to change, and which ones wouldn't? From the smart phone app, the following requirements would need to change:

- The app shall run on the latest smart phone operating systems.
- The app shall be written in Objective-C.
- The app shall fit in less than 1 megabyte of run-time memory.
- The app shall respond to each human mov in less than one second.

These requirements would need to change to:

- The system shall be built in Tinker Toy.
- The system shall fit through a standard door.
- The system shall respond to each human move in less than 30 seconds.
- ...

Just as important is to understand which requirements don't change:

- The game board shall look like:

- There shall be two players, one human and one machine.
- The only valid symbols allowed on the game board shall be X, O, and blank.
- One player shall be assigned X and the other assigned O.
- The human shall choose to play X or O for first game.
- In each subsequent game, the most recent winner shall choose to play X or O.
- When a new game starts, all cells on the game board shall be blank.
- The player assigned X shall make the first move.

- After the first move, the players shall alternate turns.
- On one player's turn, that player shall place their symbol into a blank square.
- Once played, that X or O shall remain in that cell until the end of game.
- The first player to place three of their symbols in a row, column, or diagonal shall be the winner.
- When no blank squares remain and neither player has won, the game is a draw.

Consider the requirements that did not change—they are all about a single topic, Tic Tac Toe: they are the rules of the game. They are the policies and processes to be automated. Consider the requirements that did change: they express constraints on the automation.

One kind of requirement is about the "business" being automated: policies to be enforced and processes to be carried out. The other kind of requirement is a constraint on automation. We can further differentiate the set of decisions in Figure 4.2 based on what that decision is about: business or automation technology. This is illustrated in Figure 4.7.

There are two kinds of requirement[7]:

- *Functional requirements*—Stakeholder decisions about the business[8] (to be) automated. What policies need to be enforced? In banking, policies could include "the balance of an account shall never be negative" and "an account must always have at least one customer as its owner." What processes need to be carried out? In banking, processes could include "what it means to deposit money into an account" and "what it means to transfer money from one account to another."
- *Nonfunctional requirements*—Stakeholder constraints on automation. What computing platform? What database engine? How accurate do results need to be? How quickly must results be presented? How many records need to be stored?

---

7 This ignores one other important category of requirements: "business requirements" (sometimes called project requirements). Business requirements do not constrain the product; they constrain the project. What is the budget? What is the schedule? What is the minimum acceptable rate of return on investment? And so on. Business requirements can be captured in a "project charter" and a "business case" or some similar specification. It is up to the project manager to deal with business requirements; the developers won't worry about most of them, so nothing more will be said about them in this book.

8 Again, the term "business" is used cautiously. Even in highly technical software like TCP/IP, there is still a "business." What does it mean to be a TCP connection? Can a TCP user have more than one TCP connection at the same time? What does it mean to receive a close when a TCP connection is in the established state? What do IP datagram fragmentation and reassembly mean? What happens when time to live for an IP datagram reaches zero? These decisions are independent of C, Java, or any other automation technology, including Tinker Toys. These are the "business" of TCP/IP.

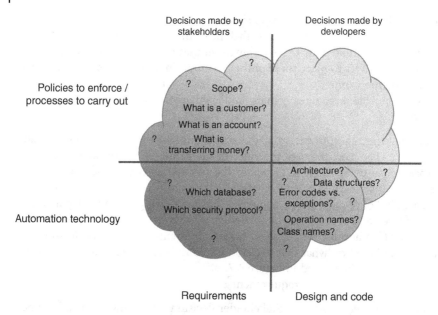

Figure 4.7 Two kinds of decisions: business versus automation technology.

Figure 4.8 relates the decisions in Figure 4.7 to the terms "functional requirements" and "nonfunctional requirements."

Functional requirements are decisions the stakeholders make about policies and processes they want automated. Nonfunctional requirements are decisions stakeholders make constraining automation technology. The decisions developers make—in light of stakeholder decisions, the requirements—are the design and the code. It is unlikely that stakeholders will let developers decide how the stakeholder's business should run, so the upper right quadrant in Figure 4.8 is empty.

4.7   Separating Functional and Nonfunctional Requirements

Figure 4.9 illustrates the problem we now have. While everyone should agree that there are two kinds of requirements, functional and nonfunctional, not everyone agrees on the criteria to separate them. If stakeholders require a particular user interface, for example, is that functional or nonfunctional? Different people have different opinions. Unfortunately, we can't make progress until this is resolved. We need an objective way of distinguishing one kind of requirement from the other.

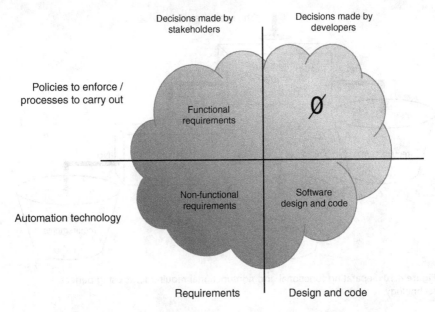

Figure 4.8 Two kinds of requirements, functional and nonfunctional.

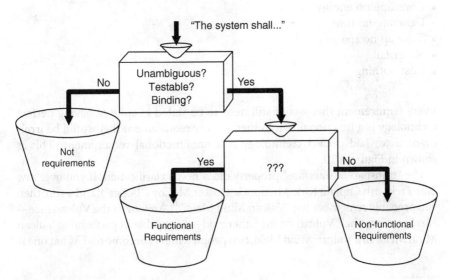

Figure 4.9 How to separate functional from nonfunctional requirements?

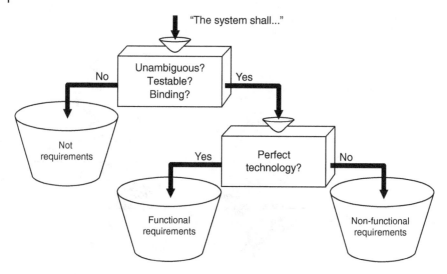

Figure 4.10 Separating functional and nonfunctional requirements using perfect technology.

The book *Essential Systems Analysis* by Steve McMenamin and John Palmer[9] introduces the concept of "perfect technology." A perfect computer would have:

- Infinite speed
- Unlimited memory
- Transparent interface
- Consume no energy
- Generate no heat
- Take up no space
- Never fail
- Cost nothing
- ...

Every requirement that would still need to be stated in spite of having perfect technology is a functional requirement. Every requirement that would be irrelevant if we had perfect technology is a nonfunctional requirement. This is shown in Figure 4.10.

The "transparent interface" property often needs clarification. If you ever saw Star Trek with Captain Kirk, Mr. Spock, Doctor McCoy ("Bones"), and so on, then you probably remember the "Vulcan Mind Meld."[10] Anyone of the Vulcan race—Mr. Spock was half Vulcan on his father's side—is capable of performing Vulcan Mind Meld. In a Vulcan Mind Meld, two people's minds become one. What one is

---

9 See [McMenamin84]. Perfect technology is also discussed in [Yourdon89].
10 See, for example, http://en.memory-alpha.wikia.com/wiki/Vulcan_mind_meld.

thinking, the other is also thinking. In terms of perfect technology, this means input/output (I/O) mechanisms like user interface screens, keyboards, mice, Web browsers, and such aren't necessary. The computer and the user's minds are one. Interface requirements are nonfunctional—intentionally, as explained in the next section. In an embedded system, sensors and actuators aren't part of functional requirements. The perfect computer already knows the pressure in Vacuum chamber 12A, and it can open and close Valve 47 by just deciding to do so.

4.7.1 An Example of Functional and Nonfunctional Requirements

Considering an automated teller machine (ATM, cash machine, bank automat, etc.), which of the following natural language requirements are functional, and which are nonfunctional?

- The ATM shall process deposit, withdraw, and balance query requests.
- The ATM shall keep transaction records online for seven days and then archive.
- The ATM shall communicate with the central office using SSL.
- The ATM shall be usable 95% of time.
- The ATM shall not allow withdrawing more than $250 per transaction.
- The ATM shall not allow withdrawing more than $500 per account in 24 hours.

You should recognize that the following are functional:

- The ATM shall process deposit, withdraw, and balance query requests.
- The ATM shall not allow withdrawing more than $250 per transaction.
- The ATM shall not allow withdrawing more than $500 per account in 24 hours.

As well, you should recognize that the following are nonfunctional:

- The ATM shall communicate with the central office using SSL.
- The ATM shall be usable 95% of time.

The requirement "The ATM shall keep transaction records online for seven days and then archive" is a common situation. Embedded in that one statement is both a functional requirement and a nonfunctional requirement. The functional requirement is "Transactions shall be remembered," while the nonfunctional requirement is "Remembered transactions shall be kept in main storage for seven days and then archived after that."

The requirement "The ATM shall not allow withdrawing more than $250 per transaction" can also be a special case depending on its justification. If the $250 limit is to minimize the bank's exposure to identity theft, then the requirement is functional. If the $250 limit is a result of size constraints on the cash box inside the ATM, then the requirement is nonfunctional. Sometimes we need to clarify a decision's rationale to properly categorize it.

4.7.2 Nonfunctional Requirements Are Still Requirements

Some people fall into a trap of thinking that nonfunctional requirements aren't real requirements—this is a misinterpretation of perfect technology. It is important to understand that nonfunctional requirements are as much requirements as functional requirements. Perfect technology is just a mental exercise that helps separate one from the other.

The implication of perfect technology is that each of the following—if required at all—are almost always nonfunctional:

- Computing machinery (CPUs, memory, networks, protocols, etc.)
- Security
- Backup and restore
- Speed, cost, capacity, reliability, maintainability
- I/O mechanisms and presentation formats
- Archiving
- ...

Functional requirements are always and only about policies and processes to be automated: policies that software needs to enforce and processes that software needs to carry out.

Appendix B gives an overview of the WebBooks 2.0 case study that is used in the remainder of this book. The following are examples of natural language functional requirements:

- Customers can browse the catalog by author, title, or subject.
- Customers use a shopping cart metaphor: add to cart, remove from cart, and proceed to check out.
- Order information includes date opened, shipping address, and quantity of each title ordered.
- An order is packable when stock on hand for each title is greater than quantity ordered.
- Customers can cancel their order as long as it has not been packed.
- Retain customer orders, even if completed or cancelled.
- Warehouse workers tell that a customer's order has been packed.
- Warehouse workers tell which orders have been shipped.
- When an order is packed, stock on hand for each title in the order is reduced by the quantity in that order.
- If stock on hand falls below a preset level for a title, a replenish order is created for the publisher.
- Replenish orders are held for 24 hours; if more copies are packed in that time, then add an equal amount to the quantity being ordered.
- Warehouse workers tell when a replenish order was received, increase stock on hand for each title by the amount reordered.
- Managers maintain the catalog.

The following are examples of nonfunctional requirements:

- Customers use a Web browser.
- Warehouse workers use dedicated terminals in the warehouse.
- Managers use dedicated terminals on their desks.
- Use existing formats for manager's reports.
- Replenish orders are emailed to publishers using an industry standard EDI format.
- Stronger security is needed, for example, two-factor authentication.
- Improve scalability.
- Improve availability.

4.8 Why Separate Functional from Nonfunctional Requirements?

Why bother separating requirements by kind? There are several important reasons:

- *Manage complexity*—By separating functional from nonfunctional requirements, one big problem becomes two smaller ones. We can first understand policy and process complexities without worrying about any automation technology. Once we've figured out the business, we can consider mapping that business onto the technology. This is classic "divide-and-conquer" complexity management.
- *Isolate areas of expertise*—Stakeholders, not technical people, are the experts in their business. Technical people, not business, are the experts in technology. Using Tinker Toy Tic Tac Toe as an example, stakeholders are the experts in Tic Tac Toe: games, boards, moves, X's and O's, three-in-a-row, etc. The technical team are the experts in Tinker Toys: dowels, spools, joints, gravity, structural stability, etc. If you give a specification with mixed functional and nonfunctional requirements to a business expert, when that business expert sees the first nonfunctional requirement, they will quit reading because they don't understand the technology.
- *Agree on the problem before building a solution*—Functional requirements, if stated completely,[11] consistently, clearly, concisely, and precisely in a semantic model, can be validated by stakeholders. Just like the blueprints for a house, stakeholders can say, "yes, that is what we want built" before time and money are wasted building the wrong thing. It is much cheaper and faster to iterate on semantic models than to iterate on code

---

11 This does not mean *all* functional requirements need to be specified, only the functional requirements relevant to the scope (to be) implemented so far. Model-based software engineering can, and sometimes should, use an agile process. This is covered in more detail in Chapter 24.

- *Enable finding an optimal solution*—One of the fundamental principles in Chapter 3 is "Avoid premature design and optimization." Separating functional requirements enables development of a semantic model: a precise specification of policies and processes to be automated. The separate nonfunctional requirements define technology constraints on solutions. Fudd's First Law of Creativity can be applied to propose and evaluate a variety of potential solutions to help find an optimal one.

Part II details how to model functional requirements. A few more comments on specifying nonfunctional requirements are presented here.

4.9 More on Nonfunctional Requirements

The nonfunctional requirements can be further separated into:

- *Nonfunctional how requirements*—Requirements that constrain use of specific automation technologies. Examples would be use of specific computing platforms (Windows™, MacOS™, Android OS™, iOS™, etc.), programming languages (Java, C++, C#, Python, etc.), compatibility with specific Web browsers (Chrome™, Safari™, Internet Explorer™, Edge™, etc.), use of given database engines (Oracle™, SQL Sever™, MySQL™, etc.), Tinker toys, and so on
- *Nonfunctional how well requirements*—Requirements that don't constrain developers to specific, named technologies. Instead, these specify "qualities of service": levels of performance that any automated solution must exhibit. Examples would be response time, throughput, accuracy, reliability, scalability, and so on.

As nonfunctional requirements are surfaced or clarified, update a "Minimum conditions of acceptance" section of the Background.[12]

4.9.1 Specifying Nonfunctional How Requirements

To unambiguously specify a nonfunctional how requirement, that requirement needs to define acceptable technology configurations. If the requirement is to use a smart phone operating system like Android OS, which versions of Android OS? All of them? Some of them? Just the latest one? As one of my former university professors said,

> *"If it's not obvious how to test it, can your specification be any good?"*
> (Dr. Ric Frankel, Seattle University)

---

12 Refer to the discussion of Figure 1.3.

Each nonfunctional how requirement needs to specify precisely which version(s) or configuration(s) of the technology is required, so testers clearly know what to test. This also makes it clear to developers what they are required to support.

4.9.2 Introducing Nonfunctional How Well Requirements

Nonfunctional how well requirements are qualities of service. Literally, how well does the software need to perform? Nonfunctional how well requirements don't constrain developers to any specific, named technology. Instead, these requirements say, "I don't care what technologies the developers use, what's important is that it performs at least this well."

Many software organizations fail to consider nonfunctional how well requirements early enough. Without upfront, explicitly stated nonfunctional how well requirements, developers make assumptions about what qualities of service are sufficient. Testers may or may not test those aspects of the system—but it's not likely because there aren't explicit requirements to test against and testers are usually too busy testing against what has been specified.

A quality of service gap between what users need and what is provided often isn't discovered until after the system goes into production. It's another case of the "Dreaded Phone Call Syndrome": "Your stupid system isn't _____ (fill in the blank) enough!" "You never told us!" "You never asked!" At this point it is usually very expensive—and sometimes even impossible—to restructure the software to satisfy the requirement.

The recommendation is to use "ISO/IEC 25010: System and software engineering – Systems and software Quality Requirements and Evaluation (SQuaRE) – System and software quality models"[13] as a starting point. Remove quality characteristics that are never relevant in your organization. Add characteristics that are unique to the kinds of software your organization produces, for example, ISO 25010 does not include scalability. Your organization should then incorporate this as a standard checklist in software requirements elicitation. Stakeholders need to be asked about all characteristics on this list and explicitly respond that there is either no requirement or say what their requirement is. This will help ensure that all nonfunctional how well requirements are surfaced and communicated, so software can be built to provide all necessary qualities of service.

4.9.3 Specifying Nonfunctional How Well Requirements

To understand how to specify nonfunctional how well requirements, we need to start with the idea of ranges of performance. Take as an example a

---

13 See [ISO11].

nonfunctional how well requirement about database capacity in terms of the number of customer records supported. Design and implementation choices by developers will lead to the maximum capacity being something or another. Maybe it's a big number, maybe it's not. It's not predetermined to be any specific level: developers influence the maximum level of performance by the technical decisions they make.

Next, understand there are economic implications over that range of performance levels. Let's say that developers were capable of building software that supported 50 billion customers. There aren't anywhere near that number of people on Earth (world population was about 7.2 billion in 2015). The system has way more capacity than any business could ever use. Further increases in level of performance don't provide additional value. This leads to the following definition:

> *"The perfection point is the most favorable level of performance, beyond which there is no additional benefit."*

For sake of argument, assume the perfection point in the banking software is 100 million customers. Assume that's the size of our bank's potential market.

Just the same, if the software were built to only support 100 customers, it would be worthless to any sizeable bank. That bank would be out of business if they could only support that few customers. This leads to the following definition:

> *"The fail point is the least favorable level of performance, beyond which there is no further reduction in benefit."*

This doesn't mean the software is worthless; maybe there are other aspects of the software that are still valuable in spite of rock-bottom performance in this characteristic. But it does mean value can't get any lower from worse performance in this characteristic. For the sake of argument, let's say the bank needs to support at least 10 million customers.

The third point is the "requirement point":

> *"The requirement point is the level of performance stakeholders feel justified asking for, based on the price they know they are paying for the software."*

For the sake of argument, let's say that based on what the bank is paying they feel justified asking for 90 million customers. Logically, the requirement point should always fall between the fail point and the perfection point.

Fail, requirement, and perfection points versus value are illustrated in Figure 4.11. Sometimes the curve is flipped vertically: a response time

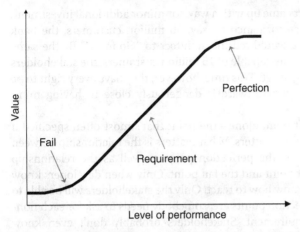

Figure 4.11 Fail, requirement, and perfection points, illustrated.

requirement would have higher value as the level of performance decreased (from 10 seconds, to 1 second, to 0.1 second, etc.).

In most organizations, if nonfunctional how well requirements are even specified at all, the developers are only given requirement points. This isn't enough for developers to know how to react. Several scenarios will be used to illustrate.

Consider the bank's capacity requirement as it stands right now; the fail point is 10 million customers, the requirement point is 90 million, and the perfection point is 100 million. The requirement point is close to the perfection point. Suppose the developers are unable to meet the requirement of 90 million customers. Say that the best they can support is 85 million. From the perspective of stakeholder expectation, it is fair to say that stakeholders have a right to be upset. They feel justified asking for 90 million and they are only getting 85 million. The question is, however, "how upset can they be?" From the perspective of value, they are getting almost as much value as they would ever be able to get. So they really shouldn't be very upset.

By the same token, let's say that with a requirement point of 90 million and a perfection point of 100 million, the project's architect has found a way to boost performance all the way up to 150 million customers. Should the architect implement this improvement? The question becomes: "how much investment is required?" and "how does that investment compare with the value at 100 million customers?" Remember that any capacity beyond 100 million customers—the perfection point—gives no additional value. It should never be assumed that increasing a level of performance is always worth the investment.

Now change the scenario and see what happens when the requirement point is close to the fail point. Assume the fail point is still 10 million and the perfection point is still 100 million, but now assume the requirement point is

20 million. If the architect came up with a way, for minor additional investment, to increase the level of performance to, say, 50 million customers, the bank would be ecstatic, and we would tell the architect to "Go for it!" By the same token, if developers were only capable of 15 million customers, the stakeholders are again justified in being upset. This time, however, they have every right to be extremely upset because the software is dangerously close to having minimal value.

It isn't the requirement point alone—the point that's most often specified if it's even specified at all—that matters. What matters is the relationship between the requirement point and the perfection point as well as the relationship between the requirement point and the fail point. Only when developers know all three points will they know how to react. Only the stakeholders will be able to say what the fail and perfection points are; somebody needs to ask for each nonfunctional how well requirement. Stakeholders probably don't even know themselves or even how to answer the question. A true engineer with a solid understanding of engineering economics can guide stakeholders through an analysis. Those stakeholder answers need to be communicated to the development team. Gilb's "Planguage"[14] can be useful for specifying nonfunctional how well requirements.

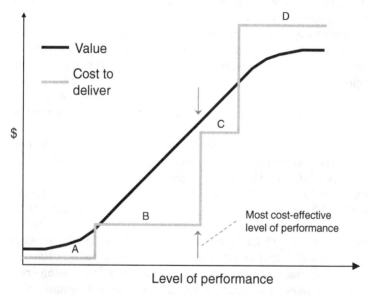

Figure 4.12 Value compared to cost of delivering that level of performance.

---

14 See [Gilb05].

Even more sophisticated economic analysis would look at the cost of delivering each level of performance. Cost is typically a step function as illustrated in Figure 4.12. Investing A covers one range of levels of performance, up to some maximum. Additional investment, to B, is required to increase the level of performance, but it opens up a new range. Further investment, to C, is required to increase the range of performance again and so on.

The most cost-effective level of performance has the largest positive gap between value and cost to deliver.

4.10 Quality Criteria

The quality criteria in Table 4.1 can be applied to all requirements-related work to identify and remove requirements defects as quickly and as cheaply as possible.

Table 4.1 Quality criteria for requirements.

Item	Criterion
RQ-1	Requirements are all—and only—decisions made by stakeholders
RQ-2	Each requirement is unambiguous: it can only be interpreted in exactly one way
RQ-3	Each requirement is testable: there is a means of demonstrating compliance or noncompliance
RQ-4	Each requirement is binding: stakeholders are willing to pay for it and are unwilling to not have it
RQ-5	All requirements have been separated by kind: functional, nonfunctional how, and nonfunctional how well
RQ-6	Functional requirements are all and only stakeholder decisions about policies to enforce and processes to carry out ("perfect technology")
RQ-7	Nonfunctional how requirements are all and only constraints on technologies: version(s) or configuration(s) is clearly specified
RQ-8	Nonfunctional how well requirements are all and only qualities of service: levels of performance an automated solution must exhibit
RQ-9	Nonfunctional how well requirements have been identified based on a checklist (possibly derived from ISO/IEC 25010) to ensure that all relevant qualities of service have been specified
RQ-10	Nonfunctional how well requirements are fully specified in terms of explicit fail, requirement, and perfection point levels of performance

4.11 Summary

IEEE's formal definition of a requirement is correct but not necessarily practical. Informally, a requirement is a decision made by someone outside a development team that is imposed on those developers. Requirements need to be unambiguous (interpretable in exactly one way), testable (compliance or noncompliance can be demonstrated), and binding (something the stakeholders want, are willing to pay for, and will be upset if they don't get). There are different kinds of requirements:

- *Functional requirements*—Constraints on business to be automated: policies to be enforced and processes to carry out
- *Nonfunctional requirements*—Constraints on automation technology. There are two further kinds: nonfunctional how—constraints on specific, named technologies—and nonfunctional how well that define necessary qualities of service

There are many advantages to separating requirements by kind; the most important is complexity management. Additional detail was provided on how to specify nonfunctional requirements. Specifying functional requirements is detailed in Part II.

5

UML Overview

This chapter gives a brief overview of the Object Management Group (OMG)—the creator and maintainer of the Unified Modeling Language (UML)—along with a short history of object-oriented development and the motivation for UML. UML is used extensively throughout this book. UML also has several useful generic facilities, such as notes, constraints, stereotypes, packages, and general dependencies, which are described here. If you are already familiar with UML, you may want to just skim this chapter.

5.1 Object Management Group (OMG®)

A good description of the OMG comes from their website[1]:

> "The Object Management Group (OMG®) is an international, open membership, not-for-profit technology standards consortium. Founded in 1989, OMG standards are driven by vendors, end-users, academic institutions and government agencies. OMG Task Forces develop enterprise integration standards for a wide range of technologies and an even wider range of industries. OMG's modeling standards, including the Unified Modeling Language (UML) and Model Driven Architecture (MDA), enable powerful visual design, execution and maintenance of software and other processes. OMG also hosts organizations such as the user-driven information-sharing Cloud Standards Customer Council (CSCC) and the IT industry software quality standardization group, the Consortium for IT Software Quality (CISQ).
>
> Our members include hundreds of organizations including software end-users in over two dozen vertical markets (from finance to healthcare and automotive to insurance) and virtually every large organization in the

---

1 See http://www.omg.org.

How to Engineer Software: A Model-Based Approach, First Edition. Steve Tockey.
© 2019 the IEEE Computer Society, Inc. Published 2019 by John Wiley & Sons, Inc.

technology industry. OMG's one organization- one vote policy ensures that every member organization- whether large or small- has an effective voice in our voting process."

5.2 Object-Oriented Development and Unified Modeling Language (UML)

Object-oriented programming can be traced back to about 1967. The language Simula 67 had most of the language features generally associated with object-oriented programming. Smalltalk-72 was an early version of the Smalltalk system that came out in 1972. Smalltalk-80 was the most widely used version. C++ traces back to about 1984 when Bjarne Stroustrup, then at Bell Labs, incorporated features of Simula 67 into C.

Object-oriented design appeared in the early 1980s, and object-oriented analysis appeared a few years later. By the early 1990s there had been an explosion of object-oriented development approaches. A catalog of object-oriented development methods published by an organization at Ft. Monmouth, New Jersey, USA, identified over 150 distinct approaches.

All of those approaches shared common elements. Not surprisingly they supported modeling of classes, objects, attributes (instance variables/member data), operations (methods/member functions), messages, and so on. There were also differences, most significantly in notation. In one approach, a circle meant one thing and a rectangle meant another thing. In a different approach, circle and rectangle meant completely different things. The various approaches also espoused different lifecycles. Some wanted you to build models in this order; others wanted you to do them in that order. Some were more iterative than others. A few did a better job of separating requirements modeling from design modeling, although the majority made no attempt.

By the mid-1990s the situation had gotten so bad that developers may have been on a project where they learned the Object-Oriented Modeling and Design (OMAD) approach,[2] but if those same developers moved to a different project that used, say, the Booch approach,[3] they had to be retrained. Each approach had an almost cult-like following and religious debates were common.

Initial work on the UML started in 1995 with the intent of "putting an end to the object oriented methods wars." The first version of UML was released in 1997. Ongoing refinement and evolution of UML continues as lessons learned from use on projects are fed back to the OMG. From a UML modeler's

---

2 See [Rumbaugh91].
3 See [Booch91].

perspective, the language has been largely stable for at least ten years. Most changes have been in how UML itself is defined (i.e., changes to the model that defines UML, the "UML meta-model").

The purpose of UML is to[4]:

> "... *provide system architects, software engineers, and software developers with tools for analysis, design, and implementation of software based systems as well as for modeling business and similar processes."*

5.3 Dialects of UML

Natural languages like English have dialects—in effect sub-languages. American English has many interesting and significant differences with UK English. "Table a motion" in parliamentary procedure in the United States means the exact opposite as it does in the United Kingdom. In the United Kingdom, it means open that topic for debate and discussion. In the United States it means put that topics aside without resolution: there is no possibility of near-term agreement so don't debate or discuss it any more. Similarly, UML as a language has at least two dialects. UML itself and the OMG do not formally recognize the notion of dialects. UML is a general-purpose modeling language suitable for a wide variety of uses. This use of the term "dialect" is an interpretation by model-based software engineering.

By far, the most common dialect is the software design dialect: using UML to describe the structure of a software solution to a business problem. A far less recognized and understood dialect of UML is for functional requirements. In this case, the thing being described is policies to enforce and processes to carry out—the semantic model. Part II details this requirements dialect of UML. Part III uses the design dialect.

This book assumes readers are already familiar with the basics of object-oriented development. For those that aren't, it may be reasonably easy to figure out from context; otherwise there are several useful books, including:

- Meilir Page-Jones' *Fundamental of Object-Oriented Design in UML*[5]—If you need an introduction to the basics of object orientation, this is a great primer. While focused on the design dialect of UML, it does a fine job of explaining the mindset of object-oriented development.
- Martin Fowler and Kendall Scott's *UML Distilled*[6]—One can't learn model-based software engineering from Fowler and Scott's book. On the other hand,

---

4 See [OMG11a].
5 See [Page-Jones00].
6 See [Fowler03].

it's a handy reference for those times when "I know what I want to say, I just don't know how to say it in UML" although the book favors the design dialect.

- The UML specification set[7]—Available from the OMG at http://www.omg.org.

5.4 Generic UML Facilities

Generic UML facilities are independent of any specific modeling context. Maybe you are modeling requirements or maybe you are modeling design, it doesn't matter. What matters is that these facilities can be used at any time. They are presented in this section because they are broadly applicable across modeling. In the discussion below, the term "model element" means something that is part of a UML model, like a class, an attribute, a state, an operation, etc.

5.4.1 Notes

The simplest of the generic UML facilities is the "note" (also called "comment"). Just as developers put comments in source code, it can be useful to make a comment on a UML diagram. UML's notation for a note, a rectangle with a folded corner, is shown in Figure 5.1.

By default, a note applies to the entire diagram. On the other hand, proximity and context may be enough to convey that the note is relevant to specific model elements. If you want to make explicit that a note applies to a particular model element, add a dotted line between the note and the model element it applies to. Do not put an arrow on the dashed line; the plain dashed line is sufficient. If you want the comment to apply to a group of model elements, draw a dashed shape around that group and dashed line to connect the note to the dashed shape as shown in Figure 5.2. The dashed shape does not need to be a rectangle. The note is interpreted as applying to all elements inside the dashed shape.

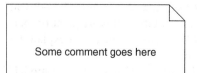

Some comment goes here

Figure 5.1 UML's notation for a note.

---

7 See [OMG11a] and [OMG11b].

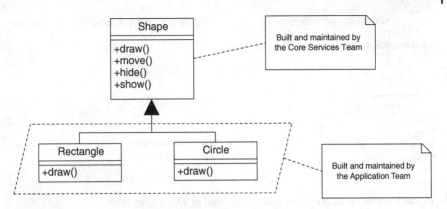

Figure 5.2 Associating notes to model elements.

Just as with comments in code, notes should follow these guidelines:

- *Comments must never contradict the thing(s) being commented on.*
- *Comments must always add useful information that is not already obvious from the thing(s) being commented on.*
- *Whenever practical, comments should explain why something looks the way it does.*

5.4.2 Constraints

Sometimes, important semantic relationships need to be maintained between two or more model elements, and it may be difficult or impossible to express those relationships in ordinary UML. As an example, at more than one major aerospace corporation, a payroll policy is:

> *"The manager of a group must be the highest paid employee in that group"*

No subordinate employee can have a salary higher than his or her manager. But it is impossible to state that policy using ordinary UML language elements like classes and attributes. UML constraints allow the modeler to specify such relationships. UML's constraint notation puts a Boolean expression (or a reference to an external policy statement) inside "{" and "}", as shown in Figure 5.3.

As with UML notes, constraints may be connected by a dashed line to model elements or groups of model elements. There is no required format for the Boolean expression. Some organizations use UML's Object Constraint Language[8]

---

8 See [OMG14].

{ some Boolean expression }   **Figure 5.3** UML's notation for constraints.

{ a reference to an external policy statement }

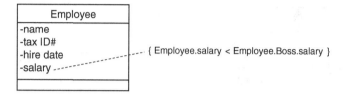

Figure 5.4 The aerospace salary policy expressed as a UML constraint.

(OCL); others find OCL too cumbersome. Figure 5.4 shows how the aerospace salary policy can be expressed using a UML constraint.

5.4.3 Stereotypes

Stereotypes let a modeler modify the meaning of UML concepts. As an example, the modeling concept "class" in a semantic model normally means "something in a business for which some software needs to be written and maintained." In some cases, it is useful or necessary to include classes in a semantic model that won't be implemented in software. Maybe this is an embedded system and we need to show the relationship between hardware elements and business elements. Rather than putting notes all over the diagram, use stereotypes instead. The stereotype notation is a short phrase between "guillemets" (pronounced "gee-may"), "«" and "»", or between double less than "<<" and greater than ">>". Figure 5.5 shows a class in a mixed hardware–software system that has been stereotyped as "«hardware»" to signify that it is a hardware element rather than something that is to be built and maintained in software.

Any kind of model element can be stereotyped: classes, attributes, operations, etc. The concepts of model-based software engineering and their meanings are defined in the meta-model for semantic modeling in Appendix L. There are also a set of predefined UML stereotypes such as "«actor»", "«include»", "«extend»", "«new»", "«destroy»", "«implement»", "«refine»", "«type»", etc.

Just creating a new stereotype alone is not necessarily sufficient. Someone reading the model might not understand what is meant by it. Much like having a legend on a map, a UML model may have a "profile" that defines local conventions and interpretations. Custom stereotypes should be precisely defined in a project—or organizational—profile. The minimal UML profile for model-based software engineering is in Appendix L. This profile extends and refines standard definitions of UML.

Figure 5.5 An example stereotype, in this case "«hardware»".

Figure 5.6 An example of UML's package notation.

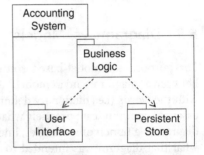

5.4.4 Packages

Packages are a model management facility and, as the name implies, simply a container. Just like folders in a desktop operating system where you can put both files and folders, packages can contain models or packages. Packages in UML even use the same file folder icon as shown in Figure 5.6.

It should be safe to assume the package named Business Logic in Figure 5.6 either contains the models of the business logic or contains other packages that themselves contain the models of interest.

Packages are useful in two important ways:

- *Complexity management*—Good packaging and naming aids abstraction and encapsulation. Each package should abstract some (presumably highly cohesive and loosely coupled) set of things and encapsulate its implementation details.
- *Work management*—Packages can help work partitioning across a project, as in "Our team will build and maintain the Business Logic, the team down the hall will build and maintain the User Interface." Chapters 6 and 11 build on this.

5.4.5 General Dependencies

A general dependency means that something in a model depends on something else, possibly in a different model. General dependencies are shown in UML as dashed lines with an arrow that points at the thing being depended on. Figure 5.6 shows two dependencies, the dashed lines from Business Logic to both User Interface and Persistent Store. Those dependencies mean that model elements inside the Business Logic package are defined in terms of elements defined in those other two packages. In the design dialect of UML, a general dependency between packages usually indicates a compilation dependency: one or more of the classes in Business Logic use operations on (send messages to) the interfaces of classes in User Interface and Persistent Store.

5.5   Diagrams vs. Models

For purposes of model-based software engineering, a distinction is drawn between a "diagram" and a "model." A diagram is a picture. A model is a picture with the words (i.e., dictionary definitions for important model elements) necessary to communicate precisely what that diagram is intended to mean. A class diagram is a bunch of rectangles, lines, etc., but the reader can't always be sure what that diagram was intended to mean unless the modeler supplements it with dictionary-like descriptions for each class, each attribute, and so on. In some cases, like use case diagrams and sequence diagrams, the diagram alone can be sufficient. In those cases, just provide the diagram. But in other cases, most notably the semantic class model, the words are indispensable.

5.6   More to UML

There is a lot more to UML than is shown in this book. Other UML facilities could prove useful on projects:

- Activity diagrams
- Deployment diagrams
- Others

These facilities—while sometimes very useful and possibly even critical—aren't necessary on all projects and are thus not required for successful use of model-based software engineering. If you find any of these other diagrams useful, by all means use them.

5.7   Summary

Object-oriented programming has existed, in one form or another, since the 1960s. The explosion of competing analysis and design methods in the late

1980s and early 1990s led to what was known as "the method wars." The OMG, formed in 1989, stepped into the fray in 1995 to drive agreement on a common modeling language for object-oriented systems. UML, the result of that agreement, was first released in 1997. Since then UML continues to evolve, but the majority of recent evolution involves how UML is defined internally—the practicing modeler doesn't need to worry about that. UML will be used extensively throughout this book. UML also has several useful generic facilities, such as notes, constraints, stereotypes, packages, and general dependencies, which can be useful across all modeling.

6

Partitioning Systems into Domains

The larger the software system, the more likely it is to encompass distinctly different subject matters. In WebBooks 2.0, customer ordering, payment, user security, scalability, and high availability are each distinctly different subject matters. Partitioning systems into domains is partly motivated by complexity management and partly by work partitioning (i.e., project management).

This chapter starts by defining domains and explains how to identify them. It then shows how to build a domain diagram that provides the top-level conceptual view of a system. The relationship between domains will be explained, along with how the "big picture" development process in Figure 1.3 relates to domains. Consistency between domain partitioning and fundamental principles in Chapter 3 is also discussed. The chapter closes with a description of how a project team should be organized around domains rather than letting an arbitrary organizational structure drive equally arbitrary software architecture.

6.1   What Is a Domain?

Sally Shlaer and Steve Mellor published most of the original work on domain separation.[1] They describe a domain:

> *"In building a typical large software system, the analyst generally has to deal with a number of distinctly different subject matters, or domains. Each domain can be thought of as a separate world inhabited by its own conceptual entities, or objects."*

In WebBooks 2.0 (see the WebBooks 2.0 Overview in Appendix B), software about Customers, Orders, Inventory, Packing, and Shipping is a very different subject matter than software about Heartbeats, Checkpoints, Failover, and

---

1 See, for example, [Shlaer90].

How to Engineer Software: A Model-Based Approach, First Edition. Steve Tockey.
© 2019 the IEEE Computer Society, Inc. Published 2019 by John Wiley & Sons, Inc.

N +M redundancy. The software development process for each subject matter may be the same (or at least similar), but the subject matters themselves are completely different.

Based on differences in vocabulary alone, it should be clear that the Web-Books 2.0 team is confronted with several distinct problems. They should separate those problems and deal with each in as much isolation as possible. We can't eliminate complexity, but we can limit how much we have to deal with at any one time. Partitioning a system into domains is an effective way of limiting complexity that needs to be dealt with at one time. Domains are separated for now and reconnected in Chapter 17.

6.2   Identifying Domains

There are many ways to identify domains in a large system. The process in this chapter is just one and works well on most systems.

6.2.1   Brainstorm Concepts

Step 1 is to create a breadth-wise list of representative concepts about which software needs to be written and maintained. Software in WebBooks 2.0 will need to be written and maintained for Customers, Orders, Credit card payment, Data centers, Load balancing, Failover, Passwords, etc. So make a list of these of concepts. Both nouns and verbs are acceptable. You don't need—or even want—to be exhaustive, which would be too much work for no benefit. Just try to be reasonably comprehensive in terms of breadth without worrying about depth. If you already have 5–10 concepts that seem related to each other, one more related concept won't make a difference.

This can be done as a brainstorming session. Write each concept on a Post-it™ or similar "sticky note" and stick it on a flip chart or whiteboard. The concepts will be rearranged into affinity groups in the next step. Simply writing each concept on a small piece of paper and putting those on a conference room table also works.

Considering WebBooks 2.0, Figure 6.1 shows a sample of concepts that could come out of brainstorming.

6.2.2   Group Concepts by "Consistent Vocabulary"

The second step is to group the concepts based on "consistent vocabulary." Consider someone who is an expert in a particular subject matter and that they would know and commonly use a particular concept, like Order. That expert would also likely know and use the concept Customer. They would also be expected to know and use concepts like Add to cart, Proceed to checkout,

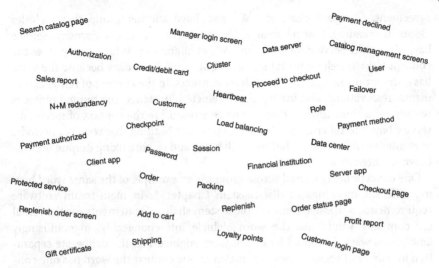

Figure 6.1 Example of brainstormed concepts for WebBooks 2.0.

Packing, and Shipping. So all of those concepts should end up in the same affinity group. This expert, however, should not be expected to know or use concepts like User, Password, Failover, Node, Financial institution, Heartbeat, Load balancing, and so on. Such a person may well use those other concepts at some point, but not in the same context as the first set of concepts. The other concepts should go into different affinity groups than the first.

Some other expert who knows and uses the concept Payment method would also know and use concepts like Debit account, Payment declined, Gift certificate, Loyalty points, and Credit account but would not be expected to know nor use concepts Failover, Node, Heartbeat, Checkpoint, Data center, and Server app. Continue grouping until each concept is in an affinity group with its related concepts. If a concept does not fit into any existing group, think about whether there are other related concepts that haven't been brought out through brainstorming. If so, list a few of those related concepts to gain confidence there really is another affinity group. If no other concepts can be found, then it could be that concept isn't significant enough and might be safe to ignore.

You may be tempted to put one concept into two or more affinity groups at the same time. It's not always clear which group some concepts belong in. One possibility is that the groups are poorly defined and need to be rearranged. Or, as often happens, the concept really does need to be in more than one group but with the understanding that it has different meanings in each of those different contexts.

As an example, assume we are working on software to automate a rental car company. We already have one affinity group that includes Renter, Daily rental rate, Weekly rental rate, Reservation, Passenger capacity, Luxury class, Rental agreement, Compact class, etc. We also have another group that includes Odometer reading, Last oil change, Customer complaint, Oil viscosity, Service bay, Mechanic, Service interval, and Wheel alignment. Which group does the concept Vehicle belong in? It belongs in both, and that's okay because the word has different meanings in each of those contexts. In the context of rental agreements, reservations, and luxury class, Vehicle represents "the thing a renter is renting for a short time so they can drive around." In the context of mechanic, service bay, and oil viscosity, Vehicle represents "a thing that requires periodic preventative maintenance, but may still break and require fixing despite preventative maintenance."

One concept being shared across groups is an example of the same word having different meanings as discussed in Chapter 1. In mainstream software requirements, a massive tome of "the system shall ..." statements for the rental car company would use the word Vehicle interchangeably, in confusingly ambiguous ways. In model-based software engineering, the deliberate separation into distinct vocabularies means that in one context the word has one consistent meaning and that meaning is different, and consistently different, in any other context. Since most people would rarely deal with more than one vocabulary at the same time, the word gets used consistently in whatever context it's being used.

Consider the concepts in Figure 6.1. Add to cart, Proceed to checkout, Packing, Shipping, and Replenish should be in one group. It should also be reasonable to group Payment method, Gift certificate, Payment authorization, Credit/debit card, Loyalty points, and Financial institution into a different group. But it should not be reasonable to group Packing and Shipping together with Loyalty points and Gift certificates. The first group is about people asking for things and getting them. The second group is about paying for goods and services. Per the fundamental principle of loose coupling, if something can be disconnected from something else, then it should be. Requesting and delivering things can be largely disconnected from paying for goods and services.

Notice that Customer and Order could belong with either of those two groups. In the context of the first, Customer represents someone who wants a set of goods and Order represents the specific goods that customer wants. In the context of the second group, Order represents goods and services that need to be paid for, and Customer represents someone responsible for making payment. Customer and Order can be in both groups because they have different meanings in both contexts.

Figure 6.2 shows the result of grouping the brainstormed concepts for Web-Books 2.0.

Each of the affinity groups from step 2 is a domain.

What if you only found one domain? On the one hand, maybe you are lucky because you might have a relatively small system that does not need domain partitioning. You may still want to further partition that one domain—or any

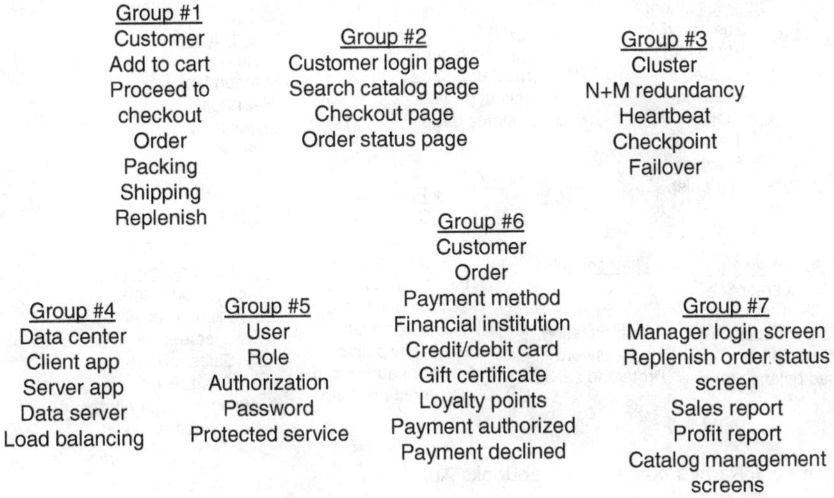

Group #1
Customer
Add to cart
Proceed to
checkout
Order
Packing
Shipping
Replenish

Group #2
Customer login page
Search catalog page
Checkout page
Order status page

Group #3
Cluster
N+M redundancy
Heartbeat
Checkpoint
Failover

Group #6
Customer
Order
Payment method
Financial institution
Credit/debit card
Gift certificate
Loyalty points
Payment authorized
Payment declined

Group #4
Data center
Client app
Server app
Data server
Load balancing

Group #5
User
Role
Authorization
Password
Protected service

Group #7
Manager login screen
Replenish order status
screen
Sales report
Profit report
Catalog management
screens

Figure 6.2 Grouped concepts for WebBooks 2.0.

domain when there is more than one—into subdomains as explained in Chapter 11. On the other hand, you may want to think carefully about how well the first two steps were done. Did you really get the breadth of concepts in brainstorming? Did you really do the affinity grouping appropriately?

As a very rough approximation, an application of about 100k source lines of code could be expected to have on the order of 5–10 domains. On average, a domain is in the range of 10–20k source lines of code. Clearly, some domains require far more lines of code and some require far less. But if your application is expected to be in the neighborhood of 50k source lines of code and you couldn't find more than one domain, then you are likely to have done the brainstorming or the affinity grouping incorrectly.

If brainstorming and affinity grouping are done by a team, it is helpful if that team represents a cross section of the disciplines involved in the project: business, technical, etc. The team members should also have good communication skills to help clarify the meaning of each term and increase the chances that it will be put into the right affinity group. This is particularly important when one concept falls in more than one domain, for example, "vehicle" in the rental car example.

6.2.3 Name the Domains

Step 3 is to give each of the affinity groups a name that reflects the scope and context of that subject matter. The name of a domain doesn't need to be a single word; a short phrase is acceptable. Group #1 from WebBooks 2.0 might be

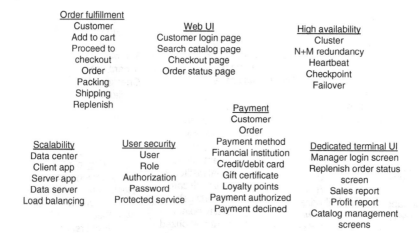

Figure 6.3 Named domains in WebBooks 2.0.

called "Order fulfillment." Group #2 might be called "Web UI." Group #3 might be called "High availability." Group #4 might be called "Scalability." Figure 6.3 shows named domains for WebBooks 2.0.

6.3   Domain Diagrams: Domains and Their Relationships

Now that domains have been identified and named, they need to be arranged to show interrelationships. One of the domains is the "reason for being" for the software. That domain represents the ultimate business the stakeholders want automated. In WebBooks 2.0, that reason-for-being domain is Order fulfillment. That reason-for-being domain is the top domain.

The remaining domains are then arranged according to "who imposes requirements on who." Order fulfillment will impose requirements on User security; User security won't impose requirements on Order fulfillment. Scalability will impose requirements on High availability, not the other way. Payment will impose requirements on Web UI; Web UI won't impose requirements on Payment. By its very nature, "imposes requirements on" is asymmetrical.

6.3.1   Domain Diagram Notation

The recommended notation for a domain diagram uses UML packages. UML's general dependency notation, a dashed line with an arrow, shows which domains impose requirements on other domains. The arrow shows the

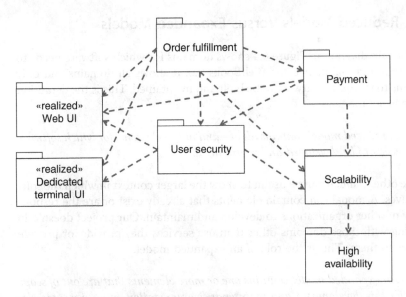

Figure 6.4 Domain diagram for WebBooks 2.0.

direction that requirements are imposed: requirements are imposed from Order fulfillment onto User security, so the dependency arrow points from Order fulfillment to User security.

Figure 6.4 shows the domain diagram for WebBooks 2.0. Use of stereotype "«realized»" will be explained below.

6.3.2 Imposing Requirements on a Domain

It is important to understand that "imposes requirements on" dependencies do not need to be designed and implemented in a client-server fashion. The higher domain might connect to a lower domain via direct procedure call or remote procedure call (RPC): this would be client-server. But a lower domain, like User security, could be client and make direct procedure calls or use an RPC interface on Order fulfillment: it could be implemented as REST, service-oriented architecture (SOA), or microservices. User security could be part of a thick client. The connection between the implementations of two domains might use inheritance: a lower domain could provide a base class that a higher domain inherits from. Template classes (or "generics") could be another way to connect one domain to another. Implementing inter-domain connections is discussed in Chapter 14.

It is also important to understand that the domain diagram should only be considered a "logical" (i.e., "conceptual") architecture. The allocation of software that implements each domain to physical processing units such as processors, processes, threads, etc. is a technology issue and will be addressed in Part III.

6.4 Reduced Models Versus Expanded Models

The domain diagram in Figure 6.4 shows domains for which software needs to be written and maintained for WebBooks 2.0. It shows all domains and only domains that require software to be built and maintained. This is the definition of a reduced model:

> *"A reduced model contains all of—and only—elements for which software needs to be developed and maintained."*

On the other hand, it can be useful to show the larger context in which the software lives. A model can contain elements that already exist or are the responsibility of other organizations to develop and maintain. Our project doesn't do anything with those domains other than use services they provide, or provide services to them. This is the role of an expanded model:

> *"An expanded model contains one or more elements that are out of scope for this development and maintenance organization, but those extra elements communicate valuable context and important relationships to what this organization needs to develop and maintain."*

The reduced model versus expanded model idea applies across all models, not just domain models. A semantic model could be reduced or expanded. A design class diagram could be reduced or expanded. Whether or not to include contextual elements—that is, to build an expanded or reduced model—can be debatable. In the end, that debate should be settled on economics. Including contextual elements comes at a cost: time and effort are needed to put those model elements in and maintain them over time. On the other hand, there may be value in communicating that larger context. Decide on a case-by case basis: what is the value of extra context compared to the cost of putting it there and keeping it up to date?

6.4.1 Preexisting Technologies

WebBooks 2.0 may make use of preexisting technologies, including HTML, Java Swing, a relational database, and so on. There could be value in showing the relationship between the domains in Figure 6.4 and those preexisting technologies, for example, Web UI will make use of HTML, while the Dedicated terminal UI might make use of the Swing UI toolkit.

If you include preexisting (i.e., out of scope) entities, you should label those elements appropriately. Mellor and Balcer [Mellor02] use the stereotype "«realized»" to identify preexisting domains. Any other appropriate stereotype, for example, "«preexisting»", could be used instead as long as that stereotype is adequately defined (e.g., in the project's or organization's profile).

6.4.2 Indeterminate Domains

Early in some projects it may not be clear if any one domain might be preexisting or not. It may be too early to decide if existing software is sufficient or if project specific software needs to be built and maintained. In this case, another stereotype, say, "«tbd»" or "«indeterminate»", could be used as long as it is adequately defined. As the project progresses and decisions are made about whether to build versus acquire externally, the domain diagram needs to be updated.

6.4.3 Domain Descriptions

If you want to provide a description for a domain, there are several options, and those options aren't mutually exclusive. You could use more than one if appropriate. The most common options are:

- A couple of sentences or a paragraph describing the scope of the domain
- The list of affinity grouped concepts that led to the identification of that domain
- A (reference to a) domain-level use case diagram[2]
- A (representative) set of requirements that have been allocated to this domain

The domain description can also play the role of Background in Figure 1.3. An example for WebBooks 2.0 is shown in Appendix C.

6.5 Quality Criteria

In addition to the overall quality criteria (Table 3.1) and naming criteria (Table 3.2),
Table 6.1 shows quality criteria for partitioning a large system into domains.

6.6 Implications of Domain Separation on Software Architecture

Each domain represents an independent service that is itself both a problem and a solution. As a problem, it defines policies and processes of (a part of) the solution for domains immediately above it. The top domain provides services to external users: automating the policies and processes the stakeholders want automated. As a solution, lower domains provide nontrivial automation technologies to the design and implementation of domain(s) above them.

---

2 Use case diagrams are presented in Chapter 7.

Table 6.1 Quality criteria for domain partitioning.

Item	Criterion
DP-1	The top domain represents the ultimate business that stakeholders want automated: it is the "reason for being" of the software
DP-2	All domains are arranged according to "who imposes requirements on who"
DP-3	The direction that requirements are imposed is clearly and correctly identified
DP-4	Domains representing preexisting entities (i.e., an expanded model) have been labeled appropriately, for example, "«realized»"
DP-5	Domains are stereotyped "«tbd»" or "«indeterminate»" only when a decision to build and maintain versus acquire have not been made

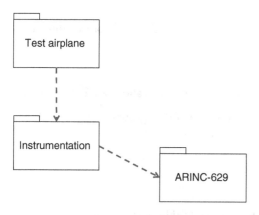

Figure 6.5 A fragment of the domain diagram for Automated Test Equipment.

Any connected pair of domains is a problem–solution pair. The higher domain describes the policies and process of a problem, and the lower domain describes part of the technology-based design of one particular solution. Each lower domain is an automation technology and is invisible to the semantic model of higher domain(s). A lower domain doesn't become relevant until design and coding of a higher domain, where the lower domain provides nontrivial mechanisms for the higher domain to map on to. A fragment of an Automated Test Equipment (ATE) system for large commercial airliners is an example; a portion of the domain diagram is shown in Figure 6.5.

6.6.1 Test Airplane Domain

The Test airplane domain is a test script interpreter. From the perspective of a factory floor mechanic who needs to test an airplane, they run a "Test," which is made up of "Blocks," which are further made up of "Steps." This is the business of the Test airplane domain, and these concepts are primary elements of the Test airplane domain's semantic model. Some "Steps" refer to "Airplane Test Points," which represent parts of the airplane that are involved in a test. An example would be a short sequence of steps in Block-9 of an ATE test script:

"110 SET Rudder to 5 degrees left
120 VERIFY Rudder is between 4.9 and 5.1 degrees left"

Recalling the transparent interface ("Vulcan mind meld") property of semantic models, each Airplane Test Point (e.g., Rudder, Engine #1, Engine #2, Flaps, etc.) represents direct control over, and direct response in return, of the airplane. At this level of abstraction, there are no wires; ATE and the airplane are "of one mind." How one actually communicates with an airplane is a responsibility of design and code, not the semantic model.

6.6.2 Instrumentation Domain

The business of the Instrumentation domain is to communicate with an airplane under test. Elements in this semantic model include instruments like "Voltmeter," "Ammeter," "Digital-to-analog converter," and "Analog-to-digital converter." One kind of instrument is an "ARINC-629 Data Point." Again, because of the transparent interface property, "ARINC-629 Data Point" represents direct access to data values on an ARINC-629 communication bus. How one actually communicates with an ARINC-629 bus is a responsibility of design and code.

6.6.3 ARINC-629 Domain

The commercial airplanes being tested are fly-by-wire and some communication between flight systems uses ARINC-629 protocol.[3] For our purposes, consider ARINC-629 to be similar to Internet Protocol (IPv6).[4] It really isn't, but explaining how ARINC-629 actually works is far too long, involved, and unnecessary. A widely known protocol like IPv6 is just as effective at illustrating: both ARINC-629 and IPv6 are nontrivial protocols. Just being able to deal with IPv6 datagrams, fragmentation, reassembly, routing, time to live, and so on represents nontrivial software. How one actually communicates with ARINC-629 device drivers is a responsibility of the design and code of the ARINC-629 domain.

---

3 See, for example, https://en.wikipedia.org/wiki/ARINC#600_Series.
4 See, for example, [IETF98].

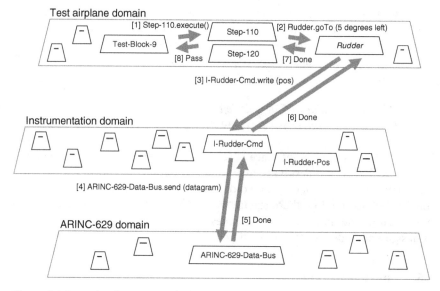

Figure 6.6 Executing Step-110 in Block-9.

6.6.4 An Example Execution Scenario: Executing Step-110

Assume a factory floor mechanic is using the ATE system to test an airplane. Test-Block-9 is being executed in a test script and the next step to execute is Step-110. Figure 6.6 overviews how Step-110 is executed in ATE software.

Block-9 knows that the next step to be executed is Step-110, so it requests that Step-110 execute

[1] Step-110.execute()

Step-110 knows it is a SET kind of step and that it needs to tell the Airplane Test Point named Rudder to move to 5° left:

[2] Rudder.goTo(5 degrees left)

Messages [1] and [2] are in the Test airplane domain; the next message crosses from Test airplane to Instrumentation. The design and implementation of Rudder converts "goTo()" into a request to an Instrument in the Instrumentation domain named I-Rudder-Cmd. The parameter "pos" is an Instrumentation domain encoding of "5 degrees left":

[3] I-Rudder-Cmd.write(pos)

The I-Rudder-Cmd object in the Instrumentation domain knows that it is of type ARINC-269-Output. More communication internal to Instrumentation domain happens, but at some point the design and implementation maps "pos" onto values in a datagram to be sent by the ARINC-629 domain:

[4] ARINC-629-Data-Bus.send(datagram)

ARINC-629-Data-Bus design and implementation finally map the send(datagram) request onto device driver calls that push the "tell the rudder to move to 5 degrees left" request onto the airplane's ARINC-629 communication bus. When ARINC-629-Data-Bus is done, it tells the requester, I-Rudder-Cmd in the Instrumentation domain, that the request has completed:

[5] Done

I-Rudder-Cmd in Instrumentation domain now knows its request has completed. There is no more for it to do, so it notifies its requestor, Rudder in the Airplane test domain, of completion:

[6] Done

Rudder in Test airplane domain now knows its request has completed. There is no more for it to do, so it notifies its requestor, Step-110, of completion:

[7] Done

Step-110 in Airplane Test domain now knows its request has completed and there is no more for it to do. This step was successful, so it returns "Pass" to Block-9:

[8] Pass

6.6.5   Another Scenario: Executing Step-120

Execution continues with the next step in Block-9, Step-120. Figure 6.7 overviews how Step-120 is executed in ATE software.

Block-9 knows that the next step to be executed is Step-120, so it requests that Step-120 execute

[1] Step-120.execute()

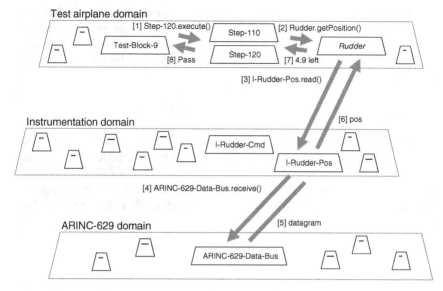

Figure 6.7 Executing Step-120 in Block-9

Step-120 knows it is a VERIFY kind of step and that it needs to ask the Airplane Test Point named Rudder what its position is:

[2] Rudder.getPosition()

Messages [1] and [2] happen within the Test airplane domain; the next message crosses from Test airplane to Instrumentation. The design and implementation of Rudder converts "getPosition()" into a request to an Instrument in the Instrumentation domain named I-Rudder-Pos:

[3] I-Rudder-Pos.read()

The I-Rudder-Pos object in the Instrumentation domain knows that it is of type ARINC-629-Input. More communication internal to Instrumentation domain happens, but at some point the design and implementation maps that onto a request to the ARINC-629 domain:

[4] ARINC-629-Data-Bus.receive()

The ARINC-629-Data-Bus design and implementation finally map the receive() request onto necessary device driver calls that read the "the rudder is at 4.9 degrees left" from the airplane's ARINC-629 communication bus. When

ARINC-629-Data-Bus is done, it returns the datagram containing the rudder position to the requester, I-Rudder-Cmd in the Instrumentation domain:

[5] datagram

The design and code for I-Rudder-Cmd in Instrumentation domain now has the ARINC-629 datagram with the rudder position embedded in it. It unpacks the rudder position. I-Rudder-Pos returns an Instrumentation domain-specific encoding to Rudder in the Airplane Test domain:

[6] pos

The design and code for Rudder converts the Instrumentation domain-specific encoding into "4.9 degrees left." The Rudder object returns this to Step-120:

[7] 4.9 degrees left

Step-120 in Airplane Test domain now knows the airplane's rudder position, so it compares it with limits because it is a VERIFY type of Step. The actual position 4.9° left is with the specified limits, so it returns "Pass" to Test-Block-9:

[8] Pass

Assuming there are more steps to execute, Test-Block-9 selects the next step and the cycle repeats:

"130 SET Rudder to 10 degrees left
140 VERIFY Rudder is between 9.9 and 10.1 degrees left"

In summary, Rudder in the Test airplane domain is mapped onto two ARINC-629 Data Points in the Instrumentation domain, one for input and the other for output. Each ARINC-629 Data Point is further mapped onto send-this-datagram or receive-that-datagram in the ARINC-629 domain, which is then mapped onto driver calls that send and receive datagrams on the airplane communication bus.

We stopped at ARINC-629 device drivers but could have gone further. On the assumption that the ARINC-629 device drivers are written in Java, consider that the Java compiler maps the semantics of source code onto the semantics of the Java virtual machine (JVM). The resident JVM implementation maps JVM byte code semantics onto physical machine semantics (registers, memory, the machine instruction set, etc.). The computer hardware maps physical machine semantics onto digital logic semantics (AND, OR, NOT, etc.). Silicon maps digital logic semantics onto conductors and semiconductors (NP junctions, PN junctions, resistors, capacitors, etc.).

Each domain, by itself, is a highly cohesive and loosely coupled subject matter. It can be considered by itself, with minimal regard to any other domain—particularly lower-level service domains that might be used in its design and implementation. Testing airplanes involves tests, blocks, steps, and airplane test points, not instrumentation or ARINC-629 protocol. ARINC-629 involves sending and receiving datagrams, not tests or JVM semantics. Binding one domain to another happens in design and code. Test airplane design and code knows about Instrumentation services. Instrumentation design and code knows about ARINC-629 sending and receiving.

6.6.6 Domain Separation in WebBooks 2.0

WebBooks 2.0 provides another set of example domains. The policies and processes of Order fulfillment (Appendix D) include Customer, Book order, Title, Medium, Publisher, and Replenish order. The design for Order fulfillment (Appendix E) describes how Customer, Book order, Title, Medium, Publisher, and Replenish order are mapped on to Client apps, Server apps, Owners, Owned datum, and Shared datum—the policies and processes of Scalability (Appendix H). The design of Scalability (Appendix I) describes how Server apps, Owners, Owned datum, and Shared datum are mapped onto Services, HA nodes, and HA clusters—the policies and processes of High availability (Appendix J). The design for High availability (Appendix K) shows how Services, HA nodes, and HA clusters are mapped onto underlying Java automation technology.

6.7 Implications of Domain Separation on Software Documentation

From a requirements allocation and traceability perspective, particularly in light of functional and nonfunctional requirements, how requirements flow into, through, and around and are created (derived) in domains needs to be explained. As an example, start with the stakeholder requirements for WebBooks 2.0.

6.7.1 Functional Requirements for a Domain

Based on requirements filtering in Figure 4.10, some stakeholder decisions would be functional requirements. Those functional requirements form the foundation of the semantic model for the Order fulfillment domain. As will be shown in Part II, those stated functional requirements are woefully incomplete. The process of building a semantic model exposes hundreds, if not thousands, of previously unstated functional requirements.

Figure 6.8 Functional requirements are captured and represented in a domain's semantic model.

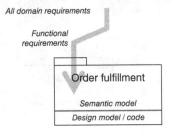

Figure 6.9 Some nonfunctional requirements are fully addressed in a domain's design and code.

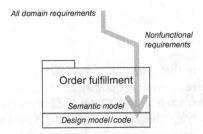

The functional requirements for Order fulfillment need to be consistent with the concepts in the affinity group: Customer, Add to cart, Proceed to checkout, Order, Packing, Shipping, Replenish, etc. Figure 6.8 illustrates how the functional requirements are fully captured and represented in the semantic model for a domain. The package representing Order fulfillment has been split into two compartments: the semantic model on top and the design model/code on the bottom. The same is true for Figures 6.9 through 6.13. This split helps emphasize where some requirements are addressed and others are created. All top-level functional requirements are addressed in the semantic model alone.

6.7.2 Nonfunctional Requirements for a Domain

All remaining requirements for that domain are, by definition, nonfunctional requirements. Figure 6.9 shows how some nonfunctional requirements are fully addressed in the design/code for Order fulfillment. A nonfunctional requirement to support at least five items in each customer order should be fully addressable in the design/code of Order fulfillment; no lower domain should be affected by that requirement.

6.7.3 Nonfunctional Requirements Flowing Through a Domain

Some nonfunctional requirements flow through the design/code of Order fulfillment: those nonfunctional requirements are partially, but not fully, satisfied

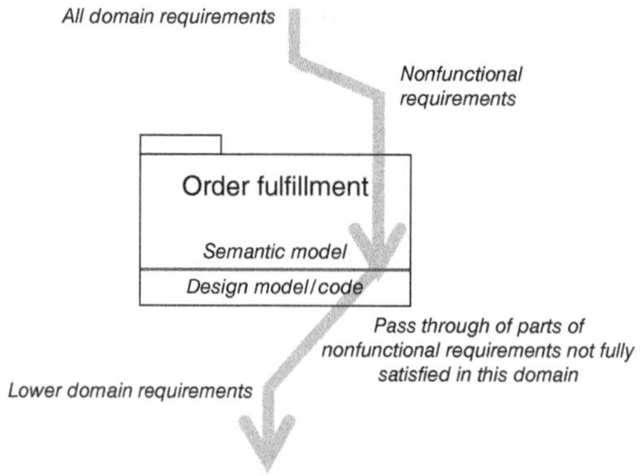

All domain requirements

Nonfunctional
requirements

Order fulfillment

Semantic model

Design model/code

Pass through of parts of
nonfunctional requirements not fully
satisfied in this domain

Lower domain requirements

Figure 6.10 Some nonfunctional requirements are partially addressed in the design/code of a domain and partially passed through to lower domains.

in that domain. Responsibility to satisfy the remainder of those requirements rests on lower domains. An example would be a requirement that all code be written in Java. Order fulfillment code would be written in Java, partially satisfying the requirement, but that requirement needs to be passed to lower domains. Scalability requirements could be another example. The design/code for Order fulfillment would be affected by Scalability (e.g., one or more classes in Order fulfillment design might extend a base class in Scalability), but most Scalability requirements would be satisfied in that domain. Requirements to deal with High availability could be partly addressed in this domain and partly in the High availability domain. This is shown in Figure 6.10.

6.7.4 Nonfunctional Requirements Bypassing a Domain

Some nonfunctional requirements bypass a domain entirely because they are only relevant to lower domains. All requirements having to do specifically with Scalability would be an example. Nothing extra needs to be done to the design/code for Order fulfillment. Scalability might be entirely implemented in that lower domain. This is shown in Figure 6.11.

6.7.5 Requirements for Lower Domains Created in a Domain

Finally, decisions made in design/code of Order fulfillment could impose new requirements on lower domains—the derived requirements idea from the aerospace community. A design decision to present Order items using a scrolling list would impose a requirement on the Web UI domain to provide a scrolling list capability. This is shown in Figure 6.12.

Requirements flowing out of and around Order fulfillment are the requirements that flow into domains immediately below, that is, domains

Figure 6.11 Some nonfunctional requirements bypass a domain entirely.

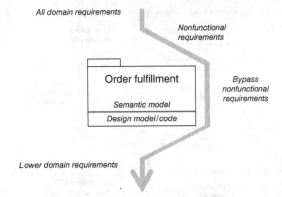

Figure 6.12 Requirements can be created (derived) in the design and code of a domain.

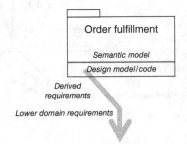

that Order fulfillment imposes requirements on Web UI, Dedicated terminal UI, Payment, Scalability, and User security. That set of requirements needs to be filtered into functional and nonfunctional requirements for each of those lower domains, and the same allocations in Figures 6.8 through 6.12 apply. Requirements that were nonfunctional to a higher domain may be functional to the lower domain. User, Role, Authentication, Password, and Protected service are nonfunctional to Order fulfillment but are functional to User security.

6.7.6 Composite View of Requirements Flow

Figure 6.13 shows a composite view of requirements flow with two adjacent domains: Order fulfillment and User security. This figure shows requirements flowing into, through, and around and being created in both domains. The requirements at the bottom of User security are (some of) the requirements flowing into Scalability. Some requirements on Scalability may be derived requirements from Order fulfillment, and some may be derived requirements from Payment.

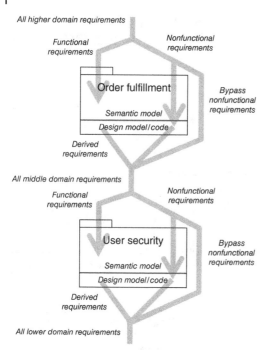

All higher domain requirements

Functional requirements

Nonfunctional requirements

Bypass nonfunctional requirements

Derived requirements

All middle domain requirements

Functional requirements

Nonfunctional requirements

Bypass nonfunctional requirements

Derived requirements

All lower domain requirements

Figure 6.13 Requirements flowing into, through, and around and being derived in a domain.

6.7.7 Recursive Design

The symmetric nature of requirements flow led Shlaer and Mellor to call this "recursive design."[5] Every domain follows this same pattern, the exception being bottom domains that address all requirements levied on them.

Figure 1.3, the "big picture" diagram, is copied in Figure 6.14.

The approach in Figures 1.3 and 6.14 is applied to each domain:

- *Each domain has its own semantic model*—The complete, consistent, clear, concise, precise, unambiguous, and validated specification of policies and processes of that domain, independent of automation technology.
- *Each domain has its own interface specification*—The top domain, Order fulfillment in WebBooks 2.0, will be (or, at least include) a specification of end-user interfaces. Each lower domain will most likely provide a programmer's guide (API specification) for how developers doing design/coding in a higher domain access services implemented in that lower domain.
- *Each domain has its own design and code*—The design and code that implement a domain shows how policies, processes, and interfaces are

---

5 See, for example, [Shlaer90].

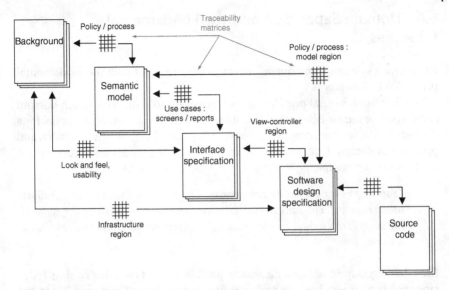

Figure 6.14 Deliverables from model-based software engineering projects.

implemented in terms of (i.e., mapped on to) lower domains and other automation technologies.

6.7.8 Packaging Multi-domain Documentation

If a team is required to deliver written (i.e., paper, or paperlike) documentation,
all documentation for one domain can be gathered into a single unit. Each unit
has traditionally been called a "volume." One project's domain diagram had
seven domains, and the team published seven volumes, one for each domain.
The semantic model chapter of each volume precisely defines policies and processes for that domain. The interface specification describes how entities external to that domain access its services. The design specification describes how
(and why) code implements those services in terms of services provided by
lower domains and underlying technologies. In WebBooks 2.0, we should
expect to publish five such volumes, one each for:

- Order fulfillment
- Payment
- User security
- Scalability
- High availability

Web UI and Dedicated terminal UI do not require documentation because they
are preexisting (i.e., «realized») technologies.

6.8 Domain Separation and the Fundamental Principles

Partitioning systems into domains needs to be consistent with the fundamental principles in Chapter 3.

The first fundamental principle is "pay attention to semantics." Each domain should be a semantic island. Part II will focus on building a semantic model for a domain so that we can completely, consistently, clearly, correctly, concisely, and precisely understand, communicate, and validate its policies and processes.

The second principle is "manage complexity." Remember:

> *"You can never eliminate complexity. The best you can do is to eliminate unnecessary accidental complexity, and manage as much of the remaining complexity as you can by reducing the amount you have to deal with at any one time."*

Each domain should isolate a distinct, separable zone of complexity, thus reducing the amount you have to deal with at any one time. When working in the Order fulfillment domain, you are only working with complexities of order fulfillment. When working in the Payment domain, you are only working with complexities of payment. The same can be said for High availability, User security, and each of the other domains.

The third principle is "use appropriate abstractions." Each domain should be identified and defined in a way that allows us to work exclusively inside that domain most of the time. When working in User security, we worry only about User security and not Payment, Scalability, or High availability. When working in Scalability, we worry only about Scalability and not User security, Payment, and so on. Entire swaths of complexity are swept aside so we can focus only on the one problem at hand.

The fourth principle is "encapsulate accidental complexity." Obviously at some point we will have design and code for each domain. The design and code for any domain (i.e., its accidental complexity) should be irrelevant from the perspective of its semantic model. The design and code are only relevant when we are concerned with automating that business. At most, the design and code of one domain will be in terms of the interface of lower domains, but never more than that. Again, entire swaths of complexity are swept aside.

The fifth principle is "maximize cohesion, minimize coupling." The primary driver of affinity grouping should be to create highly cohesive and loosely coupled domains. The "consistent vocabulary" tactic is intended to group concepts into highly cohesive clusters. In terms of coupling, from the perspective of a higher domain, a lower domain is irrelevant in the semantic model. The lower domain doesn't even appear—it doesn't become relevant—until the design of the higher domain. From the perspective of a lower domain, the higher domain will usually appear as one or more actors. One shouldn't expect to be any more loosely coupled than that.

The sixth principle is "design to invariants, design for change." Each lower domain should be a substitutable service. From the perspective of the design and code of a higher domain that depends on User security, we should be able to redefine security policies and processes without affecting the higher domain. From the perspective of higher domains that depend on Payment, we should be able to redefine payment policies and processes to include—as an obviously extreme example—payment in seashells. Such a change should have no effect on any higher domain. Each lower domain is a plug-in point within which an entirely different version of that service could be replaced with minimal disruption to the rest of the system. And if the revised domain implements the same interface, you don't even need to change any code in the higher domain. Simply compile the new code for the lower domain, link it into a new executable image, and away you go.

Any lower domain should represent a transportable service that could be used in implementing many different higher-level domains. The Payment domain, for example, should have no dependence on Order fulfillment. Given that payment is needed in any for-profit business including rental cars, there should be a reasonable chance that the Payment service built here could be reused elsewhere. The High availability service could be just as useful to a rental car company as it is to WebBooks 2.0.

The seventh principle is "avoid premature design and optimization." That principle isn't explicitly addressed in domain partitioning itself. That principle is addressed in how each domain is designed and implemented, which is presented in Part III.

6.9 Implications of Domain Separation on Organizational Structure

Melvin Conway is attributed as the source of Conway's law:

> "The structure of a software system will reflect the structure of the organization that produced it."

One example is the possibly apocryphal story of an organization that wrote a compiler for PL/1. PL/1 is a complex programming language[6]; in fact it's highly doubtful that anyone has ever built a complete PL/1 compiler. This organization divided the compilation job among 25 sub-teams. Each team claimed to be 100%

---

6 See, for example, http://en.wikipedia.org/wiki/PL/I.

successful in implementing their assigned part. In theory, all they needed to do was chain the 25 stages together, and they should have been able to put PL/1 source code in one end and get linkable object code out the other.

Unfortunately, each stage expected its input to be in one particular format and produced output in another particular format. This induced the need for 24 intermediate translators that would convert the output format of the previous stage into the input format for the next stage. One measure of the quality of a compiler is, "how many passes over any representation of the source code are needed to produce the object code?" A typical compiler uses three passes: lexical analysis, initial object code generation, and object code optimization. With 25 stages and 24 intermediate translators, this organization built a 49-pass compiler. The project was abandoned because nobody could isolate defects—there were 49 places where something could go wrong and finding where was impossible.

You are far better off using domain separation to get a solid, logical software structure, and then organize teams around that structure. Let sensible software architecture drive team structure. Don't let an arbitrary (and often politically motivated) organizational structure drive an equally arbitrary software architecture. Otherwise you risk the modern-day equivalent of the 49-pass PL/1 compiler.

6.10 Summary

A domain is a distinct subject matter about which software needs to be (or has been) written and maintained. One way to identify domains in a new development project is:

1) Brainstorm a breadth-wise set of concepts.
2) Group the concepts based on consistent vocabulary.
3) Name each group.

The domain diagram arranges domains by "who imposes requirements on who?" Just remember that "imposes requirements on" is not necessarily client-server.

Each lower domain is a nontrivial automation technology and is invisible to the semantic model of higher domains. The lower domain doesn't appear until the design and code of the higher domain, where the lower domain provides mechanisms for the higher domain to use (map on to). Requirements flow into, through, and around and can be created (derived) in domains.

Model-based software engineering applies in each domain. Each domain will have its own semantic model. Each domain will have its own interface specification. The design and code that implement the domain shows how policies, processes, and interfaces of are implemented in terms of (i.e., mapped on to) lower domains and given technologies.

Domain partitioning should be consistent with the fundamental principles in Chapter 3.

Reduced models contain all, and only, model elements for which software needs to be developed and maintained. Expanded models contain one or more model elements that are out of scope for the development and maintenance organization but communicate valuable context and important relationships. Any model can be reduced or expanded, depending on the needs of the project.

You are far better off using domain separation to get a good, solid, logical software architecture, and then organize your software team(s) around that. Let a sensible software architecture drive team structure. Don't let an arbitrary (and often politically motivated) organizational structure drive you to an equally arbitrary software architecture.

Part II

Semantic Modeling

Model-Based Functional Requirements

Part II describes how to build and maintain a semantic model. There are four components:

- *Use Case Diagram*—Scope and context: process at a high level
- *Class Model*—Policies to enforce
- *Interaction Diagrams*—Process at an intermediate level
- *State Models*—Process at a precise, detailed level

Each of these will be described. *Partitioning a Domain into Subdomains* is also described, along with a discussion of what can be done with a complete semantic model including simulation and deriving verification test cases (*Wrapping Up Semantic Modeling*).

This book overall, and Part II in particular, necessarily presents model-based software engineering sequentially. You are not required to run a project this way. You can run your project iteratively (i.e., agile), and you can develop and maintain models in parallel if you prefer. Your goal is to deliver value to stakeholders—through software—as efficiently and effectively as possible. You decide how to best accomplish that on your own projects. Chapter 24 discusses alternative software development and maintenance processes.

How to Engineer Software: A Model-Based Approach, First Edition. Steve Tockey.
© 2019 the IEEE Computer Society, Inc. Published 2019 by John Wiley & Sons, Inc.

7

Use Case Diagrams

Scope and Context

The use case diagram shows the scope and context of a (sub)domain.[1] Use cases, processes at the most coarse-grained level, present scope. Actors present context. Actors, use cases, and the relationships between them are explained in this chapter.

Generally, there will be one use case diagram for a (sub)domain.

7.1 On the Relative Unimportance of Use Case Diagramming

In designing and building houses, the first in the set of drawings is a "front elevation" as in Figure 7.1. This is from the perspective of someone outside, looking at the house. The front elevation is a convenience for the reader; it helps them see the big picture. The builder doesn't depend on the front elevation; they can build the house without it. The front elevation plays the same role in building and maintaining houses as the use case diagram plays in software: it simply overviews the scope and context of the (sub)domain being modeled.

The use case diagram helps the reader see the big picture of a (sub)domain. There's a small amount of information useful for understanding, building, and maintaining the rest of the semantic model, specifically the set of actors and use cases. But after other models have been built, nothing in the use case diagram is unique to it alone. In the end, the use case diagram repeats information in other models. The use case diagram also does not contribute to design and code (Part III). Everything needed to create and maintain the design and code is contained elsewhere, specifically the class model and state models.

It is easy to fall into a trap of overengineering use case diagrams, and they are actually not important in building and maintaining software. You can waste a lot of valuable time. Be careful not to over-invest; your time will be better spent on

---

1 Subdomains are introduced and explained in Chapter 11. You can consider only domains for now.

How to Engineer Software: A Model-Based Approach, First Edition. Steve Tockey.
© 2019 the IEEE Computer Society, Inc. Published 2019 by John Wiley & Sons, Inc.

Figure 7.1 South front elevation for the White House, Washington, DC, 1817. (Courtesy US Library of Congress. No restrictions on publication, http://www.loc.gov/pictures/resource/ppmsca.09502/)

other components of a semantic model. The goal is only to communicate scope and context. Don't be overly precise; the use case diagram is limited in how much detail it can communicate. Once scope and context are sufficiently communicated, move on to the other components.

7.2 Actor

In UML an actor is[2]:

> "... *a role played by a user or any other system that interacts with the subject*"

An actor represents the role of a person, an organization, another system, a machine, a device, and so on. For our purposes, "the subject" is the (sub)domain: the business being modeled.

---

2 See [OMG11b].

Silly Bank's loan processing business will be used to illustrate use case diagramming. The business starts with a customer applying for a loan and continues until legally mandated record retention regulations have been met. Actors in Silly Bank's loan processing business could be:

- *Customer*—A person or business who wants to borrow money from Silly Bank.
- *Loan officer*—A bank employee with authority to decide which loan applications are approved or denied.
- *Bank manager*—A bank employee with authority to decide which delinquent loans should be written off.
- *Credit bureau*—An external repository of credit history about applicants that factor into a loan officer's decision to approve or deny a loan application. The customer's financial behavior on a loan (if approved) will also be reported back to credit bureaus.

Actors are likely to—although not necessarily, as in expanded semantic models—represent automation boundaries in design. There will almost certainly be user interfaces for customer, loan officer, and bank manager, along with some kind of application programming interface (API) with credit bureaus. But remember the Vulcan Mind Meld: technical details of interfaces are irrelevant in a semantic model.

7.2.1 Actors as Roles, Not Things

When identifying actors, focus on roles, not the things playing those roles. Consider a mythical employee at Silly Bank; call her Sarah. By day, Sarah is a loan officer. She decides which loan applications to approve and which to deny. But at some point Sarah may need to borrow money to buy a car or house. How does she get her loan? She applies for it, just like everyone else. When Sarah is applying for her loan, and assuming it's approved, when she's paying it back, she's not a loan officer; she's a customer. Don't model "Sarah" or any other specific entity. Model the roles that Sarah and people like her play: loan officer, customer, and bank manager. Generally, the same real-world thing can play different roles, and different real-world things can play the same role. This is another case of applying the fundamental principle of abstraction.

Another example is a credit bureau. Finance institutions in North America use Equifax™, Experian™, or TransUnion™ for obtaining and reporting credit history. Today, a bank might use Experian so they may be tempted to model "Experian" as the actor. But what if the bank decides to switch to TransUnion or Equifax? Do you really want to change everything that refers to Experian by name? It would be much better to have the model simply refer to "credit bureau." Not only will the bank be able to easily change service providers, but also they will be able to handle more than one service provider at the same time. Again, model roles, not the things that play those roles.

7.2.2 Actor Notation

UML has two notations for actors. The most common is the "stick man" shown in Figure 7.2. The name of the actor is below the stick man.

Stick man notation is appropriate when the actor represents a human being—like a customer or a loan officer. But quite often, the thing being modeled isn't a human. It is some other system, hardware, device, etc. like the automated systems at credit bureaus. In this case, UML's class notation can be used with stereotype «actor», as shown in Figure 7.3.

UML does not prescribe either notation; you are free to use the notation you feel is most appropriate. Stick man and stereotyped class notations can be mixed on the same diagram. Readers tend to have better understanding when the stick-man-for-person and stereotyped-class-for-other-system convention is used.

7.2.3 Actor Names

Actor names tend to be nouns or noun phrases. A dictionary-like definition for each actor is also useful. That definition helps make clear what that actor is intended to represent. Both actor name and description should focus on role:

- What is that actor capable of doing?
- What are they responsible for?
- What decisions do they have authority to make?

Semantically, actors are classes. More complete discussion of how to name and describe classes can be found in the next chapter, and further detail on actor naming and description will be deferred to there.

Figure 7.2 UML's "stick man" notation for actors.

«actor»
Credit bureau

Figure 7.3 UML's «actor» stereotyped class notation.

7.2.4 Avoid Clocks as Actors

In many semantic models, particularly models for embedded systems, you may be tempted to include a clock as an actor. Don't—this is premature design. Clocks are mechanisms for measuring time. The domain should only care about policy- and process-relevant times, not how to measure or detect them. Clocks may or may not be useful in design. A number of other mechanisms for measuring and detecting time are available in design that don't involve clocks per se:

- Counting cycles on AC power
- Knowing how long it takes a certain section of code to execute
- Knowing how long it takes some external device to react
- Synchronization with some other process event
- ...

Model the business relevant times, not clocks: let designers decide the best mechanism for recognizing those times.

7.3 Use Case

As defined in UML, a use case is:

> "... the specification of a set of actions performed by a system, which yields an observable result that is, typically, of value for one or more actors or other stakeholders of the system."

Use cases represent processes that achieve some discrete, stakeholder-relevant goal. The scope of the domain is represented by a set of use cases. Some example use cases from Silly Bank loan processing could include:

- Accepting a loan application
- Originating (opening) a loan
- Processing a loan payment
- Processing a missed loan payment
- Providing loan status and payoff amount information
- ...

The UML notation for a use case is an oval with the name of the process inside. Some examples are shown in Figure 7.4.

7.4 "Participates In"

It is rare that all actors can participate in all use cases. Normally, only certain actors are allowed to participate in certain use cases. Even Silly Bank should not be silly enough to allow customers to approve their own loan applications.

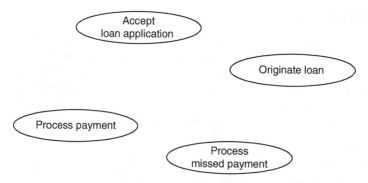

Figure 7.4 UML use case notation.

Only someone with a higher level of authority, a loan officer, should be allowed to approve or deny loan applications. This is the meaning of "participates in": specifying what actors are allowed to participate in what use cases. Participation is shown on use case diagrams as a solid line between an actor and a use case. Figure 7.5 shows a partial use case diagram for Silly Bank loan processing with several "participates-in" links.

UML allows drawing a rectangle around the use cases as well as writing the (sub)domain name in the upper right corner of that rectangle. This is optional— you are free to add the rectangle and name or leave them out. Adding the

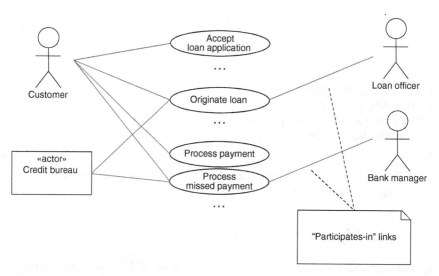

Figure 7.5 Partial use case diagram for Silly Bank with several "participates-in" links.

rectangle and name helps emphasize scope (what's inside) and context (what's outside), so it is usually a good idea to include them. Figure 7.6 shows the same partial use case diagram from Figure 7.5 with the rectangle and (sub)domain name added.

The meaning of participates in is limited. It only means that there is at least one occurrence of that use case (process) in which at least one occurrence of that actor participates. The presence of a "participates-in" link doesn't say much, but its absence does. When there is no "participates-in" link, it means that "there is no instance of this process in which any member of that actor class is ever allowed to participate"—as in "there is no instance of process payment in which a loan officer is allowed to participate." Referring to the Silly Bank savings account use case diagram in Figure 2.2, notice that a customer is not allowed to open or close Silly Savings Accounts directly. Only tellers can open and close accounts on customer's behalf.

The "participates-in" link also does not mean the actor(s) triggers that process. In Figure 7.6 it is reasonable to assume that a customer triggers acceptance of a loan application and processing of payments. But a loan officer triggers loan origination, not a customer. Customers participate in loan origination in that they sign documents as well as—obviously get the money they want to borrow. Credit bureaus participate in loan origination in that they get notice the customer has taken on new debt.

In processing a missed payment, the customer sees a reminder that they didn't pay on time, the bank manager sees a notice of missed payment, and the credit bureau sees a notice to add that missed payment to the customer's credit history. But processing a missed payment isn't triggered by any of those actors; it's triggered by time. The customer's payment was due on a certain date and it didn't arrive—that triggered the process.

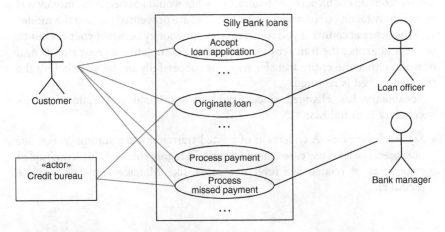

Figure 7.6 Adding the rectangle and (sub)domain name to emphasize scope and context.

The "participates-in" link also does not express any direction of information flow: is information going in, coming out, or both? The link doesn't say. Nor does the link specify the nature of the participation in terms of being optional or mandatory, nor how many instances of the actor would participate (e.g., just one credit bureau or all of them?). Some of that detail is supported by UML use case diagramming, but experience shows that it only clutters the diagram without clarifying scope and context. This also tends to violate the one-fact-one-place documentation principle in Appendix A, so it's recommended to leave that detail out.

7.5 Levels of Use Cases to Manage Big Domains

UML's use case diagram notation is space inefficient. As can be seen in Figures 7.5 and 7.6, a lot of space is taken without communicating much information. In one project, the top-level domain had 35 actors and 535 separate business processes. Clearly, it would be challenging to fit all that onto a single use case diagram even if the page was very large. There are two ways to handle this situation. One is to use levels of use cases, as introduced by Alistair Cockburn.[3]

7.5.1 Transactions

To understand Cockburn's use case levels, first consider the concept of a "transaction." A transaction represents a complete coherent atomic independent unit of work. Either the entire transaction completes successfully, or whatever partial work got done during the transaction needs to be undone. Consider transferring money from one bank account to another: what would happen if the money was successfully taken out of one account but a failure prevented putting the money into the other account? If you were transferring money between your accounts, you would expect the transfer to be treated as a complete coherent atomic unit of work: either the entire transfer happens successfully or the state before the transfer started is restored.

Vocabulary has changed since Cockburn's original publication—today's vocabulary is as follows:

- *Sky level use case*—A collection of related transactions: a summary. For our purposes, sky level use cases should represent highly cohesive, loosely coupled collections of related sea level use cases, like Manage loans or Manage accounts.

---

3 Pronounced "Coe-burn." See [Cockburn01].

- *Sea level use case*—A complete coherent atomic independent unit of work: a transaction from the perspective of the participating actor(s).
- *Mud level use case*—A fragment of a sea level use case.

The use cases identified for Silly Bank loan processing are sea level; they are transactions from the perspective of participating actors. One key property of transactions is that (unless limited by other domain constraints) there is no limit to the time between one transaction ending and another starting. Implicitly, an actor could participate in one sea level use case, go out to dinner, watch a movie, or play a round of golf—maybe even take a ski holiday—before participating in another sea level use case. In contrast, one would not expect, nor even allow, a money transfer between bank accounts to take hours or days.

Transaction boundaries—that is, "what are the sea level use cases?"—are necessarily defined by stakeholders. The semantic model is only allowed to reflect transaction boundaries defined by the business. WebBooks 2.0 stakeholders could define a transaction boundary as submitting an entire book order as a single block: shipping address, list of books and quantities, etc. On the other hand, the shopping cart metaphor, with "add to cart," "drop from cart," and "proceed to checkout" as transactions, means the WebBooks views process boundaries differently. A customer could put a book into their cart, go out to dinner and watch a movie, potentially take that ski holiday, then add another book to the cart a week or two later. They could finally decide to proceed to checkout days or weeks after that—assuming, of course, that WebBooks doesn't have a process of timing out a book order if it isn't checked out within, say, one week of the first book being put in the customer's cart.

Part of what saved the 35-actor, 535-use case project was to draw a sky level use case diagram instead of drawing all 535 sea level use cases. A sky level use case diagram communicates at least broad scope and context. A custom stereotype such as "«sky»" could be used to tag sky level use cases on the diagram. The problem with putting sky level use cases on the diagram is that while you can claim to understand context, through the actors on the diagram, you can't say the same about scope. It will be important to make a complete list of transactions, the sea level use cases, somewhere to be sure that nothing is missed in further semantic modeling, design, and code.

The other approach for dealing with the use case diagram's lack of compactness is to use a different notation. The complete scope can be simply listed in text (on separate pages than the use case diagram). List each sea level use case and the set of actors that participate. The following example is for the sea level use cases in Figure 7.5:

Accept loan application: Customer
Originate loan application: Customer, loan officer
Process payment: Customer
Process missed payment: Customer, bank manager, credit bureau

The domain with 35 actors and 535 sea level use cases had one page for the sky level use case diagram followed by about 10 pages of sea level transactions and participating actors in text. Granted, 35 actors and 535 transactions are extreme for a single domain (this domain could have benefitted from subdomain partitioning as described in Chapter 11), but you may find approaches like this useful on your own projects even if they are less extreme. You can now safely say you understand both scope and context. The actors on the sky level use case diagram show context, and subsequent pages of sea level use cases show scope.

7.6 Identifying Sea Level Event Use Cases Through Business Events

There are two kinds of sea level use case, event use cases and data use cases. Event use cases are triggered by business events. Understanding business events helps lead to a more complete set of sea level event use cases. The other kind of use case—data use cases—and how to identify them, are discussed later in this chapter.

Business events aren't explicitly represented in a use case diagram, but they play an important role in semantic modeling. A business event can be defined as:

> *"An occurrence or happening that can cause a significant, defined business response"*

Business events happen at discrete, finite moments in time. To illustrate, consider which of the following might be business events:

- Customer applies for a loan.
- Customer falls over.
- Customer makes a loan payment.
- Customer has a bad credit rating.
- System emails loan payoff acknowledgment.
- Loan table reaches maximum data capacity.
- Customer cancels their loan application.

The answers are as follows:

- *Customer applies for a loan*—Yes, this is a business event. The response is to accept and record the application.
- *Customer falls over*—Highly unlikely this is a business event, unless stakeholders happen to have a process to deal with customers falling over.
- *Customer makes a loan payment*—Yes, the response is to reduce the amount of money owed on the loan.
- *Customer has a bad credit rating*—No, this isn't a business event; it's a condition. Previous business events earned that customer their bad credit rating but having a bad rating is not a business event.

- *System emails loan payoff acknowledgment*—No, this isn't a business event either. At best, this is part of a response to a business event (in this case, the customer making a loan payment sufficient to pay off the loan). The other important issue is that emailing is nonfunctional (remember the Vulcan Mind Meld) and doesn't belong in a semantic model of banking.
- *Loan table reaches maximum data capacity*—No, this isn't a business event either. This is about automation technology and shouldn't be in a semantic model of banking. It's only relevant to software design.
- *Customer cancels their loan application*—Yes, definitely a business event. A significant, defined response of stopping the loan processing workflow would be expected.

Business events come in different flavors. You don't need to categorize them after the fact, but the intent is to help expose a more complete set of business events and surface a more complete set of sea level event use cases. Otherwise, important transactions could be missed: another "You never told us—You never asked" Dreaded Phone Call Syndrome. The other possibility is that stakeholders may not realize valuable functionality could be automated because they were never aware of the possibility.

7.6.1 Unpredictable Business Events

The first category of business events is "unpredictable." Unpredictable business events happen external to the domain and are entirely at the whim of some actor. A customer deciding to submit a loan application is entirely up to that customer. Silly Bank cannot anticipate when, or even if, any customer would ever submit a loan application. Opening a savings account and placing an order for books would be unpredictable events in other domains.

7.6.2 Timed Business Events

The second category of business events is "timed." These business events have time as the trigger. Maybe the domain needs to do something on a recurring basis: hourly, daily, or even monthly, quarterly, or annually. There aren't any recurring timed business events in Silly Bank loan processing as is, but perhaps the need to provide quarterly or annual financial summaries to corporate headquarters could be examples in a larger semantic model of banking.

A timed business event doesn't have to be recurring; a timed event could be in relation to an earlier business event. For example, legal requirements on financial data retention may cause Silly Bank to keep loan records for, say, a minimum of two years following the last business-relevant change to that loan. The timed business event is when the two-year retention period has passed because now the loan can be legally purged. But that event only happens once in the life of the loan. The need to send a replenish order to the publisher after 24 hours is an example in WebBooks 2.0 Order fulfillment.

7.6.3 Consequential Business Events

The third category of business events is "consequential." These business events aren't unexpected; the domain pretty much knows they are coming at some point because they are part of a larger workflow:

- A loan application was submitted, so the bank knows that a loan officer will eventually either approve or deny it.
- A loan application was approved, so the bank knows it will be either originated or cancelled.
- A loan was originated, so the bank expects the customer to make payments.

7.6.4 Nonoccurrence Business Events

Business events in the first three categories tend to be straightforward and obvious. Modelers usually don't miss them. The last category of business event is subtle and perhaps more important: "nonoccurrence." Some earlier business event, say, a loan being originated, can set an expectation for a consequential business event: the customer making a payment. But what if the consequential event doesn't happen: the customer never makes a payment. Of course, this specific situation is obvious and a modeler is unlikely to miss it—everybody knows about missing a loan payment. But what about:

- A customer submitted a loan application; the expected consequential business events are that a loan officer either approves or denies that application. But what if the loan officer forgets? What if they are too busy with other applications? Would it make sense to remind the loan officer that there is at least one aging application that should be taken care of?
- The loan officer approved a loan; the bank is waiting for the customer to originate it. But what if the customer never does? Did they not get the notice of approval? Did they ignore it because they got a loan with better terms from a different bank? Do they not need the money after all? Would it make sense to remind the customer to either originate the loan or cancel it?

Maybe stakeholders assume everyone already knows about aging loan applications and reminding tardy customers. Maybe they didn't tell us because—by us not asking—they thought we already knew. Or maybe they don't even know that such processes could be automated. The "nonoccurrence" category tends to expose interesting processes; deliberately considering these events makes this explicit.

7.6.5 Business Events and Completeness

By identifying business events, particularly using the categories unpredictable, timed, consequential, and nonoccurrence, we can expose a more complete set of event use cases. It should be fair to say that almost any modeler of Silly Bank's loan processing business would have easily identified the use cases of submitting applications, approving and denying applications, originating, making payments, etc. But reminding loan officers of aging applications and reminding customers about unoriginated loans is much more questionable. A few modelers might have gotten them, but most probably would not. Maybe Silly Bank didn't realize that these processes existed (and even so, very informally thus not likely to be automated) or even that such processes should exist in the first place.

7.6.6 Focus on Normal Behavior First

Another recommendation is to focus first on normal, typical, expected behavior. Answer the question "What can be expected to happen most of the time?" For Silly Bank loan processing, the most likely sequence under normal circumstances would be:

1) A loan application is submitted.
2) The application is approved.
3) The loan is originated.
4) Regular payments are made, until the final payment.
5) The record retention time passes and records are deleted.

Once normal behavior is understood, then worry about the unusual things, including the nonoccurrence business events:

- The loan application is denied.
- The loan application is not decided in time.
- An approved loan is not originated in time.
- The customer cancels an approved loan.
- The customer misses a payment.
- The loan is written off.

Paying too much attention to abnormal behavior when normal behavior isn't well understood adds complexity. Temporarily abstracting away abnormal behavior—as all good abstraction does—simplifies the job by reducing unnecessary distractions.

7.7 Business Events as Errors

In a sense, a customer missing a loan payment is a kind of error. Similarly, a loan officer not approving or denying a loan application in time is a kind of error. Both are undesirable conditions. There are economic implications of including responses to errors. The decision to include a specific response or not should be based on technical and economic considerations. Just because we found an interesting nonoccurrence event doesn't necessarily mean that a response must be in scope. Chapter 25 explains how to make an engineering decision to include such scope or not.

The semantic model—or, more precisely, the semantic modeling language—does not distinguish between desirable and undesirable behavior. All behavior is modeled using the same vocabulary: use cases, classes, associations, states, events, etc. What is versus what is not is a value judgment imposed by stakeholders. Having decided to include responses to some errors, if you want to distinguish desirable from undesirable behavior, consider that UML is colorblind. You can paint semantic model content different colors; UML ignores those colors. You could, for example, color desirable model content black and undesirable content red. Color communicates desirability to the reader, but the model (the modeling language) itself doesn't care.

7.8 Event Use Case Naming Conventions

For Silly Bank's loan processing business, Table 7.1 shows the list of business events (along with category) and corresponding responses.

There are two different styles of naming event use cases based on "Am I naming the event?" or "Am I naming the response to an event?" The more common style is to name use cases by the event (i.e., the left column in Table 7.1). This tends to be more natural in expressing scope. A potential issue is that one business event can have several, very different responses. For example, the customer makes a loan payment that's not a final payment versus a payment that does pay off the loan. Also, the same response is sometimes triggered by different business events. The alternate style is to name sea level event use cases by an action verb phrase that summarizes the response (i.e., the right column in Table 7.1). Table 7.2 proposes names for each sea level use case in Silly Bank loan processing using either the event name or response style.

Each style has advantages and disadvantages. The use case diagram for Order fulfillment (Appendix D) uses named-by-event style and the diagram for Payment (Appendix F) uses named-by-response style. Consider both and choose the style you feel is most appropriate.

7.9 Specifying Sea Level Event Use Cases

The first, and by far most important, question to ask about specifying sea level event use cases is, "Why?" Why would you want to bother specifying the details of an event use case? You maybe haven't seen yet because it comes in later

Table 7.1 Business events and responses in Silly Bank loan processing.

Business event (category)	Response
Customer submits loan application (unpredictable)	Record the submitted application
Loan officer approves loan (consequence of application)	Notify customer and credit bureau
Loan officer denies loan (consequence of application)	Notify customer and credit bureau
Loan officer originates loan (consequence of approval)	Give money to customer; notify credit bureau
Customer makes payment (consequence of origination)	Reduce amount owed, possibly closing the loan if final payment (maybe with refund if overpaid and notification to credit bureau)
Customer misses payment (nonoccurrence of making payment)	Remind customer to pay; notify credit bureau
Loan officer didn't approve or deny application (nonoccurrence of approve or deny)	Remind loan officer to decide
Customer didn't originate loan in time (nonoccurrence of origination)	Remind customer to originate
Customer cancels approved loan (consequence of approval)	Notify credit bureau
Bank manager writes off delinquent loan (consequence of too many missed payments)	Notify customer and credit bureau
Record retention time has passed (timed)	Remove loan record

Table 7.2 Naming use cases by business event versus response.

Named by event	Named by response
Submit loan application	Accept loan application
Approve loan	Register application approval
Deny loan	Register application denial
Originate loan	Process loan origination
Make payment	Process payment
Miss payment	Process missed payment
No approve/deny	Remind loan officer to decide
No loan origination	Remind customer to originate
Cancel approved loan	Register cancellation
Write off delinquent loan	Process delinquent loan write-off
Record retention time passed	Purge record(s)

chapters, but everything you would ever want to say about a sea level event use case will be captured—completely, consistently, clearly, correctly, concisely, and precisely—in the class model and state models. So whatever is said about an event use case here will also have been said—and said better—somewhere else. Be aware of the "one-fact-in-one-place" documentation principle in Appendix A: if stakeholders decide to change the details of a particular process and it gets changed in other models but not here, then there will be contradiction in the semantic model. No design or code is ever produced from use case diagrams, so the contradiction shouldn't hurt. But contradiction in models at minimum leads to confusion and wasted effort, so it should be avoided. You can avoid it by not putting such detail into use cases.

If you decide to specify sea level event use cases, the following kinds of information could be useful:

- *Triggering event(s)*—What business event(s) cause this process to happen?
- *Parameters*—What business information accompanies the event: what additional data does the process need to work with?
- *Requires*—What additional conditions need to be true (preconditions beyond just the business event occurring) before it makes sense to carry out this process?
- *Guarantees*—What changes to conditions need to be true (postconditions) on completion of the process?
- *Normal course*—What usually happens in this process?
- *Alternative course(s)*—What other things could happen that are not typical but still acceptable?
- *Exceptions*—What conditions would be unknowable when the event happened (thus could not be expressed in a requires clause) but later discovery would prevent the guarantees clause from becoming achievable?

An example of how this might be expressed for the Accept loan application use case is:

- *Triggering event(s)*—Customer submits loan application.
- *Parameters*—Customer legal name, address, tax identification number, recent employment history, recent residence history, sources of income, assets, other debt, amount of loan being requested, etc.
- *Requires*—All required loan application information is completely provided.
- *Guarantees*—A loan application has been created and is now ready to be decided by a loan officer.
- *Normal course*—None.
- *Alternative course(s)*—None.
- *Exceptions*—None.

The requires and guarantees clauses specify a sea level event use case in terms of a contract as described in Chapter 2. Again, it bears emphasizing that all of this information will be captured in the class model and state models, so be careful about investing time and effort that might end up wasted.

7.10   Sea Level Data Use Cases

Data use cases are very different from event use cases. In a data use case, something is known in the domain, and an actor needs that information to do their job. Think about Sarah, a loan officer. For Sarah to do her job of approving or denying a loan application, she needs to see the content of that application and the applicant's credit history from a credit bureau. Without that, how is she to decide?

At the same time, not every actor should have access to information on loan applications; only certain actors should be allowed access. There needs to be a use case representing access to domain information and a participates-in link for each actor class that is allowed access.

A rather obvious design (referring to Part III) would be for Sarah to log into her work account and navigate to a screen that lists all loan applications that have been submitted but not yet approved or denied. Sarah could then click on one of the loan applications, bringing up information for that application. Now she can do her job with the information provided and either click "Approve," "Deny," or "I'm not ready yet, I'll decide later" buttons at the bottom of the screen.

Why can't we just model this as an event use case? What about having a "Display loan application" event use case as shown in Figure 7.7?

A specification for the Display loan application event use case could be:

- *Triggering event(s)*—Loan officer wants to see a loan application.
- *Parameters*—None.
- *Requires*—n/a
- *Guarantees*—The loan officer sees that loan application.
- *Normal course*—n/a
- *Alternative course(s)*—n/a
- *Exceptions*—n/a

You *can* model it this way; many modelers do. But there is a risk of premature design. The key to understanding that risk is to understand the difference between push and pull communication. Modeling Sarah's interaction as an

Figure 7.7 Modeling a sea level data use case as if it were a sea level event use case.

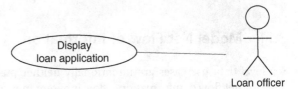

event use case is modeling it in pull form: Sarah is telling which application she wants to see, thus pulling loan application data out of the system. An alternative, push form, would be for Sarah to see the contents of a loan application appear in her email in-box or have loan application data arrive as a SMS/TXT on her smart phone. Admittedly, it's a bit of a stretch in this particular case, but in other cases it could be worth considering. Push versus pull is covered in more detail in Chapters 15 and 16.

Similarly, consider buying books at Amazon™. If you want to buy a book, the Amazon.com website allows you to search using criteria like book title, author, and/or subject. Most of the time, that is sufficient to locate the book(s) in question. This is pull communication: you enter search criteria and Amazon retrieves books that match your criteria. On the other hand, if you have ever bought a book from Amazon, then you know that you will start to receive emails saying, "People who bought the book you bought also bought this other book. You should be interested in this other book too. Click here to learn more about it." You didn't ask for that email; they just assume you want it. That email is push communication of the same information from a search (pull): giving you access to information about books that you might be interested in buying. The difference is, simply, who initiated the communication. When you enter search terms, you initiate the communication (pull). In the email case, they initiate (push).

A similar thing happened when I bought an iPod™ from the Apple website as a birthday gift for my mom. Instead of giving me an order tracking number and forcing me to ask for order status (pull), I was pleasantly surprised to see a series of emails (push):

1) The iPod you ordered just left the factory.
2) The iPod you ordered was just put on a plane in Shanghai.
3) The iPod you ordered just arrived at US Customs in San Francisco.
4) The iPod you ordered was just given to UPS for delivery.
5) The iPod you ordered was delivered by UPS.

I never had to ask; they told me whenever my order status changed.

If the semantic model specifies communication in pull terms, then you can be confident it will be designed and implemented in pull terms: the customer has to enter search criteria, Sarah has to click one from a list of undecided loan applications, or a buyer has to enter an order number. What hints are given to designers that an alternative implementation—one that users might like much better—is even possible? None at all.

7.11   Model Net Flow of Information

Sea level data use cases are intentionally neither push nor pull. They merely describe net flow of information—flow inherent in processes. Some information is known in the (sub)domain over here, and that information is needed over there. How and when it gets from here to there is irrelevant from a business perspective. That data can be pushed or pulled; the (sub)domain doesn't care as long as the data is available where it is needed no later than when it is needed.

Choosing push versus pull is a flow of control decision that needs to be based on automation technology. And we might not have enough visibility into that technology yet:

- How much data (bytes vs. kilobytes vs. megabytes, etc.) needs to be communicated?
- How fast is the communication channel?
- How expensive is it to communicate?
- How much tolerance is there for latency?
- How complex is a design that pushes information, and how complex is a design that pulls?
- ...

Even if you do know today's computing platform, can you count on that platform never changing over the service life of the software? What if stakeholders decide to port some domain to a totally different platform? What if they want to run their business on multiple platforms—platforms with very different technical characteristics—at the same time?

Push versus pull is a technology concern and has nothing to do with business process. Why model business in computing terms? Only model business in business terms. Perhaps unbeknownst to you, the same net flow of information applies to sea level event use cases. It's very easy to fall into the trap of assuming business events are pushed—because they are almost always designed and implemented that way. But that's not the only way to implement them. Sometimes it's a very inefficient way to implement them. Chapters 15 and 16 show how both event and data communication can be designed in both push and pull fashions.

The only other sea level data use case in Silly Bank loan processing is for customers and credit bureaus to have access to loan status (including payoff amount). Again, it might be implemented in a way that forces the client to ask (pull), or the information might be sent to them either periodically or on any significant change (push). That decision needs to be deferred to design.

There is nothing in standard UML notation that allows differentiation of sea level data use cases from sea level event use cases. Instead, a naming convention can be helpful. Of course you aren't required to use this convention, but it helps to name sea level data use cases with a summary of the information (typically a noun or noun phrase) followed by a question mark. This is shown in the use case diagram fragment in Figure 7.8.

Like sea level event use cases, sea level data use cases don't need to be specified in detail. If you want to specify this kind of use case, provide a summary of the information being made visible to participating actor(s). This is another possible use of BNF notation as discussed in Chapter 10.

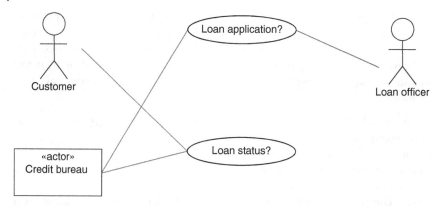

Figure 7.8 Use case diagram showing a recommended sea level data use case naming convention.

7.12 Use Cases Without Actor Participation

The "participates-in" link means one or more members of an actor class are actively involved in the process represented by a use case. The actor(s) may be the source of the triggering event, the source of necessary business information, the destination of resulting business information, and/or the destination of outgoing events. Could it ever happen that a process has no direct actor participation? The answer is yes.

Consider the timed business event "the record retention time for a loan has passed." The business response is to delete that loan. This was listed as sea level event use case "Purge record(s)" in Table 7.2. This use case could be specified using the suggested template:

- *Triggering event(s)*—Loan record retention time has passed.
- *Parameters*—None.
- *Requires*—n/a
- *Guarantees*—That loan has been purged.
- *Normal course*—n/a
- *Alternative course(s)*—n/a
- *Exceptions*—n/a

Who are the participating actors? It is a timed event and there's no clock actor. There's no required information coming in. There's no required information going out. There's no outgoing event communicated to any actor. The entire effect is internal to the domain. Nobody outside would even know it happened unless they looked. So while it may seem odd and uncomfortable at first, "free-floating" use cases aren't unreasonable. Figure 7.9 shows the complete use case diagram for Silly Bank loan processing, including the free-floating use case. At

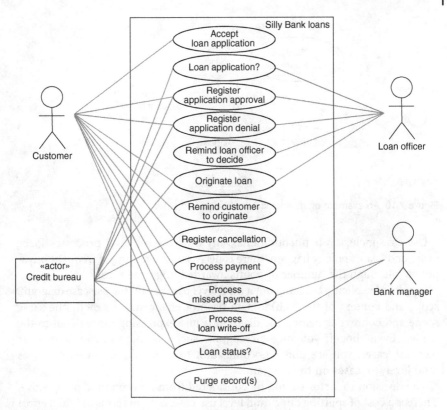

Figure 7.9 Final use case diagram for Silly Bank loan processing.

least I can say from experience that free-floating use cases don't happen very often. But they do happen and need to be allowed.

7.13 «include» Use Cases

Recalling "mud level use cases," this is one of two situations where they come in. Use case inclusion shows that a common fragment of process—the mud level use case—is shared across two or more sea level use cases. The common element of process has been factored out and expressed as a single shared fragment. Figure 7.10 shows the notation through an example of an «include»-ed use case: Awarding frequent buyer points in an order processing domain. As shown, sea level event use cases Place order and Issue apology both share that common element of process, awarding frequent buyer points.

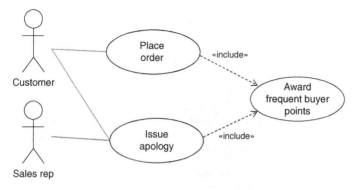

Figure 7.10 An example of an «include» mud level use case.

Use case inclusion is unconditional; any time the sea level processes Place order and Issue apology happen, there is necessarily awarding of frequent buyer points (although the number of points awarded might be zero).

In spite of explicitly breaking out a mud level use case on the use case diagram, scope and context of the (sub)domain has not changed. It's exactly the same scope and context as before; the diagram is just expressing more detail to the reader. Even though you might recognize such common elements in your own use cases, you are under no obligation to factor them out explicitly as mud level use cases on the diagram.

The decision to factor should be considered from an economic perspective. There is a cost of splitting out a mud level use case, both in terms of initial effort to create the diagram and in long-term diagram maintenance. The value of breaking out and «include»-ing a mud level use case is that it makes obvious to readers that certain process elements are shared. You need to balance the value of expressiveness against cost. When there is more value, include it. But the cost is not always warranted—particularly when this same detail will exist in other places, notably sequence diagrams and state models.

Finally, remember general dependencies and stereotypes introduced in Chapter 5. The «include» stereotype is one of several predefined stereotypes in UML. In this case, the stereotype is modifying a UML general dependency to have the special meaning of use case inclusion. This is an example of how stereotypes are used to modify the meaning of UML concepts in useful ways. The «extend» stereotype (next) is similar.

7.14 «extend» Use Cases

This is the other situation where mud level use cases come in. Use case extension shows an alternative course of action. A significant element of process—the mud level use case—is optional. The mud level use case expresses processing

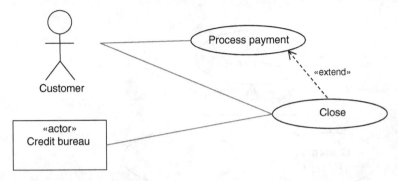

Figure 7.11 An example of an «extend» mud level use case.

that may or may not happen: sometimes it will and sometimes it won't. Figure 7.11 shows an example of an «extend»-ing mud level use case, Close, on sea level use case Process payment. As shown in the diagram, the mud level use case may happen on a Process payment, but it also may not happen.

Use case extension is optional, meaning that when Process payment happens, Close may or may not happen. Sometimes it will, and sometimes it won't.

Again, in spite of breaking out the mud level use case, scope and context of the (sub)domain has not changed. It's still the same scope and context as before; the diagram is just expressing more detail. Even though you recognize optional elements of process in use cases, you are under no obligation to break them out as mud level use cases on a diagram. This is another decision that should be considered from an economic perspective. When there is more value than cost, include it. But the cost of the added detail is not always warranted.

If you carefully compare Figures 7.10 and 7.11, it may appear that the dependency arrows are backward from what you might expect. This is actually intentional. In UML, dependency is always drawn from a model element that is incomplete to the model element that provides completion. With «include», the mud level use case is complete by itself, and the sea level use case is incomplete without the «include»-ed mud level use case. So the dependency goes from the sea level to the mud level use case. With «extend», the sea level use case is already complete by itself. The mud level use case depends on the sea level use case to give it context, so the dependency arrow is shown in the other direction.

7.15 Generalizing Use Cases

Use case generalization means there is more than one way to accomplish the same process goal. As shown in Figure 7.12, an airline gate agent may need to verify the identity of a traveler. One way to accomplish that is to check a

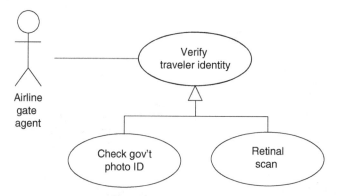

Figure 7.12 An example of use case generalization.

government-issued photo ID such as a driver's license or passport. If this is a high-tech airline, another way to verify identity could be to do a retinal scan of the traveler. Both methods accomplish the same goal of verifying traveler identity. The important thing is that the contract (requires and guarantees) of the lower-level use cases be Liskov substitutable ("require no more, and guarantee no less") with the contract of the parent use case.

Again, showing the specific use cases under the generalized use case adds detail and but also adds effort. The cost of the extra detail needs to be weighed against the benefit of showing it.

7.16 Generalizing Actors

In the same way that use cases can be generalized, actors can also be generalized. Figure 7.13 shows actor generalization.

The diagram shows that any ticket purchaser can make a reservation and cancel a reservation. In addition, a traveler is a kind of ticket purchaser that can check in for the flight. A travel agent is a kind of ticket purchaser that can also make and cancel reservations and can modify a reservation. As modeled, travel agents can't check in nor can travelers modify reservations. Actor generalization is useful for describing role-based permissions when some roles are extensions of others.

7.17 Fundamental Versus Custodial ("CRUD") Dynamics

The terms fundamental and custodial dynamics refer to how interesting and important certain processes are to stakeholders. Fundamental dynamics are those that the business is most interested in. But just like with a house or

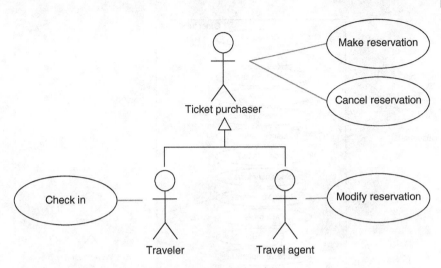

Figure 7.13 An example of actor generalization.

car, some amount of maintenance is needed. Examples of custodial dynamics in WebBooks 2.0 Order fulfillment include maintaining the set of Managers, Warehouse workers, Publishers, and the catalog of books for sale. Custodial dynamics can also be referred to as "CRUD"—an acronym for "Create, Read, Update, Delete."

Sometimes there is a lot of housekeeping—so much so that it interferes with understanding the fundamental business. Rather than clutter a semantic model with uninteresting and unimportant detail, many organizations omit custodial dynamics from the use case diagram and concentrate on just the fundamental, most interesting detail.

7.18 WebBooks 2.0 Order fulfillment Use Cases

The use case diagram for the Order fulfillment domain of WebBooks 2.0 (Appendix D) is shown in Figure 7.14. Use case diagrams for other WebBooks 2.0 domains can be found in Appendices F, H, and J.

7.19 Quality Criteria

In addition to the overall quality criteria (Table 3.1) and naming criteria (Table 3.2),

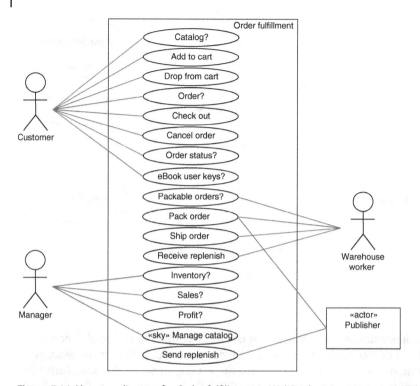

Figure 7.14 Use case diagram for Order fulfillment in WebBooks 2.0.

Table 7.3 shows quality criteria for use case diagrams.

Table 7.4 shows quality criteria for consistency between use cases and (sub) domain partitioning. If you have both use cases and (sub)domains, these additional criteria apply.

7.20 Economic Considerations

A key part of engineering is considering the economics of technical decisions. Decisions about scope and context of a domain to model, design, implement, and maintain clearly have economic implications. Semantic model content should only appear when it yields positive return on investment. Ideally, we want to be able to answer these kinds of questions:

- How long will it take and how much will it cost to deliver this scope?
- How much longer will it take and how much more will it cost if scope is added?
- How much shorter will it take and how much less will it cost if scope is removed?
- How much scope can be delivered within given constraints, for example, schedule, budget, or staffing?

Table 7.3 Quality criteria for use cases.

Item	Criterion
UC-1	The use case diagram is not overengineered: scope and context are sufficiently communicated without extra detail that is better specified elsewhere
UC-2	All—and only—relevant actors are identified (context)
UC-3	Each actor name highlights that actor's role
UC-4	All—and only—relevant use cases are identified (scope)
UC-5	All—and only—relevant "participates-in" links are identified: which actors can participate in what use cases is clearly and correctly defined
UC-6	Each sea level use cases represent a transaction from the point of view of participating actors: an atomic unit of process
UC-7	Transaction boundaries—that is, "what are the sea level use cases?"—are consistent with stakeholder need
UC-8	The full set of sea level transactions is adequately identified, including (as appropriate) custodial ("CRUD") transactions
UC-9	Only domain relevant times are modeled, not clocks
UC-10	All relevant business event types (unpredictable, timed, consequential, non-occurrence) have been considered
UC-11	Each sea level event use case is named with a business event or an action verb phrase that summarizes the response
UC-12	Each sea level data use case is named with a noun phrase that summarizes the information content being communicated
UC-13	Each sea level use case represents only net flow of information: no push or pull is expressed or implied
UC-14	If present, use case inclusion and extension have been used correctly
UC-15	If present, use case generalization has been used correctly[a]
UC-16	If shown, actor generalization has been done properly

[a] Chapter 2, Liskov substitutability: sub-use cases require no more and guarantee no less.

Table 7.4 Quality criteria for consistency between use cases and (sub)domain partitioning.

Item	Criterion
DU-1	The use case diagram shows the scope and context for a (sub)domain: the correlation of this use case diagram to that (sub)domain is clear and obvious (e.g., they have the same name)

Unfortunately, use cases tend to be highly variable in size and complexity. Unless you have a good analogy to estimate from, it will be difficult to do any better than expert judgment estimation. You may be better off waiting until you understand the class model, and any implications the proposed scope and context has on that model, before you can give meaningful estimates. More on that kind of estimation is discussed in the next chapter.

7.21 Describing Overall Workflow

The use case diagram shows scope and context. What is missing are interrelationships between transactions: the workflow perspective. The workflow perspective is also derivable from other parts of the semantic model, but again, maybe it is something that a stakeholder would find useful. If the workflow view is useful, UML's activity diagram can be used to show it. An example activity diagram for loan processing at Silly Bank is shown in Figure 7.15.

More information on activity diagrams can be found in Fowler's "UML Distilled" and the UML specification.[4]

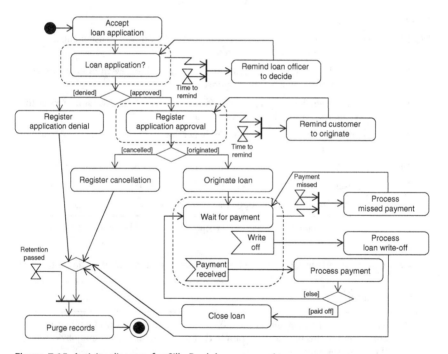

Figure 7.15 Activity diagram for Silly Bank loan processing.

---

4 See [Fowler03] and [OMG11b], respectively.

7.22   Summary

The use case diagram provides a view of (sub)domain scope and context—the big picture. Scope is represented by one or more use cases: processes at the most coarse-grained level. One or more actors represent context. The "participates-in" link specifies what actors can participate in what use cases. "Free-floating" use cases—where no actors participate—are rare but not unreasonable.

Some sea level use cases are triggered by business events. By first identifying business events, particularly using the four categories, namely, unpredictable, timed, consequential, and nonoccurrence, we can surface a more complete set of event use cases. The "nonoccurrence" category forces modelers to consider use cases that would probably otherwise be missed.

Data use cases are very different from event use cases. Something is known to the (sub)domain and an actor needs that information to do their job. Not every actor should have access to all information; only certain actors should be allowed to see it. A data use case represents access to information, and a participates-in link represents each actor that is allowed access.

Flow of information is inherent in processes. How and when information gets from here to there is irrelevant from a business perspective. Information can be pushed or pulled; the domain doesn't care as long as information is available where it is needed no later than when it is needed. Push versus pull is an automation technology concern and has nothing to do with business. Model business in business terms, not computing terms: model net flow of information.

Use case inclusion shows common elements of process being shared across several sea level use cases. Use case extension shows an alternate course of action. Use case generalization means there is more than one way to accomplish the same goal. In the same way use cases can be generalized, actors can also be generalized.

Fundamental dynamics are those that stakeholders are most interested in automating. Rather than clutter a semantic model with uninteresting and unimportant detail, many organizations omit custodial dynamics to focus on fundamental, more interesting detail.

It is easy to overengineer a use case diagram, and it is not that important to building and maintaining software. You can waste a lot of valuable time on use case diagramming. So be careful not to invest too much; time will be better spent on other components. The primary goal is to communicate scope and context. Don't worry about being overly precise; the use case diagram is limited in how much it can communicate. Once you have sufficiently communicated scope and context, then move on to other components, like the class model (next).

8

Class Models

Policies to Enforce

The use case diagram shows scope (use cases) and context (actors) for a (sub) domain: processes at a coarse-grained level. The class model defines major elements of the business and identifies important relationships that exist between those elements. The class model is a precise statement of policies to enforce across that scope and context. It specifies invariants: conditions that must always be true. The primary concepts of class modeling are:

- Class
- Attribute
- Association
- Generalization (inheritance)

A number of secondary concepts are also introduced and explained.

Unlike use case diagrams, care must be taken with class models because they are critical to design and coding (Part III). A bad job on class modeling makes design and coding much more difficult, risky, and defect prone.

8.1 Class

A class is defined in UML as[1]:

> "... *a set of objects that share the same specifications of features, constraints, and semantics.*"

A class is an abstraction for a set of business-relevant things that are subject to the same policies, processes, and constraints. It is a descriptor for a set of things with similar structure, behavior, and relationships. Simply, it is a stencil or template for a set of things that are alike. Consider your savings account at a bank: it

---

1 See [OMG11b].

How to Engineer Software: A Model-Based Approach, First Edition. Steve Tockey.
© 2019 the IEEE Computer Society, Inc. Published 2019 by John Wiley & Sons, Inc.

is a business-relevant thing in banking. My bank account is also a business-relevant thing. Someone else's bank account is also a business-relevant thing. We can abstract all of these business-relevant things—because they are alike in some sense, they are subject to the same policies, processes, and constraints—into class Bank account in a semantic model of banking.

The classes represent how the modeler chooses to abstract the (sub)domain. Different modelers may represent the same (sub)domain using different classes, based on different perspectives. The importance of being able to draw out good abstractions was discussed in Chapter 3. Strive for classes (abstractions) with high cohesion, loose coupling, consider invariants and likely variation, etc.

8.1.1 Identifying Classes

One way to identify classes is by looking for nouns and noun phrases in a description of that (sub)domain. One source of nouns might be the list of concepts that were grouped in domain partitioning. Both approaches are very rough and subject to different-words-have-same-meaning and same-words-have-different-meaning challenges, but can be a place to start.

Generally speaking, the following categories of things in (a description of) a (sub)domain are likely to be classes:

1) Actors
2) Physical things
3) Concepts
4) Roles
5) Specifications
6) Events
7) Associations

Each of these will be discussed. Just like the kinds of business events in the last chapter, this isn't a rigid classification. Instead, this is another tool to help you get started. Don't try to categorize every class into exactly one of these categories; often a class will fit into more than one category. Rather, when modeling a (sub)domain, any time a noun or noun phrase in its description matches one or more of these categories, you should have reasonable confidence it will be a class in the semantic model.

> **WARNING**
> Do not just convert use cases one-for-one into classes. A sea level use case is a process that needs to work with domain information. The class model specifies constraints on that domain information. If you force each sea level use case into a single class, then you:
>
> - Focus entirely on function, not on information constraints.
> - End up with too many classes: one per sea level use case.

- Miss important complexities of, and constraints on, information: you completely miss capturing and specifying critical policies.
- Destroy abstraction, reduce cohesion, increase coupling, etc.
- …

Don't.

1) Actor: Step one in building a class model can be to simply copy each actor from the use case diagram as a class on the class diagram. These classes should be stereotyped as "«actor»" or otherwise annotated to show they represent the same thing on the use case diagram. Customer, Loan officer, Bank manager, and Credit bureau from Silly Bank's loan processing business would be actor-stereotyped classes in its class model

2) Physical thing: These, like consequential business events in the previous chapter, are usually rather obvious: person, vehicle, power supply, aardvark, burrow, etc.

3) Concept: Something not physical (i.e., it has no mass or volume) but still relevant in the domain. Something like a "post" on social media: it doesn't have mass or volume, and yet it is fundamental to that business. A Bank account would be a concept in banking; a tax deduction, a tax credit, and a tax bracket would be concepts in personal income tax processing, and a reservation would be a concept in running an airline or a hotel. WebBooks is not interested in individual copies of the books the way a library would ("Who is borrowing copy #4 of Gone With the Wind?"). Instead, WebBooks is interested in the sets of books that have the same title ("Someone ordered three copies of Return on Software"). Title would be an example of a significant concept in WebBooks 2.0 Order fulfillment.

4) Role: How a thing is used. The physical thing could be a person where roles might be student, professor, sales person, bank manager, pilot, and so on. Another example is the long strips of concrete at airports: runways. Each has properties simply because it is a strip of concrete: length, width, maximum weight capacity, etc. that would be modeled in a Runway class representing that physical thing. Depending on weather conditions, a runway could be used for takeoffs and landings in one direction or in the opposite direction. It has properties that vary depending on how it is being used: the heading a pilot needs to fly to use that runway, the distance to the threshold, stopway, and so on. The uses (the roles) of runways could be modeled as a class "Active runway" or "Runway use."

5) Specification: Characteristics that are shared by collections of similar objects. Wingspan is not a characteristic of a single airplane per se; it's a characteristic of the kind of airplane it is. All airplanes of type Boeing 787-8 have a

length of 57 m (186 ft), a height of 17 m (56 ft), a wingspan of 60 m (197 ft), and a cruise speed of Mach 0.85. You may need to model both airplanes and airplane types in a model of an aviation domain. All cookies in the same batch were made from the same recipe; you may need to model both cookies and recipes in a semantic model of baking.

6) Event: Time—either in the past, now, or in the future—is a significant property. A dinner reservation in restaurant management, a purchase order, a course enrollment at a school, etc. could be examples of events. Book order and Replenish order could be a relevant events in WebBooks 2.0 Order fulfillment.

7) Association: Something that links or connects two or more other things. Consider a driver's license. There are characteristics of the license that don't describe the licensed driver, nor do they describe the licensing authority. They are characteristics of the connection between the licensing authority and the licensed driver: When was the license issued? When does it expire? What kinds of motor vehicles (passenger cars, heavy trucks, school busses) is that driver allowed to drive? A student's enrollment in a class at a university is another example of an association.

Again, these categories are not intended for rigorous categorization after the fact. Instead they provide practical knowledge that might otherwise only come after years of on-the-job semantic modeling experience.

8.1.2 Class Names

Classes are named using a singular noun or noun phrase. All examples above are singular nouns or noun phrases. The reason for naming a class singularly is like the relationship between a cookie cutter and cookies. The star-shaped cookie cutter can be used to make many star-shaped cookies. The bell-shaped cookie cutter can be used to make many bell-shaped cookies. The elephant-shaped cookie cutter can be used to make many elephant-shaped cookies. Similarly, class Bank account (the template) can be used to make many bank account-shaped things. Class Bank teller (the template) can be used to make many bank teller-shaped things. When naming classes, be sure to follow the naming guidelines in Chapter 3.

8.1.3 Class Notation

UML notation for a class is a rectangle divided into three compartments, as in Figure 8.1.

The top compartment holds the class name: the singular noun or noun phrase. The middle compartment is for the list of attributes (note: "instance variables" and "member data" are design and code terms) and will be explained

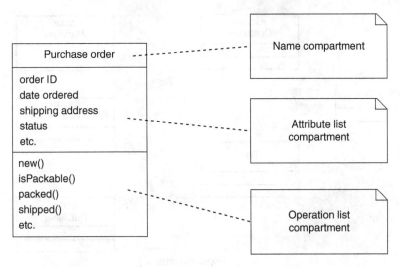

Figure 8.1 UML's notation for a class.

in the next section. The bottom compartment is for the list of operations (note: "methods" and "member functions" are design and code terms—although UML's preference to emphasize encapsulation, the term "methods" is discouraged in this context). Chapter 15 explains how operations are only relevant in design, not in semantic models. The bottom compartment will be empty in a semantic model class diagram.

A rough first approximation of classes in WebBooks 2.0 Order fulfillment domain is shown in Figure 8.2.

8.2   Attribute

The concept of an attribute does not appear to be formally defined in UML. An appropriate definition could be:

> *"a (kind of) fact about domain-relevant objects that is necessary to support one or more processes"*

An attribute represents a piece of important, useful data about objects of that class. A common and useful—but certainly not required—convention is to not capitalize attribute names and precede those names (outside of the attribute compartment on the class the diagram) with ".". Examples would be the .balance of a Bank account, the .status of a Bank account, the .overdraft limit of a Bank account, the .name of a Student, the .birthdate of a Licensed driver, and so on.

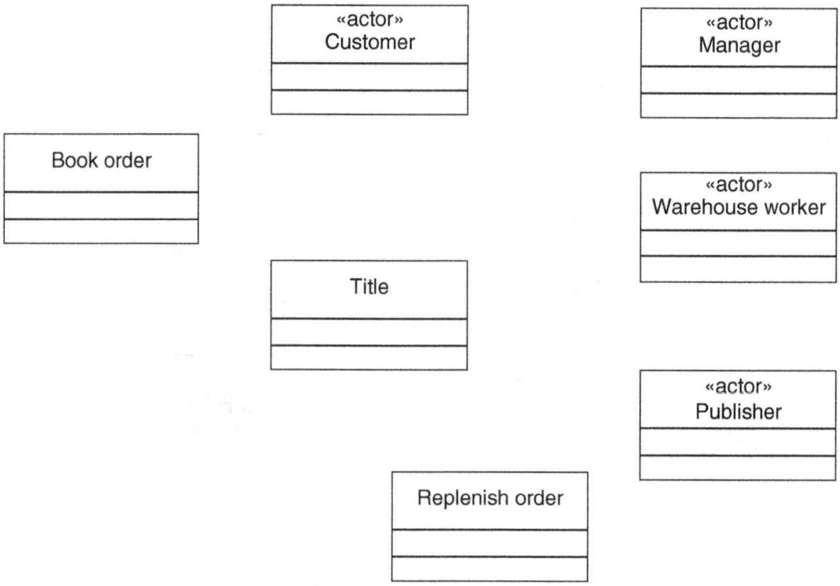

«actor» Customer

«actor» Manager

Book order

«actor» Warehouse worker

Title

«actor» Publisher

Replenish order

Figure 8.2 A rough first approximation of classes in WebBooks 2.0 Order fulfillment.

The critical idea is to capture information needed about objects to carry out sea level transactions. Ask the questions:

"When an object of class X exists, what needs to be known about it? What does it need to know about itself to adequately support the processes in scope?"

Said another way, what kinds of questions need to be answerable about potential or real-world objects in each class?

- "What is the .balance of Bank account c012166?"
- "What is the .usable length of Active runway 36L?"
- "What is the .name of Student 123456?"
- "What is the .grade point average of Student 123456?"
- "Is student 123456 on academic probation?"
- ...

8.2.1 Attribute Names

Like classes, attributes are typically named with nouns or noun phrases. Be sure to follow the naming guidelines in Chapter 3. If an attribute represents true–false (i.e., Boolean) information, it can help to name the attribute as "is <property>", as in:

- .is on academic probation for a Student
- .is waitlisted for an Enrollment
- .is enroute for a Flight
- .is overdrawn for a Savings account
- …

8.2.2 Attribute Notation

The UML notation for attributes in a class diagram is to list them by name in the middle compartment. Figure 8.3 shows proposed attributes for Order fulfillment.

8.2.3 Classes Versus Attributes

A frequent question in class modeling is, "Is it a class, or is it an attribute?" In the airplane–airplane type example, one might choose to make .airplane type an attribute of class airplane. If all any process ever cared about was "What kind of airplane is it?," that would be sufficient. However, sometimes what seems

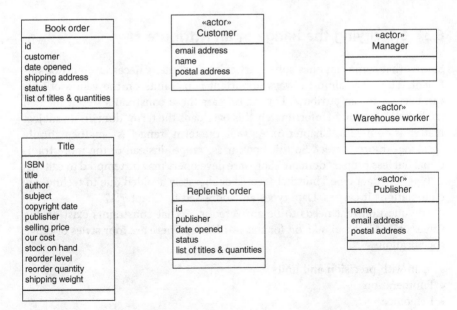

Figure 8.3 Proposed attributes for classes in Order fulfillment.

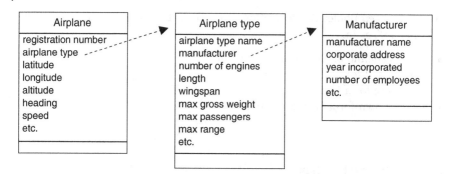

Figure 8.4 An attribute can sometimes take on its own attributes.

to be an attribute takes on its own attributes. Suppose processes cares about things like length, wingspan, maximum gross weight, cruise speed, service ceiling, manufacturer, etc. In this case, what was originally an attribute now becomes a class with its own attributes. If processes also care about characteristics of the manufacturer: corporate address, year incorporated, number of employees, etc., then what used to be the manufacturer attribute of an airplane type becomes a separate manufacturer class with its own attributes. This is shown in Figure 8.4.

8.3 Specifying the Range of an Attribute

Stating that some class has some particular attribute is necessary but not sufficient. There are almost always important constraints on the values objects can take on for an attribute. For many years these constraints were called an attribute's "domain." Unfortunately this overloads the term "domain" (a subject matter as defined in Chapter 6). As well, the term "range" is—mathematically speaking—more correct. So this book uses "range" instead of the more traditional but less proper "domain." Software developers may be tempted to call this a "type" or "data type," but that term is deliberately avoided due to technology connotations it carries. Data types are addressed in Chapter 17.

The question that needs to be answered is, "What constraints exist on the values any object can take on for this attribute?" There are four styles of range specification:

- Span with precision and units
- Enumeration
- Reference
- Unconstrained

8.3.1 Span with Precision and Units

The first style, span with precision and units, gives a lower and upper bound along with how precise values must be and in what units. The range for the .balance of a Bank account might be "USD $0 to USD $100,000 to the nearest USD cent." The span is $0–100,000, the precision is to the nearest cent, and the unit is US dollar. In a social media system, the .join date of a Member might be any date after the company went live with their first version, up to and including today, with a precision of the nearest whole day. The range of the .useable length of an Active runway might be specified as "from 500 to 30,000 feet, to the nearest 500 feet." The span is 500–30,000, the units are feet, and the precision is to the nearest 500 ft. The .pay rate of an Hourly employee might be specified as "from the prevailing legal minimum wage, up to and including $45, in Australian dollars, to the nearest whole cent." Spans are assumed to be closed intervals, that is, boundary values are included in the valid set. If open intervals are needed, they must be explicitly identified as such. Be careful with attributes that represent time in multi-time zone businesses. Is there a reference time zone like UTC, or are times considered to be local? Such issues can be critical and need to be explicitly addressed.

8.3.2 Enumeration

The second style, enumeration, specifies a list of acceptable values. The .job category of an Employee in a payroll system might be "technical, trade, office, professional, or manager." The .status of an Employee in the same payroll system might be "active, on leave, or retired." No values other than those appearing in the enumerated list are acceptable. In some cases, symbols in an enumeration will be ordered—they form a sequence. The enumeration values are an ordinal scale rather than a nominal scale in measurement theory terms[2]: enumerations are treated as unordered unless explicitly identified as ordered.

8.3.3 Reference

The third type of range specification, reference, points to an outside authority that defines the acceptable range. The .job type attribute from above might instead be "Refer to corporate policy X47G961 for the set of recognized job types." The .address of a Person in almost any business might be specified as "Anything acceptable to the U. S. Post Office or Canada Post."

---

2 See, for example, Section L.7.1 Measurement theory scale types, chapter 26 of [Tockey05], or http://en.wikipedia.org/wiki/Level_of_measurementt.

8.3.4 Unconstrained

The last style, unconstrained, means just that: the business doesn't want any constraints on values. Consider the .name of a Customer; is it reasonable or desirable to claim that somebody's name is invalid? Normally the answer should be no. A range requiring at least one vowel in last names worked fine until Suzy Ng tried to register. Another example is the Hawaiian woman with a very long last name.[3]

The entire range might be unconstrained, one side of a span with precision and units may be unconstrained, or precision may be unconstrained, as in:

- *"0 .. unconstrained kilometers, to the nearest 10 meters"*—A specified minimum but no maximum
- *"unconstrained .. 1000 kilograms, to the nearest 0.5 kilogram"*—A specified maximum but no minimum
- *"0 .. 10,000 degrees Kelvin, unconstrained precision"*—A specified minimum and maximum but no constraint on precision

The business may prefer a range to be unconstrained, but performance-for-a-price means an otherwise undesirable constraint needs to be placed in design. During design and implementation it might be necessary—economically—to impose technical constraints, but technical constraints are not inherently part of the (sub)domain and should not appear in a semantic model. Performance-for-a-price is discussed in Chapters 17 and 19.

> **WARNING**
>
> *Range specifications should not be programming language data types!* Don't specify ranges as int, float, double, long, Boolean, String, etc. These are implementation data types for a designer to choose. They are not inherent in the (sub) domain. Assigning a data type at this point is premature design. We simply don't know enough at this point to be making these kinds of decisions, particularly considering the service life of the software. So don't make these decisions now! The only exception is when the domain being modeled is, say, a compiler or a run-time system. Chapter 17 explains how and when to make design and implementation data type decisions.

8.3.5 Range Specifications and Requirements Completeness

It's important to drive the class model all the way down to range specifications for every attribute. Take, for example, the .balance of a Bank account, with a range specification of "USD $0 to USD $100,000 to the nearest USD cent."

---

3 See http://www.dailymail.co.uk/news/article-2418171/Janice-Keihanaikukauakahihuliheekahau naele-Hawaiian-woman-told-trim-long-doesnt-fit-state-ID-cards.html. See also: http://www.bbc. com/future/story/20160325-the-names-that-break-computer-systems.

Notice how that range specification is really a statement of four distinct functional requirements:

- *"The .balance for a Bank account shall be in units of USD."*
- *"The minimum value for the .balance of a Bank account shall be $0."*
- *"The maximum value for the .balance of a Bank account shall be $100,000."*
- *"The .balance for a Bank account shall be precise to the nearest cent."*

Code needs to be written to ensure each of these functional requirements is never violated in a running system. What would happen if—because nobody asked about ranges and developers only guessed—software implemented the range for a Bank account.balance to be "USD-$10,000 to $50,000 with 5 significant digits"? At some point, someone may try to have an account with a balance in the range USD −$10,000 to −$1. The software will allow it but bank policy forbids it. If a bank customer wins the lottery and tries to deposit the winnings into their account bringing .balance into the range of $50,000–100,000: this is acceptable to the bank but not allowed by the software. Finally, consider loss of precision when an account balance is rounded to five significant digits—in fact eight are required at this bank. Each of these is a case of the "Dreaded Phone Call Syndrome" just waiting to happen:

- *"Your stupid system just let an account balance to go negative."*
- *"Your stupid system just prevented a lottery winner from depositing her winnings."*
- *"Your stupid system is rounding off to five significant digits, we need eight."*

Forcing specification of attribute ranges exposes these low-level detailed requirements. The class model is incomplete without attribute ranges. The business—if any constraints exist—will need to answer when the modeler asks. Developers will create code that supports the bank's policies. We did ask, and we wrote code to match what we were told. Defects are prevented before they could ever happen. The probability of dreaded phone calls goes way down.

The range specification for an attribute is normally part of the attribute description in an attribute dictionary for the class. The range specification is not put on the class diagram because the diagram becomes too cluttered. Appendices D, F, H, and J all show examples of range specifications.

8.4 Key

A key, sometimes called an identifier, is an attribute—or a minimum set of attributes—whose value(s) can be used to uniquely identify objects in that class. Examples could be:

- The .customer id of a Customer
- The .student id of a Student
- The .ISBN ("International Standard Book Number") of a Title

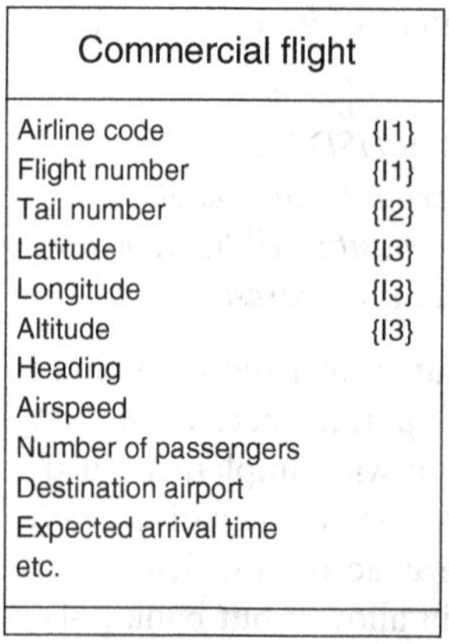

Commercial flight	
Airline code	{I1}
Flight number	{I1}
Tail number	{I2}
Latitude	{I3}
Longitude	{I3}
Altitude	{I3}
Heading	
Airspeed	
Number of passengers	
Destination airport	
Expected arrival time	
etc.	

Figure 8.5 Using "{Ix}" notation for keys.

- The .tail number of an Airplane
- The .airline code and .flight number of a Commercial flight
- ...

8.4.1 Key Notation

There is no defined UML notation for keys. You can define your own stereotype, if you wish. Options might be «key» or «pk» (as in "primary key"). Leon Starr and Mellor and Balcer[4] both use a variation of UML's constraint notation[5] "{Ix}" as shown in Figure 8.5.

As shown in Figure 8.5, there can be more than one key for a class. Also, a key can span multiple attributes. Further, the same attribute can participate in many keys although that isn't shown in Figure 8.5. A Commercial flight can be identified by:

- *It's airline code and flight number*—For example, UA 888, AA 21, CA 1521, MU 5162, etc.
- *The airplane's government-issued registration number*—Like the license (tag) number on a car, each airplane has a government-issued registration number. Airplanes in the United States have registration numbers like N6854UA; UK registration numbers are G- followed by a four-letter code, G-YMMF. Chinese registration numbers are B- followed by a four-digit number, like B-2047. The aviation industry calls this a "tail number" because it is often painted on or near the tail of the airplane.

---

4 See [Starr01] and [Mellor02], respectively.
5 See, for example, [Fowler03] or [OMG11b].

- *Its location in three-dimensional space*—As in "the airplane that is now at latitude N42 7.63, longitude W71 41.72, and altitude 37,000 feet" because only one airplane should be in a given location at a time.

8.4.2 Model Keys or Not?

Use of keys can be a subject of debate in semantic modeling. One side says that objects only need to be identifiable; the choice of any specific identification mechanism is a designer's responsibility. Making a choice now amounts to premature design. Keys may also only be relevant in implementations that involve relational databases or other persistent storage mechanisms. If the domain is implemented as memory-resident Java, C++, C#, and other objects, the built-in object reference (i.e., the "handle": the memory address of the object) could be entirely sufficient.

The counterargument is that keys aren't for the automated system; they are a necessary element of how stakeholders run their business. Imagine a credit card business that didn't deal with credit card numbers—which is, really, just a key for a credit account. A university registration and records system would certainly deal with student IDs, course IDs, and the like. The worldwide air traffic control system uses the airline code + flight number convention for commercial flights. Those keys are integral to how stakeholders run their business; to not put them in the semantic model would be a mistake. It's how the stakeholders identify and refer to specific objects in their business.

Keys can also be useful for expressing certain constraints. Consider the metamodel (a model of the semantic modeling language; see Appendix L) where Class has States and Transitions go between States. A Transition can only go between States that are *in the same Class*. Without keys it can be hard to express a states-for-a-transition-must-be-in-the-same-class constraint.

You can include keys in a class model or leave them out—as long as stakeholders who will evaluate the model for completeness and correctness agree. If you put keys in the class model, be sure to mark them using, for example, the «key» or «pk» stereotype, or the {Ix} constraint. The designer needs to be aware of the role of that attribute(s).

This debate could also be resolved by applying the perfect technology filter:

> *"If we had a perfect computer, would we still need this key in this class model?"*

If yes, because stakeholders need that key for external purposes, then it is part of how they run their business and needs to be included. Otherwise the stakeholders would deem the model incomplete. If, on the other hand, that key wouldn't be necessary given a perfect computer (i.e., any arbitrary identification mechanism would be sufficient), then leave it out.

8.5 Derived Attribute

A derived attribute is an attribute whose value can be erased and then reconstructed from other information known in the domain. The .gross pay of an Hourly employee could be erased and reconstructed from that employee's . pay rate and .hours worked. The .total cost of a Purchase order could be derived from the .quantity and .unit price of each Item ordered, plus shipping costs, and applicable sales taxes.

8.5.1 Derived Attribute Notation

UML's notation is to precede a derived attribute's name with a slash ("/"), as shown in Figure 8.6.

Beyond the graphical notation, you also need to state what the derivation policy is, that is, "what is the necessary consistency relationship between the value for this derived attribute and the values it is derived from?" You can use UML's constraint notation and include it on the class diagram as shown in Figure 8.7, or you can describe the derivation policy in the attribute dictionary.

Adding derived attributes and constraints to a class diagram will tend to clutter it. It may be better to put this detail in the dictionary. The derivation policy

Figure 8.6 UML notation for a derived attribute.

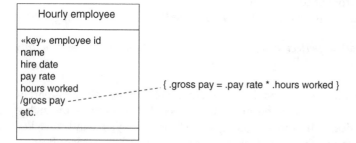

Figure 8.7 Using a UML constraint to specify a derivation policy.

can be expressed as an equation, decision table, graph, or any other non-algorithmic function. The constraint might reference an external document.

8.5.2 Model Derived Attributes or Not?

Use of derived attributes in class models can also be the subject of debate. One argument is that derived attributes imply at least some level of premature design (specifically caching of intermediate results). Showing a derived attribute may mean a designer is more likely to implement it as stored data, although it is shown in Chapter 17 that the designer has at least three alternatives. Conceptually, a derived attribute should not be interpreted as stored data. It is merely a placeholder for the derivation policy.

The important thing is that if there is a derived attribute, it must at least be marked so the designer is aware of the need to treat it different from other attributes.

8.6 Class and Attribute Normalization

Normalization is often considered a way to reduce redundancy in data structures—in particular database tables. But this vastly understates its importance. The purpose of the class model is to understand, document, communicate, and validate policies to be enforced and to help manage complexity. So a goal should be to simplify the class model into its purest, simplest, most basic (i.e., "canonical") form. This removes as much complexity as possible.

In fact, normalization can be thought of as applying high cohesion and loose coupling to class models. Consider Pike's Rule #5[6]:

> *"Data dominates. If you've chosen the right data structures and organized things well, the algorithms will almost always be self-evident. Data structures, not algorithms, are central to programming."*

Simply, "Write stupid code that uses smart data." If data is organized intelligently, functions are simplified. If data is not organized intelligently, functions become unnecessarily complex to deal with that poorly organized data. Intelligently organizing data in a semantic model vastly simplifies design and code later on.

A designer is free to, and in most cases will, de-normalize in design to meet nontrivial nonfunctional performance requirements. De-normalization is discussed in Chapter 19.

---

6 See, for example, http://users.ece.utexas.edu/~adnan/pike.html.

8.6.1 Conventional Wisdom: Normal Form Rules

The conventional wisdom on normalization involves a series of "normal form rules." A class model is considered to be in "Nth normal form" when the criteria for that level are met. Here is a brief overview of the normal form rules:

- *1st Normal Form (1NF)*—"All underlying domains[7] are atomic": no attribute represents compound information.
- *2nd Normal Form (2NF)*—"All non-key attributes are functionally dependent on key attributes": key values are sufficient to determine non-key attribute values.
- *3rd Normal Form (3NF)*—"No transitive dependencies": a non-key attribute cannot depend on anything other than a key.
- *Elementary Key Normal Form (EKNF)*—"Every non-trivial functional dependency is either the dependency of an elementary key or a dependency on a superkey.[8]"
- *Boyce-Codd Normal Form (BCNF)*—"Every non-trivial functional dependency is on a superkey."
- *4th Normal Form (4NF)*—"Every non-trivial multivalued dependency is a dependency on a superkey."
- *5th Normal Form (5NF, also called "Projection-Join Normal Form" or PJNF)*—"Every non-trivial join dependency is implied by the superkeys."
- ...

The conventional rules get very esoteric very quickly—so much so most organizations just stop at 3rd Normal Form because it's too hard to go further. But that means an as-specified class model can still cause trouble. The alternative is Domain-Key Normal Form (DK/NF).

8.6.2 Domain-Key Normal Form (DK/NF)

Ronald Fagin published "Domain-Key Normal Form"[9] in 1981. DK/NF is defined in terms of domain constraints and key constraints:

- *Domain constraint*—In our vocabulary, the range specification for an attribute. Saying the .balance of a Bank account needs to be "USD $0 to USD $100,000 to the nearest USD cent" constrains values that attribute can take on.
- *Key constraint*—In our vocabulary, this declares that some (set of) attribute(s) is a valid key for objects of that class. No two objects of that class could ever

---

7 Range specifications, in the vocabulary of this book.
8 A superkey is a set of attributes that is not necessarily minimal. See, for example, http://en.wikipedia.org/wiki/Superkey.
9 See [Fagin81].

have the same values for their key attribute(s) at the same time. If the key is a compound key, that is, it is made up of more than one attribute, then it must also be minimal (e.g., including .heading in key I3 of Figure 8.5 is not minimal: .latitude, .longitude, and .altitude are sufficient).

DK/NF says that there cannot be any constraints on information other than what are explicitly defined in range specifications and key specifications. For our purposes, we also need to consider multiplicity constraints on associations and generalizations—topics later in this chapter. Interpret DK/NF as including those constraints as well. It will be more precise to say, Range-Key-Multiplicity-Completeness Normal Form (RKMC/NF): "All relevant policies to be enforced in the (sub)domain are explicitly expressed in terms of range constraints, key constraints, multiplicity constraints, and generalization completeness constraints." Any additional (i.e., unspecified) constraints would risk insertion anomalies or deletion anomalies when an automated system implementing that class model executes.

8.6.3 Insertion Anomalies

An insertion anomaly occurs when an object created consistent with all specified range and key constraints results in an invalid (to the domain) object. That object has all attribute values within all defined ranges, and all key values are unique, yet that object would still be considered semantically incorrect—it would violate one or more policies. Consider the class diagram fragment in Figure 8.8: the range for .publisher name might be unconstrained, and the range for .publisher address might be "acceptable to the US Post Office and Canada Post."

Consider the following candidate object of class Title:

- .*ISBN*—"0-321-56149-X"
- .*title*—"Return on Software"
- .*author*—"Steve Tockey"
- .*publisher name*—"Addison-Wesley"
- .*publisher address*—"800 East 96th Street, Indianapolis, Indiana 46240"

Figure 8.8 Fragment of a class diagram for Order fulfillment.

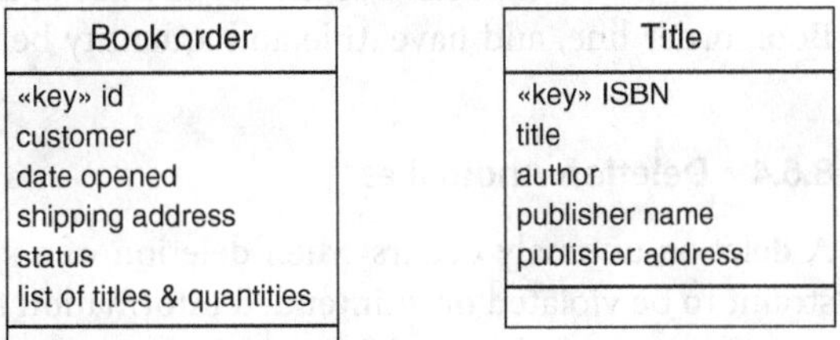

Book order
«key» id
customer
date opened
shipping address
status
list of titles & quantities

Title
«key» ISBN
title
author
publisher name
publisher address

Now consider another candidate object of class Title:

- *.ISBN*—"0-201-03801-3"
- *.title*—"The Art of Computer Programming, Volume 1: Fundamental Algorithms"
- *.author*—"Donald Knuth"
- *.publisher name*—"Addison-Wesley"
- *.publisher address*—"123 Main Street, Anytown, Iowa, 123456"

In both objects, values for .publisher name and .publisher address are valid according to the specified ranges. But note how these two objects imply that Addison-Wesley has more than one address, which would violate a policy that a publisher has only one address. The remedy is to move .publisher address to a new class, Publisher, thus constraining a single publisher to have a single address.

The list of titles and quantities attribute of class Book order is also problematic. First, what would a range specification look like?

> *"from one (title + quantity) pair to an unconstrained number of (title + quantity) pairs"*

The lower and upper bounds are somewhat reasonable, but the units are bizarre to say the least. Second, consider the following as a candidate object in class Book order:

- *.id*—"Order 47"
- *.customer*—"Joe Jones"
- *.date opened*—"21-January-2017"
- *.shipping address*—"123 Main Street, Anytown, Iowa, 123456"
- *.status*—"Open"
- *.list of titles and quantities*—"(Return on Software, 2 copies) (Gone With the Wind, 4 copies) (Return on Software, 4 copies)"

Again, a policy constraint could be violated: if a given title appears in a book order, it must only appear once. Otherwise, how should the order be interpreted? Does Joe Jones really want two copies of Return on Software (he forgot to remove the request for four)? Does he really want four copies (he forgot to remove the request for two)? Or, does he really want six copies?

The remedy is to break out the list of titles & quantities into a separate class, Book order line, and have .title and .quantity be attributes of that new class.

8.6.4 Deletion Anomalies

A deletion anomaly occurs when deletion of a single object can cause a constraint to be violated or unintended information to be lost. Given the class diagram fragment in Figure 8.8, suppose that among all objects of class Title only one of them is published by "Permanent Press." If that one object is deleted, the address of Permanent Press is lost along with it. Deleting an object of class Title should not cause information about a Publisher to be lost. Again, the remedy is to make .publisher address be an attribute of a separate class, Publisher.

8.6.5 DK/NF and the Anomalies

A class model is in DK/NF if and only if it has no insertion or deletion anomalies. Fagin goes on to prove that any class model in DK/NF is automatically in all known traditional normal forms and any other new normal form that might ever be discovered in the future. DK/NF is much simpler, more straightforward, and more reliable in addressing the problem of structuring a class model. Figure 8.9 shows an incomplete but normalized class diagram for the Order fulfillment.

Comparing the normalized class diagram to the earlier diagram in Figure 8.3, pay particular attention to how cohesion has increased and coupling has decreased:

- *Book order and Book order line have been separated*—Increasing the cohesion of each and decoupling one from the other
- *Replenish order and Replenish order line have been separated*—Increasing the cohesion of each and decoupling one from the other

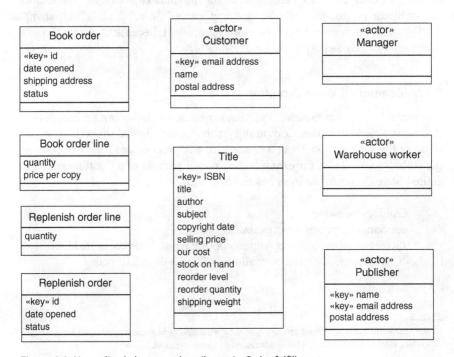

Figure 8.9 Normalized classes and attributes in Order fulfillment.

8.7   Exceptions to Class and Attribute Normalization

Strict normalization is usually critical, particularly in minimizing complexity and preventing insertion and deletion anomalies. That said, there are two exceptions that won't lead to problems. Both are presented here.

8.7.1   Null Value Exception

The first exception to strict normalization allows null values in certain ranges. Null is acceptable in a range specification when no process (sea level transaction) ever behaves differently based on presence or absence of that information. In other words, no process decisions will be made on that information being present or absent. Consider the .phone number of a Customer: some customers may have a phone and some (even today) may not. Strict DK/NF normalization would force the model to have two separate classes, Customer With Phone and Customer Without Phone, because behavior of those two classes is different.[10] However, if .phone number is only remembered for display on screens and reports, then its presence or absence is an external actor's concern. Humans are quite adept at dealing with null values; it only tends to be complex for software to manage the null cases. In the display-only/report-only case, an exception to the no null rule can be made, and the attribute range can include "not applicable," "n/a," "null," "unknown," "TBD," "will be known later," or some equivalent because it doesn't affect complexity of any sea level use case.

8.7.2   Compound Value Exception

The second exception to strict DK/NF normalization allows certain compound (i.e., nonatomic) attributes. Compound attributes are allowed when the composition of the information is not a concern to any process (sea level use case) in the (sub)domain. Take, for example, the .postal address of a Customer. In the United States, a postal address has the following structure:

<Addressee name>
<optional company or organization name>
<Street number> <Street name> <optional apartment or suite identifier>
<City name>, <State abbreviation> <5- or 9-digit ZIP code>

---

10 Anyone sufficiently advanced in class modeling would recognize the opportunity for a single superclass with two subclasses. This is addressed in Generalization, below.

The critical question is whether any sea level transaction cares separately about street names, cities, states, ZIP codes, etc. If all processes deal only with a customer's address as a "blob" (i.e., a "binary large object"), then it is acceptable to represent addresses as a single attribute. On the other hand, if any process deals with any element of an address, for example, different sales tax rates need to be applied based on .ZIP code, then the customer's address must be represented by finer-grained attributes:

- .name of a Customer
- .street address of a Customer
- .city of a Customer
- .state abbreviation of a Customer
- .ZIP code of a Customer

In fact, it is likely that if you have to deal with customer addresses then you probably also have to deal with other addresses (supplier addresses, shipper address, etc.). Abstracting addresses into a separate Address class would be preferred anyway. And for design-to-invariants/design-for-change purposes, you may need to consider international addresses. It may be reasonable that Postal Addressing becomes its own domain.

The general rule regarding normalization of compound information is simply:

> *"Represent information, as attributes, at the same level of granularity that it is dealt with by the processes (the sea level use cases)"*

If processes always deal with some particular compound information only as a blob, then it is acceptable to represent it as a blob in the semantic model. If processes deal with fragments of the information, then represent the information at the granularity of those fragments. If processes don't care if an attribute is null, then null is allowed in the class model.

8.8 Class and Attribute Descriptions

To have a well-documented class model that communicates appropriately, each class and attribute needs a description. Typical content in a class description is:

- *Basis of abstraction*—What rules or policies are common to all objects of this class?
- *Inclusion/exclusion criteria*—What rules or policies can be used to decide if some potential or real-world thing would, or would not, be a member of this class?
- *Relevance*—Why is this class important to the (sub)domain?

- *Example objects, if appropriate*—To emphasize the intent of the class, it can be helpful to show one or more real-world or potential example objects.
- *Aliases*—Other names domain experts might know it by.

8.8.1 Class Descriptions

The following are examples of reasonable class descriptions:

> *"An Hourly Employee is an employee who is closely supervised and who is paid on an hourly basis. Hourly employees are also known as 'nonexempt employees' under the Fair Labor Practices law. Contrast with Salaried Employee."*
>
> *"A cyclotron is an instrument for giving high energy to atomic particles by using electric and magnetic forces in an enclosed chamber."*
>
> *"An aardvark is a burrowing insectivorous mammal out of South Africa, with a stocky, hairy body and a long tubular snout. Aardvarks are being tracked by this Ardvo-Tracker™ system using miniaturized microwave echo locator hardware so that we can study their territorial behavior. Aardvarks are also known by their scientific name, 'Orycteropus Afer' and by the name 'aard-ay ark-vay' (in ig-pay atin-lay)."*

After writing a class description, it's a good idea to revisit the class name. Sometimes it's appropriate to refine the class name based on the description. For example, in describing class Valve in an embedded process control domain, the class description might be:

> *"A valve is a safety device which prevents dangerously high pressure from building inside a pressure vessel..."*

On reconsidering in light of that description, a better class name would be Pressure Relief Valve:

> *"A pressure relief valve is a safety device ..."*

8.8.2 Attribute Descriptions

Each attribute also needs a description defining what the modeler meant when they included it. Typical content in an attribute description is:

- The meaning of the attribute with respect to the class
- What does the information in this attribute mean to the (sub)domain?
- The attribute's range specification

The following description for the .usable length of a Runway in an aviation semantic model is a good example:

> *"The usable length is the length, in feet, of the portion of the runway that can be safely used for takeoffs and landings. The useable length of a runway is the threshold-to-threshold distance and does not include overrun, stop way, stabilized, or abandoned zones beyond the thresholds. Usable lengths are used in runway selection: arriving and departing aircraft must not be assigned to runways that are too short."*

The .pay rate of an Hourly Employee in a payroll business might be:

> *"The amount of money an hourly employee gets paid for each hour worked. Pay rate is one factor in determining the gross pay of an hourly employee"*

Many more examples of class and attribute descriptions are included in Appendices D, F, H, and J.

8.9 Association

By now, you are probably feeling that there are important connections between classes:

- Customer should be connected to Order.
- Order should be connected to Title.
- Title should be connected to Publisher.
- Replenish order should be connected to Publisher.
- ...

Associations formalize those connections and present them in a complete, consistent, clear, concise, and precise way. According to the UML specification,

> *"An association specifies a semantic relationship that can occur between typed instances. It has at least two ends represented by properties, each of which is connected to the type of the end."*

Where a class abstracts a set of domain-relevant objects, associations abstract a set of relevant connections between objects, aka "links":

- You (a customer) are linked to your account (a bank account).
- I (another customer) am linked to my account (another bank account).
- Some 3rd person (yet another customer) is linked to their account (yet another bank account).

These links are abstracted into an association, "Customer owns Bank account."

Associations in the class model exist to support processing of the form "Given an object of class X, which object or objects of class Y is it connected to?" as in "Given savings account c012166, which customer(s) owns it?" or "Given aardvark 123456, which burrow(s) does it live in?"

8.9.1   Association Notation

The UML notation for an association is a solid line between associated classes, as shown in Figure 8.10.

8.9.2   Association Names

UML does not require an association to be named; however experience shows that well-named associations contribute to understandability. Again, the primary purpose of the class model is to assist in understanding, validating, documenting, and communicating policies and for managing complexity. Being as explicit and descriptive as possible is useful.

Associations are typically named by a transitive verb phrase, such as:

- Customer *owns* Bank account.
- Commercial pilot *has type rating for* Airplane type.
- Financial institution *approves* Payment method.
- User *may play* Role.
- ...

Be cautioned that "has" and "contains" are abused association names. They appear in class models all too frequently, yet they don't add much useful information. Name an association based on the meaning of the connection. Think

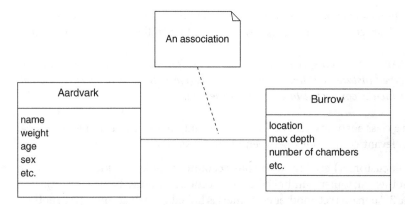

Figure 8.10 UML's notation for associations.

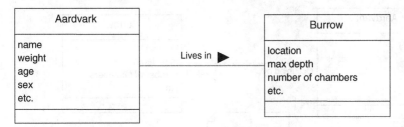

Figure 8.11 Naming associations and using UML's "taco chip."

about what the business couldn't do if it didn't know which object was connected to which other object. If the bank didn't know which Account was connected to which Customer, then the ownership of the money in that Account would be unknown—thus, "Customer *owns* Bank account."

A practical issue in natural languages like English is that they tend to be mono-directional. Saying "Customer owns Bank account" is very different than saying "Bank account owns Customer." One sentence makes sense and is the intended interpretation, and the other doesn't make sense. We don't want readers to waste time trying to figure out which is which. UML provides what is sometimes called the "taco chip" (because it has the shape of that popular Mexican food) to clarify. Figure 8.11 shows an association name and appropriate use of a "taco chip" for the association in Figure 8.10.

The taco chip itself has no meaning. It only guides the reader in understanding what the writer wants to communicate. The semantics of an association are bidirectional. If a particular customer is linked to a particular savings account, then that savings account is by definition also linked to that customer. The same holds true for all links between any customer and their corresponding savings account(s). Similarly, the association "Aardvark lives in Burrow" means that from any aardvark, we can find the corresponding burrow(s). And if we know of a specific burrow, we could just as easily find what aardvarks live in it.

An alternative form of naming associations uses the gerund (or "-ing") form of a verb. As examples:

- Owning association between customer and bank account
- Repaying association between customer and loan
- Occupying association between aardvark and burrow
- Placing association between customer and order
- …

The advantage of the gerund form is that it is less sensitive to directionality.

UML notation also allows role end names as shown in Figure 8.12. This notation solves the directionality problem; however it tends to clutter diagrams. It is a workable approach, and other than clutter it performs well.

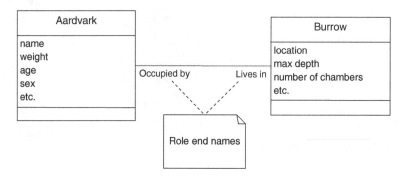

Figure 8.12 UML's role end name notation.

UML's "navigability" notation—an arrow on an association to show direction of traversal—exists, but its use is not recommended. The notation doesn't say anything useful or important from a semantic modeling perspective, and it often becomes outdated when sea level use cases are added later that traverse the association in the other direction. It's best to avoid confusion and leave navigability out.

8.9.3 Associations and Persistence

The final point about associations is that they should represent links between objects that persist beyond the sea level use case that first created them. Consider the association between Replenish order and Publisher. The link between a particular replenish order and its particular publisher is created by the sea level use case that creates the replenish order. That same link is needed later—after 24 hours—when it is time to forward the contents of that replenish order to that publisher. Without knowing the replenish order to publisher link, the replenish order would not know where to be sent.

On the other hand, consider the sea level use case where a particular warehouse worker is packing a particular book order. Of course, the link between the warehouse worker and the book order needs to exist while the order is being packed. But that link is never used by any subsequent use case. There is no other sea level use case that needs an answer to either of these questions:

- "I have a particular book order—which warehouse worker packed it?"
- "I have a particular warehouse worker—which book order(s) did that worker pack?"

If sea level use cases like those are added later, then the association needs to be made explicit. Otherwise leave it out. As shown in Chapter 17, associations cause design and code to be created. If an association is in the class model but no sea level use cases ever use it, the result is dead code: code that exists but is never executed. Keeping only associations that persist beyond the use case that created them minimizes dead code, ideally to zero.

8.10 Specifying the Multiplicity of an Association

Having established that objects are linked and that use cases need those links to carry out processes, there are almost always constraints on participation in those links. Can an aardvark not live in a burrow? Can an aardvark live in more than one burrow at the same time? Can a burrow not have any aardvarks living in it? Can more than one aardvark live in the same burrow at the same time? This is the concept of "multiplicity": constraints on participation in associations and is the constraint referred to earlier in RKMC/NF.

Matt Flavin's "Fundamentals of Data Modeling"[11] introduced anchor point analysis as a tactic to help expose the multiplicity of an association. It is based on two questions:

> *"If I were one of these, what's the minimum number of those I could be linked to?"*
> *"If I were one of these, what's the maximum number of those I could be linked to?"*

As in "If I were a bank customer, what's the minimum number of bank accounts I could own?" Could someone be a bank customer even if they didn't own any accounts? Probably yes, because having a loan could still qualify someone as a bank customer. "Could I be a customer who owned more than one account?" Almost certainly. The lower bound from bank customer to bank account is zero and the upper bound is many.

This tactic is repeated from the point of view of ("anchored at") the other participating class. "If I were a bank account, what's the minimum number of bank customers that could own me?" Could a bank account not be owned by any customer? Probably not. "Could I be a bank account that was owned by more than one customer?" Certainly, we call them joint accounts. The lower bound from bank account to customer is one and the upper bound is many.

8.10.1 Multiplicity Notation

The lower bound will usually be either zero or one, and the upper bound will usually be either one or many. UML notation for these is shown in Table 8.1.

---

11 See [Flavin81].

Table 8.1 UML notation for multiplicities.

Lower bound	Upper bound	UML notation
0	1	0..1
0	Many	*
1	1	1
1	Many	1..*

"A customer may place zero to many book orders"
"A book order must be placed by exactly one customer"

Figure 8.13 Association multiplicity on a class diagram.

Multiplicities are written on the class diagram near the intersection of the association line and the class, as shown in Figure 8.13.

Multiplicities other than zero, one, or many can be used when they represent legitimate business constraints. A passenger car, normally speaking, has at least two doors and may have up to five (a "hatchback" is often legally considered to be a door). So the lower bound is 2 and the upper bound is 5. The notation would be "2..5." Given that humans have not yet been cloned, a human has exactly two biological parents, no more and no less. The notation would be "2."

Figure 8.14 shows the class diagram for Order fulfillment with associations and multiplicities added.

8.10.2 Multiplicities and Requirements Completeness

Just as with attribute ranges, it's important to push a class model all the way down to multiplicity specifications for every association. Take the association between customers and book orders. Notice how the multiplicity is actually a concise statement of four closely related functional requirements:

- *"The minimum number of Book Orders for a Customer shall be zero."*
- *"The maximum number of Book Orders for a Customer shall be many."*
- *"The minimum number of Customers for a Book Order shall be one."*
- *"The maximum number of Customers for a Book Order shall be one."*

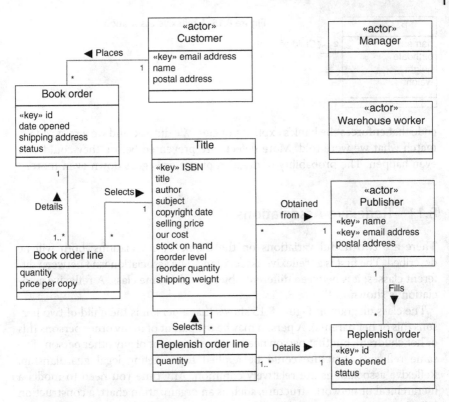

Figure 8.14 Class diagram for Order fulfillment with associations and multiplicities added.

Code needs to be written to ensure these policies aren't violated in a running system. What would happen if—because developers never asked about multiplicities, and only guessed—the software would not allow a customer to have zero book orders even though the business says that is valid? At some point, someone will try to have a customer without any book orders and the software won't allow it. It is acceptable to the business but not allowed by the software. This is another "Dreaded Phone Call Syndrome" just waiting to happen: "Your stupid system won't let us have a customer without any book orders!" Similarly, a developer may assume that because joint bank accounts are allowed, joint book orders should also be allowed despite this being a violation of policy. The moment someone in the business discovers a book order with more than one customer, some developer will get a very irate phone call.

Forcing the modeler to specify association multiplicities exposes these low-level detailed requirements. Otherwise the class model is incomplete. The business—if any constraint exists—needs to tell the modeler, although the business may not have actually thought about it yet. The developers need to write

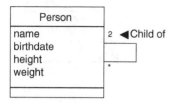

Figure 8.15 A reflexive association.

code that enforces the bank's explicit policies. We did ask, and we wrote code to match what we were told. More defects are prevented before they could ever even happen. The probability of dreaded phone calls goes down even more.

8.11 Reflexive Associations

There are two useful variations on the theme of associations; both will be described. The first is a "reflexive association." The association isn't between different classes; it is between different objects of the same class. A reflexive association is shown in Figure 8.15.

The class diagram in Figure 8.15 shows that a person is the child of two persons (his or her parents). A person may be the parent of many other persons (his or her children), but that person need not be the parent of any other person. The same reflexive structure could be applied to modeling legal guardianship. Reflexive associations are relatively common. Any time you need to model a hierarchical or network structure, such as an organization chart, a construction bill of materials, or a network topology, the best way to model it is using a reflexive association. Just be careful with multiplicities when modeling hierarchies; the root node will be the only node in a hierarchy without a parent node, so you can't say that every node has exactly one parent. Reflexive associations are also useful in representing ordering or sequencing of objects in some collection. The reflexive association for ordering can be named "Precedes," "Follows," or something similar.

8.12 Multiple Associations

The second variation is that there can be more than one association between the same classes at the same time, as shown in Figure 8.16.

There are three separate distinct associations between these two classes. Each association has a different meaning. Also, each association has different multiplicities. Multiple associations between the same classes do not happen very often, but be ready to call on it when needed. Attempting to combine all three associations into one will be difficult from a naming, and impossible from a multiplicity, perspective.

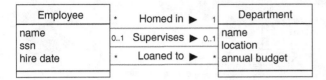

Figure 8.16 Multiple associations between the same classes.

8.13   Aggregation and Composition

If you deal with UML very long, you will run across "aggregation" and "composition." Both are intended to represent collector–collectee relationships.

8.13.1   Aggregation

Aggregation represents non-exclusive collection: the things being collected can be in more than one collection at the same time. An example could be the association between an Airway segment[12] and a Flight plan. The collectee doesn't need to be in any collector: an airway segment doesn't stop being an airway segment just because it's not in in anyone's flight plan. Any given airway segment can be contained in many flight plans at the same time. UML's notation for aggregation is a hollow diamond pointing into the class that represents the collector, as shown in Figure 8.17.

8.13.2   Composition

Composition (also called "composite aggregation" in UML 2[13]) represents exclusive collection: things being collected can be in at most one collection at a time. An example would be the association between a Motor vehicle and an Engine (e.g., "Motor Vehicle Powered By Engine"). Again, the collectee doesn't need to be collected: an engine doesn't stop being an engine just because it's not installed in a motor vehicle. However one engine can only be contained in one motor vehicle at a time. The engine can be removed from one motor vehicle and installed into another, but at any one time the engine is in at most one motor vehicle. UML's notation for composition is a solid diamond pointing into the class that represents the collector, as shown in Figure 8.18.

---

12 A straight-line path between a pair of navigational waypoints.
13 See [OMG11b].

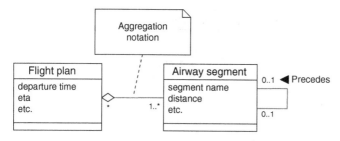

Figure 8.17 UML's notation for aggregation.

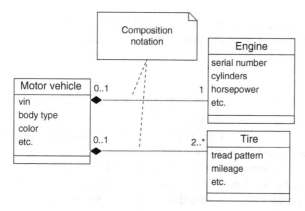

Figure 8.18 UML's notation for composition.

8.13.3 Trouble with Aggregation and Composition

It would be irresponsible to have book on modeling with UML and not at least mention aggregation and composition. However, in practice, both aggregation and composition are more trouble than they are worth. Composition is often incorrectly interpreted as "lifetime ownership": the collector manages the life-cycle of the collectees. When the collector is deleted, then all collectees are also assumed to need deletion. While easy to remember, it turns out to not be true often enough that it causes problems. Directly quoting the UML specification,

> "An association may represent a composite aggregation (i.e., a whole/part relationship). ... Composite aggregation is a strong form of aggregation that requires a part instance be included in at most one composite at a time. If a composite is deleted, all of its parts are normally deleted with it. Note that a part can (where allowed) be removed from a composite before the composite is deleted, and thus not be deleted as part of the composite."

Specifically, the phrase "if a composite is deleted, all of its parts are normally deleted with it" means that it might happen that way but it is not *required* to happen that way. The UML definition is consistent with the interpretation "when the collector is told to delete, it can unlink any or all collectees before deletion, thus leaving them undeleted."

8.13.4 Misuse of Aggregation and Composition Notation

In addition, the diamond notation is frequently misused. The design patterns[14] are usually published in UML notation. A cursory examination shows that about half of the time diamonds are used in design patterns and that use is inconsistent with defined UML semantics. Figure 8.19 shows published UML designs for both Bridge and Decorator patterns.[15]

Notice claimed aggregations between Abstraction and Implementor in Bridge pattern and between Decorator and Component in Decorator pattern. Abstractions (in Bridge pattern) are not collectors that manage collections of Implementors. Neither are Decorators (in Decorator pattern) collectors of Components—particularly because a given instance of Decorator can only be decorating exactly one Component at a time.

In my opinion, diamonds are often misused because they make diagrams look much more hip, trendy, and sexy. A class diagram with diamonds is a lot sexier than one without. However, if someone is going to publish anything using UML notation, particularly something as widely seen as a design pattern, then it should be reasonable to expect that person to have enough of an understanding

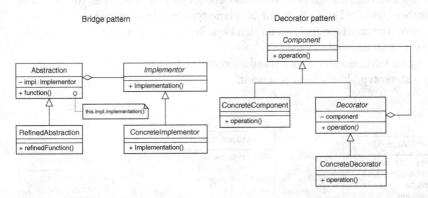

Figure 8.19 Published UML designs for Bridge and Decorator patterns.

---

14 See, for example, [Gamma95].
15 Bridge UML design is from http://en.wikipedia.org/wiki/Bridge_pattern, and Composite UML design is from http://en.wikipedia.org/wiki/Composite_pattern.

of the notation to use it correctly. This is clearly not the case in many class models.

8.13.5 Aggregation, Composition, and Analysis Paralysis

Composition and aggregation are also prime sources of "analysis paralysis." Analysis paralysis means wasting time arguing over the form of a model without changing its meaning. The look-and-feel of the model is argued endlessly, and no progress is being made on building software that automates that business.

In the end, hollow and solid diamonds say nothing beyond what is already completely, precisely, and concisely specified with plain associations and multiplicities. Just specify normal associations and multiplicities and avoid the trouble and confusion caused by the diamonds. As a modeler or model reviewer, you should be aware of these concepts and notations: you need to recognize what they are supposed to mean. But you should also be cautious and not put too much faith when you see them used by others, as they are often used incorrectly.

8.14 Foreign Key

A foreign key, sometimes called a migrated key or referential attribute, happens when a key of one class has been exported to some other class as a stand-in for an association. Attributes in one class are serving as references to objects of another class. In Figure 8.20, the .airplane type of Airplane and the .manufacturer of Airplane type are both foreign keys. Both are serving to refer to a specific object in an associated class.

Again, UML doesn't have a standard notation for foreign keys. You can make up a stereotype like «fk» if you want.

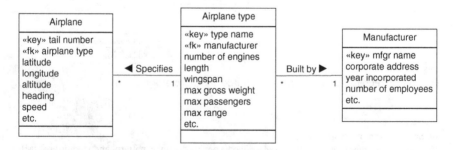

Figure 8.20 Examples of foreign keys.

8.14.1 Avoid Foreign Keys

Foreign keys should be avoided in class models. One reason is premature design: including them implies that the designer should also include them. Another reason is that they are only workable in certain situations and not others: foreign keys only work when the multiplicity is <something>:1 and not in the <something>:0..1 or <something>:1..m cases. Airplane type in Figure 8.20 cannot have a foreign key that refers to the airplanes of that type because there are many (and possibly zero) of them. That would violate normalization. If you find a foreign key in a class model, it should be removed and replaced by an explicit association with multiplicity.

8.15 Association Class

As defined in the UML specification, an association class is:

"A model element that has both association and class properties. An Association Class can be seen as an association that also has class properties, or as a class that also has association properties. It not only connects a set of classifiers but also defines a set of features that belong to the relationship itself and not to any of the classifiers."

With an association class, the concept being modeled has association (link) and class (object) properties at the same time. An object of that class not only links objects of other classes, but the link itself takes on its own important properties: attributes, participation in other associations, or significant behavior.

A Driver's license is a link in the sense that it connects the licensed person and the government entity (state, country, etc.) that is granting driving privileges. At the same time, that link has attributes of its own:

- When was that permission granted?
- When does that permission expire?
- What kind of motor vehicle(s) is this driver authorized to drive?
- Are there any extra restrictions, like wearing glasses or contact lenses?
- ...

Objects of class Driver's License can also have important states (Chapter 10):

- Valid
- Expired
- Suspended
- Revoked
- ...

A Driver's license is a good example of an association class: it has association nature at the same time it has class nature, and it may also participate on its own in associations (e.g., Driver's license *was issued by* District licensing office). The association category earlier in the discussion of identifying classes is almost always an association class because they have additional properties beyond just simple linkage.

8.15.1 Association Class Notation

Figure 8.21 shows the UML notation for an association class using airline flight reservations as the example.

8.15.2 Model Association Classes or Not?

Using association classes is not mandatory, but it is preferred. You can survive an entire modeling career without ever using an association class. The trade-off is between the modeler understanding a nontrivial modeling concept (and being able to communicate that concept to stakeholders who review the model) against building slightly larger class models using a smaller, simpler modeling vocabulary. The advantage of using an association class is that it can be more obvious and direct, and it requires fewer model elements. Figure 8.22 shows the same situation in Figure 8.21 modeled without an association class.

One reason for preferring association classes is they are more direct. The connection between travelers, flights, and reservations in Figure 8.21 should be obvious. Travelers and reservations cannot exist without flights and reservations at the same time. In Figure 8.22 there is at least a subtle implication that

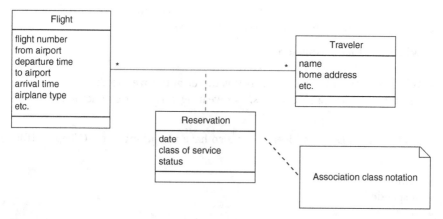

Figure 8.21 UML's notation for an association class.

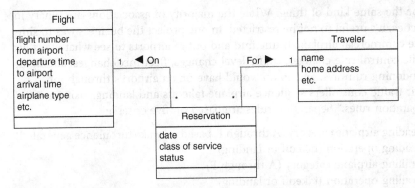

Figure 8.22 The same situation modeled without an association class.

the Reservation on flight association might be independent of the Reservation for traveler association.

The bigger reason for preferring association classes is that they are smaller, more compact models with fewer model elements. In Figure 8.21 there are three primary model elements:

- Traveler (a class)
- Flight (a class)
- Reservation (an association class)

In Figure 8.22 there are five primary model elements:

- Traveler (a class)
- Flight (a class)
- Reservation (a class)
- Reservation On Flight (an association)
- Reservation For Traveler (an association)

Fewer elements in the semantic model usually result in a smaller, simpler design, and fewer lines of code to write and maintain. Smaller designs with fewer lines of code solving the same problem are always preferred from a cost, schedule, complexity, and long-term maintenance perspective.

8.16 n-ary Association

Many (but not all) class modeling approaches restrict associations to the "binary" case: no more than two classes can be associated. In a reflexive association, there's only one participating class (e.g., Person is Biological parent of Person or Person is Legal guardian of Person), but there are two ends to the association: a kind of thing is being linked to a kind of thing, it just happens to be the same kind of thing. While the majority of associations are binary in practice, it's useful to not be restricted. In one project the business was to simulate commercial airplane traffic into and out of airports to see what effect air traffic control rule changes, traffic level changes, fleet mix changes, adding or abandoning runways, and so on would have on an airport's throughput.

Air traffic controllers sequence airplane takeoffs and landings using a set of "separation rules." Separation rules are based on five criteria:

- Leading airplane category (A through F, based on wake turbulence generated)
- Leading operation (takeoff or landing)
- Trailing airplane category (A through F)
- Trailing operation (takeoff or landing)
- Flight conditions (IFR, VFR, or SVFR)

Each of these five criteria is used in determining minimum separation. For example, if the leading operation is an Airbus A320 (Category D) taking off and the trailing operation is a Boeing 747 (Category B) landing on the same runway in VFR flight conditions, the minimum separation is 2.5 nautical miles. If the leading operation is a Boeing 747 landing and the trailing operation is an Airbus A320 landing on the same runway in IFR flight conditions, the minimum separation is 5 nautical miles.

8.16.1 n-ary Association Notation

The UML notation for n-ary associations is shown in Figure 8.23.

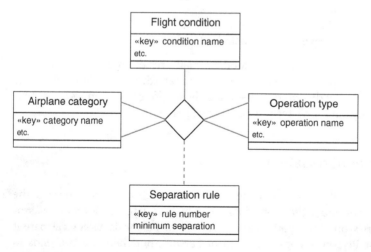

Figure 8.23 n-ary association notation.

n-ary associations are often association classes as well, and the benefits discussed earlier for association classes also apply to n-ary associations: simpler, more direct models with fewer model elements that result in smaller designs with fewer lines of code.

A problem with n-ary associations in UML is specifying multiplicities. In Figure 8.23, a given separation rule associates two airplane categories (one leading, one trailing), two operation types (one leading, one trailing), and one flight condition (either IFR, VFR, or SVFR). UML writes multiplicities on the far side of associations, but there are many such far sides: would a multiplicity written next to class Flight condition refer to the multiplicity from class Airplane category, Operation type, or Separation rule? It is often best to describe multiplicities of n-ary associations in text in an association dictionary rather than attempting to specify them on the class diagram.

8.17 Association Descriptions

In most cases a well-named association won't need any additional description. In some cases however, subtleties about the association can't be expressed on the diagram. In these cases, it is useful to include an association description. Try to answer the question "What does this association mean in business terms?"

> *"The Commercial Pilot's type rating identifies which Airplane Types that pilot can legally fly on behalf of fare-paying passengers."*

Be careful to provide only information that's not already obvious from the diagram (the "one-fact-one-place" documentation principle in Appendix A). A description of the Child of association in Figure 8.15 would probably be needed to clarify whether it is limited to biological parentage, limited to legal guardianship, or is a combination of both, as in:

> *"Person is Child of Person: This association represents only biological (i.e., genetic) parentage. Legal guardianship is not relevant in this domain."*

Association descriptions can also be particularly useful in specifying multiplicity constraints on an n-ary association because UML notation does not support this aspect of class modeling very well. The n-ary association in Figure 8.23 might be described as follows:

> *"Separation rule-Airplane category-Operation type-Flight condition: This n-ary association takes two Airplane categories (one for the leading airplane and one for the trailing airplane), two Operation types (one for*

the leading operation and one for the trailing operation), and one Flight condition. As an example, if the leading operation is an Airbus A-320 (Category D) taking off and the trailing operation is a Boeing 747 (Category B) landing on the same runway in VFR flight conditions, then the minimum separation distance is 2.5 nautical miles."

8.18   Generalization

Generalization is the semantic model equivalent of inheritance in object-oriented design and programming: it represents an "is-a-kind-of" relationship between classes. All properties of the superclass, the base class, the more general thing, apply ("are inherited") to all subclasses: the more specific, differentiated things. Figure 8.24 shows UML notation for generalization: the pyramid points into the superclass (the more general class).

Employee is a superclass of Hourly employee and Salaried employee. All properties—attributes, associations, and behavior—of Employee apply to both Hourly employee and Salaried employee. Hourly employee and Salaried employee are both kinds of Employees, but they have properties of their own. Salaried employee is a superclass of Engineer, Salesperson, and Manager.

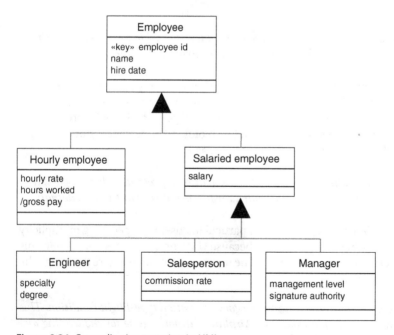

Figure 8.24 Generalization notation in UML.

All properties of Salaried employee apply to Engineer, Salesperson, and Manager. Said another way, an Engineer is a kind of Salaried employee, and a Salaried employee is a kind of Employee. The properties of Engineer are determined by combining the properties declared on Engineer with the properties declared on Salaried employee with the properties declared on Employee. Every Engineer has an .employee id, a .name, a .hire date, a .salary, a .specialty, and a .degree.

Unlike inheritance in design and programming, generalization in semantic modeling is strictly additive. Properties declared on a superclass can't be overridden as in Java, C++, C#, etc. Common or shared properties need to be pushed up a generalization hierarchy until they apply to that class and all subclasses but not to any classes above or to the side. Properties need to be pulled down until they apply to all objects of that subclass (and its subclasses) but no other classes above or to the side. Attribute .salary of class Salaried employee applies to all Engineers, Salespersons, and Managers but doesn't apply to Hourly employees nor universally to Employees.

Generalization factors out common properties so they can be declared only once. This is another case of "one fact, one place."

Some modelers will include an attribute in the superclass—sometimes called a type discriminator—as a means to represent what subclass any given object is. The class diagram in Figure 8.24 might include an .employee type attribute in Employee and a .job role attribute in class Salaried employee. The range for a type discriminator would be an enumeration of the subclasses. The range of Salaried employee.job role would be [Engineer, Salesperson, Manager]. In practice, type discriminator attributes aren't necessary and can be left out of the semantic model. If needed due to implementation technology, a designer can put them in.

8.18.1 {complete} Versus {incomplete} Generalization

One variation on generalization is whether it is "complete" or "incomplete." This is the "Completeness" constraint referred to earlier in RKMC/NF. Simply, must every superclass object also be an object of one of the subclasses? Must every Employee be either an Hourly employee or a Salaried employee? There are two possibilities. The first is that every Employee must be either Hourly or Salaried. Employee would be considered an "abstract base class" in design and programming terms. The other possibility is that objects of class Employee can exist that are neither Hourly nor Salaried. Maybe there is a third, unstated, category of Employees—say, Co-op or Intern—where there are no additional properties beyond what is already declared for the base class: Employee.

As shown by {complete} and {incomplete} constraints in Figure 8.25, all Employees are either Hourly or Salaried, but there are no other kinds of employees. However, some Salaried employees are not Engineers, Salespersons, nor

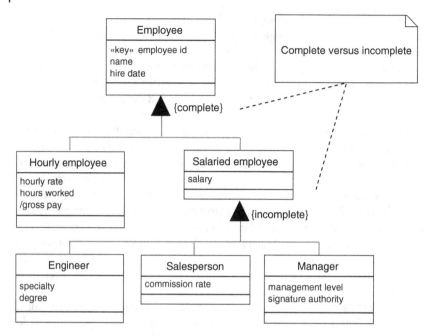

Figure 8.25 Constraints {complete} and {incomplete}.

Managers. Those other kinds of Salaried employees don't have any properties beyond what is already declared for Salaried employee. Some organizations prohibit {incomplete} generalizations; the modeler is forced to create an additional subclass (without any attributes or other properties) to explicitly represent the remaining objects not included in other subclasses. This should be considered a matter of modeling style.

8.18.2 {disjoint} Versus {overlapping} Generalization

Another variation on generalization is "disjoint" versus "overlapping." The UML notation is shown in Figure 8.26.

As used in Figure 8.26, constraint {disjoint} means that an Employee is either Hourly or Salaried and can never be both at the same time. In set theory terms, a {disjoint} generalization is a set partition. On the other hand, constraint {overlapping} is intended to mean that a Salaried Employee can be any combination of Engineer, Salesperson, or Manager, all at the same time: as in "an engineering salesperson," "an engineering manager," or "a managing salesperson." Avoid {overlapping}. Instead, the class model in Figure 8.27 shows a much better way of representing situations when constraint {overlapping} might have been used. There is no good underlying set theory equivalent to {overlapping}, and

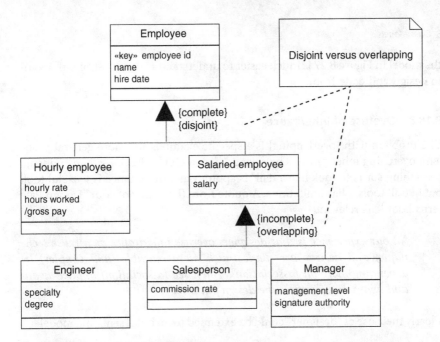

Figure 8.26 Constraints {disjoint} and {overlapping}.

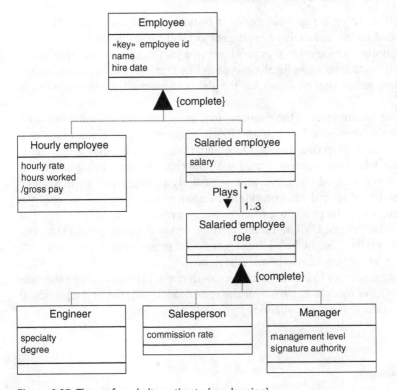

Figure 8.27 The preferred alternative to {overlapping}.

the model in Figure 8.27 is much easier to understand and more straightforward to design and code from.

8.18.3 Overuse of Inheritance

The problem with {overlapping} is a specific example of a more general problem: overusing inheritance. The saying "Give a child a hammer, and suddenly everything starts to look like a nail" is appropriate. Inheritance is a useful tool, but like all tools it has limitations. A quote from the "Gang of Four" Design Patterns book[16] is relevant:

> *"... our experience is that designers overuse inheritance as a reuse technique, and designs are made much more reusable (and simpler) by depending more on [association]. You'll see [association] applied again and again and again in the design patterns"*

Clearly their use of "designer" could be extended to include "semantic modeler."

8.18.4 Static Versus Dynamic Classification

The third variation on generalization is static versus dynamic classification. Static classification means that any given object will never change from one subclass to another. Once created as an object in a particular subclass, that object will remain in that subclass for the rest of its life. Dynamic classification, on the other hand, means that an object has the ability to morph from one subclass to another.

Consider an employee of the company in Figure 8.25, and let's call him Phred. Phred might have been hired as an Hourly employee while going to evening school for an engineering degree. On graduation, Phred is offered, and takes, a full-time job as an engineer. Phred has now changed from being an Hourly employee to a Salaried employee, and particularly an Engineer kind of Salaried employee. Phred started off as one kind of employee and morphed into another. Phred might later be promoted to manager, morphing again.

There is no defined UML notation for static versus dynamic generalization; a custom constraint might be useful. Figure 8.28 shows constraint {dynamic}, constraint {static} could also be used, if desired.

It is not mandatory to identify static versus dynamic classification on the class diagram. Other models, in particular the state model, will specify if a particular generalization is static or dynamic.

---

16 See [Gamma95].

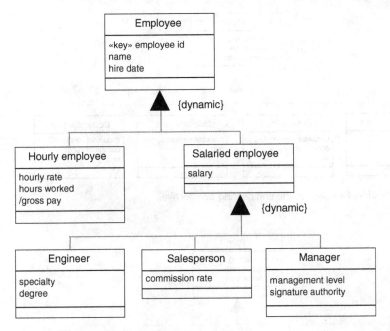

Figure 8.28 Constraint "{dynamic}" on generalizations.

8.18.5 Multiple Classification

The final variation on generalization is called multiple classification. One project was concerned with both engineering and accounting perspectives of a corporate intranet. The semantic model had a class, Part, which was the base class for a generalization in an engineering perspective. Parts were either:

- *Mechanical*—for example, a rack, shelf, support beam, etc.
- *Hardware*—for example, a router, gateway, wireless access point, desktop computer, laptop, tablet, cable, etc.
- *Software*—for example, router firmware, gateway firmware, anti-virus utility, desktop operating system, managed user application, etc.
- *Document*—for example, a service manual, installation guide, user guide, etc.

This is shown in Figure 8.29.

At the very same time, class Part was also the base for generalization in a billing perspective. From the billing perspective, a Part could be:

- *Spare*—Stored in spare parts inventory so it could be used later if needed, but no organization is being charged for it now.
- *Installed*—Being used by an organization; therefore that organization has to pay rent for it.

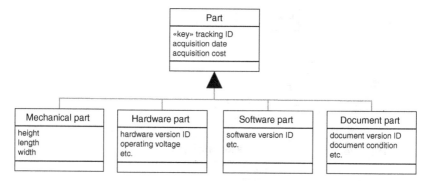

Figure 8.29 Class Part seen in the engineering perspective.

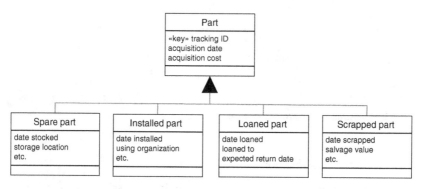

Figure 8.30 Class Part seen in the billing perspective.

- *Loaned*—Lent out to some other out-of-billing-scope organization and expected to be returned by a specified date.
- *Scrapped*—Discarded or salvaged, meaning it is no longer available for use but still needs tracking for depreciation accounting and income tax purposes.

This is shown in Figure 8.30.

8.18.6 Multiple and Dynamic Classification

The engineering and the billing dimensions exist in parallel. At the same time a given Part is Mechanical, Hardware, Software, or Document; it is also Spare, Installed, Loaned, or Scrapped. This is multiple classification and is shown in Figure 8.31.

The class model in Figure 8.31 shows both static and dynamic classification. A Hardware part cannot transform into a Software part. Once a Software part has been created, it will always be that and never become a Document part or

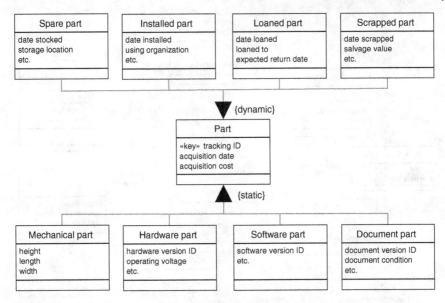

Figure 8.31 Multiple classification: class Part seen in the combined perspectives.

any other kind of part. The billing generalization is dynamic. Process defines all Parts as beginning as a Spare part. Spare parts should eventually become Installed parts and possibly later uninstalled (returning them to Spare). Spare parts could be loaned and later returned to being spare, or they could end their practical life when they become a Scrapped part.

That project was completed before domain partitioning (Chapter 6) was a recognized technique. In retrospect, if this project were redone today, the engineering and billing perspectives should be different domains. Proper domain separation might make multiple classification irrelevant. Multiple classification could be a sign that domains aren't properly separated. More cases would be needed to determine this. Until the matter is settled, you might still find the need for multiple classification even after proper domain separation. You need to be aware that this concept exists.

8.19 e-Book and Print Media in WebBooks 2.0 Order fulfillment

Suppose that WebBooks has decided to sell both e-book and print media. Some attributes of Title, such as .stock on hand and .shipping weight only apply when a title is in print format. Similarly, .product keys only apply to e-books. Further, .ISBN is unique by medium, and .prices & .costs of e-books are different for the

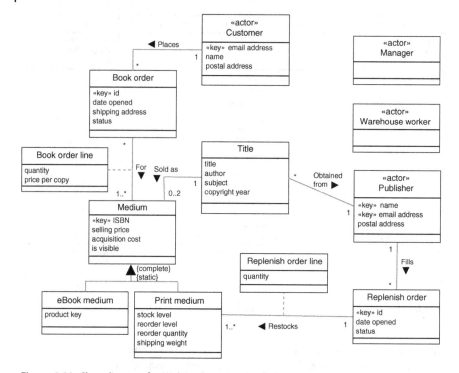

Figure 8.32 Class diagram for WebBooks 2.0 Order fulfillment, with generalization.

same title; generally the e-book is cheaper. Figure 8.32 shows a final class diagram for Order fulfillment (Appendix D) using generalization to incorporate both print and e-book media. Class models for other WebBooks 2.0 domains can be found in Appendices F, H, and J.

8.20 Quality Criteria

In addition to the quality criteria in Chapter 3, Table 8.2 shows quality criteria for class models.

One way to help verify consistency between sea level use cases and the class model is to build a "CRUD matrix." CRUD is an acronym for Create, Read, Update, Delete. List classes from the class model across the top axis of the matrix; it's usually ok to leave actor classes out. List sea level use cases down the left column. At the intersection of each use case and class, fill in C, R, U, and/or D showing that use case's access to that class. If no access, leave the cell blank. Table 8.3 shows a CRUD matrix for classes and use cases in Order fulfillment.

Table 8.2 Quality criteria for class models.

Item	Criterion
CM-1	Each class is named with a singular noun or noun phrase
CM-2	Each class has a description that clearly and adequately describes the basis of abstraction for that class
CM-3	Each attribute has a description that clearly and adequately describes the meaning of that attribute
CM-4	Each attribute has a precisely and correctly defined range: constraints on values, not programming language data types
CM-5	Each span that is an open interval is clearly identified as such
CM-6	Enumeration style range specifications clearly specify if ordering of the symbols is required or not
CM-7	Keys are specified only when they are a necessary element of how stakeholders do business. Such keys are clearly identified, so designers are aware of the role of the attribute
CM-8	All derived attributes are clearly identified, and the derivation policy is clearly and correctly specified or referenced
CM-9	The class model is in Range-Key-Multiplicity-Completeness Normal Form (RKMC/NF)[a]
CM-10	Each association is appropriately named (no "has" or "contains")
CM-11	Each association represents a connection that needs to persist beyond the sea level use case that first created it
CM-12	Unless already clear from the class diagram, each association has a description that clearly and adequately describes its meaning
CM-13	Each association has precise and correct multiplicities specified
CM-14	No foreign keys exist: all class-to-class links are represented by explicit associations
CM-15	All properties of each superclass apply to all subclasses: common or shared properties have been pushed up the generalization hierarchy until they apply to that class and all subclasses but not any classes above or to the side. Properties have been pulled down until they apply to all objects of a subclass (and its subclasses) but no other classes above or to the side
CM-16	As appropriate, {complete} or {incomplete} has been clearly and correctly used
CM-17	There are no {overlapping} generalizations: only {disjoint}
CM-18	If present, {static} or {dynamic} has been clearly and correctly used

[a] Allowing for the null and compound value exceptions described earlier.

Table 8.3 CRUD matrix for Order fulfillment.

	Book order	Book order line	Medium	Title	Replenish order	Replenish order line
Catalog?			R	R		
Add to order	C	C				
Drop from order	D	RD				
Order?	R	R	R	R		
Process checkout	UR	UR	R	R		
Process cancel	U					
Order status?	R					
Packable orders	R	R	R			
Process packing	U	U	U	R	C	CU
Process shipping	U					
Process replenish rec'd			U		RD	RD
Inventory?			R	R		
Sales?	R	R				
Profit	R	R	R			
Manage catalog			CRUD	CRUD		
Send replenish order					R	R

Check for a C, and at least one R or U in each column. If there is no C, objects of that class are never created—at least one use case is probably missing (or the population of objects in that class is static). If there is no R or U, then objects of that class are never used—at least one use case is missing, or that class is irrelevant to processes. Check for at least one C, R, U, and/or D across each row. Any use case with no C, R, U, or D isn't doing anything involving classes—either the use case is irrelevant, or more classes need to be added to the class model. CRUD analysis helps determine that if each use case and class are *necessary*, separate analysis should be done to determine if all use cases and classes are *sufficient* (i.e., complete).

Table 8.4 shows the quality criteria for consistency between use cases and class models. If you have both a class model and use cases, these additional criteria apply.

Table 8.4 Quality criteria for class model to use case consistency.

Item	Criterion
CU-1	"«actor»" stereotyped classes in the class model clearly correlate to actors in the use case diagram and vice versa
CU-2	The class model contains all—and only—classes, attributes, associations, etc. necessary to support all sea level use cases
CU-3	The classes in the class model do not map 1 : 1 to sea level use cases

8.21 Economic Considerations

As stated in the last chapter, a key part of engineering is considering the economics of technical decisions. Decisions about the scope and context of a domain to model, design, implement, and maintain clearly have economic implications.

The good news is that class models come with historical data for estimating effort. Chapter 23 explains the estimation model in detail. You can consider expanding or reducing scope in terms of its effect on the class model and re-estimate. This will give you a reasonable way to estimate cost and schedule implications of any proposed scope.

8.22 Summary

The use case diagram shows the relevant scope (use cases) and context (actors) for a (sub)domain. The class model is a precise statement of policies to be enforced across that scope and context. The class model defines major elements and important relationships that exist between those elements. Another way to think about the class model is that it describes invariants—things that need to always be true. The primary concepts of class modeling include:

- Class
- Attribute
- Association
- Generalization (inheritance)

A class is an abstraction for a set of existing or potential business-relevant things that are subject to the same policies, processes, and constraints. It is a descriptor for set of things with similar structure, behavior, and relationships. A class is a stencil or template for a set of things that are alike. Classes represent how a modeler chooses to abstract the stakeholder's business.

Attributes capture information about objects that is necessary to carry out sea level transactions. The range specification for an attribute defines constraints on values for that attribute. The four styles of range specification are:

- Span with precision and units
- Enumeration
- Reference
- Unconstrained

Forcing the modeler to specify attribute ranges surfaces low-level detailed requirements.

Some variations on the theme of attributes include keys and derived attributes.

Normalization is often considered a way to reduce redundancy in data structures, but this vastly understates its importance. Normalization is more properly thought of as applying the principle of high cohesion and loose coupling to class models. The traditional "normal form rules" can be very esoteric and impractical. RKMC/NF says that there can be no constraints on information other than what is explicitly defined by range, key, multiplicity, and completeness specifications. RKMC/NF is much simpler, more straightforward, and more reliable for properly structuring a class model.

An association abstracts a set of relevant connections between objects, aka "links." Associations in the class model exist to support processing of the form "Given an object of class X, which object or objects of class Y is it connected to?" There are almost always constraints on participation in those links. This is multiplicity: representing constraints on participation in associations. Forcing the modeler to specify association multiplicities surfaces more low-level detailed requirements. Some variations on associations include:

- Reflexive associations
- Multiple associations between the same classes
- Aggregation
- Composition
- Foreign key
- Association class
- n-ary associations

Generalization is the semantic model equivalent of inheritance in object-oriented design and programming: it represents an "is-a-kind-of" relationship between classes. Generalization factors out common properties, to declare them only once. Unlike inheritance in design and programming, generalization in semantic modeling is strictly additive—properties declared on a superclass can't be overridden in a subclass. Variations on generalization include:

- {complete} versus {incomplete}
- {disjoint} versus {overlapping}
- {static} versus {dynamic}
- Multiple classification

Unlike use case diagrams, care must be taken with class models because they are critical to later design and coding (Part III). Doing a bad job on a class model makes design and coding much more difficult, risky, and error prone.

9

Interaction Diagrams

Process at a Mid-Level

The use case diagram shows scope (use cases) and context (actors) for a (sub) domain: it identifies processes at a coarse-grained level. Interaction diagrams describe those same processes at an intermediate level, in terms of communication between objects carrying out those processes. Interaction diagrams show information flow, along with decisions and alternatives. The main elements of interaction diagramming are objects, messages, and scenarios.

Each sea level use case could have one interaction diagram although this is variable for reasons discussed in this chapter.

9.1 On the Relative Unimportance of Interaction Diagramming

Just like use case diagramming, interaction diagrams are a convenience for readers and not critical to creating or maintaining design and code. Most (if not all) interaction diagram content is derivable from class models and state models. It is easy to fall into a trap of overengineering interaction diagrams, and they are really not important in building and maintaining software. You can waste a lot of valuable time. Be careful to not invest too much; time is better spent on class modeling and state modeling.

Practically speaking, it is unlikely that interaction diagrams will be needed for every sea level use case. On the project with 35 actors and 535 sea level use cases introduced in Chapter 7, the team would have gone crazy if they had to diagram every use case. Most use cases are quite simple and don't need to be diagrammed. Usually the modeler picks the most interesting 10 to 20 sea level use cases and provides diagrams for those. Readers should be able to infer the missing diagrams from the ones provided.

How to Engineer Software: A Model-Based Approach, First Edition. Steve Tockey.
© 2019 the IEEE Computer Society, Inc. Published 2019 by John Wiley & Sons, Inc.

9.2 Basic Concepts

While a class model is organized around classes, interaction diagrams are organized around objects. Different objects, even though they are of the same class, can play different roles in a process. It can be important to illustrate those different roles, so objects representing those roles should be shown separately. In modeling of dropping a Book order line from a Book order in Order fulfillment, there can be many Order lines: the one being dropped and others not being dropped. The different roles of Book order lines—the one to be dropped versus the ones to be left alone—need to be described so objects representing each role need to be shown. As a result, naming in interaction diagrams is different than in class models. Figure 9.1 shows the three naming styles.

The modeler is free to choose the most appropriate naming style, and the styles can be mixed in a single interaction diagram.

9.2.1 Use Cases Versus Scenarios

A use case, as defined in Chapter 7, is a general pattern of interaction between actors and processes like "Pack order" where the Warehouse worker packs a Book order. Use cases are intentionally generic; they describe process at the most coarse-grained level. A scenario is a more specific interaction conforming to that general pattern. Elements that are variable in a use case can be specific in a scenario, like "Al the Warehouse worker packs Book order 47, which results in the stock on hand of Print medium Gone With the Wind falling below its reorder level, thus triggering placement of a Replenish order."

It is theoretically possible to describe any sea level use case in a single interaction diagram, but processes can be quite complex. It can be useful to break a complex sea level use case into one or more scenarios and provide interaction diagrams on that basis. Use case Pack order might be diagrammed in as many as four scenarios:

- Packing a Book order that doesn't involve replenish ordering.
- Packing an order that involves creating a new Replenish order.
- Packing an order that involves adding to an existing Replenish order, but the title needing replenishment is new to the replenish order.
- Packing an order that involves adding to an existing Replenish order, but the title needing replenishment already exists in the replenish order.

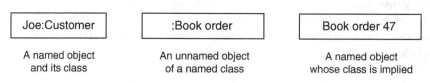

Figure 9.1 Object naming styles for interaction diagrams.

Diagramming scenarios rather than use cases leads to having more diagrams; on the other hand, each of those diagrams will be less complex. Use your best judgment in breaking use cases into scenarios for interaction diagramming.

9.3 Basic Interaction Diagram Notation

Using another simple banking business as a case study, a use case diagram with only one sea level use case: Cash a check, as shown in Figure 9.2.

The class diagram for this simple banking business is shown in Figure 9.3.

The class diagram shows Bank account as a superclass of both Checking account and Savings account. The "protected by" association is to support overdraft protection in Checking accounts. If a check is cashed against a Checking account whose .balance is insufficient, the bank will cover the check by transferring money from the protecting Savings account, as long as sufficient funds are available.

UML has two kinds of interaction diagram: sequence diagrams and communication diagrams. Both are introduced.

Figure 9.2 A use case in another simple banking application.

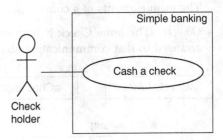

Figure 9.3 A class diagram for the simple banking application.

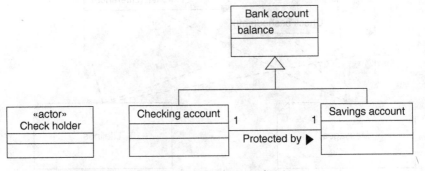

9.3.1 Basic Sequence Diagram Notation

Start by modeling one scenario: a person holds a check drawn against a Checking account. That Checking account has insufficient funds to cover the check, but the overdraft-protecting Savings account can make up the difference. The sequence diagram for this scenario is shown in Figure 9.4.

The main elements of a sequence diagram are:

- *Objects*—In this case the Check holder and the two accounts. Objects are generally arranged in a line across the top of the sequence diagram.
- *Lifelines*—Representations of participating objects over time. Lifelines usually run vertically, top to bottom.
- *Messages*—Process communication between participating objects, arranged in the order they occur in the process.

Sequence diagrams can be rotated 90° counterclockwise: objects arranged in a vertical line on the left, lifelines running horizontally, with time going from left to right. Both orientations are allowed.

9.3.2 Basic Communication Diagram Notation

Figure 9.5 shows the same scenario in communication diagram format.
The main elements of a communication diagram are:

- *Objects*—The same Check holder and two accounts. Objects are generally arranged so that communicating objects are adjacent.

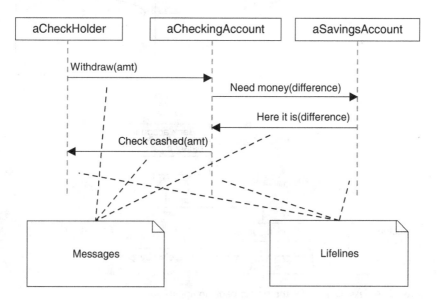

Figure 9.4 A sequence diagram for the check-cashing scenario.

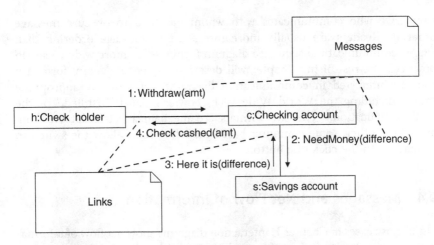

Figure 9.5 A communication diagram for the check-cashing scenario.

- *Links*—Indicating which objects communicate with which other objects. Links are solid lines between each pair of communicating objects.
- *Messages*—Process communication between participating objects, arranged near an arrow that shows the direction of information flow. Message ordering is shown using sequence numbers that precede each message.

Figures 9.4 and 9.5 show the same scenario:

1) A Check holder knows they are holding a check they now want cashed. The Checking account needs to know that to get its job done (cashing the check); so the Checking account becomes aware.
2) The Checking account knows the amount of the check is more than its .balance, so it needs help from the overdraft-protecting Savings account. The Savings account needs to know that to get its job done (making up the difference, if possible); so the Savings account becomes aware.
3) The Savings account knows it can cover the difference. The Checking account needs to know that to get its job done (giving money to the check holder); so the Checking account becomes aware.
4) The Checking account now knows it can give money to the Check holder. The Check holder needs to know that to get their job done (taking the money); so the Check holder becomes aware. The process is now completed.

Both diagrams show the same information. The difference is notation: how that information is presented. Sequence diagrams emphasize ordering of messages but tend to obscure who is communicating with who, particularly when the diagrams are larger and more complex. Communication diagrams emphasize who communicates with whom but tend to obscure message ordering. Readers are usually more interested in message ordering than who is communicating; sequence diagram format is far more widely used in practice. The rest of this chapter will describe sequence diagram format; if you are interested in communication diagrams, refer to any appropriate source including the World Wide Web, Fowler's "UML Distilled," or the UML specification.[1] The two formats are mechanically translatable from one to the other; some computer-based modeling tools allow the switch to be made with the click of a button.

9.4 Messages and Net Flow of Information

Just like use cases in Chapter 7, interaction diagrams show net flow of information (i.e., data flow), not flow of control. You may be tempted to interpret messages in Figures 9.4 and 9.5 as being pushed instead of pulled; it is a particularly hard habit to break. Perhaps you didn't notice, but the explanation of Figures 9.4 and 9.5 was intentionally carefully worded. Recall:

1) A Check holder knows they are holding a check they now want cashed. The Checking account needs to know that to get its job done (cashing the check); so the Checking account becomes aware.

That explanation intentionally did not say, "A Check holder tells the Checking account to cash the check," nor did it say, "The Checking account asks a Check holder if they would like their check cashed." It simply said that one entity knows something and another needs to know that to get its job done, so the needing entity becomes aware of what it needs to know.

Messages can be designed and coded in push mode, but it should not be a foregone conclusion. Messages in semantic models are intentionally neither push nor pull. They merely describe flow of information. That flow of information is inherent in business processes: something is known in the (sub) domain over here, and that information is needed over there to carry out the process. How and when it gets from here to there is irrelevant; that is the control flow decision. The domain doesn't care as long as information is available where it is needed no later than when it is needed. Chapters 15 and 16 show semantic model messages designed and coded in both push and pull forms.

If you are already familiar with design dialect sequence diagrams in UML, notice that there is an important difference in notation. You are probably used to seeing "activation context" bars on lifelines, as in Figure 9.6.

---

1 See [Fowler03] or [OMG11b], respectively.

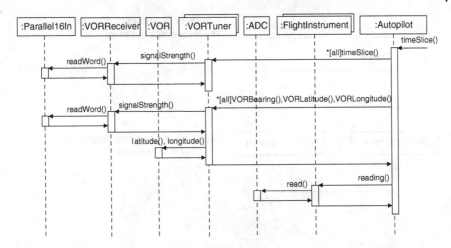

Figure 9.6 A design sequence diagram with activation context bars (flow of control).

The activation context bar means the diagram is showing control flow, not information flow. In the requirements modeling dialect, we don't model a business in computing terms; we model it in business terms.

9.5 Message Naming

Recalling sea level event use cases and sea level data use cases, the same general naming conventions apply to messages:

- *Event messages*—Describe flow of events in a process. Events are generally named with verbs or verb phrases.
- *Data messages*—Describe flow of data in a process. Data messages may be named with nouns or noun phrases and be suffixed with "?"

Figure 9.7 shows a sequence diagram for a simple sea level event use case from Order fulfillment: Cancel order.

Figure 9.8 shows a sequence diagram for a simple sea level data use case from the same domain: Customer sees book order status.

If a data message represents flow of derived attribute values, do not include the preceding "/" as on the class diagram. The fact that information is derivable is only relevant inside of that class, not outside. That detail should be encapsulated as it may be subject to change.

UML allows messages to be parameterized to indicate associated data. If you care to show it, list data in parentheses after the message name, separated by commas. Adding parameters tends to clutter and complicate sequence diagrams. Show that detail if the benefit of showing it outweighs the cost of putting it there and keeping it up to date.

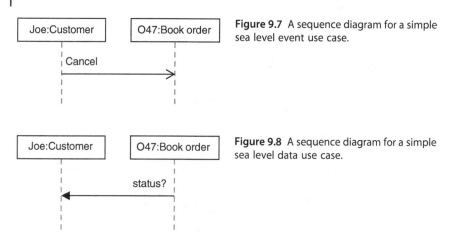

Figure 9.7 A sequence diagram for a simple sea level event use case.

Figure 9.8 A sequence diagram for a simple sea level data use case.

9.6 Which Objects Communicate?

Remember the purpose of an association is to support processing of the form:

> *"Given this object of this class, which object(s) of that class is it connected to?"*

Given a Customer, which Book orders did they place? Given a Book order, which Book order lines are in it? Given a Book order line, which Medium is it selecting? Given a Medium, which Title? And so on. In that sense, the lines of messaging in interaction diagrams should generally follow lines of association in the class diagram. Customer is associated with Book order, Book order is associated—via association class Book order line—with Medium, Medium is associated with Title, etc. So we should expect that process messaging should generally follow these same paths: Customer-Book order, Book order-Book order line, Book order line-Medium, Medium-Title, etc. We should generally not expect objects of class Customer to communicate directly with objects of class Medium. Objects of class Customer will communicate directly with objects of class Title even though they aren't associated, so it is not a hard and fast rule that an object can only communicate with its directly associated objects.

Considering the check-cashing scenario in Figures 9.4 and 9.5, which Savings account is the Checking account communicating with? Presumably, it is the one Savings account that is protecting that Checking account—as defined by association "protected by" in Figure 9.3. It might be convenient to explain that on a sequence diagram. On the other hand, there is no recognized UML notation for specifying this level of detail, and this can clutter the diagram. While that is important process detail to specify eventually, it does not need to be specified here—it can be better specified in the state model (Chapter 10).

9.7 Object Creation

Some processes call for creation of objects. These objects didn't exist before the transaction started; they were created as part of that transaction. In UML sequence diagrams, object creation is shown as in Figure 9.9. "GWTW" refers to Margaret Mitchell's classic novel "Gone With The Wind."

When the .stock on hand for a Print medium goes below the .reorder level, the Title needs to know about it to signal replenish for the corresponding Publisher. In this scenario the Publisher knows a new Replenish order needs to be created. A new Replenish order, RO9, is created as a result. Object creation is shown using two elements in a sequence diagram:

- Any object created during that transaction is below the top row.
- A message stereotyped "«new»" goes into the new object, not into its lifeline.

9.8 Object Deletion

Object deletion is shown using a bold "X" at the bottom of a lifeline, as in Figure 9.10 for the sea level use case of dropping a Book order line from a Book order.

On completion of this transaction, the selected Book order line is deleted. This notation shows the object being deleted explicitly by a separate object, the Book order in this case. Figure 9.21 shows implicit deletion: objects can delete themselves on completion of a final action.

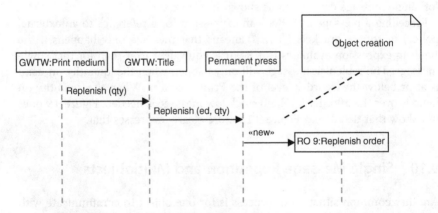

Figure 9.9 A sequence diagram showing object creation.

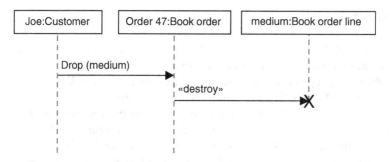

Figure 9.10 A sequence diagram showing object deletion.

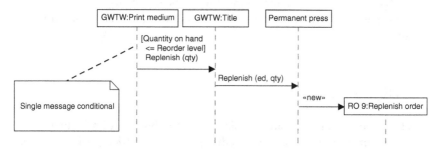

Figure 9.11 A sequence diagram showing single message conditional.

9.9 Single Message Conditional

Processes often incorporate decisions. In some cases, conditionality applies to a single message (multiple message conditional is described later). The notation for single message conditional is shown in Figure 9.11.

Preceding a message by a Boolean expression (or a reference to an external policy) in square brackets ("[", "]") means that message only happens if the Boolean expression evaluates to true. It is equivalent to if-then for that single message. The replenish message will only happen when the .quantity on hand is at or below the .reorder level of the Print medium. When the .quantity on hand is over the .reorder level, no stock low message is needed. Figure 9.9 does not show that detail, and Figure 9.11 more clearly expresses that.

9.10 Single Message Repetition and Multiobjects

Another common situation in process is for one object to communicate with not one but many objects of the same class. Take packing a Book order as an example. When an order is packed, it needs to communicate with each of

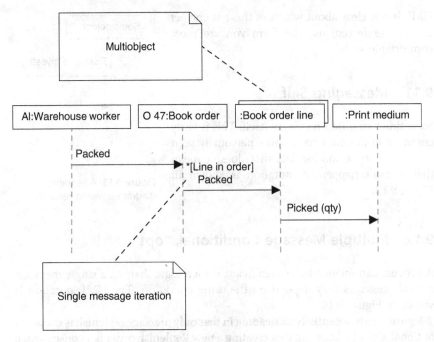

Figure 9.12 A sequence diagram showing single message repetition and multiobjects.

the Book order lines in that order, so each line can take care of its part of the packing process. This is shown in Figure 9.12.

Single message repetition is shown by preceding the repeated message with an expression between "*[" "]," as in "*[Line in Order]" in Figure 9.12. This is essentially "for all," "while-do," or "as long as." As shown in Figure 9.12, the Packed event needs to be communicated to each Book order line in the Book order that just got packed. The multiobject notation is the shadow behind the object named ":Book Order Line." This emphasizes that the message is for many objects. All of the objects represented by a multiobject play the same role in the process. If objects have different roles they need to be shown separately in the diagram.

One question about multiobjects has to do with the context of multiplicity. Specifically in Figure 9.12,

- In the context of a single Book order line, that line needs to communicate with only one corresponding Print medium. Since it's from one object to one object, Print medium can be shown as not being a multiobject.
- In the context of the overall process, one Book order has many Book order lines, and each order line has a corresponding Print medium. Many objects of class Print medium are involved in this use case, so Print medium could be shown as a multiobject.

UML is not clear about which of these is correct or even preferred; use the form you are most comfortable with.

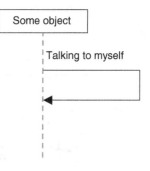

9.11 Messaging Self

Sometimes an object messages itself. This is fairly common in design. I have never personally seen this in semantic models but that doesn't mean that it can't happen. A notation is shown in Figure 9.13.

Figure 9.13 A sequence diagram showing recursion.

9.12 Multiple Message Conditional, "opt"

A process can include more significant if-then logic than on a single message: several messages may depend on the same condition. The UML notation is shown in Figure 9.14.

Figure 9.10 is potentially misleading in that only message replenish is shown as optional. Only by knowing that creating a new Replenish order is a consequence of stock going low is it apparent that other messages won't happen either. Figure 9.14 is more clear because optionality is shown for the set of messages.

9.13 Multiple Message Conditional, "alt"

Decisions sometimes need to be made among several alternatives. It's not just if-then, but it's if-then-else or switch-case. Figure 9.15 shows the UML notation for this situation.

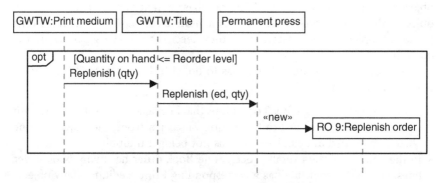

Figure 9.14 A sequence diagram showing multiple message conditional.

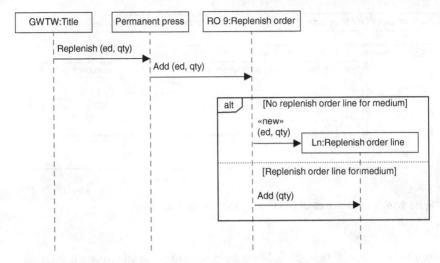

Figure 9.15 A sequence diagram showing multiple message alternatives.

When a Title needs to be replenished, the Publisher needs to add the specified quantity of the specified Print medium to a Replenish order. Two alternatives are possible:

- A Replenish order line for that Print medium doesn't exist in the Replenish order, so it needs to be created; this is shown in the top compartment of the "alt" box.
- A Replenish order line for that Print medium already exists in the Replenish order, so the order quantity for that line only needs to be increased; this is shown in the bottom compartment of the "alt" box.

If needed, there can be many compartments, one for each mutually exclusive alternative. Also, there can be any number of messages in one compartment.

9.14 Multiple Message Iteration, "loop"

In some situations the process includes iteration: looping. UML sequence diagram notation for looping is shown in Figure 9.16.

Looping has somewhat the same meaning as "for," "do-while," or "repeat-until" in programming languages: as long as the expression between the "*[" "]" is true, the loop continues. As shown in Figure 9.16, as long as a specific Book order line (there can be many in a single order) is for eBook medium, the Customer needs to receive the product key when that Book order is placed (Print medium books

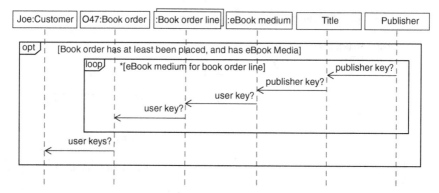

Figure 9.16 A sequence diagram showing multiple message loop.

need to be physically shipped). Looping in semantic model sequence diagrams should not actually imply serial execution as in most programming languages; the work is more properly thought of as happening concurrently.

9.15 Referencing a Separate Sequence Diagram

In some situations, it's useful to have one sequence diagram refer to another; Figure 9.17 shows how. The sequence diagram for the Pack order sea level use case references the sequence diagram for the Replenish mud level use case.

9.16 A Tactic for Developing Sequence Diagrams

A straightforward approach to developing a sequence diagram is to start by understanding the transaction as a whole. What does it require (preconditions), and what does it guarantee (postconditions)? That is, what is its contract?

Take use case Receive replenish order as an example. In this transaction, a Replenish order had earlier been sent to a Publisher to restock some set of Print media. The Publisher shipped the requested books to WebBooks, and now the crate is on the warehouse loading dock. Al the Warehouse worker sees the crate, opens the packing list, and discovers this is the set of books from Replenish Order #9. Al opens the crate, restocks the contents in appropriate warehouse locations, and then notifies the domain that the replenish order has been received. Using the template for describing an event use case (Chapter 7),

- *Triggering event(s)*—A Warehouse worker has restocked the physical books in a Replenish order from a Publisher.

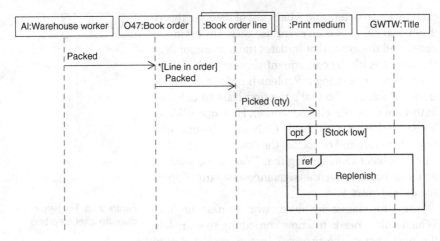

Figure 9.17 A sequence diagram showing reference to another diagram.

- *Parameters*—None.
- *Requires*—A Replenish order arrived from its publisher and physical books have been restocked.
- *Normal course*—Inventory (.stock on hand) for each Print medium in the order has been increased by the reordered quantity, and the completed Replenish order and its lines have been deleted.
- *Alternative course(s)*—None.
- *Exceptions*—None.

Step one is to look at the class diagram and drop classes that are not involved in this transaction. For Receive replenish order, dropped classes would be:

- Customer
- Book order
- Book order line
- eBook medium
- Title
- Manager

You might think that class Publisher is involved. They were, in the sense that they packed the crate and shipped it to WebBooks. But they aren't involved any longer; their involvement ended when the crate left their shipping dock. This leaves as classes directly involved in the process:

- Warehouse worker
- Replenish order
- Replenish order line
- Print medium

Step two is to determine what kind of use case this is: event or data. This is an event use case. For event use cases, find the event that initiates the transaction. For this use case, it's the consequential event of the Warehouse worker noticing a Replenish order has arrived from a Publisher. So that's the first class to consider in this use case: Warehouse worker. How many Warehouse workers are involved? Only one: the one who found the crate and restocked the Print media. So start with an object representing that Warehouse worker, let's call him Al, on the sequence diagram. This is shown in Figure 9.18.

Al:Warehouse worker

Figure 9.18 The sequence diagram after step two.

From the classes involved, who is next in line? Which object needs to know something to complete the next step of the process? In this case it should be Replenish order. How many Replenish order are involved? Only one: the one that was received. So add an object to the sequence diagram, and you might want to call it RO9: Replenish Order. You can now put in the message: Al knows the Replenish order got received and that order needs to know to get its job done. This is shown in Figure 9.19.

From the classes involved, again who is next? In this case it should be Replenish order line. How many Replenish order lines are involved? Probably many. Do they all play the same role? Yes. So this time add a multiobject to the sequence diagram. If the objects play different roles, then add one object (possibly a multiobject) for each role. You can also add the message from RO9 to the Replenish order lines that need to know they got received. This is shown in Figure 9.20.

From the classes involved, again ask who is next? In this use case, there's only one class left, Print medium. How many objects of class Print medium? Possibly many, one for each line in the Replenish order. Do they all play the same role?

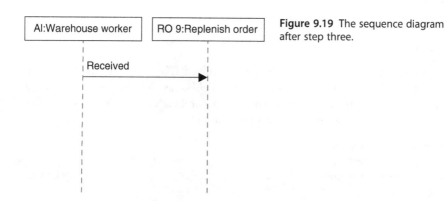

Figure 9.19 The sequence diagram after step three.

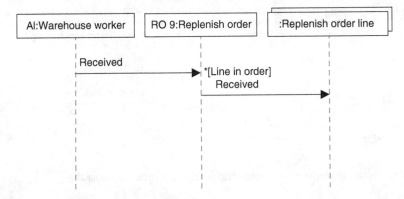

Figure 9.20 The sequence diagram after step four.

Yes, so add another multiobject to the diagram. Again, if objects play different roles, add a (multi)object for each role. Add the message from the Order lines that know they got received to the Print media that need to know they got restocked.

As described earlier for multiobjects, class Print medium could be shown as a multiobject because more than one is involved in this use case. On the other hand, there is only one Print medium for each Replenish order line, so it might be reasonable to show Print medium as a single object. UML is unclear on this point; either should be acceptable.

Finally, consider objects that might be created or deleted as a result of that process. In this use case, WebBooks wants the Replenish order and the Replenish order lines to be deleted at the end of the transaction. Adjust the sequence diagram appropriately. The complete sequence diagram for this use case is shown in Figure 9.21.

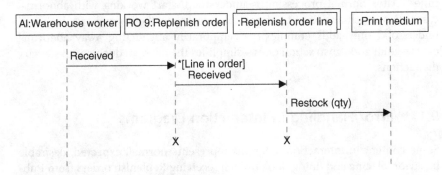

Figure 9.21 The complete sequence diagram for receiving a replenish order.

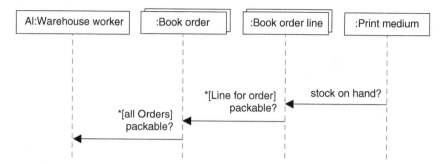

Figure 9.22 Sequence diagram for determining which Book orders are packable.

For data use cases, ask who is the ultimate destination of the information? To illustrate, take the use case Packable orders? How many Warehouse workers? Consider just the one, Al, again. Start with a single object on the sequence diagram.

Where does Al get the information? From class Book order. How many Book orders? Many. Do they all play the same role? Yes. So add a multiobject for Book order to the diagram. You can show the message between the Book order multiobject to Al now, if you want, or you can add all messages later.

Do Book orders know everything they need to know to determine packability? No, they need help from Book order lines. How many lines? Potentially many. Do all lines play the same role? Yes. So add another multiobject to the diagram.

Do Book order lines know everything they need? No. Lines for eBook media are immediately packable, but lines for Print media lines may not be, depending on inventory level. How many Print media are involved? Possibly many overall but just one per Book order line. And if there are many, they all play the same role. You can add either a single object or a multiobject to the diagram. Nothing else is needed to determine book order packability. The sequence diagram is shown in Figure 9.22.

A final recommendation about sequence diagramming is to first focus on normal behavior. Answer the question "what can be expected to happen most of the time?" After normal processing is understood, start working with abnormal cases. Too much attention to abnormal cases when the normal case isn't well understood only adds complexity. Temporarily abstracting away abnormal cases—as all good abstraction does—simplifies the job by reducing unnecessary distractions.

9.17 Error Handling in Interaction Diagrams

Some content in interaction diagrams represents normal, expected, desirable behavior: placing and filling Book orders, receiving Replenish orders from Publishers, etc. Some content may represent error handling, undesirable behavior:

like a Silly Bank Customer missing a Loan payment. There are economic implications of including error handling in a semantic model. The decision to include specific error handling or not should be based on technical and economic considerations. Chapter 25 explains how to make that an engineering decision.

The semantic model—or, more precisely, semantic modeling language—does not distinguish between desirable and undesirable conditions. All conditions are modeled using the same vocabulary: use cases, classes, associations, states, events, etc. What is desirable versus what is not is a value judgment imposed by stakeholders. Having decided to include responses, if you want to distinguish desirable from undesirable behavior, consider that UML is colorblind. You can paint semantic model content different colors; UML ignores those colors. You could color desirable model content black and undesirable content in red. Color communicates desirability to the reader; the model itself doesn't care.

9.18 Interaction Diagram Descriptions

Diagram descriptions are optional, but can be useful to explain any non-obvious aspects of a process. You are free to add a narrative to explain. Avoid implying a specific sequencing of steps when no such sequence is required. Stated or implied sequences force the designer/coder into implementing exactly that order when some other order might be more efficient.

Many example interaction diagrams for the WebBooks 2.0 case study, with brief descriptions as appropriate, can be found in Appendices D, F, H, and J.

9.19 Brokers

WebBooks 2.0 Order fulfillment (Appendix D) has Warehouse workers choose, from the set of packable Book orders, a specific order to pack. At some point, WebBooks might want to be more prescriptive about which Warehouse worker should pack which packable Book order. This is an example of a more general issue: brokering resource consumers and service providers. In this case the packable Book order is the resource consumer, and the Warehouse worker is the service provider. Many semantic models, particularly real-time/embedded and process control, need brokering.

One solution is to introduce a broker class (aka an assigner, resolver, matchmaker, controller, etc.) into the semantic model and have that class represent the policies and processes for matching resource consumers with service providers. Many variations are possible:

- How many resource consumers?
- Is the number of consumers fixed or not?

- How many service providers?
- Is the number of providers fixed or not?
- What assignment logic: first come, first served? First come, last served? Priority? Etc.

WebBooks could decide to assign the oldest packable Book order to the available Warehouse person who has waited the longest since last packing an order. The age of a packable order can already be determined from existing information: the packability status and the date the order was created. An attribute would need to be added to Warehouse worker to represent waiting time. A new broker class, possibly called Order Assigner, could have a state model representing assignment policies and processes as described in Chapter 10.

Other options are to allocate the decision logic to either the resource consumer (Book order) or to the service provider (Warehouse worker).

9.20   Cohesion and Coupling in Interaction Diagrams

Aspects of cohesion and coupling are apparent in interaction diagrams. Figure 9.21 shows a sequence diagram for the Receive replenish order use case with good (i.e., high) cohesion and (i.e., loose) coupling. Figure 9.23 shows a sequence diagram for the same use case but with bad (i.e., low) cohesion and (i.e., tight) coupling.[2]

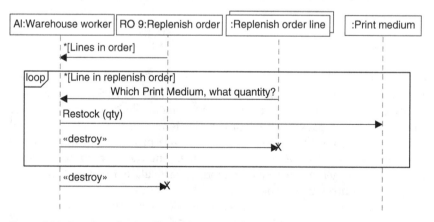

Figure 9.23 Sequence diagram for receiving a replenish order, bad cohesion, and coupling.

---

2 This is the sequence diagram manifestation of "broken modularization" as described in [Suryanarayana15].

The bad version starts with Al: Warehouse worker needing to know which Replenish order lines were in the Replenish order that just got received, so he becomes aware. For each Replenish order line,

- Al:Warehouse worker needs to know the Print medium and .quantity from that Replenish order line, so he becomes aware.
- Al:Warehouse worker knows that a Print medium needs to Restock with that quantity, so that Print medium becomes aware.
- Al:Warehouse worker knows that Replenish order line needs to be deleted, so the line becomes aware.

Al:Warehouse worker knows that Replenish order has been fully received and can also be deleted, so the order becomes aware.

Table 9.1 shows the key differences between sequence diagrams with good versus bad cohesion and coupling.

9.21 Quality Criteria

In addition to the quality criteria in Chapter 3, Table 9.2 shows the quality criteria for interaction diagrams.

Table 9.3 shows the quality criteria for consistency between interaction diagrams and use cases. If you have both interaction diagrams and use cases, these additional criteria apply.

Table 9.4 shows the quality criteria for consistency between interaction diagrams and class models. If you have both interaction diagrams and a class model, these additional criteria apply.

Table 9.1 Comparing good and bad cohesion and coupling in sequence diagrams.

Good cohesion and coupling	Bad cohesion and coupling
Process logic is distributed across classes, each providing part of the overall process. The parts are chained	Process logic is concentrated in one central "God object" that uses query–act pairs to get work done
Information and its usage are mostly co-located in the same object	Information is known in one class but is used in a different class
Lines of communication generally align with lines of association	Lines of communication don't align with lines of association
Each object is mostly only aware of classes it's associated with[a]	God object(s) knows many classes; other classes are merely dumb data containers

[a] This is the semantic model manifestation of the Law of Demeter (see, e.g., https://en.wikipedia.org/wiki/Law_of_Demeter).

Table 9.2 Quality criteria for interaction diagrams.

Item	Criterion
ID-1	The interaction diagrams are not overengineered: neither too much detail on the diagrams nor too many diagrams
ID-2	The role of each object in the interaction diagram is either obvious (e.g., from its name) or is clearly explained in a description
ID-3	Each interaction diagram shows net flow of information, not flow of control
ID-4	If a specific sequence of processing is required, then the diagram clearly reflects that requirement. If there is no sequencing requirement, the diagrams are clear that there isn't
ID-5	All diagram adornments have been used correctly: creation, deletion, multiobject, conditional, repetition, etc.
ID-6	If one interaction diagram references another, that referenced diagram exists
ID-7	The interaction diagrams have high cohesion and loose coupling

Table 9.3 Quality criteria for consistency between interaction diagrams and use cases.

Item	Criterion
IU-1	Each interaction diagram is clearly and correctly correlated with sea level use cases
IU-2	An appropriate subset of the sea level use cases are described in interaction diagrams: not too few and not too many

Table 9.4 Quality criteria for consistency between interaction diagrams and class models.

Item	Criterion
IC-1	All objects in each interaction diagram are clearly members of classes in the class model
IC-2	The lines of messaging in the interaction diagrams appropriately follow the lines of association in the class diagram

9.22 Economic Considerations

As stated in earlier chapters, a key part of engineering is considering the economics of technical decisions. Decisions about the scope and context of a domain to model, design, implement, and maintain clearly have economic implications.

Unfortunately, use cases and scenarios are highly variable in size and complexity. Unless you have a good analogy to compare with, it will be difficult to do any better than expert judgment estimation. You may be better off estimating based on the class model—and any implications proposed use cases and scenarios have on that model—to give meaningful estimates.

9.23   Summary

The use case diagram shows scope (use cases) and context (actors) for a (sub) domain: it identifies processes at a coarse-grained level. Interaction diagrams describe processes at an intermediate level: communication between objects carrying out those processes. Interaction diagrams show information flow and decisions and alternatives in processing.

Practically speaking, it is unlikely that interaction diagrams will be needed for every sea level use case. The modeler should pick the most interesting and representative subset of 10 to 20 sea level use cases and provide interaction diagrams for those. Most readers should be able to infer the missing diagrams from those provided.

Class models are structured and organized around classes; interaction diagrams are structured and organized around objects. Different objects, even though they are of the same class, can play different roles. It's important to illustrate the different roles, so objects representing those different roles should be called out separately.

UML supports both sequence and communication diagrams. Both show the same information. The difference is notation: how that information is presented to the reader. Sequence diagrams emphasize ordering of messages but tend to obscure who is communicating with who particularly when diagrams become complex. Communication diagrams emphasize who communicates with whom but tend to obscure ordering of messages. People usually care more about message ordering than who is communicating; sequence diagram format is more widely used in practice.

Interaction diagrams intentionally model only net flow of information. Messages could be designed and coded in either push or pull mode, but that is a control flow decision. The activation context bar on design dialect sequence diagrams means that diagram is showing control flow, not information flow. In the requirements dialect, business is not modeled in computing terms; it is modeled in business terms—no activation context bar is shown.

There are a number of variations on the basic theme:

- Object creation and deletion
- Single message conditional
- Single message repetition

- Multiobjects
- Messaging self
- Multiple message conditional, "opt"
- Multiple message conditional, "alt"
- Multiple message iteration, "loop"
- Referencing a separate sequence diagram

When considering use cases at this intermediate level of detail, the need for brokers could appear, and such classes should be added as necessary.

It is easy to fall into a trap of overengineering interaction diagrams, and they are not that important to building and maintaining software. You can waste a lot of valuable time on interaction diagrams. So be careful not to invest too much; your time could be better invested in other modeling.

10

State Models

Process at a Fine-Grained Level

Use case diagrams describe process at the most coarse-grained level. Interaction (sequence and communication) diagrams describe process at an intermediate level. State models specify process at the most fine-grained level, defining precise behavior of objects in a class. Two aspects of process are modeled:

- *Sequencing and timing*—Constraints on when things happen. This is modeled using states, events, and transitions.
- *Transformation*—Work being done: computation. This is modeled using actions

Each of these is described in this chapter.

Generally, each non-actor class will have a state model. Behavior of actor classes—particularly with reduced models—is normally outside the scope of a semantic model, as described in Chapter 6. A state model is for one class and precisely defines behavior of objects in that class: the cookie cutter analogy. There can never be more than one state model for a class.

State modeling is critical for design and code. Like class modeling, it's important to do well. If a bad job is done, design and coding can be much more difficult, risky, and defect prone.

The primary example used in this chapter will be class Loan in Silly Bank's Loan processing business introduced in Chapter 7. The use case diagram is shown in Figure 7.9. Figure 10.1 shows a class diagram.

10.1 Event

There is an issue of circular definitions: it's impossible to define the term event without referring to states; it's equally impossible to define the term state without referring to events. As one of my university professors once said,

How to Engineer Software: A Model-Based Approach, First Edition. Steve Tockey.
© 2019 the IEEE Computer Society, Inc. Published 2019 by John Wiley & Sons, Inc.

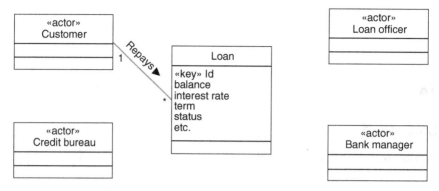

Figure 10.1 Class diagram for Silly Bank Loan processing.

> *"States are what happen between events,*
> *events are what happen between states."*

With this in mind, excuse forward references to states in explaining events. The UML definition of an event is[1]:

> *"... the specification of some occurrence that may potentially trigger effects by an object"*

An event is an occurrence or happening that can affect the state of an object—what that object is doing now or how it will react in the future. More specifically, an event may advance sequencing or timing of a process. Typical events for an object represent:

- A new object needs to be created.
- A change is needed to one or more of an object's attribute values.
- Something important happened in another object; this object needs to react.
- This object needs to be linked to, or unlinked from, another object.[2]
- Domain-relevant times: timed business events.
- An existing object needs to be deleted.

10.1.1 Finding Events

Examining sea level event use cases that involve objects in a given class can help you start the list of events for that class. Consider event messages that go into

---

1 See [OMG11b].

2 This is not necessarily an event for this object, but it could be an event for the association class representing the link between this object and another.

objects of that class. To the extent that you have interaction diagrams, they can be harvested for inbound events. Events for Silly Bank's loan class would include:

- *Application submitted*—A new Loan object needs to be created.
- *Application approved*—Something is decided by the Loan officer: approve.
- *Application denied*—Something is decided by the Loan officer: deny.
- *Loan opened*—Something is decided by the Customer: start borrowing money.
- *Payment received*—Something is decided by the Customer: make payment.
- *Payment missed*—A (sub)domain relevant time.
- *Records retention time passed*—A (sub)domain relevant time; the Loan can be deleted.
- ...

Events represent significant process happenings, as in "this (change) just happened and you need to react to it," so events are often named with a verb or verb phrase (e.g., "*something*-ed," like "payment received" or "payment missed") or a time ("at *time*" or "after *time*," like "at 2 am" or "after 24 hours").

10.1.2 Event Notation

UML notation for an event is simply a text string. The placement of that string on a state diagram will be shown later in this chapter.

Mellor and Balcer[3] suggest listing events for a class in the bottom compartment of the class diagram, stereotyped with «event», as shown in Figure 10.2. I haven't done this on a project, but it appears to make sense. There doesn't

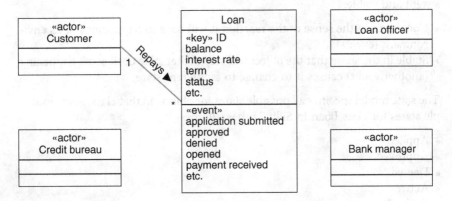

Figure 10.2 Class diagram for Silly Bank loan processing, showing events.

---

3 See [Mellor02].

seem to be any good argument against it other than a little additional effort and possibly space used on the class diagram.

An event may have parameters, and you may want to show those parameters. UML allows comma-separated parameters in parentheses after an event name. For example, "Place order (shipping address, list of books & quantities)" or "Submit loan application (application information)." Consider the value of extra detail on the diagram compared to the cost of creating and maintaining it over time. As always it is an economic decision.

Typically, events don't need descriptions; a well-chosen name conveys relevance. And that's the trick: name events by their relevance to process. If anything more needs to be said, you can include a description in an "event dictionary" for the class.

10.2 State

The UML definition of a state is:

> "... a situation during which some (usually implicit) invariant condition holds. The invariant may represent a static situation such as an object waiting for some external event to occur. However, it can also model dynamic conditions such as the process of performing some behavior (i.e., the [object] under consideration enters the state when the behavior commences and leaves it as soon as the behavior is completed)."

A state is a continuous period of time where the behavior of an object is consistent and stable:

- Consistent in the sense of the reaction it will have to happenings in its environment (events)
- Stable in the sense that the object will stay in that state until some happening (another event) causes it to change to a different state

The state model specifies all possible states for objects in that class. Some example states for class Loan in Silly Bank would be:

- Applied
- Approved
- Denied
- Active
- Paid off
- ...

All objects in a class must always be in exactly one state of that class' state model. Any one object can never be in more than, or less than, one state at any time.

Loan #d980320 might be Applied, loan #c660121 might be Paid off, and loan #s580506 might be Active.

In keeping with the issue of same words having different meanings, "state" has two distinct meanings. The meanings are similar and yet different enough to cause confusion. One meaning refers to values of an object's attributes at any moment in time. Consider loan #s580506 with .balance of $12,345. If the Customer makes a payment of $750, .balance will be reduced to $11,595. Since the value of .balance has changed, some would say this loan is in a different state.

The other meaning refers to how loan #s580506 will react to events. Since its reaction to events won't be significantly different with .balance of $12,345 than with .balance of $11,595, some would consider the loan to be in the same state. Formally, this second interpretation puts all configurations of the first interpretation that react the same way into equivalence classes and calls those equivalence classes states. Semantic modeling takes the second interpretation: the loan's reaction to events won't vary—the two configurations of .balance are in the same event–response equivalence class—the loan is in the same state.

10.2.1 State Notation

UML's notation for a state is a rectangle with rounded corners (sometimes called a "bub-tangle" because it's a hybrid of a bubble and a rectangle) with the state name inside, as shown in Figure 10.3.

The relevance of a state almost always has something to do with:

- An important (process) thing that happened in the past
- An important thing that is happening now
- An important thing that is expected to happen in the future

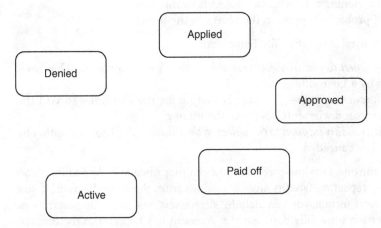

Figure 10.3 UML notation for states.

Because of this, state names tend to be (but are not exclusively):

- *Something*–ed—like "applied," "approved," or "denied"
- *Something*-ing—like "cruising" or "accelerating" in an automobile cruise controller

10.2.2 Finding States

One hint for finding states for a class is to look for attributes named ".state" or ".status". If any attributes have those names, look at their range specification. The range specification should be an enumeration; that set of values should be a first approximation of the states. Assuming class Loan in Silly Bank's class model had a .status attribute, its range would almost certainly include: Applied, Approved, Denied, Active, Paid off, etc. As a state model is refined, it may affect the attribute range.

In some cases, the state model for a class only has one state, "exists." This is not a problem if it only happens for a few classes, but be careful that it doesn't happen for too many classes. When a majority of classes in a semantic model have only the one Exists state, and just one or a few classes have very complex behavior, it suggests poor cohesion and coupling. Reexamine the allocation of process to classes; keep process elements as close as possible (i.e., in the same class) to the data (attributes) they operate on.

10.2.3 State Descriptions

If you want to write a state description, try to answer the following questions:

- What happened to get an object into this state?
- What is happening now while an object is in this state?
- What will probably happen to the object in the future?

For the Approved state of a Silly Bank loan:

- *What happened to get an object into this state*—A loan application has been approved by a Loan officer.
- *What is happening now*—The loan is waiting for the Customer to visit the bank, sign loan documents, and take the money.
- *What will probably happen to the object in the future*—The Loan will either be originated or cancelled.

Remember the one-fact-one-place documentation principle in Appendix A and avoid simply repeating what is already obvious from the state diagram. If you want to be more formal, you can include "state assertions" in a state description. A state assertion for a Silly Bank Savings Account in Chapter 2 in the Normal state could be ".balance > $0.00".

10.3   Transition

UML defines a transition as:

> *"... a directed relationship between a source vertex and a target vertex. It may be part of a compound transition, which takes the state machine from one state configuration to another, representing the complete response of the state machine to an occurrence of an event of a particular type."*

Simply, a transition specifies a valid progression in state. When an object is in a given state, process constraints won't always allow it to go directly to any other state. Normally there is a constrained progression from one state to another. A Silly Bank loan in the Applied state can go directly to the Approved state or to the Denied state, but cannot go directly to the Paid off state. An Approved loan can go directly to the Active state or the Cancelled state, but cannot go directly to the Denied state. Transitions define which progressions are allowed and, by implication, which are not.

A transition can be thought of as "if-then" process sequencing and timing:

- "If a loan is in the Applied state when the loan approval event happens, then that loan will change to the Approved state."
- "If a loan is in the Applied state when the loan denial event happens, then it will change to the Denied state."
- "If a loan is in the Approved state when the loan origination event happens, then it will change to the Active state."
- "If a loan is in the Active state when the payment missed event happens, then it will change to the Delinquent state."

10.3.1   Transition Notation

The UML notation for a transition is a solid arrow from the preceding state to the succeeding state. Transitions happen on events, the name of the event that causes that transition is written on the diagram near where the transition arrow leaves the preceding state. Make it clear which transition is paired with which event. A partial state diagram for loans at Silly Bank is shown in Figure 10.4.

It is important to understand that:

- If an object is in the preceding state when the event for a transition happens, the object will immediately transition to the succeeding state. If a loan is in the Applied state and an Approved event happens, that loan immediately transitions to the Approved state

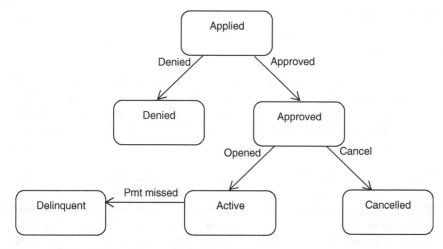

Figure 10.4 Partial state diagram for Silly Bank loans.

- If an object is in a state and there is no transition for the event that just happened, that event is ignored and disappears forever.[4] If a loan is in the Applied state and a Cancel event happens, the Cancel event is ignored and forgotten— it is as if that Cancel event never happened. Events are *not* implicitly remembered for later.

There normally isn't a need for transition descriptions—that is, a transition dictionary—because transitions are either already self-explanatory or actions (below) make them sufficiently self-explanatory.

10.3.2 Model Normal Behavior First

A practical recommendation is to model normal, typical, expected behavior first. Answer the question "what can be expected to happen most of the time?" The normal behavior for loans is from state Applied to Approved to Active to Paid off. Once normal processing is understood, then start worrying about unusual behavior like denying and cancelling. Paying too much attention to unusual cases when the normal case isn't well understood only adds complexity. Temporarily abstracting away abnormal behavior—as all good abstraction does— simplifies the job by reducing unnecessary distractions.

---

4 This is usually, but not always, true and will be refined later in this chapter.

10.4 Initial State

When an object is created, that object must—by definition—be in exactly one state. But which state? Any state? Or are there constraints on which state a new object can be in? Can a Silly Bank loan be created in the Approved state? No. Can a loan be created in the Active state? Again no. Loans can only be created in the Applied state.

UML indicates an initial state by showing a transition from a solid dot. The initial state can be more properly thought of as a pseudo-transition into the initial state[5] and would almost certainly be a "constructor" if the (sub)domain is implemented in a typical object-oriented programming language. As shown in Figure 10.5, Applied is the initial state for a loan. Any new object of class Loan must always start in this state.

Normally there will be only one initial state (i.e., one transition from the solid circle into one state) although there are occasions where UML's choice pseudo-state (a diamond as found in traditional flowcharting)[6] can be used to show transitions into different initial states based on differing business-relevant conditions.

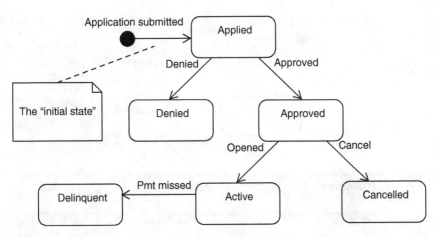

Figure 10.5 Silly Bank loan state diagram with initial state added.

---

5 See Appendix L for more detail on this.
6 See [OMG11b] or [Fowler03].

10.5   Self-Transition

The state diagram in Figure 10.5 is incomplete. The most obvious gap is, "What happens when a customer makes a payment on a loan?" Payments will only be relevant in the Active and Delinquent states. Start by considering a loan in the Active state; does receiving a payment change the state of the loan to something else? Sometimes yes: when the amount of the payment is enough to pay off the loan. But usually, no: customers rarely pay enough in one payment to fully pay off their loan, so the loan is still Active. Clearly the Payment received event can't be ignored. We will talk about computation in the section on Actions, later. For now, just show the event being recognized in the state. Figure 10.6 shows the still-incomplete state diagram for Silly Bank loans, including self-transitions for Payment received (abbreviated "Pmt Rcvd" in the diagram to conserve space).

Adding those transitions to the Loan state model now violates a necessary property: determinism. The state model in Figure 10.6 is non-deterministic. Any transition out of a given state must be associated with a unique event. There are two violations of determinism in Figure 10.6, both on event Payment Received. One violation is in the Active state and the other is in the Delinquent state. In both states, there's more than one transition out of that state on that event. A guard, next, resolves this kind of non-determinism.

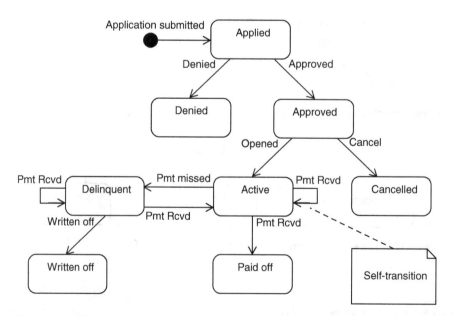

Figure 10.6 Silly Bank loan state diagram with self-transitions added.

10.6   Guard

A transition can be thought of as "if-then" sequencing and timing:

- "If a loan is in the Applied state when the loan approval event happens, then that loan will change to the Approved state."
- "If a loan is in the Approved state when the loan origination event happens, then it will change to the Active state."
- "If a loan is in the Active state when the payment missed event happens, then it will change to the Delinquent state."

A guard is like adding an "and" clause to that if-then:

- "If a loan is in the Active state when the payment received event happens *and the payment amount is not enough to pay off the loan*, then it will stay in the Active state."
- "If a loan is in the Active state when the payment received event happens *and the payment amount is enough to pay off the loan*, then it will transition to the Paid off state."

Guards are strictly Boolean expressions and cannot have side effects.

The UML notation for a guard is to append a Boolean expression (or reference an external policy) in square brackets ("[", "]"), after the event name. A guarded transition will only happen when the object is in the preceding state, the event happens, *and* the guard evaluates to true. If the object is in the preceding state, the event happens, but the guard evaluates to false, then that transition will not happen. Guards for the Payment received event for class loan are shown in Figure 10.7.

In keeping with the requirement for determinism, simply adding guards might not be enough. For a given state, guards on all transitions out of that state on the same event must be mutually exclusive. Two guard expressions for the same event out of the same state can never evaluate to true at the same time. Figure 10.8 illustrates a violation of the mutual exclusion rule.

When V is less than or equal to 100, the X to Z transition will happen on event A. When V is greater than or equal to 150, the X to Y transition will happen on A. When V in the range of 101–149, both guard conditions evaluate to true so either transition could conceivably be taken. Which one? That is non-deterministic, so the process—as modeled—isn't valid.

If the goal is to model a stochastic process, say, for discrete event simulation, model non-deterministic behavior as shown in Figure 10.9.

When event A happens, random variable V can be generated according to some defined probability density function. If the randomly generated V is in one defined range, Range1 in Figure 10.9, then the X to Y transition is taken; otherwise the X to Z transition is taken.

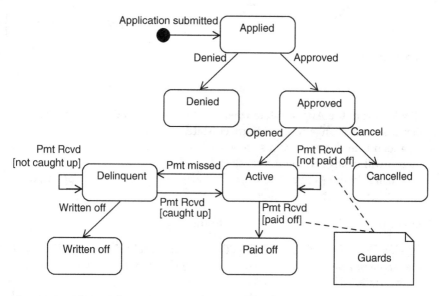

Figure 10.7 Silly Bank loan state diagram with guards added to restore determinism.

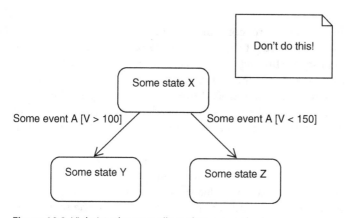

Figure 10.8 Violating the mutually exclusive guard rule.

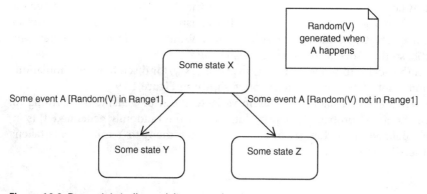

Figure 10.9 Deterministically modeling a stochastic process.

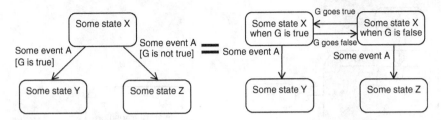

Figure 10.10 Underlying formalism for guards.

From the perspective of underlying formalisms, guards are essentially hidden states. Figure 10.10 illustrates the equivalence.

10.7 Sequential Substates

Sequential substate notation can be useful when there are common transitions to a same state on the same event from several different preceding states. Consider the state diagram on the left of Figure 10.11. Event 4 causes a common transition to state E from B, C, and D. The notation on the right of Figure 10.11 says the same thing: it doesn't matter if the object is in state B, C, or D, event 4 will cause it to go to state E. Any time the object is in superstate BCD, event 4 causes the transition to state E.

10.7.1 History Transition

UML also includes a "history transition" as illustrated in Figure 10.12.

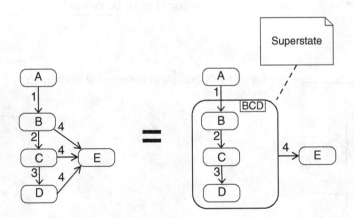

Figure 10.11 Underlying formalism for sequential substates.

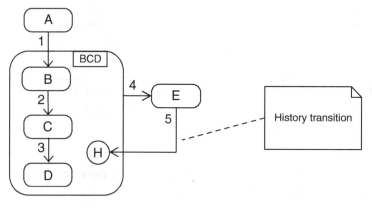

Figure 10.12 History transition on substates.

The intent of the history transition is "it doesn't matter if you went to state E from B, C, or D, but if you are in state E when event 5 happens then you return to the substate that you came from." If the object came into state E from state B on event 4, then it returns to state B on event 5 from state E.

There isn't anything wrong with using the history transition as shown in Figure 10.12; the problem is illustrated in Figure 10.13.

By introducing the transition from A to E on event 6, it is possible to be in state E without any history with respect to BCD. If the object is in state E because of the A to E transition on event 6, what should happen if event 5 occurs now? There is no history state to return to; behavior is undefined. Undefined behavior means ambiguity and ambiguity leads to the designer/developer making a guess that could be wrong: a defect. Particularly in safety-critical systems, ambiguity in requirements can have dangerous consequences and must be avoided.

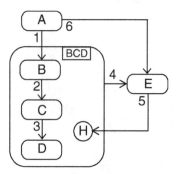

Figure 10.13 Example of the potential problem with history transitions.

10.8 Final State

Similar to initial states, processes may restrict the states that objects can be in before they can be deleted. Even Silly Bank shouldn't be silly enough to allow someone to originate a loan, take the money, and then delete the loan. Loans need to be in certain states before they can be deleted. Final pseudo-transitions would likely be mapped onto a "destructor" if the (sub)domain were implemented in object-oriented programming languages like C++ that don't have automatic garbage collection. The notation for a final state is a transition into a "bullseye" as shown in Figure 10.14. Any state in a state model can be a final state; it depends only on the domain being modeled.

A final transition may or may not have an event. According to the UML specification, when a final transition does not have an event, it means that object deletion happens when any processing (discussed in Actions, below) in that final state completes.

10.9 State–Event–Transition Completeness

Before considering state–event–transition modeling finished for a class, a very important check is to consider every possible combination of state and event. Subtle but important transitions might have been missed, and this exercise

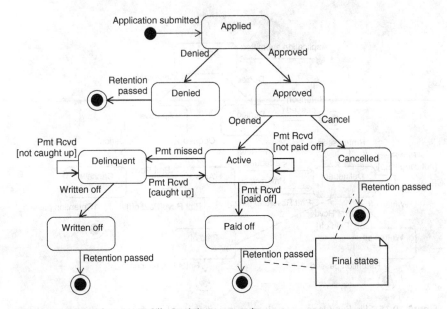

Figure 10.14 Final states in Silly Bank loan example.

helps expose them. In considering all possible state–event combinations for Silly Bank loans, the case of missing another payment even though the loan is already delinquent would be surfaced.

Other important transitions might also be surfaced by considering parameters on events:

- A loan is active but the amount of payment received is insufficient—that loan still needs to become delinquent.
- A loan is delinquent and the amount of payment is sufficient to pay the loan off (e.g., the customer refinanced with another loan)—that loan is now paid off.

This completeness step helps avoid the "Dreaded Phone Call Syndrome" where, for example, the irate user yells, "Your stupid system just let a customer miss a second payment without any penalty" or "Your stupid system just let a customer make a less than complete payment but still let the loan go from Delinquent to Active. They are still behind on their payments, the loan is still delinquent!" The developer's response, understandably, might be "But you never told us…" to which the stakeholder can easily reply, "You never asked …." This completeness check forces important questions to be asked and answered.

A revised state diagram for Silly Bank loans is shown in Figure 10.15.

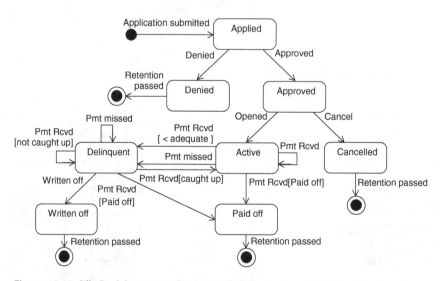

Figure 10.15 Silly Bank loan state diagram including newly surfaced transitions.

10.10 Correlating States and Attributes

A potential error in semantic modeling is associating a state model with the wrong class. There must be some kind of correlation between states in the state model and subranges of attribute values in the class model. If correlation is not there, either the state model belongs to a different class, or the class model does not have sufficient attributes.

In many cases the correlation is obvious: the set of states in the state model exactly matches the enumerated range specification of an attribute (usually) named .state or .status. Silly Bank's Loan class, above, has a .status attribute whose range specification would almost certainly be an enumeration of the states in the state model in Figure 10.15. The state model and the attributes of Loan are obviously correlated. The state model for Book order in Order fulfillment is also correlated to Book order.status this same way.

10.10.1 State Vector

In more complex cases, the correlation won't be to a single attribute. Instead, correlation will involve multiple attributes. A "state vector" makes the correlation between a state model and a set of attributes explicit and can be shown using a decision table. Table 10.1 shows an example of a state vector for a bank that has three states in the state model for Account: Closed, Opened, and Overdrawn.

Most attributes will be irrelevant for the state vector, .account Id, .date opened, and .overdraft limit do not have any influence on account state. Irrelevant attributes do not appear as columns in the state vector.

You don't need to declare explicit correlations for each state model; the correlation will be obvious in most cases. Just be sure that a correlation exists: the state model is truly describing behavior of objects in that class. That correlation can be made explicit using a state vector when it's not obvious.

Table 10.1 An example state vector correlating attribute values to states.

.status	.balance	State
Closed	Don't care	Closed
Opened	>= $0.00	Opened
Opened	<$0.00	Overdrawn

10.11   Action

The state model for a class should now be complete in terms of sequencing and timing: states, events, and transitions. But the model is almost certainly missing transformation: work to be done and computation. This is specified using actions.

Generally, actions will do some combination of:

- Compute a result from given input parameters.
- Modify (write) one or more attribute values of the containing object.
- Signal events for other existing objects to react to.
- Signal events to create new objects.
- Signal events to create new links between objects.
- Signal events to delete existing links between objects.
- Signal events to delete existing objects.
- …

There are two kinds of action: transition action and state action.

10.12   Transition Action

Transition actions are the most common. As the name implies, a transition action is work done on a state model transition. The UML notation for a transition action is to append a transition's event (and guard, if present) with a slash ("/") followed by the name of one or more actions. The complete state diagram for loans at Silly Bank, including transition actions, is shown in Figure 10.16.

10.12.1   Entry/ and Exit/ Transition Actions

Two special kinds of transition actions are "entry/" and "exit/" actions. Both involve dividing a state into two compartments. The state name goes in the top compartment; entry/ and exit/ actions (and possibly more, below) are put in the bottom compartment. Figure 10.17 shows an example of entry/ and exit/ actions in State2.

An entry/ action means "it does not matter which transition was taken to enter this state, the entry/ action(s) must happen before this state is considered entered." If an object were in State1 when eventA occurred, it would transition to State2 carrying out both action1 and action2 along the way. If the object were in State3 when eventC occurred, it would transition into State2 carrying out both action6 and action2 along the way. Entry/ actions are shorthand for having those actions appear on every transition into that state.

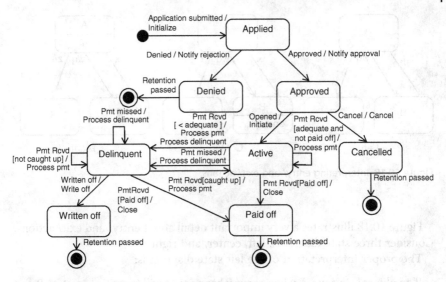

Figure 10.16 The complete state diagram for Silly bank loans.

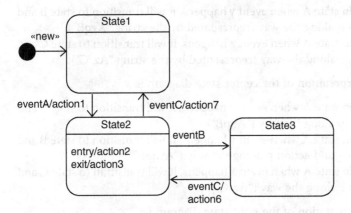

Figure 10.17 Entry/ and exit/ actions.

Exit/ actions are the opposite of entry/ actions and mean "it doesn't matter which transition is taken out of this state, this action must be done along the way." If an object is in State2 and event7 happens, the object will transition to State1 and carry out both action3 and action7 along the way. If an object is in State2 when eventB happens, it will transition into State3 and carry out action3 along the way. Exit/ actions are shorthand for having those actions appear on every transition out of that state.

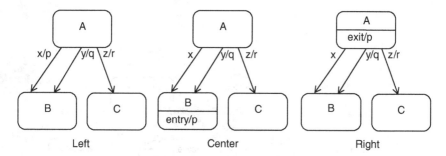

Figure 10.18 Interpreting entry/ and exit/ actions.

Figure 10.18 illustrates a very important detail about entry/ and exit/ actions. Consider three state diagrams: left, center, and right.

The proper interpretation of the left state diagram is:

- If an object is in state A when event x happens, it will transition to state B and execute action p along the way (this can be represented by the text string "AxpB").
- If an object is in state A when event y happens, it will transition to state B and execute action q along the way (represented by the string "AyqB").
- If an object is in state A when event z happens, it will transition to state C and execute action r along the way (represented by the string "AzrC").

The proper interpretation of the center state diagram is:

- If an object is in state A when event x happens, it will transition to state B and execute action p along the way ("AxpB").
- If an object is in state A when event y happens, it will transition to state B and execute action q and action p along the way ("AyqpB").
- If an object is in state A when event z happens, it will transition to state C and execute action r along the way ("AzrC").

The proper interpretation of the right state diagram is:

- If an object is in state A when event x happens, it will transition to state B and execute action p along the way ("AxpB").
- If an object is in state A when event y happens, it will transition to state B and execute action p and action q along the way ("AypqB").
- If an object is in state A when event z happens, it will transition to state C and execute action p and action r along the way ("AzprC").

Notice that the interpretation of each diagram is different. This demonstrates why you need to be careful with entry/ and exit/ actions. Undisciplined use could lead to unexpected behavior. It is certainly possible to build an incorrect

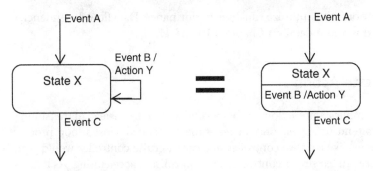

Figure 10.19 Eventname/ actions are equivalent to actions on self-transitions

semantic model—one that doesn't properly represent the stakeholder's processes; improper use of entry/ and exit/ actions is one easy way to do it.

10.12.2 Eventname/ Transition Actions

Another special kind of transition action is an "eventname/" action. This is simply a shorthand notation for a self-transition (above) and involves putting the event name, a slash, and associated action(s) into the bottom compartment of a state as shown in the right side Figure 10.19.

10.12.3 Transitions Take Essentially Zero Time

Transitions, and any transition actions, are interpreted as taking essentially zero time. Remember the perfect technology concept: the semantic model is assumed to be executing on an infinitely fast processor, so even arbitrarily complex actions take zero time to complete. If you are uncomfortable assuming zero time, then at least consider that no arguments can be made in a semantic model about action execution on one transition taking more or less time than action execution on any other transition. Always consider transitions and action execution as taking so little time that it is irrelevant in interpreting that model.

10.12.4 Order of Execution of Transition Actions

This discussion of transition actions may have implied there is an order of execution to actions: exit/ actions before transition actions and transition actions before entry/ actions. In fact, no order can or should be implied. Except where required by data flow dependencies (e.g., an output from one action is a necessary input to another), actions are assumed to execute in parallel. This means— data flow dependencies aside—the designer/developer is free to sequence actions in any order to optimize run-time performance. Data flow dependencies are discussed in more detail in Chapters 16 and 17.

10.13 State Action

As the name implies, state actions are associated with states instead of transitions. State actions tend to appear only in real-time/embedded, closed-loop process control systems, like a cruise controller in a car. A cruise controller would typically have three states: driver control, cruise control, and accelerating. As long as the car is in the cruise control state, a state action is continuously comparing actual speed to target speed (established when the controller last entered the cruise control state on a cruise event) and adjusting engine throttle accordingly.

The notation for a state action is to put the action name after "do/" in the bottom compartment of a state. Figure 10.20 shows the state diagram for a simple car cruise controller with do/ actions in both the Cruise control and Accelerating states.

State actions are continuous: as long as the object is in that state, the action is executing. A state action continues to execute until a new state is entered that does not have that action. Whenever the cruise controller is in the Cruise control or Accelerating states, the maintainSpeed action is continuously comparing actual speed to target speed and adjusting the throttle. When the cruise controller is in the Accelerating state, a separate transition action increases the target speed by some amount every second.

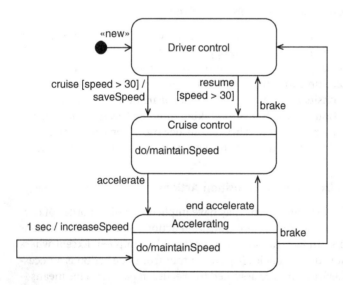

Figure 10.20 State actions in the state diagram for an automobile cruise controller.

10.14   Action Reuse

As shown in Figures 10.16 and 10.20, the same action can appear more than once in a state model. Figure 10.16 shows transition action Process pmt on four different transitions. State action maintainSpeed is reused in both Cruise control and Accelerating states of Figure 10.20. There is no limit on the number of times any one action can appear in a state model.

10.15   Transition Action and State Action Equivalence

Technically, when all actions are on transitions the state model is in "Mealy" form.[7] When all actions are on states, the model is in "Moore" form.[8] Some modeling approaches restrict state models to only Mealy, or only Moore, form. Mellor and Balcer, for example, only allow Moore form state models. Specifically, according to Mellor and Balcer, all actions must be entry/ actions. The two forms are provably equivalent: a Mealy form model can be mechanically transformed into equivalent Moore form and vice versa. Simply, continuous processing in a state can be mimicked by a self-transition with a sufficiently short timed event as shown in Figure 10.21.

Transition processing can be mimicked by having a state action that transitions on completion of one cycle of the action, as shown in Figure 10.22.

Given that both are provably equivalent, you are free to use either or both in the same state model.

10.16   Action Specifications

Just naming an action is not sufficient; an action must have a precise specification. UML does not prescribe a language for action specification; all of the following have been used:

- Requires-guarantees (contract)
- Model
- UML Action Semantics
- Pseudo-code or code fragment

Each of these is discussed below.

---

7 Named after George Mealy from his paper [Mealy55].
8 Named after Edward Moore from his paper [Moore56].

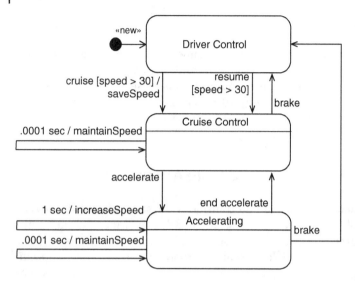

Figure 10.21 State actions in transition action form (Moore form to Mealy form).

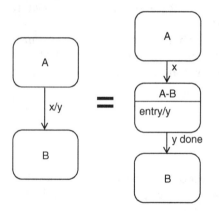

Figure 10.22 A transition action in state action form (Mealy form to Moore form).

To avoid premature design and optimization, non-algorithmic action specifications are preferred. Specifying an action in any algorithmic form virtually guarantees the designer/developer will use exactly that algorithm—which may not be optimal given nonfunctional requirements and automation technology. Pseudo-code and code fragments are clearly algorithmic. UML Action Semantics are also algorithmic, but only slightly so. Models, depending on form, might or might not be algorithmic. A decision table is non-algorithmic; a decision tree is. The only form of action specification guaranteed to be non-algorithmic is requires-guarantees (contract) form. Part III is based on actions being specified in requires-guarantees form. Consider requires-guarantees action specifications as mandatory; any of the other forms might be used as a supplement. Further discussion on this topic can be found in Chapter 20 in the section on CIMs, PIMS, and PSMs.

10.17 Specifying Actions as Requires-Guarantees (Contracts)

To avoid premature design and optimization, actions must be specified in requires-guarantees form (i.e., design by contract). An action may require certain constraints on input parameters and guarantee certain results as long as those initial constraints were met. A simple example would be the action that initializes a Silly Savings Account (transition (1) in Figure 2.9). That action has two input parameters: an opening balance and an overdraft limit. A contract for that action could be:

Requires

$0.00 <= Opening balance <= $100,000.00
$0.00 <= Maximum overdraft <= $100,000.00

Guarantees

.balance == Opening balance
.overdraft limit == Maximum overdraft

Requires conditions for input parameters can often be derived from range specifications on attributes (.balance and .overdraft limit in this example). To set the .balance and .overdraft limit properly, the input parameters for the action must be consistent with those same range specifications.

Requires-guarantees action specifications are perfectly aligned with Fudd's First Law of Creativity: the designer/developer can consider many candidate algorithms that all satisfy the contract and choose the most cost-effective one.

When action guarantees clauses (postconditions) involve events being signaled, the preferred language is:

"eventname has been signaled for object(s) via association"

The language "has been signaled *for*" instead of "has been signaled *to*" is preferred because "to" implies control flow: the action pushes the event to the destination object. Control flow is a design issue and is discussed in Chapters 15 and 16. The semantic model must only specify flow of information and "signaled *for*" says only that.

The specification of action Process delinquent in Figure 10.16 could be:

Requires
    None
Guarantees
    Payment missed has been signaled for the Customer via Repays
    Reduce credit rating (Customer) has been signaled for all Credit bureaus

10.17.1 Action Specifications in Light of Associations

Remember that associations exist to support processing of the form "given this object of class X, which object(s) of class Y is it connected to?" For example, "Given this Loan, which Customer is responsible for repaying it?" The action that processes a delinquent payment needs to notify the responsible customer and does so via the "repays" association. With event signaling, any of the following are possible:

- The event needs to be signaled for exactly one target object via an association with multiplicity that is either 1..1 or 0..1 (e.g., "Payment missed has been signaled for the Customer via Repays" where a loan is repaid by exactly one customer).
- The event needs to be signaled for all linked objects via an association with a multiplicity that is either 0..* or 1..* (e.g., "eventname has been signaled for all classname via associationname").
- The event needs to be signaled for a subset of linked objects via an association with a multiplicity that is either 0..* or 1..*. In this case, also specify selection criteria (e.g., "eventname has been signaled for all classname via associationname where selectioncriteria").
- The event needs to be signaled for all objects of an unassociated class (e.g., "Reduce credit rating (customer) has been signaled for all credit bureaus").
- The event needs to be signaled for a subset of objects of an unassociated class; again specify selection criteria (e.g., "eventname has been signaled for all classname where selectioncriteria").
- The event needs to be signaled for one (or a subset) of objects of an unassociated class, but it does not matter which object(s) it is (e.g., "eventname has been signaled for any n randomly selected TargetClass"). Note that this makes behavior specified in the model non-deterministic and should be avoided if fully deterministic behavior is important, for example, a safety-critical system.

Each relevant guarantees condition must use one of these forms.

Listing guarantees conditions in a particular sequence might also be thought of as implying an order of execution, but again this is not true. Data flow dependencies aside; guarantees conditions can be implemented in any order in design and code.

Many examples of requires-guarantees action specifications can be found in Appendices D, F, H, and J.

10.18   Specifying Actions with Models

Actions can be supplemented with specifications in the form of a model: a flow-chart, an activity diagram, a data flow diagram, a decision tree, a decision table, a mathematical formula, a control law[9], etc. The danger is that some models, like flowcharts and activity diagrams, are algorithmic and risk of biasing the designer/developer into using exactly that algorithm. Decision tables and mathematical formulas tend to be non-algorithmic and are preferred over algorithmic models.

10.19   Specifying Actions with UML Action Semantics

UML Action Semantics were first introduced in UML 1.4 and are intended to allow[10]:

- Executable (interpretable) semantic models
- Code generation from semantic models
- Formal proofs of correctness of semantic models

Some organizations want models to be fully executable.[11] Pure requires-guarantees action specifications cannot be mechanically translated into fully executable code. To make an action specification translatable, some amount of algorithmic detail is often necessary. UML's Action Semantics define an executable language that is minimally algorithmic. UML Action Semantics and action languages are described in more detail in Chapter 20.

10.20   Specifying Actions with Pseudo-code or Code Fragments

The least preferred way to specify actions is using pseudo-code or actual code fragments. Again, the risk is premature design and optimization. The pseudo-code

---

9 Control laws are frequently used in real-time embedded, closed-loop process control systems. See, for example, http://www.ni.com/white-paper/8156/en/.

10 See [Mellor98].

11 See, for example, Mellor and Balcer's "Executable UML" [Mellor02].

or code fragment will be translated or copied directly into the design and code, regardless of whether it is optimal or not.

10.21 Cohesion and Coupling Guidelines for Actions

Cohesion and coupling are pervasive properties that apply across an entire semantic model.[12] An action could have high cohesion and loose coupling or low cohesion and tight coupling. Characteristics of highly cohesive and loosely coupled actions are:

- Can read all attributes of the object the action is contained in.
- Can read all attributes of any immediately associated (i.e., linked) object.
- Can read all attributes of any object it has been given a reference as an input parameter.
- Can directly write attributes *only* of the object the action is contained in.
- Must signal an event for any immediately associated or referenced object if this action wants that object to change any of its attribute values—the other object will respond according to its current state. This applies to objects in the same class: being in the same class as the other object does not give any special privileges.
- Must represent a pure, stateless function—any persistent memory must be outside the action: as attribute values, other objects, or links with other objects.
- Data being manipulated is as close as possible to the action doing the manipulation, ideally within the same object.

10.22 Actions and Enforcing Association Multiplicities

Association multiplicities in a class model are not self-enforcing: simply stating a multiplicity constraint on an association doesn't automatically mean that constraint could never be violated. Actions must be specified in a way that maintains association multiplicity. Any action that creates or deletes any object or link must do so in a way that does not violate multiplicity constraints in the class model: at least outside the boundary of a sea level use case, a transaction. It may not be possible to specify actions so that multiplicities are never violated, but any such violation must be resolve by the end of the sea level transaction

---

12 And across design and code as well. By doing it well in the semantic model, it vastly increases the likelihood that it will also be done well in design and code.

Figure 10.23 A modified fragment of Order fulfillment's class diagram.

containing that action. Take, for example, the slightly modified fragment from Order fulfillment in Figure 10.23.

If an object of class Medium is created, part of the creation action must link it to a corresponding Title because the policies require there be exactly one Title for each Medium. That Title must either already exist or be created at the same time—possibly requiring creation of a new Publisher. If an object of class Medium is deleted, there won't be any problem in the association with Title unless that Medium was the only one for that Title. If so:

- That Title must also be deleted, or
- A new Medium must be created and linked to that Title, or
- That Title needs to be linked to some other Medium.

The last option doesn't make sense for Order fulfillment, but could make sense in some other domain with similar structure. Imagine a school where each Student must have an Advisor and each Advisor must advise at least one Student. Deleting an advisor means those students need to be re-linked to some other advisor. Deleting the last student from an advisor would require either deleting that advisor or reassigning other students from other advisors to this one.

If an object of class Title is created, there must be at least one corresponding Medium created along with it, and the link established. If a Title is deleted, then either linked objects of class Medium must also be deleted, or the linked Medium(s) must be re-linked to some other Title.

Action specifications must clearly specify behavior consistent with all multiplicity constraints.

10.23 Action Parameters

Actions in a semantic model often either (or both) require input or produce output. When a semantic model will be designed and coded by a human, precise structure of parameters does not need to be formally specified. In fact, parameters themselves may not even need to be specified. Designers can usually figure out what's needed without much difficulty. If, on the other hand, code will be generated using a model compiler (Chapter 20), then it may become important to formally specify parameters and their structures for the translator. The nature of formal parameter specification can depend on the particular model compiler being used; refer to its documentation for guidance. This discussion is a semiformal treatment of action parameters.

In some cases, a specific action does not require, or produce, parameters. An example is .mark as packed on class Book order. In this case, including parentheses on the action name should be optional. Specifically, both

Book order.mark as packed

and

Book order.mark as packed()

should be equally acceptable.

When input parameters are required, they can be specified inside of parentheses. Output parameters can be specified after a colon (":") following the closing parenthesis, as in:

Example class.example action(inputs): outputs

Generally speaking, action parameters will either be:

- *Single value*—Usually something consistent with the range of an attribute value (e.g., data to or from an attribute)
- *Object reference*—Something that points at a specific object of some class (e.g., something needs to be done to or with the referenced object)
- *Record-like structures*—A structure consisting of two or more dissimilar but related things
- *Collections*—A number of occurrences of the same kind of thing

Figure 10.24 shows a class diagram for a simplified parameter description language. Figure L.5 has a more complete diagram; this discussion simply illustrates the concept.

Primitive parameter types include all simple scalar values, as in:

- Numeric values (e.g., the number of copies of a Title being ordered, or the price of something)
- Symbols from an enumeration (e.g., Employee type as "hourly" vs. "salaried")
- A "blob" per the discussion on exceptions to strict DK/NF normalization in Chapter 8 (e.g., a postal address)

The notation for primitive types could be a simple text string. The name should suggest the role or meaning of that parameter. The initialize action on the initial transition of Publisher requires three input parameters: a publisher name, email address, and postal address. These are primitive parameter types. An example notation could be:

initialize (publisher name, email address, postal address)

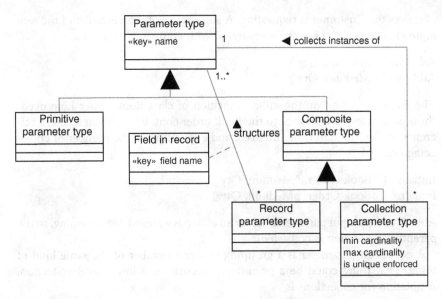

Figure 10.24 A class diagram for a simplified parameter specification language.

Another example could be a Customer seeing the status of their Book order. It's a single value from the enumerated set of the state model states:

Book order.status(): status

Primitive parameter types also include references to objects. For example, action drop line on class Book order needs a reference to the Book order line to be dropped. A notation for an object reference is to precede the referenced class name with either "^" (up arrow/caret) or "p" to signify we are talking about some kind of object reference. The example could be action Drop line on class Book order:

Book order. drop line (^Book order line)
Book order.drop line (pBook order line)

Parameters can be combined into a record-like structure.[13] A record parameter type is a composite (a grouping) of dissimilar things that belong together. The things in a record can be primitives, collections, or further sub-records. A suggested notation for records is to list the things, separated by commas, between parentheses, as in (thing1, thing2, thing3, etc.).The .add line action on Book order needs a reference to the Medium to be added and the number

---

13 See, for example, http://wiki.freepascal.org/Record.

of copies the Customer is requesting. A suggested notation is to list of the separate elements of the structure separated with comma ",":

Add line (^Medium, Qty)
Add line (pMedium, Qty)

The .initialize action on the initial transition of class Book Order Line needs three parameters: a reference to the Book order containing this new line, a reference to the Medium being ordered, and a quantity for the number of copies being ordered:

Initialize (^Book Order, ^Medium, Qty)
Initialize (pBook Order, pMedium, Qty)

Abstractly, the input parameter list for an action is a record-like grouping, so the parenthesis notation is consistent.

A collection parameter is a grouping of some number of the same kind of thing. That thing could be a primitive, a record, or a lower-level collection. A notation for collections is

min[thing-in-list]max

where

- min refers to the smallest number of elements in the grouping, typically zero or one
- thing-in-list specifies either directly or indirectly (e.g., by name or by direct specification) the kind of thing in the collection
- max refers to the largest number of elements that can be grouped according to policy/process

As examples,

0[thing]* (i.e., from zero to many occurrences of "thing"—whatever "thing" is)
5[pqr]7 (i.e., from 5 to 7 occurrences of "pqr"—whatever that is)

When a Warehouse worker is seeing the list of packable orders,

Book order.packable orders?: 0[^Book order where Book order.isPackable is true]*

When the customer sees the catalog so they can decide to create or add to a Book order,

Title.catalog? (selection criteria):
0[title, author, subject, copyright date, 1[Medium type, ISBN, selling price]*]*

When the customer sees the contents of a Book order,

Book order:

(date opened, status, shipping address, 1[title, author, subject, quantity, price per copy]*)

A complex example could be Publisher.process order placement():

Process order placement (Order Id, 1[(ISBN, Qty)]*)

where Order id is the scalar value of the order's identifier. This is followed by a collection of at least one, but possibly many composites. Each composite contains one ISBN scalar value and one Qty scalar value.

Many more examples from the WebBooks 2.0 case study can be found in the semantic models in Appendices D, F, H, and J.

10.24 Modeling "in Any Order" Events

Consider a process that requires two events to proceed; but those events could happen in either order. A vending machine will not dispense a product until both a product has been selected and enough money has been inserted. Product selection and payment can happen in either order:

- The buyer can select a product and then put in sufficient money.
- The buyer can put in sufficient money and then select a product.

Both events must happen before a product can be dispensed, but the buyer should not be required to do them in one particular order. A brute-force way to address this in a state model is shown in Figure 10.25.

This solution is not scalable. What if a process involves three events in any order? The brute-force approach for three events, A, B, and C, is shown in Figure 10.26.

Six states and 12 transitions are needed to model just the sequence-free event handling. Instead, using self-transitions and guards, a cleaner and more scalable model can be built. Figure 10.27 shows the approach for a set of four events in any order.

10.25 Error Handling in State Models

Some content in state models represents normal, expected, desirable behavior: approving loan applications, originating approved loans, paying off active loans, etc. Some content may represent failures of various sorts: missing a payment or

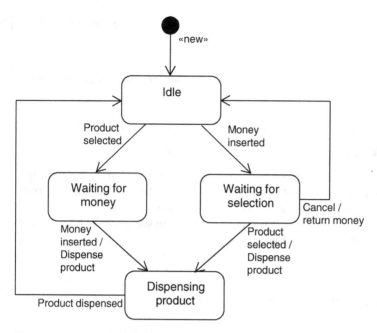

Figure 10.25 A brute-force approach to in-any-order for two events.

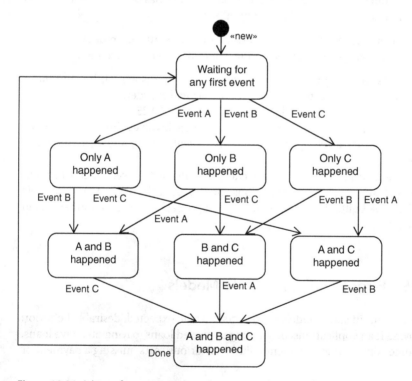

Figure 10.26 A brute-force approach to three events in any order.

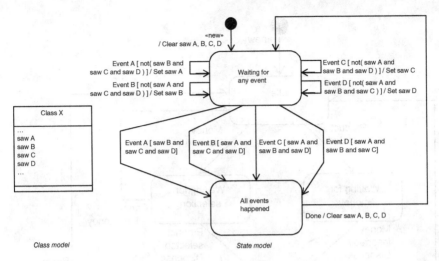

Figure 10.27 A more elegant approach to in-any-order for (in this example) four events.

cancelling an approved loan. The first step in dealing with failures in state models is to distinguish between two different kinds:

- *Business failure*—Failure (undesirable conditions) relevant to the business processes being automated
- *Mechanism failure*—Failure in one or more mechanisms being used in automating those business processes

Consider the vending machine model in Figure 10.25. Suppose the product being dispensed got jammed. The Product dispensed event would never happen and the state model would be stuck in the Dispensing product state. A more robust state model would have a timed transition out of the Dispensing product state after waiting, say, 20 seconds. This is shown in Figure 10.28.

If the Product dispensed event does not happen within 20 seconds of state entry, the vending machine transitions to the Jammed state and waits for a maintenance technician to clear the jam and reset the machine. Business failure is specified using states, events, transitions, and, possibly, actions: the same language used to specify normal behavior. The semantic model—or, more precisely, semantic modeling language—does not distinguish between desirable and undesirable behaviors. All behaviors are modeled using the same vocabulary: use cases, classes, associations, states, events, etc. What is desirable versus not is a value judgment imposed by stakeholders. If you want to distinguish desirable from undesirable behavior, consider that UML is colorblind. You can paint semantic model content different colors; UML ignores those colors. You could color desirable model content black and undesirable content in red. Color communicates desirability to the reader, but the model itself doesn't care.

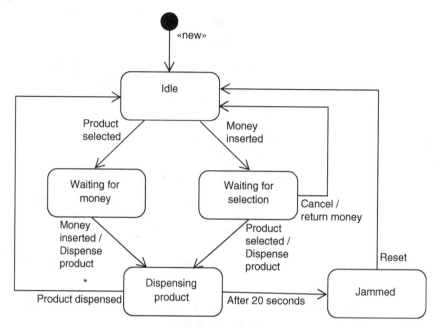

Figure 10.28 Handling business failure in a state model.

To illustrate mechanism failure, assume the vending machine software communicates via a particular protocol with a sensor that detects dispensing. Assume there has been some failure in that protocol, maybe the connection was dropped, or there was a synchronization error. Maybe the product was dispensed and the sensor was unable to register it with the vending machine software. This is not a failure in the business of the vending machine; it is a failure in the automation technology. This kind of failure should not appear in the semantic model.[14] This kind of failure needs to be handled in the design and code and should be invisible in the semantic model.

The key to distinguishing business failure from mechanism failure is perfect technology. If we had a perfect computer, would the business still need to deal with a jam in the vending machine? Yes, because jams happen in the real world where vending machines live: gravity, friction, inertia, and so on cause jams to happen. The Vulcan Mind Meld mindset means the semantic model can know whether or not the product was dispensed. Failure in an automation

---

14 More precisely, it should not appear in the semantic model of the vending machine domain. If the protocol is complex enough that it warrants being its own domain, the error would be modeled there.

mechanism—in this case a communication protocol—is not relevant to the business of the (sub)domain; it is only relevant to design and code.

Error handling has economic implications in a semantic model. The decision to include specific error handling or not should be based on technical and economic considerations. Chapter 25 explains how to make that an engineering decision.

10.26   Dynamic Classification and State Models

Remember that generalization (inheritance in semantic models, Chapter 8) can be either static or dynamic. Static classification means objects are created in one subclass and never change. The state model defined for the superclass applies (is inherited) to all subclasses equally. In dynamic classification, objects can change from one subclass to another. In this case, there will necessarily be a correlation between states in the state model and subclasses. When an object is in some particular state, then it must also be in some particular subclass. Conversely, if an object is in some particular subclass, then it must also be in some particular (subset of) state. There are at least two ways to specify the state-to-subclass correlation.

One way is to define a complete state model for the superclass. Then, via a table or some other means, correlate states in the state model to subclasses. An example is shown in Figure 10.29 and Table 10.2 for the Part class in Figure 8.29.

Another way is to specify the state model as fragments for each subclass. There is no declared superclass state model, just fragment state models defined for each subclass. This approach is shown in Figure 10.30. Use judgment to decide which is most appropriate in your situation(s).

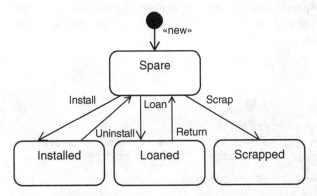

Figure 10.29 State model for the superclass and states mapped to subclasses.

Table 10.2 Correlating states to subclasses
for class Part in Figure 8.29.

Subclass	State(s)
Spare Part	Spare
Installed Part	Installed
Loaned Part	Loaned
Scrapped Part	Scrapped

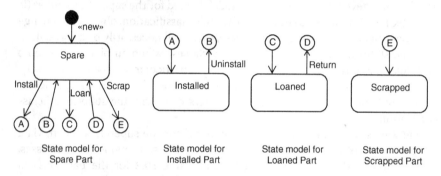

Figure 10.30 State diagram fragments for each subclass of Part in Figure 8.29.

10.27 Broker State Models

The previous chapter introduced the idea of broker classes (aka assigners, matchmakers, etc.). Figure 10.31 provides an example of the state diagram for a typical broker.

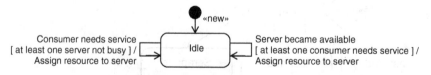

Figure 10.31 Example state diagram for a broker class.

The specification for action Assign resource to server could be:

Requires
  Nothing
  Guarantees
    Any one resource needing service has been selected
    Any one available server has been selected
    Serve (^selected resource) has been signaled for the selected server

Knowledge of concurrency design patterns can be useful in modeling brokers and other similar dynamic behaviors:

- Active object
- Monitor object
- Producer–consumer
- Leader–followers
- Reactor
- Scheduler
- ...

10.28 State–Event Matrix Notation

An advantage of state diagram notation is that it is graphic—"a picture is worth a thousand words." A disadvantage of state diagram notation is that it doesn't distinguish between events that can be safely ignored versus events that can't happen. The lack of a particular event-labeled transition out of any state—like a cancel event on a loan in the Active state in Figure 10.16—by default only means "should that event occur while the object is in that state, then nothing will change." But that might be not specific enough. The difference between safely ignorable and impossible can be crucial in safety- or mission-critical systems. Figure 10.32 shows a simplified state diagram for control of airplane landing gear in a commercial airliner.

There are two possibilities. One is that the event can happen, for example, a pilot may try to retract the gear when they are already fully retracted. The desired behavior is to just ignore it. The event happened; the acceptable response is to do nothing.

The other possibility is that due to physics or some other important constraint, that event is impossible in that state. Consider the Gear down state; If another Fully extended event were to happen, what does that mean about sensing landing gear position? Was one of the events spurious? Were both spurious? The safe thing to do is no longer assume that the landing gear is properly extended.

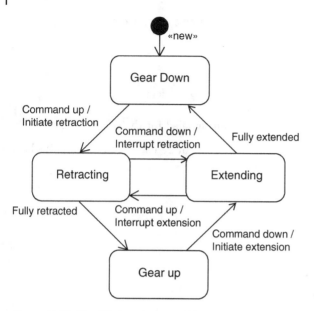

Figure 10.32 Simplified state diagram for airplane landing gear control.

Particularly in safety-critical systems like commercial airliners, the difference is significant. It's perfectly safe to ignore the first kind, but the impossible events should not be ignored in the design and code because they could be a sign of something serious, like sensor failure or fundamental implementation logic flaw. Such situations should be reported to *some*body—although it's a design decision as to whom to notify, when, and how.

A notation that distinguishes between "safe to ignore" and "not possible, and had better not happen" would be useful. There isn't any defined notation in UML, other than possibly using notes or constraints. You could explicitly show self-transitions with no actions on the "it is safe to ignore" events, but this could clutter a state diagram. Another possibility might be to add "eventName/impossible" or use stereotype "«impossible»" with the list of impossible events in the bottom compartment of a state.

Another option is to use an entirely different notation: the state–event matrix. The state–event matrix lists the states down the left column and the events across the top row of a matrix. Each cell in the matrix represents a unique state and event combination. Transition information is put into each cell. There are four possibilities:

- When it's a valid transition, write the name of the ending state (as in, if you are in the Gear up state when the Command down event happens, go to the

Extending state). If guards are relevant, those guard would need to be included in the cell.

- When that state–event combination is a final transition, write "final" in the cell.
- When that state–event combination is safe to ignore, write "ignore" in the cell.
- When that state–event is impossible, write "impossible" in the cell.

Every cell in the matrix needs to contain something, and blank cells are not allowed. Table 10.3 shows an example state–event matrix for the landing gear controller in Figure 10.32.

If the state model involves guards, the matrix needs a column for each relevant event + guard combination. Suppose a state model had event E and guards G1, G2, and G3 on various transitions for E. The state–event matrix would need at least three columns: E and G1, E and G2, and E and G3. If E is valid without any guards (i.e., sometimes E has a guard and sometimes it doesn't), then E with no guard would also need to be a column in the matrix.

Missing from the matrix are initial state, transition actions, and state action information. Those need to be specified somewhere. If a row for an explicit "does not exist" state is added, the initial state can be specified by entries in the "does not exist" row, on defined events, into appropriate new states. State actions can be written using ("do/") under the state name in the left column. Transition actions could be written in each body cell following a slash after a valid transition. Underlining the state name might be used to identify the initial state. Many options are possible; there are no standard notations. If you use a non-UML notation, be sure to define it in your profile.

By differentiating safely ignorable from impossible state–event combinations, the designer/developer of a safety-critical system can implement different behaviors for each. Situations that are safe to ignore can be designed and coded in a way that ignores them. Situations that are impossible can be designed and coded to notify some external entity that something otherwise impossible just happened (e.g., warn of a sensor failure, or throw an exception because an implementation logic error has been detected).

Table 10.3 The state model in Figure 10.32 in state–event matrix form.

	Command down	Fully extended	Fully retracted	Command up
Gear up	Extending	Impossible	Impossible	Ignore
Extending	Ignore	Gear down	Impossible	Retracting
Retracting	Extending	Impossible	Gear up	Ignore
Gear down	Ignore	Impossible	Impossible	Retracting

10.29 Modifying Sequence Diagrams to Show Object State

An interesting but nonstandard extension to UML sequence diagram notation overlays state names on object lifelines. Figure 10.33 shows an example.

This notation allows a reader to easily see the object's state both before and after the event, instead of constantly having to refer back to state diagrams.

10.30 Quality Criteria

In addition to the quality criteria in Chapter 3, Table 10.4 shows the quality criteria for state models.

Table 10.5 shows the quality criteria for consistency between state models and class models. If you have both state models and a class model, these additional criteria apply.

Table 10.6 shows the quality criteria for consistency between state models and interaction diagrams. If you have both state models and interaction diagrams, these additional criteria apply.

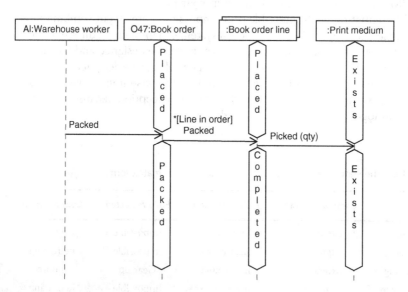

Figure 10.33 Sequence diagram with overlaid state information.

Table 10.4 Quality criteria for state models.

Item	Criterion
SM-1	Each state model has exactly one initial state that has been clearly and correctly specified
SM-2	Each object in each class must be in exactly one state at a time: an object can never be in more than or less than one state at a time
SM-3	Event(s) that apply to a given transition are clear and correct: no transitions without an event
SM-4	All, and only, valid transitions have been modeled: all events have been considered in all states
SM-5	If relevant (e.g., safety critical), safe to ignore versus impossible events are clearly and correctly specified for each state
SM-6	Each state model is deterministic: if more than one transition out of a state has the same event, their guards are mutually exclusive and span the decision space
SM-7	No history transitions appear
SM-8	Each action is clearly, precisely, and correctly specified
SM-9	If entry/ appears in any state, it correctly applies to all transitions into that state
SM-10	If eventname/ appears in any state, there are no transition out of that state with that same event
SM-11	If exit/ appears in any state, it correctly applies to all transitions out of that state
SM-12	The order of action execution is clearly and correctly specified if relevant; otherwise actions are executable in parallel
SM-13	Proper behavior does not depend on transition or action execution time
SM-14	Final states are clearly and correctly specified
SM-15	All actions are pure functions; no action depends on persistent local memory inside itself

Table 10.5 Quality criteria for consistency between state and class models.

Item	Criterion
SD-1	Each class in the class model has at most one state model
SD-2	The correlation between states and attribute values is clear and correct
SD-3	The correlation between actions and attributes is clear and correct
SD-4	Each action that creates and/or deletes also maintains multiplicities
SD-5	Few, if any, classes have just one state: "Exists"
SD-6	If dynamic classification is present, the correlation between state and subclass is clear and correct

Table 10.6 Quality criteria for consistency between state models and interaction diagrams.

Item	Criterion
SI-1	Events and data going into and out of a state model match events and data going into and out of objects on interaction diagrams

10.31   Economic Considerations

As stated in earlier chapters, a key part of engineering is considering the economics of technical decisions. Decisions about the scope and context of a domain to model, design, implement, and maintain clearly have economic implications.

Adding or removing scope in state models clearly has an impact on the time and effort needed to design, code, and maintain software. Evidence suggests that adding states isn't the primary driver of effort and cost, but adding transitions is. A state model with 5 states and 25 transitions is more work to design and implement than a state model with 10 states and 10 transitions. Unfortunately there isn't enough historical data to accurately estimate effort from just a count of transitions. Until such data exists, the best you can do is consider counts of transitions using estimation by analogy.

10.32   Summary

Use case diagrams (Chapter 7) describe process at the highest, most coarse-grained level. Interaction diagrams (sequence and collaboration, Chapter 9) describe processes at an intermediate level. State models describe process at the lowest, most fine-grained, detailed level. A state model defines precise behavior of objects in a class. Generally speaking, there will be one state model for each class that is not an actor. The state model is defined for the class but describes behavior of each object in that class.

At this fine-grained, most detailed level, two aspects of process are relevant:

- *Sequencing and timing*—Constraints on when things happen in processes. This is modeled using states, events, and transitions.
- *Transformation*—Work being done, computation in processes. This is modeled using actions.

The state model for a class is critical to design and code in Part III, so it's important to do this well. If a bad job is done on state models, later design and coding can be much more difficult, risky, and defect prone.

11

Partitioning Domains into Subdomains

Partitioning a system into domains helps manage complexity. But even after domain partitioning, more than 100 classes in one domain are still possible. Such large domains can be hard to understand and manage because of their size. As semantic models approach 40 classes, natural fracture lines tend to appear: regions of the model will specialize around subsets of the policies and processes. We can take advantage of those fracture lines to help manage complexity.

We can also partition a domain to enhance work parallelization and ease project management. Experience shows it's best to have no more than two people working on the same subject matter at the same time. Practically speaking, adding a third person to a subject matter rarely adds enough productivity to make it worthwhile. We are usually better off splitting work and doing more in parallel. So either from a complexity management or a work parallelization perspective or both, there is often value in partitioning domains. Domain and subdomain partitioning, particularly when consistent with the fundamental principles, can also help immensely in globally distributed projects that are common today. Work can be allocated to locations on a by-domain or by-subdomain basis, thus minimizing dependencies across locations. This chapter explains how to partition a domain into smaller, more manageable units: subdomains.

11.1 Subdomain Partitioning and the Fundamental Principles

When partitioning a domain into subdomains, be sure the partitioning is consistent with the fundamental principles:

- Each subdomain should abstract a single, specific topic.
- The design and implementation of a subdomain should encapsulate as much accidental complexity as possible.

How to Engineer Software: A Model-Based Approach, First Edition. Steve Tockey.
© 2019 the IEEE Computer Society, Inc. Published 2019 by John Wiley & Sons, Inc.

- Each subdomain should be highly cohesive about its single topic and loosely coupled with all other subdomains.
- Subdomain partitioning should be based on invariants and likely changes.
- Subdomain partitioning should not be influenced by premature design or optimization.

A simple but often effective guideline is:

"Partition to minimize communication across subdomain boundaries[1]"

11.2 An Example Domain to Partition

WebBooks 2.0 Order fulfillment will be used as the example. This domain is not really big enough to require—nor even necessarily benefit from—partitioning into subdomains. However it is a workable example that you are already familiar with. For reference, the domain's use case diagram is shown in Figure 11.1.

The domain's class diagram is shown in Figure 11.2.

We also focus on sequence diagrams for two use cases to illustrate the effect of subdomain partitioning. The sequence diagram for the Pack order sea level use case is shown in two figures, Figures 11.3 and 11.4, because it involves too many classes to fit in a single diagram. "GWTW" in the sequence diagrams refers to Margaret Mitchell's classic novel "Gone With The Wind." State models are unaffected by subdomain partitioning.

Finally, Figure 11.5 shows the sequence diagram for the Receive replenish sea level use case.

11.3 Partitioning a Domain

Sea level use cases and classes in Order fulfillment can be grouped into two subsets:

- Those dealing with customers and ordering: a Customer ordering subdomain
- Those dealing with replenishment of print media: an Inventory management subdomain

This is typical of the fracture lines mentioned above. One subset of use cases and classes tend to cluster around one topic, and other subsets cluster around other

---

1 Semantic models should be partitioned to minimize the *number* (i.e., kinds) of communication. Designs can be partitioned to minimize the *frequency* of communication.

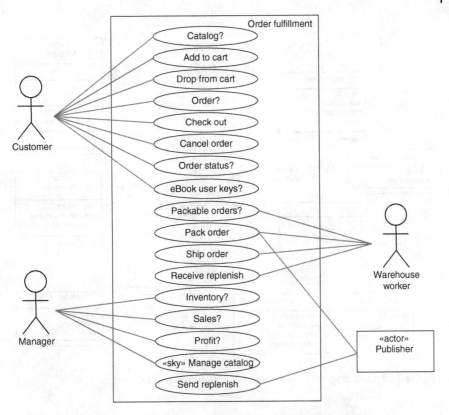

Figure 11.1 Use case diagram for WebBooks 2.0 Order fulfillment domain.

topics. There should be minimal communication between subsets. The two subsets in the Order fulfillment domain are illustrated in Figure 11.6.

As shown in Figure 11.6, subdomain boundaries fall between classes, not through classes. We don't want part of a class defined in one subdomain and the rest of it in another because that leads poor cohesion and tight coupling. Instead, by placing subdomain boundaries between classes, each class is contained entirely within a single subdomain. Coupling between subdomains is then restricted to associations and interactions that span subdomain boundaries. This coupling should be minimal given a partitioning that pays attention to abstraction, cohesion, etc.

It is not necessary to have a complete domain-level class diagram before doing any subdomain partitioning. Particularly with very large domains, subdomains may already be apparent. We can start semantic modeling at a subdomain level, just being sure to maintain consistency wherever subdomains connect.

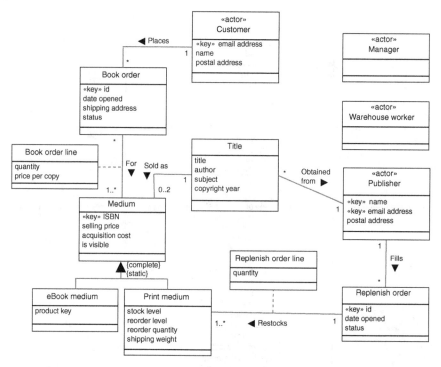

Figure 11.2 Class diagram for WebBooks 2.0 Order fulfillment domain.

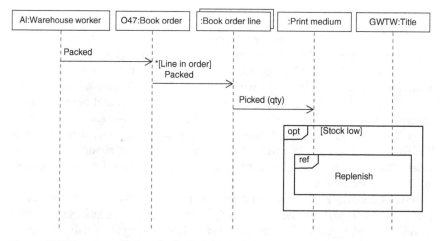

Figure 11.3 Sequence diagram for half of the Pack order sea level use case.

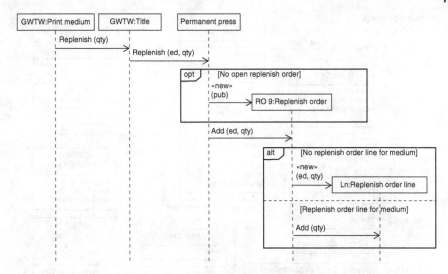

Figure 11.4 Sequence diagram for the other half of the Pack order sea level use case.

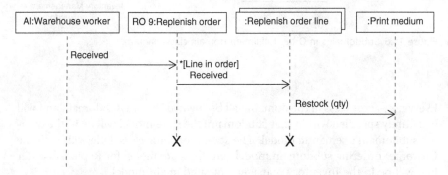

Figure 11.5 Sequence diagram for the Receive replenish received sea level use case.

11.3.1 Semantic Model for a Subdomain

The semantic model for a subdomain will have the same structure as a domain-level semantic model:

- A use case diagram
- A class model
- Relevant interaction diagrams for (a subset of) use cases
- State models for classes

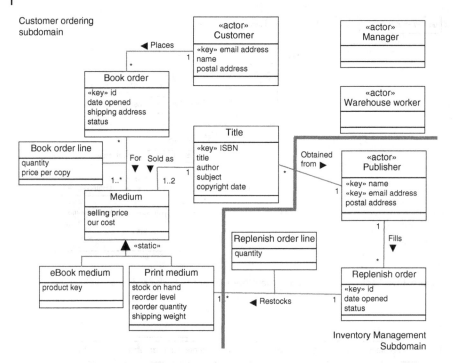

Figure 11.6 Subdomains in Order fulfillment domain class diagram.

Every non-actor class in the domain will be "owned" by one subdomain and will be entirely specified within that subdomain: the state model will be in the owning subdomain's semantic model. The state model for class Title will be in the Customer ordering subdomain model, and the state model for Replenish order line will be in the Inventory management subdomain model.

If subdomain partitioning is consistent with the fundamental principles, most sea level use cases will be contained within a single subdomain. The sea level use cases and corresponding interactions (e.g., sequence diagrams) owned within a subdomain will be specified within that subdomain's semantic model. The following use cases would be entirely within the Customer ordering subdomain:

- Add to cart
- Drop from cart
- Cancel order
- ...

The Send replenish order use case would be entirely within the Inventory management subdomain.

Only a handful of domain-level use cases should span subdomains, but these need special handling. Example use cases that span the two subdomains in Order fulfillment are:

- Pack order (when replenishing is involved)
- Receive replenish

In a similar sense to Figure 11.6, Figure 11.7 shows the subdomain boundary superimposed on the relevant portion of the sequence diagram for Pack order. Figure 11.8 shows the same for the Receive replenish.

Domain-level use cases that span subdomains need to be partitioned into the subdomains. At the domain level, consider the portion of process in each subdomain and be sure the sea level use case for that portion is in the set of use cases for that subdomain. Assume that Pack order is owned by the Customer ordering subdomain and Receive replenish is owned by the Inventory management subdomain. Request replenish should be owned by the Inventory management subdomain and Restock should be owned by the Customer ordering subdomain.

Immediately adjacent classes—classes owned by one subdomain that interact with classes owned by another subdomain—appear as actors in the other subdomain. Title will be an actor in the Inventory management subdomain, and Replenish order line will be an actor in the Customer ordering subdomain.

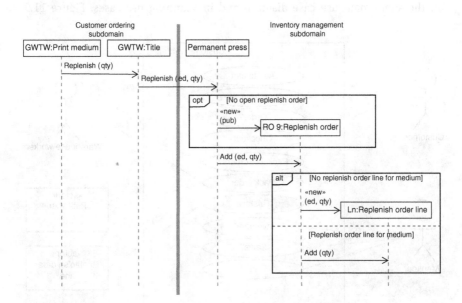

Figure 11.7 Sequence diagram for the other half of the Pack order sea level use case with subdomain boundary.

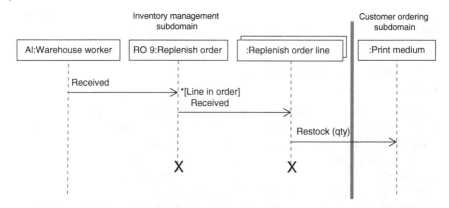

Figure 11.8 Sequence diagram for the Receive replenish sea level use case with subdomain boundary.

Domain-level actors can be shared across several subdomains; it doesn't hurt to have domain-level actors appear in more than one subdomain unless there are attributes and dynamics associated with that actor class—maintaining consistency across the subdomains becomes more difficult in that case. Warehouse worker will appear in both subdomains of Order fulfillment.

The actor representing a class in an adjacent subdomain needs to be included on the subdomain use case diagram and in spanning use cases. Figure 11.9

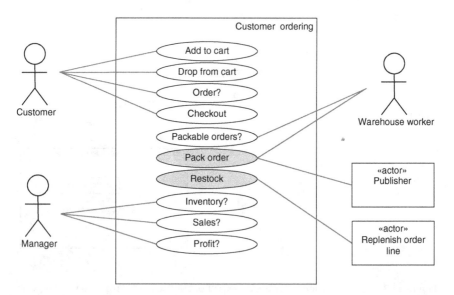

Figure 11.9 Use case diagram for Customer ordering subdomain.

shows an abbreviated use case diagram for the Customer ordering subdomain. Note the two shaded use cases, Process packing and Process restock. These represent the portion of the two subdomain-spanning use cases in the Customer ordering subdomain. Shading is only to illustrate and is not required in a real semantic model of a subdomain.

11.3.2 Customer Ordering Subdomain

Figure 11.10 shows the class diagram for the Customer ordering subdomain. Note how Replenish order line is the class in the Inventory management subdomain adjacent to Print medium. Class Replenish order does not appear because it is entirely internal to the Inventory management subdomain.

Figure 11.11 shows the sequence diagram for the Process packing use case as far as it is owned by the Customer ordering subdomain. The sequence stops when the notification is handed off to Publisher, the adjacent class in the Inventory management subdomain.

Figure 11.12 shows the sequence diagram for the Restock use case as far as it is owned by the Customer ordering subdomain. The sequence starts when the

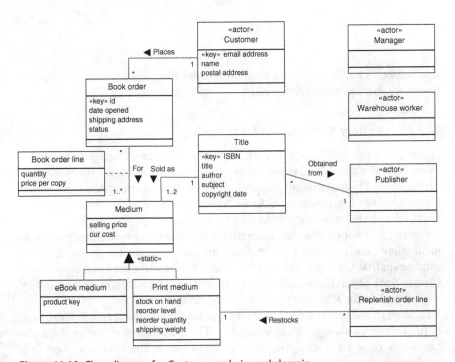

Figure 11.10 Class diagram for Customer ordering subdomain.

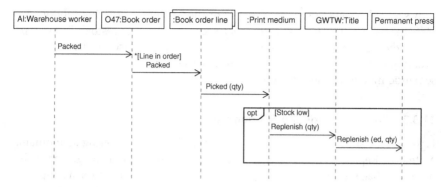

Figure 11.11 Sequence diagram for Pack order use case in Customer ordering subdomain.

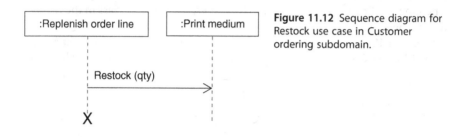

Figure 11.12 Sequence diagram for Restock use case in Customer ordering subdomain.

notification is handed off from Replenish order line, the adjacent class in the Inventory management subdomain.

11.3.3 Inventory Management Subdomain

Figure 11.13 shows the use case diagram for the Inventory management subdomain. Note the shaded use cases, Process replenish request and Process replenish received. These represent the portion of the two spanning use cases in the Customer ordering subdomain. Again, shading is only to illustrate and is not required in a real semantic model of a subdomain.

Figure 11.14 shows the class diagram for the Inventory management subdomain. Note how Title and Print medium are classes in the Customer ordering subdomain that are adjacent to Publisher and Replenish order line, respectively. Classes Book order, Book order line, Customer, etc. do not appear because they are internal to the Customer ordering subdomain.

Figure 11.15 shows the sequence diagram for the Request replenish use case in the Inventory management subdomain. The sequence starts when the notification is received from Title, the adjacent class in the Customer ordering subdomain.

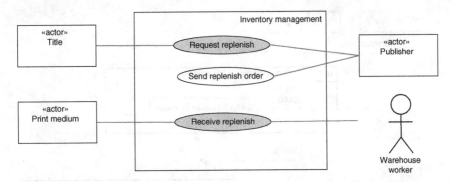

Figure 11.13 Use case diagram for Inventory management subdomain.

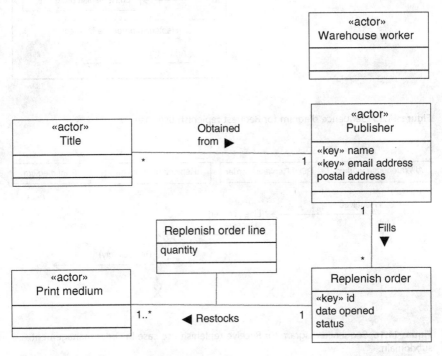

Figure 11.14 Class diagram for Inventory management subdomain.

Figure 11.16 shows the sequence diagram for the Receive replenish use case as far as it is owned by the Customer ordering subdomain. The sequence ends when the notification is handed off to Print medium, the adjacent class in the Customer ordering subdomain.

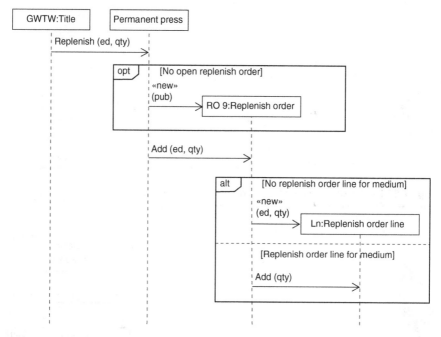

Figure 11.15 Sequence diagram for Request replenish use case.

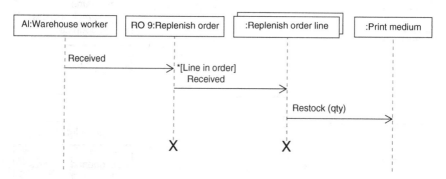

Figure 11.16 Sequence diagram for Receive replenish use case in Order management subdomain.

Interactions in any subdomain that involve classes in adjacent subdomains need to exactly match interactions in the other subdomain. As long as there is an exact match, the semantics of the interface between the two subdomains are consistent. If any change is made to interaction in either subdomain, then a corresponding change must also be made in the other subdomain.

11.4 Subdomain Diagrams

In the spirit of the domain diagram, a diagram that shows how a domain has been partitioned into subdomains would be useful. Unified Modeling Language's (UML's) package notation can represent subdomains. The relationship between adjacent subdomains is peer-to-peer, not client-server, so subdomain connections should not have arrows even though this technically violates UML notation. A subdomain diagram for Order fulfillment is shown in Figure 11.17.

If you want to provide descriptions for subdomains, there are at least two options, and they aren't mutually exclusive. You could do both if appropriate:

- A couple of sentences or a short paragraph describing the scope of each subdomain
- A (reference to a) subdomain-level use case diagram

As stated above, Order fulfillment, as is, is not big enough to require, nor even benefit from subdomain partitioning. The domain is small enough to manage in a single semantic model. However, as scope is added over time, it will necessarily grow in size and complexity. The benefit of subdomain partitioning would become more obvious:

- *Catalog subdomain*—Including Title, Medium, Print medium, and eBook medium, this becomes more of a separable package when different media types (e.g., audio books) are added. Also, if customer reviews and ratings are brought in, this subdomain grows even larger.
- *Customer ordering subdomain*—Supporting partial shipments, returned orders, recommending Titles ("Customers who ordered what you ordered also ordered Y, maybe you want to order Y too?"), etc.
- *Inventory management subdomain*—Stock levels, demand prediction, suppliers, replenishment, expanding to more than one warehouse, allowing suppliers to send partial replenish orders, third-party fulfillment,[2] etc.

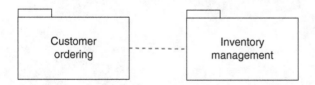

Figure 11.17 Subdomain diagram for Order fulfillment domain.

---

2 WebBooks would not stock that Title. Any order would be forwarded to a supplier who would fill that request out of their warehouse. WebBooks takes a commission on the sale; the actual shipping is done by the supplier.

11.4.1 Another Example of Subdomain Partitioning

A larger and more realistic example of partitioning into subdomains comes out of a project to automate "Atomic Vapor Laser Isotope Separation" (AVLIS).[3] Figure 11.18 shows the domain diagram for the overall AVLIS control system software.

The Process interface domain deals with instrumentation that monitors and controls separator modules: analog-to-digital converters, digital-to-analog converters, thermocouples, pressure gauges, etc. Process interface provides conversion between raw data values (typically 16-bit words) in the physical instrumentation and engineering data values (temperatures, pressures, flow rates, etc.) that Separator control works with. Process interface can be thought of as a complex View-controller service for Separator control's Model region.

The Separator control domain automates monitoring and controlling the separation process. A system operator can tell Separator control domain to Start processing, and the Separator control domain logic will pump down vacuum chambers, turn on cooling, lasers, vaporization heaters, and so on. The subdomain diagram for Separator control is shown in Figure 11.19.

Separator control subdomain descriptions are as follows:

- *Separator chamber*—The core of isotope separation; this subdomain handles overall start–stop–standby–restart–shutdown logic.
- *Vacuum subsystem*—Includes valves, pumps (both mechanical and cryogenic), and measured pressures needed to maintain a near vacuum. This subdomain supports pump-down and chamber venting processes.

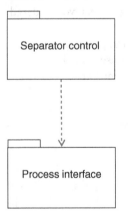

Figure 11.18 Domain diagram for Atomic Vapor Laser Isotope Separation control system software.

---

3 See, for example, http://en.wikipedia.org/wiki/Atomic_vapor_laser_isotope_separation or [Zare77].

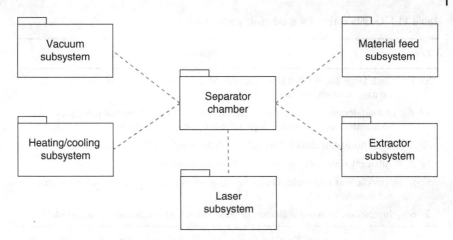

Figure 11.19 Subdomain diagram for the Separator control domain.

- *Heating/cooling subsystem*—Includes heaters along with valves and temperatures necessary to maintain the proper temperature profile and vaporization rate. This subdomain supports heat up, standby, restart, and cooldown processes.
- *Laser subsystem*—Includes logic necessary to run tunable ring dye lasers that are the key to the process. This subdomain supports turning on and turning off, making sure that the lasers are producing proper wavelengths and intensities.
- *Material feed subsystem*—Vaporization only works with a small amount of material at a time and the process starves unless a stream of new material is added. This subsystem maintains flow so the process can run for long periods.
- *Extractor subsystem*—The AVLIS process works by ionizing one isotope and not any other; the ionized isotope is electrically charged and can be extracted from the vapor stream using electromagnets. This subdomain supports turning extractor electromagnets on and off.

By breaking the Separator control domain into six subdomains, overall complexity was better managed, and software development and maintenance was parallelized.

11.5 Quality Criteria

In addition to the criteria in Chapter 3, Table 11.1 shows quality criteria for partitioning domains into subdomains.

Table 11.1 Quality criteria for subdomain partitioning.

Item	Criterion
SP-1	Each large domain has been partitioned, as appropriate for complexity management and/or work partitioning
SP-2	All subdomain partitioning is consistent with the fundamental principles: abstraction, encapsulation, high cohesion, loose coupling, etc.
SP-3	Each non-actor class is "owned by" (defined in) exactly one subdomain
SP-4	Adjacent classes appear as actors in other subdomain's semantic models
SP-5	Associations and multiplicities between adjacent classes are consistent across subdomain models
SP-6	Interaction between adjacent classes is consistent across subdomain models

11.6 Summary

Partitioning a large system into domains helps manage complexity. But even after domain partitioning, class models with more than 100 classes are possible. Such large domains can still be hard to understand and manage because of their size. As semantic models approach 40 classes, natural fracture lines tend to appear: regions of the model will specialize around subsets of the policies and processes. We can take advantage of those fracture lines to help manage complexity brought on by size. We can also partition a domain to enhance work parallelization and project management. From a complexity management or a work parallelization perspective, or both, there is often value in partitioning a large domain. This chapter explained how to partition a domain into smaller, more manageable units called subdomains.

When partitioning a domain into subdomains, be sure that each subdomain is consistent with the fundamental principles:

- Each subdomain should abstract a certain, specific topic.
- The design and implementation of the subdomain should encapsulate as much accidental complexity as possible.
- Each subdomain should be highly cohesive about a single topic and loosely coupled with the other subdomains.
- Subdomain partitioning should be based on invariants and likely changes.
- Subdomain partitioning should not be influenced by premature design or optimization.

By putting subdomain boundaries between classes, each class is owned by a single subdomain. Coupling between subdomains is then restricted to interactions that span subdomain boundaries, and this should be minimal given a good partitioning that pays attention to abstraction, cohesion, etc.

A subdomain semantic model will have the same structure as a domain semantic model with the exception of how use cases that span subdomains are handled. Use cases and corresponding interaction diagrams for sea level use cases that span subdomains need to be partitioned. An adjacent class in another subdomain will need to be included as an actor on the subdomain use case diagram and participate in the spanning use case.

Interactions that involve an adjacent class in one subdomain need to exactly match the interactions in the other subdomain. As long as there is an exact match, the semantics of the interface between the subdomains are consistent. If any change is made in one subdomain, a corresponding change must be made in the other subdomain.

The subdomain diagram shows how a domain has been partitioned into subdomains. Subdomains can be described by a couple of sentences describing scope or by a (reference to a) subdomain-level use case diagram.

12

Wrapping Up Semantic Modeling

Part II presents modeling of policies to enforce and processes to carry out independent of automation technology. Through a semantic model, we get a complete, consistent, clear, correct, concise, precise, and validated understanding of (at least part of) a "business" to be automated. This chapter completes the presentation of semantic modeling and describes what can be done with a model. In particular,

- Summary and review of the semantic model
- Organizing model content into a written specification
- Validating a model, by peer review and simulated execution
- Deriving verification test cases from a semantic model
- Translating a semantic model into natural language
- Analysis patterns versus design patterns
- Product family semantic models
- Alternate semantic model development processes
- Buy versus build: the role of semantic modeling in package acquisition[1]

12.1 Reviewing the Semantic Model

The four main components of a semantic model are:

- *Use case diagram*—Communicates scope and context of the policies and processes. Scope is captured in use cases that show process at the most coarse-grained level; context is described by a set of actors.
- *Class model*—Identifies and defines significant elements of the structure of the business as well as important relationships between those elements. The class model is a precise specification of policies to be enforced.

---

1 Sometimes referred to as COTS: "commercial off the shelf."

How to Engineer Software: A Model-Based Approach, First Edition. Steve Tockey.
© 2019 the IEEE Computer Society, Inc. Published 2019 by John Wiley & Sons, Inc.

- *Interaction diagrams*—Including either or both sequence diagrams and communication diagrams, these describe net information flow between objects. These show process at an intermediate level.
- *State models*—Precise specification of the details of process. State models fill in detail underneath interaction diagrams and give the most precise, fine-grained definition.

A semantic model intentionally describes only policy and process (i.e., functional requirements), not automation technology. It deliberately avoids bits, bytes, database tables, stored procedures, C++ classes, data files, threads, network data packets, mobile, cloud, and all other automation technologies.[2] A class in a semantic model does not necessarily represent a memory-resident Java or C++ class, a database table with stored procedures, etc. It only specifies a relevant concept that must be represented in any correct automation of that (sub)domain. Part III shows how to map the policies and processes onto automation technology. These same concepts would need to be implemented in Tinker Toys or Lego™ if that were the chosen automation technology. Avoiding technology in the semantic model reduces complexity and gives designers/developers the most freedom to be creative in designing and constructing software.

12.2 Organizing Semantic Model Content into a Written Specification

Ideally, a semantic model would be stored in an automated tool so it could be navigated in a hypertext fashion: for example, an event is signaled in an action of the state model of class A, which class responds to that event? This is an easy question for a tool to answer. Of course, a sequence diagram for the relevant use case(s) would also answer that, but we don't always make sequence diagrams for every use case. An automated tool could easily find where the event was handled and call up the state model for that class. A suitably powerful tool could even derive interaction diagrams from the state models. Unfortunately, few such tools exist today and they tend to be very expensive. Quite often project teams are requested—or required—to publish a semantic model as a paper document or some similar electronic representation like PDF.

If the goal is to organize a semantic model into some kind of paper(like) document, the following outline is known to be effective. Each level of increased indentation represents a more detailed section of model content.

---

2 Unless the model is intended to describe the policies and processes of those automation technologies, for example, a semantic model of TCP/IP.

The semantic models in Appendices D, F, H, J, and L use this structure and serve as concrete examples:

Use case diagram (and description as appropriate)
Class diagram (and description as appropriate)
Interaction diagrams (selected subset as appropriate) for each:
    Use case or scenario name
    Use case or scenario description (as appropriate)
    Sequence or communication diagram
Class dictionary for each class:
    Class name
    Class description
    State diagram (optional when only custodial behavior)
    Attribute dictionary[3]
        Attribute name
        Attribute description
        Range specification
    State and event dictionary (as needed)
    Action specifications
    Source of (for actors)
    Destination of (for actors)
Association dictionary
    Association name
    Association description
Relevant notes (optional)

The Source of and Destination of sections in this outline allow the specification of events and data that come from this actor (Source of) as well as events and data that are needed by this actor (Destination of). This is not derivable from other content in the semantic model and can be useful in automatically generating communication diagrams and test cases from the model. Examples of Source of and Destination can be found in the sample models in Appendices D, F, H, and J.

12.3 Validating a Semantic Model

The Software Quality Assurance (SQA) community has specialized vocabulary. In particular

---

3 Including derived attributes, descriptions, and derivation policies/processes, as appropriate.

- *Verification (Was it built right?)*—Gain confidence that the code is consistent with its specification, in this case the semantic model.[4] In model-based software engineering, some amount of verification testing is often needed to be confident, and the behavior of code is consistent with the behavior defined in the semantic model.
- *Validation (Was the right thing built?)*—Gain confidence that the correct product is built. Validation checks that the specification represents real stakeholder need.

Many SQA organizations focus almost exclusively on verification: testing. However, validation is equally, if not more, important. Developing software from an invalid semantic model wastes valuable time and effort. It's much quicker and cheaper (unless a model compiler is used) to fix problems in the semantic model before design and code than after. Time spent validating a model can be much less than time spent on design and code rework. Semantic models can be validated through peer review (e.g., inspection) or simulated execution. Both are discussed.

12.4 Validating a Semantic Model by Peer Review

The most common way to validate a semantic model is by peer review.[5] Simply, knowledgeable people who were not directly involved in building a model review it for completeness and correctness. Quality criteria provided in this book are intended for use in peer reviews.

Peer reviews are most effective when the reviewers "surround" the model being validated. Specifically, review participants should include:

- *Upstream suppliers*—Stakeholders who provided input (e.g., candidate functional requirements). The stakeholder's review perspective is "Does this semantic model completely and accurately represent the policies and processes I believe I communicated?"
- *Sidestream peers*—Others who did not build this model but who were capable of building it. Their review perspective is "Is this model well formed and correctly stated?" and "Does it comply with all relevant standards?"
- *Downstream consumers*—Others who will use the semantic model as input in doing their job. This includes software architects, designers, developers,

---

4 And the interface specification, Chapter 14.
5 See, for example, [Freedman90]. This intentionally includes "Inspection," a form of peer review that requires a moderator, scribe, advanced preparation against one or more checklists (quality criteria), focus on issue identification-not resolution, etc. Inspections are known to be more efficient and effective than other forms of peer review. See, for example, [Doolan92], [Fagan76], [Fagan86], [Fowler86], [Gilb93], [Strauss93], or [Wheeler96].

testers, user documentation specialists, user support staff, etc. Their review perspective is "Can I get my job done quickly and easily based on the content in this model?"

12.5 Validating a Semantic Model by Simulation

Stakeholders might not be willing to review a semantic model. It happens rarely, but when it does it needs to be dealt with. Stakeholder agreement that the model correctly represents policies and processes to be automated is essential. Another way to get agreement is by execution of the model—by hand or possibly using an automated tool[6]—against a suitably convincing set of demonstration scenarios.

Execution of a semantic model also illustrates how the model components work together to precisely define policies and processes.

There are two approaches to by-hand simulation, depending on how many simulation objects are needed. If only a few objects of any class are needed, the token-based approach is preferred. Table-based simulation is more convenient when many simulation objects are needed in a class. The token-based approach is described first.

12.5.1 Token-Based Simulation

To demonstrate token-based model simulation, we will use a small case study: the Bottle Filling Line.[7] Figure 12.1 shows a schematic overview.

This system fills bottles with liquid from a vat. Empty, unlabeled bottles are in a gravity-fed rack upstream of the vat. The filling cycle is as follows:

1) The In Gate is opened to let one bottle slide onto the Scale.
2) The Contact senses the bottle is in place.
3) Bottles are filled by weight, not volume, so the empty weight of the bottle is measured to account for variation in glass density.
4) The Valve is opened and liquid from the vat flows into the bottle, increasing weight.
5) When the weight reaches the bottle weight plus the target net weight, the Valve is closed and a label is applied.
6) The Out Gate is opened; the bottle slides down the exit chute on its way to the capper. We know a bottle has left when the Contact senses it is gone.

Our business is the control system to automate this filling line. A question frequently asked about this case study is, "Whose technology is perfect?" We

---

6 Automatic execution of a model depends on factors discussed in Chapter 20.
7 This case study is derived from [Ward86c].

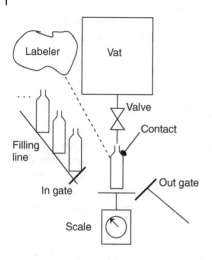

Figure 12.1 Schematic overview of the Bottle Filling Line case study.

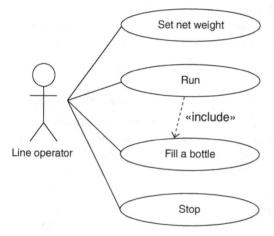

Figure 12.2 Use case diagram for the Filling Line case study.

are given factory machinery: gates, valve, scale, labeler, etc. Even if we had a perfect computer, we would still need to manage that machinery. We would also have to deal with real-world phenomena like gravity, inertia, and friction. What's perfect is only the hypothetical computer this business will execute on. That hypothetical computer is infinitely fast, has unlimited memory, and can sense all machinery inputs and control all machinery outputs directly (the Vulcan Mind Meld): we don't have to worry about instrumentation and/or communication protocols for connecting to that machinery for now; they only become relevant in design.

Figure 12.2 shows a use case diagram for the Filling Line.

The Line operator uses this system to fill bottles. The Set net weight use case allows the operator to configure the Filling Line to the size of bottle (e.g., 150 g,

355 g, 500 g, 750 g, etc.). The Fill a bottle use case fills only one bottle and then stops. The Run use case continues to fill bottles until the Line operator says Stop. The Line operator is the source of events that trigger each sea level event use case.

Figure 12.3 shows a class diagram for the Filling Line.

Figure 12.4 shows a sequence diagram for the Fill a bottle use case, which will be simulated.

It's too involved simulate every class in this model. We only simulate three core classes: Filling line, Filling station, and Bottle loader. Each of these classes is specified below. The details of the remaining classes should be straightforward and will only be implied.

Class Filling line is responsible for overall sequencing and control. Figure 12.5 shows its state diagram. The .continue attribute tells if the line is running (range is an enumeration: [yes or no]). Actions are specified directly on the state diagram.

Class Filling station is responsible for filling an empty bottle to the correct level and applying a label. Figure 12.6 shows the state diagram for Filling station. The attribute .fill net wt specifies the size of bottle to be filled; its range is [from 50.0 to 795.0 g with a precision of 0.1 g].

Class Bottle loader is responsible for moving empty bottles into the filling station and later ejecting full, labeled bottles. Figure 12.7 shows the state diagram for Bottle loader. Attribute .bottle count is the number of bottles that have been

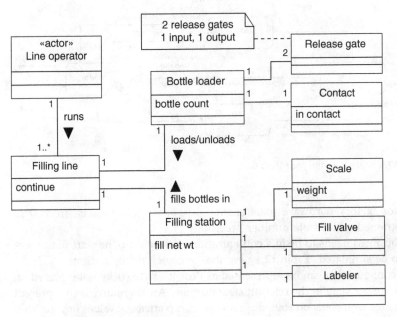

Figure 12.3 Class diagram for the Filling Line.

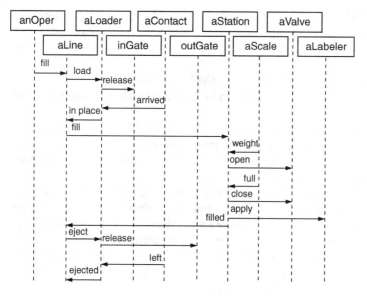

Figure 12.4 Sequence diagram for the Fill a bottle use case.

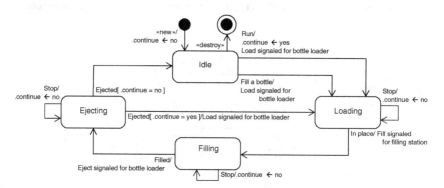

Figure 12.5 State diagram for Filling line.

filled (for factory hardware maintenance purposes); its range is [from 0 to unconstrained with whole number precision].

The business needs to be in a configuration representing the start of the scenario to be simulated. Table 12.1 describes one such configuration.

This configuration can be represented as Post-it™-style sticky notes placed on the appropriate state in the relevant state diagram. An alternative is to represent object states with coins on state diagrams and keep attribute values in your head or on paper.

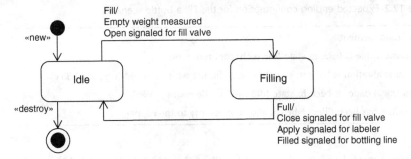

Figure 12.6 State diagram for Filling station.

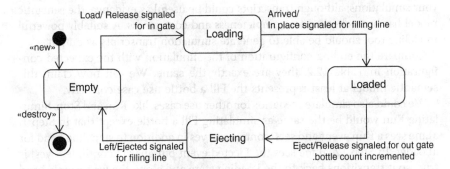

Figure 12.7 State diagram for Bottle loader.

Table 12.1 A starting configuration for simulating the Fill a bottle scenario.

Simulation element
One object of class Filling line, named aLine, in state Idle with .continue = no
One object of class Filling station, aStation, in state Idle with .fill net wt appropriate for the bottles being filled (e.g., 355 g)
One object of class Bottle loader, aLoader, in state Idle with .bottle count = 1965

When simulated execution of filling one bottle has finished, we should expect the ending configuration shown in Table 12.2. If executing the model achieves this configuration, then we can say that the semantic model correctly represents at least this use case under these specific conditions; alternate conditions will be discussed later in this chapter.

The use case starts when the Line operator (anOper) decides they want to fill one bottle. This is the first message on the sequence diagram in Figure 12.4. The

Table 12.2 Expected ending configuration for the Fill a bottle scenario.

Simulation element
The same aLine is back in state Idle with .continue = no
The same aStation is back in state Idle with .fill net wt unchanged (e.g., still 355 g)
The same aLoader is back in state Idle with .bottle count = 1966
One bottle has been filled, labeled, and is on its way to the capper

simulation starts by giving that event to object aLine, the destination object in the sequence diagram. Table 12.3 shows a step-by-step transcript; you can follow it to understand how model simulation works. You don't need to make a transcript of your simulations; although transcripts could be useful as evidence, the semantic model has been checked for completeness and correctness. A suitably powerful modeling tool should be able to generate simulation transcripts as output.

Compare the ending configuration of the simulation with the expected configuration in Table 12.2: they are exactly the same. We can now claim this semantic model at least represents the Fill a bottle use case correctly.

We could also simulate scenarios for other use cases, like Run and Stop. Simulating Run would be the same as simulating Fill a bottle except that in Step 1, aLine sees a Run event and sets .continue to yes in addition to signaling Load for aLoader. In Step 12, aLine sees the Ejected event but guard [.continue = yes] is true, so it transitions back to the Loading state and along the way signals Load for aLoader. The filling cycle (Steps 2 through 12 in Table 12.3) repeats until the .continue attribute is set to no by a Stop event (i.e., simulating the Stop use case).

12.5.2 Table-Based Model Simulation

Token-based model simulation becomes unwieldy when there are more than just a few objects in any class. The state diagram for that class gets overcrowded with tokens. The table-based approach represents each class in a table. Each table has similar structure:

- The leftmost column simulates a primary key. If the class already has a key, that attribute can be used otherwise an arbitrary key is created (often, but not always, an integer—possibly with a convenient prefix).
- Each non-key attribute becomes its own column.
- If the state model for the class has more than one state (i.e., beyond just "exists") and there is no obvious attribute (or set) representing current state,[8] then add a column to represent current state.

---

8 The "state vector" from Chapter 10.

- Add one column for each association this class participates in where the multiplicity to the other class is either __:0..1 or __:1. Association classes become their own table. Many-to-many associations use a separate correlation table to store links.

Table 12.3 Transcript of the Fill a bottle simulation.

Step	Description
1	Object aLine sees the Fill a bottle event. It's in the Idle state so it transitions from Idle to Loading and along the way signals Load for aLoader. This is the second message on the sequence diagram
2	aLoader sees the Load event. It's in the Idle state so it transitions to Loading and along the way signals Release for inGate. This is the third message on the sequence diagram
3	inGate sees the Release event so it does its job. Gravity, inertia, and friction in the real world cause an empty bottle to eventually hit the Contact so it signals Arrived for aLoader. This is the next message in the sequence diagram
4	aLoader sees the Arrived event. It's in the Loading state so it transitions to Loaded and along the way signals In place for aLine. This is the next message in the sequence diagram
5	aLine sees the In place event. It's in the Loading state so it transitions to Filling and along the way signals Fill for aStation. This is the next message in the sequence diagram
6	aStation sees the Fill event. It's in the Idle state so it transitions to Filling and along the way measures the bottle's empty weight and signals Open for aValve. These are the next two messages
7	Gravity, inertia, and friction cause liquid to flow into the bottle so it gets heavier. It's full when aScale shows an appropriate weight. This is the next message
8	aStation sees the Full event. It's in the Filling state so it transitions to Idle and along the way signals Close for aValve, Apply for aLabeler, and Filled for aLine. These are the next three messages
9	aLine sees the Filled event. It's in the Filling state so it transitions to Ejecting and along the way signals Eject for aLoader. This is the next message
10	aLoader sees the Eject event. It's in the Loaded state so it transitions to Ejecting and along the way signals Release for outGate. This is the next message
11	outGate sees the Release event so it releases. Gravity, inertia, and friction in the real world cause the bottle to eventually leave the Contact so it signals Left for aLoader. This is the next message
12	aLoader sees the Left event. It's in the Ejecting state so it transitions to Idle and along the way signals Ejected for aLine. This is the last message in the sequence diagram
13	aLine sees the Ejected event. It's in the Ejecting state and guard [continue = no] is true so it transitions to Idle with no new events to signal. There are no unhandled events, the simulation has ended with one new full, labeled bottle on its way to the capper

Filling line

name	continue	loader	filler
aLine	no	aLoader	aStation

Filling station

name	fill net wt	scale	valve	labeler
aStation	355g	aScale	aValve	aLabeler

Bottle loader

name	bottle count	in gate	out gate	contact
aLoader	1965	inGate	outGate	aContact

Figure 12.8 Starting configuration for the Fill a bottle simulation in table form.

Each simulation object is a row in the appropriate table. Column values in each row are selected as needed for the scenario(s) to be simulated. Figure 12.8 shows the same starting configuration for the Fill a bottle simulation in Table 12.1. Executing the Fill a bottle use case against this table-based representation yields the same transcript as Table 12.2. The expected ending configuration would be identical to Figure 12.8 except that the .bottle count for aLoader would be 1966.

The Bottle Filling Line may be too trivial for table-based simulation. Table-based model simulation will be demonstrated with a more substantial case study: WebBooks 2.0 Order fulfillment.

There are several approaches to simulation when a semantic model includes generalization (inheritance). For this example, assume the Collapse subclasses into superclass approach discussed in Chapter 19 because it is the easiest to visualize, understand, and work with. Simply, attributes of all subclass are absorbed into one superclass table. Depending on the subclass of a specific simulation object, some columns will be relevant and others will be empty. It may be useful to include a "type discriminator" column to show what subclass any row belongs to. Figure 12.9 shows a starting configuration for simulating Order fulfillment. Column "type" in table Medium is a type discriminator: "e" means eBook medium and "p" means Print medium.

Several rows in Figure 12.9 have been highlighted to emphasize Mary's order o3 for one copy of Gone With The Wind (GWTW) and three copies of Return on Software. This order will feature in a simulation.

Start by simulating the sea level use case Packable orders? This is a data use case so the configuration of the business won't change during the simulation; we only expect derived results. From the configuration in Figure 12.9, the first Book order ("o1") is not packable because its status is completed. The second order ("o2") is in the placed state, but asks for 20 copies of GWTW and there are only 12 on hand, so this order is not packable because of insufficient stock. The third order ("03") is packable because it is in the placed state and there is sufficient stock for both Book order lines. Table 12.4 shows the transcript for the simulation.

Customer

email	name	address
joe@a.com	Joe	123 Main
mary@b.com	Mary	421 Elm
ann@c.com	Ann	928 A St

Replenish order

id	date	status	publ
r1	14-Feb	Placed	p3

Replenish order line

id	qty	order	pMedia
l1	20	r1	m1

Book order

id	date	ship addr	status	cust
o1	12-Jan	456 B St	Cpltd	ann@c.com
o2	17-Jan	123 Main	Placed	joe@a.com
o3	21-Jan	69 C St	Placed	mary@b.com

Publisher

id	name	email	postal
p1	Addison Wesley	reorder@aw.com	address1
p2	Edgerton	more@edgerton.com	address2
p3	Macmillan	copies@macmillan.com	address3

Book order line

id	qty	price	status	order	medium
l1	1	4.50	Cpltd	o1	m3
l2	20	6.99	Placed	o2	m1
l3	1	6.99	Placed	o3	m1
l4	3	49.00	Placed	o3	m4

Title

id	title	author	subj	copyright	from
t1	GWTW	Mitchell	Drama	1936	p3
t2	P&P	Austen	Drama	pub dom	p2
t3	Rtn Sw	Tockey	Sw Dev	2005	p1

Medium

id	price	cost	type	key	on hand	reord lvl	reord qty	ship wt	sold as
m1	6.99	5.99	p		12	10	20	2.4lb	t1
m2	8.99	7.99	e	K2					t1
m3	4.50	3.50	e	K3					t2
m4	49.00	44.00	p		7	5	10	2.4lb	t3

Figure 12.9 Starting configuration for Order fulfillment simulation.

Table 12.4 Transcript of the Packable orders? simulation.

Step	Description
1	Book order o1 is not packable because its status is not Placed
2	The .stock on hand for Print medium m1 is 12, but Book order line l2 is asking for 20, so l2 is not packable
3	Book order o2 is in the Placed state; however Book order line l2 is not packable, so o2 is not packable
4	The .stock on hand for Print medium m1 is 12, and Book order line l3 is asking for 1, so l3 is packable
5	The .stock on hand for Print medium m4 is 7, and Book order line l4 is asking for 3, so l4 is packable
6	Book order o3 is in the Placed state, and both of its order lines, l3 and l4, are packable so o3 is packable

That result is exactly as expected; we can claim the semantic model properly represents order packability policies and processes.

A more complicated scenario to simulate is Pack order o3. Since that Book order requests one copy of GWTW, we expect the inventory of Print medium m1 to drop from 12 to 11. This is above the reorder level so nothing further is expected. Book order o3 also requests three copies of Return on Software and there are seven copies in stock; we expect the inventory of Print medium m4 to drop to four. The reorder level is five so we expect a Replenish order to be placed with Addison-Wesley for 10 copies. We also expect the states of Book order 03 and Book order lines l3 and l4 to change. The transcript is shown in Table 12.5.

Table 12.5 Transcript of the Pack order o3 simulation.

Step	Description
1	A Warehouse worker signals Packed for Book order o3
2	Book order o3 is in the Placed state and guard isPackable? is true so it transitions to the Packed state and along the way executes action Mark as Packed. This action signals Placed for both Book order lines l3 and l4. Trace the event signaled for l3 first[a]
3	Book order line l3 is in the Placed state so it transitions to Completed and along the way executes action Mark as packed. Book order line l3 is linked to Print medium m1, so it signals Picked(1) for m1
4	Print medium m1 is in the Exists state and sees a Picked(1) event so it self-transitions back to Exists and along the way executes action Remove from stock(1). The action reduces .stock on hand from 12 to 11. No other action is needed because the resulting stock level is above the reorder level. Return to tracing the Placed event for l4
5	Book order line l4 is in the Placed state so it transitions to Completed and along the way executes action Mark as packed. Book order line l4 is linked to Print medium m4, so it signals Picked(3) for m4
6	Print medium m4 is in the Exists state and it sees a Picked(3) event so it self-transitions back to Exists and along the way executes action Remove from Stock(3). The action reduces .stock on hand from 7 to 4. Four is below the .reorder level of five, so Replenish(10) is signaled for Title t3
7	Title t3 is in the Exists state so it self-transitions back to Exists and along the way executes action Request replenish(10). This action signals Replenish (m4, 10) to Publisher p1, Addison-Wesley
8	Publisher p1 is in the Exists state so it self-transitions back to Exists and along the way executes action Make or add to order(m4, 10). There is no open Replenish order for p1 so creation of a new Replenish order is signaled for p1 with 10 copies of Print medium m4
9	A new Replenish order, r2, is created for p1 with .date placed = today, .status = Placed, and a new Replenish order line for 10 copies of Print medium m4 is signaled
10	A new Replenish order line, l2, for 10 copies of Print medium m4 for Replenish order r2 is created. There are no more events so the simulation completes

[a] This is arbitrary. Ideally simulation would execute in parallel. Models cannot be sensitive to this kind of ordering and must behave identically under all possible execution orders.

Customer

email	name	address
joe@a.com	Joe	123 Main
mary@b.com	Mary	421 Elm
ann@c.com	Ann	928 A St

Replenish order

id	date	status	publ
r1	14-Feb	Placed	p3
r2	today	Placed	p1

Replenish order line

id	qty	order	pMedia
l1	20	r1	m1
l2	10	r2	m4

Book order

id	date	ship addr	status	cust
o1	12-Jan	456 B St	Cpltd	ann@c.com
o2	17-Jan	123 Main	Placed	joe@a.com
o3	21-Jan	69 C St	Packed	mary@b.com

Publisher

id	name	email	postal
p1	Addison Wesley	reorder@aw.com	address1
p2	Edgerton	more@edgerton.com	address2
p3	Macmillan	copies@macmillan.com	address3

Book order line

id	qty	price	status	order	medium
l1	1	4.50	Cpltd	o1	m3
l2	20	6.99	Placed	o2	m1
l3	1	6.99	Cpltd	o3	m1
l4	3	49.00	Cpltd	o3	m4

Title

id	title	author	subj	copyright	from
t1	GWTW	Mitchell	Drama	1936	p3
t2	P&P	Austen	Drama	pub dom	p2
t3	Rtn Sw	Tockey	Sw Dev	2005	p1

Medium

id	price	cost	type	key	on hand	reord lvl	reord qty	ship wt	sold as
m1	6.99	5.99	p		12	10	20	2.4lb	t1
m2	8.99	7.99	e	K2					t1
m3	4.50	3.50	e	K3					t2
m4	49.00	44.00	p		7	5	10	2.4lb	t3

Figure 12.10 Ending configuration for Pack order o3 simulation.

The ending configuration of simulating packing order 03 is shown in Figure 12.10. Mary's order o3 is still highlighted, along with the newly created Replenish order r2 for 10 copies of Return on Software from Addison-Wesley. This is exactly the configuration expected, so we can claim that the semantic model correctly represents the policies and processes of packing an order.

Generally speaking, use cases containing complex decisions are candidates for validation. There may be one execution scenario per decision outcome, or multiple decision outcomes can be combined into a single scenario—like packability of an order, as provided in Figure 12.10. Use cases in Order fulfillment that might warrant simulation include:

- Three scenarios of Process checkout: (1) a Book order that is all eBook media, (2) an order that is all Print media, and (3) an order that is a mix of eBook and Print media.
- Four scenarios of Process packing: (1) no replenish, (2) with replenish[9] and no open Replenish order, (3) with replenish and an open Replenish order without that Print medium, and (4) with replenish and an open Replenish order with that Print medium. This is the scenario simulated in Figure 12.10.

---

9 Replenish should be triggered by falling below the reorder level as well as already being below the reorder level since these behave differently.

If the semantic model can be shown to behave properly under a suitably convincing set of scenarios, then even if stakeholders refuse to review the model itself everyone should still be confident of correctness. These same demonstration test cases are also effective functional test cases that can and should be run on the implemented code.

12.6 Deriving Verification Test Cases from a Semantic Model

Validation is about confidence the semantic model accurately represents stakeholder need. Both peer review and simulated execution are effective ways of validating. Verification is about confidence that code correctly implements the semantic model, that is, policy and process semantics have been preserved in the design and code. Assuming a semantic model has been validated and code has been implemented for that model, some amount of verification testing may be necessary. If the semantic model is translated into code using a mechanical process (e.g., a model compiler, Chapter 20) and that translation process had been verified and validated, significant verification testing against the semantic model may not be necessary.

Additional vocabulary is needed to discuss verification testing. First, functional testing versus structural testing:

- *Functional (or black box) testing*—Test cases are derived from an external specification of behavior. Functional test coverage criteria[10] include boundary value coverage,[11] input domain coverage,[12] all-pairs coverage,[13] etc.
- *Structural (or white box) testing*—Test cases are derived from the structure of the design or code. Structural test coverage criteria include statement coverage, decision coverage, modified condition/decision coverage (MC/DC), all definitions coverage, all uses (reach) coverage, all define-use (D-U) paths coverage, etc.[14]

Functional testing helps show that everything in the specification has been implemented correctly in code. Unfortunately, functional testing is unlikely to reveal functionality that was implemented but not specified (e.g., back doors, Easter eggs,[15] Trojan Horses, etc.). Structural testing, because it is derived from the design and code, reveals implementation of unspecified functionality—if code for extra

---

10 Coverage criteria help determine if enough of a certain kind of testing is being done. The key to efficient and effective verification testing is to achieve some desired level of coverage (effectiveness) with the fewest possible test cases (efficiency).
11 Test the boundaries at the precision defined in the range specification.
12 See, for example, https://www.cs.ccu.edu.tw/~naiwei/cs5812/st3.pdf or [Beizer90].
13 See, for example, http://www.pairwise.org/.
14 See, for example, [Beizer90] for discussion of structural testing techniques.
15 Easter eggs are benign and often entertaining. See, for example, www.eeggs.com.

functionality exists, that code must also be tested. Structural coverage doesn't reveal functionality that was specified but never implemented. Testing to be sure that all—and only—specified functionality has been implemented requires both functional and structural testing.

Second, positive testing versus negative testing:

- *Positive testing*—Does the software do everything the specification says it should do?
- *Negative testing*—Does the software do anything the specification doesn't say it should do?

Comprehensive verification testing depends on a combination of functional and structural testing using both positive and negative test cases. Structural testing is derived from the design and code, which we don't necessarily have at this point, so it will not be addressed here. The remainder of this section will only address functional verification testing. How much verification testing is appropriate depends on the level of risk.

12.7 Economics of Software Testing: Risk-Based Testing

Any discussion of the economics of testing would be completely different if testing was free, but testing is clearly not free—there are significant costs in:

- Creating test plans and test cases
- Executing test cases (possibly including costs to acquire and maintain automated tools)
- Maintaining the test plans and test cases as the software evolves

To be sure, there will be some cost variation from one test case to another but generally speaking not very much. So consider the cost of testing to be essentially linear as shown in Figure 12.11: doubling the number of test cases should double the cost of testing. Economists talk in terms of "incremental[16] costs," in this case the cost of adding one more test case. That incremental cost is the slope of the cost of testing line.

It is impossible to test everything, even for relatively trivial software. As Boris Beizer said,[17]

> *"It only takes one failed test to show that the software doesn't work, but even an infinite number of tests won't prove that it does."*

---

16 Or "marginal" as in "marginal cost."
17 See [Beizer90].

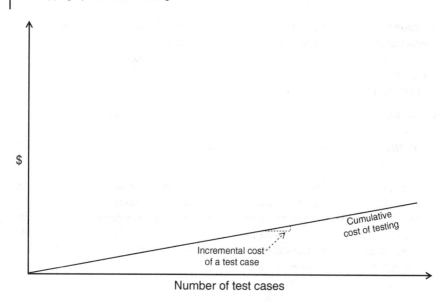

Figure 12.11 Cost of testing can be considered linear.

Consider a simple four-function—add, subtract, multiply, and divide—calculator that operates on two 5-digit integer inputs (0 to 99,999). There are 100,000 possibilities for the first input and another 100,000 possibilities for the second. There are a total of 10,000,000,000 (ten billion) possible input pairs. Taking into account the four functions means 40,000,000,000 (40 billion) test cases to exhaustively test this relatively trivial program[18]—and that considers only valid inputs. If the calculator is a desktop application, we should consider the user pressing any key on the keyboard, not just valid keys for the calculator. Scaling up to the size and complexity of the software most organizations deal with, it should be obvious how futile the goal of exhaustive testing is. Cem Kaner adds, however,[19]

> *"If you think you can fully test a program without testing its response to every possible input, fine. Give us your test cases. We can write a program that will pass all of your tests but still fail spectacularly on an input you missed. If we can do this deliberately, our contention is that we or other programmers could do it accidentally.[20]"*

---

18 Allowing both negatives and decimal point inputs expands the testing space by a factor of 2500 to 25,000,000,000,000 (25 trillion) test cases. This also ignores sequences of inputs. To truly exhaustively test this code, all possible sequences of all possible inputs need to be considered. This increases the number of test cases by N! (N factorial)

19 See [Kaner93].

20 The Intel Pentium FDIV defect—estimated to affect only 1 in 9 billion floating point divides with random parameters—could have been found with exhaustive testing. But even just nine billion test cases would have been overwhelming (see, e.g., http://en.wikipedia.org/wiki/Pentium_FDIV_bug).

Boris Beizer continues:

> *"Our objective must shift from an absolute proof to a suitably convincing demonstration."*

Why are we even testing in the first place? There must be value; otherwise it wouldn't be worth spending valuable, limited resources on. The answer comes out of the question, "What's the worst damage that could be caused by a delivered defect in this software?" If the software is a game like Angry Birds™, damage might be minimal. On the other hand, defects in software that lands a passenger airplane in heavy fog when the pilot can't see the runway until after the airplane has landed can clearly cause significant damage to the airplane, the occupants, and people and property on the ground. Damage could exceed several billion dollars. Whatever any specific software does, there is always some maximum liability. Every time an organization ships software, it exposes itself to this liability. The maximum exposure is illustrated in Figure 12.12.

Passing a test case means the software does produce the correct result for at least that tested configuration. The value of testing is that it reduces exposure and each additional passed test case buys down more exposure. The value of any test case is the probability that the element being tested is defective multiplied by the damage caused if that element failed in use. Different elements have different probabilities and different costs of failure.

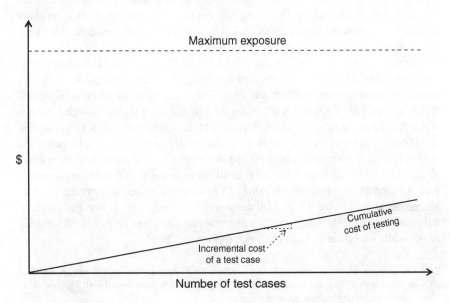

Figure 12.12 Maximum exposure from damage caused by defective software.

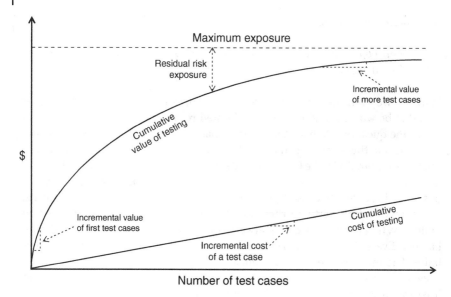

Figure 12.13 Cumulative value of testing.

In theory, all possible test cases can be sorted in order of decreasing value. If test cases are executed in order of decreasing value, the cumulative value of testing behaves as shown in Figure 12.13. The residual risk exposure at any level of testing is the difference between the maximum exposure and the cumulative value of that much testing. Reducing risk exposure to zero requires essentially infinite test cases, as already explained. There will always be residual risk exposure whenever software is shipped to users.

Many software organizations struggle to answer the question, "How much testing is enough?" The problem is they are assuming it is a technical question so they search for a nonexistent technical answer. Their mentality seems to be "If we just follow this technical approach to testing then we will have tested enough." But it is not a technical question; it doesn't have a technical answer. It is an economic question; it has an economic answer. As shown in Figure 12.13, the incremental cost of testing is essentially constant but incremental value is not. Early test cases should be highly valuable, but incremental value decreases as more test cases are run. As long as the incremental value of a test case is sufficiently greater than its incremental cost,[21] then it is a business-valuable test case. When incremental value is not sufficiently higher than incremental cost, test cases are no longer a worthwhile investment. This is shown in Figure 12.14.

---

21 Considering a minimum acceptable rate of return (MARR) as in [Tockey05], with a MARR of 21%, the incremental value of a test case must be at least 121% of its incremental cost. This is another clear application of engineering economy.

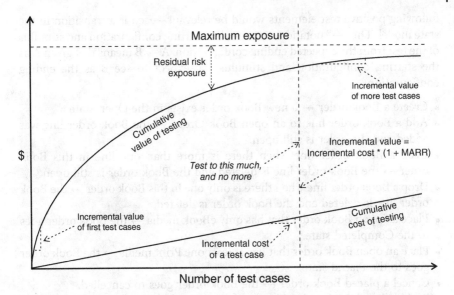

Figure 12.14 Test until the incremental value is close to the incremental cost.

It makes business sense to test things that have high probability of being defective and high cost of failure; it makes little sense to test things with low probability and cost—particularly when testing resources are severely limited. Risk-based testing considers probability and failure cost for software defects in deciding what testing should be done. The following section derives a fairly comprehensive set of test cases from a semantic model. Based on risk, more or less testing may be appropriate in practice.

12.8 Test Elements Versus Test Cases

A test case can be defined as "a specific set of inputs given to the test subject with the intent of revealing defects." A single test case can exercise many different things at the same time. So instead of deriving test cases directly from the semantic model, first derive test elements: individual, specific, detailed, testable items like a transition in a state model or the lower bound of an association multiplicity. Test elements will be assembled into test cases later.

12.8.1 Deriving Verification Test Elements from State Models

Each transition in each state model should be exercised as part of positive testing. Given the state model for class Book order in Order fulfillment, the following positive test elements would be relevant—each is a transition in the state model. The "→" notation separates the starting configuration and stimulus of the test from the expected ending configuration. A → B means that given A as the starting configuration and stimulus, we expect to see B as the ending configuration:

- Create a Book order → a new Book order exists in the Open state.
- Add a Book order line to an open Book Order → the Book order line was added and the order is still open.
- Drop a Book order line when there is more than one line in this Book order → the Book order line is deleted and the Book order is still open.
- Drop a Book order line when there is only one in this Book order → the Book order line is deleted and the Book order is deleted.
- Place an open Book order that has only eBook media → the Book order goes to the Completed state.
- Place an open Book order that has at least one Print media → the Book order goes to the Placed state.
- Cancel a placed Book order → the Book order goes to cancelled.
- Pack a placed Book order when guard isPackable? is true → the Book order goes to the Packed state.
- Ship a packed Book order → the Book order goes to the Completed state.

When a transition has a guard, consider separate test elements for when that guard is true versus when it is false. Packing a placed Book order when it is packable (sufficient inventory) does one thing; attempting to pack a Book order when there is insufficient inventory does something else (ignored because there is no transition in the state model—this would be a negative test case).

The invalid state plus event combinations are negative testing, for example, trying to pack a completed order. Subject to the "ignored" versus "impossible" discussion in Chapter 10, any ignored state plus event must be coded that way: there better not be any transition or action, and the code must not crash. Attempting to cancel a packed or completed Book order cannot affect anything. The impossible state plus event combinations should not just be ignored; some kind of notification to an appropriate entity should be generated although the details are a matter of design.[22]

12.8.2   Deriving Verification Test Elements from Action Specifications

In principle, positive testing of actions only needs to demonstrate that as long as preconditions (requires clauses) have been satisfied, then postconditions (guarantees clauses) are achieved. This can often be done with a single test element,

---

22 As relevant, this could be specified in the interface specification (Chapter 14). There is also further discussion of this in Chapters 16 and 25.

as for the Mark as placed action for Book order on the transition from Open state to Placed. The action doesn't require anything and guarantees the Placed event has been signaled for each Book order line in this Book order.

When an action contains significant decisions, have at least one test element for each decision outcome. In class Book order line, action Mark as packed on the transition from state Placed to state Completed requires nothing and has the guarantees clause:

> if linked to Print medium then picked(.quantity) has been signaled for it

Test elements should include at least two Book order lines. One should be linked to a Print medium to test the true outcome and the other to an eBook medium to test the false outcome.

To the extent that there is complex computation—while not present in Order fulfillment, shipping weight and shipping cost calculations could be an example; test elements should adequately exercise that computation.

Negative testing for actions may involve testing—if possible and appropriate—when an action's preconditions (requires clause) is not satisfied. This is negative testing with respect to the semantic model. However, if the interface specification defines required behavior under these conditions, then this would be positive testing with respect to the interface specification. The initialize action on the initial transition for Book order requires that the given address is consistent with the range of .shipping address. What if the implementation were given an invalid shipping address? Based on risk, elements for negative testing could be included.

12.8.3 Deriving Verification Test Elements from Attributes Ranges

Action specifications can have preconditions of the form

> "the given X value is consistent with the range of Y"

and a postcondition that includes

> "Y has been set to the given X"

Testing against attribute range specifications is normally relevant only on actions that write an attribute based on input from an actor. In Order fulfillment, when a Customer adds a Medium to their Book order, they need to specify the quantity of that Medium to add. It may be possible for them to specify an invalid quantity. The use case also sets the .price per copy of Book order line, but that is coming from the selected Medium, not the external Customer. Since validity of Medium.price should have been enforced when that instance of Medium was created (or last modified), we shouldn't have to do any checking in this action. We should need test elements for .quantity, not for .price per copy.

Given the style of range specification for an attribute, verification test elements are often fairly obvious. When the range is specified as:

- *Span with precision and units*—Test the limits of the span to the given precision. For example, if a .price attribute has a range of "[0.00 to 10.00 Euros to the nearest Eurocent]" positive test elements at €0.00 and 10.00, test the valid span while negative test elements at −0.01 and 10.01 test the boundary to invalid values. Pay attention to whether either end of the span is an open interval rather than a closed interval.
- *Enumeration*—Testing enumerations depends on two factors: if the enumeration is ordered and if the enumeration is the states in the state model. An unordered enumeration that is not the states might only need test elements to show that each enumerated value is properly implemented. An ordered enumeration may require additional test elements to show that proper ordering has also been implemented. When the enumeration is the states in a state model, no separate range testing is required because every value will be tested when deriving test elements from state models.
- *External reference*—Deriving test elements from an external reference depends on the nature of the referenced material, so it can't be discussed any further here. Use your knowledge of the referenced material to derive appropriate test elements.
- *Unconstrained*—By its nature, unconstrained means that verification testing isn't practical. On the other hand, truly unconstrained implementation is impossible given the limits of existing technology. To go along with stakeholder desire for "unconstrained," there is always an economic argument for some technical limit. The cost of implementation increases as the implemented range and/or precision increases; cost will outweigh benefit at some point. There will be an economically viable range and precision likely expressed as nonfunctional requirements of the form "support *at least* X." You can include test elements to demonstrate that the technical boundaries and precision are supported, but this is design dependent and not derivable from a semantic model.

12.8.4 Deriving Verification Test Elements from Derived Attributes

Testing derived attributes depends on the nature of the derivation policy. If the derivation is a mathematical formula (e.g., for Hourly employee.gross pay, it might be ".gross pay = .hours worked * .hourly rate"), then one or a few test elements verifying that the derived value is consistent with the independent values could be sufficient. If there is deliberate testing of the independent values as attributes (above), then derived attribute testing can be piggybacked on attribute range testing, that is, as one is testing Hourly employee.hours worked and .hourly rate, the effect of those changes on .gross pay can also be verified.

If the derivation involves decisions, for example, a Book order is packable only when its state is Placed and each of the Book order lines in it are also packable, then consider one test element for each decision outcome. Have at least one test element for a packable order and at least one test element for an unpackable order. Depending on risk, consider test elements that examine the different reasons for unpackability, for example, a Book order that is unpackable because of invalid status versus one that is unpackable because of insufficient inventory.

12.8.5 Deriving Verification Test Elements from Association Multiplicities

If one side of an association has multiplicity with a lower bound less than one or an upper bound greater than one (e.g., in Order fulfillment, a Customer can place zero to many Book orders but a Book order can only be placed by exactly one Customer), then there will be a range of valid alternatives. In the most general case, where the lower bound is zero and the upper bound is many, positive testable elements can be at zero, one, and many. You can verify that a Customer with no Book orders is supported, a Customer with one Book order is supported, and a Customer with many book orders is supported. Multiplicities can be tested in both an increasing and a decreasing direction as in:

- *A Customer has no Book orders, test adding one Book order to that Customer*—testing from zero to one.
- *A Customer has one Book order, test adding another Book order for that Customer*—testing from one to many.
- *A Customer has two Book orders, test removing one of them*—testing from many to one.
- *A Customer has one Book order, test removing it*—testing from one to zero.

Testing decreasing multiplicity is only valid when the semantic model allows deletion of objects in the associated class. In Order fulfillment, note that deletion of Book orders is not allowed.

Testing outside the valid range of multiplicity is negative testing, for example, trying to remove the only Customer from a Book order or trying to add another Customer to a Book order that already has one.

12.8.6 Deriving Verification Test Elements from Generalizations

Each subclass in a generalization represents a decision or alternative. Take, for example, Medium with its subclasses eBook medium and Print medium. Test elements can involve objects of the subclasses. One test element could add an eBook medium to a Book order and another could add a Print medium to a Book order.

When testing derivation of the packability of Book orders, one Book order could be entirely eBook media, another Book order could be entirely Print media, and still another Book order could be a combination of both eBook and Print media.

Testing a Book order with neither eBook or Print media would be negative testing because a Book order must have at least one Medium and Medium is {complete}—no objects of class Medium alone can exist. When a generalization is {incomplete}, a test element can consider an object that is a member of the superclass but not any of the subclasses.

12.8.7 Deriving Verification Test Elements from Information Flow

The semantic model can also be examined from a data flow perspective. Two data flow coverage techniques could be relevant:

- *All definitions*—Have at least one test case that exercises every situation where an attribute value is either set (on object creation) or modified.
- *All uses*—For each situation where an attribute value is set or modified, have at least one test case that covers the path from the value being set to each of the places where that value is used (read).

12.8.8 Assembling Verification Test Elements into Verification Test Cases

Verification testing, as described in this chapter, is system testing—at least with respect to that (sub)domain (as opposed to unit, or integration and component testing). Verification test cases will be scenarios under the (sub)domain's use cases. If not already done, make a complete list of all sea level use cases (transactions). Comprehensive verification testing needs at least one test case for each sea level use case.

Also, given your understanding of risk, decide which test elements need to appear in test cases. Exclude test elements that are too low value: probability of being broken times damage is not sufficiently greater than testing cost for that element. Putting high priority test elements into test cases may leave room for lower priority test elements to be included for free. Test elements might be rated: "must test," "nice to test if free," and "don't bother testing."

An added complication is that a theoretically viable test element may not be testable in a practical sense. Consider test elements that verify proper implementation of the range of a .grade level on a Student. If the range of the attribute is [1–12, to the whole grade], then test elements could include boundary value coverage testing: 1 and 12 as positive test elements with 0 and 13 as negative test elements. But consider a design that uses a slide bar or radio buttons for the user to select .grade levels. The slide bar or radio buttons only have limited range and can't be driven to invalid values. We can execute the positive test elements, but the negative test elements are impossible due to design choices.

The same can be said for an attribute whose range is an enumeration, for example, Employee.status with range [active, on leave, retired]. If the user interface has a pull-down list or radio buttons for selecting or an application programming interface (API) uses a type-safe enumeration, then it is impossible to test setting to any illegal value, at least through that interface. So while we might generate many test elements, design choices may make some test elements impossible to execute.

One consequence of the difference between positive and negative testing is that a single positive test case can include many positive test elements at the same time. A positive test case can test that more than one Book order line can be added to a single Book order while also testing (part of) the range of the .quantity attribute. If a positive test case fails, it should be obvious what caused the problem. Negative testing, on the other hand, should start by testing only one negative test element at a time. The rest of the test elements in that test case should be positive. A test to see if the implementation allows Print medium. stock on hand to be less than zero (presumably in a test case that is creating an object of class Print medium) should not also test if .reorder level or .reorder quantity can be set to less than one. We should expect the implementation to report that at least one of the parameters is invalid, but not necessarily report all are invalid at the same time.

A class diagram of assembling test elements into verification test cases is shown in Figure 12.15.

Descriptions for this model are as follows:

- *Testable model element*—An element in the semantic model against which code is to be verified. This could be a transition in a state model, an action, an attribute range, etc. from which test elements can be derived according to the tactics above.

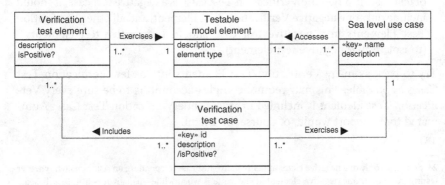

Figure 12.15 Assembling test elements into test cases.

- *Verification test element*—One of the specific, derived testable things on a Testable Model Element, like a specific transition, an action's decision outcome, a boundary value for an attribute (range), an association multiplicity test, etc. Verification test elements might represent positive or negative testing.
- *Verification test element exercises testable model element*—Each Verification Test Element exercises exactly one Testable Model Element, no more and no less. Each Testable Model Element should have at least one Verification Test Element to exercise it but will usually need more.
- *Sea level use case*—A sea level use case (transaction) in the semantic model against which code is to be validated.
- *Sea level use case accesses testable model element*—Each Sea Level Use Case should access at least one Testable Model Element and may access many. Each Testable Model Element must be accessed by at least one Sea Level Use Case (otherwise it is irrelevant and should not be in the semantic model), but may be accessed by more than one.
- *Verification test case*—A specific set of inputs given to the software with intent to reveal defects (i.e., where the code does not preserve policy or process semantics).
- *Verification test case is a scenario under a use case*—Verification testing is system testing with respect to the (sub)domain, so each Verification Test Case will be a scenario under exactly one use case, never more or less. Each use case should have at least one Verification Test Case underneath it, but generally there will be several.
- *Verification test case includes verification test element*—Each Verification Test Case has to include at least one Verification Test Element but will usually include more than one. Each Verification Test Element has to be included in at least one Verification Test Case but is sometimes included in more than one. When the Verification Test Case is a positive test case, it should include as many separate positive test elements as possible (to minimize the number of test cases). When the Verification Test Case is a negative test case, it should include only one negative Verification Test Element, and all other Verification Test Elements in a negative test case should be positive test elements[23] (to isolate that negative test element).

Try to pack as many Verification Test Elements into as few Verification Test Cases as possible. This may require complex accounting to be sure every Verification Test Element is included in at least one Verification Test Case. Automated tool support would, of course, be useful.

---

23 Start with only one negative element per negative test case. Depending on risk, consider whether testing more than one negative element at the same is worthwhile—usually it is not. Risk-based testing might require testing double negatives, triple negatives, etc.

12.8.9 Building Test Cases from Test Elements

Consider these Testable Model Elements from Order fulfillment:

- Book order's state model
- Book order.shipping address
- Book order line's state model
- Book order line.quantity

The testable elements for Book order's state model include the following:

- Initial transition → Book order is open.
- Add a line to an open order → order stays open.
- Drop a line from an open order with >1 line → line is dropped and the order stays open.
- Drop a line from an open order with =1 line → the order is deleted.
- Place an open order with only eBook media → the order becomes completed.
- Place an open order with >1 Print media → order becomes placed.
- Cancel a placed order → order becomes cancelled.
- Pack a placed order that is packable → order becomes packed.
- Ship a packed order → order becomes shipped.
- All negative test cases, for example, cancelling a completed order, shipping an open order, etc.

Book order's .shipping address is assigned from Customer input in the Initialize action, and its range specification is "[any mailing address acceptable to the US Post Office or Canada Post]." We will need two test elements, one valid shipping address (positive testing) and one invalid shipping address[24] (negative testing).

The testable elements from Book order line's state model include the following:

- Initial transition.
- Delete an open line → that line is deleted.
- Place an open line → line becomes placed.
- Pack a placed line → line becomes completed.
- All negative cases, for example, packing an open line, placing a completed line, etc.

Book order line's .quantity is assigned from Customer input in the Initialize action and its range specification is "[1 .. unconstrained, to the whole number]." We will need two test elements, one quantity = 1 (positive test) and one quantity = 0 (negative test).

---

24 See, for example, https://www.usps.com/nationalpremieraccounts/manageprocessandaddress. htm for services that can validate postal addresses.

Both of the initial transitions—assigning Book order.shipping address and assigning Book order line.quantity—are part of the Add to order use case. For this use case, one positive test case could be:

> *"Verification Test Case #1: Add one copy of Print medium Gone With The Wind (GWTW) to Customer Phred's cart with a valid shipping address when there is no open order for Phred → A new Book order for Phred with .date placed == today, .shipping address == that address, and one Book order line with .quantity == 1 and .price per copy == GWTW's .sales price"*

The upper bound of Book order line.quantity is unconstrained, so any requirement would be an economic-driven nonfunctional minimum. Whatever that minimum turned out to be, say, 100 copies, another positive test case verifying that limit is supported could be useful; however that testing is motivated by a nonfunctional requirement. While it is clearly suggested by the semantic model, that test case isn't directly derivable because it depends on information outside of the semantic model.

All positive test elements relevant to the Add to order use case are contained in at least one test case, so now consider negative test elements. The first negative test case could be:

> *"Verification Test Case #2: Add zero copies of Print medium Gone With The Wind (GWTW) to Customer Phred's cart with a valid shipping address → invalid number of copies"*

We still have the negative test element of an invalid shipping address so make another negative test case:

> *"Verification Test Case #3: Add one copy of Print medium Gone With The Wind (GWTW) to Customer Phred's cart with an invalid shipping address → invalid shipping address"*

Based on risks in Order fulfillment, it's probably not relevant to have a double-negative test case for:

> *"Verification Test Case #n: Add zero copies of Print medium Gone With The Wind (GWTW) to Customer Phred's cart with an invalid shipping address → ..."*

The expected result would almost certainly be either "invalid quantity" or "invalid address"; it is unlikely that the expected result would be that both the quantity and the shipping address are invalid.[25]

---

25 This is a case where Notification pattern (Chapter 16) could be used in design.

Verification Test Case #1 through Verification Test Case #3 include all Verification Test Elements relevant to use case Add to order.

The two final transitions both fit under use case Drop from order. In particular, two test cases are needed:

> *"Verification Test Case #4: Drop a line from an open Book order than has more than one Book order line → the selected Book order line got deleted but the rest of the Book order stayed the same"*
>
> *"Verification Test Case #5: Drop a line from an open Book order that has only one Book order line on it → the entire Book order and that Book order line are deleted"*

It's now simply a matter of looking at remaining use cases and Verification Test Elements and assembling them in a way that incorporates all relevant Verification Test Elements into the fewest possible Verification Test Cases.

12.9 Comments Regarding Acceptance Test-Driven Development

Chapter 1 identified the #1 problem in software development as vague, ambiguous, incomplete requirements. It also introduced acceptance test-driven development (ATDD) as a way to eliminate vagueness and ambiguity.[26] Each acceptance-level test case is one or more requirements written in test case language, where test case language is unambiguous.

Two important points need to be made. First, verification test cases do not need to be explicitly derived from a semantic model before code is produced, yet model-based software engineering is still at least implicitly ATDD because acceptance test cases are *derivable* before code is produced. If there is a process to generate verification test cases,[27] then simply executing that process produces acceptance test cases regardless of whether code has been produced or not. Acceptance test cases exist, at least implicitly, before code.

Second, model-based software engineering is better than ATDD because:

- Semantic models are concise and compact; acceptance test cases are not.
- Semantic models are largely graphical; acceptance test cases are not.
- Model element (class, attribute, state, etc.) descriptions provide useful detail that cannot possibly be expressed in acceptance test cases.
- Semantic modeling has explicit completeness guidelines; ATDD does not.
- Semantic models are more descriptive of the (sub)domain than acceptance test cases could ever be.

---

26 These comments also apply to behavior-driven development (BDD).

27 Using an open model compiler to derive verification test cases is introduced in Chapter 21.

- Semantic models can be executed (simulated, as above) in a way that acceptance test cases cannot. Acceptance test cases can be executed *against* code, but they cannot be executed *as* code.
- Semantic models do not perpetuate the #2 problem in software: overdependence on testing to find software defects. To an extent, ATDD does.

Instead of trying to manage requirements for nontrivial software as thousands of ATDD test cases, it is much easier to manage them as one concise, precise semantic model. Acceptance test cases can be derived from the semantic model before or after code; the order doesn't matter. Any time the semantic model is modified, ATDD test cases can be re-derived—presumably automatically.

As one of my former university professors said,

> *"If it's not obvious how to test it, can your specification be any good?"*
> (Dr. Ric Frankel, Seattle University)

It is so obvious how to test from a semantic model that verification test cases literally fall out. Therefore, a semantic model *must* be a good specification.

12.10 Translating a Semantic Model into Natural Language Requirements Documentation

For various reasons it may be necessary to translate a semantic model into natural language. Maybe the stakeholders insist on not learning Unified Modeling Language (UML) notation and they don't trust model simulation. Maybe there is a contractual requirement for natural language documentation. Not only is it straightforward, but it's also possible to do so mechanically. If you have an open model compiler (Chapters 20 and 21), it is possible to cast this as a set of production rules and have the model compiler do the work for you. The process will be illustrated using a subset of Order fulfillment; full translation would take too much time and space. Text in angle brackets ("<", ">") refers to content in the semantic model being translated.

12.10.1 Translating Use Case Diagrams into Natural Language Requirements

Starting with the use case diagram, for each actor:

- "The system[28] shall manage <actor name>s"

---

28 It could be more correct to say, "The (sub)domain shall ...."

For each use case:

- "The system shall support <use case name>".

For each participates-in link between an actor and a use case:

- "<actor name> shall be able to participate in <use case name>"

Optionally, for each unspecified participates-in link:

- "<actor name> shall not be able to participate in <use case name>"

For each "«includes»" use case relationship:

- "<included use case name> is a required part of <including use case name>"

For each "«extends»" use case relationship:

- "<extending use case name> is an optional part of <extended use case name>"

The following are examples of a portion of the Order fulfillment domain use case diagram translated to English:

> *"The system shall manage Customers*
> *The system shall manage Publishers*
> *...*
> *The system shall support Catalog?*
> *The system shall support Add to order*
> *The system shall support Drop from order*
> *...*
> *Customer shall be able to participate in Catalog?*
> *Customer shall be able to participate in Add to order*
> *Customer shall be able to participate in Drop from order*
> *...*
> *Publisher shall not be able to participate in Catalog?*
> *Publisher shall not be able to participate in Add to order*
> *Publisher shall not be able to participate in Drop from order*
> *..."*

12.10.2 Translating Class Models into Natural Language Requirements

Class models can be translated into natural language as follows. For each class (avoiding duplication with the actors, previously mentioned):

- "The system shall manage <class name>s"

For each attribute:

- "When a <class name> exists, it shall have a single value for its <attribute name>"
- "The valid values for the <attribute name> of a <class name> shall be <range specification>"

For each key:

- "The value of <key attributes> for a <class name> shall be unique"

For each derived attribute:

- "When a <class name> exists, it shall have a single value for its <derived attribute name>"
- "The value for the <attribute name> of a <class name> shall be consistent with <derivation policy>"

For each side of each association:

- "When a <near side class name> exists, it shall be linked to at least <minimum multiplicity> <far side class name>s"
- "When a <near side class name> exists, it shall be linked to no more than <maximum multiplicity> <far side class name>s"

For each subclass:

- "All requirements applying to <superclass name> shall also apply to <subclass name>"
- If the generalization is labeled "{complete}" then, "Objects of class <superclass name> shall not exist without also being one of the immediate subclasses at the same time"

The following are examples of a portion of the Order fulfillment class model translated to English:

> *"The system shall manage Customers"*
> *"When a Customer exists, it shall have a single value for its email address"*
> *"The valid values for the email address of a Customer shall be any valid email address according to relevant IETF specifications"*
> *"When a Customer exists, it shall have a single value for its name"*
> *"The valid values for the name of a Customer shall be unconstrained"*
> *"When a Customer exists, it shall have a single value for its postal address"*
> *"The valid values for the postal address of a Customer shall be any mailing address acceptable to the US Post Office or Canada Post"*
> *"The system shall manage Book Orders"*
> *"When a Book Order exists, it shall have a single value for its id"*
> *"The valid values for the id of a Book Order shall be refer to Corporate Policy CP123a, Customer Order Identification"*

"When a Book Order exists, it shall have a single value for its date ordered"
"The valid values for date ordered of a Book Order shall be a calendar date no earlier than 1-Jan-1998 and no later than today, to the whole day"
"When a Book Order exists, it shall have a single value for its shipping address"
"The valid values for the shipping address of a Book Order shall be any mailing address acceptable to the US Post Office or Canada Post"
"When a Book Order exists, it shall have a single value for its status"
"The valid values for the Status of a Customer shall be an enumeration of the states in the state model"
"When a Book Order exists, it shall have a single value for its/sales?"
"The value for the/sales? of a Book Order shall be consistent with true only when .status = placed and isPackable? = true for each Book order line in this Book order"
"When a Book Order exists, it shall have a single value for its/profit?"
"The value for the/profit? of a Book Order shall be consistent with if .status = completed then sum of profit? for each Book order line in this Book order, otherwise $0.00"
"When a Book Order exists, it shall be linked to at least 1 Customers"
"When a Book Order exists, it shall linked with no more than 1 Customers"
"When a Customer exists, it shall linked with at least 0 Book Orders"
"When a Customer exists, it shall be linked with no more than many Book Orders"
"All requirements applying to Medium shall also apply to Print Medium"
"All requirements applying to Medium shall also apply to eBook Medium"
"Objects of class Medium shall not exist without also being in one of the immediate subclasses"
...

12.10.3 Translating State Models into Natural Language Requirements

State models can be translated into natural language as follows. For each class:

- "The valid states of a <class name> shall be <list of states>"
- "When a <class name> is created, it shall start in the <initial state> state"

For each valid transition in the class state chart (including final transitions):

- "When a <class name> is in the <source state> state and sees a <event> event, it shall transition to the <destination state> state"
- If there is a guard condition on this transition then append, "but only when <guard> is true"

For each transition action:

- If the transition does not have a guard, "While transitioning from <source state> to <destination state> (in response to a <triggering event> event), <transition action> shall be completed"
- If the transition has a guard, "While transitioning from <source state> to <destination state> (in response to a <triggering event> event when <guard> is true), <transition action> shall be completed"

For each entry action:

- "Before entering <state name>, <entry action> shall be completed"

For each exit action:

- "Before leaving <state name>, <exit action> shall be completed"

For each ignored combination of state and event[29]:

- "When a <class name> is in the <state name> state, event <event name> shall be ignored"

For each activity in each state that has activities:

- "When a <class name> is in the <state name> state, <activity name> shall happen continuously"

The following is the translation of the state model for Book order in Order fulfillment into English:

> *"The valid states of a Book Order shall be Open, Placed, Cancelled, Packed, Completed"*
>
> *"When a Book Order is created, it shall start in the Open state"*
>
> *"When a Book Order is in the Open state and sees a Drop event, it shall transition to the Open state, but only if [>1 Line] is true"*
>
> *"While transitioning from Open to Open (in response to a Drop event when [>1 Line] is true), Drop line shall be completed"*
>
> *"When a Book Order is in the Open state and sees a Add event, it shall transition to the Open state"*
>
> *"While transitioning from Open to Open (in response to a Add event), Add line shall be completed"*
>
> *"When a Book Order is in the Open state and sees a Drop event, it shall transition to the final state, but only if [=1 Line] is true"*

---

29 For each impossible combination of state and event: "When a <class name> is in the <state name> state, event <event name> shall be handled as defined in the Interface Specification" or something similar.

"While transitioning from Open to final (in response to a Drop event when [=1 Line] is true), Drop line shall be completed"

"When a Book Order is in the Open state and sees a Place event, it shall transition to the Completed state, but only if [no print medium] is true"

"While transitioning from Open to Completed (in response to a Place event when [no print medium] is true), Mark as packed shall be completed"

"When a Book Order is in the Open state and sees a Place event, it shall transition to the Placed state, but only if [has print medium] is true"

"While transitioning from Open to Placed (in response to a Place event when [has print medium] is true), Mark as placed shall be completed"

"When a Book Order is in the Placed state and sees a Packed event, it shall transition to the Packed state, but only if [isPackable?] is true"

"While transitioning from Placed to Packed (in response to a Packed event when [isPackable?] is true), Mark as packed shall be completed"

"When a Book Order is in the Placed state and sees a Cancel event, it shall transition to the Cancelled state"

"When a Book Order is in the Packed state and sees a Shipped event, it shall transition to the Completed state"

"When a Book Order is in the Open state, event Cancel shall be ignored"

"When a Book Order is in the Open state, event Packed shall be ignored"

"When a Book Order is in the Open state, event Shipped shall be ignored"

"When a Book Order is in the Placed state, event Add shall be ignored"

"When a Book Order is in the Placed state, event Drop shall be ignored"

"When a Book Order is in the Placed state, event Place shall be ignored"

"When a Book Order is in the Placed state, event Packed shall be ignored"

"When a Book Order is in the Placed state, event Shipped shall be ignored"

"When a Book Order is in the Cancelled state, event Add shall be ignored"

"When a Book Order is in the Cancelled state, event Drop shall be ignored"

"When a Book Order is in the Cancelled state, event Place shall be ignored"

"When a Book Order is in the Cancelled state, event Cancel shall be ignored"

"When a Book Order is in the Cancelled state, event Packed shall be ignored"

"When a Book Order is in the Cancelled state, event Shipped shall be ignored"

"When a Book Order is in the Packed state, event Add shall be ignored"

"When a Book Order is in the Packed state, event Drop shall be ignored"

"When a Book Order is in the Packed state, event Place shall be ignored"

"When a Book Order is in the Packed state, event Cancel shall be ignored"

"When a Book Order is in the Packed state, event Packed shall be ignored"

"When a Book Order is in the Completed state, event Add shall be ignored"

"When a Book Order is in the Completed state, event Drop shall be ignored"

"When a Book Order is in the Completed state, event Place shall be ignored"

"When a Book Order is in the Completed state, event Cancel shall be ignored"

"When a Book Order is in the Completed state, event Packed shall be ignored"

"When a Book Order is in the Completed state, event Shipped shall be ignored"

...

12.10.4   Translating Action Specifications into Natural Language Requirements

Action specifications can be translated into natural language as follows. For each requires clause (precondition):

- "Action <action name> shall not occur unless all of the following are true: <requires conditions list>"

For each guarantees clause (postcondition):

- "Upon completion of <action name>, the following shall now be true: <guarantees conditions list>"

The following are examples of actions for Book order in Order fulfillment translated to English:

> *"Action Initialize shall not occur unless all of the following are true:*
> *given address is consistent with the range of .shipping address"*
> *"Upon completion of Initialize, the following shall now be true:*
> *new Book order exists with:*
> *.id properly assigned*
> *.date opened set to today*
> *.shipping address assigned as specified*
> *this book order linked to its customer*
> *one new Book order line as been created appropriately"*
> *"Action add line shall not occur unless all of the following are true:*
> *none"*
> *"Upon completion of add line, the following shall now be true:*
> *a new Book order line as been created appropriately"*
> *"Action drop line shall not occur unless all of the following are true:*
> *the referenced Book order line exists"*
> *"Upon completion of drop line, the following shall now be true:*
> *that referenced Book order line as been deleted"*
> *"Action mark as placed shall not occur unless all of the following are true:*
> *none"*
> *"Upon completion of mark as placed, the following shall now be true:*
> *place has been signaled for each Book order line in this Book order"*
> *"Action mark as packed shall not occur unless all of the following are true:*
> *none"*
> *"Upon completion of mark as packed, the following shall now be true:*
> *packed has been signaled for each Book order line in this Book order"*

Translating interaction diagrams into natural language does not have enough value to be worth investing any effort.

This discussion should make semantic modeling even more compelling. Even relatively simple semantic models like Order fulfillment expand into thousands, if not tens of thousands, of "shall" statements. Imagine how many statements would come out of a semantic model with as many as 40 classes. How easy it would be to miss one or more (or even a whole set of) important requirements? Also, with so many statements, likely randomly ordered, how hard it would be to maintain or verify consistency—that no statement contradicts another elsewhere in that collection.

It is also worth mentioning that each natural language statement implies at least one verification test case to verify that code complies with it. The value of the clarity, conciseness, and precision of the semantic modeling language should be even more obvious. Also, scalability of full ATDD becomes questionable. Remember that people who build houses gave up trying to describe them in natural language more than one hundred years ago. Houses are trivial compared to most software. So what makes you think you can be successful describing something that's orders of magnitude more complex using a natural language?

12.11   Analysis Patterns Versus Design Patterns

Design patterns[30] have been popular in the software industry for many years. Patterns represent useful, already worked-out solutions to common software problems. Many patterns truly are "design" patterns; that is, they are technology dependent:

- Adapter
- Bridge
- Strategy
- Observer (publish–subscribe)
- Singleton
- Iterator
- Proxy
- Decorator
- State (delegation)
- Data access object
- ...

On the other hand, it is important to understand that some patterns are truly "requirements patterns," they are independent of technology and entirely relevant in semantic models. Composite pattern is one of the most common

---

30 See, for example, [Gamma95].

patterns appearing in semantic models. Using reflexive associations to represent networked or tree structure semantics is also very common. Leon Starr discusses several patterns that are useful in semantic models[31]; you should familiarize yourself with those patterns if you expect to do much semantic modeling.

12.12 Product Families and Semantic Models

Chapter 3 introduced the idea of "product family development": proactive design to invariants and design for change. The discussion was in terms of "design," that is, technology dependent. Invariants and variability also apply in semantic models.

In the WebBooks case study, the Order fulfillment domain—as modeled in Appendix D—is a point solution to a point problem. It captures policies to be enforced and the processes to be carried out that WebBooks wants. But change the context a bit. Instead of us building software for WebBooks alone, consider that we are a separate company that wants to sell Order fulfillment software to anyone who wants it.

Some content in the Order fulfillment semantic model could be unique to WebBooks, for example, you can be a customer without ever having placed an order, addresses must be acceptable to the US Post Office and Canada Post, etc. Not every organization that wants order fulfillment software wants these exact policies and processes. On the other hand, much of Order fulfillment semantic model is not unique. It is generic to anyone who wants to fulfill orders:

- Customers
- Orders
- Placing orders
- Shipping orders
- Inventory
- Suppliers
- ...

If our company builds Order fulfillment software for sale, we would need to deal with core, invariant policies, and processes that apply across all possible organizations. But we would also need to acknowledge the variations that one organization will want separate from any other. It's not a product family in the technology space; it's a product family in the policy and process space.

Any variation that's technology based (i.e., nonfunctional how and nonfunctional how well) doesn't belong in the semantic model. Address that kind of variation in the design as discussed in Part III.

---

31 See [Starr96].

While there has been a fair amount of research, experience, literature, etc. on software product families,[32] how that applies in semantic models has not been fully worked out. There certainly isn't any accepted UML notation to support it.

In general, represent as much variation as possible in terms of data (i.e., in attribute values). Doing so makes configuring that aspect of product variation easy. Only represent variation in terms of model structure as a last resort. That said, structural variation in semantic models would almost certainly be required in the general case:

- Some given attribute might apply in some businesses but not others.
- The range for an attribute might be organizational specific.
- Some association multiplicities could be organizational specific.
- It is an attribute versus it is a class (as in Figure 8.4).
- An event is relevant in some organizations, but not others.
- Transitions caused by some event may vary.
- The specifics of actions (contracts) might vary.
- A dimension of inheritance may need to be {complete} in some cases but {incomplete} in others.
- ...

Any element of a semantic model could be invariant over different user organization's policies and processes: specific classes, attributes, ranges, associations, multiplicities, states, events, transitions, actions, etc. But just the same, any kind of model element could also be a variation point across those same organizations. Further research and experience is needed to work out how to best incorporate product families into semantic models. The problem hasn't been solved, but will clearly need to be solved at some point.

12.13 Alternate Semantic Model Development Processes

Part II followed a relatively top-down, outside-in process in developing semantic models. This is a workable process for most (sub)domains—about 80%—but it is certainly not appropriate for every (sub)domain. A top-down, outside-in process depends on knowing (to at least some degree of certainty) an automation boundary. But that is not always known up front. What about those cases where the automation boundary can't be known until much later in the project, and how should those (sub)domains be approached?

---

32 See, for example, https://en.wikipedia.org/wiki/Product_family_engineering.

The answer is to use a bottom-up, middle-out process instead:

1) Start by building an extended class model that is guaranteed to include all classes that might be in any implementation.
2) Build state models for classes, being sure to incorporate all processes likely to be automated.
3) Next, decide where the boundary of automation should be. This should be based on the business value of automating, the cost of automating, what is actually computable versus not (e.g., *NP* Completeness), etc.
4) Given a chosen boundary of automation, build use case diagram around that boundary.
5) Optionally, reduce the class model as appropriate.
6) Optionally, reduce the state models as appropriate.
7) Fill in as many interaction diagrams as appropriate.

The goal is to get to "done," both on semantic modeling and on the project as a whole, in the most efficient and effective manner. Use your professional judgment to decide what would be the best approach to get there.

12.14   Build Versus Buy: The Role of Semantic Models in Package Acquisition

Software is expensive to build and maintain. If you are a software vendor, selling software is your business. Of course you're going to build and maintain it—that's how you make money: by selling and supporting what you built. But many organizations' primary mission is not software. Their mission is something else, like being an airline or a retail store. Those organizations would much rather buy software than build it. In fact, buy versus build is probably the single most critical decision in the software acquisition lifecycle.

A commercial off-the-shelf software package is only useful to a buyer if it:

- Automates the policies and processes the buyer wants automated
- Is affordable

And thus "What policies and processes does the buyer want automated?" becomes a critical question. How would the buyer say? By scribbling some vague, ambiguous, woefully incomplete set of natural language statements ("The vendor product shall ...") in a massive requirements tome? Far better, the buyer should build a semantic model of what they want automated.

Next, "What policies and processes does a vendor's product automate?" Today, at best a buyer will get an equally vague, ambiguous, woefully incomplete set of natural language statements ("Our product does ..."). And that has to be teased out from all the sales and marketing hype ("Ours is by far the most superior product on the market today, blah, blah, blah...").

It would be in the best interest of a software vendor to publish their semantic model. Some might claim, "But that's proprietary." That is simply not a sensible claim. Anyone with modest intelligence can reverse engineer the policies and processes if they are only willing to invest the time and effort. Besides, the vendor had to have understood that to build a workable product in the first place. To the extent the vendor doesn't understand, there are semantic inconsistencies—then their product is defective.[33]

The vendor's intellectual property (IP) value cannot be in the policies and processes of their product's top-level domain; the IP value is in how their software implements that domain. The vendor shouldn't show the domain diagram or semantic models of lower domains unless they are relevant to how a customer uses the product. Certainly don't show the design or code for any domain— that's where the vendor's unique IP value really is.

If the vendor does think something is unique and special about their semantic model, then, at least in the United States, the vendor can patent that model. Like any other patented invention, others can see it but can't use it without appropriate licensing. So there's little danger in making a top domain semantic model visible. It's even proof that the vendor does have a complete, consistent business being automated in their product.

The buyer should be able to compare the vendor's semantic model with their own. What are the gaps? Can those gaps be tolerated? Are there reasonable workarounds? How much easier would the selection process be if the buyer could do a side-by-side semantic model comparison and gap analysis? The buyer could even publish their target semantic model in their Request for Proposal (RFP)/Request for Tender (RFT) and demand the vendor to do the gap analysis in their response.

If you are a customer looking to buy a vendor product, remember that you're the one with the money. You don't have to give the money to anyone until you are satisfied. When enough buyers demand that vendors make top domain semantic model available, and reject vendors who don't, software vendors will get the message loud and clear: no published top domain semantic model means no sale.

Clearly, every software vendor isn't going to rush out and immediately build semantic models to publish. Of course they are going to wait until enough of the customer base demands it (much to everyone's detriment). So until then, what can the buyer do? Simply use the buyer's semantic model to derive verification test cases as described earlier in this chapter. Focus on test cases for scenarios that are the most critical: How likely is there to be an important difference (or defect) in the vendor product? If there is a difference (or defect), how critical would it be? This is classic risk-based testing. The buyer should be able to get a demonstration copy of the vendor product and execute it against these

---

33 This could explain why many vendor products are so full of defects.

verification test cases. How does the demonstration copy measure up? How well does the vendor package meet the buyer's needs? How many defects in the vendor product were flushed out along the way?

Let the buyer beware: if you don't truly understand the policies and processes you want automated—because you don't have a semantic model—then you run the risk of choosing a package that doesn't meet your needs. And you probably won't (as is typical today) find out about it until well after it's too late. You've already given the vendor your money; you're unlikely to get it back. In the end, even in package acquisition—even when the buyer knows they are not going to be building the software in question, they already know they're going to buy an off-the-shelf package—there is still value in developing semantic models.

Let the vendor beware: if you're not building semantic models now, then you better start soon. When your customers realize the power of the semantic model in vendor selection decisions, they will demand to see your top domain's model. If you don't have one, you'll be out of the running: no sale. And besides, building the semantic model of your product gives you the opportunity to validate the policies and processes your product is intended to automate and be sure it actually automates them completely and consistently. You, the vendor, get a much better product—with far fewer defects—in the process.

12.15 Summary

The components in a semantic model are:

- Use case diagrams to describe scope and context of the business. This identifies process at the most coarse-grained, high-level view.
- Class model to precisely define business policies that need to be enforced.
- Interaction (sequence) diagrams to describe processes at an intermediate level.
- State models to precisely specify process at the most fine-grained level.

This chapter completes the topic of semantic modeling and describes what can be done with a model. In particular,

- Organizing model content into a written specification
- Validating a model, by peer review and simulated execution
- Deriving verification test cases from a semantic model
- Translating a semantic model into natural language
- Analysis patterns versus design patterns
- Product family semantic models
- Alternate semantic model development processes
- Buy versus build: the role of semantic modeling in package acquisition

The semantic model gives the designers/developers the expertise they need—regardless of (sub)domain—to be able to automate. Recall that code is a mapping from a semantic model of a business onto a semantic model of automation technology; therefore

> *"For software developers to be successful at automating someone's business, those developers need to understand that business at least as well as—if not better than—the business experts understand it."*

Look at a semantic model and see how well we now understand the policies and processes stakeholders want automated. Building a semantic model brings out domain knowledge in a complete, consistent, clear, correct, concise, and precise way. Key functional requirements detail that clearly would have been missing on a typical software project was exposed for everyone to see:

- Nonoccurrence business events and resulting use cases
- Attribute ranges
- Association multiplicities
- Subtle but important combinations of state and event
- ...

Failure to elicit and specify functional requirements means that either consciously or unconsciously the designer/developer ends up guessing. What's the probability of the developer guessing right? It is less than 100%, to be sure. And the result of a wrong guess is a defect in the software, now only waiting to be discovered by a tester or worse yet, a user. Testers have a hard enough time just testing what *is* specified; they are unlikely be testing what *is not* specified. The most likely result is that the user encounters these defects.

By applying the completeness hints, we even reveal incompleteness in the business expert's understanding of their own business. The most common case this happens is a particular event in a particular state (state–event completeness hint):

> *"We've been in this business for over 50 years and that's never happened. So we don't know what should be done. But now that you point it out, it is clear that it CAN happen. It's also clear that something needs to be done. Give us a week to figure it out, we'll get back to you"*

The very process of building the semantic model makes the modeler a business expert—at least to the extent of the policies and processes modeled. The semantic model represents explicit business expertise, captured in a complete, consistent, clear, correct, concise, precise, and logically organized way. It doesn't matter who built the semantic model; the model is exactly the business domain expertise that's needed to automate.

And now, on to Part III:

> *"Let's write some code!"*

Part III

Model-Based Design and Code

Part II presents semantic modeling of policies and processes, independent of automation technology. From a semantic model, we have a complete, consistent, clear, concise, precise, correct, and validated understanding of policies and processes to automate—at least the part to be automated so far. Software may of course be developed in an iterative fashion. Part III explains how to translate a semantic model and nonfunctional requirements into design and code. Chapters in Part III include:

- *Introduction to Design and Code*—Overviews translation-driven software design and code starting from a semantic model and nonfunctional requirements.
- *Designing Interfaces: Specifying Real-World Interaction*—Gives physical form to conceptual actor–domain interactions.
- *High-Level Design: Classes and Operations*—Develop a first approximation of software high-level design.
- *High-Level Design: Contracts and Signatures*—Derive operation interfaces, both syntax and semantics, in high-level design.
- *Detailed Design and Code*—Derive internal data and method structures and code for classes in high-level design.
- *Formal Disciplines of Design and Code*—Integrate science and mathematics into detailed design and code.
- *Optimization*—Optimizes design and code to satisfy the nonfunctional how well requirements while minimizing accidental complexity.
- *Model Compilation*—Automates translation of a semantic model into code: literally, self-coding documentation.

How to Engineer Software: A Model-Based Approach, First Edition. Steve Tockey.
© 2019 the IEEE Computer Society, Inc. Published 2019 by John Wiley & Sons, Inc.

- *Advanced Open Model Compilation*—How to optimize generated application code, build an open model compiler, and generate output other than application source code.
- *Wrapping Up Model-Based Design and Code*—Summarizes design and coding, including important observations on the relationship between design and code and key implications of that relationship.

13

Introduction to Design and Code

This chapter introduces designing and coding from a semantic model and non-functional requirements. Topics include:

- Comparing and contrasting semantic modeling with design modeling.
- Selecting automation technologies.
- Establishing a boundary of automation: what will and won't be automated. This continues the expanded models versus reduced models discussion from Chapter 6.
- Comparing and contrasting interface design with software design and how it affects the software design activity.
- Overviewing the software design activity.

13.1 Semantic Modeling Versus Design Modeling

All nontrivial software exists to automate a business: to enforce a set of policies and carry out a set of processes:

> *"For software developers to be successful automating someone's business, those developers need to understand that business at least as well as—if not better than—the business experts understand it."*

Semantic modeling—modeling software functional requirements—and design modeling are both modeling activities. The difference is in the goals of those models:

- The goal of semantic modeling is to capture, record, communicate, and validate a complete, consistent, clear, correct, concise, and precise statement of the policies and processes to be automated. The main concerns are managing complexity, isolating areas of expertise, enabling agreement on the

How to Engineer Software: A Model-Based Approach, First Edition. Steve Tockey.
© 2019 the IEEE Computer Society, Inc. Published 2019 by John Wiley & Sons, Inc.

problem before building a solution, and positioning developers to find an optimal solution.

- The goal of design modeling is to describe candidate solutions. The main concern is efficient use of computing resources: execution speed, memory utilization, development cost and schedule, and long-term maintenance cost and schedule.

The goals of the models are different, so the nature of the models will be different. Where semantic models are intentionally automation technology independent, design models are necessarily automation technology dependent. The semantic model is about meaning (semantics); design is about representing those semantics in technology. We should have already worked out the relevant meanings in the semantic model: What does it mean to be a customer? An account? To deposit? To withdraw? Etc.? Deciding on representation—the mapping, subject to the three constraints of completeness, preserving semantic, and meeting the nonfunctional requirements—is a much easier job. Mapping well-understood semantics onto well-understood mechanisms should be relatively straightforward. Trying to map poorly understood semantics—as is the norm in mainstream software projects—onto any technology will be challenging, regardless of how well that technology is understood.

13.2   Selecting Automation Technologies

To the extent that automation technologies (computer hardware, operating system(s), programming language(s), etc.) are not already specified in nonfunctional how requirements, this would be the time to decide:

- Processor(s)/CPU(s)
- Primary storage (memory)
- Secondary storage (disk)
- Tertiary storage (e.g., archive)
- Communication links and protocols
- Programming language(s)
- Run-time libraries
- ...

Of course, Infrastructure as a Service (IaaS), Platform as a Service (PaaS), and other cloud-based options should be considered as appropriate.

In keeping with the economics-driven spirit of software engineering, if specific automation technologies are not required, then several technically viable alternatives should be proposed and the most cost-effective one(s) selected.

13.3   Establishing a Boundary of Automation

Recall reduced versus expanded models from Chapter 6:

- Reduced models contain all of, and only, elements for which software needs to be developed and maintained.
- Expanded models contain one or more elements that are out of scope for software development and maintenance, but those additional elements are useful in communicating context about what does need to be developed and maintained.

If you have a reduced semantic model—the intent is to automate everything—the boundary of automation is already defined by the actors. Nothing more needs to be done: you already have a well-defined boundary.

You may have intended to build a reduced semantic model, but due to unforeseen budget or schedule constraints, even that can't be fully implemented. The reduced model may become an expanded model whether you like it or not. Or maybe your project is being run incrementally, designing and implementing a piece of a (sub)domain at a time.

If you have an expanded model, someone—presumably the stakeholders who are paying for the software—will need to decide what to automate and what not. Those stakeholders should have an understanding of the value of automation: it's not the technical staff's role to have that kind of knowledge although technical staff should be capable of gaining that insight over time. To make meaningful business decisions, stakeholders need to be aware of cost. That's where the technical community comes in. Having an expanded semantic model, knowing nonfunctional requirements, and using the estimation process in Chapter 23, we should be able to put reasonable price tags on alternatives, as in:

> *"If all you want is scope A, we can do that for $X in T time. If you want scope A+B, it will cost $Y and take U time. If you want scope A+B+C, it will cost $Z and take V time. It's your money being spent, what do you want us to do?"*

This is another example of true software engineering: creating a cost-effective solution to a real-world computing problem.

Once an automation boundary has been established, that boundary needs to be recorded and communicated. One option is to annotate an expanded semantic model, tagging elements that are in versus out of the reduced model's scope. You might:

- Use a custom stereotype
- Make a list of the relevant classes and/or use cases
- UML is colorblind: paint model elements different colors to reflect the decision

Another option is to copy an expanded model into an entirely new model then delete non-automated content from the copy. The problem in this case is redundancy. If changes are made to the reduced model, corresponding changes need to be made to the expanded model lest it fall out of synch. If the expanded model gets out of synch, stakeholders run the risk of losing their investment in that expanded model. Merging modified reduced model elements back into an expanded model can be nontrivial, although it does tend to be much less difficult than merging divergent code branches.

Another practical consideration could be that the organization wants a single expanded model but wants it reduced in more than one way for implementation in more than one automation technology. Select or create an approach for specifying a boundary of automation that meets the needs of your organization.

13.4 Two Kinds of Design

As illustrated by the dashed oval in Figure 13.1, there are two kinds of design: design of software interface and design of internal software structure.

The interface specification defines interfaces that real-world, external entities (real-world actors in the reduced semantic model) use to interact with the software. While the interface specification doesn't necessarily use UML, its content

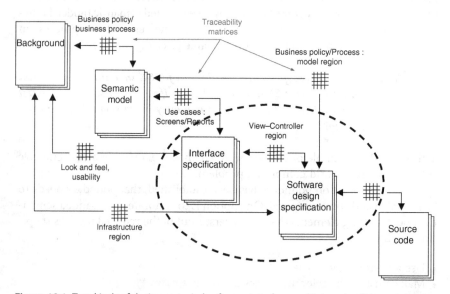

Figure 13.1 Two kinds of design: external software interface and internal software structure.

is critical for designing View-controller region (assuming a Model–View–Controller or similar highly cohesive, loosely coupled software architecture).

With a few important exceptions, the software design specification can be thought of as the classic software design you would expect to find on a typical software project that publishes design documentation. Those important exceptions will be presented later in Part III.

Design is driven at least in part by the nonfunctional requirements. There are two kinds of design; so nonfunctional requirements should be further partitioned based on the dimension of design they affect. The separation doesn't need to be explicit, that is, documented: designers only need to be aware of what nonfunctional requirements affect what parts of design. This can be managed implicitly on most projects. Recalling Figure 4.10, Figure 13.2 extends it to further filter nonfunctional requirements.

There are typically three cases:

- *Some nonfunctional requirements only affect interfaces*—A requirement like "Screen backgrounds shall be a particular shade of blue" affects look and feel of interfaces but should not affect software internal design in any significant way.
- *Some nonfunctional requirements affect only internal software design*—A requirement like "The software shall be written in Java" affects software structure (e.g., single inheritance only, not multiple inheritance) but shouldn't have a major influence on interfaces.

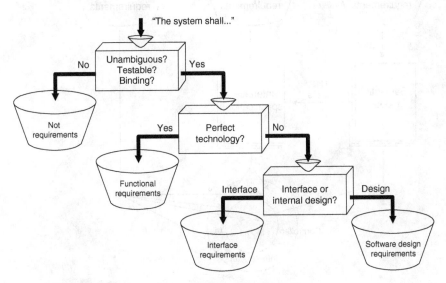

Figure 13.2 Extending the requirements filtering process.

- *Some nonfunctional requirements affect both interface and internal software design*—Requirements like "The user interface shall be Java Swing compliant" or "Client applications shall access this software via a REST API" would influence both the external interface and the internal software structure.

13.5 Overview of the Software Design Activity

Figure 13.3 shows how software activities fit together in model-based software engineering.

Part II introduced and explained semantic models. Chapter 14 shows how sea level use cases from a semantic model are combined with interface requirements to develop an interface specification. That chapter also explains how sea level use cases might also drive a service-oriented architecture (SOA), microservices, or RESTful API.

Chapter 15 shows how to derive classes and operations in high-level software design. Model region of the design is derived from the semantic model. Controller region design and code translates actions on the defined interface (e.g., mouse clicks on buttons, calls to an API, etc.) into a form that Model region

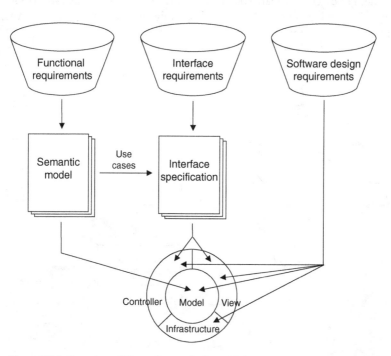

Figure 13.3 Overview of the software design activity.

is able to process. View region translates results produced by Model region to the form defined on external interfaces (e.g., displaying an output screen, printing a report, or returning a data structure from an API call). Infrastructure region provides support services that don't already exist in the run-time environment.

Chapter 16 explains how to develop signatures (syntax) and contracts (semantics) for operations in high-level design. Model region operation syntax and semantics are derived from the semantic model.

Chapter 17 shows how to derive detailed design and code. Model region classes have instance variables and methods derived from the semantic model and high-level design. View and Controller regions are driven by the interface specification, while Infrastructure region is driven as needed.

Chapter 18 explains how to bring formal, disciplined approaches into method level design and code to help avoid defects.

Chapter 19 shows how to optimize design and code to satisfy performance requirements across several levels in the design and code. A discussion of how to translate object-oriented design and code into non-object oriented is included.

Chapter 20 shows how to automate significant portions of design and code using an open model compiler: literally self-coding documentation.

Chapter 21 discusses advanced open model compilation: optimizing generated application code, how to build a model compiler along with other nontraditional uses of open model compiler technology. A brief presentation of weaknesses in UML semantics is included.

Chapter 22 summarizes Part III. This chapter also presents some important implications of the model-based software engineering process.

13.6 Summary

Semantic modeling and design modeling both involve modeling. The difference is in the intent of those models. The semantic model captures, validates, and communicates policies and processes that stakeholders want automated. Design models describe how those policies and processes are automated. The goals of the models are different, so the nature of the models is different. Where semantic models are intentionally automation technology independent, design models are necessarily automation technology dependent.

If a semantic model is not a reduced model, decisions need to be made about what will be automated and what will not. This should be driven by the value of automation in light of the cost to provide it, that is, economics.

Part of design will focus on interfaces to real-world actors and will be described in an interface specification. The other part of design is for internal structure of the software and will be captured and communicated in a software design specification.

14

Designing Interfaces

Specifying Real-World Interaction

The semantic model specifies logical (i.e., conceptual) interaction between actors and a (sub)domain. That logical interaction has to be given physical form: interface specifications define how real-world actors interact with real software. This chapter explains how sea level use cases from a semantic model are combined with nonfunctional requirements to design interfaces provided to real-world actors. Chapter 15 on initial high-level design explains that use cases in design can be a superset of use cases from the semantic model. This chapter puts interface design into the context of software development, explains the importance of usability, provides detail on designing user interfaces (UI), application program(mer) interfaces (APIs), and instrumentation interfaces in embedded systems.

14.1   Interface Design in the Context of Software Process

If a (sub)domain is developed following the sequence of chapters in this book,[1] you now have a semantic model and nonfunctional requirements. The nonfunctional requirements have also been filtered, at least implicitly, into those affecting interfaces versus software structure. No actual software design has been done yet. It might not be clear why we should be defining, designing, and agreeing on external interfaces now. The reason is to avoid wasting time building inappropriate interfaces. A real example is a nurse's record-keeping system that was built using a typical mainstream software development approach.

Nurses are required to record certain patient data: temperature, pulse rate, blood pressure, and so on. A healthcare company wanted software to allow nurses to enter that data quickly and easily into a computer. Unfortunately

---

1 Chapter 24 presents an alternate strategy that defines interfaces before developing semantic models.

How to Engineer Software: A Model-Based Approach, First Edition. Steve Tockey.
© 2019 the IEEE Computer Society, Inc. Published 2019 by John Wiley & Sons, Inc.

no member of the development team had ever seen nurses work, nor had they ever bothered to talk to any real nurses. The team simply assumed that nurses would make regular rounds to each patient in their area and then sit down at this patient records system to enter all data in order: patient by patient. In effect, they assumed nurses work in batch mode where they first gather all data and then enter it sequentially. The software was built on this assumption. It was a failure.

Nurses simply don't work that way. Just as a nurse might be sitting down for a sip of coffee, there could be an emergency in bed 204B. The nurse rushes in and helps stabilize the patient. They take patient vital signs as a last duty and head back to the station where they record that data. Before returning to the now cold cup of coffee, there might be another emergency in 208A, so it's off to stabilize another patient. Nurses work in a very interrupt-driven environment; a batch-oriented UI simply won't work.

To make matters worse, the developers didn't use any kind of Model–View–Controller[2] software architecture. UI code was tightly intermingled with business logic code. The code was so tightly coupled that it was economically inseparable. At least if they had used (some variant of) Model–View–Controller, they should have been able to redevelop View-controller to provide a revised interface. In the end, the healthcare company had to write off a $15 million investment in software that was never usable. The entire system never ran a single bit of real-world data—all because assumptions about how the system would be used were completely wrong and the software design wasn't resilient enough to adapt.

14.2 Importance of Usability

Usability is the subject of hundreds, if not thousands, of articles and books. There is simply too much to do the topic adequate justice here. That said, three important points must be made:

- *Paying attention to usability can be critical to success or failure of software as a product* —For example, the nurse's station. Also, Nancy Leveson asserts that safety is a system property that needs to consider not only the software or system but also the larger context in which it is used.[3]
- *There is a rich base of literature on usability*—A tiny sampling is shown in Table 14.1.

---

2 For example, Model–View–Presenter (MVP), Model–View–View–Model (MVVM), etc.
3 See [Leveson95].

Table 14.1 Excellent resources on usability.

Reference	Comment
[Norman90]	Donald Norman's classic *Design of Everyday Things*. Not specific to software, this covers general usability across a wide variety of products and technologies
[Nielsen00]	Jakob Nielsen is a luminary in software usability and has published numerous articles and books
[Cooper04]	Alan Cooper's classic *The Inmates Are Running the Asylum*
[Cooper03]	The sequel to *The Inmates ...*, *About Face* goes into detail about using "persona" to drive usability

- *Usability, particularly software usability, needs to be treated as its own discipline*—There is too much depth and breadth for any one person to be truly expert in both software development and usability. Expertise in each separate discipline will be needed on most modern software projects.

Tables 14.3–14.6 provide quality criteria specifically addressing usability.

14.3 Whose Interface Is It?

The most basic issue in interface design is whether this (sub)domain provides the interface, or something else provides the interface to this (sub)domain: who is client and who is server? When a (sub)domain is server, this team is responsible for negotiating the interface with the client(s). In WebBooks, Order fulfillment provides interfaces to Customers, Warehouse workers, and Mangers. Interfaces for these actors need to be designed within Order fulfillment. On the assumption that Order fulfillment is client and Payment is server, Payment needs to provide an interface (presumably, an API) to Order fulfillment. Assuming Order fulfillment and Payment are clients of Scalability, Scalability needs to define an API for those domains to use.

When your (sub)domain is client and another is server, the burden is on the other team to provide the interface for your software—your team doesn't provide the interface. Order fulfillment has an interface to Publishers so it can place Replenish orders. Publisher software provides the interface to Order fulfillment. Order fulfillment software needs to be written to that interface(s), not the other way. The Order fulfillment team shouldn't need to do any work defining an interface to Publishers.

14.4   Net Flow of Information and Push Versus Pull at Interfaces

Chapter 7, on use cases in semantic modeling, introduced the idea of "net flow of information." That same philosophy—modeling information flow not control flow—carried through interaction modeling (Chapter 9) and state modeling (Chapter 10). The motivation was a need to understand policies and processes, free of any and all automation technology: abstracting technology complexities away to focus purely on essential complexities.

Interface design, on the other hand, is necessarily technology dependent. Flow of control is critical. The interface designer needs to consider implications of control flow on each sea level use case. Should an actor push an event into a (sub)domain?

- Should Customer push an Add to cart into Order fulfillment?
- Should Customer push a Proceed to check out?

Or, should a (sub)domain pull the event from the actor?

- Should Order fulfillment software query Customers periodically asking if they would like to Add to cart or Proceed to checkout?

It probably makes more sense to have WebBooks Customers push Add to cart events into Order fulfillment. On the other hand, it might make sense to periodically query a Customer when their shopping cart isn't empty and they haven't proceeded to checkout in a reasonable time: "There are books in your shopping cart and you haven't checked out in four weeks. Do you want to proceed to checkout now?" This would mean pulling the Proceed to checkout event from the Customer as their response to this query.

Similarly, we might implement a Customer seeing the status of their Book order as pull; they use a query screen any time they want to know. Or we might push order status to the Customer either periodically or when a significant change happens (e.g., "your iPod order has just arrived in US Customs in San Francisco" as described in Chapter 7). Any sea level use case in a semantic model could be implemented in push or pull terms. In some cases it is advantageous to implement both push and pull. Let the user push, but ask (pull) if they haven't pushed in a reasonable time. Conscious, technically viable, and economically sound decisions need to be made.

14.5   Two Kinds of Actor

As discussed in Chapter 7, there are two kinds of actor: humans and other software/systems. This leads to two kinds of interface specification. When the actor is a human, the interface specification defines a UI in one or a combination of forms: user's manuals, low- or high-fidelity UI prototypes, wire frames, dialog maps, etc.

When the actor is other software or systems, the interface specification will often define an application programming interface (API) although this isn't necessarily so. A (sub)domain might be implemented as a framework: client software connects to the (sub)domain by inheriting from one or more base classes. Either way, client developers need to know how to connect their software to the (sub)domain providing services. Even with a framework there will probably be operation calls, the connection mechanism needs to be described in sufficient detail. A client developer must be able to create their design and code solely from the (sub)domain's interface specification. There must be no reason for the client developer to need to look at server code.

14.6 Dealing with Collections

Sea level use cases often involve collections of information. In Order fulfillment, use case:

- *Catalog?* provides a Customer with a collection of Titles and associated Media, presumably matching that Customer's selection criteria for title, author, subject, etc.
- *Order?* provides a Customer with the content of a specific Book order: order data plus a collection of Book order line and associated Media information.
- *Packable orders?* provides a Warehouse worker with the collection of packable Book orders that involve Print Media based on current inventory levels.
- *Inventory?* provides a Manager with a collection of information about inventory levels for Print media.
- ...

Take the Catalog? use case as one example. Assume the interface is implemented in pull fashion—a Customer requests a list of Titles and Media satisfying given selection criteria. A collection of information matching that criteria is returned. The collection could contain any number of items, particularly if the Customer specified broad criteria: "Show me all Titles and Media on the subject of Software Engineering."

The collection might be given to the client as a single large data block. Interface designers tend to call this approach "chunky" because the interface is organized around one or a few large blocks of data. At the other end of the spectrum, the collection might be provided in terms of Iterator pattern as shown in Figure 14.1. As described here, it is a code-level API. A user might be given a screen with a "Next" button that behaves the same way: get the next item from the collection.

Client code accesses the collection one item at a time using code similar to Code Sample 14.1. The interface could be an iterator (i.e., expose those four operations), or the interface could return an iterator object for client code to use. Another alternative is the "smart for()" in Java, "for(AClass anObject: aCollection) { ... }."

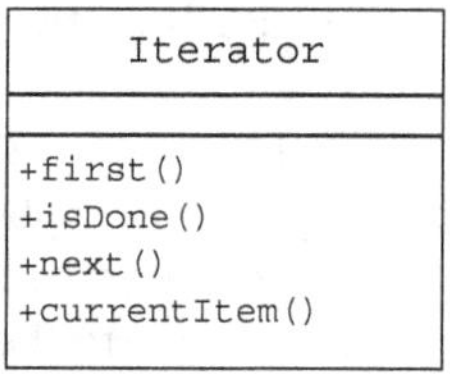

Interface designers tend to call this approach "chatty" because it is organized around many small units.

Iterator
+first()
+isDone()
+next()
+currentItem()

Figure 14.1 Iterator pattern interface.

An interface involving a collection could be anywhere on the chunky to chatty spectrum: organized around larger or smaller blocks. Google™ returns search results one page at a time, with up to 12 results per page. Amazon.com™ returns search results one page at a time, with up to 12 results per page. On Facebook™, news feeds appear as a single large collection but are delivered to the user in blocks.

Code Sample 14.1 Using Iterator Pattern to Access Items in a Collection Sequentially

```
public class SomeClient {
  ...
  public void dealWithSomeCollection() {
    ...
    Iterator myIterator = SomeCollection.createIterator()⁴;
    ...
    myIterator.first();
    while( !myIterator.isDone() ) {
      ItemType thisItem = myIterator.currentItem();
      // process thisItem as appropriate
      myIterator.next();
    }
  }
}
```

---

4 In this context, "SomeCollection.createIterator()" is a Factory that returns iterator objects (see, e.g., https://en.wikipedia.org/wiki/Factory_(object-oriented_programming)).

The decision to communicate collections in chunky, chatty, or intermediate blocks depends on technical and economic criteria such as:

- Minimum, average, and maximum size of one item in that collection.
- Minimum, average, and maximum number of items in that collection.
- Cost of gathering the items in that collection.
- Likelihood a client will need all of the items. A WebBooks Manager may want the entire inventory versus a Google user will usually find what they need in the first page or two. Facebook assumes users only want their most recent history.
- Cost of establishing a communication channel between client and server.
- Cost of one instance of communication between client and server, for example, latency.
- Increase in cost of communication as the number of items per instance of communication increases.
- ...

Technical constraints and economic considerations should drive intelligent design decisions.

14.7 User (Human) Interface Design

When an actor represents a human being, the interface specification needs to define a UI. The specification itself can take many forms, including but not limited to any combination of:

- User guide or user manual
- Storyboard
- Pencil-and-paper sketches (i.e., low-fidelity prototypes[5])
- Machine-based screen and report prototypes (i.e., high-fidelity prototypes)
- Narrative (text) descriptions for sea level use cases
- ...

14.8 Task Analysis

Task analysis examines both the work and the larger work environment to better understand the context of the software and its requirements—particularly UI requirements.[6] Task analysis results are not requirements themselves;

---

5 See, for example, [Rettig94].
6 More information on task analysis can be found in, for example, [Drury87].

instead they are rich contextual information from which requirements and interface design hints can be extracted.

"Task" is intended to distinguish this analysis from "goals" and "actions":

- *Goal*—Why the user is using the system: "BigBank customers use automated teller machines (ATMs) to access and manage their money."
- *Task*—What a user is trying to accomplish in a given interaction: "Pat wants to transfer money from her savings account to her checking account."
- *Action*—How the user physically interacts to accomplish the task: "1) Pat swipes her card 2) Pat enters her PIN 3) Pat selects Transfer 4) Pat identifies the account to transfer from 5) Pat identifies the account to transfer to, 6) ..."

The focus is on tasks: what the user is trying to accomplish? Tasks in task analysis correspond to sea level (transaction) use cases in the semantic model.

A full task analysis can be very comprehensive and detailed, but at minimum addresses characteristics of user classes (actors), tasks (sea level use cases), and the interaction between user classes and tasks. Full task analysis should consider both average and variation. The characteristics presented here are just a starting point. Some may be irrelevant for your software, and others not listed might be very relevant. Modify the set of characteristics to match your product's needs.

14.8.1 Survey of User Classes

The first section in a task analysis is a survey of user classes, that is, human actors in the semantic model:

- What level of education do they have (preexisting skills and knowledge)?
- How familiar are they with the business and/or product?
- How familiar are they with the (proposed) implementation technology?
- What are their relevant work habits and preferences?
- What are their relevant physical characteristics? (e.g., age, height, colorblindness, etc.)
- What are their dispositions and/or personality types?
- ...

A task analysis was done on a system being built by a Wall Street investment house. Their original vision was to build a Web front end for both investors and investment advisors (employees of the investment house) to access and manage investor accounts. This summary of that task analysis will involve just two user classes (actors):

- *Investor*—Characteristics of investors are very broad. Essentially this represents a cross section of the adult population of North America. Most importantly, they have widely varying familiarity with the business of investing and investment management along with widely varying familiarity with Web UI. Some are very familiar, but most have little business or technical knowledge.
- *Investment advisor*—Characteristics are much narrower. Typical investment advisors have a college degree (usually in business or finance), and they are intimately familiar with investing and investment management. They are also comfortable working with computers and Web interfaces.

14.8.2 Survey of Tasks

The second section in a task analysis report is a survey of tasks, that is, sea level use cases in the semantic model):

- What level of competence is required to complete each task successfully?
- What level of creativity is required to complete it successfully?
- What level of attentiveness is required to complete it successfully?
- Are there any time constraints?
  - For example, can't be done any quicker than... can't take any longer than...
- Is there any inter-task sequencing?
  - For example, this task can't start until some earlier task has finished.
- What are relevant task-related errors? For each:
  - Probability of...
  - Consequence of...
  - Need error prevention, error detection, and/or error handling?
- ...

The investment management system had many tasks: open an investment account, deposit money into an account, withdraw money from an account, transfer money from one account to another, reallocate money in an account to different securities, etc. For our purposes consider only the task of reallocating money in an account. This task requires basic math skills. There is no need for significant creativity, and only a moderate degree of attention is needed. There are no relevant time constraints. Inter-task sequencing requires only that the account be open and have some minimum amount of money. Kinds of mistakes include selecting a wrong percentage for allocation or moving funds into an incorrect security.

14.8.3 User Classes and Tasks

The third section of the task analysis report is a survey of user classes performing tasks:

- How often do members of this user class perform that task?
- What is the relative importance of that task to this user class?
- Is the user under time pressure when they do it?
- How does the user learn to do it?
- What is the relevant environment where the task is performed?
  - Temperature (hot/cold)
  - Humidity (dry/wet)
  - Light (bright/dim)
  - Noise (quiet/loud)
  - Other people (public/private)
  - ...
- Are there other useful tools or resources that users have available?
- ...

In the investment management project:

- *An investor reallocates money in their account*—This happens infrequently, typically less than once per year. It is very important to the investor when they are doing it but unimportant otherwise. They are under no time pressure when they do it, and they learn by trial and error. They will normally do this either in an office or home environment: indoor, well lit, warm, relatively quiet, etc.
- *An investment advisor reallocates money in an account*—This happens frequently, as often as several times a day. It is very important to the investment advisor: it's their job. There may not be any business-imposed time pressure, but if the advisor is paid on commission, then the more they can do, the more they are paid, so there is implicit pressure. They learn by taking a training course on the company's software. They will do this work in an office environment.

14.8.4 Benefit of Task Analysis

The investment company's original plan was to build one Web interface that all users, investors and investment advisors alike, would use. The task analysis made it obvious how misguided that plan was. If the interface were simple enough for a typical investor, it would be too slow and cumbersome for an investment advisor. If the interface is streamlined enough for an investment advisor, the typical investor would be overwhelmed. The task analysis led to redirecting the project to build two separate UI: a step-by-step basic interface for investors and a streamlined interface for investment advisors. It was much better to discover that before significant investment in code, rather than after—like the nurse's station project. A task analysis of the nurse's station system should have revealed the software team's incorrect assumptions before significant design or code had been developed.

An interesting follow-on question—which can also be addressed through task analysis—is: what would happen if the investment company decided to create a mobile app? Instead of using a relatively large screen in a warm, well-lit, indoor environment, imagine the challenge of reallocating funds using a smart phone screen in the back of a freezing taxicab that's speeding down a bumpy back road because the investment advisor is late for a flight. Different conditions may easily lead to very different interface requirements and designs.

Another project that benefited from task analysis was a data acquisition and process control system for a high-technology metal refining process. The refining process itself deals with extremely dangerous materials. A task analysis of the entire refining process was done, and the results are used to determine which process steps should be automated and which should be done manually. Computers are great at paying attention but horrible at creativity. Humans are great at creativity but are unable to pay close attention for long periods. Tasks scoring high on attention and low on creativity were selected for automation; the remaining tasks were left to manual processing.

14.9 Dialog Map

A dialog map[7] is an alternate use of the Unified Modeling Language (UML) state model notation described in Chapter 10. Instead of describing behavior of objects in a semantic model class, the dialog map describes behavior of a UI. Table 14.2 shows how state model concepts are mapped onto UI design.

Table 14.2 State model concepts mapped onto user interface design.

State model concept	User interface representation
State	Application screen or window
Event	User action
Transition	Change from one screen to another
Guard	Additional flow control logic

---

7 See, for example, [Wiegers03] or [Horrocks99].

Figure 14.2 shows a fragment of a dialog map for an automated teller machine (ATM).

As shown, when the ATM is turned on, the UI displays a welcome screen. When the customer swipes their card, the ATM displays an "Enter your PIN" screen. When the user has entered a PIN, it is validated against the master account number on the swiped card (via secure communication to the bank's back-end servers). Assuming the PIN is valid for the master account, the user is shown the "Select Transaction" screen so they can choose one of several options:

- Query the balance in an account.
- Deposit money into an account.
- Withdraw money from an account.
- Transfer money from one account to another.

If the user selects "Withdraw money," they will be shown a screen listing each account under the master account. They are prompted to select the account they want to withdraw from. Once the account has been selected, the user is shown another screen where they enter and validate the amount to be withdrawn. The cloud in Figure 14.2 is not part of dialog map notation; it only represents continuing dialog that is too involved for this example. After validating the amount to withdraw, the ATM shows a "Working" screen while it accesses the secure network to perform the withdraw. Assuming success, the ATM will give the user their money then show a "Do you want another transaction?" screen.

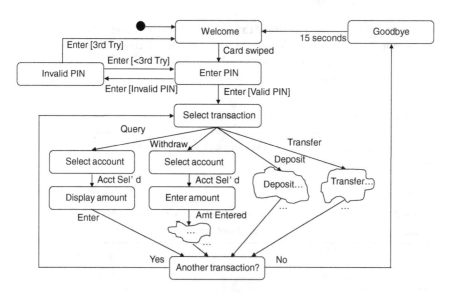

Figure 14.2 A fragment of a dialog map for an automated teller machine.

If there was a problem with the requested withdraw—the user asked for more money than was in the account, or the request would put the account over a maximum withdraw limit in 24 hours—the dialog map would show the user being given a "Sorry, your withdraw could not be completed. Here is why…" screen. After the user acknowledges the error, the ATM shows the "Do you want another transaction?" screen.

If the user wants another transaction, the ATM returns to the "Select Transaction" screen. If the user says no, the ATM displays a "Thank you for using our ATM, Goodbye" screen for 15 seconds before returning to the Welcome screen for the next customer.

The dialog map can be supplemented with state model actions to identify points where accesses to Model region (in the Model–View–Controller sense) happen. After gathering account and amount information along the withdraw dialog path, View-controller region code implementing this dialog map will give a "withdraw amount X from account Y" request to Model region (the bank's back-end systems). The response—success or failure—is returned to the ATM.

To transfer money, the user needs to go through a longer dialog to specify necessary business information:

- The account the money should be transferred from
- The account the money should be transferred into
- The amount to be transferred

After gathering this information across several screens, again View-controller region code gives a "transfer this much money from this account to that account" request to Model region—the bank's back-end servers—and waits for the response. There will typically be many points in a dialog map that involve submitting requests to Model region and reacting to responses that come back.

Figure 14.3 shows a sample dialog map for the Customer interface in the Order fulfillment domain of WebBooks.

Figure 14.4 shows the same dialog map annotated to relate sections to use cases in the semantic model.

Besides being useful for getting agreement on UI flow, Chapter 17 shows how a dialog map can drive detailed design and code in View-controller region. A dialog map is also an excellent resource for testing (refer to the section on deriving verification test elements from state models in Chapter 12). At a minimum, a UI should be tested along each transition in the dialog map (i.e., decision coverage of the state model). Based on risk, also consider testing all possible user actions in all possible UI states: What if the user presses the Confirm button while the ATM is processing a request? What if the user swipes their card again in the middle of a balance query? Those actions should be ignored but was code written so it actually does ignore them? Consider using state–event matrix notation instead of state chart notation, as discussed in Chapter 10. This can better ensure completeness of the dialog map as well as differentiate between

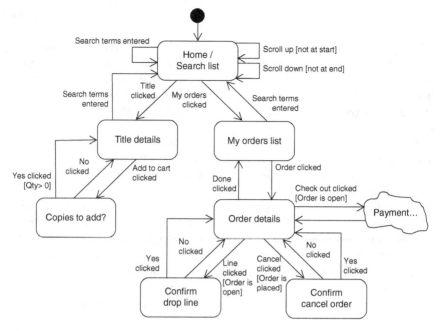

Figure 14.3 Sample dialog map for Customer user interface in Order fulfillment.

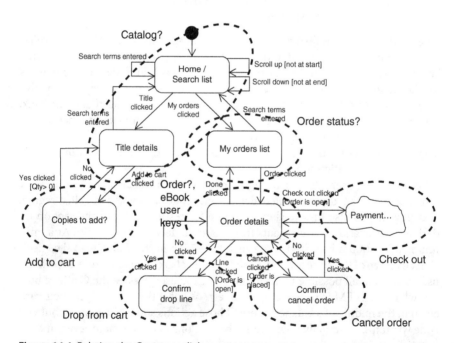

Figure 14.4 Relating the Customer dialog map to use cases.

actions to ignore (e.g., clicking a disabled button) and impossible actions (e.g., no such button is on that screen).

14.10   User Interface Prototype

It may be useful to prototype proposed UI. Prototypes can be cheap and easy to build, and user feedback can be incorporated sooner and with less effort. There are two approaches to UI prototyping:

- *High-fidelity prototypes*—Using specialized tools or code to simulate precise look and feel of a UI
- *Low-fidelity prototypes*—Pencil-and-paper sketches, as in Figure 14.5

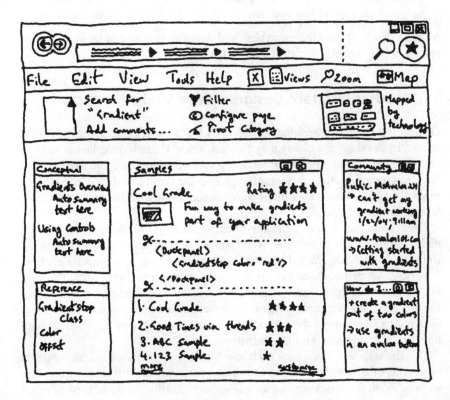

Figure 14.5 A low-fidelity user interface prototype for some sample screen.

Low-fidelity prototypes[8]:

- Are faster to build (lower effort and cost)
- Can be evaluated sooner
- Are easier to change
- Lead to more substantial user feedback

When evaluating any UI prototype,

- *Make sure real users do the evaluation*—Include both experienced and inexperienced users.
- *Have users try to complete realistic tasks*—Rettig explains how this can be done even with low-fidelity prototypes.
- *Ask specifically, "Does this prototype ..."*
  - ... include all capabilities you expected to see?
  - ... present them in a way you want to see them? How logical and complete is navigation? Can you think of easier ways to get your work done?
  - ... include capabilities you don't really need, want, or understand?

More information on UI prototyping and usability testing can be found in, for example, [Nielsen94], [Rubin94], or [Wiegers03].

14.11   User Interface Design, a Case Study

One project used a process for designing UI that is worth discussing. The team started by developing a dialog map for each actor. Users were called in to evaluate the flow of each proposed interface. Issues were identified and fixed. After a few short iterations, the users were happy with the flow represented in the dialog maps. The agreed-on dialog maps were pinned to the middle of walls in a conference room.

The second step was to draft low-fidelity prototypes for each screen in each dialog map. Screen prototypes were pinned on the same wall, surrounding the respective dialog map. The team used colored yarn to connect each low-fidelity screen prototype to its corresponding state in the dialog map. The yarn helped reviewers quickly jump between the dialog map's definition of flow and the prototype for that screen. Again users were called in to evaluate this level of design. After a few more short iterations, the users were happy with both general flow in the dialog map and low-fidelity screen layouts.

The last step was to replace each low-fidelity prototype with a high-fidelity prototype, maintaining the screen-to-dialog-map linkage with yarn. Again users were called in for review and again a few short iterations were needed to reach agreement.

---

8 See, for example, [Rettig94].

This approach was particularly effective in allowing users to progressively review and comment on the evolving interface design rather than confronting them with an essentially completed design at the end. This process should be broadly applicable.

14.12 User Guide Documentation

If your goal is to organize user documentation into some kind of paper(like) document, the following outline is an effective way to accomplish that. Each level of increased indentation represents a more detailed section of document content. Appendix E and part of Appendix G use this structure and serve as examples.

General Information
    Introduction to this interface
    How to start and stop this software or interface
    Seeing what options are available
    Selecting an option
    How to correct mistakes (e.g., delete and/or undo)
    Using the help facility (if one exists)
Guide to individual sea level use cases (organized by workflow if possible)
    Described from the point of view of the user
    Include error prevention, detection, and correction
"Don't Do's"
    Known actions resulting in unsatisfactory responses, if any
Glossary

14.13 API Design

Actors are not always humans, particularly with lower-level service (sub)domains. The Payment domain in WebBooks 2.0 is an example; it's a service domain for Order fulfillment. High availability is a service domain to Scalability.

Just as complexity needs to be managed and controlled elsewhere, complexity should also be managed and controlled in API design. Overly complex APIs place unnecessary burdens on developers who need those services. Overly complex APIs also place unnecessary burdens on the developer(s) who will build or maintain View-controller region design and code for a (sub)domain. Design an API to be simple enough for client developers to get their job done quickly and easily, in light of the economics of the project and product.

Usability is as important in API design as it is in UI:

> *"... API design—the public interfaces we provide in the libraries we create, with the express intent of exposing features and functionality to developers who call our code—is just as important as UI design."*
> (Brandon Satrom, Web Standards Sherpa)

> *"APIs cannot be designed without an understanding of their context."*
> (Michi Henning, ZeroC)

> *"Programmers are people, too"*
>
> (Ken Arnold)

If not already imposed by nonfunctional requirements, the first decision in API design is the technology to be used. Common API technologies include[9]:

- *Direct function call*—Clients make direct calls to functions in the same address space. Direct function call has the advantage of being simple (developers already know how to do it) and it is the fastest of all API technologies. On the other hand, this tends have limited scalability.
- *Remote procedure call (RPC)*—Clients make calls to functions in different address spaces, possibly on different computers. The main advantage of RPC is that it is more scalable than direct function call. Modern RPC implementations hide most communication complexity. In the early days of RPC, the developer had to write marshaling and de-marshaling code. Today this is usually generated by an Interface Definition Language (IDL) compiler. The main disadvantages are slower performance, somewhat higher complexity, and some technical limitations (e.g., possibly no pointer or by-reference parameters) compared to direct function call.
- *Service-oriented architecture*[10] *(SOA)*—SOA is a special case of RPC and is used widely enough to warrant mentioning. The primary advantages of SOA are scalability, location independence, and implementation independence. The primary disadvantages are performance and possible security compromises. Microservices is an adaptation of SOA that emphasizes smaller, more highly cohesive, more loosely coupled interfaces.
- *Representational State Transfer (REST)*—REST[11] is based on four principles: layered client-server, statelessness of servers, use of cache, and uniform interface between components (often HTTP's Get, Head, Post, Put, Patch, and

---

9 See, for example, [Daigneau12].
10 See, for example, [Daigneau12]. This is evolving into "microservices."
11 See, for example, [Fielding00].

Delete). REST is the most scalable API technology[12] but has the disadvantage of communication complexity being pushed into the payload, as well as possible performance and security compromises.

- *Framework*—The client makes use of a (sub)domain's services through subclassing base classes, generic (i.e., template) classes, etc.

If a particular API technology is not mandated by nonfunctional how requirements, the choice of technology should be driven by economics rather than what's the newest, hippest, trendiest, sexiest, looks-great-on-a-resume technology.

A number of other issues may be relevant in designing APIs, including:

- Exposing class constructors versus factory methods
- Synchronous versus asynchronous communication
- Returning error codes versus throwing exceptions, which is discussed in more detail in Chapter 16
- Version management as the API evolves over time, for example, is backward compatibility a requirement?
- …

Each of these issues needs proper consideration in the design of any specific API; however most details are beyond the scope of this book.

14.13.1   API Security

Depending on API visibility, that is, local to a single machine, on a secure intranet, on an unsecured intranet, or wide open to the Internet, API security could be a major concern. A recommended approach for addressing API security is as follows:

1) Start with a known threat catalog such as from the Web Application Security Consortium (WASC).[13]
2) Add or remove threats as appropriate for your software and its environment.
3) Assess the risk of each relevant threat: How likely is an attack from that direction? How damaging could that attack be if successful?
4) For threats with high enough risk exposure to warrant mitigation, research the latest defense strategies on the Web. The Web usually has the most current strategies, as they are constantly evolving.

---

12 A good example of a REST API can be found at https://developer.paypal.com/docs/api/.
13 See [WASC10]. The Open Web Application Security Project (OWASP) 2013 Top 10 List (https://www.owasp.org/index.php/Top_10_2013-Top_10) is more limited and specific to Web applications but identifies the top 10 most common and dangerous security holes.

14.13.2   API Documentation

If your goal is to organize API documentation into some kind of paper(like) document, the following outline is an effective way to accomplish that. Each level of increased indentation represents a more detailed section of document content. Part of Appendix G and Appendices I and K use this structure and serve as examples. The PayPal API documentation[14] and Facebook API documentation[15] follow roughly this outline:

General Information
    Introduction to this API
    How to connect/access this API
    Exported constants
    Exported types
    Exported variables (e.g., environment variables)
    Exported function/operation signatures and contracts
        Parameters and types
        Return value(s) and type(s)
        Errors and exceptions
    Exported files
Guide to individual sea level use cases (organized by workflow if possible)
    From point of view of client
    Include error prevention, detection, and correction
"Don't Do's"
    Known actions resulting in unsatisfactory responses, if any
Appendix explaining API design decisions[16]

Code samples are an extremely useful and valuable part of API documentation: case studies, demos, tutorials, a "Getting started guide," etc. Provide easy-to-clone, real-world examples:

> *"Example code should be exemplary. If an API is used widely its examples will be the archetypes for thousands of programs. Any mistakes will come back to haunt you a thousand fold"*
>
> (Joshua Bloch, Google)

---

14 See https://developer.paypal.com/docs/api/.
15 See https://developers.facebook.com/docs.
16 Knowing why an API was developed the way it was helps new client developers understand it faster.

As an example of designing and documenting an API, consider the Payment domain in WebBooks. Most Payment use cases involve user (Customer) interaction:

- Process add payment method
- Process edit payment method
- Process drop payment method
- Process payment
- Payment status?
- Process method time out
- Process decline
- Process drop c/d account

The UI for these use cases needs to be defined—as described earlier in this chapter—for example, in some combination of a dialog map, UI prototype, user's manual, etc.

Two Payment use cases involve a combination of user interaction and API interaction with Order fulfillment:

- Process cancel payment
- Process approve

The UI part of these use cases also needs to be defined alongside of the above. Order fulfillment interaction needs to be specified in an API; an example is shown below.

Two Payment use cases involve only API interaction with Order fulfillment and also need to be specified in a client domain API:

- Process create payment
- Process refund

Of course, other information needs to be included in the full API specification, but Code Sample 14.2 shows an example design for a Payment API from the perspective of that API itself. This is the interface the client domain designer/developer will be calling when they need Payment domain services.

API documentation needs to explain that when the client domain wants to make the payment, up to two steps are needed:

1) If a Payment object doesn't already exist, one needs to be created. A previous attempt at payment may have been made, and a Payment object representing the status of that earlier failed attempt could still exist (with various Payment methods for various amounts in various states).
2) Once the Payment object exists, call operation processPayment() with the (possibly changed) amount of purchase. The amount could have changed from a previous attempt (e.g., the Customer could have added or dropped products, or changed quantities).

Code Sample 14.2 Relevant Code for the Payment API

```
public class¹⁷ Payment {

  public Payment ( Purchase aPurchase, Customer aCustomer ) {
    // constructor for Payment objects
    // requires
    //   aPurchase <> null
    //   aCustomer <> null
    // guarantees
    //   new Payment exists
    //   total due == $0.01 (as an initial default)
    //   payment status == PREPARING
      ...
  }

  public boolean processPayment ( double amount ) {
    // this operation manages all of the payment interaction
    // requires
    //   amount > $0.00
    // guarantees
    //   if pre ( payment status ) == PREPARING
    //      then total due == amount
    //            if this payment was processed successfully
    //                  payment status == AUTHORIZED and returns true
    //               otherwise returns false
    //      otherwise nothing changes and returns false
      ...
  }

  public void refund ( ) {
    // this allows a customer to undo a previously approved Payment
    // requires
    //   none
    // guarantees
    //   if pre ( payment status ) == AUTHORIZED
    //     then all Payment methods have been refunded
    //         payment status is REFUNDED
    //     otherwise <some error is reported to a system operator>
      ...
  }
}
```

---

17 "public interface Payment" could be a more appropriate alternative.

The processPayment() operation returns true when payment has been success-fully processed; otherwise it returns false (meaning the Customer cancelled that payment). Use case Refund involves simply calling operation refund() on the API. An example of how client code using the Payment API might look is shown in Code Sample 14.3.

Code Sample 14.3 Example Code Showing Client Domain Use of the Payment API

```
public class ClientDomainPurchase {

  // other client domain purchase data relevant to the application
  ...
  private Payment myPayment;

  public ClientDomainPurchase ( ... ) {
  // the constructor for the client domain purchase object
  // requires
  //   tbd depending on the application
  // guarantees
  //   tbd depending on the application
    ...
   myPayment = null;
    ...
  }


  public void payForPurchase ( ... ) {
  // this is the client domain operation that wants to get payment
  // requires
  //   tbd depending on the application
  // guarantees
  //   tbd depending on the application
    ...
   if ( myPayment == null ) {
     myPayment = new Payment ( this, myCustomer ) ;
   }
   if ( myPayment.processPayment ( amountOfPurchase ) ) {
     // Payment was successful, handle it as needed
     ...
   } else {
```

```
  // Payment was not successful, handle it as needed

  ...
 }
 ...
}

public void refundPurchase ( ) {
// this is the client operation that needs to make a refund
// requires
//   tbd depending on the application
// guarantees
//   tbd depending on the application

 ...
 myPayment.refund();

 ...
 }

}
```

Notice how the Payment constructor and operation processPayment() combine to implement several Payment domain use cases in the semantic model:

- *Process create payment*—Construct a Payment then call processPayment()
- *Process approve*—When processPayment() returns true
- *Process cancel payment*—When processPayment() returns false

Operation refund() implements the entirety of the Process refund use case in the semantic model.

14.14   Handling Interface Errors

Regardless of interface technology, UI or API, users/clients can make mistakes:

- Leaving required input blank or null
- Using inappropriate (e.g., out of range) values
- Using values that are inconsistent with each other... (e.g., password not appropriate for user name, return flight date earlier than outbound flight date on airline reservations, etc.)
- Requesting a function/operation that's inappropriate at this time
- ...

Error prevention and error handling strategies for UI include the following:

- Position recurring UI elements consistently on all screens.
- Use "progressive disclosure" to provide just enough information and feedback to complete the task along with links to more information when requested.
- Adequately separate clickable/selectable items from each other.
- Avoid putting the most commonly clicked items next to each other.
- Provide slide bars, radio buttons, pull-down lists, etc. when input needs to come from a limited range or input set.
- Pre-populate input fields with default values.
- Use range checking on numeric input fields.
- Disable buttons when inappropriate to click.
- When reporting an error, make clear what went wrong and suggest how to fix it.
- Offer an appropriate facility to undo or go back.
- ...

Some example error prevention and error handling strategies for APIs include the following:

- Use strong typing where appropriate.
- Substitute the closest legal value when given out of range input.
- Use a neutral value when given out of range input.
- ...

Given the set of errors that clients could make along with candidate error prevention and handling strategies, refer to Chapter 25 on the economics of error handling to decide what, if anything, should be done at the interface.

14.15 Packaging the Interface Specification

In terms of packaging interface specifications, interfaces can be specified as one document per actor, or all interfaces could be specified as sections in a single document. Practically speaking it is often better to create separate specification documents for each actor because approval, configuration management, and change control needs often vary.

14.16 Quality Criteria

In addition to the quality criteria (Table 3.1) and naming criteria (Table 3.2), the quality criteria in Table 14.3 can be applied to all interface design-related work to identify and remove interface defects as quickly and as cheaply as possible.

The quality criteria in Table 14.4 address general usability for all interfaces. These criteria apply independent of the interface being a UI or an API.

The quality criteria in Table 14.5 address usability guidelines specifically for UI.

The quality criteria in Table 14.6 apply to API designs.

Table 14.3 Quality criteria for overall interface design.

Item	Criterion
IO-1	Interface functionality is consistent with the actors and use cases in the semantic model
IO-2	The interface provides appropriate configuration, backup and restore, performance monitoring and tuning, and other use cases
IO-3	Chunkiness versus chattiness of collections is appropriate
IO-4	The interface adequately addresses security
IO-5	All relevant nonfunctional requirements are satisfied by the interface
IO-6	The interface is not artificially constrained by nonexistent requirements
IO-7	Using only the interface specification, a client can understand how to use the software to perform all functions they need it to perform

Table 14.4 Quality criteria for general usability.

Item	Criterion
US-1	The interface is specified from the point of view of the client of the software as opposed to the point of view of the software itself
US-3	The interface makes it as easy as possible for clients to get their work done
US-4	The interface makes reasonable attempts to prevent clients from making mistakes
US-5	The interface supports appropriate responses to mistakes clients are likely to make
US-6	Clients would not be unpleasantly surprised by anything on the interface
US-7	The interface allows advanced clients to take appropriate shortcuts
US-8	As appropriate, the interface offers a simple and consistent mechanism for reversing actions (undo or back up)

Table 14.5 Quality criteria for user interfaces.

Item	Criterion
UI-1	The interface allows the user to easily assimilate information being presented
UI-2	The interface does not depend on color alone to convey important information
UI-3	The user can easily determine what state the software is in
UI-4	The user can easily determine what actions are possible in each state
UI-5	The user can easily determine what actions are required to perform their intended task
UI-6	All user to system dialogs provide a means for the user to determine progress and know when the dialog is complete
UI-7	The interface allows the user to feel in control of the software, as opposed to the user feeling that the software is controlling them
UI-8	The interface minimizes user short-term memory load (e.g., by recalling previously entered information)

Table 14.6 Quality criteria for APIs.

Item	Criterion
AP-1	Appropriate API technology is used (direct function call, RPC, SOA, microservices, REST, framework, etc.)
AP-2	The API encapsulates (e.g., contracts are clearly and correctly specified for every visible function)
AP-3	The choice of collections versus arrays versus iterators is appropriate
AP-4	The choice of constructors versus factory methods is appropriate
AP-5	The choice of error codes versus exceptions is appropriate
AP-6	The choice of synchronous and asynchronous interaction is appropriate
AP-7	Appropriate code examples are provided
AP-8	The provided code examples are good examples
AP-9	There is sufficient explanation of why the API looks the way it does
AP-10	The version of the API is appropriately identified

14.17 Summary

The semantic model specifies logical (i.e., conceptual) interaction between actors and a business. That logical interaction needs to be given physical form in design. Interface specifications define how real-world actors interact with real software. This chapter explained how sea level use cases from a semantic model combine with relevant nonfunctional requirements to define interfaces that software will provide to real actors. This chapter put interface design into the context of software development processes, explained the importance of usability, and provided detail needed to design UI and APIs from semantic models and nonfunctional requirements.

15

High-Level Design

Classes and Operations

This chapter describes how an initial high-level software design for a (sub) domain can be derived from a semantic model and its corresponding interface specification. That initial high-level design consists of classes, operations, and dependencies. Operation syntax (signatures) and semantics (contracts) will be derived in the next chapter. Chapters 15–19 explain manual derivation of design and code; Chapters 20 and 21 describe automatic derivation using open model compilers. Even if you use a model compiler, you should still be familiar with Chapters 15–19 as model compilers simply automate the same basic process.

15.1 Comments on High-Level Design

First and foremost, Chapters 15–17 only describe one way to translate a semantic model and interface specification into design and code. These chapters should be considered an existence proof that translation can be done:

> *"There are many ways to translate any Semantic model and Interface specification into design and code—many aren't even object oriented."*

Hard performance constraints in some embedded systems can preclude implementing in an object-oriented programming language. Derivation of non-object-oriented design and code are discussed in Chapter 19.

Second, to help avoid premature design and optimization, develop the initial high-level design in the simplest, most straightforward way possible. Make design decisions in a way that—under similar design circumstances—you would expect the majority of other designers in your organization to make substantially the same decisions. The high-level design produced by this process is only a first approximation. Optimization is discussed in Chapter 19.

How to Engineer Software: A Model-Based Approach, First Edition. Steve Tockey.
© 2019 the IEEE Computer Society, Inc. Published 2019 by John Wiley & Sons, Inc.

Finally, this initial high-level design should be considered logical, not necessarily physical. Allocation of classes and operations to computational elements—processors, processes, tasks, threads, etc.—has not been done. If final implementation involves more than a single thread in a single process on a single CPU, classes and operations should be allocated to computational elements to maximize parallelization and minimize the cost of inter-element communication. Partitioning domains into subdomains (Chapter 11) minimizes the kinds of communication; this partitioning should minimize the occurrence (frequency) of communication.

Another perspective on logical versus physical design is thin client versus thick client in multitier implementations. It should make sense to allocate View-controller region[1] to the tier closest to the user. Model (and Infrastructure) region would be allocated to the lower tier(s). From a simplicity, understandability, cohesion, and coupling perspective, this would be the most obvious, straightforward design. On the other hand, technical and economic considerations could lead to differing allocations:

- *Thin client*—The tier closest to the user would have some, but not all View-controller region classes. Other View-controller region classes would be on lower tier(s). All Model and Infrastructure region classes would be on the lower tier(s).
- *Thick client*—The tier closest to the user would have all View-controller region classes and some Model (and possibly Infrastructure) region classes. Remaining Model (and Infrastructure) region classes would be on lower tier(s).

Thin client versus thick client becomes particularly relevant to WebBooks if they later develop a mobile app. How much functionality belongs on the mobile device versus how much belongs on back-end servers is a significant driver of performance, availability, reliability, and so on.

Unified Modeling Language's (UML's) deployment diagrams[2] can be useful for specifying allocation of logical design to computational elements but are not discussed in this book.

---

1 The name Model–View–Controller implies View and Controller are separable. They can often be separated in embedded systems where input functionality is easily separable from output functionality. With user interfaces the separation is much less clear, often to the point of being meaningless. Is class Button a Controller element because something happens when clicked? Or is it a View element because it appears on a screen and looks different when it is enabled versus disabled? In practice, it seems best to treat user interface View and Controller as one combined region: View-controller.

2 See, for example, [OMG11b] or [Fowler03].

15.2 UML Notation for High-Level Design

The concept of language dialects, as related to UML, was introduced in Chapter 5. Part II, on semantic modeling, uses a functional requirements dialect of UML. Part III uses the design dialect. Skim or skip this section if you are already familiar with UML for software design.

15.2.1 Design Use Case Diagrams

There may be benefit in providing a design use case diagram. Just like in semantic models, the design use case diagram describes scope and context. But instead of describing scope and context of policies and processes alone, the design use case diagram shows scope and context of implementation (i.e., design and code). Design use cases can be a superset of semantic model use cases. Use cases relevant in design may be irrelevant to policies and processes:

- *Configuration*—Use cases to configure the implementation into specific installations
- *Backup and restore*—Use cases to save and recover system state, to not lose important user data or configuration information
- *Performance monitoring and management*—Use cases to monitor, and possibly tune, an installation's performance
- ...

And, just like in semantic modeling, it is easy to overengineer use case diagrams in design.

15.2.2 Design Class Diagrams

A design class diagram shows the main structural elements, and important relationships, of the computing solution. High-level design classes will normally be a superset of semantic model classes. Cohesion and coupling should usually drive the high-level design to some variation of Model–View–Controller style although this is not required. Performance considerations may override cohesion and coupling concerns. Classes in Model region often correlate with classes in the semantic model. Classes in View-controller region implement the interfaces defined in the interface specification.

Model–View–Controller (and its relatives), as defined, is sufficient for many self-contained desktop applications and mobile applications. However, as software scales up in size and complexity, the need for a new region tends to emerge: Infrastructure. This region provides services that aren't available in a preexisting execution environment. Examples could be:

- Configuration/start-up service
- Error logging service

- Interprocess(or) communication service
- Multitasking/multi-threading service
- Data distribution service
- Fixed-point math service
- ...

A postal address service and a sophisticated string matching service to support catalog searches might be useful Infrastructure region services in the high-level design of Order fulfillment.

Unlike semantic models, design class diagrams don't show associations. Instead, they show dependencies between classes. When class A uses features on the interface of class B, the design shows a dependency as a dashed arrow pointing from A to B. Generalizations (inheritance) in design class diagrams use the same notation as semantic models although the semantics differ. Subclass features in semantic models should not override superclass features; they should only supplement. Overriding superclass features is common practice in design.

The middle compartment of a design class may show instance variables (member data) and types (e.g., int, float, double, char, String, Date, Customer, Medium, etc.). The bottom compartment may show operations (member functions), possibly including return types. UML supports writing an operation's full signature in the bottom compartment, but this usually takes up too much space and is rarely done in practice. Just an operation's name is usually sufficient on a design class diagram; the signature and contract can be precisely specified elsewhere.

Features—instance variables and operations—on design class diagrams can be annotated to express visibility:

- *An instance variable or operation preceded by "-" means private*—That feature is not visible outside the boundary of that class implementation; it is encapsulated.
- *An instance variable or operation preceded by "+" means public*—That feature is visible outside the boundary of that class implementation.
- *An instance variable or operation preceded by "#" means protected*—That feature is visible within the class it is defined on and in subclasses of that defining class.

Design also has class (or static) variables and operations. Instance (i.e., member) data and operations apply to each object in the class. Class (static) variables and operations apply only once, for the entire class. Think of the class itself as an object named by that class name that has global visibility in the (sub)domain. Class variables and class operations are the data and function of that class-as-an-object.

Class features are underlined in UML design notation. Figure 15.1 shows UML design notation for a sample class with public, private, instance, and class (static) features. Any abstract class or feature can be given the constraint "{abstract}" or be written in *italics*. More examples of design class diagrams appear later in this chapter and in Appendices E, G, I, and K.

BankAccount
-countOfOpenAccounts:int
-totalDeposits:double
-balance:double
-status:boolean
+numberOfOpenAccounts()
+totalValueOfDeposits()
+BankAccount()
+open(openBalance)
+deposit(amount)
+withdraw(amount)
+balance()
+close()

Figure 15.1 A design class with public, private, instance (member), and class (static) features.

15.2.3 Design Sequence Diagrams

Sequence diagrams in design show flow of control: activation context bars, synchronization, etc. Examples of design sequence diagrams appear later in this chapter. Generally speaking, end-to-end execution of a sea level use case in design sequence diagrams starts with Controller region objects decoding what the real external actor wants done. Model region objects carry out the business process (possibly involving Infrastructure region). View region objects present the business result to a real actor.

The rest of high-level design documentation doesn't belong on UML diagrams. For each class,

- *Class description*—What is the role of this class in design? What is its heritage: is it implementing one or more classes from the semantic model (Model region) or interface specification (View-controller region), or is it a support service (Infrastructure region)? To the extent that a design class or feature is part of a design pattern,[3] the role of that class in that pattern should be described.
- *Public interface*—Exported, externally visible constants, types, variables, operation signatures (syntax: input parameters and types, return parameters and types, exceptions, etc.), and semantics (contracts). Operation signatures and contracts for Model region are derived in Chapter 16. Public variables should be avoided due to encapsulation and coupling concerns.

15.3 Deriving Design Classes for Model Region

To be consistent with the fundamental principles, we normally expect the top-level design for a (sub)domain to be Model–View–Controller or some variant. The first step[4] in deriving a high-level design for a (sub)domain is to simply

---

3 See, for example, [Gamma95].

4 The steps don't need to be done in exactly this order. You can re-sequence or work in parallel. Describing them in this order is a convenience.

make a Model region design class for every class in the semantic model, including actors. Actors play a special role in design that will be explained later. Don't show dependencies between classes yet; they will be added as the high-level design progresses. Include semantic model generalizations as design inheritance in this step. Figure 15.2 shows the high-level design in Model region for WebBooks 2.0 Order fulfillment as derived from the class diagram in Figure 8.32 (also Figure D.2) after this first step.

15.3.1 Addressing Dynamic Classification

Order fulfillment domain includes one generalization but it is static: an EBook-Medium will never change into a PrintMedium or vice versa. If WebBooks sells some given Title in print form and then decides later to sell it in e-book form, a new instance of Medium is created. On the other hand, semantic models may include dynamic classification. Figure 15.3 shows a simplified version of the dynamic classification example in Figure 8.28. It is almost certain that at least one employee who hired in as an hourly employee would eventually become a salaried employee. That person is the same employee, but they are now a different kind of employee.

Mainstream object-oriented programming languages like Java, C++, and C# do not support dynamic reclassification. Once a Java object has been instantiated as a concrete subclass, it must remain that subclass for the rest of its life.

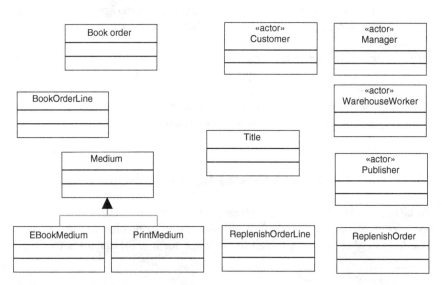

Figure 15.2 High-level design for Order fulfillment Model region after the first step.

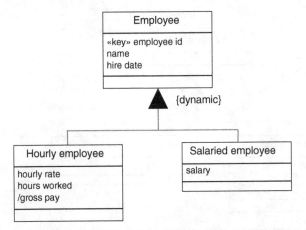

Figure 15.3 Example of dynamic classification in a semantic model.

It can never become an object of a different subclass. There are two ways to design from dynamic generalization in a semantic model. The specifics at the detailed design and code level are discussed in Chapter 17.

15.3.2 Collapse Inheritance Hierarchy

The simplest way is to collapse the inheritance hierarchy. Subclasses Hourly employee and Salaried employee are absorbed into superclass Employee. All differences become hidden; the internal implementation of Employee is responsible for taking care of everything. This is shown in Figure 15.4.

Employee
-id
-name
-hireDate
-salary
-hourlyRate
-hoursWorked
-grossPay

Figure 15.4 Collapsing subclasses to implement dynamic classification in high-level design.

15.3.3 State (aka Delegate) Pattern

An alternative is to use State (sometimes called Delegate) design pattern.[5] All invariant properties of the superclass in the semantic model are implemented in the design base class. Dynamic, state-specific properties are implemented in delegate subclasses. When a design base class object is asked to do something that doesn't depend on subclass, it handles it by itself. Any time the base object is asked to do something state specific, it hands that off to the current state

---

5 See, for example, https://sourcemaking.com/design_patterns/state.

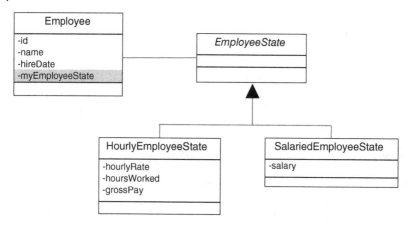

Figure 15.5 Using State pattern to implement dynamic classification in high-level design.

delegate. Figure 15.5 shows the high-level design using State pattern. Instance variable myEmployeeState holds a reference to the delegate. The delegate base class should be abstract.

15.3.4 Associations Become Design Classes

The second step is to add a design class for every association in the semantic model. Associations play a special role in design that is described in Chapter 17. For now, they are placeholders for work that needs to be done; we are just not ready to do that work yet. More design context is needed to avoid inappropriate design decisions and prevent premature optimization.

Be careful with association classes in the semantic model: don't generate two design classes. If the class perspective was already translated in the first step, don't generate another class for the association perspective in the second step. Figure 15.6 shows Order fulfillment Model region design as derived from the semantic model after the second step. Added design classes for semantic model associations are shaded to emphasize the difference with Figure 15.2. Book order line and Replenish order line are association classes that already represent the For and Restocks associations in the semantic model, but For and Restocks do not appear as design classes.

15.4 Deriving Operations for Model Region

The third step is to translate messages in the semantic model into operations on the interface of Model region design classes. Remember that messages in semantic models only describe information flow, not control flow. We

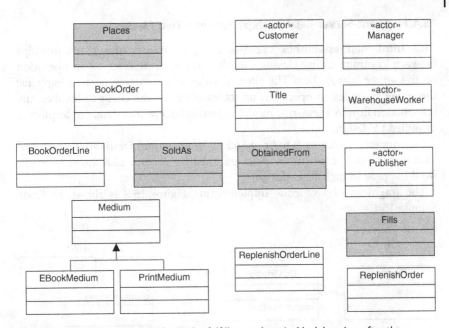

Figure 15.6 High-level design for Order fulfillment domain Model region after the second step.

Figure 15.7 A simple, generic semantic model sequence diagram.

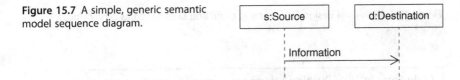

intentionally avoid control flow in semantic models; we are forced to make control flow decisions[6] in design.

To illustrate, consider the simple, generic semantic model sequence diagram in Figure 15.7. This diagram shows s:Source being the producer of Information and d:Destination being the consumer. Information could either be data (e.g., an attribute or derived attribute of Source) or event (e.g., signaled in an action in the state model of Source); it doesn't matter. What matters is that Source and Destination interact in the semantic model and high-level design has to implement that interaction.

---

6 This is an example of the "latest responsible moment" decision philosophy and supplements the data flow versus control flow discussions in a semantic model (see Chapters 7, 9, and 10).

15.4.1 Client-Server Relationships Between Two Classes

This third step establishes client-server (i.e., master–slave) relationships between communicating classes and allocates each message to an operation on the server (slave) class. The client decides when communication happens; the server provides an operation on its interface for the client to invoke. Any information flow in a semantic model, regardless of event or data, can be pushed or pulled in design.

One design alternative is to have Source be client and Destination be server. This is the "push" control flow referred to earlier. Figure 15.8 shows how this would appear in high-level design.

The fragment of Java code implementing Figure 15.8 is shown in Code Sample 15.1.

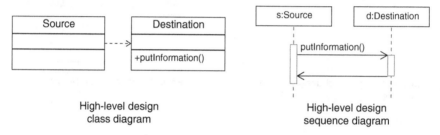

High-level design
class diagram

High-level design
sequence diagram

Figure 15.8 High-level design for Source as client and Destination as server ("push").

Code Sample 15.1 Pushing Information from Source to Destination

```java
public class Source {
  ...
  private Destination myDestination;
  ...
  public void someOperation() {
    // determine current value for Information
    InfoType info = ...
    // push Information into myDestination
    myDestination.putInformation( info );
  }
}

public class Destination {
  ...
```

```
public void putInformation( InfoType info ) {
  // use Information

  ...
  }
}
```

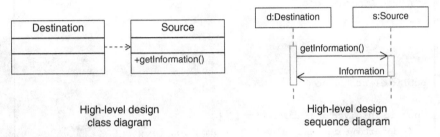

Figure 15.9 High-level design for Destination as client and Source as server (pull).

The other design alternative is to have Destination be client and Source be server. This is the "pull" control flow referred to earlier. Figure 15.9 shows how this would appear in high-level design.

The fragment of Java code implementing Figure 15.9 is shown in Code Sample 15.2.

15.4.2 Client-Server Relationships Between Three or More Classes

If the semantic model has three classes and two messages, the number of design alternatives doubles. This is shown in Figures 15.10–15.14. Objects of class B are responsible for converting X's into Y's.

Code for Figures 15.11–15.14 should be clear except possibly alternative 4 in Figure 15.14. This alternative represents concurrent execution of A and C accessing a common, shared B.

If still another class and message are added to the semantic model, the number of design options doubles again to eight. Adding yet another class and message further doubles the number of design options to 16. The number of high-level design options for any semantic model is on the order of two to the power of n where n is the number of communicating classes. Again, recall Fudd's First Law of Creativity:

> "The fact that hundreds, or even thousands, of candidate designs can be derived from a single semantic model allows designers to consider many alternatives and decide which might be most appropriate given the non-functional requirements and hardware & software environment"

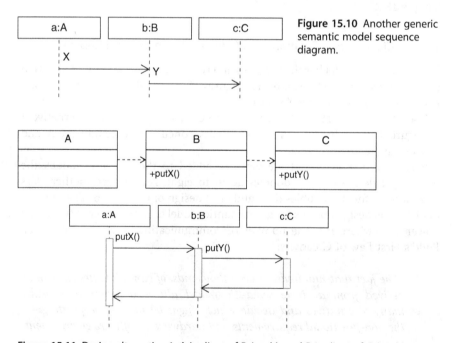

Figure 15.10 Another generic semantic model sequence diagram.

Figure 15.11 Design alternative 1: A is client of B (push), and B is client of C (push).

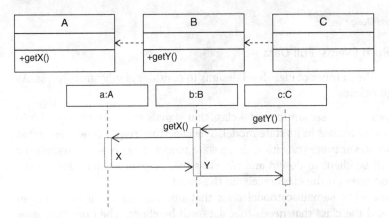

Figure 15.12 Alternative 2: C is client of B (pull), and B is client of A (pull).

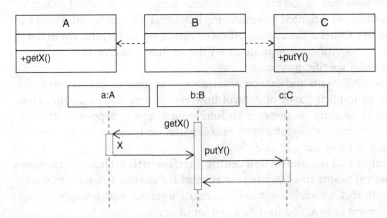

Figure 15.13 Alternative 3: B is client of A (pull), and B is client of C (push).

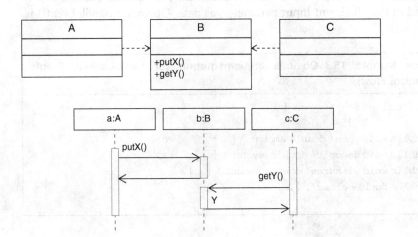

Figure 15.14 Alternative 4: A is client of B (push), and C is client of B (pull).

15.4.3 Push Events, Pull Data

In practice, the number of high-level designs to consider is substantially less. As general guidelines,

- *Push events*—The semantic model class that signals an event will signal it in one or more actions in its state model. The class that responds will have that event on one or more transitions in its state model. The class that signals the event will be client in design and the class that responds will be server: the operation goes on the class receiving the event.
- *Pull data*—The semantic model class that provides data will be server in design and the class that needs that data will be client. The operation goes on the class that has the (possibly derived) attribute.

These guidelines lead to the most synchronous design that is easiest to implement in most object-oriented programming languages. Of course, this is not the only possibility. Other more asynchronous designs are possible, and any of those other designs might be appropriate given the technical and/or economic circumstances of a specific project.

Even allocating events and data communications to separate operations in the design has an implicit flavor of control flow versus data flow. Consider class BankAcoount needing to respond to four events: open, deposit, withdraw, and close. The most straightforward implementation (pushing events) would be as shown in Code Sample 15.3.

Code Sample 15.3 is a control flow centric interface in that it has separate control (i.e., entry) points to communicate each of the events. Contrast this with Code Sample 15.4, which has a data flow centric interface with a single control point. The event is specified in data as an input parameter.

In Code Sample 15.4, control flow itself (the invocation) only communicates that some account-relevant event has occurred. The specific event is represented in the aBAEvent input parameter, as data. Operation handleEvent() is,

---

Code Sample 15.3 Obvious Implementation for BankAccount Events (Control Flow)

```
public class BankAccount {
    ...
    public void open ( double amount ) { ... }
    public void deposit ( double amount ) { ... }
    public void withdraw ( double amount ) { ... }
    public double close () { ... }
}
```

Code Sample 15.4 Less Obvious Implementation for BankAccount Events (Data Flow)

```
public enum BAEvent { OPEN, DEPOSIT, WITHDRAW, CLOSE };

public class BankAccount {
  ...
  public double handleEvent ( BAEvent aBAEvent, double amount ) { ... }
}
```

---

of course, not very cohesive. On the other hand, technical and/or economic constraints could make this design better than others. For instance, in remote procedure call (RPC), having fewer different types of calls—and encoding the desired function as a parameter—is sometimes preferred. This example also helps illustrate that control flow and data flow are very different concepts and that understanding that difference opens the door to many alternative, possibly more appropriate designs.

The remainder of this chapter follows the "push events, pull data" guidelines. Chapter 16 shows contrasting signatures and contracts for pulled events and pushed data, that is, what happens when these guidelines are not followed.

It is also important to understand that notation used in this chapter implies direct function calls: an operation on one class directly invokes an operation on another class. Conceptually, that is fine for now. Actual invocation may use RPC, service-oriented architecture (SOA), microservices, REST, or any other mechanism.

15.5 Deriving Operations in Model Region for Order fulfillment

This section derives Model region operations for several sea level use cases in Order fulfillment, one at a time. Start with use case Packable orders? The semantic model sequence diagram is shown in Figure 15.15.

In deriving the design for this use case,

- *First consider the stock level? message between Print medium and Book order line*—We determine this is data because .stock level is an attribute of Print medium. According to the guidelines, the destination, Book order line, will

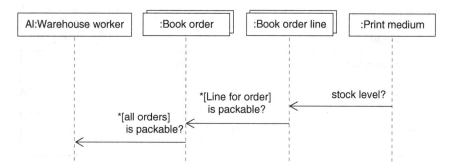

Figure 15.15 Semantic model sequence diagram for use case Packable orders?

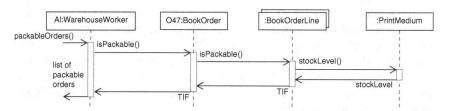

Figure 15.16 Design sequence diagram for use case Packable orders?

be client. The source, Print medium, will be server. The operation goes on the server so we put a stockLevel()[7] operation on class PrintMedium.

- *Next, consider is packable? between Book order line and Book order*—This is also data because is packable? is a derived attribute of Book order line. So BookOrderLine becomes server and gets an isPackable() operation on its interface.
- *Finally, is packable? between Book order and Warehouse worker*—This is also data; is packable? is a derived attribute of Book order. So BookOrder becomes server and gets an isPackable() operation on its interface.

A design sequence diagram for this use case is shown in Figure 15.16.

The high-level design, including dependencies, incorporating this first use case is shown in Figure 15.17. Technically, the dependency should be from BookOrderLine to PrintMedium but is shown between BookOrderLine and Medium. Later interaction will involve BookOrderLine to Medium dependencies; this is just a shortcut for now. Added operations are shaded in the diagram.

---

7 Different naming conventions are possible. Some organizations would name the operation as "getStockLevel()".

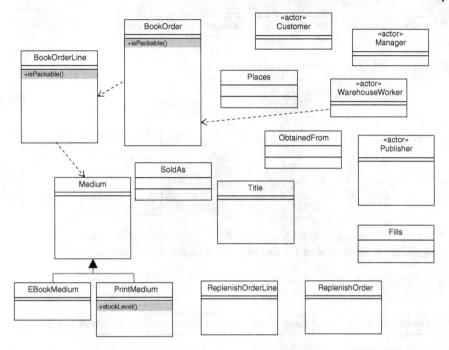

Figure 15.17 Model region high-level design for use case Packable orders?

15.5.1 Pack Order Use Case

Next consider use case Pack order; the semantic model sequence diagram for the first part of the use case is shown in Figure 15.18.

In deriving the design according to the guidelines,

- *Consider the Packed message between Warehouse worker and Book order—*
  We can determine this is an event because Packed causes a transition on the state model of Book order. The source of the event, Warehouse worker, becomes client, and the destination, Book order, becomes server. So we put a packed() operation on class BookOrder.
- *Next, consider Packed between Book order and Book order line—*This is also an event, which causes a transition on the state model of Book order line. So BookOrderLine becomes server and gets a packed() operation on its interface.
- *Finally, the Picked message between Book order line and Print medium—*This is also an event, so PrintMedium becomes server and gets a picked() operation on its interface.

A design sequence diagram for this use case is shown in Figure 15.19.

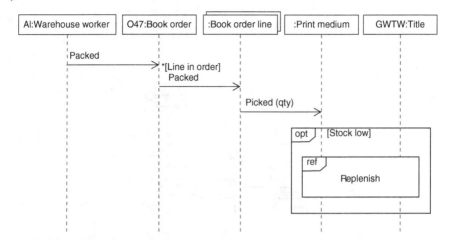

Figure 15.18 Semantic model sequence diagram for part of use case Pack order.

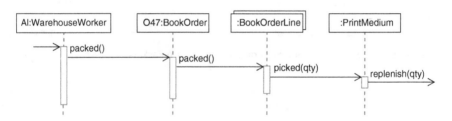

Figure 15.19 Design sequence diagram for part of use case Pack order.

15.5.2 Extending Use Case Replenish

The pack order sequence diagram (Figure 15.18) only covers the first part of the sea level use case. The Replenish extending use case sequence diagram is shown in Figure 15.20.

Each message in the extending use case is also an event and needs to be pushed. The high-level design, including dependencies, after incorporating both pack order and replenish use cases is shown in Figure 15.21. The operation name "ctor()" is shorthand for a constructor.

Notice that interaction between:

- PrintMedium and Title involves association SoldAs
- Title and Publisher involves association ObtainedFrom
- Publisher and Replenish order involves association Fills

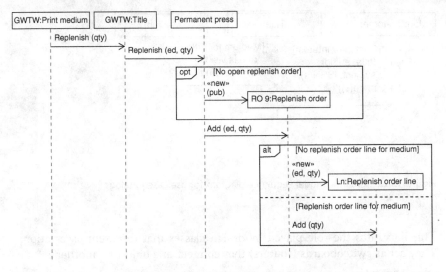

Figure 15.20 Semantic model sequence diagram for extending use case Replenish.

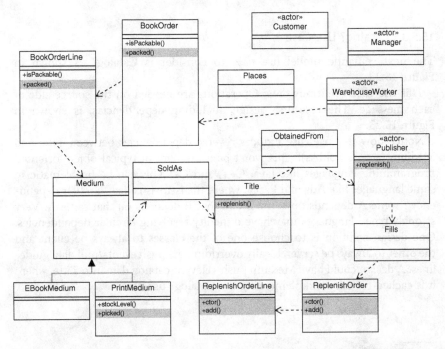

Figure 15.21 Model region design incorporating use case Pack order with Replenish.

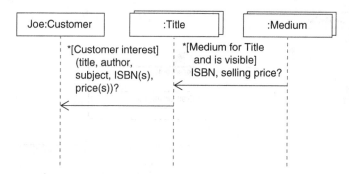

Figure 15.22 Semantic model sequence diagram for use case Catalog?

This illustrates the role played by design classes that represent associations. They act as switchboards (routers) that connect one object to another[8]:

- Which Title is for this PrintMedium? SoldAs knows that
- Which Publisher is for this Title? ObtainedFrom knows that
- Which Replenish orders are for which Publisher? Fills knows that

15.5.3 Catalog? Use Case

The next semantic model use case to consider is Catalog? as shown in Figure 15.22.

This use case is entirely data. Operations are needed on the source side of each message. The resulting design, including dependencies, is shown in Figure 15.23.

Notice how this use case induces reverse dependencies between Title and Medium (across SoldAs). This won't be a problem in typical object-oriented programming languages like Java, C++, and C#. This can be problematic in some languages like Ada and Pascal where the issue is called "circular dependency": some A depends on some B and that B depends on that same A. Very strongly typed languages may have difficulty resolving circular dependencies. One design solution is to choose one of the classes to always be client and the other to always be server, locally overriding the push events/pull data guidelines. A design could have Medium push-relevant catalog data into Title, where it is cached for use in implementing the Catalog? use case.

---

8 Or objects (plural) if the multiplicity of the association is greater than one in that direction (e.g., Publisher fills zero to many Replenish orders).

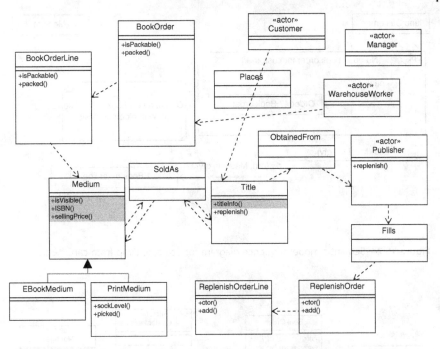

Figure 15.23 Model region design incorporating use case Catalog?

An alternative design solution, if supported by the language, is to separate A's interface from A's implementation and B's interface from B's implementation. Even a strongly typed compiler should not have a problem with A's implementation depending on B's interface and B's implementation depending on A's interface.

15.5.4 Add to Cart Use Case

The next use case to incorporate is Add to cart, as shown in Figure 15.24.

This is mostly event communication so most messages will be pushed. The high-level design incorporating this use case is shown in Figure 15.25.

15.5.5 Drop from Cart Use Case

The next semantic model use case is Drop from cart as shown in Figure 15.26.

Again, this is essentially event communication so most operations go on destination classes. The high-level design incorporating use case Drop from cart is shown in Figure 15.27.

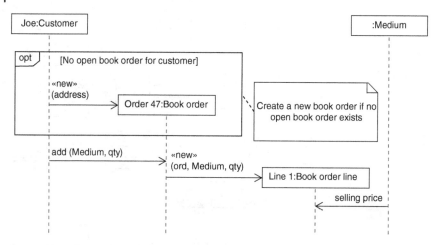

Figure 15.24 Semantic model sequence diagram for use case Drop from cart.

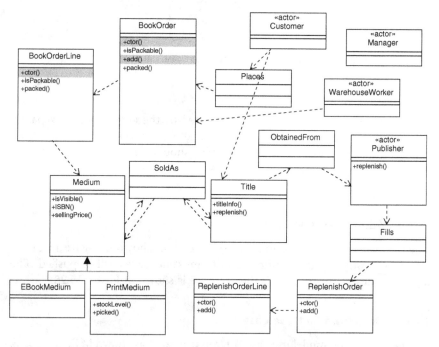

Figure 15.25 Model region design incorporating use case Add to cart.

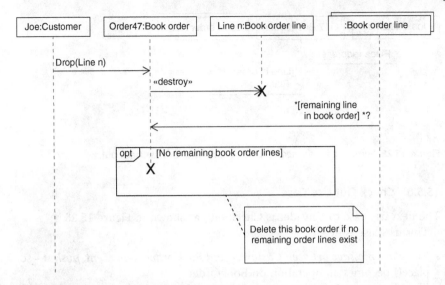

Figure 15.26 Semantic model sequence diagram for use case Drop from cart.

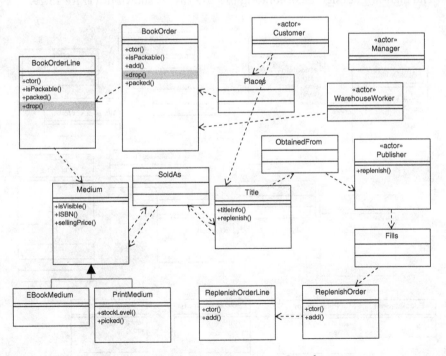

Figure 15.27 Model region design incorporating use case Drop from cart.

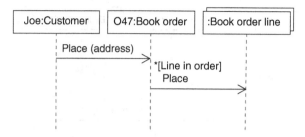

Figure 15.28 Semantic model sequence diagram for use case Check out.

15.5.6 Check Out Use Case

The next use case to consider is Check out, as shown in Figure 15.28. This use case is event:

- *The place message between Customer and Book order is an event, push it*—so place() becomes an operation on BookOrder.
- *The place message between Book order and Book order line is an event, push it*—so place() becomes an operation on BookOrderLine.

The high-level design incorporating this use case is shown in Figure 15.29.

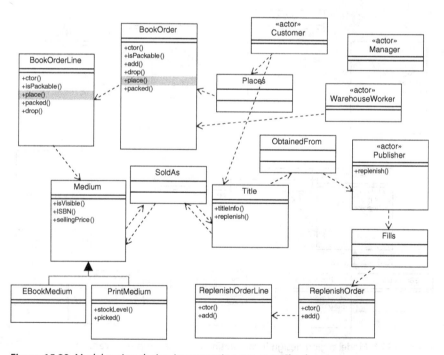

Figure 15.29 Model region design incorporating use case Check out.

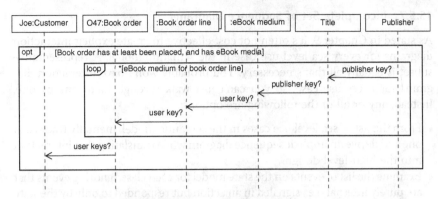

Figure 15.30 Semantic model sequence diagram for use case eBook user keys?

The final use case to consider by itself is eBook user keys? as shown in Figure 15.30.

This use case is data, where the high-level design incorporating this use case is shown in Figure 15.31.

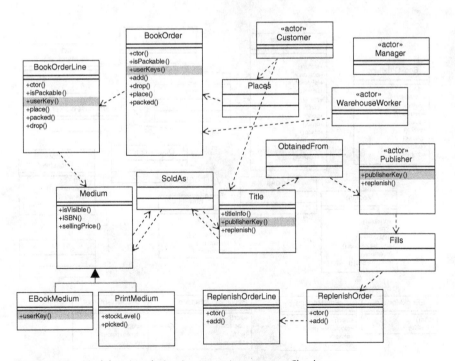

Figure 15.31 Model region design incorporating use case Check out.

15.5.7 Incomplete Set of Sequence Diagrams

As stated in Chapter 9, it's often not cost effective to create explicit interaction diagrams for every sea level use case in the semantic model. A representative subset is usually all that's necessary. You probably won't have interaction diagrams for every use case, so you can't just walk through them one by one. Instead, any or all of the following are options:

- From the list of sea level use cases in the semantic model, mentally trace each one and derive an implicit sequence diagram while translating that interaction into the high-level design.
- Examine the list of events on the state model for each class, ignoring events that are purely internal (i.e., signaled in an action but responded to only by the state model of that same object—that event never leaves that object), and add an operation to the interface of the high-level design for each non-internal event.
- Look for access to attributes and derived attributes by other objects and classes. For each, provide a "getter" operation.

Some combination of these hints should get you very close to a complete set of operations for Model region design classes.

Figure 15.32 shows an initial design for Model region of Order fulfillment, incorporating all sea level use cases.

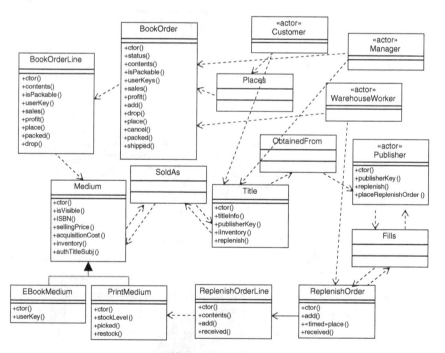

Figure 15.32 Initial high-level design for Model region of Order fulfillment.

15.6   High-Level Design for View-Controller Region

Step 4 is designing View-controller region. In (sub)domains with nontrivial interfaces, View-controller region is a translator. Controller region senses happenings on the interface (e.g., a user enters a number into field 4 on screen 21 and then clicks button 7) and translates those happenings into syntactically complete business requests (e.g., a bank customer wants to transfer some amount of money from their savings account to their checking account). Controller region passes that syntactically complete request into Model region: "transfer $X from savings account Y to checking account Z."

Model region caries out the business process, in this case first semantically validating the request:

- Are both accounts open?
- Is there enough money in the savings account?
- Has more than $250 been withdrawn from the savings account in the last 24 hours?
- ...?

If all semantic validations pass, Model region executes the transfer. The output of Model region will either be "that request was valid and has been completed, here is the result" or "that request was invalid and here is why."

View region receives either of those two results. If View region receives a success result, then, for example, it puts up screen 29 telling the user: "Your transfer was successful, would you like a printed receipt?" If View region receives a failure result, then, for example, it may put up screen 41 saying: "Your transfer failed" along with a user-readable translation of the error code ("the savings account doesn't have enough money," "your request would cause more than $250 to be transferred out of that account in 24 hours," etc.).

In cases where the interface is trivial (e.g., an API that simply exposes a subset of Model region operations), View-controller region will be a façade that "wraps" Model region. The API for Payment domain in Chapter 14 is an example.

15.7   High-Level Design for a User Interface View-Controller Region

View-controller region design for a user interface (UI) will be described from three different perspectives:

- Single-user desktop application
- Distributed client-server application
- Web application

While WebBooks is required to provide a Web UI for customers, it will still be designed from each of these perspectives to provide a contrast between approaches. The design for a single-user desktop application will be shown first. Again, keep in mind that these designs should be considered existence proofs that systematic design can be done. The specific design on any project could vary from what is described here.

15.8 High-Level Design for Single-User Desktop View-Controller Region

Figure 15.33 shows a relatively brute-force (in the sense that each screen is hard-coded as a class, a more elegant, data-driven design appears later) design of View-controller region for the Customer UI in Order fulfillment, assuming it is implemented as a desktop application. Each user screen in the Customer's interface is coded as a separate View-controller region class. The Customer class implements the screen sequencing logic defined in the Dialog map. In this design, the actor is client of both View-controller and Model regions. Customer pulls user input from View-controller region and pushes business requests into Model region.

Conceptually, the Model region to View-controller region boundary splits actors: Customer in Figures 15.33 and 15.34. Actor classes are gateways between Model region and View-controller region. Similarly, Figure 15.34 shows how UI

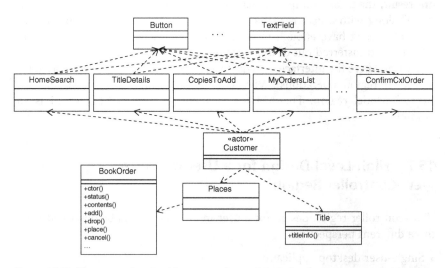

Figure 15.33 First approximation View-controller region design for Customer user interface.

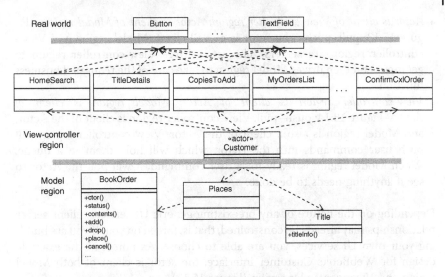

Figure 15.34 Model region, View-controller region, and real world.

widgets visible on the screen are gateways between software and the real world. The user enters data into a text field and clicks on a button to make their request, as defined in the interface specification. View-controller region decodes that request and passes it—via the Actor gateway—into Model region where the request is processed. The response from Model region causes the Actor to drive View-controller region in presenting the result to the user.

A general issue in designing View-controller region for a UI is the client-server relationship between the actor straddling the Model region to View-controller region boundary and Model region and View-controller region code. Refer back to Figures 15.11–15.14 on the three classes with two messages in various combinations of push versus pull. These are also design options regarding View-controller to Model region control relationships. In all cases below, consider A to represent View-controller region, B to represent the Actor, and C to represent Model region:

- *View-controller region is client of Actor; Actor is client of Model region*—Figure 15.11: push–push. View-controller region is overall client, the Actor is server, and the Actor is client of Model region. View-controller region code calls the actor, which then calls Model region.
- *Model region is client of Actor; Actor is client of View-controller region*—Figure 15.12: pull–pull. Model region is overall client; the Actor is client of View-controller region. Model region asks the actor for input, and the actor asks View-controller region. Decoded input is returned via the actor to Model region.

- *Actor is client of View-controller region; Actor is client of Model region*—Figure 15.13: pull–push. The actor is overall client; Model region and View-controller region are servers. The actor drives View-controller region to get input and then drives Model region to take care of the requested business function.
- *View-controller region is client of Actor; Model region is client of Actor*—Figure 15.14: push–pull. View-controller region is client of the Actor, and Model region is also a client of the Actor. View-controller region will push user commands into the Actor, which will hold them in a queue. When Model region is ready for a user command, it will poll the Actor to see if anything needs to be done.

Depending on the nature of any preexisting generic UI services, client-server relationships may already be constrained, that is, forced on you. If you are building your own UI services, you are able to choose. As noted, in the example design for WebBooks Customer interface, the actor is client of both Model region and View-controller region (Figure 15.13).

More specifically, View-controller region design in Figure 15.34 should include an abstract base class, possibly called UIScreen. Each user screen-specific class derives from it. The abstract base class was not shown in Figure 15.34 because it clutters the diagram with little benefit. A fragment of the high-level design for Customer UI screens including UIScreen is shown in Figure 15.35.

Base class UIScreen implements the common structure of UI screens. This includes screen headers and footers, standard screen elements and backgrounds, etc. The constructor on UIScreen initializes the common elements.

Each concrete subclass implements one user screen in the Customer UI. Instance variables in a concrete subclass play one of two roles:

- *(References to) screen-specific widgets*—for example, the scroll up and scroll down buttons on the HomeSearchList screen or the Ok/Submit button on the CopiesToAdd screen
- *Screen-specific dynamic content*—such as the search criteria, the displayed results on the HomeSearchList screen, and the quantity selected on the CopiesToAdd screen

The constructor on a concrete screen class extends the base class constructor and implements screen-specific initialization like instantiating screen-specific widgets and setting screen-specific dynamic content to default values. Each concrete screen class also has:

- *Instance variable setters for screen-specific dynamic content*—To allow display content to be initialized before the screen is activated

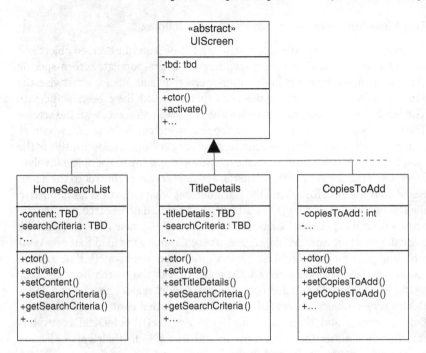

Figure 15.35 A fragment of View-controller region design showing UIScreen.

- *Instance variable getters for screen-specific dynamic content*—To allow the actor to retrieve screen content like the selected quantity from the Copies-ToAdd screen

The activate() operation on each concrete screen manages screen-specific behavior:

- *Enforce ranges on input values*—Like the selected quantity on the Copies-ToAdd screen.
- *Enable and disable buttons as appropriate*—The Ok/Submit button on the CopiesToAdd screen might be disabled when the user field for selecting the quantity to add does not hold a valid value (e.g., negative, null, zero, etc.).
- *Implement local screen-specific behavior*—Like scroll up and scroll down on the HomeSearchList (assuming a scrolling widget does not already exist).
- *Deciding when to return to the actor*—Knowing when required input is complete and the user pressed a Continue or Submit button.

An additional deactivate() operation is needed in non-garbage-collecting languages like C++. The operation releases all screen resources (e.g., local widgets). Garbage-collecting languages like Java take care of that automatically.

This View-controller region design works as follows:

- On start-up, a Customer object constructs a HomeSearchList screen object and then uses setSearchCriteria() and setContent() to pre-populate screen-specific dynamic content (presumably to user-specific default values; otherwise the generic default values set in the constructor would have been sufficient). The actor then calls activate() to allow the real user to interact with the screen.
- The HomeSearchList screen waits for the real-world customer to take whatever action they want: selecting new search criteria or clicking on a specific title in the search list. When the customer makes an action requiring Actor object involvement, like entering new search criteria, activate() returns control to the actor.
- Based on the reason for return, the actor decides what to do next (as defined in the Dialog map). Assuming the customer had entered new search criteria, the actor would use getSearchCriteria() to retrieve those new criteria, fetch the matching content from Model region, use setContent() to load that new content into the HomeSearchList screen, and then reactivate() that screen. Assuming the customer selected a specific title in the search list, the actor would fetch required detailed content from Model region, construct a Title-Details screen object, use setTitleDetails() to push that content into the Title-Details screen, and then call TitleDetails.activate(). TitleDetails.activate() returns when either the user wants to add that title to their cart or enters new search criteria, as defined in the Dialog map.
- Assuming TitleDetails.activate() returned because the user wanted to add that title to their cart, actor Customer would create and initialize a CopiesToAdd screen and then call its activate(). CopiesToAdd.activate() would return when the customer hit either the Yes (with a valid quantity) or No button. If Yes was hit, the actor would now know to submit a BookOrder.add(selectedTitle, selectedQuantity) to model. In either case, Yes or No, the CopiesToAdd screen has done its job and can be deactivate()-ed if in a non-garbage-collecting language. The Customer actor object would then activate() the TitleDetails page as defined in the Dialog map.

15.8.1   A More Elegant View-Controller Design

A more elegant View-controller design would use an abstract Screen Interpreter class that manages user screens based on data descriptions—"Interpreter" or "Data-driven" architectural style—as shown in Figure 15.36. Cost, schedule, long-term maintenance, and other economic and technical criteria would need to be considered to decide if the brute-force or more elegant design is more cost effective on any specific project.

Either way, brute force or elegant, design for View-controller region is essentially "glue code" that binds an actor to generic services (UI toolkit widgets in this case) in a way that supports the UI defined in the interface specification.

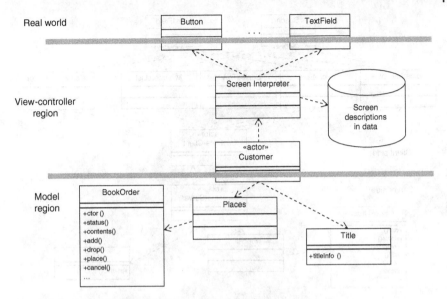

Figure 15.36 A more elegant View-controller region design.

15.8.2 Recursive Design in View-Controller Region

Most designs for View-controller region use preexisting generic widget services like Java Swing, AWT, and so on. In some cases, however, generic widget services are needed but don't already exist. Two cases are possible:

- *View-controller region services can be built on the fly because they aren't difficult*—For example, they won't take more than a few days to build.
- *View-controller region generic services will be provided by a nontrivial domain that needs to be built*—You may have already recognized this when you did domain partitioning in Chapter 6, but sometimes this can be a surprise later in the project.

Hopefully you would have recognized the need for generic UI services from the beginning, so you would have identified it as a domain. But one doesn't always recognize up front. Sometimes the team gets surprised. Don't panic; just manage it as its own domain and move on. This is recursive design in action.

15.9 High-Level Design for Distributed Client-Server View-Controller Region

The designs in Figure 15.33 and 15.36 would be sufficient for a single-user desktop application. If the View-controller region design is for a distributed client-server application (or, e.g., an app running on a smart phone or tablet), class

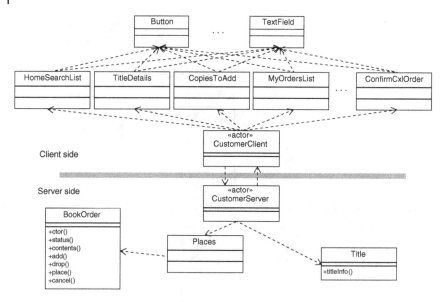

Figure 15.37 View-controller region design for client-server Customer user interface.

Customer in Figure 15.33 could be split to provide true client-server architecture. One part of Customer becomes client-side logic. This would almost certainly include the screen sequencing logic in the Dialog map. The other part of Customer becomes a server-side portal, CustomerServer, that provides the API for CustomerClient to invoke. This is shown in Figure 15.37.

The server-side portal API could be RPC, SOA, microservices, or REST depending on which is most cost effective in the long run.

Depending on project organizational structure, Model region team might publish an API for CustomerServer if View-controller region is developed and maintained by some other team. If the entire domain is being designed, coded, and maintained by the same team, the high-level design for Customer-Server might be sufficient (i.e., as internal documentation).

Finally, Figure 15.38 shows a View-controller region design when the application uses Web pages as actually required in WebBooks 2.0. A few differences between this and previous designs are worth mentioning:

- *Each user screen is a separate, self-contained Web page*—Each page is presumably implemented in HTML or some other appropriate technology.
- *Screen-to-screen sequencing logic (the Dialog map) is embedded in the individual pages*—For example, when the user clicks on the Yes button on the CopiesToAdd page, it links back to the TitleDetails page as defined in the Dialog map.

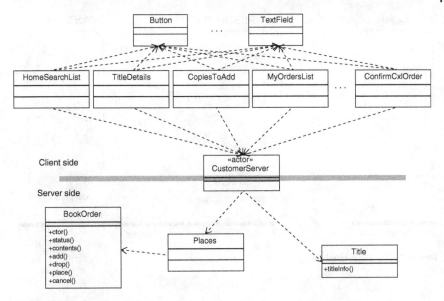

Figure 15.38 View-controller region design for client-server Customer user interface.

- *Each page is a client of the CustomerServer actor*—This is View-controller region as client of Actor and Actor as client of Model region as shown in Figure 15.11. The real user pressing the Yes button on the CopiesToAdd page also sends an add(selectedTitle, selectedQuantity) request to the CustomerServer.

15.10 High-Level Design for an API View-Controller Region

When the (sub)domain provides an API (direct function call, RPC, SOA, micro-services, REST, etc.), Controller region parses incoming requests and data and passes decoded requests to Model region. Model region does the business work, and the result comes out the other side. View region takes over and translates Model region's output into responses as defined in the interface specification. In the simplest case, View-controller region is just a wrapper or façade[9] for Model region. The API for Payment domain (presented in both Chapter 14 and Appendix G) is an example of a simple wrapper or façade.

---

9 See, for example, https://en.wikipedia.org/wiki/Facade_pattern.

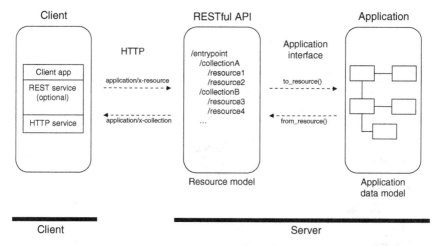

Figure 15.39 High-level design for a REST application.

In more complex cases, View-controller region needs to map the published API onto Model region's internal API (as implemented at actor classes). In very complex cases involving SOA, microservices, or REST, View-controller region design and code can do quite a lot of work. Figure 15.39 shows a high-level architecture for a generic REST application.

Figure 15.40 shows how the architecture in Figure 15.39 could relate to Model–View–Controller regions and the real world. In thin client or thick client architectures, the boundaries could be different.

REST services depend on mechanisms in the Resource Model that receive a request, evaluate the request's meaning (Controller region), and route it to procedures that implement the requested behavior (Model region). A "Front Controller" can coordinate with "Service Controllers"—classes with one or more public methods (aka request handlers) that execute the business task and coordinate access to resources (files, documents, images, etc.).

Rules, known as "routing expressions," can define which request handler should be invoked for which kind of request. Routing expressions typically precede each Web method in the service controller and are interpreted by the front controller. When a Web server receives a request, the framework selects and invokes the appropriate handler by evaluating various elements of the request against these expressions. More information on service controllers can be found at http://www.servicedesignpatterns.com/RequestAndResponseManagement/ServiceController.

There are several styles for implementing service controller code (see, e.g., http://www.servicedesignpatterns.com/WebServiceImplementationStyles). One style, "Data Source Adapter" attempts to minimize the amount of custom code

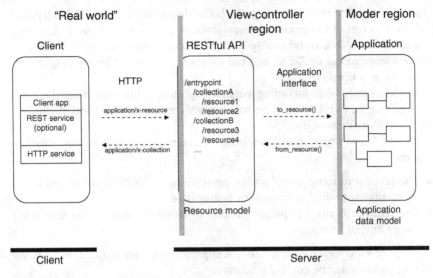

Figure 15.40 Relating high-level REST design to Model–View–Controller.

needed (see, e.g., http://www.servicedesignpatterns.com/WebServiceImplementationStyles/DatasourceAdapter). Many platforms support this approach. The trade-off is high coupling to Model region.

The book *Service Design Patterns*[10] discusses View-controller region design patterns useful in Web API projects although most patterns are not specific to Web APIs and are more broadly applicable.

15.11 High-Level Design for a Real-Time/Embedded View-Controller Region

With real-time embedded software, View-controller region code implements the interface to sensor and actuator hardware. Protocols like SCADA,[11] IEEE 488,[12] IEEE 1588,[13] Fieldbus,[14] ARINC 429,[15] and so on are used to interact with sensor and actuator hardware. Part of Controller region speaks the appropriate

---

10 See [Daigneau12].
11 See, for example, https://en.wikipedia.org/wiki/SCADA.
12 See, for example, https://en.wikipedia.org/wiki/IEEE-488.
13 See, for example, http://www.embedded.com/design/connectivity/4007485/Basics-of-real-time-measurement-control-and-communication-using-IEEE-1588-Part-1.
14 See, for example, https://en.wikipedia.org/wiki/Fieldbus.
15 See, for example, https://en.wikipedia.org/wiki/ARINC_429.

device protocol to read "raw" (e.g., 16-bit analog-to-digital or 8-bit binary flag) values. The rest of Controller region translates the raw values into engineering units, for example, a 16-bit analog-to-digital value represents a process temperature measurement of 225°C and the fourth bit in a set of binary flags means some valve is open.

Model region takes incoming engineering units values and does the work needed (e.g., control laws). Control outputs computed by Model region are handed off to View region.

Part of View region translates outgoing engineering unit values into raw values:

- The request to ramp a process temperature up to 250°C is translated into a 16-bit digital-to-analog output for heater hardware.
- The request to close a specific process valve means clearing bit 6 of some binary output controller.

The rest of View region code speaks the appropriate device protocol to push raw output values into the control hardware.

In embedded code with truly tight performance constraints, an alternative is to map all engineering units in Model region into equivalent raw units and do all Model region computations in raw units. This avoids raw-to-engineering and engineering-to-raw conversions that can sometimes be computationally complex.

Controller region and View region design and code could be simple or complex, depending on the nature of the hardware protocol(s) and the complexity of raw-to-engineering and engineering-to-raw conversions. To the extent that instrumentation protocols or conversion algorithms are nontrivial, domain separation can be used: the semantics of a protocol and/or a raw-engineering-raw conversion service can be modeled as a separate domain.

15.12   High-Level Design for Infrastructure Region

The last step, Step 5, is to design classes in Infrastructure region. This depends entirely on the "service gap": what services are needed by Model region and View-controller region that aren't already part of the existing computing environment?

- If none, Infrastructure region is empty.
- If only trivial services are needed, they can be designed and implemented as part of the same domain.
- If complex services are needed, again, recursive design can be used to address those complexities separately.

Table 15.1 Quality criteria for high-level design.

Item	Criterion
HD-1	The high-level design is consistent with all relevant nonfunctional how requirements
HD-2	The high-level design encapsulates appropriately
HD-3	Relevant, non-obvious design decisions are clearly described and justified
HD-4	Model region classes are consistent with semantic model (classes and associations)—the correlation is either obvious or sufficiently explained
HD-5	Model region operations are consistent with messages in the semantic model
HD-6	View-controller region classes are necessary and sufficient to support interfaces specified in the Interface specification
HD-7	Infrastructure region classes and operations are necessary and sufficient
HD-8	Design interaction (sequence) diagrams are consistent with the high-level design class diagram
HD-9	Design interaction (sequence) diagrams are consistent with use cases in the Interface specification
HD-10	Pushing versus pulling of events and data are appropriate given relevant technical and economic factors

15.13   Quality Criteria

In addition to the overall quality criteria (Table 3.1) and naming criteria (Table 3.2), the quality criteria in Table 15.1 can be applied to high-level design-related work to identify and remove defects as quickly and as cheaply as possible.

15.14   Summary

This chapter explained how an initial high-level software design for a (sub) domain can be derived from a semantic model and its corresponding interface specification. That initial high-level design consists of classes, operations, and dependencies. Operation syntax (signatures) and semantics (contracts) will be derived in the next chapter. This and the next several chapters explain manual (i.e., human) derivation of design and code; Chapters 20 and 21 explain automatic derivation using open model compilers. Even if you use a model compiler, you should still want to understand these chapters as model compilers simply automate similar processes.

16

High-Level Design

Contracts and Signatures

Chapter 15 explained how to derive classes and operations in the high-level design for a (sub)domain. This chapter continues with derivation of operation signatures (syntax) and contracts (semantics). Technically, these are partial signatures. Parameters will be identified, but types will not be determined until the next chapter. In Model region, these are derived from the semantic model. Topics in this chapter include:

- High-level design as a deliberate encapsulation barrier
- Deriving contracts and signatures for Model region pulled data
- Deriving contracts and signatures for Model region pushed events
- Defensive programming and Design by contract
- Defensive programming and Trust boundaries
- Handling operation contract-level errors
- Deriving class invariants for Model region
- Deriving contracts and signatures for Model region pulled events
- Deriving contracts and signatures for Model region pushed data
- Contracts and signatures in View-controller and Infrastructure regions
- Documenting the initial high-level design
- Quality criteria

16.1   High-Level Design as a Deliberate Encapsulation Barrier

In model-based software engineering, high-level design represents a deliberate, intentional encapsulation barrier. Everything in high-level design is public within the (sub)domain. If a developer is working on the detailed design or code of Customer and Customer uses operations on the interface of Order, that developer should know everything they need about Order from its high-level design. Order's operation syntax (signatures) and semantics (contracts) must

How to Engineer Software: A Model-Based Approach, First Edition. Steve Tockey.
© 2019 the IEEE Computer Society, Inc. Published 2019 by John Wiley & Sons, Inc.

be visible to Customer's developer. There must be no reason for Customer's developer to know—or even care how Order is implemented:

> *"Develop <u>to</u> an interface, not <u>through</u> an interface"*

Using interfaces in high-level design instead of classes[1] would make it harder to break this intentional encapsulation barrier. This also makes unit testing easier by only needing a mock object—or "test double"—to implement that same interface.

16.2 Deriving Contracts and Signatures for Model Region Pulled Data

Following the guidelines in the previous chapter, data messages in semantic models are normally pulled in Model region. The server class, the source of that data, provides an operation on its interface. Several variations on pulling data are presented:

- Operations implementing access to attributes
- Operations implementing derived attributes
- Operations with input parameters
- Operations returning collections

The simplest case of an operation implementing pulled data represents read access to a semantic model attribute. The signature for this kind of operation does not have any input parameters. It has only one output parameter (again, the actual data type may not be determined until the next chapter), the attribute value being read. The contract will not require anything and guarantee that it returns the attribute value. In Order fulfillment (see Figure 15.32), PrintMedium.stockLevel(), Medium.ISBN(), and BookOrder.status() are examples of attribute read accesses. Code Sample 16.1 shows a signature and contract for PrintMedium.stockLevel().

Code Sample 16.2 shows a signature and contract for Medium.ISBN(). BookOrder.status() would look very similar to both of these.

16.2.1 Derived Attributes

An operation that exposes a derived attribute value, such as BookOrder.isPackable() or BookOrderLine.isPackable(), is slightly more complex. The signature

---

1 For example, in Java, "public interface BookOrder {...}" instead of "public class BookOrder {...}".

Code Sample 16.1 Signature and Contract for PrintMedium.stockLevel()

```
public class PrintMedium extends Medium {

 public int stockLevel() {
 // requires
 //  none
 // guarantees
 //  returns .stockLevel for this print medium
  ...
 }
}
```

Code Sample 16.2 Signature and Contract for Medium.ISBN()

```
public class Medium {

 public ISBNtype ISBN() {
 // requires
 //  none
 // guarantees
 //  returns .ISBN of this medium
  ...
 }
}
```

---

of this kind of operation also has no input parameters. It also has only one output parameter, the derived value. Again, the contract will require nothing and guarantee that it returns the derived value. Code Sample 16.3 shows a signature and contract for BookOrderLine.isPackable().

Code Sample 16.4 shows a signature and contract for BookOrder.isPackable().

In Code Samples 16.3 and 16.4, the guarantees clause summarizes the intent of the derivation policy (i.e., the derivation function). For proof of correctness (see Chapter 18) or other formal analysis purposes, it might be more useful to have the derivation policy itself as the guarantees clause.

16.2.2 Derived Attributes with Input Parameters

In some cases an operation implementing a derived attribute needs input parameters. Manager.sales() and Manager.profit() both need the date range over

---

Code Sample 16.3 Signature and Contract for BookOrderLine.isPackable()

```
public class BookOrderLine {

  public boolean isPackable() {
  // requires
  //  none
  // guarantees
  //  returns true when packable, false when not packable
   ...
  }
}
```

Code Sample 16.4 Signature and Contract for BookOrder.isPackable()

```
public class BookOrder {

  public boolean isPackable() {
  // requires
  //  none
  // guarantees
  //  returns true when packable, false when not packable
   ...
  }
}
```

---

which sales or profit is to be derived. A signature and contract for Manager.sales() is shown in Code Sample 16.5; the signature and contract for Manager.profit() is very similar.

16.2.3 Returning Collections Instead of Values

In some cases an operation implementing a derived attribute returns a collection rather than a single value. Customer.catalog(), Customer.order(), and WarehouseWorker.packableOrders() are examples in Order fulfillment. The chunky versus chatty topic in the section on dealing with collections in Chapter 14 applies here. Customer.catalog() could return search results as follows:

Code Sample 16.5 Signature and Contract for Manager.sales()

```
public class Manager {

 public double sales ( Date startDate, Date endDate ) {
 // requires
 //  startDate is in valid range
 //  endDate is in valid range
 //  startDate is not later than endDate
 // guarantees
 //  returns the total book order sales between those dates
  . . .
 }
}
```

- *One single, possibly very large block*—i.e., chunky
- *One result at a time, as in Iterator pattern*[2]—i.e., chatty
- *Intermediate-sized blocks*—e.g., up to 12 results per block, similar to Amazon.com

Code Sample 16.6 shows a chunky design for Customer.catalog().

Code Sample 16.7 shows a chatty design of Customer.catalog().

Code Sample 16.8 shows an intermediate design of Customer.catalog() that returns results in blocks of, for example, up to 12 books per block.

Code Sample 16.6 Chunky Signature and Contract for Customer.catalog()

```
public class Customer {

 public SearchResults catalog ( SearchCriteria criteria ) {
 // requires
 //  none (i.e., search criteria can be null)
 // guarantees
 //  returns data for all books in the catalog
 //    that match those criteria
  . . .
 }
}
```

---

2 See, for example, Figure 14.1.

Code Sample 16.7 Chatty Signature and Contract for Customer.catalog()

```
public class Customer {

  public void catalog( SearchCriteria criteria ) {
  // initializes the search to the given search criteria
  //   i.e., plays the role of Iterator.first()
  // requires
  //   none (i.e., search criteria can be null)
  // guarantees
  //   a search has been initialized using the given criteria
   ...
  }

  public boolean isDone() {
  // requires
  //   none
  // guarantees
  //   returns true when no more books match the search criteria
   ...
  }

  public void next() {
  // requires
  //   none
  // guarantees
  //   moves to the next book that matches the search criteria
   ...
  }

  public SearchResult currentItem() {
  // returns the currently referenced book
  //   i.e., plays the role of Iterator.currentItem()
  // requires
  //   !this.isDone()
  // guarantees
  //   returns data for the current matching book
   ...
  }

}
```

Code Sample 16.8 Intermediate Signature and Contract for Customer.catalog()

```
public class Customer {

 public void catalog( SearchCriteria criteria ) {
 // initializes the search with the given search criteria
 //   i.e., plays the role of Iterator.first()
 // requires
 //   none (i.e., search criteria can be null)
 // guarantees
 //   a search has been initialized using the given criteria
  ...
 }

 public boolean isDone() {
 // requires
 //   none
 // guarantees
 //   returns true when no more books match the search criteria
  ...
 }

 public void nextBlock() {
 // requires
 //   none
 // guarantees
 //   moves to the next block of books that
 //     match the search criteria
  ...
 }

 public SearchResults currentItems() {
 // returns the next block of up to 12 search results
 // requires
 //   !this.isDone()
 // guarantees
 //   returns a block of up to 12 books from the catalog that
 //     match the search criteria
  ...
 }

}
```

The decision to return collections in chunky, chatty, or intermediate-sized blocks should be based on the same relevant technical and economic factors listed in Chapter 14. If chatty or intermediate blocks are used, the high-level design diagram needs to be updated to reflect that decision. And if not already obvious, the justification for that decision should be included in design documentation.

16.3 Deriving Contracts and Signatures for Model Region Pushed Events

Following guidelines in the previous chapter, event messages in semantic models are normally pushed. The server class, the destination of that event, provides an operation on its interface. Signatures and contracts for operations implementing pushed events can be nontrivial. Fortunately, they follow a general pattern. Once you understand that pattern, applying it to a specific event becomes straightforward. The general pattern is presented first, followed by discussion of variations along with examples from Order fulfillment. Figure 16.1 illustrates the general pattern: design for any specific event should be no more complex than this.

Start with the upper left quadrant of Figure 16.1, a semantic model sequence diagram. As shown, objects of ClassX will respond to event1 and event2. Not shown are other sequence diagrams for ClassX: creation, deletion, and so on.

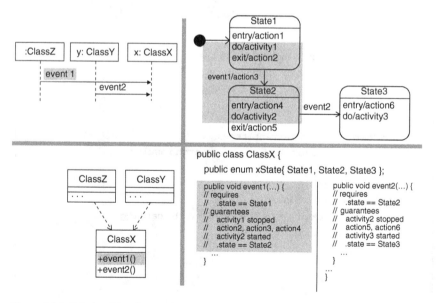

Figure 16.1 Relationship of operation contract to state model, a generic, nontrivial case.

The upper right quadrant is a state model for ClassX in a semantic model. When an object of ClassX is in state1 and it sees an event1, then it transitions to State2. Along the way it carries out several business process elements:

- Stopping state action(s) in State1 ("do/activity1")
- Performing exit action(s) while leaving State1 ("exit/action2")
- Performing transition action(s) while going from State1 to State2 ("/action3")
- Performing entry action(s) on entering State2 ("entry/action4")
- Starting state action(s) in State2 ("do/activity2")

On completing these actions (remember that semantic model actions take essentially zero time to complete), the object of ClassX is now in State2.

The lower left quadrant is high-level design following the push events recommendation:

- ClassX in the semantic model (upper half) became ClassX in the high-level design (lower left quadrant).
- ClassY in the semantic model became ClassY in the design.
- ClassZ in the semantic model became ClassZ in the design.
- event1 is an event in the semantic model so it gets pushed in design: ClassZ is client, ClassX is server, and an operation named event1() goes on ClassX.
- event2 is an event in the semantic model so it gets pushed in design: an operation named event2() goes on ClassX.

The lower right quadrant is the interface for ClassX, showing partial contracts for event1() and event2(). Signatures will be derived later. Operation event1() in design needs to represent the same semantics as event1 in the state model. Trace backward from operation event1() through shaded operation event1() on the design class diagram in the lower left quadrant through shaded message event1 in the sequence diagram in the upper left quadrant to the shaded transition in the state model in the upper right quadrant. In the state model, event1:

- Is only responded to when the ClassX object is in State1
- Carries out the shaded business processes in the upper right quadrant
- Leaves that ClassX object in State2

Code Sample 16.9 shows partial contracts for ClassX.event1() and event2() based on Figure 16.1.

16.3.1 Including State Model Actions

Contracts for actions in the semantic model also affect a containing operation's contract. Assume contracts on the actions in the state model in the upper right quadrant are the following:

- action2 requires pr1 and pr2 while guaranteeing po1 and po2.

Code Sample 16.9 Partial Contracts for ClassX.event1() and event2()

```
public class ClassX {

 public void event1() {
 // requires
 //   .state == STATE1
 // guarantees
 //   activity1 has stopped
 //   action1, action2, and action3 have been done
 //   activity2 has started
 //   .state == STATE2
   ...
 }

 public void event2() {
 // requires
 //   .state == STATE2
 // guarantees
 //   activity2 has stopped
 //   action5 and action6 have been done
 //   activity3 has started
 //   .state == STATE3
   ...
 }

}
```

- action3 requires pr3 and po2 while guaranteeing po3 and po4.
- action4 requires pr4 while guaranteeing po5.

Notice that requires condition po2 of action3 is a guarantees condition of action2. This will be relevant in determining requires conditions for operation event1(). Figure 16.2 shows action contract dependencies using classic data flow diagram notation.[3]

While po2 is a requires condition for action3, it can't be a requires condition for the operation because it is a guarantees condition of action2. Requires conditions for event1() need to include pr1, pr2, pr3, and pr4. Guarantees conditions for event1() need to include po1, po2, po3, po4, and po5. If po2 was

---

3 See, for example, [DeMarco79], [Yourdon75], or [Yourdon89].

Figure 16.2 Contract dependencies for action2, action3, and action4.

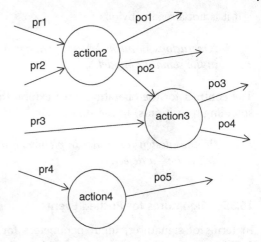

not needed outside of action3, then guarantees conditions for operation event1 would only include po1, po3, po4, and po5. Code Sample 16.10 shows a more complete contract for ClassX.event1() that includes action requires and guarantees conditions from state model actions in the semantic model.

There could be more than one transition in a class' state model caused by a given event. The contract for a pushed event operation would need to consider all valid starting states, all relevant action preconditions, all relevant action postconditions, and all relevant ending states.

Code Sample 16.10 A More Complete Contract for ClassX.event1()

```
public class ClassX {

  public void event1() {
  // requires
  //   .state == STATE1
  //   pr1, pr2, pr3, pr4
  // guarantees
  //   activity1 has stopped
  //   po1, po2, po3, po4, po5
  //   activity2 has started
  //   .state == STATE2
    ...
  }

}
```

If it is not already obvious,

> *"Operations for pushed events in design implement state model transitions in the semantic model."*

The contract for the operation must exhibit the same semantics as the corresponding transition(s) in the state model[4]:

> *"If the design or code implements any other semantics, it is—by definition—a defect."*

16.3.2 Signatures for Pushed Events

In terms of signatures, input parameters for an operation implementing a pushed event will be the union of the input parameters of the transition actions—subject to data flow dependencies, above. If action parameters are explicitly specified in the semantic model, this should be easy—at least in terms of the number and names of the parameters. If action parameters aren't specified, it can be more work for the designer to determine them: the designer/developer would need to figure out the parameters on their own from the action specifications.

Building on the event1() example, assume the following:

- Requires condition pr1 is a constraint on input parameter anA of action2.
- Requires condition pr2 is a constraint on input parameter aB of action2.
- Requires condition pr3 is a constraint on input parameter aC of action3.
- Requires condition pr4 is a constraint on input parameter aD of action4.

Operation event1() would need input parameters anA, aB, aC, and aD in its signature.

The guarantees conditions of these actions refer to:

- Changing attribute values of this object
- Signaling events for other objects or associations
- Changing the state of this object, as appropriate

Thus, event operations do not return output parameter(s), although this could be revised based on error handling, below.

A full signature and contract for ClassX.event1() is shown in Code Sample 16.11.

---

4 Subject to Liskov substitutability: the design could require less and guarantee more than the transition in the semantic model. This will be discussed below, in the section on error handling.

Code Sample 16.11 Full Signature and Contract for ClassX.event1()

```
public class ClassX {

 public void event1 ( A anA, B aB, C aC, D aD ) {
 // requires
 //   .state == STATE1
 //   pr1 (anA is ...), pr2 (aB is ...), pr3 (aC is ...), pr4 (aD is ...)
 // guarantees
 //   activity1 has stopped
 //   po1, po2, po3, po4, po5
 //   activity2 has started
 //   .state == STATE2
  ...
 }

}
```

16.3.3 Variations on the Theme

Variations in semantic model content affect the contract of an event operation in high-level design. These variations will be presented along with examples from Order fulfillment. The first variation is the number of valid start (transition-from) states:

- *None (i.e., an initial transition)*—No starting state is declared in the operation requires clause. The guarantees clause declares that a new object exists in the initial state.
- *One*—That starting state is declared in the operation requires clause. Nothing need be declared in the guarantees clause.
- *Many*—The list of valid start states, joined by "or," are declared in the operation requires clause. Nothing specific need be declared in the guarantees clause.

The second variation is whether or not there is a guard on any transition:

- *No guard*—There is no effect on the operation contract.
- *Guard*—The guard is "and"-ed with the relevant start state in the requires clause of the operation. Nothing specific need be declared in the guarantees clause.

The third variation is the number of ending states from valid transition(s) in the state model:

- *None (i.e., a final transition)*—Nothing need be declared in the operation requires clause. The guarantees clause declares that the object goes out of existence. Alternatively, the object could be "marked for delete" as described for Silly Bank Accounts in Chapter 2 and expanded below.

- *One*—The operation guarantees clause declares the object is in that ending state.
- *Many*—The operation guarantees clause takes the form of if-then or switch-case that declares the appropriate end state given the corresponding start state(s) and guard(s).

The fourth variation is the number of actions on a transition in the state model—including exit/, transition, and entry/ actions:

- *None*—There is no effect on the operation contract.
- *One*—The requires conditions of that action are "and" joined with any other requires clause conditions for the operation. The guarantees conditions of the action are "and" joined with any other guarantees clause conditions for the operation.
- *Many*—The requires conditions of all actions are "and" joined with other requires conditions for the operation, subject to data flow dependencies. The guarantees conditions of all actions are "and" joined with any appropriate guarantees conditions for the operation, subject to dependencies.

16.4 Deriving Contracts and Signatures for Pushed Events: Concrete Examples

As concrete examples, start with BookOrder.cancel() and BookOrder.shipped(). Both represent single transitions from a single start state, with no guards and no actions. The cancel transition is only appropriate when the Book order is in the placed state and leaves the order in the cancelled state. A signature and contract for BookOrder.cancel() is shown in Code Sample 16.12.

Code Sample 16.12 Signature and Contract for BookOrder.cancel()

```
public class BookOrder {

  public void cancel() {
  // requires
  //   .state == PLACED
  // guarantees
  //   .state == CANCELLED
    ...
  }

}
```

Similarly, the shipped transition is only appropriate when the Book order is in the packed state and leaves the order in the completed state. A signature and contract for BookOrder.shipped() is shown in Code Sample 16.13.

As an example of guards and transition actions, consider BookOrder.packed (). The operation transitions from the placed state to the packed state but is guarded with "isPackable?." The transition also has the action "Mark as packed" with no input parameters. A signature and contract for BookOrder.packed() is shown in Code Sample 16.14.

Operation BookOrder.place() is an example of one start state, Open, with transitions to multiple end states. When the Book order contains Print media,

---

Code Sample 16.13 Signature and Contract for BookOrder.shipped()

```
public class BookOrder {

 public void shipped() {
 // requires
 //   .state == PACKED
 // guarantees
 //   .state == COMPLETED
  ...
 }

}
```

Code Sample 16.14 Signature and Contract for BookOrder.packed()

```
public class BookOrder {

 public void packed() {
 // requires
 //   .state == PLACED and this.isPackable()
 // guarantees
 //   packed has been signaled for each line in this order
 //   .state == PACKED
  ...
 }

}
```

the transition is to Placed, and when there are no Print media, the transition is to Completed. Transition action "Mark as placed" is carried out on both transitions. Action "Mark as placed" takes an address as an input parameter. A signature and contract for BookOrder.place() is shown in Code Sample 16.15.

To correlate this example with Figure 16.1, Figure 16.3 shows the state model for class Book Order with the relevant transitions shaded similar to the upper right quadrant of Figure 16.1.

Figure 16.4 shows the signature and contract for BookOrder.place() annotated to emphasize its relationship with Figure 16.3, similar to Figure 16.1.

Constructors implement initial transitions in state models. Constructor contracts require no start state and guarantee a new object exists in the specified initial state. There will almost always be an initialization action on that transition, and input parameters could be relevant. Code Sample 16.16 shows a signature and contract for the constructor of Book order.

Code Sample 16.17 shows a signature and contract for the constructor of Book order line.

Destructors logically implement final transitions in state models. Destructor contracts may require a start state(s) and guarantee the object has been (at least logically) deleted. Code Sample 16.18 shows a signature and contract for ReplenishOrder.received().

When designing and coding in garbage-collecting languages like Java, remember that final transitions aren't necessarily correctly designed this way. Run-time

---

Code Sample 16.15 Signature and Contract for BookOrder.place()

```
public class BookOrder {

 public void place ( Address anAddress ) {
  // requires
  //   .state == OPEN
  //   anAddress is in range of .shippingAddress
  // guarantees
  //   .shippingAddress == anAddress
  //   place has been signaled for each line in this order
  //   if this order contains any print media
  //     then .state == PLACED
  //     otherwise .state == COMPLETED
   . . .
 }

}
```

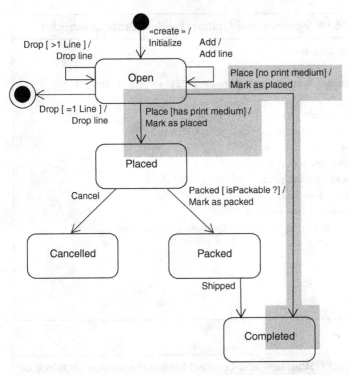

Figure 16.3 State model for Book order, annotated for transitions on the Place event.

```
public void place ( Address anAddress ) {

// requires

//    .state == OPEN                                        ← Start state

//    anAddress is in range of .shippingAddress            ← Action requires condition

// guarantees

//    .shippingAddress == anAddress                         ← Action guarantees conditions
//    place has been signaled for each line in this order

//    if this order contains any print media

//        then .state == PLACED                             ← End state (accounting for guard)

//        otherwise .state == COMPLETED

    ...
}
```

Figure 16.4 Signature and contract for BookOrder.place() annotated to match Figure 16.3.

Code Sample 16.16 Signature and Contract for BookOrder Constructor

```
public class BookOrder {

  public BookOrder( Customer aCustomer, Address anAddress ) {
  // requires
  //   aCustomer is not null
  //   anAddress is in range of .shippingAddress
  // guarantees
  //   a new BookOrder exists with:
  //     .id properly assigned
  //     .dateOpened == today
  //     .shippingAddress == anAddress
  //     this Book order is linked to Customer (via Places)
  //     .state == OPEN
    ...
  }

}
```

Code Sample 16.17 Signature and Contract for BookOrderLine Constructor

```
public class BookOrderLine {

  public BookOrderLine( BookOrder anOrder, Medium aMedium, int qty ) {
  // requires
  //   anOrder not null
  //   aMedium not null
  //   qty in range of .quantity
  // guarantees
  //   a new BookOrderLine exists with:
  //     .quantity == qty
  //     .dateOpened == today
  //     .pricePerCopy == aMedium.sellingPrice()
  //     this Book order line linked to anOrder and aMedium
  //     .state == OPEN
    ...
  }

}
```

Code Sample 16.18 Signature and Contract for ReplenishOrder.received()

```
public class ReplenishOrder {

 public void received() {
 // requires
 //  .state == PLACED
 // guarantees
 //   received has been signaled for each line in this order
 //   this Replenish order has been deleted
  ...
 }

}
```

---

objects don't actually get deleted until their reference count is zero and the garbage collector reclaims memory. As long as any other object holds a reference to
this object, the other object could treat this object as still valid because this operation leaves this object's state in its last business value. A safer, more semantically correct design would add a state, say, "MARKEDFORDELETE" to signify
that the business object has been logically deleted, but the run-time object has
not yet been deleted.

Code Sample 16.19 shows a signature and contract for ReplenishOrderLine.
received(), with an additional state to address garbage collection.

**Code Sample 16.19 Safer Signature and Contract for ReplenishOrderLine.
received()**

```
public class ReplenishOrderLine {

 public void received() {
 // requires
 //  .state == OPENED
 // guarantees
 //   restock(.quantity) has been signaled for linked PrintMedium
 //   .state == MARKEDFORDELETE
  ...
 }

}
```

16.5 Defensive Programming and Design by Contract

Defensive programming is generally interpreted as intentionally developing robust code that is able to gracefully handle all possible situations. An operation that prevents—or at least handles—buffer overflow on an input string would be considered more defensive than an operation that does not. The less defensive operation might fail with an array index out of bounds, or it may expose security vulnerabilities allowing a malicious hacker to inject executable code and take control of the software.

In design by contract terms, defensive programming can be thought of as "not requiring anything." An operation that requires nothing must be able to gracefully handle all possible situations it could ever encounter. The defensive operation would be robust, capable of protecting itself against intentional or unintentional misuse. Contracts derived so far in this chapter are not defensive—unless they already happen to require nothing as in Code Sample 16.1 through Code Sample 16.4. Contracts that require anything do not protect themselves from intentional or unintentional misuse.

A designer can choose to make a non-defensive operation more defensive. Start with the signature and contract for event1() from Code Sample 16.11, above. It is in its least defensive form (i.e., it requires the most). The signature and contract for ClassX.event1() is repeated in Code Sample 16.20.

Code Sample 16.20 Least Defensive Contract for ClassX.event1()

```
public class ClassX {

 public void event1 ( A anA, B aB, C aC, D aD ) {
 // requires
 //  .state == STATE1
 //  pr1 (anA is ...), pr2 (aB is ...), pr3 (aC is ...), pr4 (aD is ...)
 // guarantees
 //  activity1 has stopped
 //  po1, po2, po3, po4, po5
 //  activity2 has started
 //  .state == STATE2
  ...
 }

}
```

16.5.1 Spectrum of Defensiveness

Several contracts with varying levels of defensiveness will be presented. Code Sample 16.21 shows the most defensive contract for event1(); it does not require anything. Options for the "otherwise some TBD response" will be presented later in this chapter in the discussion of error handling.

It is reasonably common to at least handle an object not being in the proper starting state. Code Sample 16.22 shows a slightly defensive contract that checks for proper starting state.

Other alternatives involve more or fewer action requires conditions being required versus in the if() part of the guarantee. For example, Code Sample 16.23 shows a moderately defensive contract with a combination of action preconditions as operation requires conditions and as conditions in the if() part of the guarantee.

Consider operation BookOrder.cancel() in Code Sample 16.12. It requires .state == PLACED and guarantees .state == CANCELLED. This is the least defensive contract—client code could call BookOrder.cancel() on a Book order that isn't in the Placed state. A more defensive contract is shown in Code Sample 16.24.

Operation BookOrder.place() in Code Sample 16.15 is another example to consider. Code Sample 16.25 shows a moderately defensive contract.

Code Sample 16.26 shows a fully defensive contract for BookOrder.place().

Code Sample 16.21 Most Defensive Contract for ClassX.event1()

```
public class ClassX {

  public void event1 ( A anA, B aB, C aC, D aD ) {
  // requires
  //   none
  // guarantees
  //   if pre (.state) == STATE1
  //       pr1 (anA is ...), pr2 (aB is ...), pr3 (aC is ...)
  //       pr4 (aD is ...)
  //   then activity1 has stopped
  //       po1, po2, po3, po4, po5
  //       activity2 has started
  //       .state == STATE2
  //   otherwise some TBD response
  ...
  }

}
```

Code Sample 16.22 A Slightly Defensive Contract for ClassX.event1()

```
public class ClassX {

 public void event1( A anA, B aB, C aC, D aD ) {
 // requires
 //  pr1 (anA is ...), pr2 (aB is ...), pr3 (aC is ...), pr4 (aD is ...)
 // guarantees
 //  if pre(.state) == STATE1
 //    then activity1 has stopped
 //       po1, po2, po3, po4, po5
 //       activity2 has started
 //       .state == STATE2
 //    otherwise some TBD response
  ...
 }

}
```

Code Sample 16.23 A Moderately Defensive Contract for ClassX.event1()

```
public class ClassX {

 public void event1( A anA, B aB, C aC, D aD ) {
 // requires
 //  pr3 (aC is ...), pr4 (aD is ...)
 // guarantees
 //  if pre(.state) == STATE1, pr1 (anA is ...), pr2 (aB is ...)
 //    then activity1 has stopped
 //       po1, po2, po3, po4, po5
 //       activity2 has started
 //       .state == STATE2
 //    otherwise some TBD response
  ...
 }

}
```

Code Sample 16.24 A Defensive Contract for BookOrder.cancel()

```
public class BookOrder {

 public void cancel() {
 // requires
 //   none
 // guarantees
 //   if pre(.state) == PLACED
 //     then post(.state) == CANCELLED
 //     otherwise some TBD response
  ...
 }

}
```

Code Sample 16.25 A Moderately Defensive Contract for BookOrder.place()

```
public class BookOrder {

 public void place( Address anAddress ) {
 // requires
 //   anAddress is in range of .shippingAddress
 // guarantees
 //   if pre(.state) == OPEN
 //     then .shippingAddress == anAddress
 //        place has been signaled for each line in this order
 //        if this order contains any print media
 //          then .state == PLACED
 //          otherwise .state == COMPLETED
 //     otherwise some TBD response
  ...
 }

}
```

Code Sample 16.26 A Fully Defensive Contract for BookOrder.place()

```
public class BookOrder {

   public void place ( Address anAddress ) {
   // requires
   //   none
   // guarantees
   //   if pre (.state) == OPEN and
   //      anAddress is in range of .shippingAddress
   //   then .shippingAddress == anAddress
   //      place has been signaled for each line in this order
   //      if this order contains any print media
   //         then .state == PLACED
   //         otherwise .state == COMPLETED
   //   otherwise some TBD response
   ...
   }

}
```

16.5.2 Defensive Programming and Liskov Substitutability

When an operation implements a pushed event, valid transition start states and
all relevant requires conditions from actions must be expressed either as operation contract requires conditions or as conditions in the guarantees' if() clause.
Semantics of the operation must be the same as the transition(s) in the state
model. Observe that all more defensive contracts are Liskov substitutable with
less defensive contracts:

> *"Each more defensive contract requires less and guarantees more than any
> less defensive contract and is therefore substitutable for that less defensive
> contract—but not the other way around"*

16.5.3 Benefits and Costs of Defensive Programming

The obvious benefit of defensive programming is less fragile, vulnerable, unse-
cure software. It is generally in your best interest to be as defensive as you can. It
is also likely to be in the users' best interest, too. Less obvious, however, may be
the cost of being defensive. Complexity, run-time performance, and project cost
and schedule consequences of being defensive can be significant:

- *Increased structural complexity*—Decision logic to check for and handle invalid conditions increases structural complexity (see Appendix N) in method

code: if there are N requires conditions, then there may need to be as many as N separate decisions (e.g., in right start state, parameter1 in its range, parameter2 in its range, etc.). If the method is already complex, additional defensiveness can push it over structural complexity limits.

- *Increased run time*—Checking for, and acting on, invalid conditions has performance implications. At a minimum, code determining valid from invalid situations needs to be executed on every call. Checking for the right start state on events is relatively trivial, so it's usually reasonable to at least test that. Checking that a pointer parameter is not null is also trivial, but checking that a large data structure is fully internally consistent could consume a lot of potentially scarce computing resources.
- *Increased development and maintenance cost and schedule*—Designing, developing, and maintaining code to recognize and handle invalid conditions adds expense and time, possibly consuming enough resources to affect the team's ability to meet cost and/or schedule constraints.

If the cost of defensive programming is affordable, it makes sense to apply. But it's not always affordable; the overhead of defensive programming can be too high. One organization mandates 100% defensive programming in all operations; their production code continually suffers performance problems as a result. Already scarce CPU cycles are wasted checking the same parameters over and over when operation x() calls y(), which then calls z(),with the same parameter. The decision to be more or less defensive needs to be based on relevant technical and economic factors.

16.6 Defensive Programming and Trust Boundaries

A compromise between fully defensive programming and its negative consequences is to establish trust boundaries. A trust boundary marks a place in design where the critical change is how well we know—and therefore trust—code (i.e., developers) on the other side. Consider a project using a Model–View–Controller architectural style. Assume the developers working on Model region have been working together for years. Everyone trusts each other to behave professionally: documentation is kept consistent with code, contracts are kept consistent with method implementations, potentially unsafe changes to contracts are negotiated, and so on. Publishing contracts that require more than nothing is reasonable because everyone knows about contracts and honors them.

Assume another team of developers new to the organization is responsible for View-controller region. The Model region team doesn't know those developers and cannot fully trust them yet. The Model region team can program defensively at the boundary between Model region and View-controller region. Actor classes on the border of Model region are designed as defensively as possible; internal classes are not defensive to minimize performance and complexity consequences.

The Model region team may not be able to relax every boundary contract to require nothing, but the more they can the better off everyone will be. This may be particularly true if someone later decides to make the application a REST, SOA, or microservice with an API on the Internet. The code is as defensive as can be at the Model region boundary, but doesn't suffer performance or complexity consequences of being defensive in every single operation. Trust boundaries can be established at (sub)domain boundaries.

Being minimally defensive gives code that is fast and simple but also inherently unsafe. On the other hand, being defensive is safe but more complex and slower. Trade-offs are available:

- Selective application of defensiveness in terms of trust boundaries
- Degrees of defensiveness in terms of if() and "otherwise" in contract guarantees

If a design is suitably defensive at a trust boundary, little to no defensiveness might be needed inside that boundary.

16.7   Handling Contract-Level Errors

This section identifies options to consider to be more defensive in handling contract-level errors, mostly by adding behavior in the "otherwise" part of the guarantee's if() clause. Use this section in conjunction with Chapter 25 to make decisions for specific operations:

- Use this section to identify candidate error handling approaches.
- Discard technically infeasible approaches.
- Use the economic decision process in Chapter 25 to identify options with adequate economic justification.
- Design and implement the most cost-effective option(s).

16.7.1   Preventing Errors

The first error handling strategy in Chapter 25 is "prevent"—do something to guarantee the error can never occur. It is possible to prevent some contract requires conditions from being violated, specifically conditions having to do with input parameter values. A technique for input parameters with enumerated ranges in the semantic model is to represent them in design and code using a type-safe enumeration.[5] An example would be an operation that takes

---

5 "Type-safe" means the language enforces that range. In C, "#define NORMAL = 1; #define OVERDRAWN = 2; int accountStatus; accountStatus = NORMAL;" uses enumeration but is not type-safe because accountStatus can still be assigned any other int value.

a calendar month parameter as an input, requiring it to be one of the 12 - calendar months of the year. Instead of representing calendar month as an int, char, String, or similar, represent it with a Java enum as shown in Code Sample 16.27.

The compiler, linker, and run-time system prevent aMonth from ever being outside of the valid set, guaranteeing the operation requires condition would never be violated.

A similar technique can be used when the programming language supports subranges (e.g., Pascal and Ada). This allows scalar values to be protected in the same way as type-safe enumerations. This is shown for Pascal in Code Sample 16.28.

Code Sample 16.27 Declaring and Using a Type-Safe Enumeration in Java

```java
public enum MonthName { JAN, FEB, MAR, APR, MAY, JUN,
                        JUL, AUG, SEP, OCT, NOV, DEC };

public class SomeClass {

 public void someUsefulOperation ( MonthName aMonth ) {
 // requires
 //   aMonth is a valid month name
 // guarantees
 //   something useful has happened with aMonth
 ...
 }

}
```

Code Sample 16.28 Examples of Declaring and Using Pascal Subranges

```pascal
type
 ZeroToNinetyNine = 0 .. 99;
 AthroughF = 'A' .. 'F';

procedure someProcedure ( aNumber: ZeroToNinetyNine,
                          aLetter: AthroughF )
 begin
 ...
 end
```

Code Sample 16.29 Wrapping a Preexisting Type

```
public class WebBooksDate extends Date {

  public static Date earliestDate = new Date( 1998, 1, 1 );

  public WebBooksDate( int year, int month, int day ) {
  // requires
  //   year > 0
  //   month in range 1 .. 12
  //   day in range 1 .. max day, appropriate given the month
  // guarantees
  //   returns a WebBooks date between earliestDate and today
  //     input dates before earliestDate return earliestDate
  //     input dates after today return today
    . . .
  }
  . . .
}
```

The third technique requires more effort but could still be cost effective. This technique wraps standard types like int, float, double, Date, etc. with application code to enforce range limits. Code Sample 16.29 shows a partial wrapper for the standard Date class in Java that could enforce the date range in the Order fulfillment semantic model.

If design and code use a mechanism that prevents a condition from ever being violated, that condition can be removed from operation contracts. If a condition cannot be prevented from being violated, it is the responsibility of client code to ensure no violation ever happens, or the server operation must be defensive and handle it.

In theory, it is possible to do Petri Net[6] analysis of state models in the semantic model to verify that invalid object starting states could never be encountered. Even so, it could be best to retain start state conditions because client code could be improperly modified at some point, changing the Petri Net analysis. Without complete Petri Net reanalysis, a defect could exist without anyone knowing.

---

6 See, for example, https://en.wikipedia.org/wiki/Petri_net.

16.7.2 Handling Errors

Assuming violation of a contract requires condition cannot be prevented, an alternative is to be defensive and express that element in the if() part of the guarantees.[7] This implies that while that specific condition is undesirable, it is not unexpected. This also calls for some form of error handling should that condition ever be violated, that is, the "otherwise" part of the if(). As explained in Chapter 25, there are three dimensions to error handling:

- What to do, if anything
- Who to notify, if anyone
- Continue or stop

The following elaborates on these dimensions at the level of errors relative to operation contracts.

16.7.3 What to Do, if Anything

The first dimension of choice is what to do, if anything. Given operation contracts as presented above, the two kinds of errors client code could make are as follows:

- Calling an operation when the target object is not in the right start state.
- Calling an operation with invalid input parameters, for example, an input parameter out of range or input parameters out of synch with each other. Each value alone may be acceptable, but they conflict with each other in a business significant way.

Candidate error handling strategies if an operation is called when the object isn't in the right start state (considering guards) include but are not limited to the following:

- Remember events that are safe to ignore versus events that are impossible (Chapter 10). If it is a safely ignorable event, then just ignore it.
- Return to some previously known safe state (e.g., a "rollback" of some sort).
- Assume a reasonable alternative (i.e., "closest legal") start state and transition from there.
- Go to an appropriate default state.
- Introduce a "failed" state into the design and transition to there.

---

7 Recall the "buy information" strategy in Chapter 25. A possible additional approach might be to offer a pre-validation function that only checks for appropriateness of the call. Only call the actual do-the-work operation if the pre-validation operation says it's OK to.

All options beyond ignoring safely ignorable events introduce semantic differences between the modeled policies and processes and the design and implementation. According to the underlying theory of modeling, behavior under these circumstances is undefined, so the freedom exists to design and implement some behavior. Just be aware that such behavior is beyond the semantic model.

Candidate error handling strategies when an operation is called with invalid (i.e., out-of-range or out-of-synch-with-each-other) parameters include but are not limited to:

- *Substitute a neutral value*—If the parameter is used in addition, substitute zero. If the parameter is used in multiplication or division, substitute one, etc.
- *Substitute the closest legal value*—An example is the constructor for Web-BooksDate in Code Sample 16.29.
- *Substitute the same value as was passed in the last invocation.*
- *Return the same value that was returned in the last invocation.*

16.7.4   Who to Notify, if Anyone

The second dimension of error handling is notification. If something effective can be done (above), then notification may not be necessary. However, if nothing can be done, or if what was done isn't a full recovery, then some kind of notification is recommended. There are two candidate kinds of entities, either of which or both, that could be notified:

- *Client*—for example, upward in the execution call stack
- *Some other third party*—for example, a user or system operator

If the choice is to notify the client, there are two mutually exclusive approaches:

- *Data flow-based notification*—for example, return an error code
- *Control flow-based notification*—for example, throw an exception

16.7.5   Data Flow-Based Notification

Figure 16.5 is a flowchart showing decision criteria and options for data flow-based error notification. The numbered keys (in hexagons) refer to following descriptions of important aspects of the decision process.

1) *When to provide notification?*—Immediate notification means the client gets direct status in the operation's return parameter(s). Notification does not need to be immediate; it can be deferred to a later time as explained below.

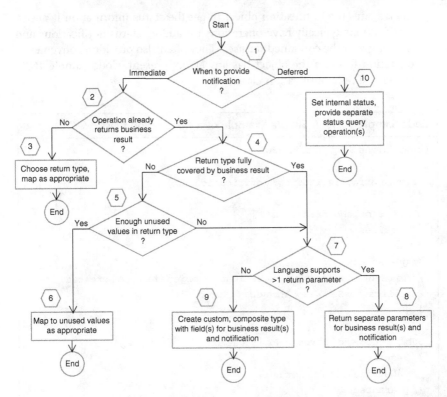

Figure 16.5 Decision criteria and options for data flow-based error notification.

2) *Operation already returns business result?*—An operation implementing attribute access or a derived attribute would return a business result, but not all operations need to return a business result. An operation non-defensively implementing a pushed event doesn't return any business result to the client.

3) *Choose return type; map as appropriate*—The return type is free for use; choose an appropriate type based on the number and kind of distinct notifications that need to be communicated. Simple binary success or failure can be communicated using a Boolean. Success versus several distinct failures can be communicated with an enumeration, int, char, or string. Some cases benefit from returning an item count.[8] With Notification pattern,[9] a notification object collects zero or more status notifications. Each processing failure adds a status notification to the object. On return, the client

---

8 The client calls the operation with a list of X known items to be processed. The operation returns the number of successfully processed items, Y. If X == Y, then the operation completed successfully.
9 See [Fowler04].

interrogates the notification object to get the status information it needs. Notifications typically have operations for adding status notifications and iterating over the contained statuses. They often also provide a convenience operation to tell if the object has any errors present. Code Sample 16.30 shows a simple notification class.

Code Sample 16.30 A Simple Example of a Notification Class

```java
public class SimpleNotification {

 private ArrayList<String> notificationSet;

 public SimpleNotification() {
 // requires
 //   none
 // guarantees
 //   an empty (successful) notification object has been created
  notificationSet = new ArrayList<String>();
 }

 public void add( String aNotification ) {
 // requires
 //   aNotification is not null
 // guarantees
 //   aNotification has been added
  notificationSet.add( aNotification );
 }

 public boolean containsNotification() {
 // requires
 //   none
 // guarantees
 //   returns true when any notification messages exist
 //       otherwise returns false
  return ( notificationSet.size() != 0 );
 }

 // operations to provide client access to list of errors
 //   goes here. Presumably they would use Iterator pattern
  ...

}
```

4) *Return type fully covered by business result?*—When an operation does return a business result, that result might or might not use the entire return type. There may be free, business-unusable values that can be used to communicate errors. An operation that converts a text string to a floating point number, convertToFloat(), would use the entire return type, float. All numbers are in the output range; no number could be returned to signal a conversion error. Java's NaN ("Not a Number") could be used, but most other languages do not support such a mechanism. Constructors return the memory address of the newly constructed object, so no unused values are available. A square root function, for example, java.lang.Math.sqrt(), returns the positive square root of the input parameter. Any negative return value could be used to communicate an error.

5) *Enough unused values in return type?*—Just because unused values exist in the return type doesn't guarantee enough of them exist to communicate all distinct error status return values.

6) *Map to unused values as appropriate*—When enough unused values exist in the return type, simply map the distinct errors onto available return values.

7) *Language supports >1 return parameter?*—Some languages like Java allow only one explicit return parameter from an operation. Some languages allow explicit in/out/in-out parameters (e.g., Pascal and Ada). Some languages provide call-by-reference[10] parameters, which can be used in an operation to modify a parameter in a way that the client can see that modification.

8) *Return separate parameters for business results(s) and notification*—If the language supports multiple return values, simply return the business value(s) and error notification(s) in separate parameters. Again, this can be done explicitly via out or in-out parameters or implicitly via call-by-reference parameters.

9) *Create custom composite type with fields for business result(s) along with notification*—A custom composite type with fields for each kind of business data and each kind of error notification can be created and populated by the operation. The composite type is passed back to the client as a single return parameter.

10) *Set internal status; provide separate status query operation(s)*—Execute the operation, saving any error status in one or more local variables. Provide one or more other operations that allow clients to query the saved error status when they are ready for it.

Code Sample 16.30 shows a simple notification class. Notification classes allow the server operation to collect many errors and return them all at the same

---

10 See, for example, https://en.wikipedia.org/wiki/Evaluation_strategy#Call_by_reference.

time—as opposed to the typical approach of just failing on the first one. This can be particularly useful in user interfaces because users find it frustrating to be notified of an error, fix that error, and then be told of another error. Why wasn't the user notified of all errors the first time?

Code Sample 16.31 shows how a server operation, in this case BookOrder.add(), can use the notification class in Code Sample 16.30. This operation is now able to communicate more than one failure to the client. The client—in this case the Customer actor—has the option to communicate more than just one error to

---

Code Sample 16.31 Using the Simple Notification Class

```
public class BookOrder {

  public Notification add ( Medium aMedium, int qty ) {
  // requires
  //  none
  // guarantees
  //  if pre (.state) == OPEN and aMedium <> null and qty > 0
  //    then one new BookOrderLine has been added to this order
  //      and returns a notification with zero errors
  //    otherwise returns a notification showing all errors
    result = new SimpleNotification ();
    if ( state != BOStatus.OPEN ) {
     result.add ( "BO.add (): Initial order state != Open" );
    }
    if ( aMedium == null ) {
     result.add ( "BO.add (): Invalid Medium" );
    }
    if ( qty <= 0 ) {
     result.add ( "BO.add (): Invalid quantity" );
    }
    if ( !result.containsNotification () ) {
     // do BookOrder.add () logic here[11]
    }
    return result;
  }

}
```

---

11 In principle, should there be any failure(s) recognized in code implementing the transition logic (e.g., in EBookMedium.makeUserKey() or below), notifications could be appended to this notification object.

the actual user. In general, this example should have had target object state and input parameter validity pre-verified in View-controller region code. Book Order.add() should be inside of a trust boundary and not require programming this defensively, which is only an illustration of the use of notification classes.

16.7.6   Control Flow-Based Notification

Instead of notifying the client using a data flow-based mechanism, notification can use a control flow-based mechanism. Three different control flow-based notification mechanisms are discussed:

- Exception
- Callback
- Goto

The first, exception, is by far the most common control flow notification mechanism in modern programming languages.[12] There are five primary elements to exceptions, two on the server operation side and three on the client operation side.

The server operation side has a keyword like Java's "throw" to specify the departure point from normal control flow. Languages supporting exceptions usually have a predefined set of standard exceptions,[13] and application code can also extend a preexisting exception class like Java's RunTimeException to communicate more detailed error and context information to the client operation. Code Sample 16.32 shows subclassing a generic exception class to provide additional status or context information back to the client.

Code Sample 16.33 shows an example of using Java exceptions[14]: both predefined exception InvalidArgumentException and custom InvalidAddressException from Code Sample 16.32.

The client operation side of exceptions has keywords like Java's "try," "catch," and "finally." The try keyword specifies the beginning of the exception-sensitive execution block; any exception thrown inside this block (and not successfully handled in lower-level code) is directed to the immediately following catch block(s) for handling. If the exception is not successfully handled at this level (i.e., there is no catch block specified for that exception), the search for an exception handler continues with the next higher try–catch block (i.e., in operations that were clients of this operation, if none are found, then execution stops with a fatal "Unhandled exception"). The optional finally block is for processing that must be accomplished regardless of whether the try block completed

---

12 An interesting alternative view can be found at http://www.gigamonkeys.com/book/beyond-exception-handling-conditions-and-restarts.html.

13 See, for example, http://www.tutorialspoint.com/java/java_builtin_exceptions.htm.

14 This example shows Java's "unchecked exceptions." For a discussion of "checked exceptions," see, for example, https://en.wikipedia.org/wiki/Exception_handling#Checked_exceptions.

Code Sample 16.32 Extending Java's Built-in Exception Class

```java
public class InvalidAddressException extends RunTimeException {

  private Address badAddress;
  private int failureCode;

  public InvalidAddressException( Address anAddress, int failCode ) {
  // requires
  //  none
  // guarantees
  //  a new InvalidAddressException exists with
  //    .badAddress set to the offending address
  //    .failureCode set to failCode
   super();
   badAddress = anAddress;
   failureCode = failCode;
  }

  public String getBadAddress() {
  // requires
  //  none
  // guarantees
  //  returns the offending address as a string
   return badAddress.asString();
  }

  public Address getFailureCode() {
  // requires
  //  none
  // guarantees
  //  returns the failure code
   return failureCode;
  }

}
```

---

successfully. An example of finally block processing would be releasing resources that may have been allocated in the try block. Code Sample 16.34 shows a possible example of client code that could use the BookOrder constructor in Code Sample 16.33 and deal with the exceptions thrown.

Code Sample 16.33 An Example of Throwing Exceptions

```
public class BookOrder {

  public BookOrder( Customer aCustomer, Address anAddress ) {
  // requires
  //   none
  // guarantees
  //   if aCustomer is not null and address is valid
  //     then a new BookOrder exists with:
  //       ...
  //     otherwise
  //       throws InvalidArgumentException when aCustomer is null
  //       throws InvalidAddressException when address is invalid
    if ( aCustomer == null ) {
      throw( new InvalidArgumentException( "Customer is null" ) );
    }
    if ( !anAddress.isValid() ) {
      throw( new InvalidAddressException( anAddress,
                                          anAddress.failureCode() ) );
    }
    // normal processing goes here
  }

}
```

In languages such as C++, it is possible to pass a pointer to a function as a parameter on the operation being called. The server operation code can invoke the referenced function via that pointer, not necessarily caring what that called function does.[15] In control flow-based error notification, the client can pass a pointer to an error handling function to be called by the server operation if an error occurs. Code Sample 16.35 shows pseudo-code demonstrating abstractly how callbacks can be used.

It should not be a foregone conclusion that a semantic model will always be designed and implemented in a high-level programming language. Tight

---

15 Although the called functions had better be Liskov substitutable with some expected, nominal contract.

Code Sample 16.34 An Example of Catching Exceptions

```
public class SomeExampleClass {

  public void createOrder( Customer aCustomer, Address anAddress ) {
  // requires
  //  none
  // guarantees
  //  if the customer and address are valid
  //    then a new order has been created
  //    otherwise
  //      if aCustomer was null it was handled some way
  //      if anAddress was invalid it was handled some other way
    try {
      // assume that some resources X and Y are allocated here
      BookOrder newOrder = BookOrder.new ( aCustomer, anAddress );
      // some possible other processing might be here
    } catch( InvalidArgumentException e ) {
      // code to handle the null customer goes here
    } catch( InvalidAddressException e ) {
      // code to handle the invalid address goes here
      //  access to offending address and failure code
      //  provided through e.getBadAddress() and e.getFailureCode()
    } finally {
      // release resources x and y here
    }
  }

}
```

---

performance or other technical constraints may lead to design and implementation in languages like C or even an assembly language. There is no exception mechanism in lower-level programming languages; control flow-based error notification can be based on simple goto or jmp instructions. Be aware of Edsger Dijkstra's famous "Go To Statement Considered Harmful"[16] and use goto and jmp with appropriate caution.

---

16 See [Dijkstra68].

Code Sample 16.35 A Pseudo-code Example of Callbacks

```
someClientA():
 doSomething( parameter1, errorHandler1() )


errorHandler1():
 // handle type 1 errors appropriately

someClientB():
 doSomething( parameter2, errorHandler2() )

errorHandler2():
 // handle type 2 errors appropriately

doSomething( someType parameter, function errorHandler() ):
 // process the parameter here
 if ( !someKindOfError )
 then // proceed normally
 else errorHandler()  // this is the callback invocation
```

16.7.7   Error Codes Versus Exceptions

By far the two most common (and contentiously argued) alternatives for error notification are error codes and exceptions. An almost religious fervor surrounds each, with various zealots claiming theirs to be the one, the only, the true way. In fact, both mechanisms have their place. It simply isn't an always one versus always the other matter. There are cases when the designer doesn't have a choice because one isn't even available. For example, constructors can't return error codes, and exceptions can't be thrown across some networks. Table 16.1 contrasts error codes and exceptions as objectively as possible to help designers make informed, technically viable, and economically prudent choices.

16.7.8   Third-Party Notification

In addition to, or instead of, notifying a client operation using either data flow- or control flow-based mechanisms, the server operation has the option of notifying a third party such as a user or system operator. Again, that notification could be immediate (e.g., printing out an error message or displaying an error dialog box) or deferred (e.g., logging an error message to a log file). Make third-party notifications as specific, clear, concise, and actionable as possible.

Table 16.1 Objectively contrasting error codes and exceptions.

Perspective	Error codes	Exceptions
Availability	Virtually universal	Not supported in all languages and technologies (e.g., remote procedure call [RPC])
Developer familiarity	Virtually universal	Not all developers know or are comfortable using
Effect on control flow	Combines normal and fail, but locality makes it easy to inspect for error handling code in client	Separates normal from fail so clean flow on no error. Error handling code may be distant, so harder to inspect[a]
Effect on data flow	Combines error notification with business results: can force complex return type or deferred notification	Return values are always and only business results
Effect on run time	More expensive when an error doesn't occur; less expensive when one does	Less expensive when an error doesn't occur; more expensive when one does (e.g., instantiate exception object)
Propagation[b]	Requires explicit propagation: visible to intermediate levels	Automatic propagation: invisible to intermediate levels
Capacity to communicate error and context	Limited, unless developer builds complex return type, but that's much more work	Rich, easy to extend Exception base class and include as much extra information as desired
Ease of forgetting	Forgetting to check error codes can cause subtle and hard-to-trace failures later	Forgetting to catch exceptions causes obvious, easy-to-trace failures now ("Unhandled exception")
Ease of ignoring	Easy to ignore checking for error codes	Hard to ignore; requires explicit exception swallowing code[c]
Effect on class count	None, unless developer creates custom notification class(es)	Custom exception classes increase class count

[a] Joel Spolsky said, "I consider exceptions to be no better than goto's, and goto's have been considered harmful since the 1960." See http://www.joelonsoftware.com/items/2003/10/13.html.
[b] Said another way, error codes only communicate directly to the immediate client; exceptions can communicate to any arbitrary higher level that has the appropriate catch block defined.
[c] As in "try { X() } catch (*) { //do nothing };"

The recipient must know enough about what happened, and why it happened, to be able to take appropriate, effective action.

Be very careful with third-party notification when data contained in the system needs to be protected for security or privacy reasons. Including data that needs to be protected means that the notification or error log also needs to be adequately protected by either encryption or access control. More than one organization has experienced a security breach by logging critical data without adequate protection.[17]

16.7.9 Continue Versus Stop

The last dimension of error handling is to continue or not. Continuing is appropriate if any actions taken above were sufficient to repair or satisfactorily recover from the error or if the error is safely ignorable. If the error can't be repaired or recovered and isn't safely ignorable, then stopping in-process work may be needed. If stopping is needed, the scope of what to stop also needs to be decided, depending on the nature of the policies and processes being automated. Options include stopping:

- Action
- Transition or operation
- Use case or transaction (i.e., rollback)
- Workflow (sequence of transactions)
- Subdomain
- Domain
- Whole system

16.7.10 Summary of Contract-Level Errors

To summarize, the above tactics handle operation contract-level errors mostly by adding behavior in the "otherwise" clause of the guarantee's if():

- What to do, if anything
- Who to notify, if anyone
- Continue or not

Use these tactics to generate as many alternatives as are reasonable, throw away technically infeasible alternatives, and then use the economic decision process in Chapter 25 to find the most cost-effective solution (which may be a combination). Finally, whatever error handling choices are made need to be expressed in the operation's contract because they alter operation semantics in a way that needs to be communicated to the client (developer).

---

17 See, for example, http://www.bbc.com/news/business-43995168.

16.8 Deriving Class Invariants for Model Region

As defined by Bertrand Meyer,[18] design by contract includes "class invariants." Requires conditions and guarantees conditions are specific to operations. A few operations might share common requires or guarantees conditions, for example, BookOrder constructor and BookOrder.place() might both require input parameter anAddress to be valid. On the other hand, class invariants apply universally, across all operations. They are implicit pre- and post-conditions for every operation. These invariants reflect internal object (instance) level policies that must be true at the beginning and end of every operation:

- Range specifications for attributes
- Key uniqueness
- Derived attribute policies
- Constraints on generalizations (inheritance)

In addition to the explicit requires and guarantees conditions in each operation's contract, each operation must expect some invariants to hold when the operation is invoked as well as ensure those same invariants hold when the operation completes (unless the relevant execution context is being stopped and either roll back to previous safe, valid system state or quitting altogether, i.e., a fatal error).

Some class invariants also apply universally, but not at the level of a single operation. Instead, these apply to transactions (sea level use case):

- Association multiplicities to associated classes

Take the Order fulfillment sea level use case of adding a Medium to a Book order when no open order exists for that customer. Both a new Book order line and a new Book order need to be created. One of the multiplicity constraints is that a Book order line cannot exist without being connected to a Book order. Another constraint is that no Book order can exist without at least one Book order line. Most software executes sequentially, meaning that either the new Book order, or the new Book order line, will be constructed first. Whichever is constructed first cannot have as a guarantee that the other exists because that other has not yet been created. Association multiplicity constraints may be temporarily violated while a sea level use case/transaction is executing; however when any transaction starts, as well as by the time it finishes, all multiplicity constraints must hold.

---

18 See, for example, [Meyer92] or [Meyer97].

Class invariants for Model region can be derived from the semantic model. Using class Book order as a specific example, class invariants are as follows:

- Attribute .id shall be referred to Corporate Policy CP123a, "Customer Order Identification."
- Attribute .id shall be unique for each Book order.
- Attribute .date opened shall be a calendar date no earlier than January 1, 1998, and no later than today, to the whole day.
- Attribute .shipping address shall be any mailing address acceptable to the US Post Office or Canada Post.
- Attribute .status shall be one of the states in the state model.
- Derived attribute .isPackable shall be true only when .status == placed and isPackable? == true for each Book order line in this Book order.
- Derived attribute .sales shall be that if .status == completed then sum of sales? for each Book order line in this Book order, otherwise $0.00.
- Derived attribute .profit shall be that if .status == completed then sum of profit? for each Book order line in this Book order—otherwise $0.00.
- Each Book order shall be linked to exactly one Customer.
- Each Book order shall be linked, via Book order lines, to at least one but possibly many Medium.

Class invariants for Book order line are as follows:

- Attribute .quantity shall be 1, unconstrained, to the whole number.
- Attribute .price per copy shall be $0.00, unconstrained in US dollars, to the whole cent.

  Derived attribute .isPackable shall be always true if this Book order line refers to eBook medium. If this Book order line refers to Print medium, true only when .quantity >= print medium.stock on hand.
- Derived attribute .sales shall be quantity * .price per copy.
- Derived attribute .profit shall be quantity * (.price per copy – Medium.our cost).
- Each Book order line shall be linked to exactly one Book order.
- Each Book order line shall be linked to exactly one Medium.

Class invariants for Medium are as follows:

- Attribute .ISBN shall be either ISBN-10 and ISBN-13 format as defined by www.isbn-international.org.
- Attribute .ISBN shall be unique for each Medium.
- Attribute .selling price shall be $0.00, unconstrained in US dollars, to the nearest whole cent.
- Attribute .acquisition cost shall be $0.00, unconstrained in US dollars, to the nearest whole cent.
- A Medium doesn't have to be linked, via Book order lines, to any Book order but can be linked to many.

- Each Medium shall be linked to exactly one Title.
- Each Medium shall either be an eBook Medium or a Print Medium.[19]

Class invariants for eBook Medium are as follows:

- Attribute .product key shall see Engineering Memo PQR789.
- All properties of Medium shall apply to eBook Medium.

Every class invariant is simply a design restatement of a policy expressed in the semantic model.

16.9   Deriving Contracts and Signatures for Model Region Pulled Events

In some cases the guideline on pushing events needs to be overridden due to technical or economic constraints—some events need to be pulled. Consider use case Pack order as an example. The semantic model sequence diagram for the first part of the use case is shown in Figure 16.6.

For contrast with the pulled version below, the design sequence diagram following Chapter 15's pushed event recommendation is shown in Figure 16.7.

Figure 16.8 shows the same part of the use case designed entirely in pull form instead of push.

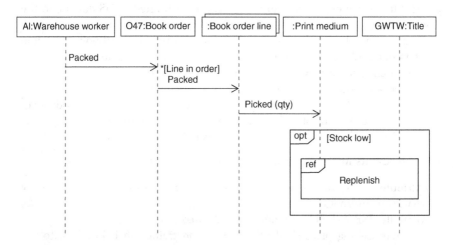

Figure 16.6 Semantic model sequence diagram for part of use case Pack order.

---

19 Because this generalization is «complete». Incomplete generalizations would say, "A
<superclass> doesn't have to be any of <list of subclasses>".

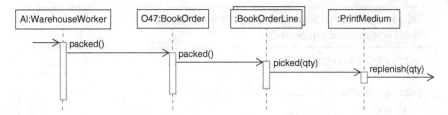

Figure 16.7 Design sequence diagram for part of Pack order in push form.

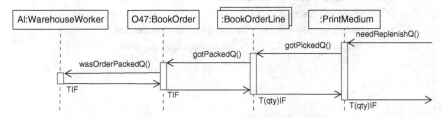

Figure 16.8 Design for same part of Pack order in pull form.

Start with the replenish(qty) message between Title and Print medium in the semantic model (see Figure 15.17) being implemented in pull form in Model region as operation PrintMedium.needReplenishQ().[20] The corresponding design object of class Title is asking if it needs to place a replenish order with the Publisher.

To determine if this PrintMedium needs replenishment, it needs to know if any BookOrderLines linked with it got picked since they were last asked. If any linked line did get picked, .stockLevel needs to be reduced by the quantity packed: the Remove from stock (qty) action on the state model. The linked Title needs to be told (via the return parameter) how many, if any, copies need to be replenished. Code Sample 16.36 shows a signature and contract for PrintMedium.needReplenishQ().

For a BookOrderLine to determine if it got packed since it was last asked, it needs to be in the Placed state and determine if its corresponding BookOrder got packed since the last time that order was asked. If the BookOrder did get packed since last asked, this BookOrderLine needs to transition to the Completed state—doing action Mark as Packed along the way—and signal the quantity picked (via the return parameter). Code Sample 16.37 shows a possible signature and contract for BookOrderLine.gotPickedQ().

---

20 In the eventNameQ() naming convention used here, the Q represents a question mark that can't be used in operation names in most programming languages, that is, ClassName.eventName?().

**Code Sample 16.36 Signature and Contract for
PrintMedium.needReplenishQ()**

```
public class PrintMedium {

  public int needReplenishQ() {
  // requires
  //   none
  // guarantees
  //   for all linked order lines packed since last asked
  //      .stockLevel is reduced by quantity for each line picked
  //   returns number of copies that need to be replenished
  //      0 means none needed, i.e., no orders got packed
   ...
  }

}
```

Code Sample 16.37 Signature and Contract for BookOrderLine.gotPickedQ()

```
public class BookOrderLine {

  public int gotPickedQ() {
  // requires
  //   none
  // guarantees
  //   if pre( .state ) == PLACED &&
  //      this order got packed since last asked
  //   then post( .state ) == COMPLETED
  //        returns .quantity
  //   otherwise returns 0
   ...
  }

}
```

For a BookOrder to determine if it got packed since it was last asked, it needs to be in the Placed state and determine if any WarehouseWorker packed it since they were last asked. Operation WarehouseWorker.wasOrderPackedQ() would presumably call View-controller code to ask actual warehouse workers if any of them had packed that order. If this BookOrder does discover that it had been packed, it needs to do two things:

- Change its state to Packed.
- Set up to notify—exactly once—each linked BookOrderLine that it got packed.

Code Sample 16.38 shows a possible signature and contract for BookOrderLine. gotPackedQ().

Each operation in the pulled event design implements the same process semantics as the pushed event version and, of course, as the semantic model. The only difference is that the flow of control has been reversed. As a result of the reversal, on the other hand, logic to implement some operations gets significantly more complex. For example, BookOrder needs to remember which BookOrderLines have been notified and which have not—lines must be notified exactly once. Generally, pulled events lead to increased complexity.

Pulling an event can be a local decision; it doesn't need to affect all other operations in that use case. Figure 16.9 shows a design sequence diagram for Pack order where only the Packed message between Book order and Book order line is pulled and all other events are pushed.

Code Sample 16.38 Signature and Contract for BookOrderLine.gotPacked()

```
public class BookOrder {

  public bookean gotPackedQ ( BookOrderLine aLine ) {
  // requires
  //   aLine not null
  // guarantees
  //   if pre ( .state == PLACED ) &&
  //      this order got packed since it was last asked
  //   then post ( .state ) == PACKED
  //      set up to notify each line exactly once
  //   if aLine needed notification and
  //      had not been notified yet
  //   then it has been marked as being notified
  //      and true is returned
  //   otherwise false is returned
  ...
  }

}
```

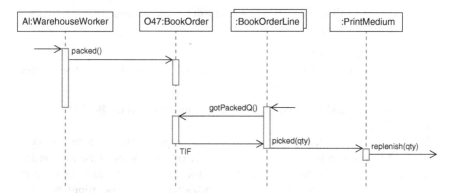

Figure 16.9 Design sequence diagram for Pack order, with only one event pulled.

16.10 Deriving Contracts and Signatures for Model Region Pushed Data

In some cases the guideline on pulled data needs to be overridden due to technical or economic constraints—some data needs to be pushed. Consider use case Packable orders? as an example. The semantic model sequence diagram is shown in Figure 16.10.

For contrast with the pushed version, the design sequence diagram following Chapter 15's pulled data recommendation is shown in Figure 16.11.

Figure 16.12 shows the same use case designed entirely in push form instead of pull.

Assume that .stockLevel for some PrintMedium changed because it was either picked by a Book order line that got packed or restocked by a Replenish order line that got received. On that change, the operation that modifies .stockLevel should call this.stockLevelChanged() to notify all linked BookOrderLines of the updated stock level. Code Sample 16.39 shows a possible signature and contract for PrintMedium.stockLevelChanged().

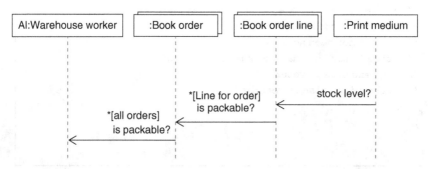

Figure 16.10 Semantic model sequence diagram for use case Packable orders?

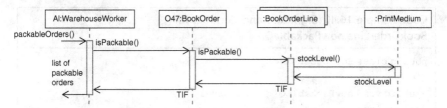

Figure 16.11 Design sequence diagram for use case Packable orders? in pull form.

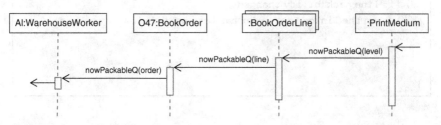

Figure 16.12 Design for packable orders? use case in push form.

Code Sample 16.39 Signature and Contract for PrintMedium.stockLevel-Changed()

```
public class PrintMedium {

 public void stockLevelChanged() {
 // requires
 //   none
 // guarantees
 //   all book order lines linked to this Print medium
 //     have been notified of the new .stockLevel
 ...
 }

}
```

When a Book order line linked with that PrintMedium[21] is notified of the updated stock level, it needs to recompute its packability. Code Sample 16.40 shows a possible signature and contract for BookOrderLine. nowPackableQ().

---

21 Any BookOrderLine associated with an EBookMedium is always packable.

Code Sample 16.40 Signature and Contract for BookOrderLine.nowPackableQ()

```
public class BookOrderLine {

  public void nowPackableQ( int newLevel ) {
  // requires
  //   none
  // guarantees
  //   if line packability changed
  //     then the linked Book order has been notified
    ...
  }

}
```

Code Sample 16.41 Signature and Contract for BookOrder.nowPackableQ()

```
public class BookOrder {

  public void nowPackableQ( BookOrderLine aBookOrderLine ) {
  // requires
  //   aBookOrderLine <> null
  // guarantees
  //   if .state == PLACED && order packability changed
  //     then warehouse workers have been notified
    ...
  }

}
```

When a BookOrder has been notified of change to packability of one of its BookOrderLines, that Book order needs to recompute its packability. A Book Order is only packable when it is in the Placed state and all of its linked order lines are also packable. Code Sample 16.41 shows a possible signature and contract for BookOrder.nowPackableQ().

On change to Book order packability, the Warehouse worker user interface needs to be updated to communicate the new status. Either:

- Either the Book order's packability status would be pushed through View-controller region to the actual warehouse workers—continuing the push data theme.
- Or View-controller region would pull order packability from the WarehouseWorker actor —pulling the status the rest of the way to the actual warehouse workers.

Each operation in the push data design implements the same process semantics as the pull data version (and, of course, as the semantic model). The only difference is that flow of control has been reversed. As a result of the reversal, on the other hand, logic to implement an operation may get more complex. For example, BookOrder needs to cache a local copy of BookOrderLine packability. Generally, pushing data leads to increased complexity.

Pushed data can be implemented using publish/subscribe (i.e., Observer pattern[22] or Implicit invocation[23]). WarehouseWorkers could subscribe to BookOrders, BookOrders could subscribe to the BookOrderLines they contain, and BookOrderLines could subscribe to their linked PrintMedium. Any change to . stockLevel for a Print medium could cascade via a series of publish/subscribe updates.

Just like with pulled events, pushed data can be a local decision; it doesn't need to affect all operations in the use case. Figure 16.13 shows a design sequence diagram for Packable orders where only the isPackable message between Book order and Book order line is pushed and all other data are pulled.

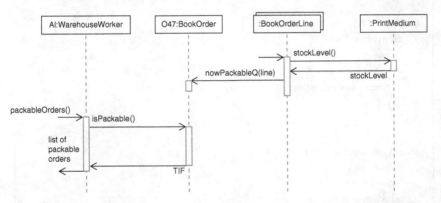

Figure 16.13 Design sequence diagram for Packable orders, with only one data message pushed.

22 See, for example, http://en.wikipedia.org/wiki/Observer_pattern.
23 See, for example, http://en.wikipedia.org/wiki/Implicit_invocation.

16.11   Contracts and Signatures in View-Controller and Infrastructure Regions

To the extent that design and code needs to be developed in View-controller and Infrastructure regions, classes and operations were identified in Chapter 15. The syntax and semantics of those operations depends on a variety of factors:

- Simple versus complex interface functionality
- Simple versus complex infrastructure services
- Whether or not recursive design (Chapter 6) is used
- ...

If View-controller or Infrastructure region is complex and being developed using recursive design, then although that design is outside of Model region for this domain, it is designed as Model region in its own domain. Operation signatures and contracts would be derived when that (sub)domain is designed. On the other hand, the classes and operations should be simple enough that developing signatures and contracts is not difficult (otherwise recursive design should be used).

   Code Sample 16.42 shows partial signatures and contracts for class UIScreen from Figure 15.35.

Code Sample 16.42 Partial Signatures and Contracts for UIScreen

```
public class UIScreen {

 public UIScreen( ) {
 // requires
 //   none
 // guarantees
 //   common screen elements have been initialized
  . . .
 }


 public EventType activate( ) {
 // requires
 //   none
 // guarantees
 //    returns when a relevant user event has occurred
  . . .
 }

}
```

Code Sample 16.43 shows partial signatures and contracts for class Copies-ToAdd from Figure 15.35.

Code Sample 16.43 Partial Signatures and Contracts for CopiesToAdd

```
public class CopiesToAdd extends UIScreen {

  public CopiesToAdd( ) {
  // requires
  //   none
  // guarantees
  //   a Copies to add screen has been initialized
   ...
  }

  public EventType activate( ) {
  // requires
  //   none
  // guarantees
  //   returns when a relevant user event has occurred
   ...
  }

  public void setCopiesToAdd( int defaultQuantity ) {
  // requires
  //   defaultQuantity > 0
  // guarantees
  //   copiesToAdd == defaultQuantity
   ...
  }

  public int getCopiesToAdd( ) {
  // requires
  //   none
  // guarantees
  //   returns the value in copiesToAdd
   ...
  }

}
```

16.12   Documenting the Initial High-Level Design

Remember that everything so far is only the first draft of the design; don't go overboard finalizing documentation yet. The important thing is to have notes about what came from where (when not already obvious) along with client-server decisions and why they were made that way—particularly when the push events/pull data guidelines weren't followed. Class interfaces can be affected by optimization (Chapter 19), so just be sure you don't forget how you got to this point.

16.13   Quality Criteria

In addition to the overall quality criteria (Table 3.1) and naming criteria (Table 3.2), the quality criteria in Table 16.2 can be applied to all initial high-level design-related work to identify and remove defects as quickly and as cheaply as possible.

Table 16.2 Quality criteria for designing contracts and signatures.

Item	Criterion
SC-1	Contracts and (partial) signatures are consistent with all relevant nonfunctional how requirements
SC-2	Trust boundaries are clearly identified and appropriate given relevant technical and economic factors
SC-3	Published class interfaces are consistent with the high-level design diagram
SC-4	Published class interfaces maintain encapsulation
SC-5	Considering trust boundaries, complexity, and performance constraints, design is appropriately defensive: contracts require as little as possible
SC-6	Error handling is clear and appropriate given relevant technical and economic factors
SC-7	All logged error data is either noncritical or appropriately protected
SC-8	Anything already enforced by compiler, linker, or run-time system is not specified in a contract
SC-9	Any functionality dealing with collections is appropriately chunky versus chatty given relevant technical and economic factors
SC-10	Model region operation contracts and (partial) signatures are consistent with the semantic model
SC-11	View-controller region contracts and signatures are consistent with Interface specifications
SC-12	Infrastructure region contracts and signatures are consistent with necessary services
SC-13	All relevant, non-obvious design decisions are clearly described and justified

16.14 Summary

Chapter 15 explained how to derive part of the high-level design for a (sub) domain: classes and operations. Derivation of high-level design continues in this chapter with operation contracts (semantics) and partial signatures (syntax). For Model region, these were derived from the semantic model. Topics in this chapter include:

- High-level design as a deliberate encapsulation barrier
- Deriving contracts and signatures for Model region pulled data
- Deriving contracts and signatures for Model region pushed events
- Defensive programming and design by contract
- Defensive programming and trust boundaries
- Handling operation contract-level errors
- Deriving class invariants for Model region
- Deriving contracts and signatures for Model region pulled events
- Deriving contracts and signatures for Model region pushed data
- Operations and signatures in View, Controller, and Infrastructure regions
- Documenting the high-level design

17

Detailed Design and Code

This chapter gets down to the nuts and bolts of software: lines of code. This is where earlier claims of "literally self-coding documentation" are substantiated. This chapter shows how to use the semantic model, interface specification, and high-level design to drive detailed design and code for a (sub)domain. We write executable software to meet the needs of stakeholders—software that automates policies and processes—with specified interfaces.

Following a few initial comments on detailed design, this chapter presents data design before algorithm design. Data design topics include:

- Implementing attributes in Model region
- Implementing associations in Model region
- Data access object pattern
- Implementing derived attributes in Model region

Algorithm design topics presented in this chapter include:

- Completing operation signatures: parameter and return types
- Designing and implementing methods[1] in Model region
- Designing and implementing dynamic classification
- Connecting domains
- Detailed design and code in View-controller region for a user interface (UI)
- Detailed design and code in View-controller region for an API or embedded
- Detailed design and code in Infrastructure region
- Handling method-level errors
- A few comments on code comments
- Wrapping up method-level design and code
- Detailed design and code documentation

---

1 Remember "operation" is functionality visible on the interface of a class. "Method" (also known as member function) refers to private encapsulated code that implements an operation's functionality.

How to Engineer Software: A Model-Based Approach, First Edition. Steve Tockey.
© 2019 the IEEE Computer Society, Inc. Published 2019 by John Wiley & Sons, Inc.

17.1   Comments on Detailed Design

Remember the deliberate encapsulation barrier: everything in high-level design is visible within the (sub)domain. If a developer is working on the detailed design and code of Customer and that code uses operations on the interface of Order, then that developer should know everything they need about Order from its high-level design. Order's operation syntax (signatures) and semantics (contracts) must be defined and available to Customer's developer. There must be no reason for Customer's developer to know—or even care—how Order is implemented:

> *"Develop to an interface, not through an interface"*

Everything in detailed design and code for one class that uses other classes should be accomplished entirely via published interfaces of those other classes. And everything in detailed design and code for a class should be kept private within that class (subject to performance issues to be discussed in Chapter 19).

Second, to help avoid premature optimization, develop initial detailed design and code in the simplest, most straightforward way possible. Make decisions in a way that—under similar design circumstances—you would expect the majority of other designers in your organization to make substantially the same decisions. The detailed design and code produced in this chapter is only a first approximation. Optimizing design and code—as needed—is discussed in Chapter 19.

17.2   Implementing Attributes in Model Region

Each attribute in the semantic model[2] needs to be represented in design and code by an instance variable (also known as "member data." C# implementations can use private or public properties as appropriate) of an appropriate data type: int, float, double, char, String, Date, etc. Based on the attribute's meaning, use, and range defined in the semantic model, along with an understanding of the data types available in the programming language and any custom types you are willing to implement on your own, decide how to represent each attribute.[3] Consider what the information is used for in the semantic model. Is it used mostly in computation? Or, is it mostly just stored and retrieved for actors?

In Order fulfillment, Title.copyright year is only used for presentation on user screens and reports. It's an example of store and retrieve. No computation is

---

2 In the *reduced* semantic model, to be precise.
3 Section L.7 discusses some issues on measurement theory and data types.

ever done on it, so it could easily be represented using String. The range of Title. copyright year also includes "public domain," String would be very convenient for representing both kinds of values. Title.author and Title.subject are used for catalog searches and for display on screens and reports: that's mostly store and retrieve. On the other hand, there is some computation. Representing .author and .subject using String is probably also appropriate.

Print medium.stock level is processed (added, subtracted, and compared to Book order line.quantity), so representing it in numeric form would be more appropriate. Precision is to the whole number, so int would be better than float or double. Attribute Print medium.stock level could be represented as a String, if you really wanted. String could be used in a way that preserves business semantics, but it would be much harder to do necessary computations. It would also be inefficient from a computing perspective. Print medium.shipping weight could also be a mixed-use attribute. In some cases it is shown on screens and reports. If used in calculating shipping charges, it would be used in computation. Computing shipping charges isn't in the current version of Order fulfillment but could be added later. Keep in mind that the difference in vocabularies would likely drive Shipping to be another domain.

Generally speaking, an attribute whose range specification is:

- *Span with precision and units*—Is represented by a numeric type: int, float, double, etc.
- *Enumeration*—Is represented as a type-safe enumeration if available in the programming language. Boolean can be used if there are only two values. If type-safe enumeration is not available and there are more than two values, int, char, or String are alternatives.
- *Reference*—Depends on the nature of the referenced specification but will normally be represented by either numeric, type-safe enumeration, char, or String.
- *Unconstrained*—Technical and economic factors must be considered to provide a cost-effective representation that is as close to unconstrained as affordable.

17.2.1 Implementing Span with Precision and Units

Silly Savings Account.balance has a range specified as a span with precision and units: USD $0–100,000 to the nearest USD cent. In Java, that range could be represented by float—but that would be risky given loss of precision on large numbers. Silly Bank needs to track balances to the penny; using float could be a problem for very rich people. Double would be more appropriate but may also suffer from lack of precision. It might be best to develop (or acquire from some other source) a Money or Currency type that uses fixed precision. The same can be said for .overdraft limit, it should also be represented by either double, Money, or Currency.

17.2.2 Implementing Enumerations

The states of a Silly Savings Account are an enumeration: Normal and Overdrawn. Java supports type-safe enumeration; the most straightforward implementation would be

```
public enum SillyStatus { NORMAL, OVERDRAWN };
```

If the programming language doesn't support type-safe enumeration, alternative implementations could be as follows:

- *int*—for example, 0 = overdrawn and 1 = normal
- *char*—as in "o" = overdrawn and "n" = normal
- *String*—"overdrawn" and "normal"

There are only two enumerated values in the semantic model so .status could be represented using a Boolean: TRUE = normal, FALSE = overdrawn.

The states of a Silly Bank loan are: applied, approved, active, paid off, denied, cancelled, delinquent, and written off. Again, type-safe enumeration would be most appropriate:

```
public enum SillyLoanStatus { APPLIED, APPROVED, ACTIVE,
                PAIDOFF, DENIED, CANCELLED,
                DELINQUENT, WRITTENOFF };
```

Types int, char, and String are also possible but should only be used if type-safe enumeration is not available. Boolean is not appropriate because there are more than two values.

17.2.3 Implementing References

As stated earlier, this depends on the nature of the referenced specification. The .name of a Silly Bank Customer could be represented as a String. Of course, if supported by the language, you are free to create your own custom types. Given the need to limit date ranges, Java's existing Date class can be wrapped as described in Chapter 16. Class String can be wrapped to provide support for address validation. These custom wrapped classes can be considered part of Infrastructure region.

17.2.4 Implementing Unconstrained

If an attribute's range specification is "unconstrained," it would be cost prohibitive to implement in a truly fully unconstrained way. It will be necessary to introduce technology constraints. These are not business constraints; the business already said they didn't have any. They probably don't even want any constraints. But to implement the attribute in a truly unconstrained way will cost more than stakeholders are willing to pay.

This is another situation where engineering economy comes into play. Given project cost and schedule constraints, nonfunctional requirements, and implementation technology choices, how few technology constraints *can* be imposed within reasonable cost, schedule, and performance limits? Switching an instance variable from float to double is essentially no cost to a developer but might have performance implications because double precision takes more compute time and uses more memory.

Whatever technology constraints do get imposed need to be communicated to stakeholders[4]:

> *"We know you wanted unconstrained names for customers, but that implies names of arbitrary length (i.e., up to infinite) and script (e.g., including Klingon and Romulan). We don't think you can afford that. So we recommend a limit of 128 characters and Unicode because we think that gives you the most reasonable price-performance. We need to be certain these technical constraints are OK with you..."*

Stakeholders must be allowed to negotiate price–performance trade-offs and either ask for lower cost or schedule (but accept necessarily lower performance) or higher performance (but accept necessarily higher cost or schedule).

17.2.5 Explaining Representation Choices

If the representation chosen for an attribute isn't obvious, be sure to explain what was done and why—either in detailed design documentation or in code comments. If you didn't have any better idea and just did it that way because it seemed reasonable, say so. Saying "I didn't have any better ideas" or "it seemed reasonable at the time" gives a maintainer explicit permission to change it later.

Unless there is some overriding reason otherwise, instance variable names in detailed design and code should match as close as possible the attribute names in the semantic model. This makes correlation and consistency obvious. Where correlation is not obvious, be sure to explain how and why the name had to change.

Figure 17.1 shows possible representations for attributes in Order fulfillment as mostly existing Java types with a few custom types.

---

4 Remember the Hawaiian woman with a very long last name: http://www.dailymail.co.uk/news/article-2418171/Janice-Keihanaikukauakahihuliheekahaunaele-Hawaiian-woman-told-trim-long-doesnt-fit-state-ID-cards.html.

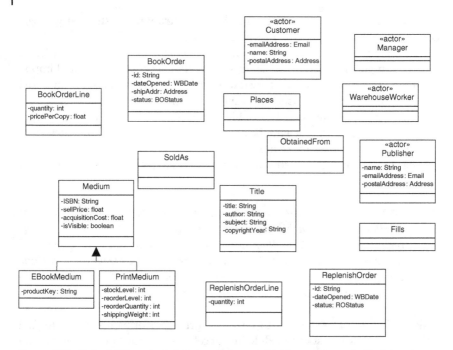

Figure 17.1 Order fulfillment attributes as instance variables and types in Model region.

17.3 Implementing Associations in Model Region

When the semantic model was first translated into high-level design, associations became placeholder classes. There are two approaches for representing associations, depending on implementation technology: memory-resident objects versus a persistence layer (e.g., relational database). Both will be described.

17.4 Implementing Associations in Memory-Resident Objects

If the design is based on memory-resident objects, that is, implemented in Java, C++, C#, etc., associations will normally be merged as object references into one, the other, or both (for binary associations) associated classes. Client-server relationships usually determine which class the association is merged into. From the point of view of the client, four server multiplicities are typical:

- One client object to exactly one (1) server object
- One client object to zero or one (0..1) server object

- One client object to one or many (1..*) server objects
- One client object to zero or many (*) server objects

17.4.1   -to-exactly-one

When the multiplicity to the server object is -to-exactly-one (i.e., the lower and upper bounds are both 1), simply add an instance variable to the client class. This instance variable holds the reference to that one linked instance of the server class. In Order fulfillment, the Obtained from association between Title and Publisher is an example. The first approximation design in Figure 15.32 shows Title as client of Publisher. The multiplicity is exactly one Publisher for each Title. The most straightforward design would be to add an instance variable, .pObtainedFrom,[5] to Title. That instance variable refers to the one corresponding instance of Publisher.

That client-to-server multiplicity is always -to-exactly-one so the instance variable must always refer to one and only one valid object of the server class, that is, .pObtainedFrom can never be null; it will always reference exactly one Publisher. Any method on Title that needs to traverse the Obtained from association can do so via .pObtainedFrom, knowing that it will never be null.

Try to name the client-side instance variable as close as possible to the association name in the semantic model. It was easy for Title Obtained from Publisher. It might be more difficult in some cases, depending on the name in the semantic model. If that same association were named, "Publisher Sells Title" or "Publisher Supplies Title," it would not make sense to name the Title instance variable .pSells or .pSupplies. On the other hand, both association names are easily reversible, "Title Sold by Publisher" or "Title Supplied by Publisher," meaning the instance variable in Title could be named .pSoldBy or .pSuppliedBy and still clearly correlate to the association in the semantic model. This is where the gerund ("-ing," in Chapter 8) form of association naming could be superior.

17.4.2   -to-zero-or-one

When the multiplicity to the server class is -to-zero-or-one, that is, the lower bound is 0 and upper bound is 1, still add an instance variable to the client class. This instance variable holds the reference to the linked object of the server class. Consider "Wall socket powers Operating appliance." One Wall socket can power zero or one Operating appliance, and one Operating appliance can only be powered by one Wall socket. If Wall socket is client and Operating appliance is server, add a .pPowers instance variable to WallSocket.

---

5 Preceding names by "p" can be a useful convention.

The minor complication is that the instance variable can be null. WallSocket methods that access the linked Operating appliance need to protect that access with

```
if ( pPowers != null ) then ...
```

17.4.3   -to-one-or-many

When the multiplicity to the server class is -to-one-or-many (i.e., the lower bound is 1 and upper bound is many), the client instance variable will be a collection. That collection holds a set of references to all currently linked server objects. Consider "Landlord Manages Apartment" with one Landlord managing at least one but possibly many Apartments and one Apartment managed by exactly one Landlord. When Landlord is client, add a .pManages instance variable. Client-to-server accesses across the association will either involve all linked server objects, or a mechanism may be needed to select a subset (e.g., "all apartments in Building X"; this should be obvious from action specifications in the semantic model). The lower bound of Landlord to Apartment is 1, so the collection will never be empty. An empty collection violates policy, indicating a defect in design or code.

17.4.4   -to-zero-or-many

When the multiplicity to the server class is -to-zero-or-many, that is, the lower bound is 0 and upper bound is many, again add the instance variable to the client for the collection of references to currently linked server objects. An example would be Customer places Book order in Order fulfillment. The semantic model says a Customer doesn't have to place any Book orders but can place many. Customer is client, so add .pPlaces as an instance variable. Client-to-server access across .pPlaces will again either address all linked Book orders, or a mechanism may be needed to select a relevant subset. The lower bound on server multiplicity is 0, so .pPlaces can be empty.

In the latter two cases (-to-one-or-many and -to-zero-or-many), Iterator pattern[6] can be used to hide the collection implementation from client method code. Iterator pattern works equally well with the -to-zero-or-many and -to-one-or-many cases. Client code is identical, regardless of the collection being empty or not. Current versions of Java also support an "enhanced for() loop" that allows simple traversing of collections, as in

```
for( BookOrder anOrder: pPlaces ) { ... }
```

---

6 See, for example, https://en.wikipedia.org/wiki/Iterator_pattern. Also, see Figure 14.1.

17.4.5 Bidirectional Client-Server Links

Some designs have bidirectional client-server links. This happens twice in the high-level design for Order fulfillment (Figure 15.32):

- Publisher fills Replenish order
- Title sold as Medium

In these cases, simply apply the above guidelines to each of the client-server relationships. Specifically, for Publisher fills Replenish order,

- *When Replenish order is client and Publisher is server (in use case Place replenish order: notifying the publisher after the 24 hour hold)*, one Replenish order can only be filled by -to-exactly-one Publisher, and ReplenishOrder gets a .pFilledBy instance variable that's a single, non-null reference to the one Publisher. ReplenishOrder methods traversing this association (e.g., .placeOrder()) would use this reference.
- *When Publisher is client and Replenish order is server (in use case Make/add to replenish order)*, one Publisher can have -to-zero-or-many Replenish orders, and Publisher gets a ".pFills" instance variable that is a collection of references to Replenish orders. Publisher methods that traverse .pFills should use Iterator pattern or enhanced for().

When a Replenish order is deleted after being received, design and code need to make sure the reference to it is also removed from Publisher.pFills; otherwise there will be a memory leak.

Similarly, for association Sold as,

- *When Medium is client and Title is server (in use case Pack order involving replenishment)*, one Medium can only be -to-exactly-one Title, and Medium gets a ".pIsFormOf" instance variable that's a single non-null reference to that one Title. Medium methods that traverse .pIsFormOf would simply use this reference.
- *When Title is client and Medium is server (for use case Catalog)*, one Title has -to-one-or-many Media, and Title gets a ".pSoldAs" instance variable that is a collection of references to Media. Title methods that traverse .pSoldAs should use Iterator pattern. This particular association is a special case, since there will not be more than two Media for any Title (one eBook and one Print). It might be better to implement the association as separate .pSoldAsPrint and . pSoldAsEBook instance variables (either, or both, of which could be null).

17.4.6 Association Classes

The last situation to consider is an association class in the semantic model:

- In association "Book order for Medium"—Book order line is the association class. BookOrder is client of BookOrderLine and BookOrderLine is client of Medium.

- In association "Replenish order for Medium"—Replenish order line is the association class. ReplenishOrder is client of ReplenishOrderLine and ReplenishOrderLine is client of Medium.

With association classes, break the association dimension into two separate design links, one from the overall client to the association class as server and another from the association class as client to the overall server. In Book order for Medium, Book order is overall client. BookOrder gets a .pFor instance variable that's a collection of one to many references to BookOrderLine. BookOrderLine is client of Medium, and each BookOrderLine will only have one Medium. BookOrderLine gets a .pFor reference that will never be null. Handling Replenish order for Print medium is identical with only the names being slightly different.

In some cases the association class is overall client and the associated classes are servers. This is the easiest case because the association class only needs to have the one never-null reference to each of the objects being associated. As a contrived example, if BookOrderLine were overall client, then it would get .pForBookOrder and .pForMedium instance variables referencing the two objects it is linking.

Figure 17.2 shows instance variables for Order fulfillment, including references for associations. The instance variables representing associations are

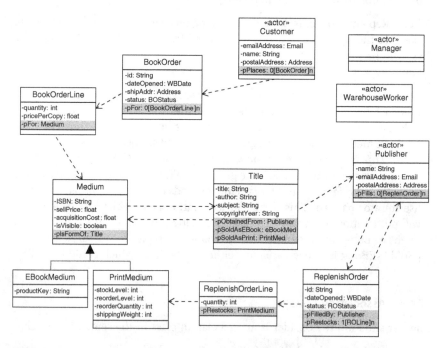

Figure 17.2 Instance variables for Order fulfillment, including associations—memory resident.

shaded in the diagram. The notation "-places: 0[BookOrder]n" is not standard UML and is intended to communicate that instance variable .pPlaces is a set of zero to many (references to) instances of BookOrder.

One final point on associations in memory-resident implementations is that each association in the semantic model turns into actual detailed design and code:

> *"If dynamic-only connections (e.g., "Warehouse worker Packs Book order" as discussed in Chapter 8) are modeled as associations in the semantic model then there will be dead, unused design and code"*

Unless you want to pollute your system with dead code, remembering that complexity is your enemy and this would clearly be unnecessary complexity, don't model dynamic connections as associations in the semantic model. Specifying dynamic connections in state model actions and, possibly, sequence diagrams alone is entirely sufficient.

17.5 Implementing Associations in a Persistence Layer

If the design is based on a persistence layer, for example, a relational database,[7] each semantic model class becomes a database table in design. Each attribute in the semantic model becomes a column in the corresponding table. Choose column data types as appropriate per the discussion earlier of memory-resident objects.

17.5.1 Keys

If a class in the semantic model already has an appropriate key, use that as the key for the database table. If there isn't an explicit key, or the explicit key is inappropriate (e.g., a multi-attribute key in the semantic model but high performance is required, so a single valued key is needed in design), then create an arbitrary key for that table. Consider class Commercial Flight from Chapter 8. If the key were specified as "Latitude, Longitude, and Altitude" in the semantic model, performance using this as the key in a relational database could suffer. An arbitrary key, for example, AirplaneId, might be

---

7 This section addresses using a relational database as the persistence layer. Technical or economic constraints may drive use of a hierarchical (see, e.g., https://en.wikipedia.org/wiki/Hierarchical_database_model) or network (see, e.g., https://en.wikipedia.org/wiki/Network_model) database. Those alternatives are not explicitly discussed here because they are much less likely to be used in practice. You should be able to derive those from this relational design.

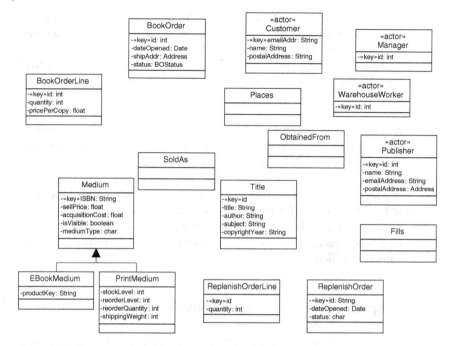

Figure 17.3 First approximation relational database schema considering only attributes and keys.

needed to satisfy performance requirements. That key is internal, invisible to the business.

Figure 17.3 shows a first approximation relational database schema for Order fulfillment considering only attributes and keys (no associations, yet).

17.5.2 Foreign Keys

Relational databases use foreign keys to represent semantic model associations. Placement of foreign keys is driven by a combination of multiplicity and normalization. Compound data fields should be avoided—a specific database engine might not even support compound values—so collecting a set of foreign keys in a single column is ill advised. Client-server relationships can be irrelevant in database designs.

The important variations on association multiplicities, and recommended implementations, are:

- *One-to-one (e.g., On-duty navigator pilots Ship at sea)*—It shouldn't matter where the foreign key goes; it could go on either side. Navigator could have a foreign key pointing to Ship and/or Ship could have a foreign key pointing to

Navigator. Depending on performance needs, it may be worth putting foreign keys on both sides.

- *One-to-zero-or-one (e.g., Wall socket powers Operating appliance)*—The foreign key should generally go on the -to-one side (Operating appliance). Performance might suggest putting it on the other side (Wall socket), but that means it might be null. Putting foreign keys on both sides might be useful for performance reasons. For example, Wall socket has a foreign key pointing to Operating appliance, and Operating appliance has a foreign key pointing to Wall socket.
- *Zero-or-one-to-zero-or-one (e.g., Batch of chocolate is cooking in Vat)*—Ideally this should be treated the same as the many-to-many case using a correlation table (possibly naming that correlation table using the gerund ("-ing") form). This can also implemented using a foreign key in Batch pointing to Vat and a foreign key in Vat pointing to Batch, as long as null cases are properly handled.
- *One-to-one-or-many (e.g., Landlord manages Apartment)*—The many side should get the foreign key pointing to the one side: Apartment should get a foreign key pointing to Landlord.
- *One-to-zero-or-many (e.g., Variable in code is declared to be of Type)*—The foreign key should go on the many side, and Variable should get a foreign key pointing at Type.
- *Zero-or-one-to-one-or-many (e.g., Administrative assistant supports Manager)*—Ideally this would also be done with a correlation table, but could be done by putting a foreign key pointing to Administrative assistant in Manager as long as nulls are properly treated.
- *One-or-many-to-one-or-many (e.g., Author writes Book), one-or-many-to-zero-or-many (e.g., Member Volunteers on Committee), zero-or-many-to-zero-or-many (e.g., Student Attends Course)*—All of these are treated the same using a correlation table. The correlation table is a separate table that is most likely keyed by the concatenation of the keys of the linked tables.

The general rule is to place foreign keys so they point at a table that has a -to-exactly-one multiplicity. If multiplicity is -to-zero-or-one, a foreign key can be used, but access needs to be protected for the null case. Many to many or biconditional (zero or anything to zero or anything) should use a correlation table.

17.5.3 Association Classes

When the semantic model has an association class, use a correlation table in design—as in the many-to-many case. The correlation table can be keyed by the concatenation of the keys of the linked tables. There will also be non-key fields for attributes in the semantic model. Book order line is an association class in Order fulfillment's semantic model. As shown in Figure 17.4, it is implemented as a table keyed by bookOrderId and mediumID but also has quantity as a non-key field.

Figure 17.4 shows a second approximation relational database schema for Order fulfillment. Database columns that implement associations are shaded in the diagram.

Note that Figure 17.4 includes an inheritance relationship: Medium is superclass with EBookMedium and PrintMedium as subclasses. Most relational databases do not support inheritance. Chapter 19 on optimization includes a section on design and implementation in lower-level (i.e., non-object-oriented) languages. Three options are presented:

- Collapse subclasses into superclass
- Distribute superclass
- Link classes

Choose the most cost-effective option considering the service life of the system.

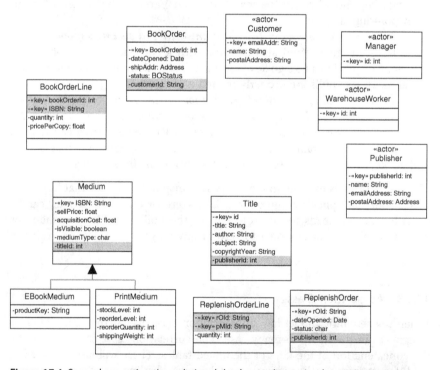

Figure 17.4 Second approximation relational database schema, implementing associations.

17.6 Data Access Object Pattern

Data access object pattern[8] can be useful when memory-resident business objects need to be synchronized with rows in a relational database table. Data access object pattern combines the benefits of memory-resident objects with services of a relational database:

- The database can serve as an object persistence mechanism.
- Business objects can be shared across several applications via the database.
- The database can provide transaction semantics.[9]

Figure 17.5 shows generic Data access object pattern. The classes in Data access object pattern are:

- *BusinessObject*—A memory-resident business object that needs synchronization with a corresponding row in a database table
- *DataSource*—The API to the database (e.g., SQL)
- *DataAccessObject*—Hides the specifics of DataSource and its API from BusinessObject
- *TransferObject*—A container for passing data between BusinessObject and DataAccessObject

Figure 17.6 shows Data access object pattern applied to class BookOrder in Order fulfillment.

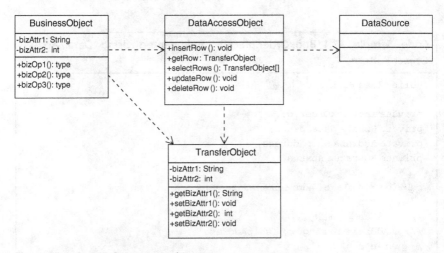

Figure 17.5 Generic Data access object pattern.

---

8 See, for example, http://www.oracle.com/technetwork/java/dataaccessobject-138824.html.
9 See, for example, https://en.wikipedia.org/wiki/Transaction_processing. Specifically, begin transaction, commit, rollback, and end transaction.

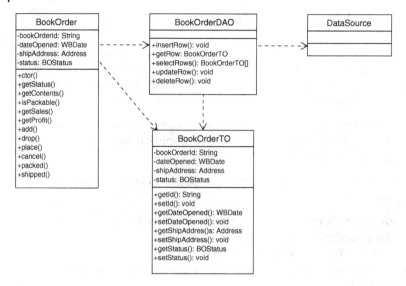

Figure 17.6 Data access object pattern applied to class BookOrder.

Code Sample 17.1 shows a partial implementation of BookOrder.place() in terms of Data access object pattern, as designed in Figure 17.6.

Code Sample 17.1 BookOrder.place() Implemented Using Data Access Object Pattern

```
public class BookOrder {

  private int bookOrderId;
  private WBDate dateOpened;
  private Address shipAddress;
  private BOStatus status;

  public void place( Address anAddress ) {
  // requires
  //   .status == OPEN
  //   anAddress in range of .shipAddress10
  // guarantees
  //   this order was pre-synchronized with the reference state
  //   .shipAddress = anAddress
  //   place() has been signaled for each line in this order
  //   if this line contains any print media
```

---

10 Assuming Address enforces "acceptable to the US Post Office and Canada Post," this is guaranteed via use of Address as the data type for both, that is, this violation is prevented.

```
//    then .status == PLACED
//    otherwise .status == COMPLETED
//    the reference state has been synchronized with any changes
// fetch the reference state from the database row
BookOrderTO aBookOrderTO = BookOrderDAO.getRow( bookOrderId );
status = aBookOrderTO.getStatus();[11]
// the memory-resident business object is now in synch with DB
//
// code for the place() business process goes here
//
// now re-synch the reference state with this new state[12]
aBookOrderTO.setStatus( status );
BookOrderDAO.updateRow( bookOrderId, aBookOrderTO );
// DB is now in synch with the memory-resident business object
  }

}
```

A client object—in this case, Customer—invokes BookOrder.place(). Figures 16.3 and 16.4 in the previous chapter show how the contract for BookOrder.place() relates to the transition in the semantic model. As shown in Code Sample 17.1, when BookOrder place() is invoked:

1) The memory-resident BookOrder uses `BookOrderTO aBookOrderTO = BookOrderDAO.getRow( bookOrderId )` to fetch the reference state of the business object from DataSource. This assumes Book orders are shared across other applications and this memory-resident object doesn't hold the reference state. If this memory-resident object does hold the reference state, steps 1–3 aren't necessary.

2) BookOrderDAO fetches the corresponding row from the BookOrder database table (SQL "`select * from table BookOrder where rowId = bookOrderId`"). Given the result of the SQL select, BookOrderDAO populates aBookOrderTO and passes aBookOrderTO back to the memory-resident BookOrder business object.

3) The BookOrder business object updates its instance variables as necessary, based on aBookOrderTO. Now it is in synch with the reference state in the database.

---

11 .bookOrderId and .dateOpened don't need to be synchronized because they are static with respect to business processes: once established, they never change. .shipAddress will be overwritten in this operation, anyway. Only .status needs to be synchronized.

12 For performance reasons, this step might be optional: "if (somethingChanged) then …" to avoid unnecessarily database accesses when nothing changed in the memory-resident business object.

4) The .place() business process on the memory-resident BookOrder runs according to business semantics, possibly changing the state of the memory-resident business object.

5) If the .place() business operation was successful (and, possibly, only if it modified the state of the memory-resident business object), the memory-resident BookOrder updates aBookOrderTO with its current state and tells BookOrderDAO to update the row via `BookOrderDAO.updateRow( bookOrderID, aBookOrderTO)`.

6) BookOrderDAO uses aBookOrderTO to make an SQL update (e.g., "`update * from table BookOrder where rowId = bookOrderId`"), which pushes the updated row data back into the database.

If you hand code a Data access object or two, you quickly realize how much code is derivable from the business object and the Data source. It is straightforward to generate both Data access object code and Transfer object code; some commercial products provide this capability.

There are significant syntactic and semantic differences in SQL implementations.[13] Data access object pattern can support running the application on multiple database products in spite of these differences. Where portability across multiple SQL implementations is needed, apply Bridge pattern[14]: the Data access object is Implementor and Data source-specific Data access objects are Concrete implementors. If Bridge is used, Factory method pattern[15] is useful for creating appropriate Data source-specific Data access objects.

17.7   Implementing Derived Attributes in Model Region

When implementing derived attributes from the semantic model,[16] first be sure to fully understand the derivation policy. The derivation policy must be either defined or referenced in the semantic model. That derivation policy should ultimately be in the form of a function: an output (call it the "dependent variable") representing the derived attribute in the semantic model and one or more inputs (call them "independent variables"). The value of the dependent variable is constrained to be in the prescribed relationship (the derivation policy) with the values of the independent variables.

A simple example is the .gross pay of an Hourly employee in a payroll business.[17] Derived attribute .gross pay (the dependent variable) is constrained to be equal to the .pay rate times the .hours worked (two independent variables).

13 See, for example, http://troels.arvin.dk/db/rdbms/.
14 See, for example, https://en.wikipedia.org/wiki/Bridge_pattern.
15 See, for example, https://en.wikipedia.org/wiki/Factory_method_pattern.
16 Assuming memory-resident objects and pull data form because that is the most common. Both persistence layer and push data forms should be derivable from this discussion.
17 See, for example, Figure 8.7.

There are at least three alternatives for detailed design and code, which will be discussed below:

- Compute on demand
- Compute on update and store
- Deferred update

17.7.1 Compute on Demand

Compute on demand means don't store the derived (dependent) variable as an instance variable with an accessor (getter) operation. Instead, provide an operation that derives the value whenever a client requests it. The method implements the derivation policy, returning the computed dependent value. This is shown in Code Sample 17.2 for Hourly employee.gross pay.

Code Sample 17.2 A Derived Attribute Implemented Using Compute on Demand

```java
public class HourlyEmployee {

  private double payRate;
  private double hoursWorked;


  ...


  public void setPayRate( double newPayRate ) {
   payRate = newPayRate;
  }


  public void setHoursWorked( double newHoursWorked ) {
   hoursWorked = newHoursWorked;
  }


  public double grossPay() {
   return payRate * hoursWorked;
  }


  ...


}
```

17.7.2 Compute on Update and Store

Compute on update and store means storing the dependent value as an instance variable. When any independent value changes, the derivation function updates the stored dependent value. The stored dependent value is always up to date.[18] Whenever a client requests the derived value, the accessing operation simply returns the stored value. This is shown in Code Sample 17.3 for Hourly employee.gross pay.

Code Sample 17.3 A Derived Attribute Implemented Using Compute on Update and Store

```java
public class HourlyEmployee {

  private double payRate;
  private double hoursWorked;
  private double grossPay;

  . . .

  public void setPayRate ( double newPayRate ) {
    payRate = newPayRate;
    grossPay = payRate * hoursWorked;
  }

  public void setHoursWorked ( double newHoursWorked ) {
    hoursWorked = newHoursWorked;
    grossPay = payRate * hoursWorked;
  }

  public double grossPay () {
    return grossPay;
  }

  . . .

}
```

Compute on update and store is easy when all dependent variables are local to the same object. A potential challenge can be recognizing when nonlocal independent value changes. Code needs to recognize change in a value that's a property of another object. If you want to use compute on update and store, you would probably need a publish/subscribe mechanism (i.e., Observer pattern) to recognize changes to nonlocal independent variables.

---

18 Within the performance capabilities of the system.

17.7.3 Deferred Update

Immediate recomputation on change of any independent variable isn't strictly required. The strict requirement is only that derivation happens before the next client access to the dependent variable. Deferred update takes advantage of this by adding a clean–dirty flag. Whenever the dependent value is recomputed and stored, that flag is set to "clean," meaning the dependent variable is consistent with the independent variables. If any independent variable changes, the flag is set to "dirty." If a client asks for the dependent value when the flag is "dirty," the derived value is recomputed and stored, the flag reset to "clean," and the newly recomputed value is returned to the client. This is shown in Code Sample 17.4 for Hourly employee.gross pay. The constructor would need to initialize the clean–dirty flag. Also, this option is somewhat silly in this specific case, but becomes more reasonable as the derivation becomes more computationally expensive.

Code Sample 17.4 A Derived Attribute Implemented Using Deferred Update

```java
public class HourlyEmployee {

  private double payRate;
  private double hoursWorked;
  private double grossPay;
  private boolean grossPayIsUpToDate;  // the clean-dirty flag

  . . .

  public void setPayRate( double newPayRate ) {
    payRate = newPayRate;
    grossPayIsUpToDate = false;
  }

  public void setHoursWorked( double newHoursWorked ) {
    hoursWorked = newHoursWorked;
    grossPayIsUpToDate = false;
  }

  public double grossPay() {
    if ( !grossPayIsUpToDate ) {
      grossPay = payRate * hoursWorked;
      grossPayisUpToDate = true;
    }
    return grossPay;
  }

  . . .

}
```

17.7.4 Decision Criteria

The choice should be based on relevant technical and economic factors. A number of technical factors could be considered:

- How frequently do independent variables change?
- How much does it cost to fetch the independent variables, particularly if they are not local (i.e., in another object)?
- How much does it cost to compute the dependent variable from the independent variables?
- How much does it cost to store the computed dependent variable?
- How frequently is the derived value (dependent variable) needed by clients?
- What is the client's tolerance for lateness following a request for the derived value?
- ...

In compute on update and store and deferred update, publish/subscribe (observer pattern) can further complicate design and code. The effect on cost and schedule for both development and long-term maintenance should be considered. And again, unless design choices are obvious, the rationale should be included in design documentation.

Order fulfillment has the following derived attributes:

- BookOrder.isPackable()
- BookOrder.sales()
- BookOrder.profit()
- BookOrderLine.isPackable()
- BookOrderLine.sales()
- BookOrderLine.profit()

It probably makes sense to implement all of them using compute on demand:

- It is the simplest design and code
- The independent variables don't change very often
- It's not expensive to re-compute the derived values when needed
- The derived values are not used very often by clients (except BookOrder. isPackable(), but even that doesn't require very high performance)

17.8 Completing Operation Signatures: Parameters and Return Types

Operation signatures are a design topic, but final discussion of signatures was deferred to here because it tends to depend on instance variable representation (data type) decisions. Instance variable data type decisions are better talked about here than in any earlier chapter. So, while parameter and return types aren't a detailed design topic, the discussion was postponed to make logical sense.

Generally, input parameter and return types should be the same as the type chosen for corresponding instance variables:

- If the instance variable is type int, then input parameters and return values associated with that instance variable should also be type int. PrintMedium.stockLevel would be an example in Order fulfillment.
- If the instance variable is type double, then parameters associated with that instance variable should also be type double (SillySavingsAccount.balance and overdraftLimit, etc.).
- If the instance variable is type String, then parameters associated with that instance variable should also be type String (Title.subject).
- ...

There can, of course, be exceptions. The instance variable might use one type, while a corresponding parameter might use a different type. This is possible as long as the programming language supports automatic type conversion (e.g., float to double) or code is added to handle necessary conversions.

17.9 Designing and Implementing Methods in Model Region

Each operation in Model region has a contract: semantics are defined. Now it's just a matter of designing and implementing method code to satisfy those contracts. The final part of detailed design and code in Model region is to choose algorithms and implement methods for each operation. The choice can be nontrivial. Selection criteria include:

- Run-time performance
- Accuracy and precision
- Complexity
- ...

Remember that data flow dependencies are the only constraints on sequencing individual lines of code. When there are no data flow dependencies, actions and action algorithms can be designed and coded in any sequence and can even be done in parallel. Mainstream programming languages necessarily serialize execution. Even if execution could be done in parallel, code is generally forced into serial implementation whether we like it or not—unless we explicitly parallelize: threading, tasking, and multiprocessing. Most developers are so used to serializing design and code that it becomes almost second nature. We often have difficulty even seeing, let alone taking advantage of, opportunities for parallelization.

If an action is specified as an algorithm in the semantic model, then translation into detailed design and code could be trivial depending on the action specification language and how easily it can be translated into the target programming language. In the extreme case, an action might already be specified as a code fragment; all that needs done is to just copy that fragment into code. The next chapter provides more detail on how to develop method-level detailed design and code when actions are specified in contract form.

When the same action appears more than once on the state model for a class, consider implementing it as a private function, calling it from the method code of the public operations.

Pay particular attention to cases where associations are implemented with double linking (e.g., Title sold as Medium, Publisher fills Replenish Order in Order fulfillment). Care needs to be taken with object references on both sides. For example, when a ReplenishOrder is created, it needs to set its reference to the Publisher, and Publisher needs to add a reference to that new ReplenishOrder to its list. When a ReplenishOrder is deleted, its reference to the Publisher goes away automatically; however the reference to the deleted ReplenishOrder also needs to be removed from the collection in Publisher.

The next chapter presents a technique, Programming by intent, that can be useful in developing nontrivial method code.

17.10   Designing and Implementing Dynamic Classification

```
┌─────────────────────────┐
│       Employee          │
├─────────────────────────┤
│ -id                     │
│ -name                   │
│ -hireDate               │
│ -employeeType           │
│ -salary                 │
│ -hourlyRate             │
│ -hoursWorked            │
├─────────────────────────┤
│ +ctor()                 │
│ +name()                 │
│ +hireDate()             │
│ +convertToSalaried()    │
│ +convertToHourly()      │
│ +setSalary()            │
│   ...                   │
│ +grossPay()             │
│ +setHourlyRate()        │
│ +setHoursWorked()       │
│   ...                   │
└─────────────────────────┘
```

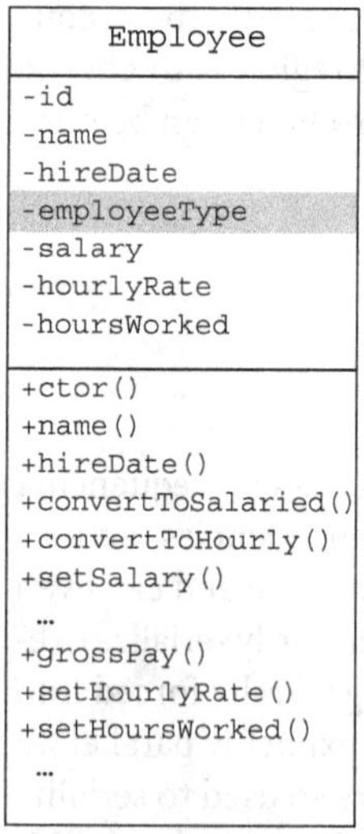

Figure 17.7 Collapsed dynamic classification with a type discriminator.

Chapter 15 presented options for implementing dynamic classification in the semantic model in terms of high-level design. Two options were presented:

- Collapse inheritance hierarchy
- State (aka delegate) pattern

The detailed design for both is described here.

17.10.1   Collapse Inheritance Hierarchy

From an attribute perspective, all instance variables in subclasses are moved into in the base class. You may need to add a "type discriminator" instance variable to indicate the business type of each run-time instance. Instance variable .employeeType in Figure 17.7 is a type discriminator for the Employee dynamic classification example in Chapter 15.

The method-level code follows standard patterns:

- *Constructor*—The constructor will need to implement all normal functionality expected of a constructor. In addition, if the starting subtype is defined in the class's semantic model state model, it also needs to initialize the constructed object to being in the right state by setting the type discriminator instance variable. If the start subtype is not predetermined, then presumably it would be passed in as an input parameter (e.g., "`Employee newEmployee = new Employee( String aName, EmployeeType newEmployeeType, etc.);`") and the constructor would act accordingly. If parameters differ by subclass, constructors with different signatures can be used.

- *State invariant methods*—Any superclass method whose behavior is invariant with respect to the subclasses is unaffected. An example is .name(), which doesn't behave any differently for Hourly versus Salaried employees.
- *State variant methods*—Any method whose behavior depends on subclass needs to include decision logic, for example, if-then when there are only few possibilities, or switch-case might be preferred when there are many. An example is .setSalary(), where operation only applies to Salaried employees and must not have any effect on an Hourly employee other than generating some kind of appropriate error response. In some cases, it may be appropriate to just ignore the request.
- *State changing methods*—Any method whose behavior changes the subtype of the object needs to update the type discriminator. It also needs to assign values to instance variables that have become relevant because of the type change (presumably supplied as input parameters, but some could be set to established default values). As a matter of safety, any instance variable that became inappropriate because of the type change should be set to some known value (e.g., zero if it is numeric, an empty string if it is a String, null if it is a reference). The example is convertToSalaried().

All of these are shown in a partial implementation of Employee in Code Sample 17.5.

Code Sample 17.5 Partial Implementation of Collapsed Employee Class

```
public enum EmployeeType { HOURLY, SALARY };

public class Employee {

  private String name;
  private EmployeeType employeeType;
  private double salary;
  private double hourlyRate;
  private double hoursWorked;

  . . .
```

```
 public String name () {
  return name;
 }

 public void convertToSalaried ( double startingSalary ) {
  if ( employeeType != EmployeeType.SALARY ) {
   employeeType = EmployeeType.SALARY;
   salary = startingSalary;
   hourlyRate = 0.0;
   hoursWorked = 0.0;
  } else {
   // some kind of TBD error
  }
 }

 public void setSalary ( double newSalary ) {
  if ( employeeType == EmployeeType.SALARY ) {
   salary = newSalary;
  } else {
   // some kind of TBD error
  }
 }

 public double grossPay ( ) {
  if ( employeeType == EmployeeType.HOURLY ) {
   return payRate * hoursWorked;
  } else {
   // some kind of TBD error
   return 0.0;
  }
 }

 ...

}
```

17.10.2   State (aka Delegate) Pattern

From an attribute perspective, all instance variables stay in the subclass they were originally declared. The state delegate reference plays the role of the type discriminator. Instance variable myEmployeeState in Figure 17.8 is a type discriminator for Employee.

The method-level logic also follows standard patterns:

- *Constructor*—The constructor will implement all normal functionality expected of a constructor. In addition, if the starting subtype is defined in

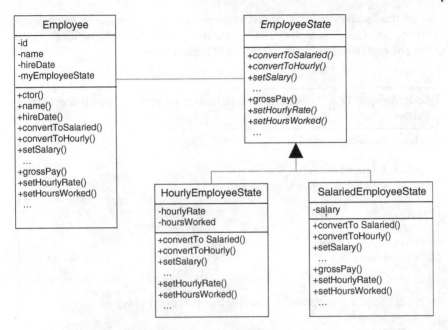

Figure 17.8 Dynamic classification using State pattern.

the class's semantic model state model, it also needs to instantiate the state delegate and assign the delegate pointer. If the start subtype is not predetermined, then presumably it would be passed in as an input parameter and the constructor would act accordingly.

- *State invariant methods*—Any base class method whose behavior is invariant with respect to the subclasses is unaffected. An example is .name(), which doesn't behave any differently for Hourly versus Salaried employees.
- *State variant methods*—Any method whose behavior depends on subclass is forwarded to the state delegate. An example is .setSalary(), where operation only applies to Salaried employees and must not have any effect on an Hourly employee other than generating some kind of appropriate error response. In some cases, it may appropriate to just ignore the request (i.e., the delegate can implement it by doing nothing). Default behavior can be implemented in the delegate base class and overridden as appropriate in delegate subclasses.
- *State changing methods*—Any method whose behavior changes the state of the object needs to instantiate the new delegate and overwrite the delegate reference. The example is .convertToSalaried(). Implementation in non-garbage-collecting languages can be more difficult—old State delegate objects must be explicitly deleted. In multi-threaded applications, care must be taken in methods that change state.

All of this is shown, for a partial implementation of Employee using State pattern, in Code Samples 17.6 (Employee), 17.7 (EmployeeState), 17.8 (HourlyEmployeeState), and 17.9 (SalaryEmployeeState).

Code Sample 17.6 Partial Implementation of Employee Class Using State Pattern

```java
public class Employee {

  private String name;
  private EmployeeState myEmployeeState;

  . . .

  public String name() {
    return name;
  }

  public void convertToSalaried( double startingSalary ) {
    myEmployeeState =
      myEmployeeState.convertToSalaried( startingSalary );
  }

  public void setSalary( double newSalary ) {
    myEmployeeState = myEmployeeState.setSalary( startingSalary );
  }

  public double grossPay() {
    return myEmployeeState.grossPay()
  }

  . . .

}
```

Code Sample 17.7 Partial Implementation of EmployeeState Class

```java
public abstract class EmployeeState {

  . . .

  public abstract EmployeeSalaryState convertToSalaried(
                          double startingSalary );
```

```
public abstract void setSalary( double newSalary );

public double grossPay() {
  // some kind of TBD error
  return 0.0;
}

...


}
```

Code Sample 17.8 Partial Implementation of HourlyEmployeeState Class

```
public class HourlyEmployeeState {

  private double hourlyRate;
  private double hoursWorked;
  ...
  public void convertToSalaried( double startingSalary ) {
   return new SalaryEmployeeState( double startingSalary );
  }
  public void setSalary( double newSalary ) {
    // some kind of TBD error
  }

  public double grossPay() {
    return payRate * hoursWorked;
  }
  ...

}
```

Code Sample 17.9 Partial Implementation of SalaryEmployeeState Class

```
public class SalaryEmployeeState {

  private double salary;
  ...
```

```
public void convertToSalaried( double startingSalary ) {
  // Already a salaried employee, some kind of TBD error
  return this;
}

public abstract void setSalary( double newSalary ) {
    salary = newSalary;
}


. . .


}
```

17.11   Connecting Domains

Domain separation helps manage complexity in large systems via fundamental principles of abstraction, encapsulation, cohesion, coupling, etc. At some point, however, separated domains need to be connected. This is that point.

Remember that lower-level service domains are invisible to the semantic model of any higher domain. In design and code, however, a lower-level service domain is exactly that: a nontrivial service to be used in design and implementation of the higher domain. Typically, methods implementing operations in the higher domain make use of services (classes and operations) in lower domains. Domain connections in WebBooks 2.0 are shown in the domain diagram in Figure 6.4:

- Order fulfillment to Payment, Scalability, User security, Web UI, and Dedicated terminal UI
- Payment to Scalability, User security, and Web UI
- User security to Scalability, Web UI, and Dedicated terminal UI
- Scalability to High availability

How to connect one domain to another is specified in the server domain's interface specification. Client domain methods needing service domain functionality need to be designed and coded in terms of that interface. To be specific, code in Order fulfillment that needs to connect to Payment must do so using the Payment API defined in the Payment domain interface specification. All code that needs Scalability must access it as described in the Scalability domain interface specification. Scalability code that needs to be highly available does so by using the API in the High availability domain interface specification. Appendices E, G, I, and K show examples of how domains connections can be documented:

- The interface specification describes how clients of that domain connect to its implementation
- The high-level and detailed design describe how the implementation of that domain is connected to the domain(s) it is built on.

17.12   Detailed Design and Code in View-Controller Region for a User Interface

Detailed design for View-controller region for a UI involves two general topics. The first topic is the method-level design and code for the screen/window objects (e.g., classes in Figure 15.35). These should be straightforward given operation contracts and signatures developed in the previous chapter. The same should be true for detailed design and code of a generic screen interpreter class such as shown in Figure 15.36, although inherently such a class would be more complex.

The remaining topic is the detailed design and code for the actor class. The main job of the actor class is to implement the decision logic in the Dialog map (e.g., class Customer in Figure 15.34; an example dialog map is shown in Figure 14.3). Again, since the operation signatures and contracts have already been worked out in previous chapters, the detailed design and code for operations on the actor class should be straightforward.

One option to consider when the actor is client of both Model region and View-controller region, and the programming language supports function pointers, is to implement the Dialog map as a state–event matrix and a table-based interpreter. State-event matrix notation is discussed in Chapter 10 (specifically Table 10.3); implementing a table-based interpreted is discussed in Table 20.3 and Code Sample 20.15.

17.13   Detailed Design and Code in View-Controller Region for an API or Embedded

When the (sub)domain has a simple API, detailed design and code in View-controller region can be easy. View-controller region is simply a façade[19]

---

19 See, for example, https://en.wikipedia.org/wiki/Facade_pattern.

around Model region. The actors themselves are wrappers. In WebBooks 2.0 Payment domain, there are only four connection points:

- Create a payment (returns approved or denied).
- Modify a payment (returns approved or denied).
- Cancel a payment.
- Request a refund.

Payment domain is an example of a simple wrapper API. There is no complexity in View-controller region for that domain.

On the other hand, View-controller region for some APIs could be quite complex—particularly in the case of SOA, microservices, or REST. If View-controller region detailed design and code can be developed in a person-week or so, it probably makes sense just to invest the time in designing, coding, and testing and be done with it. If the job will be any bigger, apply recursive design: make it its own domain.

When a (sub)domain is for an embedded application that deals with input and output instrumentation, View-controller handles converting input signals in raw (i.e., device) units into engineering units for Model region and output signals in engineering units from Model region into raw units. View-controller region might also need to handle addressing instrumentation input/output channels. The same basic idea applies: if View-controller region can be designed, coded, and tested in a person-week or so, just go ahead and get it done.

On the other hand, raw-to-engineering and engineering-to-raw conversions can be quite complex. Also, input/output channel addressing can be nontrivial. If View-controller region for an embedded application can't be completed in a person-week or so, then recursive design would be appropriate: make units conversion and/or channel addressing its own Instrumentation domain.

17.14 Detailed Design and Code in Infrastructure Region

Infrastructure region may be either nonexistent or relatively trivial—maybe involving a couple of application-specific wrapped system classes like Address and WebBooksDate in Order fulfillment. Just like View-controller region, if the detailed design, coding, and testing for Infrastructure region can be done in a person-week or so, then just get it done. There are cases, however, when Infrastructure services become complex enough to warrant recursive design. Lower-level service domains, like Scalability and High availability in WebBooks 2.0, can be considered complex Infrastructure services where recursive design was applied.

17.15 Handling Method-Level Errors

The previous chapter dealt with operation-level errors: invalid invocations of one form or another. There is still an issue of errors within the method that implements an operation. Some common method-level errors and error handling strategies are discussed in this section.

Typical method-level errors include:

- *Resource is not available*[20] *when needed*—The semantic model takes a pure technology-free perspective; there are infinite resources. Operation contracts derived solely from semantic models do not address potentially scarce resources: memory,[21] disk space, file or table size limits, write-locked output file, network capacity or connectivity, etc.
- *Security violation*—A method needs access to a secure service and does not have sufficient permission.
- *Internal computational error (e.g., overflow, underflow, divide by zero, etc.)*— Most of these should already be avoided by proper operation contracts. On the other hand, not paying attention to order of operations in some computations could lead to these in spite of having appropriate contracts.
- ...

Again the questions of what to do, who to notify, and whether or not to continue apply. Use the economic decision-making process in Chapter 25 to find the most cost-effective approach. Finally, whatever error handling choices are made must be incorporated into the operation's contract if they alter semantics of the operation in a way that needs to be communicated to the client (developer).

17.16 A Few Comments on Code Comments

Useful and appropriate code comments are invaluable in communicating important information to maintenance developers. Unfortunately, too many developers are either too lazy to comment code in the first place or too lazy

---

20 "We should be careful about anything that we have to ask for before we can use it. It might not be available." (Pete Becker)

21 See Pete Becker's description of callouts for one possible approach: http://www.petebecker.com/js/js199902.html.

to keep comments up to date. The following principles separate useful from useless code comments:

- *Comments shall never contradict design or code*—If the design or code changes in a way that invalidates a comment, then that comment must be updated or deleted.
- *Comments shall always add useful information*—Comments must never simply repeat code (e.g., "i++ // add 1 to i"), but the information in the comment must not already be obvious from the code.
- *As often as practical, comments shall explain why the code looks the way it does*—One reason code cannot be self-documenting is that it can't explain way it looks the way it does. Method- or class-level explanations can often be captured in comments.

The next chapter presents a technique, Programming by intent, which helps lead to useful and appropriate method-level comments.

17.17   Wrapping Up Method-Level Design and Code

Operations in systems developed under model-based software engineering tend to be small, highly cohesive, and loosely coupled. Similarly, methods to implement those operations also tend to be small, highly cohesive, and loosely coupled. Designing and coding methods is normally not a challenge. The exception would be an operation with a simple contract but a very complex algorithm like calculating the next move in an automated chess game. In these cases, pay attention to structural complexity (as discussed in Appendix N) and the fundamental principles in driving appropriate use of private methods for the class (e.g., the extract method refactoring[22]).

17.18   Detailed Design and Code Documentation

When representation choices for attributes and associations are obvious, nothing needs said in detailed design documentation—particularly if there is a an overall statement like "Unless explicitly stated otherwise, design decisions should be assumed to have been made because they seemed reasonable at the time." The same holds for methods: given the high-level design, such as classes, operations, signatures, and contracts, most method implementation choices will be obvious and straightforward. Only in exceptional cases when

---

22 See, for example, http://refactoring.com/catalog/extractMethod.html.

Table 17.1 Quality criteria for detailed design and code.

Item	Criterion
DC-1	Every semantic model attribute has been mapped to data that accurately represents its specified range
DC-2	Every semantic model association is appropriately implemented, considering multiplicity, client-server relationship, and persistent versus memory resident
DC-3	Method-level design and code are specified for every operation in the high-level design
DC-4	Behavior of method-level code is consistent with the specified contract for each operation in the high-level design
DC-5	Each instance variable is accessed by at least one method
DC-6	Linkages to lower-level service domains are clear, correct, and consistent with that service domain's interface specification
DC-7	All detailed design and code has minimum structural complexity (cyclomatic complexity, depth of decision nesting, fan out, etc.)
DC-8	Method-level error handling is technically feasible and economically appropriate
DC-9	All relevant, non-obvious detailed design and code decisions are clearly described and justified

a non-obvious detailed design was chosen, provide a description of what was done and why it was done that way.

17.19 Quality Criteria

In addition to the overall quality criteria (Table 3.1) and naming criteria (Table 3.2), the quality criteria in Table 17.1 can be applied to all detailed design and code-related work to identify and remove defects as quickly and as cheaply as possible.

17.20 Summary

This chapter substantiates the claim of "literally self-coding documentation." Ignoring optimization for now,

- *The semantic model precisely specifies policies that need to be enforced and processes that need to be carried out*—Model region code needs to enforce exactly those policies and carry out exactly those processes (i.e., preserve those semantics), but there isn't much room for Model region code to be very different than it is.

- *The Interface specification defines the form for all of the external interfaces*— View-controller region code must implement exactly those interfaces, but there isn't much room for View-controller region code to be very different than it is.

By the time development gets this far, the structure of the code has pretty much been predetermined. Because the specifications looks like P, then the code pretty much has to look like Q; not many alternatives are possible.

Topics presented in this chapter include:

- Implementing attributes in Model region
- Implementing associations in Model region
- Data access object pattern
- Implementing derived attributes in Model region
- Completing operation signatures: parameter and return types
- Designing and implementing methods in Model region
- Designing and implementing dynamic classification
- Connecting domains
- Detailed design and code in View-controller region for a UI
- Detailed design and code in View-controller region for an API or Embedded
- Detailed design and code in Infrastructure region
- Handling method-level errors
- Some comments on comments
- Wrapping up method-level design and code
- Detailed design and code documentation
- Quality criteria

18

Formal Disciplines of Design and Code

Engineering uses science, mathematics, and practice to generate technically viable solutions to a real-world problem, together with engineering economy to select the most cost-effective solution. This chapter presents a disciplined, formal science and mathematics of method (i.e., member function) level design and code, addressing:

- Programming by intent
- Assertions
- Software proofs of correctness
- Intend-act-prove-assert format

These disciplines increase the probability that candidate solutions—detailed design and code for a method—really solve that problem completely and correctly.

18.1   Programming by Intent

Code exists to fulfill some intent. Unfortunately, code can only tell you what it does, not what it is intended to do. Deriving intent from code can be difficult, if not impossible. Programming by intent[1] makes intent explicit. Programming by intent is not necessary or even appropriate for every method; simple methods are straightforward enough that this may not add value. On the other hand, nontrivial methods benefit greatly.

Figure 18.1 is a flowchart for programming by intent. Numbers in hexagons refer to descriptions of important aspects of the process. An example of applying the process is presented below. The starting point is an operation interface—the syntax (signature) and semantics (contract)—for a method to be designed and coded. The intent of the method is to turn contract requires conditions (preconditions) into guarantees conditions (postconditions). Class

---

1 Programming by intent is a refinement of the Pseudocode Programming Process in [McConnell04] and is only loosely related to Simonyi's Intentional Programming [Simonyi95].

How to Engineer Software: A Model-Based Approach, First Edition. Steve Tockey.
© 2019 the IEEE Computer Society, Inc. Published 2019 by John Wiley & Sons, Inc.

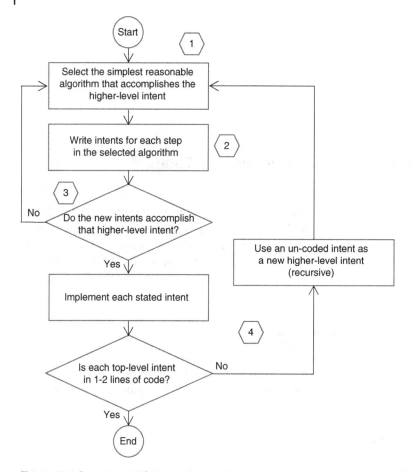

Figure 18.1 Programming by intent process.

invariants are implicitly included in the contract. Class invariants may be temporarily violated inside a method, but they are given to be true when the operation is called and must be true again by the time the method (or, in some cases, transaction) completes.

1) *Select the simplest reasonable algorithm that accomplishes the higher-level intent*—Programming by intent is a recursive process: given some higher-level intent, how can it be satisfied in terms of lower-level intents? Don't worry about optimization yet, that's covered in the next chapter. For now, just satisfy the higher-level intent as simply as practical

2) *Write intents for each step of the selected algorithm*—Capture this lower level of intent as comments, indented from the higher-level intent. All new steps should be at the same level of abstraction. Decisions (if-then-else) and loops (for, do-while, etc.) are changes in level of abstraction. Just express the intent

of a decision or loop for now, not its internal logic. Lower levels will be added later, as needed.

3) *Do the stated intents accomplish that higher-level intent?*—Review the new intents to be confident they satisfy the higher intent: "If I am successful at accomplishing lower-level intents Q, R, S, and T will I have accomplished the higher-level intent, P?" If not, abandon that algorithm, and go back to step 1 to choose another algorithm

4) *Implement each stated intent*—If a stated intent can be implemented in a line of code or two, then fill in that code beneath the intent, keeping the intent as a comment. If any intent cannot be accomplished in a line or two of code, rescope the problem to be accomplishing that intent and recursively apply the programming by intent process. An alternative to elaborating the lower intent inside this method is to package it as a private function, that is, the extract method refactoring[2]

18.1.1 IRR() Example

Programming by intent will be demonstrated using an operation that calculates the internal rate of return (IRR) of a cash flow stream. The IRR of a cash flow stream is the interest rate, i, where the present worth (PW(i)) equals zero.[3] The operation interface—signature (syntax) and contract (semantics)—is shown in Code Sample 18.1.

Code Sample 18.1 The Interface, Syntax and Semantics, for Operation IRR()

```
public class CashFlowStream {

  public double IRR() {
  // requires
  //   n/a
  // guarantees
  //   if IRR is meaningful for this cash flow stream
  //     then its IRR is returned
  //     otherwise CashFlowStream.IRR_ERROR is returned
    // Programming by intent will be used to fill in the method body
  }

}
```

---

2 See, for example, http://c2.com/cgi/wiki?ExtractMethod.
3 A complete discussion of IRR can be found in chapter 8 of [Tockey05] or in any other engineering economy book. See also, https://en.wikipedia.org/wiki/Internal_rate_of_return.

18.1.2   IRR() Example: First Cycle

Start at step 1, the intent is to turn requires conditions into guarantees conditions. The simplest reasonable algorithm to accomplish that is explained on Page 118 of Return on Software.[4] This is a case of "it seemed reasonable at the time"; almost any *N*th order polynomial root solver would work. Include a comment to that effect as an implementation note; otherwise maintainers may waste valuable time trying to understand why that algorithm was chosen over some other.

Step 2 of programming by intent says write intents, at the same level of abstraction, as comments for the selected algorithm. Code Sample 18.2 shows the intents for the top-level steps of the algorithm as comments. For the rest of this example, added or modified content will be shown in *italics*.

Step 3 says review the intents. If we are able to accomplish each of those intents, then clearly we will have satisfied the intent of IRR(): we would fulfill its contract. Step 4 says fill in code below intents where possible and recursively apply the process for any nontrivial intent.

Code Sample 18.2 The Highest-Level Intent(s) for the Selected Algorithm

```
public class CashFlowStream {

   public double IRR () {
   // requires
   //   n/a
   // guarantees
   //   if IRR is meaningful for this cash flow stream
   //     then its IRR is returned
   //     otherwise CashFlowStream.IRR_ERROR is returned
   // implementation notes
   //   uses the algorithm described on page 118 of Return on Software
   //     any root solver could have been used, this was convenient
    // Only calculate IRR if this cash flow stream is well-formed
    // otherwise return an error
   }

}
```

According to the definition of IRR(), a cash flow stream is well formed only when:

---

4 See [Tockey05].

- The first nonzero cash flow instance is negative.
- There is only one sign change after that first nonzero cash flow instance.
- The PW(0%) is greater than $0.00.

These properties guarantee that the cash flow stream has exactly one IRR. When multiple roots exist, there is no rational way to decide which of them is the IRR. Assume a PW(i) operation already exists on CashFlowStream. The other two criteria are nontrivial to compute; consider writing private helper functions instead of elaborating in-line. Those functions would be examples of the extract method refactoring. The result after the first complete cycle—minus recursion for lower-level complexities—is shown in Code Sample 18.3.

Code Sample 18.3 Code Under the Highest-Level Intent(s)

```java
public class CashFlowStream {

  // status value for returning an error on IRR calculations⁵
  public static final double IRR_ERROR = -999999.99;

  public double IRR() {
  // requires
  //   n/a
  // guarantees
  //   if IRR is meaningful for this cash flow stream
  //     then its IRR is returned
  //     otherwise CashFlowStream.IRR_ERROR is returned
  // implementation notes
  //   uses the algorithm described on page 118 of Return on Software
  //     any root solver could have been used, this was convenient
    // Only calculate IRR if this cash flow stream is well-formed
    if( this.firstNonZeroCashFlowIsNegative() &&
      this.onlyOneSignChange() &&
      this.PW( 0.0 ) > 0.00 ) {
      // calculating IRR is non-trivial, recursively apply PbI here
    } else {
      // not a well-formed CFS, return an error
      return CashFlowStream.IRR_ERROR;
    }
  }

}
```

---

5 IRR can never be negative so we can use an error code in the return value as discussed in Chapter 16. The designer could have chosen to throw an exception, although they did not define the contract that way.

18.1.3 IRR() Example: Second Cycle

We are now at step 1 with a new intent: calculating the IRR of a well-formed cash flow stream. Continuing with the algorithm, the next level intents are shown as comments in Code Sample 18.4. This completes step 2 of the second cycle.

Code Sample 18.4 Second Level Intents for the Selected Algorithm

```
public class CashFlowStream {

  // status value for returning an error on IRR calculations
  public static final double IRR_ERROR = -999999.99;

  public double IRR() {
  // requires
  //  n/a
  // guarantees
  //  if IRR is meaningful for this cash flow stream
  //    then its IRR is returned
  //    otherwise CashFlowStream.IRR_ERROR is returned
  // implementation notes
  //  uses the algorithm described on page 118 of Return on Software
  //    any root solver could have been used, this was convenient
   // Only calculate IRR if this cash flow stream is well-formed
   if ( this.firstNonZeroCashFlowIsNegative() &&
     this.onlyOneSignChange() &&
     this.PW( 0.0 ) > 0.00 ) {
    // start Estimated IRR at 0%
    // start Step Amount at +10%
    // iteratively narrow Estimated IRR until PW() close to $0.00
    // done narrowing, return Estimated IRR
   } else {
    // not a well-formed CFS, return an error
    return CashFlowStream.IRR_ERROR;
   }
  }
}
```

Assuming the published algorithm is correct, no review (step 3) is needed. We are now at step 4. Some intents in Code Sample 18.4 are simple enough to accomplish in a single line of code; however one intent is complex. The current detailed design and code is shown in Code Sample 18.5.

Code Sample 18.5 Code for the Second Intents

```java
public class CashFlowStream {

  // status value for returning an error on IRR calculations
  public static final double IRR_ERROR = -999999.99;
  // how close PW() at Estimated IRR needs to be to $0.00
  private static final double MAX_DIFFERENCE = 0.01;

  public double IRR() {
  // requires
  //   n/a
  // guarantees
  //   if IRR is meaningful for this cash flow stream
  //     then its IRR is returned
  //     otherwise CashFlowStream.IRR_ERROR is returned
  // Implementation notes
  //   uses the algorithm described on page 118 of Return on Software
  //   any root solver could have been used, this was convenient
   // Only calculate IRR if this cash flow stream is well-formed
   if( this.firstNonZeroCashFlowIsNegative() &&
     this.onlyOneSignChange() &&
     this.PW( 0.0 ) > 0.00 ) {
    // start Estimated IRR at 0%
    double estimatedIRR = 0.;
    // start with Step Amount at +10%
    double stepAmount = 10.;
    // iteratively narrow Estimated IRR until PW() close to $0.00
    do {
     // refine Estimated IRR by one iteration
    } while ( Math.abs ( currentPW ) > MAX_DIFFERENCE )
    // done narrowing, return Estimated IRR
    return estimatedIRR;
   } else {
    // not a well-formed CFS, return an error
    return CashFlowStream.IRR_ERROR;
   }
  }

}
```

Code Sample 18.6 Third Level Intents for the Selected Algorithm

```
public class CashFlowStream {

  // status value for returning an error on IRR calculations
  public static final double IRR_ERROR = -999999.99;
  // how close PW() at Estimated IRR needs to be to $0.00
  private static final double MAX_DIFFERENCE = 0.01;

  public double IRR() {
  // requires
  //   n/a
  // guarantees
  //   if IRR is meaningful for this cash flow stream
  //     then its IRR is returned
  //     otherwise CashFlowStream.IRR_ERROR is returned
  // Implementation notes
  //   uses the algorithm described on page 118 of Return on Software
  //     any root solver could have been used, this was convenient
    // Only calculate IRR if this cash flow stream is well-formed
    if ( this.firstNonZeroCashFlowIsNegative() &&
       this.onlyOneSignChange() &&
       this.PW( 0.0 ) > 0.00 ) {
      // start Estimated IRR at 0%
      double estimatedIRR = 0.;
      // start with Step Amount at +10%
      double stepAmount = 10.;
      // iteratively narrow Estimated IRR until PW() close enuf $0.00
      do {
        // refine Estimated IRR by one iteration
          // save the previous PW at the old Estimated IRR
          // move the Estimated IRR by the Step Amount
          // calculate the new PW at the new Estimated IRR
          // if the new PW is farther from $0.00 than the old
          //   then cut Step Amount in half and switch direction
      } while ( Math.abs( currentPW ) > MAX_DIFFERENCE )
      // done narrowing, return Estimated IRR
      return estimatedIRR;
    } else {
      // not a well-formed CFS, return an error
      return CashFlowStream.IRR_ERROR;
    }
  }

}
```

18.1.4   IRR() Example: Third Cycle

The remaining intent is to refine the estimated IRR by one iteration. The algorithm in the book provides the detail (step 1) so steps 2 and 3 are to put the lower-level intents in as comments and review. Again assume the algorithm is correct; the result is shown in Code Sample 18.6.

Step 4 is to fill in the code. All intents are simple enough to accomplish, so we are done. Minor backtracking was needed to initialize local variable currentPW. Such minor backtracking is common.

18.1.5   IRR() Example: Final Code

The final code for IRR() should be as shown in Code Sample 18.7.

Code Sample 18.7 Final Code for IRR() Using Programming by Intent

```
public class CashFlowStream {

    // status value for returning an error on IRR calculations
    public static final double IRR_ERROR = -999999.99;
    // how close PW() at Estimated IRR needs to be to $0.00
    private static final double MAX_DIFFERENCE = 0.01;

    public double IRR() {
    // requires
    //   n/a
    // guarantees
    //   if IRR is meaningful for this cash flow stream
    //      then its IRR is returned
    //      otherwise CashFlowStream.IRR_ERROR is returned
    // Implementation notes
    //   uses the algorithm described on page 118 of Return on Software
    //      any root solver could have been used, this was convenient
    //   // initialize currentPW to PW( 0.0 )
    double currentPW = this.PW( 0.0 );
    // Only calculate IRR if this cash flow stream is well-formed
    if( this.firstNonZeroCashFlowIsNegative() &&
        this.onlyOneSignChange() &&
        currentPW > 0.00 ) {
    // start Estimated IRR at 0%
    double estimatedIRR = 0.;
    // start with Step Amount at +10%
    double stepAmount = 10.;
```

```
// iteratively narrow Estimated IRR until PW() close enuf $0.00
do {
  // refine Estimated IRR by one iteration
  // save the previous PW at the old Estimated IRR
  double lastPW = currentPW;
  // move the Estimated IRR by the Step Amount
  estimatedIRR = estimatedIRR + stepAmount;
  // calculate the new PW at the new Estimated IRR
  currentPW = this.PW( estimatedIRR );
  // if the new PW is farther from $0.00 than the old
  if ( Math.abs ( currentPW ) > Math.abs ( lastPW ) ) {
    // then cut Step Amount in half and switch direction
    stepAmount = -stepAmount / 2.0;
  }
} while ( Math.abs ( currentPW ) > MAX_DIFFERENCE )
// done narrowing, return Estimated IRR
return estimatedIRR;
} else {
// not a well-formed CFS, return an error
return CashFlowStream.IRR_ERROR;
}
}
}
```

Programming by intent may appear simplistic, but it would be deceptively so:

- The focus on intent makes creating detailed design and code much easier.
- The focus on intent makes reviewing detailed design and code much easier.
- All detailed design and code under any intent is focused on accomplishing exactly that one intent, leading to high cohesion and loose coupling at the line of code level. While not specifically applicable in IRR(), lines of code in a method can be sequenced in any order that doesn't violate the data flow dependencies of the algorithm, that is, otherwise apparently random re-sequencing of code can often still function correctly, while cohesion and coupling at the line of code level has been destroyed.
- Comments explain the code's intent; they are guaranteed to be useful comments.
- Explicit documentation of intent makes maintaining detailed design and code much easier.

18.2 Assertions

Many programming languages support assertions: run-time verification of properties expected to be true during execution. In Java's assertion syntax,[6]

```
assert expression1: expression2;
```

Expression1 is a Boolean specifying what is expected to be true at that point. Expression2 is optional in Java (i.e., "`assert expression1;`" is acceptable) and if present should be used to communicate more detail about the failed expectation. Several example Java assertions are shown in Code Sample 18.8.

Code Sample 18.8 Several Example Java Assertions

```
assert grossPay == hoursWorked * payRate;
assert grossPay == hoursWorked * payRate: "incorrect grossPay!";
assert grossPay == hoursWorked * payRate:
            grossPay + " != " + hoursWorked " * " payRate ;
assert aCustomer != null;
assert aCustomer != null: "aCustomer is null!";
assert aMedium != null: "aMedium is null!";
assert quantity > 0: "quantity is not greater than zero!";
assert quantity > 0: quantity + " is not greater than zero!";
```

As long as expression1 evaluates to true, that condition holds and execution continues. When expression1 evaluates to false, execution stops with an AssertionError exception. The result of expression2, if present, is passed to AssertionError's constructor, making it available for inspection in the exception object.

18.2.1 Assertions != Error Handling

Assertions are often confused with error handling but are fundamentally different. Error handling is for situations that are undesirable but in some sense expected. A user entering an invalid user name and password combination in a security domain is undesirable but expected. Clearly it needs to be handled. A Customer inadvertently selecting a quantity of zero when they want to add a Medium to a Book order would also be undesirable but expected in a system like WebBooks 2.0. If View-controller region doesn't already prevent or handle

---

6 See, for example, http://docs.oracle.com/javase/7/docs/technotes/guides/language/assert.html.

it, Model region will need to handle it because some customer will surely make that mistake at some point.

Assertions, on the other hand, are executable verification of design correctness properties, including—but not exclusively—contracts. When an assertion fails, it is not a run-time error; it is run-time recognition of design or code incorrectness. Never catch AssertionError exceptions; the only way to address an assertion failing is to modify code to correct the problem. Similarly, Expression2 is expected to never be seen outside the development or test team, so it doesn't need to be end user friendly.

18.2.2 Assertions and Design by Contract

In theory, each condition in the requires clause of an operation's contract can be asserted just after method entry (i.e., immediately after the opening curly brace, "{"). Each condition in the guarantees clause can be asserted just before the method exits (i.e., immediately before any explicit or implicit return like the final curly brace, "}"). Code Sample 18.9 shows the signature and contract for an operation that computes the square root of an input parameter, along with assertions consistent with that contract.

Code Sample 18.9 Example Operation Contract, with Consistent Assertions

```
public double squareRoot ( double inputValue ) {
// requires
//   inputValue >= 0.0
// guarantees
//   abs( inputValue - (squareRoot * squareRoot) ) <= someDelta
//      i.e., squareRoot squared is sufficiently close to inputValue
  assert inputValue >= 0.0: "Negative input to squareRoot () ";
  ... // code to calculate the square root goes here
  assert abs( inputValue - (squareRoot * squareRoot) ) <= someDelta:
                                "Error calculating squareRoot";
  return squareRoot;
}
```

18.2.3 Assertions and Class Invariants

In object-oriented systems, class invariants can be asserted as well. Class invariants are assumed to be true when an operation is invoked.[7] Specifically, the opening assertion(s) in any (non-constructor) method can be the union of class

---

7 Subject to the limitation on multiplicity constraints in the middle of a transaction in Chapter 16.

invariants and operation requires conditions. For a constructor, the object didn't exist at the point of invocation, so no class invariants could possibly be true for the object being constructed—the only valid assertion elements would be contract requires conditions.

Class invariants must also be true when the operation completes. Specifically, closing assertion(s) in any (non-destructor) method can be the union of class invariants and operation guarantees conditions. A read-only operation (a getter or derived attribute method) should not affect the state of the object, so it should not affect class invariants. In reality, however, a coding error could unintentionally alter state and violate a class invariant. Asserting class invariants on the way out of a read-only method can still be useful because it would help identify where the developer made a subtle mistake in method code.

18.2.4 Assertions and Fault Isolation

Assertions are extremely useful for fault isolation. If an entry assertion (e.g., "Negative input to squareRoot()") fires, then it is the client's problem—they are not honoring the contract (or the contract and the assertions have gotten out of synch). Client design and code need to be corrected to repair the violation. If a class invariant assertion fires on entry, code prior to calling this operation behaved incorrectly.

If an exit assertion (e.g., "Error calculating squareRoot") fires, the problem is inside this method: it was given appropriate input but failed to achieve what was expected. The same can be said about a class invariant assertion firing on exit: the method violated a constraint and needs to be repaired.

18.2.5 Assertions Are Not Always Useful

Assertions can't always be used because some correctness properties are not computable in reasonable time or not even computable at all (e.g., $\mathcal{NP}$-complete[8]). Consider a function to balance a binary tree.[9] An exit assertion that the method properly balanced the input tree would be at least as expensive as the work done by the method. So while it is beneficial to have assertions for conditions that can be computed economically, don't expect assertions can be created for every condition.

Assertions can also be trivial. Code Sample 18.10 shows a trivial assertion that could, and almost certainly should, be omitted.

---

8 See, for example, https://en.wikipedia.org/wiki/NP-complete.
9 See, for example, https://en.wikipedia.org/wiki/Binary_tree.

Code Sample 18.10 A Trivial Assertion That Should Be Omitted

```
...
// start the Item count at 0
itemCount = 0;
assert itemCount = 0: "itemCount is not zero";
...
```

An assertion immediately after an explicit return statement would never be executed and should also be omitted.

18.2.6 Assertions and Performance

A disadvantage of assertions is that they can affect execution speed and memory use even when not computationally complex. To compensate, most languages that support assertions also support turning them on and off—either as a compile or run-time option. When assertions are enabled, they behave as if-then-else statements: "if (!expression1), then throw new AssertionError(expression2), otherwise continue executing." When assertions are disabled, they are treated as comments or NOPs,[10] often with little or no effect on either execution speed or memory use.

Generally, assertions should be enabled in development and test environments. After sufficient testing there should be enough confidence that design and code are correct so assertions can be disabled for production. Disabling assertions in production won't adversely affect performance. If failure does occur in production, try to re-create that failure with assertions enabled in the test environment.

Performance testing must be done with production-equivalent code, that is, assertions disabled if they are disabled in production. On the other hand, full performance testing should be deferred until functional tests are essentially complete.

18.2.7 An Assertion Mistake

A common but dangerous mistake is putting functionality with necessary side effects into an assertion expression: the assertion expression does work the rest of the method needs for correct behavior. Code Sample 18.11 shows an example of incorrectly depending on side effects of an assertion expression.

---

10 NOP == "No operation," that is, do nothing.

Code Sample 18.11 Code That Depends on Assertion Expression Side Effects

```
public class SomeClass {

 public void someOperation( ) {
 // requires
 //  A
 // guarantees
 //  Z
  assert A;
  ...
  assert b.allocateResource( c ); // this assertion is dangerous!
  ...
  assert Z;
 }

}
```

When assertions are disabled, the entire assertion statement is ignored. This method would execute correctly when assertions are enabled but could fail when assertions are disabled because the resource would not be allocated:

> *"Assertion expressions must be free of necessary side effects. Method behavior must be identical with assertions enabled or disabled"*

More precisely, method behavior with assertions disabled must be Liskov substitutable with method behavior when assertions are enabled: it can require no more and guarantee no less.

Code Sample 18.12 shows how to handle assertions when expression side effects are necessary.

Code Sample 18.12 Code That Does Not Depend on Assertion Expression Side Effects

```
public class SomeClass {

 public void someOperation( ) {
 // requires
 //  A
 // guarantees
 //  Z
  assert A;
  ...
  boolean success = b.allocateResource( c );
```

```
    assert success; // this assertion is not dangerous
    ...
    assert Z ;
  }

}
```

Kudrjavets et al.[11] report a strong correlation between use of assertions and a significant reduction in post-release defects. In two different releases of two different code bases each having nonuniform distribution of assertions, regions of code with more assertions had statistically fewer post-release defects. Also, assertions revealed defects that testing was unable to reveal. It is unlikely that the presence of assertions alone caused this difference. A more likely explanation is that proper use of assertions requires thinking about code at a detailed semantic level. Developers who can use assertions properly are probably more capable and are thus more likely to write correct code.

18.3 Software Proof of Correctness: Revealing the True, Formal Nature of Code

Most developers simply don't understand how immensely formal and logical code is—or, said more appropriately—needs to be. By approaching code from the perspective of proving it correct, the true, formal, logical nature of code is revealed. As Edsger Dijkstra said,[12]

> "One should not first make the program and then prove its correctness, ... On the contrary: the programmer should let correctness proof and program grow hand in hand."

18.3.1 Proofs of Correctness Versus Testing

Testing demonstrates proper behavior *only for the specific test cases that were passed*. The following quote by Cem Kaner is appropriate[13]:

---

11 See [Kudrjavets13].
12 See [Dijkstra72].
13 See [Kaner93].

> *"If you think you can fully test a program without testing its response to every possible input, fine. Give us your test cases. We can write a program that will pass all of your tests but still fail spectacularly on an input you missed. If we can do this deliberately, our contention is that we or other programmers could do it accidentally."*

Code written without contracts and attention to simplicity and provability would naturally be susceptible to semantic inconsistencies: defects. Exhaustive testing of even simple code like the four-function calculator in Chapter 12 is impossible. When scaled up to typical applications, it is insane to think that testing could ever be anywhere close to comprehensive:

> *"Depending on testing alone to reveal software defects—to demonstrate code correctness—is a hopelessly lost cause."*

By proving code correct, there is less dependence on testing. Proven code *cannot give anything other than the right answer*. Testing actually becomes a way of validating the proof: if properly selected test cases pass (e.g., test cases achieve decision coverage[14]), then it is highly likely that the proof is correct, so you can be confident the code is correct for *all* cases, not just the cases that were tested.

Finally, optimization, in the next chapter, needs to start with design and code that are known to be correct. It makes no sense to optimize defective code. Simply

> *"Optimizing wrong code still gives you wrong code, you are merely getting the wrong answer faster or using fewer other critical resources."*

18.3.2 Introducing Software Proofs of Correctness

A proof is[15]:

> *"Establishing the validity of a statement esp. by derivation from other statements in accordance with the principles of reasoning."*

A software proof of correctness establishes validity of code. It demonstrates that method code implements a contract completely, correctly, and without unintended side effects.

Any section of code that terminates (e.g., a method) can be thought of as a mathematical rule for a function that converts an initial state into a final state. It doesn't matter if that function is actually "mathematical" or not:

---

14 See, for example, https://en.wikipedia.org/wiki/Code_coverage.
15 See [Websters86].

- *Matrix inversion program*—Transform an input matrix into an inverted output matrix
- *Payroll program*—Transform input payroll data into employee paychecks

The function defined by any such code is a set of ordered pairs—starting states Si and ending states Ei:

$$(S1, E1), (S2, E2), ..., (Sn, En)$$

The structured theorem, derived from Böhm and Jacopini,[16] states:

> *"There exists a structured program for any problem that permits a flow chart-able solution. Structured programs define a natural hierarchy among parts, which are repeatedly nested into larger and larger parts, by sequence, selection, and iteration."*

Each part is a sub-hierarchy that can be executed independently of its surroundings. Any such part can be described by a specification that has no control properties, only the effect it has on the program's state:

{ precondition } function { postcondition }

Or in plain English

> *"If precondition is true before the function is executed, then postcondition will be true after."*

18.3.3 Propositions

A proposition is[17]:

> *"An expression in language or signs of something that can be believed, doubted, or denied or is either true or false."*

Software proofs of correctness involve inserting propositions, as comments, around every executable line of code. Those propositions are statements about the state of execution expected to be true at that point. Propositions:

- *Are usually named*—for example, P: ..., Q: ..., R: ..., S: ....
- *May be stated in terms of other propositions*—for example, X: Y and Z.
- *May be implicit*—Many propositions may be true at a given point in a proof, but usually only propositions pertinent to that point are stated explicitly.

---

16 See [Boehm66].
17 Also [Websters86].

Code should be written so that every line can be verified only by reference to lines already written and not to lines not yet written. Each proposition must be consistent with prior propositions and executable statements, based on propositional calculus[18] and the semantics of the programming language. The proof of a method starts with the operation's requires clause and class invariants. The proof is expected to end with operation's guarantees clause[19] and class invariants.

18.3.4 A Small Example Proof

Code Sample 18.13 shows an example proof of correctness for BookOrderLine. packed(). Proof propositions are embedded as comments and highlighted in **underlined bold**.

Code Sample 18.13 A Simple Proof of Correctness

```
public class BookOrderLine {

  private int quantity;
  private float pricePerCopy;
  private Medium isFor;
  private BOLState state;

  public void packed() {
  // requires
  //   .state == Placed
  // guarantees
  //   if linked to Print medium
  //     then picked( .qty ) has been signaled for it
  //   .state == Completed
    // { P0: class invariants and .state == PLACED }
    if( for instanceof PrintMedium ) {
      // { P1: P0 and linked media type == PrintMedium }
      isFor.picked( quantity );
      // { P2: P1 and picked( quantity ) has been signaled }
    }
    // { P3: P0 and if linked to PrintMedium
    //          then picked( quantity ) has been signaled }
    state == BOL_State.COMPLETED;
    // { P4: class invariants and
    //       if linked to PrintMedium
```

---

18 See, for example, https://en.wikipedia.org/wiki/Propositional_calculus.
19 Or, more correctly, something that is at least Liskov substitutable.

```
//      then picked ( quantity ) has been signaled
//      and . state == COMPLETED }
}

}
```

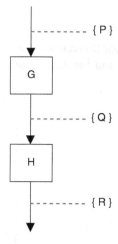

Figure 18.2 Proofs involving sequence, graphically.

Software proofs of correctness are presented in terms of the kinds of code constructs to be proven: sequence, invocation, selection, and iteration.

18.4 Proofs Involving Sequence

In this context, sequence means a series of lines without decision logic, that is, straight-line execution. The proof rule for sequences is

$$\frac{(\{P\}G\{Q\},\{Q\}H\{R\})}{(\{P\}GH\{R\})}$$

or, semiformally,

"If executing G when P gives Q and executing H when Q gives R then executing G followed by H when P gives R."

Figure 18.2 shows this graphically.

Code Sample 18.14 shows how the proof sequence in Figure 18.2 would look in code.

Code Sample 18.14 Proof for Sequence in Code

```
public class SomeClass {

 public void someOperation () {
  ...
  // { P: ... }
  G;
  // { Q: ... }
  H;
  // { R: ... }
  ...
 }

}
```

As a concrete example, Code Sample 18.15 shows the proof sequence for ReplenishOrderLine's constructor.

Code Sample 18.15 Proof for Sequence Using ReplenishOrderLine Constructor

```
public class ReplenishOrderLine {

  private int quantity;
  private PrintMedium restocks;
  private ROL_State state;

  public ReplenishOrderLine( PrintMedium aPrintMedium, int aQuantity
) {
    // requires
    //   aPrintMedium is not null
    //   aQuantity is consistent with range of .quantity
    // guarantees
    //   a new ReplenishOrderLine exists with:
    //     .quantity == aQuantity
    //     this line linked to its PrintMedium
    //     .state == Open
    // { P0: aPrintMedium not null, aQuantity in range,
    //       and a new ReplenishOrderLine exists }
    quantity = aQuantity;
    // { P1: P0 and .quantity == aQuantity }
    restocks = aMedium;
    // { P2: P1 and this line linked to its PrintMedium }
    state = ROL_State.OPEN;
    // { P3: P2 and .state == Open }
  }

}
```

18.5 Proofs Involving Invocation

When a line of code to be proven is—or contains—an operation invocation (i.e., a function call, a message), elements of the proof proposition preceding that line need to be mapped into the requires clause of the called operation's contract. The guarantees clause of the called operation's contract drives the proof proposition following the line of code being proven. Figure 18.3 shows this graphically for a line of client code that needs a square root calculated and a server operation that calculates square roots.

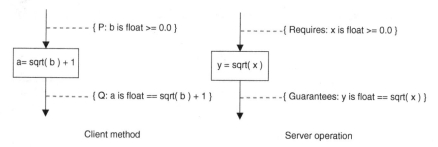

Figure 18.3 Proofs involving invocation, graphically.

The proof requires several steps:

1) *Relevant elements of the preceding proof proposition (P) are mapped onto actual parameters of the client-side call*—"b is float >= 0.0" is mapped onto the b parameter of the sqrt() call on the client side.
2) *Actual parameters on the client side are mapped onto formal parameters of the server operation*—Actual parameter b where "b is float >= 0" is mapped on to formal parameter x; therefore "x is float >= 0.0."
3) *Formal parameters on the server operation are mapped onto contract requires clause elements of the server operation*—Because "x is float >= 0.0," the requires side of the contract on the server operation is satisfied.
4) *The guarantees clause of the server operation is mapped back to the client side*—"y is float == sqrt(x)" is mapped as the function result on the client side, so the result of the call is "sqrt() result is float == sqrt(x)." Given that x == b, the result of the call is "sqrt() result is float == sqrt(b)."
5) *The remainder of the client-side expression is evaluated*—The value on the right side of the assignment in the line of code to be proven has to be "result is float == sqrt(b) + 1." This is assigned to variable a; therefore proposition Q must be "a is float == sqrt(b) + 1."

A second concrete example illustrates how side effects in the server operation affect the proof. Assume the server operation is Stack.push() as shown in Code Sample 18.16.

Code Sample 18.16 Contract for Function Being Invoked

```
public class Stack {

    ...

    public int push( double value ) {
    // requires
    //   none (the stack is initialized in its constructor)
```

```
// guarantees
//   value has been added to the top of the stack
//   returns size of (i.e., number of elements in) the stack
  ...
}

}
```

Assume Code Sample 18.17 needs to be proven, specifically the italicized line of code—we need to derive proof proposition R.

Code Sample 18.17 Proof for Invocation in Code

```
public class SomeClass {

  private Stack s;

  public void someOperation ( ) {
  // requires
  //   s has been initialized
    ...
    // { P: s is a stack of 0 .. n doubles }
    double d = 100.0;
    // { Q: s is a stack of 0 .. n doubles, d is double == 100.0 }
    int size = s.push( d ); // need to prove this line of code
    // { R: we need to derive this proposition }
    ...
  }

}
```

To derive proof proposition R,

1) *Relevant elements of the preceding proof proposition, Q, are mapped onto actual parameters of the client-side call*—Proposition element "s is stack of 0 .. n doubles" is mapped onto s in "s.push()"; proposition element "d is double == 100.0" is mapped onto actual parameter d in the call.
2) *Actual parameters on the client side are mapped onto formal parameters of the server operation*—"s is stack of 0 .. n doubles" is mapped onto the Stack being push()-ed onto; "d is double == 100.0" is mapped onto formal parameter value, so logically, "value is double == 100.0."

3) *Formal parameters on the server operation are mapped onto contract requires clause elements of the server operation*—Push doesn't require anything; however class invariants are assumed. So, logically, the first proposition in the push() method would be "P: all class invariants of Stack, and value is double == 100.0."

4) *The guarantees clause of the server operation is mapped back to the client side*—"Value has been added to the top of stack" and "returns size of (number of elements in) the stack" are mapped onto (i.e., they drive) an intermediate client-side proposition "s is a stack of 1 .. n+1 doubles and number of elements in s was returned/"

5) *The remainder of the client-side expression is evaluated*—The return value is assigned to variable size; therefore "size is int == number of elements in s." The side effect is "s is stack of 1 .. n+1 doubles."

The proof proposition R that follows the invocation must therefore be as shown in *italics* in Code Sample 18.18.

Code Sample 18.18 Example Proof for Invocation in Code

```
public class SomeClass {

  private Stack s;

  public void someOperation( ) {
  // requires
  //   s has been initialized
    ...
  // { P: s is a stack of 0 .. n doubles }
  double d = 100.0;
  // { Q: s is stack of 0 .. n doubles, d is double == 100.0 }
  int size = s.push( d );
  // { R: s is a stack of 1 .. n+1 doubles, d is double == 100.0,
  //     size is int == number of items in stack s }
    ...
  }

}
```

18.6 Proofs Involving Selection

In this context, selection refers to a non-looping decision like if-then-else. Switch-case and try-catch-finally are special cases and are treated separately below. The proof rule for selection is

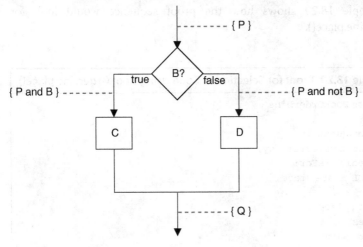

Figure 18.4 Proof involving selection, graphically.

$$\frac{(\{P \, and \, B\} \, C \, \{Q\}, \{P \, and \, not \, B\} \, D \, \{Q\})}{(\{P\} \, if \, B \, then \, C \, else \, D \, \{Q\})}$$

Figure 18.4 shows this graphically.

Code Sample 18.19 shows how the proof sequence in Figure 18.4 would look in code.

Code Sample 18.19 Proof for Selection in Code

```
public class SomeClass {

 public void someOperation() {
  // { P }
  if( B ) {
   // { P and B }
   C
   // { Q }
  } else {
   // { P and not B }
   D
   // { Q }
  }
  // { Q }
  ...
 }

}
```

Code Sample 18.20 shows how the proof sequence would look for BookOrderLine.place().

Code Sample 18.20 Proof for Selection in Code Using BookOrderLine.place()

```
public class BookOrderLine {

  private int quantity;
  private float pricePerCopy;
  private Medium isFor;
  private BOL_State state;

  public void place () {
  // requires
  //   .state == Open
  // guarantees
  //   if linked Medium is EBookMedium
  //     then .state == Completed
  //     otherwise .state == Placed
   // { P0: class invariants and .state == Open }
   if ( isFor instanceof EBookMedium )
     // { P1: P0 and linked medium is EBookMedium }
     state = BOL_State.COMPLETED;
     // { P2: P1 and .state == Completed }
   } elseif {
     // { P3: P0 and linked medium is not EBookMedium }
     state = BOL_State.PLACED;
     // { P4: P3 and .state == Placed }
   }
   // { P5: class invariants and
   //      if linked Medium is EBookMedium
   //        then .state == Completed
   //        otherwise .state == Placed }
  }

}
```

18.6.1 Proofs Involving Switch-Case

Proofs involving switch-case statements are one special case of proofs involving selection. This is shown graphically in Figure 18.5.

Code Sample 18.21 shows how the switch-case proof in Figure 18.5 would look in code.

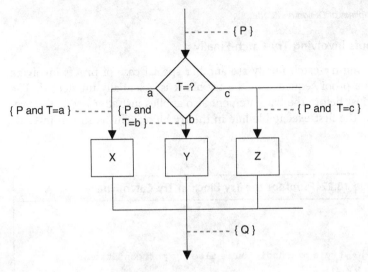

Figure 18.5 Proof for switch-case.

Code Sample 18.21 Proof for Switch-Case in Code

```java
public class SomeClass {

  public void someOperation() {
    ...
    // { P }
    switch( T ) {
     case a:
       // { P and a }
       X;
       // { Q }
       break;
     case b:
       // { P and b }
       Y;
       // { Q }
       break;
     case c:
       // { P and c }
       Z;
       // { Q }
       break;
    }
    // { Q }
    ...
  }

}
```

18.6.2 Proofs Involving Try-Catch-Finally

Proofs involving try-catch-finally are another special case of proofs involving selection. The proof sequence in the try block is essentially unaffected. The proposition just before the try statement also applies just after and is the precondition for the first executable line in the try block. This is shown in Code Sample 18.22.

Code Sample 18.22 Proof for the Try Block in Try-Catch-Finally

```
 . . .
// { P }
try {
   // { P } ← try's precondition is also its postcondition
   int x = y / z;
   // { Q: P and x is int == y / z }
   int a = b / c;
   // { R: Q and a is int == b / c }
    . . .
}
```

One important aspect of proofs involving try-catch-finally is the proof within the catch block. When code in the try block doesn't call any lower-level operations and there is only one line where a particular exception could be thrown, the postcondition assertion of the catch statement can easily be determined: it will be the precondition of the line that caused the exception to be thrown. This is shown in Code Sample 18.23.

Code Sample 18.23 Proof for a Catch Block in Try-Catch-Finally

```
   . . .
// { P }
try {
   // { P }
   int x = y / z;
   // { Q: P and x is int == y / z }
    . . .
} catch ( ArithmeticException e ) {
   // { P } ← P must still be true here
   System.out.println( "Divide by zero in ..." );
    . . .
}
```

The complication is when more than one line of code can throw that same exception, either as separate lines in the try block or embedded in operations called from the try block. The same exception thrown by multiple lines is shown in Code Sample 18.24.

Code Sample 18.24 Another Proof for a Catch Block in Try-Catch-Finally

```
. . .
// { P }
try {
  // { P }
  int x = y / z;
  // { Q: P and x is int == y / z }
  int a = b / c;
  // { R: Q and a is int == b / c }
  . .
} catch ( ArithmeticException e ) {
  // { S: P or Q } ← Which division caused it: z or c?
  System.out.println( "Divide by zero in ..." );
  . . .
}
. . .
```

The other important aspect of proofs involving try-catch-finally is the optional finally block. When present, this block is executed regardless of success or failure of the try block. The postcondition for the finally statement has to be the last postcondition of the try block union-ed with the postcondition of each catch block, as shown in Code Sample 18.25.

Code Sample 18.25 Proof for the Finally Block in Try-Catch-Finally

```
. . .
// { A }
try {
  // { A }
  X;  // assume X could throw Exception1
  // { B }
  Y;  // assume Y could throw Exception2
  // { C }
} catch ( Exception1 e1 ) {
  // { A )
  System.out.println( "Exception1 in ..." );
```

```
    . . .
    // { D }
  } catch ( Exception2 e2 ) {
    // { B }
    System.out.println( "Exception2 in ..." );
    . . .
    // { E }
  } finally {
    // { C or D or E ) ← one of C, D, or E must be true here
    . . .
  }
  . . .
```

The following quote from Damian Katz is very insightful, particularly regarding exceptions[20]:

> *"The much bigger problem in software reliability is not how we communicate errors, it's the state we are in after the error happens."*

18.7   Proofs Involving Iteration

In this context, iteration means code that loops: for-next, repeat-until, do-while, etc. The proof rule for iteration is

$$\frac{(\{P\}G\{Q\},\{Q \text{ and } B\}H\{Q\})}{(\{P\}G; \text{while } B \text{ do } H\{Q \text{ and not } B\})}$$

Figure 18.6 shows this graphically.

The elements of the loop and its proof are:

- G is loop initialization.
- H is the loop body.
- Q is the loop invariant.
- B is the loop (termination) condition.

18.7.1   Loop Invariant

Loop invariants are probably the most difficult part of software proofs of correctness. Think of them as conditions that must be true at the beginning and end of each pass through the loop. A hint for finding a loop invariant is to look

---

20 See http://damienkatz.net/2006/04/error_code_vs_e.html.

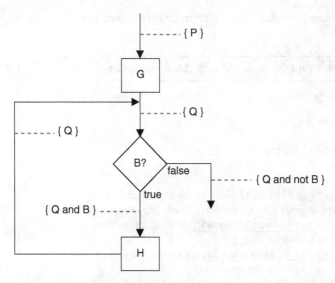

Figure 18.6 Proof involving iteration.

at that loop's postcondition; the loop invariant will be similar. The difference will be that the loop's postcondition will have all of the loop's work done, while the loop invariant expresses some of the loop's work having been done and some still remaining. As an example, imagine a loop's postcondition is

```
// { R: have calculated umptyfratz for all n items }
```

The loop invariant should be something like

```
// { Q: have calculated umptyfratz for k items, where 0<=k<=n }
```

The items from 0 to k have been calculated; the items from k + 1 to n have not. The loop termination condition, not B, should be k == n.

18.7.2 Loop Body

The loop body, H, has two distinct jobs although not necessarily in this order:

- Modify the loop variable that drives the loop condition, B, causing the loop to eventually terminate. Modifying the loop variable will temporarily invalidate the loop invariant, Q.
- Do the work necessary to reestablish Q based on the modified loop variable.

Proof involving iteration uses proof by induction.[21] Code Sample 18.26 shows how the proof sequence in Figure 18.6 would look in terms of Java's

---

21 See, for example, https://en.wikipedia.org/wiki/Mathematical_induction.

built-in iterator for class ArrayList. Proof statements are shown as comments in **underlined bold**.

Code Sample 18.26 Proof for Iteration with Java's ArrayList

```
public class SomeClient {
  ...
  private ArrayList<ItemType> itemCollection;
  ...
  public void dealWithSomeItemCollection() {
    ...
    // { P: … }
    // the following line of code is loop initialization, G
    Iterator<itemType> myIterator = itemCollection.iterator();
    // { Q: 0.. n items have been processed } ← loop invariant, Q
    while ( myIterator.hasNext() ) {
      // { R: Q and there is at least one unprocessed item (i.e., B) }
      ItemType thisItem = myIterator.next();
      // { S: R and thisItem is the next item in collection }
      ... // process thisItem as appropriate. This is the loop body, H
      // { T: Q and thisItem has been processed }
    }
    // { U: Q and all items have been processed (i.e., not B) }
    ...
  }
}
```

Code Sample 18.27 shows how the proof sequence could look for BookOrder. packed(). Proof statements are shown as comments in **underlined bold**.

Code Sample 18.27 Proof for Iteration in Code

```
public class BookOrder {

  private String id;
  private BO_State state;
  private ArrayList<BookOrderLine> isFor;

  public void packed() {
  // requires
  //   .status == placed
  // guarantees
  //   if this.isPackable()
  //     then packed has been signaled for each line
```

```
//      and status == packed
//   otherwise nothing
 // { P0: class invariants and .status == PLACED }
 if ( this.isPackable() ) {
   // { P1: P0 and this Book order is packable }
   // the following line is loop initialization, G
   Iterator<BookOrderLine> boLine = isFor.iterator();
   // { P2: P1 and boLine is new iterator over order lines }
   // { Q: P1 and 0..n lines were signaled } ← loop invariant
   while ( boLine.hasNext() ) {
     // { P3: Q and there are more lines to signal (i.e., B) }
     BookOrderLine thisLine = boLine.next();
     // { P4: P1 and thisLine is next line in collection }
     thisLine.packed(); // ← this is H
     // { P5: Q and .packed() has been signaled for thisLine }
   }
   // { P6: Q and all lines have been signaled (i.e., not B) }
   status = BO_State.PACKED;
   // { P7: P6 and status == packed }
 } else {
   // { P8: P0 and this order is not packable }
   // nothing
 }
 // { P9: if this.isPackable()
 //      then packed has been signaled for each line
 //           and status == packed
 //      otherwise nothing }
}

}
```

18.7.3   Proofs of for() Loops

In practice, developers don't only write while() loops. There are more direct ways of writing loops; the most common is the for() loop. The proof of a for() loop is simply a special case. Figure 18.7 shows this graphically.

Code Sample 18.28 shows how the proof sequence in Figure 18.7 would look in code.

18.8   A Complete Proof of Correctness

Code Sample 18.29 is the complete proof of correctness for CashFlowStream. IRR(). Proof statements are shown as comments in **<u>underlined bold</u>**.

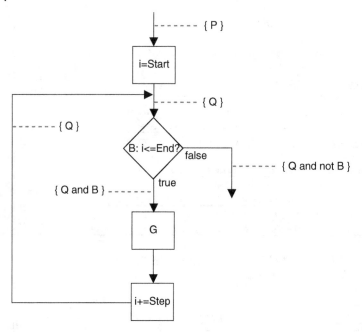

Figure 18.7 Proof of a for() loop, graphically.

Code Sample 18.28 Proof of a for() Loop in Code

```
public class SomeClass {

  public void someOperation() {
    ...
    // { P }
    for( int index = startValue, i <= endValue, i += stepValue ) {
    // { Q and index <= endValue }
      G;
      // { implicit "index += stepValue" happens here }
    }
    // { Q and index > endValue }
    ...
  }

}
```

Code Sample 18.29 Proof of Correctness for CashFlowStream.IRR()

```
public class CashFlowStream {

  // status value for returning an error on IRR calculations
  public static final double IRR_ERROR = -999999.99;
  // how close PW() at Estimated IRR needs to be to $0.00
  private static final double MAX_DIFFERENCE = 0.01;

  public double IRR() {
  // requires
  //   n/a
  // guarantees
  //   if IRR is meaningful for this cash flow stream
  //     then its IRR is returned
  //     otherwise CashFlowStream.IRR_ERROR is returned
  // Implementation notes
  //   uses the algorithm described on page 118 of Return on Software
  //     any root solver could have been used, this was convenient
    // { P0: Class invariants for CashFlowStream }
    // initialize currentPW to PW( 0.0 )
    double currentPW = this.PW( 0.0 );
    // { P1: P0 and currentPW is double == PW( 0.0 ) of this CFS }
    // Only calculate IRR if this cash flow stream is well-formed
    if( this.firstNonZeroCashFlowIsNegative() &&
      this.onlyOneSignChange() &&
      this.PW( 0.0 ) > 0.00 ) {
      // { P2: P1 and computing IRR is meaningful }
      // start Estimated IRR at 0%
      double estimatedIRR = 0.;
      // { P3: P2 and EstimatedIRR is double == 0. }
      // start with Step Amount at +10%
      double stepAmount = 10.;
      // { P4: P3 and stepAmount is double = 10. }
      // iteratively narrow Estimated IRR until PW() close to $0.00
      do {
        // { P5 (Loop Invariant): P0 and
        //   estimatedIRR is double >= 0. converging on actual IRR
        //   abs( stepAmount ) is double <= 10. }
        // refine Estimated IRR by one iteration
        // save the previous PW at the old Estimated IRR
        double lastPW = currentPW;
        // { P6: P5 and lastPW is double == currentPW }
        // move the Estimated IRR by the Step Amount
        estimatedIRR = estimatedIRR + stepAmount;
        // { P7: P6 and estimatedIRR has moved in
```

```
//        the direction & size of stepAmount }
// calculate the new PW at the new Estimated IRR
currentPW = this.PW( estimatedIRR );
// { P8: P7 and currentPW is double == PW at estimatedIRR }
// if new estimatedPW is farther from $0.00 than old
if( Math.abs( currentPW ) > Math.abs( lastPW ) ) {
  // then cut Step Amount in half and switch direction
  // { P9: P8 and estimatedIRR is farther from $0.00 }
  stepAmount = -stepAmount / 2.0;
  // { P10: P9 and stepAmount is reversed and halved }
}
// { P5 (Loop Invariant) : P0 and
//   estimatedIRR is double >= 0. converging on actual IRR
//   abs( stepAmount ) is double <= 10. }
} while( Math.abs( currentPW ) > MAX_DIFFERENCE )
// { P11: P5 and currentPW is within MAX_DIFFERENCE of $0.00
//          (not B, the loop termination condition) }
// done narrowing, return Estimated IRR
return estimatedIRR;
// { P12: P0 and well formed CashFlowStream and
//                 estimatedIRR was returned }
} else {
// { P13: P0 and not well formed CashFlowStream }
// not a well-formed CFS, return an error
return CashFlowStream.IRR_ERROR;
// { P14: P0 and not well formed CashFlowStream and
//          CashFlowStream.IRR_ERROR was returned }
}
// { P15: P0 and if this is a well formed CashFlowStream
//        then IRR was returned
//        else CashFlowStream.IRR_ERROR was returned }
}

}
```

18.8.1 Value of Software Proofs of Correctness

Like programming by intent, a software proof of correctness is not necessary or even appropriate for every method. Simple methods can be straightforward enough that a proof may not add value. When a method is nontrivial, and particularly when defects could cause serious damage, a proof of correctness could be well worth the investment. We should even question whether proofs are an extra investment. The effort needed to prove code correct could easily be less than the effort needed to debug it later, particularly if a defect is discovered months, or even years after the code was last seen by developers. Why not develop software in a way that minimizes the probability of defects in the first place:

- The level of thinking needed to write correct code is the same level of thinking needed to prove it correct.
- The level of thinking needed to fully determine the cause of some failure, that is, debugging, is the same level of thinking needed to prove it correct.
- The level of thinking needed to fully verify a defect has been eliminated is the same level of thinking needed to prove that code correct.

Why not just use that level of thinking by proving the code correct from the start? Time spent in up-front proof can be much less than time wasted later debugging poorly written, incorrect code. Remember that rework percentage, R%, is over 60% in typical software organizations. Proving method code correct *cannot* take this much time

Code doesn't always need to be *proven*, but it should always be *provable*. Always write code to make proving it as easy as possible. Consider the properties of a well-written mathematical proof:

- Minimum number of steps.
- Clear, logical progression from one step to the next.
- Every step is necessary.
- All steps are sufficient.

These same properties apply to well-written code. The process of creating a good software proof leads to good code. Conversely, creating good code makes it inherently provable.

18.9   Intend-Act-Prove-Assert Format

Intend-act-prove-assert format combines design by contract, programming by intent, proofs of correctness, and assertions into one unified package. That package leverages the strengths of each, giving appropriate emphasis to semantics in method-level design and code.

With intend-act-prove-assert format, every step in method code is a triple or quadruple:

- *Intend*—As a comment, what intermediate goal is to be accomplished? This is from programming by intent and brings in the advantages of that approach.
- *Act*—The line of code expected to accomplish that intent.
- *Prove*—As a comment, the proof proposition. This is the postcondition for the executable code immediately before and the precondition for the next intend-act-prove-assert set.

```
public class SomeClass {

    public void someOperation() {
    // requires
    //    A
    // guarantees
    //    Z
        // { P0: Class invariants and A }          ← Class invariants and requires proposition
        assert this.classInvariants()&&A();        ← Class invariants and requires assertion
        // intent of line 1
        line1;
        // { P1: A with semantic of line1 }        ← First intend-act-prove-assert set
        assert AWithSemanticOfLine1();
        // intent of line 2
        line2;
        // { P2: P1 with semantic of line2 }        ← Second intend-act-prove-assert set
        assert P1WithSemanticOfLine2();
        ...
        // intent of line m
        linem;
        // { Pm: P1 with semantic of linem }        ← Second to last intend-act-prove-assert set
        assert P1WithSemanticOfLinem() );
        // intent of line n
        linen;
        // { Pn: Class invariants and Z }           ← Last intend-act-prove-assert set
        assert this.classInvariants() && Z();       ← Class invariants and guarantees proposition
    }                                               ← Class invariants and guarantees assertion
}
```

Figure 18.8 An abstract example of intend-act-prove-assert format.

- *Assert*—An optional, formal, executable statement of correct state of execution and proof at that point.

The first intend-act-prove-assert set uses the operation's contract requires conditions and class invariants as its precondition. The last set needs at least class invariants and the operation's contract as its postcondition (per Liskov substitutability, it could guarantee more). This is shown abstractly in Figure 18.8. Assume this.classInvariants() is private method that returns true only when the class invariants hold.

18.9.1 An Example of Intend-Act-Prove-Assert

Code Sample 18.30 shows CashFlowStream.IRR() in intend-act-prove-assert format. Some assertions are omitted because they do not add value. In practice, it makes sense to assert contract requires and guarantees, class invariants, and significant internal decisions (if-then-else, switch-case, loop—particularly loop invariants). Assertions for assignment statements usually don't add enough value to make them worthwhile. Also, an assertion immediately following a return statement could never be executed.

Code Sample 18.30 CashFlowStream.IRR() in Intend-Act-Prove-Assert Format

```
public class CashFlowStream {

  // status value for returning an error on IRR calculations
  public static final double IRR_ERROR = -999999.99;
  // how close PW() at Estimated IRR needs to be to $0.00
  private static final double MAX_DIFFERENCE = 0.01;

  public double IRR() {
  // requires
  //   n/a
  // guarantees
  //   if IRR is meaningful for this cash flow stream
  //     then its IRR is returned
  //     otherwise CashFlowStream.IRR_ERROR is returned
  // Implementation notes
  //   uses the algorithm described on page 118 of Return on Software
  //   any root solver could have been used, this was convenient

    // { P0: Class invariants for CashFlowStream }
    assert this.classInvariants();

    // initialize currentPW to PW( 0.0 )
    double currentPW = this.PW( 0.0 );
    // { P1: P0 and currentPW is double == PW( 0.0 ) of this CFS }

    // Only calculate IRR if this cash flow stream is well-formed
    if( this.firstNonZeroCashFlowIsNegative() &&
      this.onlyOneSignChange() &&
      this.PW( 0.0 ) > 0.00 ) {
     // { P2: P1 and computing IRR is meaningful }

      // start Estimated IRR at 0%
      double estimatedIRR = 0.;
      // { P3: P2 and EstimatedIRR is double == 0. }

      // start with Step Amount at +10%
      double stepAmount = 10.;
      // { P4: P3 and stepAmount is double = 10. }

      // iteratively narrow Estimated IRR until PW() close to $0.00
      do {
        // { P5 (the Loop Invariant): P0 and
        //   estimatedIRR is double >= 0. converging on actual IRR
        //   abs( stepAmount ) is double <= 10. }
        assert this.classInvariants() &&
```

```
           estimatedIRR >= 0.0 &&
           Math.abs( stepAmount ) <=10.0;


    // refine Estimated IRR by one iteration
     // save the previous PW at the old Estimated IRR
     double lastPW = currentPW;
     // { P6: P5 and lastPW is double == currentPW }


     // move the Estimated IRR by the Step Amount
     estimatedIRR = estimatedIRR + stepAmount;
     // { P7: P6 and estimatedIRR has moved in
     //        the direction & size of stepAmount }


     // calculate the new PW at the new Estimated IRR
     currentPW = this.PW( estimatedIRR );
     // { P8: P7 and currentPW is double == PW at estimatedIRR }


     // if new estimatedPW is farther from $0.00 than old
     if( Math.abs( currentPW ) > Math.abs( lastPW ) ) {
       // then cut Step Amount in half and switch direction
       // { P9: P8 and estimatedIRR is farther from $0.00 }
       stepAmount = -stepAmount / 2.0;
       // { P10: P9 and stepAmount is reversed and halved }


     }
     // { P5 (Loop Invariant): P0 and
     //   estimatedIRR is double >= 0. converging on actual IRR
     //   abs( stepAmount ) is double <= 10. }
     assert this.classInvariants() &&
             estimatedIRR >= 0.0 &&
             Math.abs( stepAmount ) <=10.0;

  } while( Math.abs( currentPW ) > MAX_DIFFERENCE )
  // { P11: P5 and currentPW is within MAX_DIFFERENCE of $0.00
  //              (the loop termination condition) }


  // done narrowing, return Estimated IRR
  return estimatedIRR;
  // { P12: P0 and well formed CashFlowStream and
  //                 estimatedIRR was returned }

} else {
  // { P13: P0 and not well formed CashFlowStream }
  // not a well-formed CFS, return an error
  return CashFlowStream.IRR_ERROR;
  // { P14: P0 and not well formed CashFlowStream and
  //          CashFlowStream.IRR_ERROR was returned }
```

```
    }
    // { P15: P0 and if this is a well formed CashFlowStream
    //         then IRR was returned
    //         else CashFlowStream.IRR_ERROR was returned }

    }

}
```

With intend-act-prove-assert format, the intent, the code, the proof of correctness, and assertions to validate code and proof at run time are all embedded in the method:

- Intents are expressed as useful comments.
- Lines of code show how each intent is accomplished.
- The proof is represented by propositions.
- When code is executing with assertions enabled, code and proof are continuously verified at run time.
- Should any assertion fail, defects in both code and proof can be quickly isolated to just a few lines of code.

18.10   Quality Criteria

Table 18.1 shows the quality criteria for programming by intent.
Table 18.2 shows the quality criteria for assertions.
Table 18.3 shows the quality criteria for software proofs of correctness.

Table 18.1 Quality criteria for programming by intent.

Item	Criterion
PI-1	Each nontrivial method uses explicit programming by intent
PI-2	All intents at any one level are at the same level of abstraction
PI-3	All lower-level intents accomplish the corresponding higher intent
PI-4	Each intent is implemented in either a line of code or two or is recursively decomposed using programming by intent or an extracted method

Table 18.2 Quality criteria for assertions.

Item	Criterion
AS-1	Assertions are not used when error handling is more appropriate
AS-2	Error handling is not used where assertions are more appropriate
AS-3	AssertionError exceptions are never caught
AS-4	Where appropriate, assertions include class invariants
AS-5	Assertions are included when economically computable
AS-6	No trivial assertions appear
AS-7	No assertions immediately after return statements
AS-8	Assertion expressions are free of required side effects (behavior identical whether assertions enabled or not)

Table 18.3 Quality criteria for software proofs of correctness.

Item	Criterion
PC-1	Proof of correctness is used where appropriate
PC-2	Each executable line of code is surrounded by propositions
PC-3	The first proposition in each method is the operation's contract requires clause, with class invariants if appropriate
PC-4	The last proposition in each method is at least the operation's guarantees clause (Liskov substitutable), with class invariants if appropriate
PC-5	All stated propositions pertinent to the proof at that point
PC-6	All pertinent propositions are stated in the proof at that point
PC-7	Each proposition is consistent with the prior propositions and the semantics of the programming language
PC-8	Parameters and return values are correctly mapped for invocation
PC-9	Semantic at client invocation is consistent with contract at server operation, including side effects
PC-10	Each loop invariant (Q) is consistent with that loop's postcondition
PC-11	Each loop body (H) addresses the termination condition (B), explicitly or implicitly (e.g., in a for loop)
PC-12	Each loop body (H) reestablishes the loop invariant (Q)
PC-13	Even if method code is not explicitly proven, it is written to be easily provable

18.11   Summary

Engineering uses science, mathematics, and practice to generate a set of technically viable solutions to a real-world problem, together with engineering economy to select the most cost-effective one. This chapter presented a disciplined, formal science and mathematics of method-level design and code.

Programming by intent makes a developer's intent in (i.e., reason for) writing code explicit, separate from the mechanics of the code itself. Comments explicitly explain code's intent; they are guaranteed to be useful comments that make creating, reviewing, and maintaining detailed design and code much easier. Also, the detailed design and code under any intent is focused on accomplishing exactly that intent, leading to high cohesion and loose coupling at the line of code level.

Assertions are run-time verification of design correctness, including—but not exclusively—operation contracts. When an assertion fails, it is not a run-time error; it is run-time recognition of design or code incorrectness. The only way to handle an assertion firing is to modify code to correct the problem.

A software proof of correctness establishes the validity of code. It demonstrates that code implements a contract completely, without unintentional side effects. Also, by approaching code formally, from the perspective of proving it correct, the true, formal, logical nature of code is revealed. Software proofs of correctness involve inserting propositions, typically as comments, around every executable line of code. Those propositions are statements about the state of execution expected to be true at that point.

By proving code correct, you depend much less on testing. Proven code cannot give anything other than the right answer. Testing becomes simply a way of exercising the proof: if properly selected test cases pass, then it is highly likely that the proof is correct, so you can have high confidence the code is correct for *all* cases, not just the ones that were tested.

Intend-act-prove-assert format combines design by contract, programming by intent, proofs of correctness, and assertions into one complete, unified package. That package leverages the strengths of each, giving complete and appropriate emphasis to semantics in method design and code.

These formal disciplines increase the probability that a candidate solution— detailed design and code for a method—really does solve that problem. This way, we won't waste time on method design and code that wasn't going to work in the first place.

19

Optimization

If a (sub)domain is developed following the sequence of chapters in this book, code written so far should compile and execute correctly—where "correctly" is defined by the semantic model and interface specification. If premature design and optimization have been avoided, that design and code will be as simple as possible. On the other hand, one or more nonfunctional how well requirements might not be satisfied, or the design and code could be suboptimal. This chapter presents ways to improve performance.

Unfortunately, improving performance necessarily increases accidental complexity and increases development and maintenance cost, schedule, and probability of defects. The goal will be to maximize the value of design and code performance with minimum investment in optimization, without breaking functionality in the process. This chapter presents an engineering process for optimization and overviews several design and code optimization techniques. This chapter is intended to survey optimization techniques, including:

- High-level design optimization: usage matrix, horizontal and vertical split, horizontal and vertical merge
- Detailed design and code optimization: higher-performance algorithms, semantics preserving transforms, bypassing encapsulation
- SQL optimization
- Programming language optimizations: design and implementing in a lower-level language
- Run-time environment optimizations: tune operating system, tune database, tune network
- Hardware optimization: higher-performance hardware, distribute across more processors, special-purpose hardware
- Solidifying optimizations

The techniques in this chapter are by no means exhaustive. A complete discussion of software optimization would require a full book all by itself.

Other techniques not presented here can and should be considered where appropriate. Key messages in this chapter are as follows:

- Optimization can, should, and often must be done.
- Optimization necessarily increases accidental complexity: increasing cost, schedule, and the likelihood of defects.
- The value of any optimization needs to be considered in light of its cost over the expected service life of the software.
- Non-obvious design and code optimizations need to be explained and justified.

19.1 An Engineering Approach to Optimization

To qualify as an engineering approach, that approach must consider value in light of cost over an appropriate planning horizon. Figure 19.1 copies Figure 4.12 and shows value and cost of delivering different levels of performance for a generic nonfunctional how well requirement. See Chapter 4 for the complete discussion of how business value changes over levels of performance. Cost is usually a step function: each successive optimization has a cost but enables performance up to some new, higher maximum. The most cost-effective level of performance for any nonfunctional how well requirement maximizes the positive difference between value and cost to deliver.

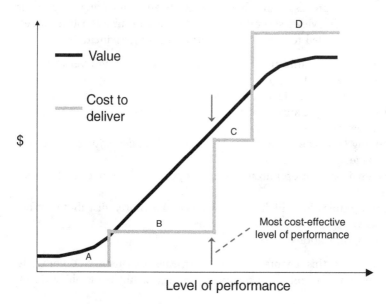

Figure 19.1 Value compared to cost of delivering that level of performance.

One interesting element of Systems Engineering is finding an overall minimum investment that yields the highest value of overall performance. Stakeholders might agree to relax the requirement point on one nonfunctional how well requirement in exchange for a significant increase in level of performance on another. For example, they might be willing to accept a 1.5% reduction in reliability in exchange for a 25% improvement in response time. Or they might be willing to accept 2% degradation in response time for a 20% improvement in reliability.

The following process is derived from Jon Bentley's classic "Writing efficient programs"[1] and is shown in Figure 19.2. Numbers in hexagons refer to later descriptions of important aspects of the process.

1) *Start*—Start with the simplest design and code that implements the semantic model and provides specified interfaces. The semantic model defines correct behavior; previous chapters translated that into the cleanest, most straightforward model region design and code. View-controller region code was driven by the specified interfaces. At this point, the justification for why

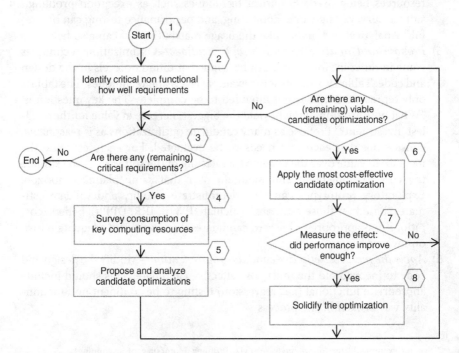

Figure 19.2 An engineering process for optimization.

---

1 See [Bentley82].

design and code look the way they do should be: "Assuming performance is not an issue, this is the simplest, most straightforward, and obvious implementation."

2) *Identify critical nonfunctional how well requirements*—In some cases, the requirement point for a nonfunctional how well requirement is not being met. In other cases, there is potential for significant increase in value from small investment in optimization. Both of these are the "critical" nonfunctional how well requirements.

3) *Are there any (remaining) critical requirements?*—If no, optimization is finished. Any further optimization would only add unnecessary complexity: increasing cost, schedule, and likelihood of defects without adequate return on that investment. If yes, there is more optimization to do.

4) *Survey consumption of key computing resources*—What computing resources drive the level of performance for the critical nonfunctional how well requirements? Key resources might include CPU speed, storage capacity (cache, primary, secondary (e.g., online disk), tertiary (e.g., offline disk, CD-ROM, etc.)), network bandwidth, and so on. How efficiently are those resources being used? Empirical techniques such as execution profiling,[2] storage surveys,[3] network monitoring, and performance testing can be useful.[4] Analytical techniques like the usage matrix (below) can also help.

5) *Propose and analyze candidate optimizations*—Optimization techniques come in different forms and can be applied at different levels in the design and code. Table 19.1 shows some example levels and techniques. The table is only representative; it is not intended to be complete. The key question is, "What optimization(s) might yield the biggest increase in value for the smallest investment?" Propose as many candidate optimizations as is reasonable, considering that each one needs to be evaluated. For each, estimate the increase in value over the expected service life of the software. Also estimate the cost to implement and maintain over that same planning horizon. Exploratory prototypes can help demonstrate viability and validate estimates. Based on those estimates, calculate PW(i), IRR, DPP(i), benefit/cost ratio, etc. as appropriate. Discard candidates that don't yield adequate return on investment.

6) *Apply the most cost-effective candidate optimization*—Modify the design and code to incorporate the most cost-effective candidate. This should include appropriate functional (i.e., regression) testing to be confident no functionality was broken in the process

---

2 See, for example, https://en.wikipedia.org/wiki/Profiling_(computer_programming).

3 How many bytes are needed to represent one object of some class in that medium (can you use a sizeOf() function)? How many objects of that class are expected? Multiplying size by population gives an approximate consumption for that class. Add these up for all classes to calculate a total.

4 See, for example, [Molyneaux14] or any other good book on software performance testing.

Table 19.1 Example levels and techniques for optimization.

Level	Example techniques
High-level design	Usage matrix Horizontal and vertical split Horizontal and vertical merge
Detailed design and code	Higher-performance algorithm Semantics preserving transform Bypass encapsulation
Programming language	Design and implement in a lower-level language
Run-time environment	Tune operating system Tune database Tune network
Hardware	Higher-performance hardware[a] Distribute across more processors Special-purpose hardware (e.g., graphics processor)

[a] For example, faster CPU, more storage, and higher network bandwidth, ...

7) *Measure the effect: did performance improve enough?*—Through performance testing or other appropriate means, be certain of enough improvement to warrant keeping that optimization. If not, abandon it and try the next candidate

8) *Solidify the optimization*—If performance improved enough, solidify it in design and code. Solidification is discussed below.

19.1.1 Optimizing at Different Levels

Optimizations can be applied at different levels in design and code. Table 19.1 surveys optimization levels and shows some example techniques available at each level. Some techniques appear at more than one level. This table is only intended to illustrate common optimizations, not be a precise taxonomy.

19.2 Usage Matrix

When considering high-level design optimization for a (sub)domain, two skills can be useful:

- Determining where to optimize the high-level design
- Deciding how to optimize it

	Class1	Class2	Class3	...	Classn	Totals
UC1	10 * 1 * 5 = 50	10 * 3 * 5 = 150	10 * 0 * 5 = 0		10 * 0 * 5 = 0	> 200
UC2	5 * 1 * 1 = 5	5 * 3 * 1 = 15	5 * 25 * 1 = 125		5 * 0 * 1 = 0	> 145
...						
UCm	5 * 1 * 3 = 15	5 * 0 * 3 = 0	5 * 25 * 3 = 375		5 * 0 * 3 = 0	> 390
Totals	> 70	> 165	>500		> 0	

Figure 19.3 Sample fragment of a usage matrix.

An empirical approach to determining where to optimize would involve profiling execution of running code, looking for class-level and use case-level performance bottlenecks. An analytical alternative called a usage matrix[5] is shown in Figure 19.3 and explained below.

Sea level use cases (transactions) are listed down the left column of the matrix. Design use cases (system configuration, backup, restore, performance monitoring, etc.) can be included if appropriate, but design use cases tend not to drive overall performance and can usually be ignored. Design classes are listed across the top row. The focus is normally on Model region classes although Infrastructure and View-controller region classes can be included if they significantly influence performance.

Each cell in the matrix holds the formula

*Frequency * Instances * Priority*

- *Frequency*—The average number of occurrences of that use case per unit of a reference time. That reference time can be a second, a minute, an hour, a day, etc. as appropriate for the (sub)domain. Be sure to use the same reference time for all use cases; don't mix per-minute frequency on some use cases with per-hour or per-day frequency on others. The example in Figure 19.2 shows UC1 occurring on average 10 times per unit time where UC2 averages 5
- *Instances*—The average number of objects of that class involved per occurrence of that use case. The example in Figure 19.2 shows each occurrence of UC1 involves on average one instance of Class1, three instances of Class2,

---

5 See [Inmon87].

and no instances of Class3 or Classn. UC2 involves on average one instance of Class1, three instances of Class2, fifteen instances of Class3, and no instances of Class4

- *Priority*—The relative execution priority of one sea level use case compared to others. As shown in Figure 19.2, UC1 has relative priority 5, UC2 has priority 1, and UCm has priority 3. Said another way, UCm has three times the execution priority of UC2; UC1 has five times the execution priority of UC2.

If accurate estimates of any factor are not available, consider using ranges of estimates or sensitivity analysis.[6] When all frequency, instance, and priority values are determined, multiply to compute the cell values. Write the sum of each row in the right column. Write the sum of each column in the bottom row. Finally, scan the bottom row and right column looking for unusually high values. The largest row total (>390) in Figure 19.2 is more than double other row totals. Optimizations along use case UCm are likely to give the best improvement. Similarly, the largest column total (>500) is for Class3. Optimization involving Class3 is likely to give the best improvement.

19.3 High-Level Design Optimizations

Having identified, either empirically or analytically, a place in a (sub)domain high-level design that might benefit from optimization, the question now becomes how to optimize. Four alternatives will be presented:

- Horizontal split
- Vertical split
- Horizontal merge
- Vertical merge

These techniques come from Bill Inmon and were originally intended for relational databases (i.e., database de-normalization). Your high-level design might involve a relational database as a persistence layer.[7] Even if your design uses entirely memory-resident objects, these same optimizations can still be useful.

19.4 High-Level Design Optimization: Horizontal Split

Horizontal split, shown in Figure 19.4, moves a subset of objects from one collection (a class, a set, a table, etc.) into a separate collection with identical structure.

---

6 See, for example, chapter 23 of [Tockey05].
7 Remember Data access object pattern discussed in Chapter 17.

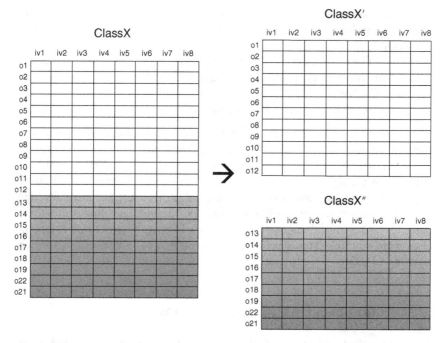

Figure 19.4 Horizontal split, conceptually.

ClassX represents the collection before optimization. Each row represents one object; each column represents one instance variable. In horizontal split, the objects (rows) are conceptually sorted into two or more groups based on relevance to performance. The unshaded set on the top represents performance-critical objects, while the shaded set at the bottom represents non-performance-critical objects. This optimization splits ("horizontally") ClassX into two separate classes (tables), ClassX′ and ClassX″. ClassX″ could be moved to lower-performance, lower-cost technology. Data archiving is a real-world example of a horizontal split.

19.4.1 Horizontal Split in Order fulfillment

Consider class BookOrder in Order fulfillment. It should be reasonable to assume that Open, Placed, and Packed orders would be important for performance, while Cancelled and Completed orders—that still need to be remembered—wouldn't. Original class BookOrder could be split horizontally as shown in Figure 19.5.

HighPerformanceBookOrder is for Open, Placed, and Packed orders and could be kept in main memory (possibly cache) or in higher-performance

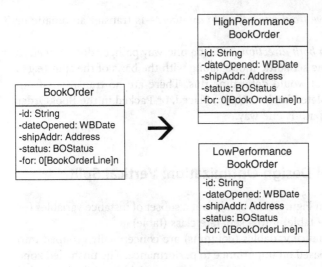

Figure 19.5 BookOrder, horizontally split.

front-end servers. LowPerformanceBookOrder holds Completed and Cancelled orders and could be kept in lower-performance back-end servers or even serialized (e.g., XML) and saved on external media.

Horizontal split doesn't necessarily result in separate classes; it can just create separate collections. Whether you make separate classes or separate collections depends on implementation technologies.

This optimization "de-clutters" storage: performance-critical objects are separated from noncritical objects that need to be retained but would hinder performance or cost too much to keep in higher-performance technology. Even when split classes are kept in technology of the same performance, if you already know what kind of object you are looking for, for example, "Find BookOrder #12345 and we already know it's an open order," searches can be quicker because the search space is reduced: a smaller population of objects needs to be scanned.

Beyond the obvious increase in accidental complexity, disadvantages of this optimization include:

- *Multiple search spaces when subset isn't known*—For example, "Find BookOrder #54321 but we don't know if it is open or closed" means you may have to search both high- and low-performance sets. The mechanism to search two locations, and the time involved, could be significant.
- *When do objects move from one subset to another?*—Is it immediate (e.g., on change to Completed or Cancelled for BookOrder)? Or, does it happen on some periodic basis (e.g., nightly)?

- *How do objects move from one subset to another?*—Is transfer automatic or manual?
- *Can objects move in both directions?*—Is it a one-way path, or does it need to be bidirectional? The semantic model along with the basis of the split (e.g., . state in BookOrders) would determine this. There are no transitions from Cancelled or Completed back to Open, Placed, or Packed in the BookOrder state model so the path is one way.

19.5   High-Level Design Optimization: Vertical Split

Vertical split, shown in Figure 19.6, breaks out a subset of instance variables (or columns in a database table) into a separate class (table).

In vertical split, instance variables (columns) are conceptually grouped into two or more subsets based on importance to performance. The unshaded zone on the left represents performance-critical instance variables, while the shaded zone on the right represents noncritical data. This optimization splits ClassY into separate classes (tables): ClassY' and ClassY''. ClassY'' could be moved to lower-performance, lower-cost storage. The "link" instance variable in Figure 19.6 represents a mechanism for connecting one part of pre-split objects to the other, if necessary. Given an object in ClassY', it may be necessary to find its counterpart in ClassY''. For memory-resident objects, this could be the object reference (memory address). If splitting a database table, the key of ClassY could be used in both ClassY' and ClassY''. If the link isn't needed, it can be left out.

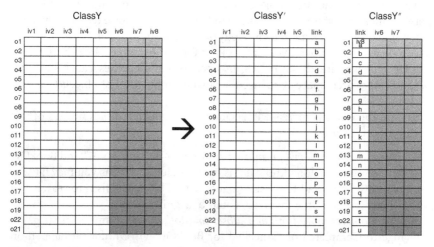

Figure 19.6 Vertical split, conceptually.

19.5.1 Vertical Split in Order fulfillment

In Order fulfillment, consider class Title before introduction of Medium (i.e., assume WebBooks sells print media only. See, for example, Figure 8.14). For serving Web pages to Customers who are browsing the catalog, it should be reasonable to assume that .author, .title, .subject, and .selling price would be important while inventory management attributes like .stockOnHand, .reorderLevel, etc. would not. Figure 19.7 shows how class Title could be split vertically.

HighPerformanceTitle, with only customer web page-relevant data, could be kept in front-end servers, while inventory data could be moved to lower-performance back-end servers.

This optimization also works by "de-cluttering." Performance-critical data are separated from other data that need to be retained but would otherwise get in the way (e.g., cost too much to keep in higher-performance technology). The footprint is smaller; more objects can be packed into the same space. This reduces the amount of high-performance storage needed.

Beyond the obvious increase in accidental complexity, disadvantages of this optimization include the following:

- *Objects exist in more than one place*—When creating or deleting an object, the action needs to happen in more than one place. Consider the potential for damage if only a partial object is created or an object is only partially deleted.

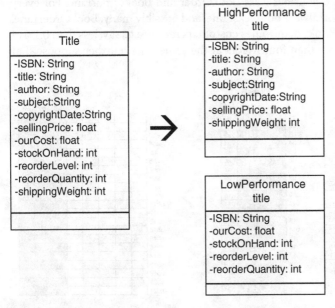

Figure 19.7 Title, before introduction of Medium, vertically split.

- *Space taken by the link*—Even if, as in the case of a vertically split table, the key of ClassY is used in both ClassY' and ClassY", there is still storage consumed by the second occurrence of that data. This could be significant when ClassY has a large population and/or a complex key.

19.5.2 High-Level Design Optimization: Vertical Merge

Vertical merge, shown in Figure 19.8, is the opposite of vertical split. It appends instance variables of one class (or columns in a database table) to those of another. Previously separate classes become a single class.

ClassA and ClassB in Figure 19.5 represent separate classes. ClassB's instance variables are shaded to highlight how they appear after the merge. In this example there must be a one-to-one unconditional association between ClassA and ClassB: for every object of ClassA, there is exactly one object of ClassB and vice versa. This is implemented by the .myB and .myA instance variables. However this does not need to be the case. There could be a -to-zero-or-many association: for every object of ClassA, there could be zero to many objects of ClassB. There should at least be *some* association between ClassA and ClassB or it doesn't make sense to merge them.

19.5.3 Vertical Merge in Order fulfillment

In Order fulfillment, consider class BookOrder and BookOrderLine. For every BookOrder there will always be at least one, and possibly many, BookOrderLine. Suppose that WebBooks determines customers rarely (e.g., say, less than 0.1% of the time) order more than four Media at the same time. Further suppose that

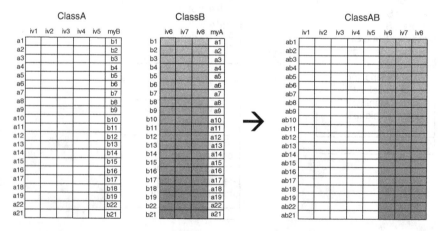

Figure 19.8 Vertical merge, conceptually.

interviewing those few customers who do order more than four Media reveals they would not be upset if they had to split over more than one BookOrder. BookOrderLine could be merged into BookOrder as shown in Figure 19.9.

When .lnXquantity == 0, .lnXpricePerCopy == 0.0, and .lnXfor == null, it means that line X is empty. The BookOrder constructor would initialize instance variables for the four embedded lines. Whenever an order line is added, the next set of .lnXquantity, .lnXpricePerCopy, and .lnXfor are filled in. Those same instance variables would need to be reset if that line is dropped.

Vertical merge makes sense only when classes being merged are associated in some way. Vertical merges are also much easier in some cases than others, depending on association multiplicity:

- *-to-one*—easy, which is shown in Figure 19.8
- *-to-zero-or-one*—slightly more difficult because of the null case

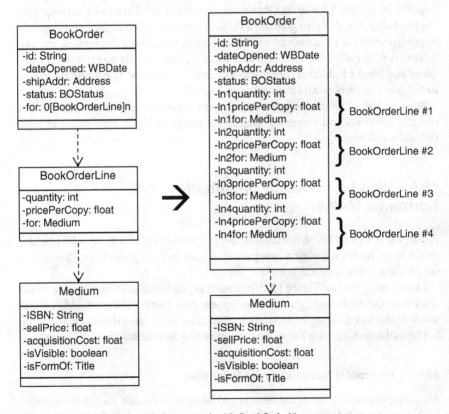

Figure 19.9 BookOrder vertically merged with BookOrderLine.

- *-to-one-or-many*—a bit more difficult, which is shown in Figure 19.9 with a fixed upper bound
- *-to-zero-or-many*—the most difficult case, where both the many case and the null case need to be addressed

Associations without significant attributes, state, or action were vertically merged in Chapter 17. Associations Places, Sold as, Obtained from, and Fills in Order fulfillment are examples (see Figure 8.32). All associations in a semantic model are implicitly association classes: the class dimension of the ordinary associations is insignificant and can be ignored in design and code. Figure 19.9 shows merging a full-blown association class (its class dimension is significant)—namely, you get the reference (.lnXfor in Figure 19.6) along with instance variables of the association class. The practical details were discussed in Chapter 17 on "Implementing associations" for both memory-resident and persistence layer implementations.

This optimization improves performance by reducing hops from one class to another. In the un-optimized case, to go from a Title to its Publisher requires hopping from that Title to its ObtainedFrom and from there to its corresponding Publisher. Similarly, to go from a Publisher to its ReplenishOrder(s) requires hopping from that Publisher to its Fills and from there to its ReplenishOrder(s). Access is direct after the vertical merge, that is, from a Title directly to its Publisher and from a Publisher directly to its ReplenishOrders. The direct reference to the associated object(s) is essentially cached.

Beyond the obvious increase in accidental complexity, this optimization reduces cohesion and increases coupling: a merged class is now doing at least two different jobs.

19.6 High-Level Design Optimization: Horizontal Merge

As shown in Figure 19.10, horizontal merge appends objects in one class (table) to those in another. Originally separate classes (tables, collections) become a single class (table, collection).

ClassC and ClassD in Figure 19.10 represent separate classes. ClassD's objects are shaded on the left to highlight how they appear post-merge. There should be some similarity between ClassC and ClassD. It wouldn't make sense to horizontally merge ReplenishOrderLine with BookOrder because the two classes are so different.

19.6.1 Horizontal Merge in Order fulfillment

An example from Order fulfillment could be to horizontally merge BookOrder with ReplenishOrder and BookOrderLine with ReplenishOrderLine. This is shown in Figure 19.11.

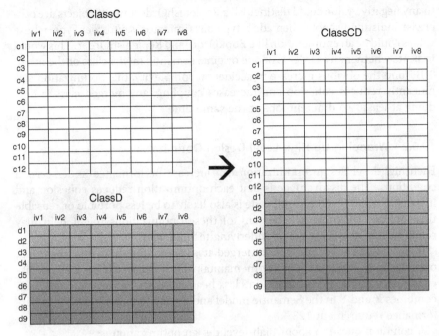

Figure 19.10 Horizontal merge, conceptually.

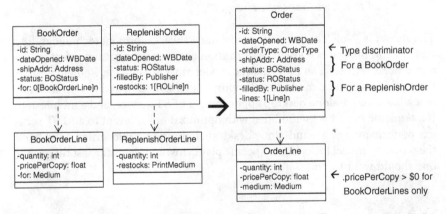

Figure 19.11 Example horizontal merge.

Horizontal merge may require a "type discriminator" instance variable to distinguish business objects of one merged class from the other. If there are obvious preexisting differences, such as an instance variable would be null for one and not the other, distinguishing is already easy. In Figure 19.11, .pricePerCopy is only relevant for BookOrderLines and must be positive. Setting .pricePerCopy to any negative value could distinguish a ReplenishOrderLine. If objects are otherwise indistinguishable, then add a type discriminator, say, .orderType, whose values could be an enumeration like BookOrder and ReplenishOrder. This would indicate whether any Order is of one original semantic model class or the other.

Beyond the obvious increase in accidental complexity, this optimization significantly reduces cohesion and increases coupling: any merged class is now doing at least two different jobs at the same time.

19.6.2 Wrapping Up High-Level Design Optimization

Each high-level design optimization can increase performance under certain conditions. The disadvantage is that each optimization reduces cohesion and increases coupling. Optimized code is also likely to be less portable or reusable than before. To know whether any of these optimizations might help may require detailed knowledge of underlying technologies.

If any design classes are split or merged, it is very important to document that optimization; otherwise long-term maintainability suffers. This can be discussed in a "heritage" comment in class headers, as in "// Heritage: this class combines X and Y in the Semantic model and was done to be able to meet performance requirement 123."

A common question about high-level design optimization is:

> *"As we modify the design class diagram, do we also modify the semantic model to reflect that same change?"*

The answer is "No!" The semantic model must always represent technology-free policies and processes. Design optimization cannot and must not affect policy and process semantic, so the semantic model must not change. Remember that one goal of a semantic model is to support implementation in different technologies, like a stand-alone desktop application, a REST service, and a mobile app. If a semantic model were modified with optimizations relevant to a REST service, performance as a stand-alone desktop application could suffer. Modifying the semantic model locks it into specific platforms, and that's the last thing anyone should want to do.

19.7   Detailed Design and Code Optimization

Optimizations in this section apply to detailed design and code, that is, within a method. Two general approaches will be discussed:

1) Higher-performance algorithms or data structures
2) Semantics preserving transforms

An additional approach, bypassing encapsulation, is not available in all languages and is only mentioned briefly. Specifically, "friend"[8] in C++ allows code in one class direct access to member data and functions in another class. Direct access might also be available in some languages through reflection.[9] Bypassing encapsulation can increase performance by reducing execution overhead but at the cost of significantly increasing coupling.

19.7.1 Higher-Performance Algorithms or Data Structures

The most effective way to improve performance in critical methods is to use higher-performance algorithms and data structures. Bubble Sort[10] is simple but may not perform well, particularly with large collections. When many items need sorting, a higher-performance algorithm like QuickSort[11] could be better. For searching, linear search is simple but slow. Binary searches and hash tables[12] tend to be much faster. At the detailed design and code level, these kinds of optimizations are preferred over semantics preserving transforms. Try these before resorting to semantics preserving transforms.

19.7.2 Semantics Preserving Transforms

A semantics preserving transform[13] is defined as:

> *"... takes as input a high-level language program (which incorporates efficient algorithms and data structures) and produces as output a program in the same language that is suitable for compilation into efficient code."*

Table 19.2 overviews categories of semantics preserving transforms; more detail on each category is provided below. The first two categories focus on data, and the rest focus on methods.

Use semantics preserving transforms only if performance of critical methods is still inadequate even after implementing high-performance algorithms and data structures.

---

8 See, for example, http://www.cprogramming.com/tutorial/friends.html.
9 See, for example, https://en.wikipedia.org/wiki/Reflection_(computer_programming).
10 See, for example, https://en.wikipedia.org/wiki/Bubble_sort.
11 See, for example, https://en.wikipedia.org/wiki/Quicksort.
12 See, for example, https://en.wikipedia.org/wiki/Hash_table.
13 See [Bentley82].

Table 19.2 Categories of semantics preserving transforms.

Category	General strategy
Trading time for space	Conserve storage by compressing data into smaller space, at the cost of more work to retrieve it
Trading space for time	Save time by making information faster to retrieve, but at the cost of using more space
Loop transforms	Modify looping code to take less time
Logic transforms	Modify Boolean computation to take less time
Procedure transforms	Modify function call structure to take less time
Expression transforms	Modify mathematical expressions to take less time
System-dependent efficiencies	Take advantage of characteristics specific to the automation technology

19.7.3 Trading Time for Space Transforms

Table 19.3 overviews trading time for space transforms. These transforms conserve storage by compressing data into fewer bits but require more work (i.e., time) to retrieve it.

19.7.4 Trading Space for Time Transforms

Table 19.4 overviews trading space for time transforms. These transforms save time by making information faster to retrieve, at the cost of using more bits.

Table 19.3 Trading time for space transforms.

Semantics preserving transform	Description
Data compression	Reduce or eliminate repeating, insignificant, and/or irrelevant data. JPEG image format[a], MP3 audio format[b], and run-length encoding[c] are examples
Interpreter	Encode information into abstract units and use an interpreter (i.e., expander) to unpack as needed. The Java virtual machine[d] uses byte codes instead of machine language instructions. TurboTax makes extensive use of interpretation (i.e., it is driven by configuration data tables)

[a] See, for example, https://en.wikipedia.org/wiki/JPEG.
[b] See, for example, https://en.wikipedia.org/wiki/MP3.
[c] See, for example, https://en.wikipedia.org/wiki/Run-length_encoding.
[d] See, for example, https://en.wikipedia.org/wiki/Java_virtual_machine or [Lindholm14].

Table 19.4 Trading space for time transforms.

Semantics preserving transform	Description
Data structure augmentation	Reduce access time by moving data closer to where it is needed or supplement structures to access data more easily. Indexing a database table[a] and vertical merge are examples
Store precomputed results	Instead of recomputing something every time it is asked for, compute only when necessary. Functions implemented with table lookup and the compute on update and store implementation of derived attributes are examples
Caching	Store frequently accessed data in a closer and/or higher-performance technology
Lazy evaluation	If the result of an expensive computation might not be used, then don't compute it until it is actually needed. The compute on demand implementation of derived attributes is an example

[a] See, for example, http://www.programmerinterview.com/index.php/database-sql/what-is-an-index/.

19.7.5 Loop Transforms

Most execution time is spent in loops of one sort or another; they can be good targets for optimization. Table 19.5 overviews loop transforms.

Table 19.5 Loop transforms.

Semantics preserving transform	Description
Code motion out of loops	Invariant computations in a loop can be safely moved outside and done only once[a]
Combining tests	Reduce the number of tests performed in a loop by simulating some exit conditions by others. An example would be using a sentinel value[b]
Loop unrolling	Reduce loop overhead by having each cycle do more work[c]
Transfer-driven loop unrolling	Some assignments in a loop can be removed by repeating code and changing variable use. An example appears below
Loop fusion	When two nearby loops operate on the same elements, they can be fused into one loop that does the work of both[d]

[a] See, for example, https://en.wikipedia.org/wiki/Loop-invariant_code_motion.
[b] See, for example, https://en.wikipedia.org/wiki/Sentinel_value.
[c] See, for example, https://en.wikipedia.org/wiki/Loop_unrolling.
[d] See, for example, https://en.wikipedia.org/wiki/Loop_fusion

Code Sample 19.1 is initial Pascal code that will demonstrate transfer-driven loop unrolling.

Code Sample 19.2 shows the result after applying transfer-driven loop unrolling. Notice in the second half of the loop that variables p and q have swapped roles.

Code Sample 19.1 Initial Code to Demonstrate Transfer-Driven Loop Unrolling

```
{ Insert node newNode into a sorted linked list
  Assumes front and back sentinels on both ends of the list }
p := listAnchor;
q := p^.next;
while q^.value <= newNode^.value
  do begin
      p := q;
      q := q^.next; { Note: p always follows q }
      end;
newNode^.next := q;
p^.next := newNode;
```

Code Sample 19.2 Final Code Demonstrating Transfer-Driven Loop Unrolling

```
{ Insert node newNode into a sorted linked list
  Assumes front and back sentinels on both ends of the list }
p := listAnchor;
startPoint:
  q := p^.next; { q is ahead of p }
  if q^.value <= newNode^.value
    then begin
        newNode^.next := q;
        p^.next := newNode;
        goto endPoint;
        end;
  p := q^.next; { p is now ahead of q, they have swapped roles }
  if p^.value <= newNode^.value
    then begin
        newNode^.next := p;
        q^.next := newNode;
        goto endPoint;
        end;
  goto startPoint;
endPoint:
```

19.7.6 Logic Transforms

Table 19.6 overviews logic transforms. These target logical expressions, such as are found in if() statements, while() statements, etc. The goal is to achieve the same outcome quicker.

A monotone function only moves in one direction.[14] Consider Code Sample 19.3, which determines if the sum of values in some large array is greater than a specified threshold. When all values in the array are known to be positive, variable sum is monotone: it is non-decreasing.

Because array values can never be negative, as soon as sum exceeds thresholdValue, the loop can be abandoned. This avoids all remaining iterations. The short-circuit version is shown in Code Sample 19.4.

Table 19.6 Logic transforms.

Semantics preserving transform	Description
Short-circuit monotone functions	When the outcome of a function can be determined early, stop computing as soon as that outcome has been determined. This is demonstrated below
Reorder tests	Arrange logical tests so that inexpensive and often successful tests precede expensive and rarely successful tests to avoid computing the expensive tests
Precompute logical functions	A logical function over a small finite domain can be replaced by a lookup table. This is a special case of storing precomputed results

---

Code Sample 19.3 Initial Code to Demonstrate Short-Circuit Monotone Function

```
double total = 0.0;
for( int i = 0; i < arrayTop; i++ ) {
  total = total + hugeArray[ i ];
}
return( total > threshold );
```

---

14 "Mono" = one, "tone" = direction.

Code Sample 19.4 Final Code Demonstrating Short-Circuit Monotone Function

```
double total = 0.0;
int i = 0;
while ( i < arrayTop && total <= threshold ) {
  total = total + hugeArray[ i ];
  i++;
}
return ( total > threshold );
```

19.7.7 Procedure Transforms

Table 19.7 overviews procedure transforms. These transforms target function call structure to reduce execution time.

Pascal Code Sample 19.5 will be used to demonstrate the exploit common cases optimization.

Table 19.7 Procedure transforms.

Semantics preserving transform	Description
Collapse procedure hierarchy	Treat a function as a macro, avoiding call overhead[a]
Exploit common cases	Code a function to handle all cases correctly and common cases efficiently; this is shown below
Remove tail recursion	If the final action of a function is to call itself recursively, replace that call by a loop[b]
Remove return address from stack	If a function contains only one recursive call to itself, the call can be replaced by iteration while keeping track of call depth

[a] See, for example, http://refactoring.com/catalog/inlineMethod.html.
[b] See, for example, http://www.refactoring.com/catalog/replaceRecursionWithIteration.html.

Code Sample 19.5 Initial Code to Demonstrate Exploit Common Cases

```
function Fibonacci ( N: integer ) : integer;
 var
  F: integer;
 begin
  case N of
   1: F := 1;
   2: F := 1;
   otherwise: F := Fibonacci ( N-1 ) + Fibonacci ( N-2 );
  end;
 Fibonacci := F;
end;
```

Assuming the most common cases involve x less than or equal to 10, Code Sample 19.6 shows the exploit common cases optimization.

Code Sample 19.6 Final Code Demonstrating Exploit Common Cases

```
function Fibonacci ( N: integer ) : integer;
 var
  F: integer;
 begin
  case N of
   1: F := 1;
   2: F := 1;
   3: F := 2;
   4: F := 3;
   5: F := 5;
   6: F := 8;
   7: F := 13;
   8: F := 21;
   9: F := 34;
   10: F := 55;
   otherwise: F := Fibonacci ( N-1 ) + Fibonacci ( N-2 );
  end;
 Fibonacci := F;
end
```

19.7.8 Expression Transforms

Table 19.8 overviews expression transforms.

Code Sample 19.7 will be used to demonstrate exploit algebraic identities optimization.

Computing a square root is relatively expensive. If x and y are nonnegative, sqrt(x) can only be less than y when x is less than y squared. Squaring y is much less expensive than computing the square root of x. Calculating the natural log of a and b separately will be more expensive than calculating the natural log of (a * b), as long as a * b cannot lead to numeric overflow. Code Sample 19.8 demonstrates the exploit algebraic identities optimization.

Table 19.8 Expression transforms.

Semantics preserving transform	Description
Compile time initialization	A version of store precomputed results that, when possible, computes at compile time
Exploit algebraic identities	If an expression is expensive to compute, replace it by an equivalent expression that is cheaper to compute. This is demonstrated below
Eliminate common sub-expressions	If a sub-expression is evaluated more than once with none of its variables altered, reevaluations can be avoided by storing the first result
Pair computations	If two related expressions are frequently evaluated together, combine them in a procedure that evaluates both at the same time

---

Code Sample 19.7 Initial Code to Demonstrate Exploit Algebraic Identities

```
// assume x, y, a, and b are never negative
if ( sqrt ( x ) < y ) { ... }
z := ln ( a ) + ln ( b );
```

Code Sample 19.8 Final Code Demonstrating Exploit Algebraic Identities

```
// assume x, y, a, and b are never negative
if ( x < y * y ) { ... };
z := ln ( a * b );
```

Code Sample 19.9 Initial Code to Demonstrate Pair Computations

```
function MaxX( I, N: integer ): integer;
 var
  J, M: integer;
 begin
  M := X[I];
  for J := I+1 to N
   do if M < X[J]
      then M := X[J];
   MaxX := M;
 end;

function MinX( I, N: integer ): integer;
 var
  J, M: integer;
 begin
  M := X[I];
  for J := I+1 to N
   do if M > X[J]
      then M := X[J];
   MinX := M;
 end;
```

Code Sample 19.9 shows Pascal code that will demonstrate the pair computations optimization.

If calling MinX() or MaxX() means it is highly likely the other will be called as well, both functions can be paired into a single function. Code Sample 19.10 shows code demonstrating the pair computations optimization.

Code Sample 19.10 Final Code Demonstrating Pair Computations

```
procedure MinXMaxX( I, N: integer; var MinX, MaxX: integer );
 var
  J: integer;
 begin
  MinX := X[I];
  MaxX := MinX;
  for J := I+1 to N
   do begin
```

```
        if MaxX < X[J]
          then MaxX := X[J];
        if MinX > X[J]
          then MinX := X[J];
  end;
```

19.7.9 System-Dependent Efficiencies

All above semantic preserving transforms are largely independent of programming language, compiler, and computing hardware. However, in most high-level languages, functionally equivalent programs can have very different costs. As a specific example, in at least one implementation of Basic, GOTO, and GOSUB use a linear search from the front of the source code. It can be far more efficient to put frequently called subroutines at the front of the program rather than at the end, as is typical style. This is illustrated in Code Sample 19.11.

Code Sample 19.11 A System-Dependent Optimization: Placement of Subroutines

```
1 GOTO 1000
100 REMARK *** SUBROUTINE FIND() ***
. . .
190 RETURN
200 REMARK *** SUBROUTINE SORT() ***
. . .
290 RETURN
1000 REMARK *** THE REAL START OF THE PROGRAM ***
1010 PRINT
1020 PRINT "DEMONSTRATION PROGRAM"
. . .
1240 GOSUB 200
. . .
1620 GOSUB 100
. . .
9999 END
```

19.7.10   Semantics Preserving Transforms Versus Refactoring

Some semantics preserving transforms are identical to refactoring.[15] Collapse procedure hierarchy is the same as Fowler's inline method. The difference is intent:

- *Semantics preserving transform*—improve performance, at the cost of increasing necessary accidental complexity
- *Refactoring*—reduce unnecessary accidental complexity, possibly taking a small but acceptable reduction in performance

Both must be "semantics preserving"; the modified code is expected to have identical behavior—semantics—as before. If anything other than structure and performance changed, the modification did not preserve semantics and may have introduced a defect (i.e., if the semantic difference is enough to matter). The same can be said for all optimizations at all levels: semantics—behavior—must not change; only code structure and performance can change.

19.7.11   Wrapping Up Semantics Preserving Transforms

A modern compiler can apply many of the semantics preserving transforms automatically. On the other hand, even the best optimizing compiler cannot apply all optimizations. Required knowledge in some cases is simply not available to the optimizer. For example, short-circuiting the monotone function in Code Sample 19.4 is based on knowing the array values are never negative. Also, not all compilers have good optimizers. Developers often need to apply some degree of semantics preserving transform.

In one project, loop unrolling made the difference between meeting and not meeting a critical performance requirement. The size of the CPU's instruction cache drove the optimum loop unrolling factor to be 34. If developers had manually unrolled that loop by, say, a factor of 8, a compiler would not have been able to unroll by 34. The best it could have done would be to unroll by a further factor of four, giving a total unrolling of 28. Starting with the simplest possible code gives the compiler the most opportunities to do all optimizations it is capable of. If that is enough, you are done. If it is not enough, then—and only then—is it the developer's turn.

Generally, when dealing with performance-critical code, developers should:

- *Know the compiler*—What optimizations can it do? What optimizations can't it do? Which language constructs encourage optimization? Which language constructs discourage optimization?
- *Know the cost of each language construct*—This can be derived empirically by measuring running programs, such as experimental prototypes. This might

---

15 See, for example, [Fowler99].

also be derived analytically by examining object code generated by the compiler in light of the CPU's instruction timing.

- *Know the computing environment*—CPU speed(s), caching strategies, paging, database peculiarities, network peculiarities, etc.

A very interesting real-world case of optimization involves inlining functions (collapse procedure hierarchy) in the Linux kernel.[16] It is generally recognized that inlining reduces run time because it avoids the overhead of making a function call. On the other hand, inlining replicates the function body each time that function is referenced. This makes the executable code bigger, and a bigger executable leads to more CPU instruction cache misses. A set of Linux network functions were originally tagged as inline. Many of those functions expanded to over 100 bytes of machine code each. A cache miss can cost more than a function call: removing the inline tag leads to the Linux kernel running 3% faster.

19.8   SQL Optimization

Some (sub)domains are implemented using a relational database. Those that do should consider how optimal the SQL statements are. Optimal SQL can significantly outperform suboptimal SQL. Particularly when working with large-scale data, even a minor SQL change can have a dramatic effect on performance. Of course, more can be said on SQL optimization than is in this section. Markus Winand[17] provides a good general reference.

One goal of SQL optimization is to avoid unnecessary work by not accessing rows that do not affect the result. Some specific guidelines include the following:

- *Order joins carefully*—Put tables with fewer rows earlier in the join order.
- *Index where appropriate*—Avoid full-table scans when it is more efficient to get needed rows through an index. If a table is used mostly for searching, consider adding more indexes. A separate index that fetches the few hundred rows that are needed can be faster than an index that fetches thousands of rows, many of which are not needed.
- *Select only columns needed*—Avoid select * unless all column data is really needed. Not only does this copy and move less data, but more of the relevant content can be cached.
- *Use partitioned views.*
- *Table variables and temporary tables can be more efficient than one large source table.*
- *Set operations tend to execute faster than loops (i.e., fetch cursors).*

---

16 See https://lwn.net/Articles/82495/.
17 See [Winand12].

- *Implement a query as a stored procedure*—Stored procedures are often pre-compiled and can execute faster.
- *Be careful with mixed type expressions*—Implicit type conversion can be costly.
- ...

RDBMSs often have product-specific features that outperform standard SQL. Vendors depend on these features for product differentiation. Many product-specific books and papers are available.[18] On the one hand, taking advantage of a product-specific feature can significantly improve performance. On the other hand, it will limit portability. To the extent a product-specific feature can be encapsulated in a Data access object, you can get the benefit of improved performance without harming portability.

19.9 Design and Implement in a Lower-Level Language

Many developers work in environments that either don't support or even allow object-oriented development. According to a 2017 survey by IEEE Spectrum, C was the second most popular programming language.[19] But that does not make this book is irrelevant. Teams can—and have—built semantic models, translated to object-oriented designs, and then further translated into equivalent structured (i.e., procedural) designs for implementation in C, Pascal, COBOL, etc. The process for translating object-oriented design and code into structured design and code is shown in Figure 19.12. Each step is explained in detail below. This also gives insight into compilers and run-time systems for object-oriented languages—the CPU is not object oriented, so a conversion to procedural has to happen at some point.

19.9.1 Erase Class Boundaries

Start with an object-oriented design and code that may or may not have been optimized as described earlier in this chapter; the design can still be further optimized later. Classes are explicit in the object-oriented design and code; they will be implicit in the structured version. Naming conventions and code structuring guidelines help retain the original class identity for units of code. One useful naming convention is to add a prefix on public elements in the structured design to refer to the original class from the object-oriented design. Table 19.9 shows example prefixes for Order fulfillment.

---

18 See, for example http://docs.oracle.com/cd/A87862_01/NT817CLI/server.817/a76992/sql.htm.
19 See http://spectrum.ieee.org/computing/software/the-2017-top-programming-languages.

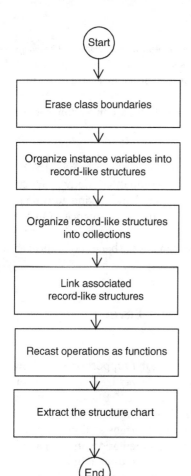

Figure 19.12 Translating object-oriented design and code into structured design and code.

Table 19.9 Example class prefixes for Order fulfillment.

Item	Prefix
Book order	BO_
Book order line	BL_
Customer	CU_
Manager	MA_
Medium	MD_
eBook medium	EM_
Print medium	PM_
Publisher	PB_
Replenish order	RO_
Replenish order line	RL_
Title	TL_
Warehouse worker	WW_

A code structuring guideline is to put source code for a class into files named by that class. For example, for C code, BO_BookOrder.h and BO_BookOrder.c, BL_BookOrderLine.h and BL_BookOrderLine.c, MD_Medium.h and MD_Medium.c, CU_Customer.h and CU_Customer.c, etc.

19.9.2 Organize Instance Variables into Record-Like Structures

The second step is to organize the instance variables for each class in the object-oriented design into record-like structures (i.e., `struct` in C, `record` in Pascal). Instance variables representing semantic model associations (i.e., object references) require special treatment and are addressed later. Code Sample 19.12 shows candidate Pascal record structures for two classes in Order fulfillment.

Code Sample 19.12 Example Pascal Record-Like Structures

```
{ in file BO_BookOrder.pas }
type
  { enumerated type for states in state model }
  BO_status = ( BO_Open, BO_Placed, BO_Packed, BO_Completed,
          BO_Cancelled );

  BO_BookOrder = record
    { attribute instance variables }
    id: string;
    dateOpened: string;
    shippingAddress: string;
    status: BO_status;
  end;


{ in file BL_BookOrderLine.pas }
type
  { enumerated type for states in state model }
  BL_status = ( BL_Open, BL_Placed, BL_Completed );

  BL_BookOrderLine = record
    { attribute instance variables }
    quantity: integer;
    pricePerCopy: real;
    status: BL_status;
  end;
```

19.9.3 Organize Record-Like Structures into Collections

The next step can be to organize the record-like structures into collections that gather the objects in that class. This is not always necessary, but is required when any functionality needs to traverse all objects in a class. In Order fulfillment, determining which orders are packable for Warehouse workers requires visiting all Book orders. Catalog searches require visiting all Titles. No use case requires visiting all Book order lines, so this step is not needed for that class.

A number of options are available; this list is not necessarily exhaustive:

- Array
- Linked list—possibly singly or doubly linked as appropriate
- Tree
- Hash table
- Records in a flat file on a disk
- Rows in a database table—possibly indexed

Typical criteria for selecting one type of collection over another are shown in Table 19.10.

To minimize accidental complexity, the same choice for all classes in a (sub) domain would be preferred, but performance considerations might lead to different choices for different classes. Assume for this demonstration that Book order will be put into a singly linked list. A more realistic implementation would use trees or hash tables for performance reasons, but that complicates this

Table 19.10 Possible selection criteria for collection types.

Decision criterion	Discussion
How many run-time objects?	If there are relatively few run-time objects, then a simpler collection like an array might be preferred over a more complex collection like a hash table or tree
Static versus dynamic population?	A static population of run-time objects might suggest static allocation (e.g., fixed size array), whereas a dynamic population argues for a more flexible collection like linked list, hash table, tree, or database table
Uniform versus nonuniform access?	If some objects are accessed more frequently than others, it can make sense to use a linearly searchable collection and place frequently accessed objects near the front. Uniform access would suggest using a collection with more balanced performance like a tree or hash table
Memory resident versus persistent?	If objects need to persist or be shared outside the application, then a database or flat files might be preferred. Otherwise, memory-resident objects perform much faster
—	—

example. Code Sample 19.13 shows Book order implemented as a linked list and includes an initializer for that list.

Code Sample 19.13 Collection of BookOrders Implemented in Pascal as a Linked List

```pascal
{ in file BO_BookOrder.pas }
type
  { enumerated type for states in state model }
  BO_status = ( BO_Open, BO_Placed, BO_Packed, BO_Completed,
          BO_Cancelled );

  BO_BookOrder = record
    { attribute instance variables }
    id: string;
    dateOpened: string;
    shippingAddress: string;
    status: BO_status;
    { link to the next Book order in the list }
    nextBookOrder: ^BO_BookOrder;
  end;

var
  firstBookOrder: ^BO_BookOrder;
  lastBookOrder: ^BO_BookOrder;

{ Class initializer }
procedure BO_InitializeBookOrderClass;
  { requires
    none
  guarantees
    the Book Order class (linked list) has been initialized
  }
begin
  firstBookOrder := null;
  lastBookOrder := null;
end;
```

One consequence of choosing the collection type is to either determine or at least constrain object reference mechanisms. If you chose,

- *Array*—The most obvious reference would be the array index.
- *Flat file* or *database table*—Typically would use a key.
- *Linked list, tree, hash table*—The most obvious would be a pointer (memory address).

A question to answer is whether or not references need to be human readable. A machine convenient reference like a memory address or array index would execute fast, but stakeholders may require an externally human-readable key like customerID or bookOrderID. A class like BookOrderLine isn't directly referenced externally, so a purely internal reference like a pointer should be sufficient. Even if stakeholders require a human-readable key, it does not prevent you from also using a machine convenient reference for performance.

19.9.4 Link Associated Record-Like Structures

The next step is to link the record-like structures to support associations in the semantic model. Those links may have already been implemented in the object-oriented design (e.g., as described in Chapter 17); you can revisit the linking structures now and modify as appropriate.

Book order line in the semantic model is an association class between Book order and Medium. Based on client-server messaging, the object-oriented design in Figure 17.2 links BookOrder to BookOrderLine and then BookOrder-Line to Medium. Each BookOrder can have one to many BookOrderLines. That link is represented in the design as a collection of BookOrderLine references in BookOrder in an instance variable named .pFor. Each BookOrderLine is linked to one Medium. That link is represented in the object-oriented design as a single Medium reference in BookOrderLine.pFor. The job is to now represent the same kind of linking in the structured design and code.

The earlier decision was to represent BookOrders as a linked list, so it would make sense to also represent collections of BookOrderLine as a linked list. We don't need a single list of all order lines, just a list of order lines for each Book order. Each BookOrderLine only needs a single reference to the corresponding Medium. The same decision—and the same decision criteria—about how to reference instances from the previous step applies. Code Sample 19.14 shows the record-like structures extended to represent associations.

Code Sample 19.14 Partial Pascal Code for Association Linking in Order fulfillment

```pascal
{ in file BO_BookOrder.pas }
  type
  { enumerated type for states in state model }
  BO_status = ( BO_Open, BO_Placed, BO_Packed, BO_Completed,
                BO_Cancelled );
```

```
BO_BookOrder = record
  { attribute instance variables }
  id: string;
  dateOpened: string;
  shippingAddress: string;
  status: BO_status;
  { link to the next Book order in the list }
  nextBookOrder: ^BO_BookOrder;
  { association participation instance variables }
  pForFirstOrderLine: ^BL_BookOrderLine;
  pForLastOrderLine: ^BL_BookOrderLine;
end;


{ in file BL_BookOrderLine.pas }
type
  { enumerated type for states in state model }
  BL_status = ( BL_Open, BL_Placed, BL_Completed );

  BL_BookOrderLine = record
  { attribute instance variables }
  quantity: integer;
  pricePerCopy: real;
  status: BL_status;
  { link to the next book order line in the list }
  nextLine: ^BL_BookOrderLine;
  { association participation instance variables }
  pFor: ^MD_Medium;
end;
```

19.9.5 Recast Operations as Functions

The next step is to recast each operation in the object-oriented design as a function in the structured design. Use the appropriate class abbreviation in each function name: this not only ties the function back to the original class, but it can also be necessary to avoid name clashes. Object-oriented programming languages support polymorphism, but C, Pascal, etc. do not: function names must be globally unique.

Each function will also need an additional parameter—a reference parameter—to point it at a specific instance. While ultimately a style issue, a common convention is to put the reference parameter first. The data type of the reference parameter depends on the object reference decision earlier. When the reference parameter is a human-readable identifier, it can be useful to have a

utility function to convert that identifier into a corresponding machine convenient reference.

Code Sample 19.15 for BookOrder and Code Sample 19.16 for BookOrder-
Line show partial Pascal code for all instance variables as well as functions that
implement relevant portions of use cases:

- isPackable()
- addToCart()
- packOrder()

Code Sample 19.15 Partial Pascal Code for Book Order

```
{ in file BO_BookOrder.pas }
  type
    { enumerated type for states in state model }
    BO_status = ( BO_Open, BO_Placed, BO_Packed, BO_Completed,
                  BO_Cancelled );

    BO_BookOrder = record
      { attribute instance variables }
      id: string;
      dateOpened: string;
      shippingAddress: string;
      status: BO_status;
      { link to the next Book order in the list }
      nextBookOrder: ^BO_BookOrder;
      { association participation instance variables }
      pForFirstOrderLine: ^BL_BookOrderLine;
      pForLastOrderLine: ^BL_BookOrderLine;
    end;

var
  firstBookOrder: ^BO_BookOrder;
  lastBookOrder: ^BO_BookOrder;

{ Class initializer }
procedure BO_InitializeBookOrderClass;
  { requires
      none
    guarantees
      the Book Order class (linked list) has been initialized
  }
  begin
    firstBookOrder := null;
    lastBookOrder := null;
  end;
```

```
{ Constructor }
function BO_newBookOrder( anAddress: address ): ^BookOrder;
 { requires
   BookOrder class has been initialized
   anAddress is consistent with range of .shipping address
   sufficient memory exists for the new instance
 guarantees
   one new Book order exists with .id set, .date == today,
     .shipping address == an address, and .state == Open
   reference to newly created order has been returned
 }
 var
  newBookOrder: ^BO_BookOrder;
 begin
  New( newBookOrder );
  { initialize attribute instance variables }
  newBookOrder^.id := newBookOrderId();
  newBookOrder^.dateOpened := System.Today();
  newBookOrder^.shippingAddress: anAddress;
  newBookOrder^.status := BO_Open;
  { null out the pointer to the next book order }
  newBookOrder^.NextBookOrder := null;
  { initialize association participation instance variables }
  newBookOrder^.pForFirstOrderLine := null;
  newBookOrder^.pForLastOrderLine := null;
  { add this to the linked list of Book Orders }
  if ( firstBookOrder = null )
   then firstBookOrder := newBookOrder;
  if ( lastBookOrder <> null )
   then lastBookOrder^.NextBookOrder := newBookOrder;
  lastBookOrder := newBookOrder;
  return newBookOrder;
 end;


  ...


function BO_isPackable( aBookOrder: ^BO_BookOrder ): Boolean;
 { requires
   aBookOrder <> null
  guarantees
   true only when .state is Placed and each line is packable
 }
 var
  packable: Boolean;
  nextBookOrderLine: ^BL_BookOrderLine;
 begin
```

```
    packable := ( aBookOrder^.state = BO_Placed );
    nextBookOrderLine := aBookOrder^.pForFirstOrderLine;
    while( nextBookOrderLine <> null )
     begin
      packable := packable AND BL_isPackable( nextBookOrderLine );
      nextBookOrderLine := nextBookorderLine^.nextLine;
     end;
    return packable;
   end;

...

procedure BO_add( aBookOrder: ^BO_BookOrder,
            aMedium: ^MD_Medium,
            qty: integer );
  { requires
    aBookOrder <> null
    aMedium <> null
    qty is consistent with the range of book order line .quantity
   guarantees
    if state was Open --> one new book order line has been added
  }
   var
    newBookOrderLine: ^BL_BookOrderLine;
   begin
    if( aBookOrder^.state = BO_Open )
     begin
      newBookOrderLine := BO_NewBookOrderLine( aMedium,
                                               qty );
      if( aBookOrder^.firstBookOrderLine = null )
       then aBookOrderLine.firstBookOrderLine :=
                        newBookOrderLine;
      if( aBookOrder^.lastBookOrderLine <> null )
       then aBookOrder^.lastBookOrderLine^.nextLine :=
                        newBookOrderLine;
      aBookOrder^.lastBookOrderLine := newBookOrderLine;
     end;
   end;

  procedure BO_packed( aBookOrder: ^BO_BookOrder );
   { requires
     aBookOrder <> null
    guarantees
     if .state was Placed and this order is packable -->
      packed has been signaled for each line (via For)
      and .state == Packed
```

```
      }
      var
       nextBookOrderLine: ^BL_BookOrderLine;
      begin
       if( aBookOrder^.state = BO_Open AND
          BO_isPackable( aBookOrder ) )
         then begin
             nextBookOrderLine := aBookOrder^.firstBookOrderLine;
             repeat
               BL_Place( nextBookOrderLine );
               nextBookOrderLine := nextBookOrderLine^.nextLine;
             until( nextBookOrderLine = null );
             aBookOrder^.state = BO_Packed;
           end;
      end;

...
```

Code Sample 19.16 Partial Pascal Code for Book Order Line

```
{ in file BL_BookOrderLine.pas }
 type
  { enumerated type for states in state model }
  BL_status = ( BL_Open, BL_Placed, BL_Completed );

  BL_BookOrderLine = record
    { attribute instance variables }
    quantity: integer;
    pricePerCopy: real;
    status: BL_status;
    { link to the next Book order line in the list }
    nextLine: ^BL_BookOrderLine;
    { association participation instance variables }
    pFor: ^MD_Medium;
  end;

{ Constructor }
function BL_newBookOrderLine( aMedium: ^MD_Medium,
                                  qty: integer ): ^BL_BookOrderLine;
  { requires
    aMedium <> null
    qty is consistent with range of .quantity
    sufficient memory exists for the new instance
  guarantees
```

```
        one new book order line exists with:
          .quantity == qty
          .pricePerCopy == aMedium.sellingPrice()
          linked to the referenced Medium
          reference to newly created order line has been returned
    }
    var
     newBookOrderLine: ^BL_BookOrderLine;
    begin
     New( newBookOrderLine );
     { initialize attribute instance variables }
     newBookOrderLine^.quantity := qty;
     newBookOrderLine^.pricePerCopy := sellingPrice( aMedium );
     newBookOrderLine^.status := BL_Open;
     { null out the pointer to the next book order line }
     newBookOrderLine^.nextLine := null;
     { initialize association participation instance variables }
     newBookOrderLine^.pFor := aMedium;
     return newBookOrderLine;
    end;

...


    function BL_isPackable( aBookOrderLine: ^BL_BookOrderLine ):
  Boolean;
      { requires
        aBookOrderLine <> null
      guarantees
        true only when this order line is packable
          (i.e., refers to eBook medium, or
             print medium.stockLevel >= .quantity)
      }
    var
     packable: Boolean;
    begin
     packable := MD_isPrintMedium( aBookOrderLine^.pFor );
     if ( not packable )
      packable := ( PM_stockLevel( aBookOrderLine^.pFor ) >=
                    aBookOrderLine^.quantity );
     return packable;
    end;

...


  procedure BL_packed( aBookOrderLine: ^BL_BookOrderLine );
    { requires
```

```
    aBookOrderLine <> null
 guarantees
   if .state was Placed
    if linked to Print Medium
      then picked( .quantity ) has been signaled for it
     .state == Completed
 }
 begin
  if ( aBookOrderLine^.state = BL_Placed )
   then begin
      if ( MD_isPrintMedium( aBookOrderLine^.pFor ) )
        then PM_picked( aBookOrderLine^.pFor );
        aBookOrderLine^.state := BL_Completed;
      end;
  end;

. . .
```

19.9.6   Extract the Structure Chart

If you use appropriate naming conventions and code structuring guidelines, the object-oriented nature of the code should still be readily apparent even though the code is written in a non-object-oriented programming language. The object-oriented design diagram should be sufficient as a high-level design diagram. On the other hand, it might be useful to extract a more traditional structure chart diagram.[20] If a structure chart diagram is needed, start with the main function, and then arrange all remaining functions in a who-calls-who hierarchy. The challenge in any nontrivial system will be the size of the structure chart, as they tend to grow quite large.

19.9.7   Dealing with Inheritance

A complication in translating object-oriented design to structured design is inheritance. Languages like C, Pascal, etc. don't support inheritance so it needs to be simulated. In Order fulfillment, inheritance exists between Medium, eBookMedium, and PrintMedium. Several options are available; three are discussed in this section. Another alternative not presented here is to use function pointers in the record-like structure.

---

20 See, for example, https://en.wikipedia.org/wiki/Structure_chart or [Page-Jones88].

19.9.8 Dealing with Inheritance: Collapse Subclasses into Superclass

One option is to collapse the subclasses into the superclass data structure. This is effectively a vertical merge as described earlier in this chapter. If supported by the language, something like C's union or Pascal's "variant record" overlays the varying parts, reducing memory use—which could be important when memory is constrained.

This is also where a type discriminator becomes very important. There might be no other way for functions to know what subclass they are dealing with. A flag embedded in the data structure becomes critical. The record-like structure for Medium, eBook medium, and Print medium using the collapse option are shown in Code Sample 19.17.

Code Sample 19.17 The Collapse Option for Dealing with Inheritance

```
{ in file MD_Medium.pas }
 type
  MD_MediumType = ( eBookMedium, PrintMedium );

  EM_EBookMedium = record
   { attribute instance variables for eBook Medium }
   productKey: string;
  end;

  PM_PrintMedium = record
   { attribute instance variables for Print Medium }
   stockLevel: integer;
   reorderLevel: integer;
   reorderQuantity: integer;
   shippingWeight: integer;
  end;

  MD_Medium = record
   { attribute instance variables for Medium }
   ISBN: string;
   sellPrice: real;
   acquisitionCost: real;
   isVisible: Boolean;
   case mediumType: MD_MediumType of
     eBookMedium: EM_EBookMedium;
     PrintMedium: PM_PrintMedium;
   end;
   { association participation instance variables }
   pIsFormOf: ^TL_Title;
  end;
```

This approach tends to be simplest and gives generally uniform access time to objects, that is, performance is generally not affected by what subclass the object belongs to. On the negative side, this implementation can lead to wasted (i.e., holes in) memory—particularly when `union` or "variant record" isn't used.

19.9.9 Dealing with Inheritance: Distribute the Superclass

A second option is to distribute the superclass (base class) into the subclasses as shown in Code Sample 19.18.

Code Sample 19.18 The Distribute Option for Dealing with Inheritance

```
{ in file EM_EBookMedium.pas }
 type
  EM_EBookMedium = record
   { attribute instance variables for Medium }
   ISBN: string;
   sellPrice: real;
   acquisitionCost: real;
   isVisible: Boolean;
   { attribute instance variables for eBook Medium }
   productKey: string;
   { association participation instance variables }
   pIsFormOf: ^TL_Title;
   end;


{ in file PM_PrintMedium.pas }
 type
  EM_EBookMedium = record
   { attribute instance variables for Medium }
   ISBN: string;
   sellPrice: real;
   acquisitionCost: real;
   isVisible: Boolean;
   { attribute instance variables for Print Medium }
   stockLevel: integer;
   reorderLevel: integer;
   reorderQuantity: integer;
   shippingWeight: integer;
   { association participation instance variables }
   pIsFormOf: ^TL_Title;
   end;
```

This has the advantage of more efficient use of memory as well as search times being reduced when the subtype is already known. If it is already known that the book with .ISBN == 0-321-22875-8 is a Print medium, there is no need to search eBook medium. On the other hand, if the subtype is not known, then both subclasses might need to be searched. This also increases duplicate code for superclass functions, for example, EM_sellPrice() and PM_sellPrice() are both needed yet have virtually identical code.

19.9.10   Dealing with Inheritance: Link All Classes

A third option is to leave all record-like structures as separate entities and link them with pointers. This is shown in Code Sample 19.19.

Code Sample 19.19 The Link Option for Dealing with Inheritance

```
{ in file EM_EBookMedium.pas }
 type
  EM_EBookMedium = record
   { attribute instance variables for eBook Medium }
   productKey: string;
   { reference to base Medium }
   pMedium: ^MD_Medium;
  end;


{ in file PM_PrintMedium.pas }
 type
  EM_EBookMedium = record
   { attribute instance variables for eBook Medium }
   stockLevel: integer;
   reorderLevel: integer;
   reorderQuantity: integer;
   shippingWeight: integer;
   { reference to base Medium }
   pMedium: ^MD_Medium;
  end;


{ in file MD_Medium.pas }
 type
  MD_MediumType = ( eBookMedium, PrintMedium );

  MD_Medium = record
   { attribute instance variables for Medium }
```

```
ISBN: string;
sellPrice: real;
acquisitionCost: real;
isVisible: Boolean;
{ reference to either eBook Medium or Print Medium }
case mediumType: MD_MediumType of
  eBookMedium: ^EM_EBookMedium;
  PrintMedium: ^PM_PrintMedium;
end;
{ association participation instance variables }
pIsFormOf: ^TL_Title;
end;
```

Most object-oriented compilers and run-time systems use this third option because it tends to use memory most efficiently and also tends to minimize run time. On the disadvantage side, it is the most complex because of the number of pointers in use.

19.9.11   Comments on the Derived Structured Design

If a structured design is derived from an object-oriented design, that design is almost certain to be better—in terms of the fundamental principles: abstraction, encapsulation, cohesion, coupling, etc.—than a traditionally developed structured design. In object-oriented design the fundamental principles are easier to observe and enforce. In deriving the structured design, you are essentially just ignoring information you already have (class boundaries).

When developing structured design and code the traditional way, knowledge of the classes is less obvious or probably missing entirely, so it is a lesser (potentially nonexistent) driver of good design partitioning. This is why converting object-oriented design and code to structured design and code is so straightforward: known information is being ignored. This is also why converting traditional structured design and code into object-oriented design and code is so difficult: information (good class partitioning) didn't exist and that knowledge can be hard to create.

19.9.12   Going even Lower

In some cases, even implementing in structured languages like C, Pascal, etc. carries too much overhead. It's not unheard of for critical functions or even entire (sub)domains to be implemented in assembly language. One team had to develop a solver for systems of simultaneous linear equations under extremely tight constraints: very limited memory with a slow CPU. Design and coding was done first in plain FORTRAN to verify algorithm correctness. The FORTRAN code was then hand-assembled into the production application. The resulting assembly code both ran correctly and met all performance constraints.

19.10   Run-Time Environment Optimization

Performance can be significantly affected by run-time environment configuration. Operating systems, databases, and networks are often highly configurable and can be tuned to perform better given the nature of applications. Each will be briefly discussed.

19.10.1   Tune the Operating System

A number of parameters may be available for tuning an operating system, such as:

- System versus nonsystem memory allocation
- Default stack sizes (kernel stack, user stack, thread stack)
- Default shared memory size
- Virtual memory size versus physical memory available
- Various OS caches (thread cache, file descriptor cache, etc.)
- Various queue sizes (I/O queue, event queue, etc.)
- Number and size of I/O buffers
- Maximum I/O block size
- I/O file allocation size
- Scheduler parameters (minimum run time, maximum wait time, etc.)
- RAID levels and configuration
- ...

19.10.2   Tune the Database

Database installations are often highly configurable and tunable:

- Index critical tables (covered earlier)
- Adjust cache sizes
- ...

Transaction logs and temporary spaces are heavy consumers of I/O and affect performance for all database users. Placing these appropriately is crucial. Frequently joined tables and indexes should be placed so that when requested, they can be retrieved simultaneously from separate disks. Frequently accessed tables and indexes are often placed on separate disks to balance I/O and reduce read queuing.

Tuning the DBMS can involve setting the recovery interval (time needed to restore the state of data to a particular point in time), assigning parallelism (breaking up work from a single query into tasks assigned to different computers), and network protocols used to communicate with database consumers.

It is much faster to access data in memory than from disk, so maintaining a sizeable cache helps functions run faster. The same consideration should be given to working space. Caching execution plans and procedures means that they are reused instead of being recompiled every time they are needed. It can be important to take as much memory as possible while leaving enough for other processes and the operating system without excessive paging.

Processing resources are sometimes assigned to specific activities to improve concurrency. On a server with eight processors, six could be reserved for the DBMS to maximize use of processing resources. Debnath[21] provides an interesting approach to database tuning.

19.10.3 Tune the Network

A number of parameters may be available for tuning a network, such as:

- Connection time-out
- Default send and receive transfer sizes
- Default IP window size
- Logical interfaces per physical interface
- Delayed acknowledgement time
- TCP TIME-WAIT
- TCP maximum RST segments per unit time
- TCP connection's minimum and maximum retransmission time-out (RTO)
- Default maximum UDP socket datagram size
- Default maximum UDP socket receive buffer size
- ...

19.11 Hardware Optimization

One simple, but possibly expensive, way to improve performance is to invest in higher-performance computing infrastructure (hardware):

- Faster CPU
- More memory
- Higher bandwidth network
- Special-purpose hardware, like a graphics processor
- ...

Another approach is to distribute the computation across more processors, that is, parallelization. Availability of relatively inexpensive cloud computing

---

21 See [Debnath08].

infrastructures makes this increasingly feasible. Ian Foster provides a good explanation of how to develop parallel programs.[22] At the highest level, Foster's process involves four steps:

1) Partition the computation into as many (kinds of) small units as possible.
2) Understand the communication needs between each of the (kinds of) units.
3) Agglomerate units into higher-level computational elements that localize computation with data and minimize the need for communication with other elements.
4) Allocate the resulting computational elements to the available processing resources.

19.12   Solidify Optimizations

Any nontrivial, non-obvious optimization worth keeping is also worth documenting to support long-term maintenance. Remember that software maintainers need answers to two critical questions:

- *What is this code intended to do?*
- *Why does this code look the way it does?*

Depending on the scope of the code in question, the first question can be answered:

- *For Model region code*—The semantic model defines what the code is intended to do.
- *For View-controller region code*—The interface specification defines intent.
- *For any method on a class*—The operation contract defines it.
- *For lines of code in a method*—If programming by intent was used, this will also be explicit.

Done properly, model-based software engineering automatically answers the first question. Answering the second question should be the primary role of design and code documentation:

> *"Design and code documentation should be more about why the code looks the way it does than about how the code looks."*

When optimizing, performance improves but necessarily at the cost of increased accidental complexity: with negative effects on cost, schedule, and defects. Document each optimization:

---

22 See [Foster95].

- *What* changed in the design and/or code?
- *How* it changed? How is the after-code structure related to the before-code structure?
- *Why* it changed? What critical aspect(s) of performance drove this optimization?

Similarly, if you have any sense that any of your design decisions are "clever," it becomes very important to explain your cleverness:

- *What* clever thing did you do?—What did the design and code look like before? What does it look like after?
- *Why* did you do that clever thing?—What is the benefit over having done it in a more obvious, straightforward way? Why is this way better?

You should not even consider effort invested in design and code documentation as "for someone else's benefit." Code has a particular habit of following its developer around for a very long time—even when that developer moves to another project or even another organization. Instead, think of design documentation as reminding yourself of the critical details so that when it does resurface five or ten years in the future, you will be reminded of your rationale. You will be able to maintain that code much more easily. You're not documenting for someone else's benefit, but you're documenting for your own future benefit.

19.13 Quality Criteria

In addition to the overall quality criteria (Table 3.1) and naming criteria (Table 3.2), the quality criteria in Table 19.11 can be applied to all optimized design and code-related work to identify and remove defects as quickly and as cheaply as possible.

Table 19.11 Quality criteria for design and code optimization.

Item	Criterion
OP-1	The set of optimizations are sufficient: all relevant nonfunctional how well requirements are satisfied
OP-2	Every optimization is necessary: the increase in value from improved performance is adequately higher than lifetime cost
OP-3	The behavior—the semantic—of the design and code has not been changed by any optimization: that is, no defects were introduced
OP-4	If not already obvious, each optimization is clearly documented in terms of what got changed, how it got changed, and why it got changed

19.14 Summary

This chapter presents an engineering process for optimization and overviews design and code optimization techniques. This chapter surveys general concepts and techniques, including:

- High-level design optimization: usage matrix, horizontal and vertical split, horizontal and vertical merge
- Detailed design and code optimization: higher-performance algorithms, semantics preserving transforms, bypassing encapsulation
- SQL optimization
- Programming language optimizations: design and implementing in a lower-level language
- Run-time environment optimizations: tune operating system, tune database, tune network
- Hardware optimization: higher-performance hardware, distribute across more processors, special-purpose hardware
- Solidifying optimizations

The techniques in this chapter are by no means exhaustive. A complete discussion of optimization would require an entire book on its own. Other techniques can and should be considered where appropriate. Key messages in this chapter are as follows:

- Optimization can, should, and often must be done.
- Optimization necessarily increases accidental complexity: driving up cost, schedule, and the likelihood of defects.
- The value of any optimization needs to be considered in light of its cost over the expected service life of the software.
- Non-obvious design and code optimizations need to be explained and justified.

Unfortunately, improving performance necessarily increases accidental complexity and increases development and maintenance cost, schedule, and defects. The goal will be to maximize the value of the design and code with minimum investment in optimization—and without breaking functionality in the process.

19.14.1 Code Is Still a Mapping

Despite optimization, the design and code for a (sub)domain is still a mapping from policy and process semantics onto automation technology semantics that must:

- Be sufficiently complete
- Preserve semantic
- Now, satisfy all nonfunctional how well requirements

Also, that design and code should also have the least possible complexity.

20

Model Compilation

Chapters 15–19 described by-hand translation of semantic models into executable code. Generating code from UML models is as old as UML, which was introduced in 1997. That said, the majority of UML-based code generators only translate from design models[1]: a designer makes a class diagram in UML's design dialect and a tool turns that into code frames. Generated code is usually limited to class headers, variable declarations, and operation signatures. Most tools are unable to generate any more than that. This chapter explains how to translate a semantic model to fully executable code. This is much more powerful.

Topics in this chapter include:

- Open versus closed model compilers
- Regular versus irregular mappings
- Computation Independent Models (CIMs), Platform Independent Models (PIMs), and Platform Specific Models (PSMs)
- UML Action Semantics
- Open model compilation, in detail
- A brief review of programming language evolution
- Quality criteria

20.1 Open Versus Closed Model Compilers

In addition to translating only from design, mainstream model compilers—both UML and not—are "closed": they follow a predetermined, hardwired process in generating the code. A closed compiler can only generate what it

---

1 Whenever the term "round trip," that is, model-to-code and code-to-model, is used in describing a tool, that tool is necessarily a design dialect tool. Semantic model-to-code is practical, as described in this chapter. Code-to-semantic model is not possible in the general case; the reason should be apparent after understanding this chapter.

How to Engineer Software: A Model-Based Approach, First Edition. Steve Tockey.
© 2019 the IEEE Computer Society, Inc. Published 2019 by John Wiley & Sons, Inc.

knows how to generate, and that might not be appropriate for any number of reasons. If you don't like the code generated by a closed compiler, you only have two choices:

- *Edit the generated code*—You now risk those edits being overwritten the next time code is generated. Even if you are careful not to overwrite, you still need to manually edit the generated code to apply the modifications to that next generation.
- *Don't use a model compiler, but generate code by hand*—You miss the benefits of model compilation.

An open model compiler puts the translation process entirely under your control:

> *"If you don't like the code generated by an open model compiler, don't modify that code. Instead, modify the compiler to have it generate code you do like[2]"*

Sally Shlaer and Steve Mellor[3] pioneered open model compilation as an extension to their object-oriented analysis method.[4] Their key insight was to focus on the design *process* rather than the design *product*. Their goal was to move the mechanical, repeatable parts of software design and coding out of a developer's head and into a machine. This chapter provides an in-depth description of open model compilation.

20.2   Regular Versus Irregular Mappings

As already explained, Model region code is a mapping from a semantic model of policies and processes to a semantic model of automation technology. Any mapping satisfying the three properties—sufficiently complete, preserves semantics, and satisfies nonfunctional requirements—is a correct program.[5] Many correct programs can exist for a given policy and process semantic model and automation technology pair. Instead of looking at a single correct program, consider all

---

2 Optimizing application code is discussed in Chapter 21.
3 Then at Project Technologies, Inc.
4 Best described in [Shlaer88] and [Shlaer91].
5 More precisely, it is correct with respect to that semantic model of policies and processes.

possible correct programs. Consider how regular or irregular the mappings within a single correct program might be:

- *Regular mapping*—One kind of element in the policy and process semantic model is always mapped the same way onto the automation technology (e.g., model class to Java class, model attribute to Java instance variable, association to instance variable, model event to Java operation, etc.).
- *Irregular mapping*—One kind of element (e.g., class) in the policy and process semantic model is sometimes mapped one way onto the automation technology and sometimes mapped another way (e.g., to Java classes in some cases, to Java interfaces in other cases, and to Java instance variables in still others).

When mappings are regular, they can be described through a set of production rules of the form "A ➜ B + C" (i.e., "Things of type A in a policy and process semantic model are mapped onto things of type B followed by things of type C in the automation technology"). A mapping does not actually need to be completely regular to be described by production rules. Regularity simply reduces the number of production rules needed and removes potential non-determinism about what rule to apply when more than one could be applied. Table 20.1 summarizes, at a high level, regular mappings described in Chapters 15–19.

The heart of an open model compiler is a production rule interpreter, as shown in Figure 20.1.

The rule interpreter simply applies a defined set of production rules to a semantic model to generate source code. If you don't like the generated code, don't edit it and risk overwriting later. Instead, edit the production rules to direct the model compiler to generate better code. Open model compilers have existed since the 1990s and have been used in complex, high-performance, mission- and life-critical real-time embedded applications including high-speed telephone switching systems and medical devices.

Table 20.1 High-level semantic model to technology mappings in Chapters 15–19.

Semantic model element	Is mapped onto technology element
Class	Class and/or database table
Attribute	Instance variable and/or field in table
Association	Instance variable and/or field in table
Derived attribute	"Getter" (pull) operation
Data message	"Getter" (pull) operation
Event message	"Put-er" (push) operation
State model transition	Operation contract and method

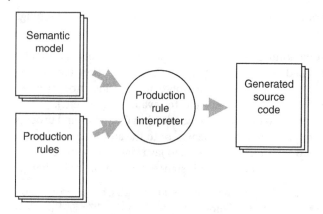

Figure 20.1 A production rule interpreter is the heart of an open model compiler.

20.3 CIMs, PIMs, and PSMs

A critical aspect of model compilation involves the terms Computation Independent Model, Platform Independent Model, and Platform Specific Model. These terms originate in OMG's Model Driven Architecture (MDA).[6] As implied,

- *CIM*—A purely semantic model, devoid of any and all automation technology. Semantic models are CIMs. The terms mean the same and will be used interchangeably throughout this chapter. Unfortunately, CIMs cannot be mechanically translated into fully executable code for reasons explained below.
- *PIM*—A PIM contains sufficient guidance to produce fully executable code while still being generic enough to be translated into a variety of computing platforms.
- *PSM*—A PSM is targeted for execution in one specific technology environment, for example, Java on a single-user desktop versus distributed C# versus C++ on a mobile device.

As stated, it is not possible to mechanically generate fully executable code— down to assignments, if-then-else, loops, returns, etc.—from a CIM. There are two reasons. First, there is no practical, general mechanical way to translate any arbitrary attribute range into an appropriate run-time data type. The range of the .balance of a Bank account at Silly Bank is specified as "from USD $0 to USD $100,000,000 to the nearest USD $0.01." It is not possible[7] to reliably convert any statement like this into, say, a choice of double or a special Money

---

6 See, for example, [Truyen06].
7 More precisely, it is not possible today. It is not clear that it could ever be possible.

or Currency type. The range of Customer.name in Order fulfillment is specified as "unconstrained"; how can a program recognize that String might be appropriate? Human involvement is needed.

The second reason is that action specifications in a CIM are non-algorithmic. As described in Chapter 10, action specifications should be in design by contract (i.e., requires-guarantees) form. Choice of an algorithm would, in general, depend on characteristics of the automation technology. Selecting an appropriate algorithm, given only a contract, is also non-computable. Human involvement is needed here, too.

When a person translates a semantic model into code, they can and do make nontrivial technology decisions—often without even noticing. With a model compiler, the CIM needs to be supplemented with data type guidance for attributes and algorithm guidance for actions. This CIM-plus-guidance is the PIM. Algorithms can be specified in an abstract but computationally complete "action language" as explained below.

A less important but still significant issue is reduced versus expanded models. A reduced model contains only elements intended for automation; every element in a reduced semantic model is to be translated. An expanded model includes model elements that provide a larger context for understanding policies and processes. The model compiler needs to know which elements of an expanded model to translate and which to not. A PIM can also inform the compiler which elements need translation.

20.3.1 PIM Overlays

PIM content needed to compile a CIM should be separable and managed apart from its semantic model. One reason is that many people who work with semantic models don't need and may be distracted by PIM content. Domain experts normally don't care about automation technology issues like data types and algorithms. Another reason is that it allows one CIM to have different overlays for different purposes. The same semantic model can be translated:

- Using PIM overlay A and production rule set 1 into a self-contained desktop application
- Using PIM overlay A and rule set 2 into a self-contained mobile application
- Using PIM overlay B and rule set 3 into a REST service
- Using PIM overlay C and rule set 4 into a distributed system with a mobile front end and a REST back end

PIM content can be used to guide optimization as discussed in Chapter 21. It can also encode choices in a product family CIM: use range X for attribute 58, multiplicity Y for association 66, and treat generalization 73 as {complete}. PIM content could be significantly different from one product family instance to the next. Separating PIM content into overlays allows independent

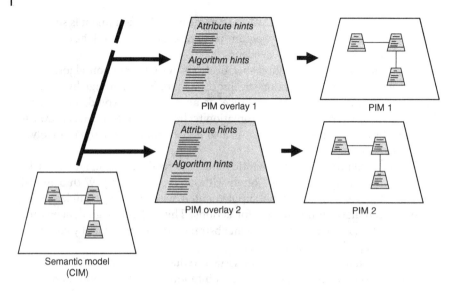

Figure 20.2 Separating PIM content into overlays on a semantic model.

maintenance of one CIM and separate overlays for each translation scenario as illustrated in Figure 20.2.

If a CIM is modified, for example, to extend scope, adapt to a change in policies or processes, and fix a CIM-level problem that snuck into production, it could be as simple as running the revised CIM through the model compiler with each PIM overlay plus rule set combination to generate revised implementations for each target platform. Some CIM changes, like extending scope, often require corresponding modification of PIM overlays.

20.4   UML Action Semantics

UML's "Action Semantics" are an abstract, computationally complete, minimally algorithmic "language" that has been carefully defined to allow actions to be translated into programming languages without over-constraining to a specific platform.[8] Action semantics are necessarily algorithmic; however control structures like for-next, while-do, and repeat-until found in typical programming languages are usually intentionally absent. Data in action semantics form are only specified in terms of, for example, values and collections. When a model compiler needs to translate a collection, it is free to translate it into a memory-resident array, linked list, database table, records in a flat file

---

8 See, for example, [Mellor98].

on a disk, etc. It is also free to generate code that traverses that collection with a for-next, while-do, repeat-until, Iterator pattern, etc.

For various technical and nontechnical reasons, the OMG initially decided it was not appropriate to standardize action language syntax. This gave tool builders full freedom to define their own. Syntax can be textual or graphical; it doesn't matter as long as there is a clear mapping of that syntax onto the action language semantics. One advantage of vendor compliance is the ability to export a model from one tool and import it into another. Even though action language syntax may be completely different between the tools, action specifications have exactly the same meaning in both so they are shareable.

A number of action language syntaxes have existed for years. Some of these action languages predate the OMG Action Semantics specification and might not fully comply with the standard. On the other hand, these early action languages have proven sufficient and useful on many real projects. The earliest example of concrete action language syntax would probably be Shlaer–Mellor Action Language (SMALL) and That Action Language (TALL). Other action languages include Executable UML,[9] Object Action Language (OAL), Action Specification Language (ASL), Platform Independent Action Language (PAL), and PathMATE Action Language (PAL). Starr's Concise Relational Action Language (SCRALL)[10] is a graphical language. The OMG adopted the Action Language for Foundational UML (Alf),[11] which is similar to Java, in 2013. Code Samples 20.1 and 20.2 show action language implementations of action Mark as Placed on class Book order. Both code samples contain for-next loops. The key is that these loops do not imply serial execution as in typical programming language. Action semantics explicitly support parallel execution.

Code Sample 20.1 Action BookOrder.markAsPlaced()in Executable UML

```
entry/
  self.shippingAddress = anAddress;
  select many lines from instances of BookOrderLine
                where selected.orderId == this.id;
  for each aLine in lines
    generate placed() to aLine;
  end for;
  generate orderIsPlaced() to customer
```

---

9 SMALL, TALL, and Executable UML are described in [Mellor02].
10 See [Starr01].
11 See [OMG13]. More information on Alf can be found at: http://www.slideshare.net/seidewitz.

Code Sample 20.2 Action BookOrder.markAsPlaced()in Alf

```
public place ( in anAddress: Address ) {
  this.shippingAddress = anAddress;
  for ( aLine in this.isFor ) {
    aLine.place ();
  }
}
```

20.5   Open Model Compilation, in Detail

Figure 20.3 shows the complete picture of open model compilation.
Each component in Figure 20.3 is described in more detail:

- *Semantic model (CIM)*—A technology-free model of policy and process semantics as developed in Part II. Appendices D, F, H, and J are example CIMs.
- *Attribute and action hints (PIM overlay)*—Additional guidance the model compiler needs for mapping attributes onto run-time data types along with action semantics for generating method body code. If the semantic model is an extended model, this would also inform the compiler which CIM

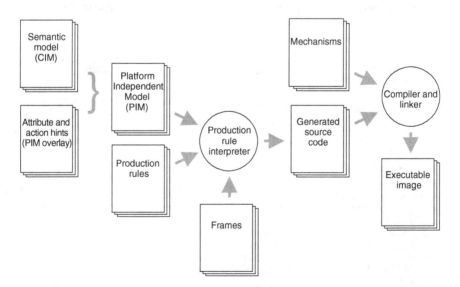

Figure 20.3 Complete picture of open model compilation.

elements need translation and which do not. If the CIM is a product family model, option selections are also specified.

- *PIM*—A CIM combined with a PIM overlay, which is the input actually translated by the model compiler.
- *Production rules*—A set of rules for the interpreter to apply in generating application source code. Each rule is a precise description of how elements in a PIM are mapped onto automation technology.
- *Frames*—Partially generic and partially tagged units of code that provide a structure into which application-specific code is injected. Mellor and Balcer[12] don't distinguish between production rules and frames, calling both "archetypes." It is not critical to distinguish between the two.
- *Production rule interpreter*—The heart of an open model compiler. Using the PIM, production rules, and frames as input, the interpreter generates the application source code.
- *Generated source code*—Compilable application-specific source code created by the production rule interpreter.
- *Mechanisms*—Application-independent code providing generic services. An event queue service and an error logging service would be typical examples. This code is specific to the target platform but independent of applications being generated. This code is usually written by hand, but is written only once and can be reused across many different PIMs.

20.6 A Nontrivial Example of Code Generation

Full translation of a complete PIM can involve hundreds of production rules and is too complex to step through from beginning to end. This section presents a proof-of-concept demonstration via partial translation of class Book order into Java. This demonstration concentrates on Book order's CIM attributes and state model, assuming events are pushed per guidelines in Chapter 15.

20.6.1 Example Frame

Code Sample 20.3 is a partial frame for generating Java. Like mechanisms, this is handcrafted code that is application independent, written once, and reused many times. The difference between mechanisms and frames is that a frame can appear many times in generated code; mechanisms are services that appear only once. Italicized text preceded with "#" refers to production rules that are described below. Quotes identify static template content apart from production rules; any text in quotes carries through unchanged into generated source code.

---

12 See [Mellor02].

Code Sample 20.3 A Partial Frame for Generating into a Java Class

```
"package " #DOMAIN_NAME ";"
"public class " #CLASS_NAME " {"
"public enum " #CLASS_NAME "_states { " #STATE_ENUM_LIST " };"
#ATTRIBUTE_INSTVAR_LIST
#CONSTRUCTOR_OPERATION
#PUSHED_EVENTS_OPERATION_LIST
#TRANSITION_ACTION_PRIVATE_METHOD_LIST
"}"
```

The complete frame for translating a CIM class into Java is much bigger. This example does not implement associations, getters for attributes, derived attributes, state actions, generalizations, and so on. These increase the size of the example without helping demonstrate the concept any better, so they are left out. See Appendix M for a more complete set of production rules and a Java class frame. The Java class frame is labeled "Class.#JAVA_CLASS_FRAME." A frame for generating C++ or C would obviously look different.

20.6.2 Production Rule *#DOMAIN_NAME*

The first production rule simply assigns the CIM's (sub)domain name as the Java package name. In practice, production rules need to be declared more formally to be interpretable. That formality interferes with this demonstration so rules in this chapter are defined semiformally.

Production Rule: #DOMAIN_NAME

```
#DOMAIN_NAME →
  (String) Domain.formattedDomainName()
```

This rule formats the (sub)domain name (in this case "Order fulfillment") into a text string with appropriate capitalization, no unacceptable characters (e.g., spaces, commas, hash/pound signs, and other non-alphanumerics), etc. Domain name "Order fulfillment" would be formatted as "OrderFulfillment." Domain name "*My Domain #1!*" would be formatted as "MyDomain1." The result of applying each production rule will be underlined to help contrast with the previous step, as shown in Code Sample 20.4 after applying *#DOMAIN_NAME* to Book order. This rule is trivial, but it starts the demonstration with a very simple, easy-to-understand first step.

Code Sample 20.4 Code After #DOMAIN_NAME Has Been Applied

```
package OrderFulfillment;
public class #CLASS_NAME {
public enum #CLASS_NAME_states { #STATE_ENUM_LIST };
#ATTRIBUTE_INSTVAR_LIST
#CONSTRUCTOR_OPERATION
#PUSHED_EVENTS_OPERATION_LIST
#TRANSITION_ACTION_PRIVATE_METHOD_LIST
}
```

20.6.3 Production Rule *#CLASS_NAME*

The second production rule assigns the CIM class name to the generated Java class.

Production Rule: #CLASS_NAME

```
#CLASS_NAME →
   (String) Class.formattedClassName()
```

This rule formats the CIM class name (in this case "Book Order") into a text string with appropriate capitalization, no unacceptable characters, etc. Class name "Book order" is formatted as "BookOrder." A CIM class named "My Class 1, 2, 3!" would be formatted as "MyClass123." This is also a simple rule; the result is shown in Code Sample 20.5.

20.6.4 Production Rule *#STATE_ENUM_LIST*

This is a more substantial production rule that reveals one key to open model compilation: production rules can iterate over a set of CIM elements. This rule

---

Code Sample 20.5 Code After #CLASS_NAME Has Been Applied

```
package OrderFulfillment;
public class BookOrder {
public enum BookOrder_states { #STATE_ENUM_LIST };
#ATTRIBUTE_INSTVAR_LIST
#CONSTRUCTOR_OPERATION
#PUSHED_EVENTS_OPERATION_LIST
#TRANSITION_ACTION_PRIVATE_METHOD_LIST
}
```

Code Sample 20.6 Code After #STATE_LIST Has Been Applied

```
package OrderFulfillment;

public class BookOrder {

  public enum BookOrder_states { DOESNTEXIST, OPEN, PLACED,
                                 PACKED, COMPLETED, CANCELLED };
#ATTRIBUTE_INSTVAR_LIST
#CONSTRUCTOR_OPERATION
#PUSHED_EVENTS_OPERATION_LIST
#TRANSITION_ACTION_PRIVATE_METHOD_LIST
}
```

---

generates an enumeration entry for each state in the CIM state model. To be consistent with Java style, state names are capitalized as part of formatting.

Production Rule: #STATE_ENUM_LIST

```
#STATE_ENUM_LIST →
  foreach aState in this class's state model {
    (String) aState.formattedENUMName() + ", " +
  }
```

Recalling the issue regarding when Java objects are really deleted versus "marked for delete" in Chapter 2,[13] this model compiler adds a hidden state called "Doesn't Exist." This hidden state, when combined with the visible states for Book order, yields Code Sample 20.6.

20.6.5 Production Rule *#ATTRIBUTE_INSTVAR_LIST*

This rule generates private instance variable definitions for each attribute in the CIM class. The rule fetches each attribute's run-time type from the PIM overlay.

Production Rule: #ATTRIBUTE_INSTVAR_LIST

```
#ATTRIBUTE_INSTVAR_LIST →
  foreach anAttribute in this class {
    "private " +
    (String) PIM_overlay.runTimeType( anAttribute ) + " " +
    (String) anAttribute.formattedAttributeName() + ";"
  }
```

---

13 A Java object only goes out of existence when no other Java object references it and the garbage collector reclaims the memory.

Code Sample 20.7 Code After #ATTRIBUTE_INSTVAR_LIST Has Been Applied

```
package OrderFulfillment;

public class BookOrder {

  public enum BookOrder_states { DOESNTEXIST, OPEN, PLACED,
                                 PACKED, COMPLETED, CANCELLED };

  private String id;
  private Date dateOpened;
  private Address shippingAddress;
  private BookOrder_states state;

#CONSTRUCTOR_OPERATION
#PUSHED_EVENTS_OPERATION_LIST
#TRANSITION_ACTION_PRIVATE_METHOD_LIST
}
```

The result of applying *#ATTRIBUTE_INSTVAR_LIST* is shown in Code Sample 20.7. Formatting—indentation and blank lines—in generated code samples is not necessarily automatic. Output formatting must be explicitly encoded into frames and production rules (provided the rule interpreter supports it). Some formatting in this proof of concept has been added manually to enhance readability. Readability of generated code should not be an issue in practice, however, for the same reason that developers need not be concerned with readability of object code output by a Java, C#, C++, or C compiler.

20.6.6 Production Rule *#PUSHED_EVENTS_OPERATION_LIST*

The production *rule #CONSTRUCTOR_OPERATION* is skipped for this example and is only shown for context. Consider it to be a special case of *#PUSHE-D_EVENTS_OPERATION_LIST*. The pushed events rule is an even more substantial rule that generates a Java operation interface and method body for each event in the CIM state model. This production rule reveals another key to open model compilation: production rules can be embedded within production rules.

Production Rule: #PUSHED_EVENTS_OPERATION_LIST

```
#PUSHED_EVENTS_OPERATION_LIST →
  foreach anEvent in this class' state model {
    "public void " +
```

```
      (String) anEvent.formattedEventName() +
      "(" + #OPERATION_FORMAL_PARAMETERS + ") {"
      #EVENT_METHOD_BODY +
      "}"
  }
```

Assume that *#OPERATION_FORMAL_PARAMETERS* is applied at the same time. Given what's already shown and what follows, it should be apparent that generating formal parameters for an operation interface is a solvable problem. The result of applying both rules is shown in Code Sample 20.8.

Code Sample 20.8 Code After #PUSHED_EVENTS Has Been Applied

```
package OrderFulfillment;

public class BookOrder {

  public enum BookOrder_states { DOESNTEXIST, OPEN, PLACED,
                    PACKED, COMPLETED, CANCELLED };

  private String id;
  private Date dateOpened;
  private Address shippingAddress;
  private BookOrder_states state;

#CONSTRUCTOR_OPERATION

  public void add( Medium aMedium, int qty ) {
      #EVENT_METHOD_BODY
  }

  public void drop( BookOrderLine aLine ) {
      #EVENT_METHOD_BODY
  }

  public void place( Address anAddress ) {
      #EVENT_METHOD_BODY
  }

  public void packed() {
      #EVENT_METHOD_BODY
  }

  public void shipped() {
```

```
      #EVENT_METHOD_BODY
   }

   public void cancel() {
      #EVENT_METHOD_BODY
   }

#TRANSITION_ACTION_PRIVATE_METHOD_LIST
}
```

20.6.7 Production Rule *#EVENT_METHOD_BODY*

This production rule reveals another key to open model compilation: production rules can be conditional. Based on any number of relevant factors, a rule can direct the interpreter to emit different code to deal with important variations in translation.

Production Rule: #EVENT_METHOD_BODY

```
#EVENT_METHOD_BODY ➜
   foreach aTransition triggered by this event {
      "if( state == " +
      (String) class.formattedClassName() +
      "_states." +
      (String) transition.formattedStartState() +
      #OPTIONAL_GUARD + " ) {"
      #TRANSITION_ACTIONS_LIST
      if( aTransition.startState() != aTransition.endState() ) {
         "state = " +
         (String) class.formattedClassName() +
         "_states." +
         (String) aTransition.formattedendState() + ";"
      }
      "}"
      if there is another transition triggered by this event
         " else "
   }
```

Production rule *#OPTIONAL_GUARD* is also shown. Note that guard text in generated code doesn't have to be generated from the CIM. Like run-time types for attributes, source code for guard implementations can be extracted from the PIM overlay.

Production Rule: #OPTIONAL_GUARD

```
#OPTIONAL_GUARD →
  if ( aTransition.hasGuard() ) {
    " && " +
    (String) PIM_overlay.guardCondition( aTransition.guard() )
  }
```

The result of applying both *#EVENT_METHOD_BODY* and *#OPTIONAL_-GUARD* is shown in Code Sample 20.9.

Code Sample 20.9 Code After #EVENT_METHOD_BODY Has Been Applied

```
package OrderFulfillment;

public class BookOrder {

  public enum BookOrder_states { DOESNTEXIST, OPEN, PLACED,
                                 PACKED, COMPLETED, CANCELLED };

  private String id;
  private Date dateOpened;
  private Address shippingAddress;
  private BookOrder_states state;

#CONSTRUCTOR_OPERATION

  public void add( Medium aMedium, int qty ) {
    if ( state == BookOrder_states.OPEN ) {
      #TRANSITION_ACTION_LIST
    }
  }

  public void drop( BookOrderLine aLine ) {
    if ( state == BookOrder_states.OPEN && !has1Line() ) {
      #TRANSITION_ACTION_LIST
    } else if ( state == BookOrder_states.OPEN && has1Line() ) {
      #TRANSITION_ACTION_LIST
      state = BookOrder_states.DOESNTEXIST;
    }
  }

  public void place( Address anAddress ) {
    if ( state == BookOrder_states.OPEN && !hasPrint() ) {
      #TRANSITION_ACTION_LIST
      state = BookOrder_states.COMPLETED;
    } else if ( state == BookOrder_states.OPEN && hasPrint() ) {
      #TRANSITION_ACTION_LIST
```

```
                   state = BookOrder_states.PLACED;
      }
}

public void packed() {
   if ( state == BookOrder_states.PLACED ) {
      #TRANSITION_ACTION_LIST
      state = BookOrder_states.PACKED;
   }
}

public void shipped() {
   if ( state == BookOrder_states.PACKED ) {
      #TRANSITION_ACTION_LIST
      state = BookOrder_states.COMPLETED;
   }
}

public void cancel() {
   if ( state == BookOrder_states.PLACED ) {
      #TRANSITION_ACTION_LIST
      state = BookOrder_states.CANCELLED;
   }
}

#TRANSITION_ACTION_PRIVATE_METHOD_LIST
}
```

20.6.8   Production Rule *#TRANSITION_ACTIONS_LIST*

This rule translates each action on a CIM transition into a call to a private method that implements the action's functionality.

Production Rule: #TRANSITION_ACTIONS_LIST

```
#TRANSITION_ACTIONS_LIST →
  foreach anAction on this transition {
    "this." +
    (String) snAction.formattedActionName() +
    "(" + #ACTION_ACTUAL_PARAMETERS + ");"
  }
```

Assume *#ACTION_ACTUAL_PARAMETERS* is also solvable. The result of applying both *#TRANSITION_ACTION_LIST* and *#ACTION_ACTUAL_-PARAMETERS* is shown in Code Sample 20.10. As should be expected, Foreach

Code Sample 20.10 Code After #TRANSITION_ACTION_LIST Has Been Applied

```
package OrderFulfillment;

public class BookOrder {

  public enum BookOrder_states { DOESNTEXIST, OPEN, PLACED,
                                 PACKED, COMPLETED, CANCELLED };

  private String id;
  private Date dateOpened;
  private Address shippingAddress;
  private BookOrder_states state;

#CONSTRUCTOR_OPERATION

  public void add( Medium aMedium, int qty ) {
     if( state == BookOrder_states.OPEN ) {
       this.addLine( aMedium, qty );
     }
  }

  public void drop( BookOrderLine aLine ) {
     if( state == BookOrder_states.OPEN && !has1Line() ) {
       this.dropLine( aLine );
     } else if( state == BookOrder_states.OPEN && has1Line() ) {
       this.dropLine( aLine );
       state = BookOrder_states.DOESNTEXIST;
     }
  }

  public void place( Address anAddress ) {
     if( state == BookOrder_states.OPEN && !hasPrint() ) {
       this.markAsPlaced( anAddress );
       state = BookOrder_states.COMPLETED;
     } else if( state == BookOrder_states.OPEN && hasPrint() ) {
       this.markAsPlaced( anAddress );
       state = BookOrder_states.PLACED;
     }
  }

  public void packed() {
     if( state == BookOrder_states.PLACED ) {
```

```
      this.markAsPacked();
      state = BookOrder_states.PACKED;
   }
}

public void shipped() {
   if( state == BookOrder_states.PACKED ) {
      state = BookOrder_states.COMPLETED;
   }
}

public void cancel() {
   if( state == BookOrder_states.PLACED ) {
      state = BookOrder_states.CANCELLED
   }
}


#TRANSITION_ACTION_PRIVATE_METHOD_LIST
}
```

will not generate code when a set of items is empty. Some method bodies don't have any transition actions: there weren't any on that transition in the CIM state model.

20.6.9 Production Rule #TRANSITION_ACTION_PRIVATE_METHOD_LIST

This production rule implements each transition action as a private method.

Production Rule: #PRIVATE_TRANSITION_ACTIONS

```
#TRANSITION_ACTION_PRIVATE_METHOD_LIST →
   foreach aTransitionAction on this class {
      "private void " +
      (String) aTransitionAction.formattedActionName() +
      "(" + #ACTION_FORMAL_PARAMETERS + ") {" +
      #ACTION_BODY +
      "}"
   }
```

Assume *#ACTION_FORMAL_PARAMETERS* generates the formal parameters list for a private method. None of the code generated above will change from here on, so it is skipped to conserve space. The result of applying both rules is shown in Code Sample 20.11.

Code Sample 20.11 Code After #TRANSITION_ACTION_PRIVATE_METHOD_ LIST and #ACTION_FORMAL_PARAMETERS Have Been Applied

```
package OrderFulfillment;

public class BookOrder {

  // previously generated code is skipped to save space

  private void initializer( Customer aCustomer, Address anAddress ) {
    #ACTION_BODY
  }

  private void addLine ( Medium aMedium, int qty ) {
    #ACTION_BODY
  }

  private void dropLine ( BookOrderLine aLine ) {
    #ACTION_BODY
  }

  private void markAsPlaced ( Address anAddress ) {
    #ACTION_BODY
  }

  private void markAsPacked() {
    #ACTION_BODY
  }
}
```

20.6.10 Production Rule *#ACTION_BODY*

Production rule *#ACTION_BODY* can expand an action's implementation in any one of several ways. From the model compiler's perspective, the simplest is to just extract a Java code snippet from the PIM overlay. As long as that snippet is written consistent with the production rule set's naming conventions, that snippet will fit into the generated code. Method body code generation can be as simple as just copying text.

Simple version of #ACTION_BODY
```
#ACTION_BODY →
  (String) PIM_overlay.actionBody( action )
```

On the other end of the spectrum, the action body in the PIM overlay could be written in an action language: Alf, Executable UML, SMALL, TALL, ASL,

SCRALL, etc. This requires the model compiler to have a set of production rules to compile that action language. A complete Alf parser is available,[14] and further language implementations are in progress. In theory, a model compiler could copy Alf and then hand it off to an existing Alf compiler for post-processing.

20.6.11 Closing the Nontrivial Example

As stated, this demonstration did not generate complete code for a CIM class. A number of elements required for complete implementation were left out. One example is entry/ and exit/ actions. On the other hand, it is not difficult to add them. Starting with production rule *#EVENT_METHOD_BODY* above, only two additions are needed (underlined below):

Production Rule: #EVENT_METHOD_BODY Modified for entry/ and exit/ Actions

```
#EVENT_METHOD_BODY →
  foreach aTransition triggered by this event {
    "if ( state == " +
    (String) class.formattedClassName () +
    "_states." +
    (String) aTransition.formattedStartState () +
    #OPTIONAL_GUARD + " ) { "
    #EXIT_ACTION_LIST
    #TRANSITION_ACTION_LIST
    #ENTRY_ACTION_LIST
    if ( transition.startState () != transition.endState () ) {
      "state = " +
      (String) class.formattedClassName () +
      "_states." +
      (String) aTransition.formattedEndState () + "; "
    }
    "}"
    if there is another transition on this event
      " else "
  }
```

Production rule *#EXIT_ACTION_LIST* follows. Rule *#ENTRY_ACTION_LIST* rule is virtually identical; simply replace all occurrences of "exit" with "entry."

---

14 See http://lib.modeldriven.org/MDLibrary/trunk/Applications/Alf-Reference-Implementation/dist/.

Production Rule: #EXIT_ACTION_LIST

```
#EXIT_ACTION_LIST →
  foreach anExitAction on state being exited {
    "this." +
    (String) anExitAction.formattedActionName() +
    "(" + #ACTION_FORMAL_PARAMETERS + ");"
  }
```

20.6.12   Complete Source Code for Class BookOrder

Code Sample 20.12 shows complete source code for class BookOrder[15] generated by an open model compiler built for this book. The free demonstration
semantic model editor and open model compiler are available online at
http://www.construx.com/howtoengrsw/. This is the actual generated code,
with only minor formatting to fit into book pages. All code, including contracts
and assertions, was generated by the production rules shown in Appendix M.

Code Sample 20.12 Complete Generated Code for Book Order

```
package OrderFulfillment;

  // generated 2017/07/26 21:59:50 by JAL open model compiler v4.9

public class BookOrder {

  public enum BookOrder_states { DOESNTEXIST, OPEN, PLACED, PACKED,
                                 COMPLETED, CANCELLED };

  // Attribute instance variables

    private String id;
    private Date dateOpened;
    private Address shippingAddress;
    private BookOrder_states state;

  // Association participation instance variables

    private Customer placedBy;
    private ArrayList<BookOrderLine> selectsMedium;
```

---

15 Ignoring, for now, connections to other domains like Payment, Scalability, and User security.

```
// Constructor

  public BookOrder( Address anAddress ) {
  // requires
  //  anAddress is consistent with range of .shippingAddress
  // guarantees
  //  --> new order exists w/ id, date, address and state == open
    assert( anAddress != null );
    placedBy = null;
    selectsMedium = new ArrayList<BookOrderLine>();
    this.initializer( anAddress );
    state = BookOrder_states.OPEN;
    bookOrderSet.add( this );
  }


// Attribute getters

  public String id() {
  // requires
  //  none
  // guarantees
  //  returns the id
    return id;
  }

  public Date dateOpened() {
  // requires
  //  none
  // guarantees
  //  returns the date opened
    return dateOpened;
  }

  public Address shippingAddress() {
  // requires
  //  none
  // guarantees
  //  returns the shipping address
    return shippingAddress;
  }

  public BookOrder_states state() {
  // requires
  //  none
  // guarantees
```

```
  //  returns the state
    return state;
  }


// Derived attributes

  public boolean isPackable() {
  // requires
  //   none
  // guarantees
  //   true only when state is placed and each line is packable
    boolean thisOrderisPackable =
                  ( state == BookOrder_states.PLACED );
    for ( BookOrderLine aLine: selectsMedium ) {
      thisOrderIsPackable &= aline.isPackable();
    }
    return thisOrderIsPackable;
  }

  public double sales() {
  // requires
  //   none
  // guarantees
  //   returns total dollar sales of this order
    double totalSales = 0;
    if ( state == BookOrder_states.COMPLETED ) {
      for ( BookOrderLine aLine: selectsMedium ) {
        totalSales += aline.sales();
      }
    }
    return totalSales;
  }

  public double profit() {
  // requires
  //   none
  // guarantees
  //   returns total dollar profit of this order
    double totalProfit = 0;
    if ( state == BookOrder_states.COMPLETED ) {
      for ( BookOrderLine aLine: selectsMedium ) {
        totalSales += aline.profit();
      }
    }
    return totalProfit;
```

```
}

public String userKeys() {
// requires
//   none
// guarantees
//   returns user keys for eBook media
   String userKeySet = "";
   if( state != BookOrder_states.OPEN &&
      state != BookOrder_states.CANCELLED ) {
      for( BookOrderLine aLine: selectsMedium ) {
         userKeySet += aline.userKey();
      }
   }
   return userKeySet;
}


// Pushed events

public void add( Medium aMedium, int qty ) {
// requires
//   state == open, aMedium not null
//   qty consistent w/ range of .quantity
// guarantees
//   state was open --> new Book order line has been created
   assert( aMedium != null ): "aMedium was null";[16]
   assert( qty > 0 ): "qty was <= zero";
   if( state == BookOrder_states.OPEN ) {
      this.addLine( aMedium, qty );
   }
}

public void drop( BookOrderLine aLine ) {
// requires
//   state == open and >1 line and a Line exists in BookOrder
//      -- or --
//   state == open and =1 line and a Line exists in BookOrder
// guarantees
//   state was open and >1 line --> referenced line
//                                  has been deleted via For
//      -- or --
```

---

16 This only demonstrates it is also possible to generate assertions. Not all possible assertions were included.

```
//  state was open and =1 line --> referenced line
//                    has been deleted via For
//    and state == Doesn't exist
  if ( state == BookOrder_states.OPEN && hasMLines() ) {
    this.dropLine ( aLine ) ;
  } else if ( state == BookOrder_states.OPEN && !hasMLines() ) {
    this.dropLine ( aLine ) ;
    state = BookOrder_states.DOESNTEXIST;
    bookOrderSet.remove ( this ) ;
  }
}

public void place ( Address anAddress ) {
// requires
//   state == open and no print media and
//     anAddress is consistent w/ range of .shippingAddress
//     -- or --
//   state == open and has print media and
//     anAddress is consistent w/ range of .shippingAddress
// guarantees
//   state was open and no print media -->
//           .shipping address == anAddress,
//           place has been signaled for each line via For
//           and state == completed
//     -- or --
//   state was open and has print media -->
//           .shipping address == anAddress,
//           place has been signaled for each line via For
//           and state == placed
  assert ( anAddress != null ) ;
  if ( state == BookOrder_states.OPEN && !hasPMedium() ) {
    this.markAsPlaced ( anAddress ) ;
    state = BookOrder_states.COMPLETED;
  } else if ( state == BookOrder_states.OPEN && hasPMedium() ) {
    this.markAsPlaced ( anAddress ) ;
    state = BookOrder_states.PLACED;
  }
}

public void packed () {
// requires
//   none
// guarantees
//   state was placed -->
//           packed has been signaled for each line via For
//           and state == packed
```

```
    if ( state == BookOrder_states.PLACED && isPackable() ) {
      this.markAsPacked();
      state = BookOrder_states.PACKED;
    }
  }

  public void shipped() {
  // requires
  //   none
  // guarantees
  //   state was packed --> state == completed
    if ( state == BookOrder_states.PACKED ) {
      state = BookOrder_states.COMPLETED;
    }
  }

  public void cancel() {
  // requires
  //   none
  // guarantees
  //   state was placed --> state == cancelled
    if ( state == BookOrder_states.PLACED ) {
      state = BookOrder_states.CANCELLED;
    }
  }


// Private transition actions

  private void initializer( Address anAddress ) {
  // requires
  //   anAddress is consistent w/ range of .shippingAddress
  // guarantees
  //   new book order exists with id, date, address set
    assert ( anAddress != null );
    id = this.helperNewID();
    dateOpened = new Date();
    shippingAddress = anAddress;
  }

  private void addLine( Medium aMedium, int qty ) {
  // requires
  //   aMedium is not null
  //   qty is consistent w/ range of .quantity
  // guarantees
  //   new Book order line has been created
    assert ( aMedium != null ): "aMedium was null";
    assert ( qty > 0 ): "qty was <= zero";
    BookOrderLine newLine = new BookOrderLine( aMedium, qty );
```

```
        }

        private void dropLine( BookOrderLine aLine ) {
        // requires
        //   a Line exists in this BookOrder (via For)
        // guarantees
        //   referenced Book order line has been deleted via For
          assert( aLine != null ): "a line is null";
          aLine.destroy();
        }

        private void markAsPlaced( Address anAddress ) {
        // requires
        //   anAddress is consistent w/ range of .shippingAddress
        // guarantees
        //   .shipping address == anAddress
        //   place has been signaled for each line in this order via For
          assert( anAddress != null ): "an address is null";
          shippingAddress = anAddress;
          for( BookOrderLine aLine: selectsMedium ) {
            aLine.place();
          }
        }

        private void markAsPacked() {
        // requires
        //   none
        // guarantees
        //   packed has been signaled for each line in this order via For
          for( BookOrderLine aLine: selectsMedium ) {
            aLine.packed();
          }
        }


    // PIM overlay helper code

      private static int lastId = 0;

      private String helperNewId() {
      // requires
      //   none
      // guarantees
      //   returns a string for the next Book Order.id
        lastId++;
        return "Book Order #" + Integer.toString( lastId );
      }

      private boolean hasPMedium() {
```

```
// requires
//   none
// guarantees
//   returns true only when this order has any print media
  boolean hasPrintMedium = false;
  for( BookOrderLine aLine: selectsMedium ) {
    hasPrintMedium = hasPrintMedium || aLine.hasPrintMedium();
  }
  return hasPrintMedium;
}

private boolean hasMLines() {
// requires
//   none
// guarantees
//   returns true only when this order has more than one line
  return selectdMedium.size() > 1;
}

// All class members accessor

  private static ArrayList<BookOrder> bookOrderSet =
                      new ArrayList<BookOrder>();

  public static ArrayList<BookOrder> allBookOrders() {
  // requires
  //   none
  // guarantees
  //   returns (reference to) ArrayList<> of class members
    return bookOrderSet;
  }


// Association participation link and unlink services

  // link and unlink services for: <places

    public void linkPlaces( Customer aCustomer ) {
    // requires
    //   aCustomer <> null
    // guarantees
    //   both this and aCustomer are linked to each other
      assert( aCustomer != null );
      placedBy = aCustomer;
    }

    public void unlinkPlaces( Customer aCustomer ) {
```

```
        // requires
        //  aCustomer <> null
        // guarantees
        //  this and aCustomer are unlinked
          assert ( aCustomer != null );
          placedBy = null;
        }

    // link and unlink services for: for>

      public void linkItemIn ( BookOrderLine aBookOrderLine ) {
      // requires
      //  aBookOrderLine <> null
      // guarantees
      //  both this and aBookOrderLine are linked to each other
        assert ( aBookOrderLine != null );
        selectsMedium.add ( aBookOrderLine );
      }

      public void unlinkItemIn ( BookOrderLine aBookOrderLine ) {
      // requires
      //  aBookOrderLine <> null
      // guarantees
      //  this and aBookOrderLine are unlinked
        assert ( aBookOrderLine != null );
        int index = selectsMedium.indexOf ( aBookOrderLine );
        if ( index != -1 ) {
          selectsMedium.remove ( index );
        }
      }

  }
```

The executable code requires 55 rules; the remaining rules generate contracts, assertions, and other run-time checks. Underlining was added after translation to show code that came from the PIM overlay rather than the CIM; the reason will be explained later.

Ignoring blank lines but including comments, source code for class BookOrder is 324 lines. Ignoring comments, it is 175 lines. Only 85 lines have PIM overlay content (underlining); but many of those are type declarations: code generated for dynamically typed languages like Python or Smalltalk, would have even less underlining. The significant non-model generated PIM overlay code is in methods that implement actions, derived attributes, and helper functions. In class BookOrder, that is 55 lines, or 18% of the total non-blank, non-comment code. Clearly, different model compilers could produce different percentages.

Table 20.2 Summarizing generated code for several classes in Order fulfillment.

	BookOrder	BookOrderLine	ReplenishOrder	ReplenishOrderLine	Total
Non-blank, with comments	324	233	221	184	962
Non-comment	171	119	119	89	498
Any PIM content	85	33	34	19	171
Significant PIM content	55	19	28	10	112
Percent of total (%)	32	8	13	5	12

On the other hand, this provides a nontrivial data point. Generated code for several classes in Order fulfillment is summarized in Table 20.2.

Code generated for several domains reveals an average of about 20% of the code having significant PIM content. Notice how much less source code needs to be written by a developer. Most source code comes directly from policy and process semantics. Repeatable parts of design and coding have been automated:

> *"Why waste a developer's time and effort doing what a machine can do? Why not invest that time and effort in things a machine can't do, like building new semantic models, creating PIM overlays, and building & maintaining production rules, frames, and mechanisms?"*

As a proof of concept, this should be sufficiently convincing that full, automatic, mechanical translation from a CIM, via a PIM overlay, into executable code is entirely possible, realistic, practical, and enormously useful.

20.6.13 Breadth-First Versus Depth-First Code Generation

This demonstration used a breadth-first strategy; each production rule was applied sequentially. This helps illustrate how each production rule works, independent of the others. This is very inefficient in practice. A real open model compiler uses a depth-first strategy, immediately applying rules embedded in rules. Depth-first translation is significantly more efficient. One measure of goodness for a compiler is the number of passes it makes over any representation of the input. Mainstream language compilers typically use three passes: parsing, initial code generation, and optimization. If production rules are applied breadth-first, the number of passes must be at least the number of rules, for example, with 150 rules there must be at least 150 passes. Depth-first translation is done in a single pass.

20.6.14 Generating View-Controller Region Code

The proof of concept showed how an open model compiler translates a CIM class into code, but that was only for Model region of a Model–View–Controller–Infrastructure style software architecture. Only Model region code could ever be generated from a CIM. Semantic models don't have any user interface (UI) detail—intentionally—no View-controller region code could ever be generated. But that doesn't mean View-controller region code can't be generated by some other means.

First, remember that some code implementing an actor can be derived from a Dialog map as shown in Chapter 17. The Dialog map is a state model and this proof of concept focused on translating state models; you should be well on your way to creating a set of production rules to produce actor code from a Dialog map.

Second, given a suitable machine-readable description language for UI screens, production rules to map that language into code can also be written. As long as the language is complete and precise enough, for example, it allows definition of button name and location, text field name, etc., and as long as UI elements are linkable to a corresponding element on a Dialog map or CIM actor API, then code that puts a UI element on a screen and links it to the actor API can also be generated.

The key question is, however, "is it worth the extra effort to generate UI code?" Depending on how often UI are built or modified, effort needed to make View-controller region generate-able might or might not be a good investment. This is another economic—that is, engineering—decision.

20.6.15 Generating Infrastructure Region Code

It's also possible to generate Infrastructure region code. The User security, Scalability, and High availability domains in WebBooks 2.0 are service domains whose code can be generated from their semantic models. In a Model–View–Controller–Infrastructure architecture sense, these domains should be considered Infrastructure region from the perspective of Order fulfillment as Model region. Mechanisms, as shown in Figure 20.3, can also be considered Infrastructure region code although they are usually hand written.

20.7   A Brief Review of Programming Language Evolution

Open model compilation is simply stepping up to the next rung on the ladder of programming language evolution. A brief review of programming language evolution helps put this into perspective. Start with machine languages.

20.7.1   To the Computer, It's All Ones and Zeros

Code Sample 20.13 is a machine language program that runs in a real (albeit dated) computer. The program starts at memory address 000 010 000 000.

Code Sample 20.13 Sample Machine Language Code	
Memory Address	Memory Contents
000 000 001 000	000 000 000 000
000 010 000 000	111 011 100 000
000 010 000 001	001 010 001 100
000 010 000 010	011 000 010 000
000 010 000 011	001 100 001 000
000 010 000 100	111 100 101 000
000 010 000 101	101 110 001 011
000 010 000 110	110 000 100 110
000 010 000 111	110 000 100 001
000 010 001 000	101 010 000 111
000 010 001 001	111 011 000 000
000 010 001 010	101 010 000 011
000 010 001 011	111 110 000 101
000 010 001 100	000 010 001 101
000 010 001 101	000 011 001 000
000 010 001 110	000 011 000 101
000 010 001 111	000 011 001 100
000 010 010 000	000 011 001 100
000 010 010 101	000 011 001 111
000 010 010 010	000 010 100 000
000 010 010 011	000 011 010 111
000 010 010 100	000 011 001 111
000 010 010 101	000 011 010 010
000 010 010 110	000 011 001 110
000 010 010 111	000 011 000 100
000 010 011 000	000 010 100 001
000 010 011 001	000 000 000 000

Even if you were already familiar with that computer, you would still have a hard time figuring out what this code does—let alone write another program in a similar way (i.e., entirely as ones and zeros). On the other hand, this is the only code a computer actually understands. This is how developers wrote code for many years. Some developers can—and to a limited extent—still do this kind of programming.

20.7.2 Second Generation: Assembly Languages

Code Sample 20.13 is for a specific computer. Without that machine (or an emulator), you can't execute the program except by hand—and that requires understanding the computer's instruction set. Code Sample 20.14 shows the same program, but in a language that represented a great improvement over machine language when introduced. Instead of coding in ones and zeros, the advancement was to use a symbolic representation: assembly language. While some details of this code are probably still obscure, you should have a much better chance of figuring out what it does. The two columns on the left represent memory address and memory contents in octal (base 8). The source code is to the right of the two numeric columns—this sample is the output from the

---

Code Sample 20.14 Sample Assembly Language Code

```
                    *10
0010 0000 AINDEX,  0000          / AUTO-INDEX REGISTER

                    *200
0200 7340 START,   CLA CLL CMA   / SET AC REGISTER to -1
0201 1214          TAD HPNTR     / MAKE START ADDRESS OF STRING
0202 3010          DCA AINDEX    / PUT THAT INTO AUTO-INDEX REGISTER
0203 1410 NXTCH,   TAD I AINDEX  / GET THE NEXT CHARACTER
0204 7540          SNA           / AT END OF STRING YET?
0205 5613          JMP I OSRETN  / YES, RETURN TO OPERATING SYSTEM
0206 6046          TLS           / NO, PRINT THIS CHARACTER
0207 6041          TSF
0210 5207          JMP .-1       / WAIT FOR TERMINAL TO FINISH
0211 7300          CLA CLL       / CLEAR REGISTER FOR NEXT CHARACTER
0212 5203          JMP NXTCH     / GO TO GET THE NEXT CHARACTER
0213 7605 OSRETN,  7605          / OPERATING SYSTEM RE-ENTRY POINT
0214 0215 HPNTR,   HELLOW
0215 0310 HELLOW,  "H            / THE STRING TO PRINT
0216 0305          "E
```

```
0217 0314          "L
0220 0314          "L
0221 0317          "O
0222 0240          "              / SPACE CHARACTER
0223 0327          "W
0224 0317          "O
0225 0322          "R
0226 0314          "L
0227 0304          "D
0230 0241          "!
0231 0000          0              / NULL CHARACTER TO TERMINATE
         $
```

assembler, not the input. This is in PAL-8 Assembler for Digital Equipment Corporation's PDP-8 family of computers.

The advantages assembly language has over machine language include:

- Higher level of abstraction—developers express code in familiar mnemonics instead of ones and zeros
- Clarity
- Reduction in the kinds of coding mistakes that can be made, for example, miscalculating a memory address, miscalculating an offset, using the wrong instruction code, etc.
- Scalability—much bigger programs can be written and maintained
- ...

The net effect was an increase not only in code quality but in developer productivity as well.

These improvements did not come without cost:

- A translation step is needed between the developer's view of code and the computer's view.
- That translation step can be automated, but requires a nontrivial translator.

20.7.3 Third Generation: High-Level Compiled Languages

There has long been a dream of "programs that write programs." In theory, one could just describe requirements to a computer and it would produce a running application. The first widely used programming language was FORTRAN where the name stands for "FORmula TRANslator." COBOL, "COmmon Business Oriented Language," was originally intended for nontechnical (i.e.,

---

Code Sample 20.15 FORTRAN II Code for Hello World

```
      WRITE ( 1,100 )
100 FORMAT ( "HELLO WORLD!" )
      STOP
      END
```

---

business) people to develop and maintain code. The idea behind this generation of languages was to express intent in terms of familiar statements like mathematical formulas and generate assembly or machine code from that. For example,

```
Y = A * X ** 2 + B * X + C
```

This one line of FORTRAN source code could translate into hundreds, or even thousands, of assembly or machine language instructions (depending on whether the machine has hardware floating point or not). This code more clearly represents what a developer wants done. It's more in the problem space and less in the solution space.

Code Sample 20.15 shows the same functionality as Code Sample 20.14 in FORTRAN II. Even if you never wrote FORTRAN II in your life, the function should still be pretty obvious.

Again, when introduced, this generation of languages represented a major improvement over assembly language:

- Even higher level of abstraction and clarity.
- Portability—code can run on any computer with an appropriate compiler; code is no longer tied to one specific machine architecture.
- Input/output (I/O) device independence, writing to a console, line printer, card punch, and tape/disk file are equally easy—each would require very different code in assembly language.
- Further reduction in the kinds of coding mistakes that can be made—inappropriate register allocation, misunderstanding memory organization, etc.
- Scalability—even bigger programs can be written and maintained.
- Developers write less actual code; the compiler takes care of repeatable, mundane details: I/O device specifics are hidden, register allocation, memory allocation, translation of characters into binary code, etc. Repeatable parts of implementation are less error prone because they are automated.
- ...

The net result was a further increase not only in code quality but in developer productivity as well.

But again, these improvements did not come without cost:

- An even bigger translation step is needed between the developer's view of the code and the computer's view. That translation step can be automated, but requires an even more complex translator.
- Run-time overhead—the program takes up more memory and may execute slower than a native, functionally equivalent assembly or machine-code implementation.
- The translator is closed; if you don't like the generated assembly/machine code, your only hope is to hand-assemble. Many developers had to, and some still do, hand translate (or write code in a lower-level language) for that reason.

20.7.4 Modern Languages

Modern programming languages, like Java, C++, C#, Python, etc., continue this tradition of abstracting away more mechanism complexities. In this generation of languages, the advances are less in the core programming language and more in surrounding libraries like the collection classes, stream types, graphics libraries, UI toolkits, threading libraries, etc. Again, these increase abstraction and portability: the developer writes less code, and the compiler and run-time system take care of more. Code Sample 20.16 shows the same functionality in Java.

Code Sample 20.16 Java Code for Hello World

```java
public class HelloWorld {
  public static void main( String[] args ) {
    System.out.println("Hello, World!");
  }
}
```

20.7.5 Compilable Semantic Models

Figure 20.4 shows the same functionality in compilable semantic model form, that is, with a PIM overlay. The semantic model is actually significantly more powerful than the Java version in Code Sample 20.16. It not only says "Goodbye," but as many objects of class HelloWorld can be instantiated as desired.

Open model compilation is simply stepping up to the next rung on the ladder of programming language evolution. The advantages include (these are not necessarily limited to model compilation):

- Even more abstraction and clarity.
- Complete separation of functional from technical complexity.

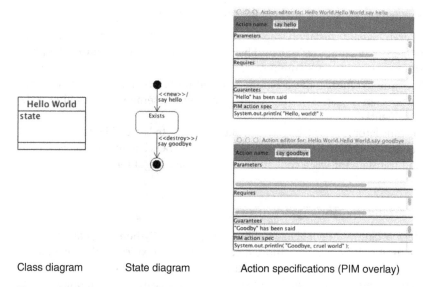

Class diagram   State diagram   Action specifications (PIM overlay)

Figure 20.4 Semantic model of Hello World.

- CIM completeness criteria and guidelines help avoid injecting requirements defects.
- Further reduction in the kinds of coding mistakes that can be made—attribute range errors, bidirectional associations, state model implementation, etc.
- CIM correctness means source code correctness.
- Developers write even less code; more is generated.
- Repeatable parts are less error prone because they are automated.
- One CIM, many translated implementations.
- Total control over generated code, for example, performance tuning, technology change, etc.
- Scalability: domain separation and subdomain partitioning mean extremely large systems can be developed and maintained efficiently and effectively.
- Portability: abstract action languages like ALF can translate into Java, C++, C#, Python, etc.
- Semantic models are far more reusable than source code in mainstream programming languages.[17]
- ...

---

17 The myth of source code reuse is discussed in Chapter 22.

With model compilation, the actual code that needs to be written by developers is reduced to:

- Reusable mechanisms, frames, and production rules in the compiler and run time
- Type declarations in PIM overlays
- Action semantics language algorithms in PIM overlays
- Class-level helper functions like guard implementers and derived attribute implementers in PIM overlays

The net result is again an increase not only in code quality but in developer productivity as well. Remember Shlaer and Mellor's goal of moving mechanical, repeatable parts of software design and coding out of a developer's head and into a machine: that is essentially what open model compilation is doing. It's doubtful that we will ever see programs that write programs without any human intervention at all. But the closer we can get, the better off we will be.

As with the earlier generations, there are costs:

- An even bigger translation step is needed. That translation step can be automated, but requires a complex translator.
- Run-time overhead—the program takes up more memory and may execute slower than a native, functionally equivalent Java, C++, C, Python, and other implementation.
- Model editors and open model compilers can be expensive, but that one-time, up-front investment needs to be compared to long-term value of reduction in both development staff and time to market. An estimation model is provided in Chapter 23 that quantifies cost and schedule for model-based software engineering projects both with and without model compilers.
- Up-front investment in production rules, frames, and mechanisms may be needed. A minimum of about 60 rules are needed to get any executable code; some domains may require over 300 production rules to produce efficient generated application code.
- May be hard to debug generated code without a semantic model-level debugger
- ...

20.8 Quality Criteria

Table 20.3 shows quality criteria for open model compilation.

Table 20.3 Quality criteria for open model compilation.

Item	Criterion
MC-1	The semantic models (CIMs) have been appropriately validated
MC-2	All necessary PIM overlay content is present: run-time data types, action specifications, reduced/expanded tags, product family choices
MC-3	Action specifications are at least Liskov substitutable with contracts
MC-4	PIM overlay choices are efficient: nonfunctional requirements (specifically how well) will be satisfied
MC-5	PIM overlay content is compatible with the production rule set(s)

20.9 Summary

Once an open model compiler has been developed and validated, notice how much easier developing new software becomes:

- *There are new policies and processes to automate*—Create and validate a semantic model (CIM), then create the PIM overlay content, compile it, and run it.

Notice how much easier maintaining existing software becomes:

- *There is a change to policies and/or processes*—Revise the semantic model, revise PIM overlay content as needed, run the revised PIM through the model compiler, and you now have a faithful implementation of that modified business. Any time a semantic model is changed, it doesn't matter how much it changed; simply recompile it, and the resulting code is a proper implementation of that revised model, provided necessary PIM overlay content is in place.
- *There is no change to policies and processes, just a need to improve some nonfunctional aspect of the code*—Revise relevant production rule(s), frames, and/or mechanisms as described in the next chapter. Run the existing semantic model(s) through the improved model compiler, and you now have an improved implementation of that same business. You are also guaranteed that in all possible cases where the improvement could have been applied, it was applied.

Further, many mappings from a single semantic model are possible. By using a different set of production rules, frames, and mechanisms, we can produce a wide variety of semantically equivalent implementations of the same policies and processes in very different execution environments (e.g., C++, C#, C, Pascal, etc.). The translation from object-oriented design to structured design (to Pascal code in the example) in Chapter 19 also follows a set of definable translations. It is possible to translate from a CIM with an appropriate PIM overlay—simply using a different set of frames, production rules, and mechanism—into C or Pascal instead of Java. PIM and C compilers have existed for many years. Some organizations use open model compilers to translate PIMs into hardware description languages like VHDL and RTL.

21

Advanced Open Model Compilation

This chapter builds on open model compilation presented in the last chapter, discussing topics such as:

- Optimizing application code
- Building a new open model compiler on an existing rule interpreter
- Generating output other than application source code
- Building a new production rule interpreter
- Weaknesses in UML semantics

21.1 Optimizing Generated Application Code

If an open model compiler generates code that satisfies all nonfunctional how well requirements, nothing more need be done. Project staff should focus on building and maintaining CIMs and PIM overlays. But what if generated code does not satisfy nonfunctional how well requirements? Or, what if substantial return on investment can be realized from further optimization? The point of an open model compiler is to be just that: open. This section discusses modifying an open model compiler to improve performance of generated code.

Before modifying an open model compiler, be sure to understand what application code should be optimized. Profile execution of running applications to find performance bottlenecks. Only now, unlike in Chapter 19, don't modify application source code. Instead, modify the open model compiler. Optimization can be incorporated into open model compilation in several ways, which are described. Unlike Chapter 19 where optimization tends to be localized, optimization in an open model compiler tends to improve performance across entire applications because it is applied wherever possible, not just where a developer explicitly applied it.

How to Engineer Software: A Model-Based Approach, First Edition. Steve Tockey.
© 2019 the IEEE Computer Society, Inc. Published 2019 by John Wiley & Sons, Inc.

21.1.1 Improve Mechanisms

The simplest form of optimization is to improve mechanisms. One example might be an event queuing service. Maybe the existing implementation is straightforward but slow. An improved implementation can be linked into generated applications, and performance should increase anywhere the queuing service is used. Another example might be a memory management service. Going from garbage collecting only when needed to incremental garbage collection could lead to better overall application performance.

21.1.2 Improve Frames and Production Rules

The next level of optimization involves modifying frames and production rules. In one organization, a very simple model compiler translated CIM classes into C and used linear search to find target objects in a linked list. Modifying frames and production rules to use binary search increased execution speed by a factor of 10. A later modification to hash tables led to even better performance.

As another example, when the state model for a CIM class has many transitions on a single event, performance can be affected by the long series of if-then statements as shown in Code Sample 21.1. This code would be generated by production rule *#EVENT_METHOD_BODY* in the previous chapter.

Code Sample 21.1 Long Chains of If-Then-Else Can Be Inefficient

```
public void someEvent ( ParameterType aParameter ) {
    if ( status == ClassName_states.S1 ) {
        #TRANSITION_ACTION_LIST
        status = ClassName_states.S2
    } else if ( status == ClassName_states.S3 ) {
        #TRANSITION_ACTION_LIST
        status = ClassName_states.S4
    } else if ( status == ClassName_states.S5 ) {
        #TRANSITION_ACTION_LIST
        status = ClassName_states.S6
    } else if ( status == ClassName_states.S7 ) {
        #TRANSITION_ACTION_LIST
        status = ClassName_states.S8
    } else if ( status == ClassName_states.S9 ) {
        #TRANSITION_ACTION_LIST
        status = ClassName_states.S10
    }
}
```

Generating code that uses switch-case instead of a long chain of if-then-else might execute more efficiently. This is shown in production rule *#EVENT_-METHOD_BODY_AS_SWITCH_CASE*. This requires, however, that either no transition has a guard or guards be implemented in a modified *#TRANSITION_ACTIONS_LIST_AS_SWITCH_CASE* rule. This is, of course, source code compiler dependent. A compiler is free to implement switch-case using a jump table or as a chain of if() {} else if() {} else if() {} ....

Production Rule: #EVENT_METHOD_BODY_AS_SWITCH_CASE

```
#EVENT_METHOD_BODY_AS_SWITCH_CASE →
  "switch (state) {" +
  foreach transition triggered by this event {
    " case " + (String) class.formattedClassName() + "_states." +
    (String) transition.formattedStartState() + ":" +
    #TRANSITION_ACTIONS_LIST +
    if ( transition.startState() != transition.endState() ) {
      "state = " +
      (String) class.formattedClassName() +
      "_states." +
      (String) transition.formattedendState() +
    }
    "break;" +
  }
  "}"
```

Potentially more efficient method body code would be generated, as shown in Code Sample 21.2.

Another frame and rule optimization also involves generating code from CIM state models. Instead of generating if-then-else or switch-case, it is sometimes better to use a table-driven interpreter. State model behavior can be encoded in data as shown in Table 21.1.

Table interpreter code can be included in either a frame or as a mechanism. Code Sample 21.3 shows operation doEvent() that interprets a state model from the matrix based on a currentState instance variable and the event that was just recognized.

Production rules in a model compiler can generate the data for the state–event matrix from the CIM state model. An example rule, *#POPULATE_STATE_EVENT_TABLE*, is shown.

Production Rule: #POPULATE_STATE_EVENT_TABLE

```
#POPULATE_STATE_EVENT_TABLE →
  foreach aState on class {
  foreach anEvent on class {
    "table[ " + (string) aState.name() + ", " +
            (string) anEvent.name() + " ].endState = " +
```

Code Sample 21.2 Switch-Case Can Be Much More Efficient Than If-Then-Else

```
public void eventName ( ParameterType aParameter ) {
  switch (status) {
    case ClassName_states.S1:
      #TRANSITION_ACTION_LIST
      status = ClassName_states.S2;
      break;
    case ClassName_states.S3:
      #TRANSITION_ACTION_LIST
      status = ClassName_states.S4;
      break;
    case ClassName_states.S5:
      #TRANSITION_ACTION_LIST
      status = ClassName_states.S6;
      break;
    case ClassName_states.S7:
      #TRANSITION_ACTION_LIST
      status = ClassName_states.S8;
      break;
    case ClassName_states.S9: {
      #TRANSITION_ACTION_LIST
      status = ClassName_states.S10;
      break;
    }
  }
}
```

Table 21.1 A State model encoded as data in a state–event matrix.

	Event1	Event2	Event3	EventN
State1	action1(), State2	Impossible	Impossible	Ignore
State2	Ignore	–, State2	Impossible	–, State1
State3	action2(), StateN	Impossible	action3(), State1	Ignore
StateN	Ignore	Impossible	Impossible	action4(), State3

```
if ( behavior ( aState, anEvent ).type = transition ) {
  (String) behavior ( aState, anEvent ).toState() + ";" +
  "table[ " + (string) aState.name() + ", " +
  (string) anEvent.name() + " ].action = " +
  (String) behavior ( aState, anEvent ).action() + ";" +
} else {
```

Code Sample 21.3 An Operation and Method for Interpreting State Models as Tables

```
public void doEvent ( Event anEvent ) {
// requires
//   state-event matrix data has been populated
//   currentState is in the set of valid states for the class
//   anEvent is in the set of valid events for the class
// guarantees
//   the appropriate CIM transition, if any, has been executed
  if ( table [ currentState, anEvent ] .endState != ignore ) {
   if ( table [ currentState, anEvent ] .endState != impossible ) {
    if ( table [ currentState, anEvent ] .action != null ) {
      this.execute ( table [ currentState, anEvent ] .action ) ;
    }
    currentState = table [ currentState, anEvent ] .endState;
   } else {
   // handle it as an impossible state + event combination
   //   e.g., throw an exception, log an error, ...
   }
  }
}
```

```
    if ( behavior ( aState, anEvent ) .type = impossible ) {
      "table [ " + (string) aState.name () + ", " +
      (string) anEvent.name () + " ] .toState = impossible;" +
    } else {
      "table [ " + (string) aState.name () + ", " +
      (string) anEvent.name () + " ] .toState = ignore;" +
    }
    "table [ " + (string) aState.name () + ", " +
    (string) anEvent.name () + " ] .action = null;"
  }
 }
}
```

Code Sample 21.4 shows the code that would be generated by this rule for the state model in Table 21.1.

21.1.3 Marking

The next form of optimization is called "marking" or "coloring." In this approach, a developer adds directives to the PIM overlay to guide production rules into translating one way instead of another. One example involves

Code Sample 21.4 Generated Code for the Table-Driven State Model in Table 21.1

```
table[ State1, Event1 ].endState = State2;
table[ State1, Event1 ].action = action1();
table[ State1, Event2 ].endState = impossible;
table[ State1, Event2 ].action = null;
...
table[ State1, EventN ].endState = ignore;
table[ State1, EventN ].action = null;
table[ State2, Event1 ].endState = ignore;
table[ State2, Event1 ].action = null;
table[ State2, Event2 ].endState = State2;
table[ State2, Event2 ].action = null;
...
table[ State3, Event1 ].endState = StateN;
table[ State3, Event1 ].action = action2();
..
table[ StateN, EventN ].endState = State3;
table[ StateN, EventN ].action = action4();
```

generating code for derived attributes. Remember that derived attributes can be implemented in at least three different ways:

- Compute on demand
- Compute on update and store
- Deferred update

Action semantics code implementing a derivation policy is independent of these strategies. A developer could mark their choice in the PIM overlay. The production rule that generates derived attribute code could query the PIM overlay and generate accordingly, as shown in production rule *#DERIVED_ATTRIBUTE*. This rule defaults to compute on demand if no marking is found. Mark-sensitive production rules should either assume a default marking or report a compiler error if no marking can be found.

Production Rule: #DERIVED_ATTRIBUTE
```
#DERIVED_ATTRIBUTE →
  if( PIM overlay marks this derived attribute as ONUPDATE ) {
    #DERIVED_ATTRIBUTE_COMPUTE_ON_UPDATE
  } else {
    if( PIM overlay marks this derived attribute as DEFERRED ) {
      #DERIVED_ATTRIBUTE_DEFERRED_UPDATE
```

```
  } else {
    #DERIVED_ATTRIBUTE_COMPUTE_ON_DEMAND
  }
}
```

Another example could be to mark some CIM classes as persistent and others as nonpersistent. When the model compiler encounters a class marked nonpersistent, it can generate memory-resident Java, C++, C#, etc. When a class is marked persistent, the model compiler can generate SQL DDL for the database table as well as a memory-resident business object and corresponding Data access object. This is shown in the following pair of production rules. Note that *#IMPLEMENTATION_CLASS* defaults to nonpersistent if the PIM overlay does not specify.

Production Rule: #COMPILE_MODEL

```
#COMPILE_MODEL →
  foreach aClass in model {
    #IMPLEMENTATION_CLASS
  }
```

Production Rule: #IMPLEMENTATION_CLASS

```
#IMPLEMENTATION_CLASS →
  if ( PIM overlay marks this class as persistent ) {
    #SQL_TABLE_DEFINITION_DDL
    #PERSISTENT_BUSINESS_OBJECT
    #DATA_ACCESS_OBJECT
  } else {
    #NON_PERSISTENT_BUSINESS_OBJECT
  }
```

All markings should be in the PIM overlay layer, not in the CIM. Different target platforms could require different markings for the same CIM element. Optimal implementation of a derived attribute on one target platform might be compute on demand and deferred update on another. If the marking is in the CIM, only one marking could be found for that derived attribute, so only one implementation strategy could ever be used for all production rule sets applied to that CIM.

Applying markings in a PIM overlay is appropriate when the open model compiler already knows how to react. If an open model compiler doesn't support a particular marking, production rules will need to be added or modified. For example, if the existing compiler only generates memory-resident Java objects, a new set of rules needs to be added to support producing database tables, memory-resident business object, and Data access object code.

21.1.4 Smart Rules

The last, and most complex, form of optimization uses smart rules, or "alternate mapping rules." This encodes decision logic into production rules themselves. Marking is driven externally: someone outside the PIM decides which markings to apply and the model compiler reacts as instructed. With smart rules, the model compiler itself makes decisions with no help from outside. These rules say, essentially, "under this set of conditions translate this way, otherwise translate that way." This approach requires the ability to process possibly complex decision logic in the production rule interpreter.

A simplistic model compiler might generate a public getter operation for every CIM attribute whether or not that attribute is ever accessed outside the class.

Production Rule: #ATTRIBUTE_GETTERS_LIST

```
#ATTRIBUTE_GETTERS_LIST →
  foreach( anAttribute on class ) {
    #ATTRIBUTE_GETTER
  }
```

A smarter model compiler would only generate a public getter operation for attributes that are accessed outside of the class.

Production Rule: #SMART_ATTRIBUTE_GETTERS_LIST

```
#SMART_ATTRIBUTE_GETTERS_LIST →
  foreach( anAttribute on class ) {
    if( anAttribute is read by some action in some other class) {
      #ATTRIBUTE_GETTER
    }
  }
```

Generating unused attribute getter code is not an issue in environments with source code optimizers that eliminate dead code before run time. But not all environments are that sophisticated, particularly those targeting deeply embedded code on low-cost, low-performance hardware. Smart rules can be critical in these situations.

Another example of smart rules could build on the earlier if-then versus switch-case versions of rule *#EVENT_METHOD_BODY*. The if-then and switch-case production rules could be embedded in a smart rule that chooses based on the number of transitions in the CIM state model. This is shown in rule *#SMART_EVENT_METHOD_BODY*.

Production Rule: #SMART_EVENT_METHOD_BODY

```
#SMART_EVENT_METHOD_BODY →
  if( anEvent causes less than 3 transitions ) {
    #EVENT_METHOD_BODY_AS_IF_THEN
```

```
} else {
  #EVENT_METHOD_BODY_AS_SWITCH_CASE
}
```

The production rule set demonstrated in the proof of concept (see Appendix M) generates separate private method code for implementing actions. Depending on the source code compiler and run-time system, it might be better to generate action code in-line in the method implementing the transition, that is, avoid the private method calls. Choice of in-line might also depend on the number of separate invocations made to that private action (i.e., in-line only if three or fewer invocations). A smart rule could scan the state model and decide to in-line or not on an action-by-action basis. Keep in mind, however, that this could easily depend on the source code compiler and run-time system.[1] The source code compiler might already be capable of inlining, duplicating that functionality in the model compiler would be wasted effort.

21.2 Building a New Open Model Compiler on an Existing Rule Interpreter

In some cases, no amount of optimizing an existing open model compiler is sufficient to generate application code that meets performance criteria. Or the need may be to generate code for an entirely different platform. In these cases, the only option—other than abandoning model compilation—is to build a new model compiler.

First, consider building a new open model compiler on an existing rule interpreter; building a new production rule interpreter will be discussed below. As long as the existing rule interpreter supports all capabilities needed by the new production rules, it is sufficient. New production rules, frames, and mechanisms may be enough to generate efficient code or target a new platform. Shaded components in Figure 21.1 are needed to build a new open model compiler on an existing rule interpreter.

21.2.1 Reducing the Semantic Modeling Language

An open model compiler is not necessarily required to implement the entire semantic modeling language (i.e., the entire metamodel in Appendix L). A compiler only needs to support the subset of the language intended for use in CIMs and PIM overlays. Perhaps none of your semantic models ever use state actions; it would then be safe to leave state actions out of your new

---

1 See, for example, https://lwn.net/Articles/82495/.

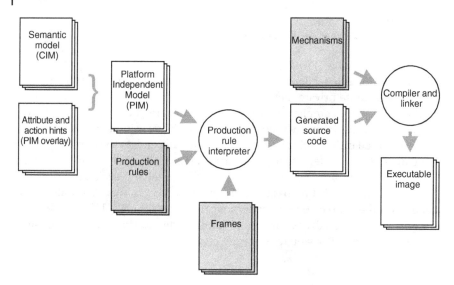

Figure 21.1 Shaded components are needed for a new compiler on an existing interpreter.

compiler. The same is true for other language elements like generalization, dynamic classification, etc.

As a matter of good practice, however, a model compiler that doesn't implement the complete semantic modeling language should at least generate some kind of notification (i.e., a model compiler error) when a model being translated contains unsupported language elements. Otherwise, a model with any of those unsupported elements could lead to silent failure. The compiler won't generate code for the unsupported elements, so the code can't behave as the modeler intends. Significant time could be wasted figuring out that the reason is simply modeling language elements unsupported by that model compiler.

21.2.2 Getting Started

One good way to start is to hand translate one or more classes into the kind of code you want generated. Start with one very simple class and work up from there. A very simple class could have:

- One attribute with a range defined as a span plus range and precision
- One state, "Exists"
- A creation event ("«new»") and initial transition with an initializer action that sets that non-state attribute to some arbitrary value
- A self-transition on an update event that modifies the non-state attribute
- A deletion event ("«destroy»") and final transition that deletes the object

The sidebar shows a concrete example of such a class.

1. Simple Class

This is an example of a very simple semantic model class that can be used as a starting point for by-hand translation and later as a test case for generated code from a new open model compiler. This helps provide an anchor point for deriving mechanisms, frames, and production rules. The state diagram is shown in Figure 21.2.

1.1 Attribute Descriptions

x: an arbitrary attribute.
    Range: [0 .. unconstrained, to the whole number]
State: the state of this object. It only has one state, exists.
    Range: [the set of states in the class' state model, only "Exists"]

A7.4.3.2 State and Event Descriptions

None

A7.4.3.3 Action Specifications

```
initializer ():
    requires
        none
    guarantees
        new object of Sample class exists with .x == 0

modify x ( new x ):
    requires
        new x is in range of .x
    guarantees
.x == new x
```

Code Sample 21.5 shows an example of hand-generated code for Simple class. On one hand, you will eventually have to consider all relevant kinds of CIM and PIM overlay content you intend to compile, so make sure your set of sample classes covers that breadth. On the other hand, putting too many complexities into too few samples can make this step very difficult. Aim for a balance between a small set of samples without too much added complexity from one to the next.

21.2.3 Determining Mechanisms and Frames

Once you have derived enough sample code by hand, look for references to common services that only need written once. Examples could be error logging, event queuing, message distribution, data distribution, memory

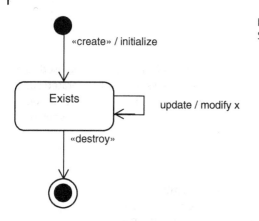

Figure 21.2 State diagram for Simple class.

Code Sample 21.5 By-Hand-Generated Code for Simple Class

```java
package SomePackage;

public class SimpleClass {

  // Class description

    // Simple class from Chapter 21

  public enum SimpleClass_states { EXISTS, DOESNTEXIST };

  // Attributes
    private int x;
    private SimpleClass_states state;

  // Association participation instance variables

    // none

  // Constructor
    public SimpleClass() {
    // requires
    //   none
    // guarantees
    //   state was Doesn't Exist ➜ .x == 0 and state == Exists
      this.initializer();
      state = SimpleClass_states.EXISTS;
      assert( x == 0 ) : "initializer failed";
      simpleClassSet.add( this );
    }
```

```
// Attribute getters
  public int x() {
  // requires
  //  none
  // guarantees
  //  returns the x
    return x;
  }

  public SimpleClass_states state() {
  // requires
  //  none
  // guarantees
  //  returns the state
    return state;
  }


// Derived attributes
  // none


// Pushed events
  public void update( int newX ) {
  // requires
  //  state == Exists and new x is consistent w/ range of .x
  // guarantees
  //  state was Exists --> .x == new x
    assert( newX >= 0 ) : "invalid new x";
    if( state == SimpleClass_states.EXISTS ) {
      this.modifyX( newX );
    }
    assert( x == newX ) : "assignment failed";
  }

  public void destroy() {
  // requires
  //  none
  // guarantees
  //  state was Exists --> state == Doesn't exist
    if( state == SimpleClass_states.EXISTS ) {
      state = SimpleClass_states.DOESNTEXIST;
    }
  }

// Private transition actions
  private void initializer() {
```

```
    // requires
    //   none
    // guarantees
    //   .x == 0
      x = 0;
      assert ( x == 0 ) : "initializer failed";
    }

    private void modifyX ( int newX ) {
    // requires
    //   new x is consistent w/ range of .x
    // guarantees
    //   .x == new x
      assert ( newX >= 0 ) : "invalid new x";
      x = newX;
      assert ( x == newX ) : "assignment failed";
    }

  // PIM Overlay helper code
    // none

  // All class members accessor
  private static ArrayList<SimpleClass> simpleClassSet =
                    new ArrayList<SimpleClass>();

  // Association participation link and unlink services
    // none

}
```

management, threading, tasking, and so on. These write-once services are mechanisms. After mechanisms have been identified, the next level are static but repeating structures in the application code (e.g., once per class, once per thread, etc.). These are typically incorporated into frames. The key to determining if some application code is mechanism or frame is that mechanisms exist only once in an application's code base and frames appear more than once.

21.2.4 Determining Production Rules

After mechanisms and frames have been identified, examine the remaining hand-translated application code. Reverse engineer production rules from that remainder by comparing your hand-coded samples to the metamodel in

Appendix L. Look for patterns. Find the translation steps needed to get from a CIM + PIM overlay to your hand-generated code. This is where production rules live. It may help to first express those patterns as informal rules, just to get a sense of the translation process. Once comfortable with the informal rules, formalize those into the production rule interpreter's rule language.

Appendix M shows a set of production rule for a simple open model compiler to give an example of what production rules can look like. These rules generate code essentially identical to Code Sample 21.5.

You may want to establish a style guide for production rules. Here is a small sample of guidelines, and you can of course modify these to suit your environment:

- *Use an appropriate naming convention for production rules*—Each rule will translate from a single metamodel class: the kind of thing it is mapping from. Each rule maps to a particular construct in the automation technology. A rule can be named by the combination of the kind of thing it is mapping from and the kind of thing it is mapping to. Examples are Attribute.#DEFINE_INST_-VAR, Attribute.#GETTER, Class.#JAVA_CLASS_FRAME, Event.#EVENT_-METHOD_BODY, Parameter.#FORMAL_PARAMETER, etc. Appendix M follows this convention
- *Minimize syntactic (structural) complexity of each rule*—Avoid rules with many, or deeply nested, steps. Avoid rules that invoke many other rules. Structural complexity is discussed in Appendix N and applies to production rules as well.
- *Pay attention to the fundamental principles*—Each rule should abstract one mapping concept, be highly cohesive, loosely coupled from other rules, etc.

Given that design documentation in by-hand-translated projects should emphasize why the code looks the way it does, the productions rules in open compiler should also have explanation of why: why map this way and not some other way? This can be critical to enable long-term, cost-effective maintenance of an open model compiler.

21.2.5 Implementing Production Rules

Once formally defined, production rules can be implemented incrementally. This allows you to observe how generated code progresses with each added rule. The complete code generation process can be very complex, involving hundreds of rules. Incremental implementation can help.

A top-down strategy starts from big things, that is, frames, with some or all embedded rules commented out (e.g., as an output text string, not executed as a reference to a separate rule). As each successive rule is enabled, start with a stub version that only puts a marker in generated code where that rule would do its expansion. The marker might be some variant of the production rule's name. This allows you to see where the rule will inject its content into the generated code so you can make sure it is in the right place. The proof of concept in Chapter 20 did this: it started with the top-level rule and successively enabled lower-level rules, one at a time.

After you are confident that rule placement is correct, enable the full rule (i.e., have it generate what it is supposed to). Successively add rules until all have been incorporated.

A bottom-up strategy starts from the most detailed things (typically names of things like states, events, etc.), making sure that code generated for those is correct. Next, incorporate higher-level rules that make use of these lower-level rules. Build throwaway frames that use only the lower-level rules until those lower rules have been shown correct. When everything is working at that level, move up a level by creating a new throwaway frame and enabling new rules, one at a time, in place of previous throwaway frames.

These two strategies are not mutually exclusive; they can be used in combination. Some parts of a new model compiler might be built top-down, while others might be built bottom-up.

21.2.6 Verifying a New Open Model Compiler

After a new open model compiler is built, it should be verified.

1) Start with a few simple test models:
   First, an empty model (no classes at all)
   Second, a model with one class, a few attributes, only one state, a few events, for example, Simple class from above
   Then, test in manageable increments up to your full CIM + PIM content.
   Have test models that exercise rule boundary values (zero, one, many, etc.).

2) When you are confident through those simple test models:
   Generate code for your hand-coded classes and compare: is it the same?

3) Compile one or more production CIM + PIM overlays and execute them:
   Use an appropriate set of verification test cases (e.g., as in Chapter 12).
   Does behavior of generated code match expected results?

If your production CIM + PIM overlays cover the breadth of what you need to compile and all application-level verification test cases are passing, then you should have confidence that your new model compiler is working properly.

21.3 Generating Output Other Than Application Source Code

An open model compiler isn't limited to generating only application source code; it can also be put to other valuable uses. Several useful alternatives are presented in this section, but there are probably more that haven't even been though of yet. If you want to support these kinds of uses, you won't be able to do it without building new production rules, although mechanisms may be unnecessary.

21.3.1 Generating Formal Documentation

One alternate use of an open model compiler is as a document production facility to publish formal, formatted specification documentation. Simply, define production rules that output model content interspersed with appropriate formatting directives (e.g., HTML or other formatting tags). The example semantic models in Appendices D, F, H, and J show one possible target for formal document output.

21.3.2 Generating Natural Language Documentation

Another non-code use of an open model compiler can be to mechanically translate a semantic model into natural language as described in Chapter 12. The same open model compiler that generates application source code can also generate massive tomes of "The system shall ..." statements if stakeholders demand that kind of documentation. Beware that even a relatively modest semantic model can generate hundreds of pages of natural language statements. The following are a sampling of production rules that generate "shall" statements instead of code.

```
#NATURAL_LANGUAGE_REQUIREMENTS_SPECIFICATION →
  #INTRODCUTION
  #CLASS_DICTIONARY_LIST
  #ASSOCIATION_DICTIONARY_LIST
  #ANY_OTHER_CONTENT

#CLASS_DICTIONARY_LIST →
  foreach aClass in model {
    "This domain shall manage " + (String) aClass.name() + "s"
    #ATTRIBUTE_DICTIONARY_LIST
    #STATE_DICTIONARY_LIST
    #EVENT_DICTIONARY_LIST
    #TRANSITION_DICTIONARY_LIST
    #ACTION_DICTIONARY_LIST
  }

#ATTRIBUTE_DICTIONARY_LIST →
  foreach anAttribute in aClass {
    "When a " + (String) aClass.name() +
```

```
    " exists, it shall have a single value for its " +
    (String) anAttribute.name() +
    #ATTRIBUTE_RANGE_DEFINITION
}


#ATTRIBUTE_RANGE_DEFINITION →
    "Valid values for the " +
    (String) anAttribute.name() + " of a " +
    (String) aClass.name() + " shall be " +
    #ATTRIBUTE_RANGE_SPECIFICATION²


#STATE_DICTIONARY_LIST →
    "The acceptable states for a " +
        (String) aClass.name() + " shall be: " +
    foreach aState in aClass {
    (String) aState.name() + ", "
    }


#EVENT_DICTIONARY_LIST →
        "Objects of class " + (String) aClass.name() +
        " shall respond to: " +
        foreach anEvent in aClass {
            (String) anEvent.name() + ", "
        }
        foreach anEvent in aClass {
            #TRANSITION_DICTIONARY_LIST
        }


#TRANSITION_DICTIONARY_LIST →
        foreach aTransition triggered by anEvent {
            "When an object of class " + (String) aClass.name() +
            " is in state " +
            (String) aTransition.fromStateName() + " and " +
            (String) aTransition.fromEventName() + " occurs " +
            #OPTIONAL_GUARD +
            #TRANSITION_ACTIONS_LIST +
            if( aTransition.startState() != aTransition.endState() ) {
                " That object shall end in state " +
                (String) aTransition.endStateName() +
            }
        }
```

---

2 This rule is a bit complicated because it needs to deal with span with units and precision, enumeration, by-reference, and unconstrained ranges. The details aren't specified here but are clearly solvable.

```
#OPTIONAL_GUARD →
  if( aTransition.hasGuard() ) {
    " when " +
    (String) aTransition.guardName() +
    " is true " +
  }


#TRANSITION_ACTIONS_LIST →
  if( aTransition has at least one action ) {
    " The following actions shall happen: " +
    foreach anAction on aTransition {
      (String) anActionName() + ", "
    }
  }
```

Additional rules are needed to generate the complete set of "The system shall…" statements as shown in Chapter 12. Rules above do not generate natural language statements for:

- Action contracts
- Keys
- Derived attributes
- Associations
- Generalizations
- Impossible transitions
- …

Clearly, such rules can be created. This should again serve as a proof of concept that full, automatic, mechanical translation from a semantic model into natural language documentation is entirely possible, realistic, and—in some, possibly limited, cases—even useful.

21.3.3 Generating Verification Test Cases

Another non-source code use of an open model compiler is to generate verification test cases as described in Chapter 12. The first part of the process, generating test elements, is mechanical and can be described in production rule form.

Production Rule: #STATE_MODEL_TEST_ELEMENTS

```
#STATE_MODEL_TEST_ELEMENTS →
    Foreach aState in aClass
        Foreach anEvent in aClass
            if( at least one transition from aState on anEvent )
                then #TRANSITION_POSITIVE_TEST_ELEMENTS
                else #STATE_EVENT_NEGATIVE_TEST_ELEMENT³
```

---

3 This rule does not distinguish ignored from impossible transitions as discussed in Chapter 10.

Production Rule: #TRANSITION_POSITIVE_TEST_ELEMENTS

```
#TRANSITION_POSITIVE_TEST_ELEMENTS →
    foreach aGuard on aState and anEvent
        'Given starting state == ' + aState + ',' +
        ' when event ' + anEvent + ' happens,' +
        if aGuard != TRUE
            ' while guard ' + aGuard + ' is true ' +
        if any transition actions have requires clauses
            foreach aRequires on union of transition actions
                ' and condition ' + aCondition + ' is true'
        'The expected result is ending state == ' +
            aTransition.toState +
        if any transition actions have guarantees clauses
            foreach aGuarantees on union of transition actions
                ' and condition ' + aCondition + ' is true'
```

Production Rule: #STATE_EVENT_NEGATIVE_TEST_ELEMENT

```
#STATE_EVENT_NEGATIVE_TEST_ELEMENT →
    foreach aGuard on aState and anEvent
        'Given starting state == ' + aState + ',' +
        ' when event ' + anEvent + ' happens,' +
        if aGuard == TRUE
            ' while guard ' + aGuard + ' is false ' +
        'Nothing can have changed (i.e., this is ignored)' +
```

Full generation of all possible test elements according to Chapter 12 would require many more production rules; however this should again illustrate the nature of these rules. Assembling the test elements into a minimal set of test cases might best be done by a separate program, outside of the model compiler rule set.

21.3.4   Computing Semantic Model Structural Complexity Metrics

Still another use is to create a set of production rules that compute structural complexity metrics for a semantic model. The nature of complexity metrics production rules could be to assign variables representing metrics values to zero. Then, while traversing the model, whenever something countable is discovered, increment the appropriate counter.

One example could be to compute the cyclomatic complexity of the state model for a class. Just like the flowchart for a method, the state model for a class is also a directed graph, and its cyclomatic complexity can be computed. Insofar as cyclomatic complexity has already been positively correlated with defects in method-level code; it is conceivable that defects in the logic of a semantic model class might be correlated with the cyclomatic complexity of its state model (this has not been researched yet; at this point it is a suggestion and not a statement of fact).

To compute the cyclomatic complexity of a state model, add one to the number of transitions out of each state beyond the first transition. The following production rule zeros, calculates, and then outputs the cyclomatic complexity for a given class.

Production Rule: #STATE_MODEL_CYCLOMATIC_COMPLEXITY

```
#STATE_MODEL_CYCLOMATIC_COMPLEXITY →
  Vg = 0
  foreach aState in aClass {
    set outgoingTransitionCount = 0
    foreach aTransition out of aState {
      outgoingTransitionCount++
    }
    if ( outgoingTransitionCount > 1 ) {
      Vg = Vg + outgoingTransitionCount - 1
    }
    "Cyclomatic complexity of " +
        (String) aClass.name() + "'s state model is " +
        (String) Vg
```

To support this kind of rule, the production rule interpreter needs to support local variable computation inside rules. If that isn't available in your production rule interpreter, an alternative is to have rules output a stream of tokens. A post-processor can scan those tokens to compute the metric values.

Production Rule:
#STATE_MODEL_CYCLOMATIC_COMPLEXITY_TOKEN_STREAM

```
#STATE_MODEL_CYCLOMATIC_COMPLEXITY_TOKEN_STREAM →
  "// State model = " + (String) aClass.name()
  foreach aState in aClass {
    "//   State = " (String) aState.name()
    foreach aTransition out of aState
      " +1 // for " + (String) aTransition.fromStatename() +
      " + " + (String) aTransition.onEventName() +
      if ( aTransition.hasGuard() ) {
        " when " + aTransition.guardName()
      }
      " -1 // because only those >1 count"
    }
  }
```

The above rule will generate the following token stream for Book Order's state model.

```
// State model = Book Order
//   State = Not exists
  +1 // for Not exists + create
  -1 // because only those >1 count"
//   State = Open
  +1 // for Open + Add
  +1 // for Open + Drop when >1 line
  +1 // for Open + Drop when =1 line
  +1 // for Open + Place when no print medium
  +1 // for Open + Place when has print medium
  -1 // because only those >1 count"
//   State = Placed
  +1 // for Placed + Packed when isPackable?
  +1 // for Placed + Cancel
  -1 // because only those >1 count"
//   State = Packed
  +1 // for Packed + Shipped
  -1 // because only those >1 count"
//   State = Completed
```

A state model where no state has more than one outgoing transition has cyclomatic complexity 1. Adding all of the +1 and −1 tokens yields a sum of 5 for Book order. Cyclomatic complexity is that sum plus 1 or 6. So the cyclomatic complexity of Book order's state model is 6. Cyclomatic complexity for Book order line's state model is 3. Replenish order and Replenish order line both have state models with cyclomatic complexity 2.

Other possible structural complexity metrics include:

- If/when/otherwise/etc. decision logic in action guarantees clauses is also indicative of decision complexity.
- There might be something in the number of associations a class participates in (akin to fan-out).
- There might be something in the number of other classes that actions in one class signal.[4]
- …

A production rule set can be defined to compute and export virtually any metric about semantic models that a researcher might eventually discover is useful. Again, it's just another production rule set.

---

4 Similar to fan-out and to coupling between objects (CBO) in the Chidamber–Kemerer metrics set, see [Chidamber94]. Lorenz and Kidd [Lorenz94] presents another proposed set of complexity metrics for object oriented systems. See also the discussion of structural complexity in Appendix N.

21.4 Building a New Production Rule Interpreter

An earlier section discussed building a new open model compiler—new mechanisms, frames, and production rules—assuming an existing production rule interpreter already supports everything needed. But what if available production rule interpreters don't support everything needed? As examples,

- Parameter passing or other communication from one production rule to another
- Local (to rules) variables and computations, possibly to support smart rules
- Complex decision logic to support smart rules
- ...

Mechanisms and frames are simple text substitution so they should rarely, if ever, be a problem. On the other hand, you may need to build your own rule interpreter. Another possibility is that no rule interpreter is available on the platform where you want to compile models.

Step one in building a production rule interpreter can be to determine the kinds of production rules you need to interpret. Pay attention to what is different about these production rules that is not supported by any existing production rule interpreter. Since you are defining a new interpreter, you are free to define the production rule syntax. Backus–Naur Form (BNF)[5] or syntax diagrams ala Jensen and Wirth[6] are ways to describe production rule syntax. Aim for a LALR(1) grammar[7] in your rule syntax; they are easiest for a parser to work with.

Step two can be to build a semantic model of the production rule interpreter. Analyze the rule set(s) you want to interpret. Look for invariants and variants among those rules. Represent rule-level invariants as classes and variants as attributes and associations. Modeling the business of the production rule interpreter: you are making a rule interpreter CIM. Figure 21.3 shows a semantic model class diagram for a very simple production rule interpreter to illustrate what such a semantic model can look like.

An overview of the classes in Figure 21.3 is as follows:

- *Meta-Class*—A class in the metamodel of the (subset of the) semantic modeling language being compiled. Specifically, this refers to classes in Figures L.2, L.3, L.4, and L.5 of the metamodel in Appendix L.

---

5 See, for example, https://en.wikipedia.org/wiki/Backus%E2%80%93Naur_form.
6 See [Jensen07].
7 The LR stand for left to right: sentences are parsed left to right. LA stands for look ahead: the parser needs to look ahead in the token stream. The (1) means look ahead is no more than one token: only the next token is needed to guide parsing. See, for example, https://en.wikipedia.org/wiki/LALR_parser.

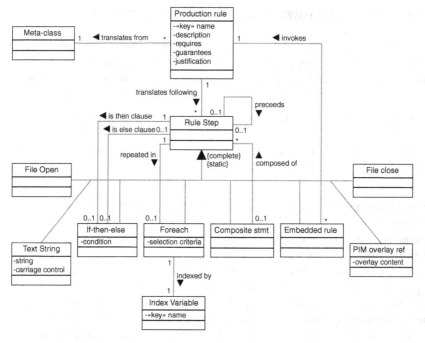

Figure 21.3 Semantic model class diagram for a simple production rule interpreter.

- *Production Rule*—A rule that translates from some aspect of the metaclass into application source code. The production rules in Appendix M are examples of this class. The attributes of production rule allow the rule developer to add a description, a rule contract, and an explanation of why that rule looks the way it does.
- *Rule Statement*—Production rules are generally compound, that is, they are made up of a sequence of elements: statements.
- *File Open*—The model compiler needs to output source code files, so those files will need to be opened for write. Note that if you are building an environment that executes models in an interpreted (rather than compiled) manner, then this may not be required
- *Text String*—Directs the production rule interpreter to emit a constant string of source code text.
- *If-Then-Else*—Directs the interpreter to make a decision: under some circumstances behave one way and under other circumstances behave a different way. An If-Then-Else statement must have a Then clause but does not require an Else clause.
- *Foreach*—Directs the interpreter to iterate over a set of elements defined by the selection criteria. A Foreach statement repeatedly applies the referenced Rule statement to each element in the selected set.

- *Index Variable*—Defines (the name of) the variable that will reference the one current item from the selected set being iterated over.
- *Composite Statement*—Gives the production rule developer the ability to embed statements in a higher-level statement: for example, the Then clause of an If-Then-Else is defined in the class model to be a single Rule statement. By allowing Rule statements to be compound, the Then clause can consist of a sequence of lower-level Rule statements.
- *Embedded Rule*—Gives the ability for one production rule to refer directly to another.
- *PIM Overlay Ref*—Specifies that necessary content is not coming from the semantic model, the CIM, but it is coming from the PIM overlay.
- *File Close*—Just as output files need to be opened, they also need to be closed after the output has been generated.

Step three involves designing and coding the rule interpreter. Assuming a Model–View–Controller architectural style, the semantic model will become Model region in the interpreter design. You will need a rule parser to convert from the external representation into the internal representation in the implemented rule interpreter. This parser is in View-controller region. Instead of hand coding the production rule parser, consider using a parser generator along the lines of LEX.[8]

You may also need a parser for the semantic model and PIM overlay to be translated. If the semantic model and PIM overlay are coming from an external representation, a parser is necessary. Again, use a parser generator if possible, rather than writing one by hand. On the other hand, if your production rule interpreter lives inside a model editor environment, it won't need to parse models. It just needs to access model content as defined by that larger environment, for example, some form of SQL.

21.4.1 Compiling Your Production Rule Interpreter

One option is to design and code the new rule interpreter by hand. Alternatively, if you have access to an existing production rule interpreter, why not take advantage of it? At least in theory, you could develop your production rule interpreter CIM and then build a PIM overlay for the existing open model compiler. Run your production rule interpreter PIM through that model compiler. The output will be an application that implements your production rule interpreter on that compiler's target platform. This is shown in Figure 21.4; the shaded elements are your new production rule interpreter.

If the generated implementation of your new production rule interpreter is sufficient, you are done. But if your new production rule interpreter is intended to run on different platform, then go back to your interpreter CIM and build a

---

8 See, for example, https://en.wikipedia.org/wiki/Lex_(software).

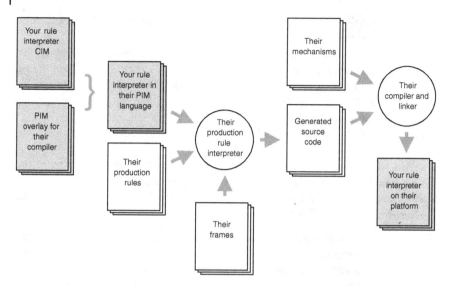

Figure 21.4 Compiling your new rule interpreter on an existing open model compiler.

new PIM overlay. This time target the platform you want to compile in. Run this second CIM plus PIM overlay through your open model compiler on the other platform. The output this time will be the production rule interpreter in your target environment. This is shown in Figure 21.5; again shaded elements are your new interpreter.

Move the generated code for the new production rule interpreter to the target environment. Compile and link with the mechanisms and, after appropriate testing, you are ready to compile production models.

21.5 Quality Criteria

Table 21.2 shows quality criteria for optimizing an open model compiler so that it generates better application source code.

Table 21.3 shows quality criteria for building a new open model compiler on an existing production rule interpreter.

Table 21.4 shows quality criteria for building a new production rule interpreter.

21.6 Weaknesses in UML Semantics

One final but very important point about UML, models, semantic modeling, and model compilation is on weaknesses in published UML semantics. Partly due to

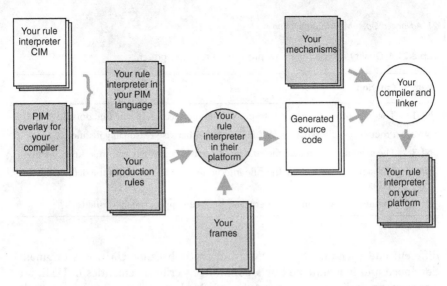

Figure 21.5 Compiling your rule interpreter on your new open model compiler.

Table 21.2 Quality criteria for optimizing an open model compiler.

Item	Criterion
OC-1	Application performance has been profiled to understand bottlenecks
OC-2	All markings are in a PIM overlay layer, not in a CIM
OC-3	If markings in a PIM overlay are important to performance, production rules that respond to those markings are present
OC-4	Production rules sensitive to markings either assume a default marking or report a compiler error if no marking is found
OC-5	Optimizations don't duplicate what is already available in the source code compiler/object code optimizer/linker chain
OC-6	Optimizations have been appropriately documented
OC-7	The optimized model complier has been appropriately tested

Table 21.3 Quality criteria for a new open model compiler on an existing interpreter.

Item	Criterion
NC-1	The subset of semantic model language and PIM overlay is adequate
NC-2	The compiler generates appropriate notification when unsupported elements appear in the model being compiled
NC-3	Appropriate production rule style guidelines have been followed
NC-4	Any exceptions to production rule style guidelines have been appropriately justified
NC-5	Production rules have documentation explaining why they look the way they do
NC-6	The new open model compiler has been appropriately verified

Table 21.4 Quality criteria for a new production rule interpreter.

Item	Criterion
NI-1	The new production rule interpreter supports necessary rule functionality
NI-2	Production rule syntax is LALR(1) unless otherwise reasonably justified
NI-3	The semantic model for the rule interpreter is consistent with rule functionality
NI-4	The semantic model for the rule interpreter is consistent with the defined rule syntax
NI-5	The new production rule interpreter has been appropriately verified

different end-user intents for UML and partly because UML was originally developed and is maintained by a committee,[9] critical semantics in UML are either intentionally or unintentionally undefined or weakly defined. UML itself, as a language, has many built-in ambiguities.

UML, as it is defined in the specification set, it is not precise enough for model-based software engineering. For example, M. von der Beeck[10] presents nineteen different interpretations for state charts alone. Examples include:

- *Self-triggering—Can a transition happen without an event?*
- *Negated trigger events—Can the nonoccurrence of an event be implicitly considered an event?*
- *Instantaneous states—Can a state be entered and exited at the same time?*
- *Parallel execution of transitions—Is it allowed?*
- *Determinism—Is it required or not?*
- *Priorities for transition execution—Can some transitions be of higher priority than others?*
- *Do transitions take zero time, or nonzero, finite time?*
- *...*

For model-based software engineering—model validation and translation (both by hand and using a model compiler), there must be *exactly one* interpretation of a semantic model. Published UML semantics are inadequate to provide that single interpretation. Practical, real-world UML modeling, including the approach defined in this book, necessarily require supplementing existing UML semantics. For example, transitions in a semantic model are defined to take essentially zero time.

The metamodel and UML profile for model-based software engineering is in Appendix L. UML by itself is too loosely defined to support full semantic

---

9 The infamous quote "A camel is a horse designed by a committee" seems appropriate.
10 See [von der Beeck94].

modeling and model compilation. Extra effort needs to—and has—been applied to fill semantic gaps in UML.

21.7 Summary

This chapter builds on open model compilation presented in the last chapter, discussing advanced topics such as:

- Optimizing application code
- Building a new open model compiler on an existing rule interpreter
- Generating output other than application source code
- Building a new production rule interpreter
- Weaknesses in UML semantics

Open model compilation may even set a path for job specialization in future software organizations:

- *Those who know semantic modeling*—professionals who specialize in building CIMs
- *Those who know PIM Overlay language(s)*— professionals who will fill in necessary content to make CIMs fully compilable
- *Those who know model compilers*—professionals who build and maintain open model translation environments: production rule sets, frames, mechanisms, and possibly production rule interpreters

22

Wrapping Up Model-Based Design and Code

Part III presents translation of a semantic model, an interface specification, and a set of nonfunctional requirements into design and code. That design and code are expected to automate the policies and processes in the semantic model, provide the specified interfaces, and satisfy the nonfunctional requirements. Many different implementations of a single semantic model and interface specification are possible. Part III is only intended to show that translation is possible: documentation *can* be literally self-coding. This chapter wraps up model-based design and code and covers:

- Summarizing model-based design and code
- Comparing and contrasting semantic and design models
- Organizing design documentation into written specifications
- Design versus code: what's the difference?
- Verification testing of design and code
- Product family design
- The myth of source code reuse

22.1 Reviewing Model-Based Design and Code

The chapters in Part III are:

- *Introduction to Design and Code*—Overviews translation-driven software design and coding starting from a semantic model and nonfunctional requirements.
- *Designing Interfaces: Specifying Real-World Interaction*—Gives technological form to conceptual actor interactions. A semantic model might say Customers can order books and a nonfunctional requirement might say Customers will use a Web interface. This designs Web pages for Customers to use when ordering books. If an actor represents other software, the interface would be an API specification, that is, a developer's guide.

How to Engineer Software: A Model-Based Approach, First Edition. Steve Tockey.
© 2019 the IEEE Computer Society, Inc. Published 2019 by John Wiley & Sons, Inc.

- *High-Level Design: Classes and Operations*—Creates a first approximation of software high-level design. Model region classes and operations are derived from the semantic model. View-controller region classes and operations are derived from the interface specification. Infrastructure region is designed as needed.
- *High-Level Design: Contracts and Signatures*—Derives operation signatures (syntax) and contracts (semantics) for Model region classes. Develops the same level of design for View-controller and Infrastructure regions.
- *Detailed Design and Code*—Designs internal data (i.e., instance and class variables) and method structures (algorithms) for each design class, down to lines of code.
- *Formal Disciplines of Design and Code*—Integrates science and mathematics into method-level design and coding, including programming by intent, assertions, software proofs of correctness, and intent-act-prove-assert format. This chapter highlights the true, formal nature of code and shows how detailed design and code defects can be avoided.
- *Optimization*—As necessary and appropriate, optimize design and code to satisfy all nonfunctional how well requirements and provide maximum value through performance while minimizing accidental complexity.
- *Model Compilation*—Automate translation of a semantic model into executable code: literally, self-coding documentation
- *Advanced Open Model Compilation*—Optimize generated application code, build an open model compiler, and generate output other than application source code.

22.2   Comparing and Contrasting Semantic and Design Models

The semantic model is expected to be a complete, consistent, clear, concise, precise, unambiguous, and validated description of (some portion of) a "business" to automate. It specifies policies to enforce and processes to carry out. A semantic model is about meaning. Design and code, on the other hand, are about representing that meaning in automation technology. As long as design and code map policy and process semantics onto technology semantics in a way that:

- Is sufficiently complete
- Preserves policy and process semantics
- Satisfies all nonfunctional requirements

then that design and code *must* be a well-behaved computer program that automates those policies and processes in terms of that automation technology.

One goal of model-based software engineering is to simplify development and maintenance by separating policy and process complexity from technical complexity. On one hand, understand the intricacies of the policies and processes to be automated. Make sure a semantic model—as large and complex as it might be—completely, consistently, clearly, correctly, concisely, and precisely defines the policies to enforce and the processes to carry out. On the other hand, as a separate activity with a completely different mindset, map those policy and process semantics onto automation technology semantics. Essential complexity is in one place, and accidental complexity in another: they are as separate as they could ever be.

This is abstraction in action, in this case abstracting automation technology complexities away from policy and process complexities. It also abstracts policy and process complexities away from automation technology complexities. It doesn't matter what a given multiplicity constraint in a semantic model might mean to the stakeholders, but what matters from an automation perspective is simply that we can represent any arbitrary multiplicity constraint wholly, completely, precisely, and efficiently. It also doesn't matter what a given transition in a state model might mean to the stakeholders, but what matters from an automation perspective is simply that we can represent any arbitrary transition wholly, completely, precisely, and efficiently. As Shlaer and Mellor said (slightly paraphrased),

> *"Separate the technology from the business.*
> *And, separate the business from the technology."*

Mapping well-defined, well-understood policy and process semantics onto automation technology semantics can be straightforward. An arbitrarily large and complex semantic model can be translated in a deliberate, systematic way into design and code. Done properly, model-based software engineering completely separates complexities of policies and processes being automated from complexities of automation. This is key to "turning one big problem into two smaller ones," which is a major advantage of model-based software engineering.

22.3 Documenting Design in a Written Specification

Design documentation is mostly relevant only for projects that do not use a model compiler. With a model compiler, most of the design is implicit in the production rules. Most design should not need to be explicitly documented except, as discussed in Chapter 21, where production rules are documented to explain why they look the way they do. Also, detailed design (algorithm and instance variable) documentation can be embedded as comments in a PIM layer.

Ideally, when a model compiler is not used, design documentation would be stored in an automated tool so it could be navigated in hypertext fashion: for example, a message is sent from a method of class A—which class receives that message (i.e., implements that operation)? This is easy for a tool to answer. A design sequence diagram could also answer it, but we usually don't make sequence diagrams for every design use case. An automated tool could easily find where that message is received and bring up that class. We may be requested—or required—to publish manually derived design as a paper (or similar electronic representation) document.

If the goal is to organize and present (sub)domain design in some kind of paper(like) document, the following outline is known to be effective. Each level of increased indentation represents a more detailed section of document content. Design documentation examples in Appendices E, G, I, and K use this structure.

Design use case diagram, and diagram description as appropriate
Design class diagram, and diagram description as appropriate
Design interaction diagrams (a selected subset, as appropriate), for each:
    Use case or scenario name
    Use case or scenario description, as appropriate
    Sequence or communication diagram
Class dictionary, for each design class[1]:
    Class name
    Class description
        Include heritage: what this class represents[2]
        Include its role in any design patterns, if applicable
        Justify any non-obvious class-level design decisions
    Class interface
        Exported constants, types, etc.
        Public operations[3]
            Syntax: parameter name, role, data type
            Semantic: contract
Relevant design notes (optional, as appropriate)

---

1 To the extent that you can take advantage of tools like JavaDoc or Doxygen, do so.
2 In terms of semantic model content, interface specification content, or infrastructure content.
3 Treat things like C# "properties" and Eiffel "features" as public operations.

Keeping in mind the deliberate encapsulation barrier, high-level design should be separated in some appropriate way from detailed design:

For each design class:
    Static and instance variables (i.e., member data)
        What does it mean?
        Where did it come from?
        Why does it look the way it does?
    Static and instance method implementations (i.e., member function)
        What does it mean?
        Where did it come from?
        Why does it look the way it does?
    Relevant notes (optional)

22.4 Design Versus Code: What's the Difference?

The software industry has long treated design and code as separate and distinct entities. Design documentation—if it even exists—is in one place and the code is somewhere else entirely. We need to realize that design and code are not two separate things. In fact, design simply describes the same policy-and-process-semantic-to-automation-technology-semantic mapping as code does; it's just a more coarse-grained description:

> *"Design and code are not two different things,*
> *they are just different views of the same thing"*

Fine-grained detail in source code—like semicolons and curly braces—is necessary to support compilation.[4] But that same fine-grained detail is not important—and detracts from—communicating larger structures of the mapping to humans. Fine-grained detail can be, and simply is, ignored in design to focus on important, larger-grained structures.

22.5 Knuth's Literate Programming

If design and code are separated, then they will naturally tend to get out of synch. Why not keep them *in the same place*? We need a development environment that integrates design and code into a single, unified entity. Donald Knuth's "literate programming"[5] is an example. Quoting Knuth,

---

4 For example, LALR-1 parsability, context-free grammars, etc.
5 See [Knuth92] or https://en.wikipedia.org/wiki/Literate_programming.

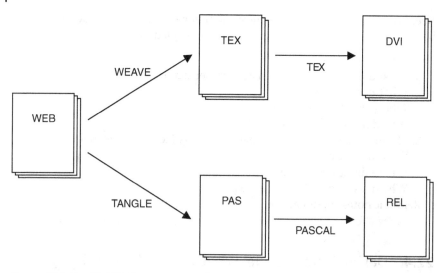

Figure 22.1 Knuth's WEB literate programing system.

"Let us change our traditional attitude to the construction of programs. Instead of imagining that our main task is to instruct a <u>computer</u> what to do, let us concentrate rather on explaining to <u>human beings</u> what we want a computer to do."

Figure 22.1 overviews Knuth's WEB literate programming system:

The WEB is the unified design-and-code entity created by developers. It is an integrated structure of code fragments and descriptive text, along with formatting and layout directives. The WEAVE tool prepares a WEB for presentation to a reader. In Knuth's implementation, the document production chain uses the TeX formatter.[6] TeX is not WYSWYG ("What You See Is What You Get") like modern word processing environments; authoring in Knuth's WEB is analogous to writing HTML. Modern implementations of literate programming can generate PDF or HTML. TANGLE extracts the source code and prepares it for compilation. In Knuth's implementation the programming language is Pascal; TANGLE extracts a .pas file from which the Pascal compiler creates the relocatable (.rel) object code for linking into a complete application. Modern implementations work with Java, C, C++, Ruby, etc. Some literate programming tools are programming language independent.

Figure 22.2 shows a mock-up of a top-level project screen for a modern literate programming tool that could support model-based software engineering.

---

6 See, for example, https://en.wikipedia.org/wiki/TeX.

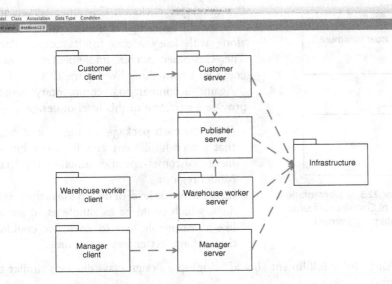

Figure 22.2 Top-level of WebBooks 2.0 design and code in literate programming form.

Figure 22.2 is an implementation view and would necessarily have accompanying commentary, either in this same window or trivially reachable from here. The commentary for this top-level view should explain the following:

- This is the topmost design view of WebBooks 2.0.
- Customer Client is a Web client running on a customer's computer, presumably a desktop machine in their home or office, or on a mobile device. Further, Customer Client implements both customer-related Order fulfillment domain and Payment domain user interfaces (UIs).
- Manager Client and Warehouse Worker Client are client UIs on dedicated terminals inside WebBooks facilities.
- Customer Server, Manager Server, and Warehouse Worker Server are corresponding server sides, each implementing Order fulfillment domain functionality. Customer Server also implements Payment domain functionality.
- A Publisher Client is not needed because all communication with publisher APIs is contained within Publisher Server. There is no need for a UI.
- Infrastructure implements User security, Scalability, and High availability domains as well as any other small-scale support services like performance (e.g., service-level agreement) monitoring and tuning.
- Why this was chosen as the top-level architecture for the system, which could be as simple as "It seems reasonable, we don't have any better ideas."

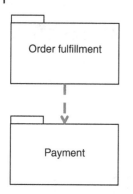

Figure 22.3 Implementation view of Customer Server in literate programming.

If a developer clicks on Customer Server, the IDE should bring up its implementation view along with (easy access to) its commentary. The Customer Server implementation view could look something like Figure 22.3.

Again, accompanying commentary would provide a narrative of this level of design:

- Overview each package, noting in particular that Order fulfillment and Payment implement customer-specific functionality (i.e., Model region).
- Justify why this level of design looks the way it does, which could be as simple as "it seems like a reasonable way to do it, we couldn't think of any better way at the time."

Clicking Order fulfillment should bring up a design class diagram similar to Figure 22.4.

Again, the diagram is the implementation view and accompanying commentary would explain and justify important decisions that drive this design, for example, any de-normalization, use of Data access object pattern, etc. Clicking class BookOrder could bring up something like Code Sample 22.1.

Each `<<italicized tag>>` is a hyperlink. Clicking on the bottom hyperlink would return to the class diagram in Figure 22.4. Clicking on the `<<BookOrder.place()>>` tag could bring up something like Code Sample 22.2.

Again, italicized texts are hyperlinks and clicking the bottom hyperlink returns to class BookOrder in Code Sample 22.1. Clicking the `<<BookOrder.mark as placed()>>` link could bring up something similar to Code Sample 22.3.

Again, clicking the bottom link returns to Figure 22.2, while clicking `<<BookOrderLine.placed()>>` could bring up BookOrderLine.placed() as shown in Code Sample 22.4.

A more complex method, like CashFlowStream.IRR() in Code Samples 18.1 through 18.7, could be described using multiple levels of decomposition. Each level would have the same implementation plus commentary format. Instead of expanding code in place as shown in Code Samples 18.1–18.7, literate programming could hyperlink each level. Assertions and proof propositions could appear at any level; each level could form an intent-act-prove-assert block.

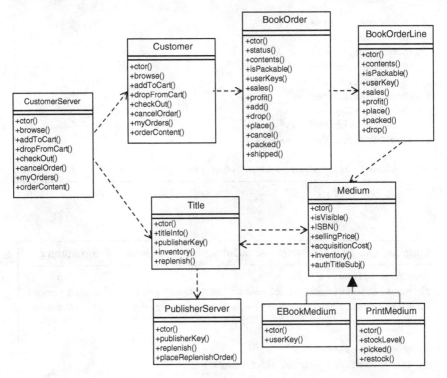

Figure 22.4 Implementation view of Order fulfillment in literate programming.

Code Sample 22.1 Class BookOrder in Literate Programming

```
BookOrder
Directly implements class Book Order in the semantic model. There were no
other important design decisions that warrant justification; this class
looks the way it does because it seems reasonable.

<<BookOrder>> =
public class BookOrder {

  <<BookOrder instance variables>>

  <<BookOrder.constructor()>>
  <<BookOrder.status()>>
  <<BookOrder.contents()>>
  <<BookOrder.isPackable()>>
```

```
<<BookOrder.userKeys()>>
<<BookOrder.sales()>>
<<BookOrder.profit()>>
<<BookOrder.add()>>
<<BookOrder.drop()>>
<<BookOrder.place()>>
<<BookOrder.cancel()>>
<<BookOrder.packed()>>
<<BookOrder.shipped()>>
}
this class is defined in package <<OrderFulfillment>>
```

Code Sample 22.2 Operation BookOrder.place() in Literate Programming

```
BookOrder.place()
This operation directly implements the "place" event on the state model
of Book Order.⁷ Nothing special was done here; we didn't have any better
ideas than this.

<<BookOrder.place()>> =
public void place( Address anAddress ) {
// requires
//   anAddress is consistent w/ range of .shippingAddress
// guarantees
//   this order has been marked as placed
//   if this order has print media in it
//     then state == placed
//     else state == completed
  if( state == BookOrder_states.OPEN ) {
    <<BookOrder.mark as placed()>>
    if( <<BookOrder.has print media()>> ) {
      state = BookOrder_states.PLACED;
    } else {
      state = BookOrder_states.COMPLETED;
    }
  }
}
this operation is called by <<Customer.placeOrder()>>
this operation is defined in class <<BookOrder>>
```

---

7 Ideally, this would be a hyperlink to Book order's state model in the semantic model for Order fulfillment.

Code Sample 22.3 Method BookOrder.markAsPlaced() in Literate Programming

```
BookOrder.markAsPlaced()
This private method directly implements the "mark as placed" action on
the state model of Book Order.⁸ Nothing special was done here; we didn't
have any better ideas than this.

<<BookOrder.mark as placed()>> ==
private void markAsPlaced( Address anAddress ) {
// requires
//   anAddress is consistent w/ range of .shippingAddress
// guarantees
//   .shipping address == anAddress
//   placed() has been signaled for all BookOrderLines in this order
  shippingAddress = anAddress;
  for( BookOrderLine aLine: forOrderLines ) {
    aLine.<<BookOrderLine.placed()>>
  }
}
this method is called by <<BookOrder.place()>>
this method is defined in class <<BookOrder>>
```

Code Sample 22.4 Operation BookOrderLine.placed() in Literate Programming

```
BookOrderLine.placed()
This operation directly implements the "placed" event on the state model
of Book Order Line.⁹ Nothing special was done here; we didn't have any
better ideas than this.

<<BookOrderLine.placed()>> =
public void place() {
// requires
//   none
// guarantees
//   if state was Open and this line is linked to a print medium
```

---

8 Ideally, this would also hyperlink to Book order's state model in the Semantic model for Order
fulfillment.
9 Ideally, this would also hyperlink to Book order line's state model in the semantic model for Order
fulfillment.

```
//    then state == Placed
//    else state == Completed
if( state == BookOrderLine_states.OPEN &&
      <<BookOderLine.hasPrintMedium()>> ) {
   state = BookOrderLine_states.PLACED;
  } else if( state == BookOrderLine_states.OPEN &&
      !<<BookOrderLine.hasPrintMedium()>> ) {
   state = BookOrderLine_states.COMPLETED;
  }
}
this operation is called by <<BookOrder.markAsPlaced()>>
this operation is defined in class <<BookOrderLine()>>
```

22.5.1 Linear Text Versus a Web of Design Content

The only difference between Knuth's original WEB and the above example is that here all elements are hyperlinked: clicking a link brings you immediately to that element. Knuth's WEB mimics paper documentation and is strictly linear: page 1, page 2, page 3, and so on. Code is, to an extent, also linear, for example, the code within a single class. But developers don't always reason about design and code in strictly linear fashion. The conceptual structure of software is also partly a network: a design class diagram is a network of interconnected classes, and a domain diagram for a large system is a network of domains. The logical structure of software is also partly hierarchical: a nontrivial method like IRR() has multiple levels of abstraction and decomposition that are typically represented by indentation in source code.

It is difficult, if not impossible, to take a complex information base that is partly network and partly hierarchical in structure and present it in one single, meaningful linear path. Literate programming with hyperlinks acknowledges that those inherent network and hierarchical structures have significance to developers and maintainers. Instead of forcing arbitrary linearization, literate programming with hyperlinks gives developers and maintainers the opportunity to go inside the design and code and wander to their heart's content. Developers and maintainers can follow any hyperlinked path for any reason that happens to be relevant at that time.

Also, in hyperlinked literate programming, the only way to get to the code is through the design. Design and code can't get out of synch because they are one single, unified holistic entity. Changing one necessarily changes the other. Since they are in the same place, there is no extra effort to update one when updating the other. Both can, should, and must be updated at the same time. They are guaranteed to stay in synch.

22.6 Verification Testing of Design and Code

It does not matter if design and code were developed by hand or generated by a model compiler: the design and code must preserve policy and process semantics and support the specified interfaces. Some level of verification testing against the semantic model and interface specification could be warranted; the depth and breadth of testing should depend on risk as described in Chapter 12. Opportunities for verification testing are explained in this section, and you will need to decide which are, or are not, warranted on your project.

22.6.1 Unit Test Against Operation-Level Semantics (Contracts)

Each operation is expected to have an explicit contract that defines its semantics. The method-level implementation can be tested against that contract. Depending on risk, unit test cases could be developed to achieve:

- Input domain coverage[10]
- Boundary value coverage[11]
- All-pairs coverage[12]

Even though we are testing detailed design and code, these test cases are still considered functional (i.e., "black box") because internal method implementation should be invisible (i.e., encapsulated).

If appropriate, unit test cases can be run under a code coverage analysis tool to be sure that appropriate structural (i.e., "white box") coverage has been achieved[13]:

- Statement coverage
- Decision (branch) coverage
- Modified condition/decision coverage (MCDC)

If an operation being tested calls (i.e., "sends messages to") any other operation or private method, you should use a mock object (i.e., "stub" or "test double") to be sure any test incidents are due to the method being tested and not an artifact of other production code that happened to be called.

---

10 See, for example, https://www.cs.ccu.edu.tw/~naiwei/cs5812/st3.pdf or [Beizer90].
11 Test boundaries at the precision defined in the corresponding range specification.
12 See, for example, http://www.pairwise.org/.
13 See, for example, https://en.wikipedia.org/wiki/Code_coverage.

Sidebar on Unit Testing

According to the strict definition of unit testing,

"A unit is the smallest isolate-able piece of software.[14]*"*

Strictly speaking, testing an operation without using mock objects is not unit testing: it is integration testing and unit testing combined. The practical issue is the value of unit testing in terms of fault isolation compared to the cost in terms of creating and maintaining necessary mock objects. In strict unit testing—meaning use of mock objects—if a defect is discovered, it must be in the method being tested, and it can be nowhere else. This is very precise fault isolation. On the other hand, every operation called from the one being tested requires a mock to achieve unit testing's required isolation. The cost of creating and maintaining mocks could be higher than the value of increased fault isolation.

This is another economic (i.e., engineering) decision. When the value of increased fault isolation sufficiently exceeds the cost of developing and maintaining mock objects, it makes sense to do strict unit testing. Where value does not sufficiently exceed cost, it doesn't make economic sense. Instead, combining unit and integration testing is more appropriate.

The point of this sidebar is to simply raise awareness that what many organizations call "unit testing" (i.e., using automated test frameworks like JUnit, NUnit, CPPUnit, PyUnit, etc.) is not actually unit testing according to the strict definition. Most often, it is unit testing and integration testing combined. On the other hand, if whatever testing an organization is doing makes economic sense, then it is appropriate to do it that way.

22.6.2 Integration Test a Single Class

One level of integration testing is to be sure that a class behaves—as a whole—the way it should. Positive test cases can exercise each transition in the state model. Depending on detailed design and risk, negative test cases covering invalid combinations of state and event might be appropriate. If code generation rules like those in Chapter 20 (and Appendix M) are used, any invalid event in any state is automatically ignored and not worth testing. Specific test cases to address impossible event + state pairs could be useful.

To the extent that class-level integration tests can be combined with operation-level unit tests, you can get the same coverage from fewer test cases, thus maintaining test effectiveness through coverage and increasing test efficiency by using fewer test cases.

---

14 See, for example, [Beizer90].

22.6.3 Integration Test One Class to Another Class

When single classes have been tested and can be trusted, the next level of integration testing—again, depending on risk—could be to integrate and test pairs of classes. The goal is to verify the interface between those classes is implemented properly. A calling operation might give a parameter in units of meters, while the called operation might expect that parameter to be in centimeters. Unit testing either operation alone would not reveal this defect; only integration testing of both can reveal it.

22.6.4 (Sub)domain Functional Testing

At a minimum, the (sub)domain functional test cases derived in Chapter 12 could be appropriate. Additional testing to the level of incorporating every test element as described in Chapter 12 could be appropriate if warranted by risk. This testing might be done through the external interface(s) (i.e. include executing View-controller region code) or may focus entirely on Model region code (e.g., use a testing tool like Fit[15]).

22.6.5 Usability and/or Interface Tests Against the Interface Specification

Depending on risk, interface testing (including usability testing) against the interface specification(s) could be appropriate. If the interface has a dialog map, consider positive testing of all transitions and negative testing for event + state combinations that are not meaningful but still technically possible (the implementation of the interface may make it impossible to produce some given event in some given UI state).

22.6.6 Performance Testing Against Nonfunctional How Well Requirements

To the extent that nontrivial nonfunctional how well requirements exist, some amount of performance testing might be warranted to be confident of meeting required qualities of service.

22.6.7 Summarizing Verification Testing of Design and Code

Remember

> *"If it's not obvious how to test it, can your specification be any good?"*
> (Dr. Ric Frankel, Seattle University)

---

15 See, for example, https://en.wikipedia.org/wiki/Framework_for_integrated_test.

It *is* obvious how to test it, so the semantic model and interface specification on a model-based software engineering project *must* be good specifications.

22.7 Design and Code for Product Families

Chapter 3 introduced "design to invariants and design for change" and "product families." Chapter 12 extended that in the context of semantic modeling: addressing variants and invariants in policy and process. When dealing with product family software, we likely also need variants and invariants in design and code. Specific techniques in design and code include:

- *Separate common from variable functionality*—conditional compilation, inheritance, and aspect-oriented design as examples
- *Hide variation behind abstract interfaces*—for example, design patterns like Proxy, Adapter, Factory method, Data access object, etc.
- *Configuration files, preferences, or registries.*
- *Dependency injection*[16]
- ...

Consider the following questions: "Who, when, and how does someone select something in a range of a technology variation? Does a developer select it in code? Does a configurer select it at link time? Is it a load time decision? Does a user decide at run time?" Consider who should make each variation decision, and when should they make it (i.e., should they be able to change their mind? If so, when and how?). In making design-for-change decisions, consider how much flexibility is offered by implementing the choice that way. Does that choice adversely affect performance? Make cost-effective decisions about variation points in design and code.

22.8 The Myth of Source Code Reuse

Much like the myth of self-documenting code, another common myth in the software industry is that source code is reusable. The simple fact that we see so little source code reuse should be enough to seriously question this assertion. If source code really were so reusable, then *someone* should have figured out how to do it by now: we have had more than 50 years to figure it out.

---

16 See, for example, https://en.wikipedia.org/wiki/Dependency_injection.

On the other hand, consider that source code reuse depends on all of the following being true:

- *Policy and process semantics that you want automated must be compatible[17] with policies and processes automated in any source code you intend to reuse*—Any incompatibility in policy or process semantics means the source code does the wrong thing. At a minimum, this means you must be able to compare semantic models of code you might want to reuse and the functionality you need.
- *Automation technology in any code you intend to reuse needs to be similar enough to your available technology* (in the nonfunctional how requirements sense)—This isn't always an issue and might be helped by using higher-level programming languages. But this can still be a significant impediment if the source code you want to reuse isn't written in a language you need it in.
- *Performance of any code you intend to reuse needs to meet your performance requirements* (in the nonfunctional how well requirements sense)—The source code has to provide adequate qualities of service: speed, accuracy, reliability, etc.

Realizing that code is a mapping means accepting that code can be incredibly sensitive to automation technology, particularly depending on criticality of the nonfunctional requirements. This is why source code reuse is only possible under far more limited circumstances than most people in and around our industry want to assume.

On the other hand, semantic models are very reusable. In a series of Automated Test Equipment (ATE) projects for major, complex safety-critical products at one manufacturer, the top domain semantic models across all versions are almost identical. The company saved significant time and money on the follow-on ATE projects by simply making a few minor modifications to already existing top domain semantic models.

I propose the following as a ranking of the reusability of software work products (aside from reuse of an entire application, e.g., very few developers ever write the development tool chain they use—they reuse entire applications written by others. But again, this isn't source code reuse):

1) Semantic models
2) Design patterns and architectural styles
3) Source code

---

17 In the Liskov substitutability sense, policy and process semantics in code to be reused can require no more and guarantee no less than the policy and process semantics I want automated. How likely is this to happen in practice?

22.9 Summary

Part III presented translation of a semantic model, along with nonfunctional requirements, into design and code. That design and code are expected to automate the policies and processes in the semantic model, provide the specified interfaces, and satisfy the nonfunctional requirements. Many different implementations of a single semantic model and interface specification are possible. Part III is only intended to prove that translation is possible: documentation *can* be literally self-coding. This chapter wraps up model-based design and code and covers:

- Summarizing model-based design and code
- Comparing and contrasting semantic and design models
- Organizing design documentation into written specifications
- Design versus code: what's the difference?
- Verification testing of design and code
- Product family design
- The myth of source code reuse

Recall the ultimate goal of model-based software engineering:

> *"... change the nature of programming from a private, puzzle solving activity to a public, mathematics based activity of translating specifications into programs ... that can be expected to both run and do the right thing with little or no debugging."*

The public, mathematics-based nature of model-based software engineering should now be clear: semantic models are translated into design and code that can be expected to both run and do the right thing with little or no debugging.

Part IV, "Related Topics," is next. This includes an estimation model, development and maintenance processes, the economics of error handling, and the arguments against model-based software engineering.

Part IV

Related Topics

Part I covers foundations: problems plaguing the software industry, root causes of those problems, the nature of code, fundamental principles, kinds of requirements, introducing UML, and partitioning large systems into domains.

Part II covers semantic modeling: precise, concise specification of policies to be enforced and processes to be carried out, presumably (but not necessarily) in software. Partitioning large domains into subdomains and use of semantic models for simulation and deriving test cases are also presented.

Part III covers design: starting with well-defined policy and process semantics and nonfunctional requirements, map those policy and process semantics onto automation technology semantics. Much of that mapping process can be automated (i.e., in an open model compiler).

Part IV puts all these pieces together for real-world projects, covering topics such as:

- *Estimation*
- *Development and Maintenance Process*
- *Economics of Error Handling*
- *Arguments Against Model-Based Software Engineering*

How to Engineer Software: A Model-Based Approach, First Edition. Steve Tockey.
© 2019 the IEEE Computer Society, Inc. Published 2019 by John Wiley & Sons, Inc.

23

Estimation

A key part of engineering is considering the economic consequences of technical decisions. Decisions about the scope of policies and processes to model, design, code, and maintain clearly have economic implications. On the one hand, some given additional scope should provide benefit by either increasing an organization's revenue or decreasing its costs ("cost avoidance" in engineering economy). On the other hand, that same scope requires investment to develop and maintain. There is never any guarantee that the benefit of any scope will adequately compensate for its cost. Scope should only be included when it is affordable and provides sufficient return on investment. A true software engineer—one capable of performing economic analysis—may guide the stakeholders in an analysis, but it is ultimately up to stakeholders to determine the benefit of proposed scope.

It is up to the development community to determine cost. We need to be able to answer questions like:

- How long will it take and how much will it cost to deliver some given scope?
- How much longer will it take and how much more will it cost if scope is added?
- How much shorter will it take and how much less will it cost if scope is removed?
- How much scope can be delivered within given constraints, for example, schedule, budget or staffing?

This chapter describes how to estimate model-based software engineering projects. This process and its productivity factors are derived from real projects in varied disciplines including real-time/embedded, scientific and engineering, business data processing, etc.

"Warning! Your results may vary!"

How to Engineer Software: A Model-Based Approach, First Edition. Steve Tockey.
© 2019 the IEEE Computer Society, Inc. Published 2019 by John Wiley & Sons, Inc.

Circumstances unique to your project or organization could invalidate some or all of this process or productivity factors. It is normally safe to start here, but you need to confirm and update your estimates based on your own experience. You don't need to wait to the end of a project to confirm estimates. Schedule performance index (SPI) and cost performance index (CPI) from earned value[1] on plan-based projects or velocity and sprint or release burn down[2] on agile projects can validate estimates while a project is running.

23.1 Estimation, Commitment, Uncertainty, and Risk

A full discussion of software estimation is too big for a single chapter; entire books have been written on the topic.[3] That said, a few fundamental concepts underlie effective estimation.

23.1.1 Why Estimate?

First and foremost, we don't estimate just for the sake of estimation. We estimate to support making decisions—decisions that need to be made when crucial information isn't available. A decision like "Should we do this project at all?" almost certainly depends on how long it would take and how much it would cost. If we did that project, at the end we would know exactly how long it took and exactly how much it cost. But by then it would be too late to make the decision because the project has already been done. When a decision needs to be made before crucial information is known, that decision needs to be based on an estimate. If the decision is to not do something, the actual outcome will never be known. If Project X were never done, nobody would ever know for sure how long it would have taken or how much it would have cost:

> *"Estimates are for making decisions when crucial information can't be known until after that decision is made, if ever"*

23.1.2 Good Enough, Not Good Enough, and Too Good Estimates

Given that estimates are for making decisions, those estimates don't need to be perfect. They only need to be good enough to make the right decision. Assume for some Project X that "If it would take any more than 12 months, then it's too long and we won't do it." Project X might be estimated to take at least 14 months, so the

---

1 See, for example, https://en.wikipedia.org/wiki/Earned_value_management.
2 See, for example, https://www.scrumalliance.org/community/articles/2014/february/velocity.
3 See, for example, [Stutzky05] and [McConnell06].

decision would be to not do it. If the project had actually been done, it might have taken 30 months. Despite underestimating by more than a factor of two, that estimate led to making the right decision—don't do Project X—so it was "good enough."

An estimate that is "not good enough" risks making a wrong decision. For Project X, "If it will take any more than 18 months, then it's too long and we won't do it." An estimate of at least 14 months could lead to deciding to do the project, and an actual outcome of 30 months would almost certainly mean it was the wrong decision.

An estimate can also be "too good"—meaning additional time and money were spent on the estimate without changing the decision. Once it has been determined that Project X will take at least 14 months and the no-go point is 12, any more time spent refining that estimate is wasted. The decision to not do Project X can already be made safely.

Decisions over the course of a project vary widely. Early decisions tend to be few but broad in consequence:

- Should we do a project at all?
- How should this project be coordinated with related projects?
- How much budget needs to be allocated?
- How should the project be staffed?
- ...

Later decisions tend to be many but localized:

- When should the product marketing campaign start?
- Should resources be shifted off this project and onto another?
- Should some given scope be added or removed at this point in the project?
- Will this user story fit into the next sprint, or does it need to be decomposed?
- ...

"Good enough" varies by decision; an estimate good enough for a project go-no-go decision is almost certainly too coarse to make a resource reallocation decision. If the estimator doesn't know the intended decision(s), then how can they know how good their estimate needs to be? Estimators need to ask decision makers what decisions are to be made (unless it's already obvious). Further, estimators need to make clear to the decision maker: "This estimate is good enough for making decisions A, B, and C, *and no others*." If the decision maker wants to make other decisions, they need to check back with the estimator. The estimator reserves the right to change the estimate to support other decisions.

23.1.3 Estimates Versus Commitments

Estimates and commitments are not the same:

> *"An estimate is not a commitment!"*

An estimate should represent an equal chance of doing better as doing worse. Suppose an estimator is confident that some work will take at least one month to accomplish. Suppose they are also confident that same work will not take any more than three months. If they are confident that the work is as likely to take more than two months as less than, then the estimate should be "two months." A good (i.e., unbiased) estimator will overestimate (the actual outcome is better than estimate) as often—and by as much—as they underestimate (the actual outcome is worse than estimate).

A commitment is a statement by those who will do the work that they will try their best to do no worse than that. It would not make sense to commit to an estimate that, by definition, has only a 50% chance of being met: commitments would only be met half of the time. A reasonable commitment needs to include an allowance for uncertainty and contingencies for risks. In engineering economy (e.g., [Tockey05]), risk is quantifiable and uncertainty is not. In project management, risk is project specific and uncertainty is not. Caution: Use of These Terms Varies by Context.

23.1.4 Uncertainty

In this context, uncertainty is generic to all projects in an organization. It is driven by the nature of the projects and the environment in which they are done: the kinds of software being built and maintained, the stakeholder's ability to make decisions, the software process, etc. Uncertainty can be measured: developing and using a cone of uncertainty for plan-based (e.g., waterfall and its variants) projects is discussed in [Tockey05]. Figure 23.1 shows a schedule cone of uncertainty for a real software organization.[4] This graph shows measured uncertainty for schedule estimates as a function of schedule progress through their plan-based projects. Specifically, if a project in this organization were estimated to take 10 months at 10% of the way into the project, it can be reasonably expected to take no less than about 9 months, be as likely to take more than as less than about 17.5 months, and take no more than about 26 months. A project estimated to take 10 months 75% of the way in should be expected to take no less than about 8 months, take as likely more than as less than about 11 months, and take no more than about 14 months.

Uncertainty can be measured on agile projects[5] by recording actual velocities (the sum of initial estimates of all planned work that was completed in that sprint) at the end of each of a series of sprints. Velocities may need to be normalized to account for changes in staffing or sprint duration. Standard deviation can be computed from any two or more normalized velocity measurements. The

---

4 A cone of uncertainty calculator and user's guide can be found at http://www.construx.com/ Thought_Leadership/Books/Return_on_Software_Tools/.
5 See Chapter 24 for my definition of agile development.

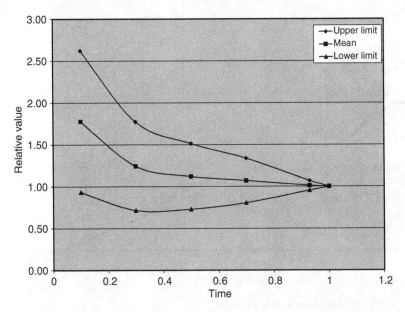

Figure 23.1 A schedule cone of uncertainty for a real software organization.

standard deviation formula can be found on the Web using any search engine, but the easiest way may be to use the STDEV() function in your favorite spreadsheet. As an example, assume normalized velocities for seven sprints of a project were, in order, 42, 51, 39, 48, 45, 41, and 50. Average velocity over those seven sprints is 45.1, and standard deviation is 4.7.

The planning velocity for the next sprint should be a running average of the three or four most recent sprints. Using those same velocities, the four most recent sprints were 48, 45, 41, and 50, so the planning velocity for the next sprint should be 46. After computing planning velocity, add and subtract two standard deviations. For the next sprint, this would be $46 + 2 * 4.7 = 55$ and $46 - 2 * 4.7 = 37$. Connect those three points, 55, 46, and 37, on the first day of the sprint to zero on the last day of the sprint as shown in Figure 23.2.

As long as actual sprint burn down stays between the upper and lower limits; variation from ideal burn down is probably random and should not cause concern. If actual burn down crosses either limit line, then it is statistically significant and should be dealt with:

- *Crossing the upper limit means sprint scope should be reduced*—The product owner should decide which unfinished sprint backlog items to push back to the product backlog. Don't push any more than would drive work remaining below the lower limit.

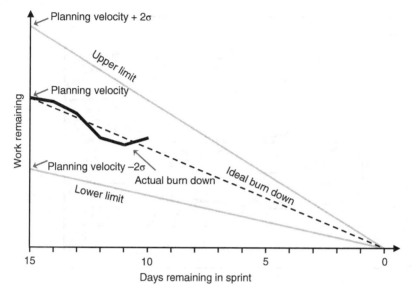

Figure 23.2 Sprint burn down with uncertainty.

- *Crossing the lower limit means sprint scope can be added*—The product owner should decide which product backlog item(s) to pull forward into this sprint. Don't pull any more than would drive work remaining over the upper limit.

Measured uncertainty can also be applied to release burn down, as introduced in Figure 23.3 for a scope-driven release. Release will not happen until the entire release backlog has been completed, as opposed to a schedule-driven release where release happens on a defined date regardless of how much release backlog has been completed.

Figure 23.3 shows three sprints completed. Release is as likely to happen before the end of Sprint 10 as it is to finish after. Best-case finish can be projected using average velocity plus two standard deviations per sprint; the team can reasonably expect to finish no earlier than the end of Sprint 9. Worst-case finish can be projected using average velocity minus two standard deviations per sprint; the team can reasonably expect to finish no later than the end of Sprint 11.

Release scope is not always constant and may grow for a variety of reasons. If the project has a history of scope growth, then average, best-case, and worst-case growth rates can also be calculated and projected as shown in Figure 23.4.

When scope growth is considered, this release is as likely to finish before as after the end of Sprint 13. The release has little chance of finishing before the end of Sprint 11 and could possibly take until the end of Sprint 15.

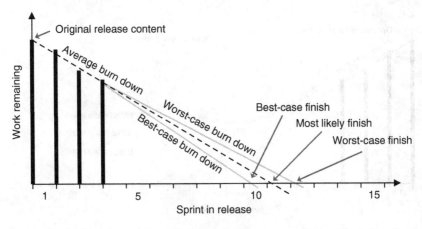

Figure 23.3 Release burn down with uncertainty for a scope-driven release.

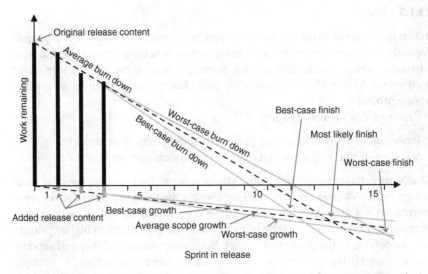

Figure 23.4 Release burn down for a scope-driven release, considering scope growth.

Some releases are driven by schedule instead of scope. The goal is to deliver as much as possible within that time. This is shown in Figure 23.5 for an eight-sprint release. Work remaining at the end of Sprint 8 is again estimated using average velocity plus and minus two standard deviations per sprint. The product owner needs to understand how much functionality can reasonably be delivered in the available time. Of course, scope growth can also be considered as in Figure 23.4.

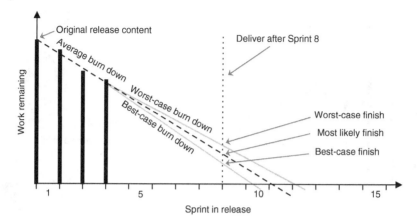

Figure 23.5 Release burn down with uncertainty for a schedule-driven release.

23.1.5 Risk

In this context, risk is unique to the project being estimated. Maybe this project depends on some other project delivering certain functionality on time and with adequate quality. Maybe this project is using a new technology they've never used before. Maybe a key team member might leave. Those are all issues specific to one project.

Each risk can be analyzed for:

- *Probability*—How likely is the project to suffer harm from a risk?
- *Severity*—If that risk does materialize, how much damage will it do?

Ideally, probability would be estimated as a percent, for example, the new technology has a 45% chance of not working the way the team hopes, or the key team member has a 10% chance of leaving. Severity would ideally be estimated in terms of its effect on either schedule or cost based on which has higher priority (e.g., as defined in the project's charter). In these terms, probability and severity are expressed using ratio scales.[6] An "expected value of risk exposure"—simply called "risk exposure" from here on—can be calculated for each risk by multiplying probability by severity as shown in Table 23.1.

More likely, the team is unable to quantify probability in percent and severity in time or money. Instead, probability and severity could be expressed using ordinal scales, for example:

- *Probability*—Almost certain, Probable, Even, Unlikely, Remote
- *Severity*—Catastrophic, Critical, Serious, Marginal, Negligible

---

6 See, for example, chapter 26 of [Tockey05], Appendix L, or http://en.wikipedia.org/wiki/ Level_of_measurement.

Table 23.1 Risks with ratio-scaled probabilities, severities, and calculated risk exposures.

Risk	Probability (%)	Severity (months)	Risk exposure (months)
Other team doesn't deliver	25	6	1.5
New technology doesn't perform	45	4	1.8
Key team member leaves	10	8	0.8

Table 23.2 Risks with ordinal-scaled probability and severity.

Risk	Probability	Severity
Other team doesn't deliver	Unlikely	Critical
New technology doesn't perform	Even	Serious
Key team member leaves	Remote	Catastrophic

This is shown in Table 23.2.

23.1.6 Asset

Like risks, assets are unique to a project. Unlike risks, assets are positive, not negative. The Project Management Institute[7] refers to these as "negative risks," but this term is difficult for many to grasp, so "asset" is used instead. Some call this an "opportunity." Instead of suffering harm, an asset can work in a project's favor. One asset might be an ability to reuse a significant portion of the semantic model from another project. Another asset might be that the team may be able to hire a star developer and the extra productivity will help them finish sooner.

Similar to risks, each asset should be analyzed for probability and benefit:

- *Probability*—How likely is the project to gain from this asset?
- *Benefit*—If the asset does help, how much will it help?

Ideally, asset probability would be estimated as a percent, for example, the team has a 75% chance of being able to reuse the earlier semantic model, or a 40% chance of being able to hire that star developer. Benefit would be estimated in terms of its positive effect on schedule or budget. The project might save

---

7 See the Guide to the Project Management Body of Knowledge [PMI13].

Table 23.3 Assets with ratio-scaled probabilities, benefits, and calculated gain.

Asset	Probability (%)	Benefit (months)	Gain (months)
Reuse earlier model	75	2	1.5
Hire star developer	40	1	0.4

Table 23.4 Example assets with ordinal-scaled probabilities and benefits

Asset	Probability	Benefit
Reuse earlier semantic model	Probable	Significant
Hire star developer	Even	Moderate

two months from model reuse and one month from the star developer. In these terms, probability and benefit are again expressed using ratio scales. An "expected value of asset gain"—simply called "gain" from here on—can be calculated for each asset by multiplying probability by benefit as shown in Table 23.3.

More likely, probability and benefit would be expressed using ordinal scales:

- *Probability*—Almost certain, Probable, Even, Unlikely, Remote
- *Benefit*—Extreme, Significant, Moderate, Marginal, Negligible

This is shown in Table 23.4.

Using risks and assets to derive commitments will be explained later in this chapter.

23.1.7 Effort Versus Schedule

Effort represents an amount of work to be done; schedule represents how long that work will take. In some cases more than one person can work in parallel, meaning schedule could be less than effort. For example, some unit of work is 5 person-weeks[8] of effort and two people will work on it full time, so it is reasonable to expect it to take about 2.5 calendar weeks of schedule. On the other hand, distractions (e.g., working on multiple projects at the same time, supporting products in the field, assisting marketing, etc.) and forced wait states could drive schedule to be greater than effort. Some other unit of work might be 2

---

8 One person-week is one person working for one week, that is, about 40 hours.

person-weeks of effort, but the person working on it can only allocate one third of their time, so it is reasonable to expect that work to take about 6 calendar weeks of schedule.

Baking bread provides good examples of forced wait states. The steps in making bread are:

1) Mix the ingredients.
2) Knead the dough.
3) Let the dough rise.
4) Punch down the dough, knead it again, and form it into loaves.
5) Let the loaves rise in baking pans.
6) Bake the loaves in the oven.
7) Let the loaves cool.

While making bread, the baker is forced to wait during both rise stages (steps 3 and 5) as well as when the bread is baking and cooling (steps 6 and 7). The baker can do nothing except wait. The duration for baking bread is several hours; the baker's actual effort over that time may only be an hour or two. Critical path dependencies and the need for external approval of work products are examples of forced wait states on software projects.

23.2 Estimating Nominal Effort and Nominal Schedule

The terms "nominal effort" and "nominal schedule" are very important in estimation. "Nominal" means the project is not being pressured to finish quickly, nor is it being pressured to finish cheaply. Schedule can be traded for effort, as described below. The nominal configuration of the project means there is no trading: the project is in its most comfortable configuration.

23.2.1 Estimating Nominal Effort

Nominal effort, in person-months,[9] for model-based software engineering projects can be estimated based on the number of classes in the semantic model(s):

Effort = 0.3 – 0.7 person-months per class in the semantic model(s)

This covers technical work starting once (sub)domains have been identified through developer testing of code. Tested (sub)domain code should be ready

---

9 One person-month is one person working for one month: about 21.75 person-days or 174 person-hours. Person-days in a person-month do not include weekends, holidays, etc. You may need to adapt this depending on your own organization.

for integration with other (sub)domains. This also assumes not using a model compiler: design, coding, and testing are done by hand. Effort reduction from model compilation is discussed below. Any other work such as:

- Development and approval of Background documentation[10]
- Domain and subdomain partitioning
- Integrating adjacent (sub)domains and integration testing
- System testing
- Deployment (i.e., transferring the product from developers to users)
- User acceptance testing
- Project management
- Etc.

are not included. That additional work also needs to be accounted for but is not covered in this formula because it is specific to an organization or a project.

Reasonably accurate class counts for (sub)domains can be available relatively early. You do not need complete semantic model(s) to have confidence that a class count is reasonable. Class counts for semantic models are generally accurate to within 10% of final count in the first 10% of the effort on that (sub) domain. On a (sub)domain with 6 person-months of effort, a reasonably accurate class count should be available after spending a little more than one half person-month on semantic modeling. If accurate enough class counts aren't available, you can still use this formula with best-case, most likely, and worst-case counts. For example, the project will finish with at least X, most likely Y, and no more than Z classes. Class counts can also be estimated before any significant work is done on a project or (sub)domain using expert judgment or by-analogy estimation.[11]

The 0.3–0.7 person-months per class productivity factor range is derived from a variety of real-world projects and represents the learning curve. Use 0.7 person-months per class when the team has been trained in model-based development (e.g., they have read and understand this book, or they have attended a seminar) but do not have hands-on, real-world project experience.[12] Use 0.3 person-months per class when the team is fully proficient. Developers tend to start at 0.7 person-months per class and ramp to 0.3 over the course of developing about four (sub)domains. For example, their first (sub)domain might take 0.7 person-months per class, the second (sub)domain might take 0.5, the third might take 0.4, and the fourth and beyond might take 0.3.

---

10 See Figure 1.3.
11 As described in chapter 22 of [Tockey05].
12 Teams in this situation should be given access to someone who does have hands-on experience to help keep the project from going astray.

When a project has inexperienced staff and there are more (sub)domains than team members, each person will probably work on more than one (sub)domain, so adjust estimates accordingly. A project with 35 subdomains and seven developers should expect each developer to work on an average of five subdomains. Each developer should reach full productivity by the end of that project.

The Order fulfillment semantic model (Appendix D) has 12 classes. Beginner productivity of 0.7 person-months per class means 8.4 person-months to produce code ready to integrate with other (sub)domains. Full productivity means 3.6 person-months to reach this same point. A semantic model with 30 classes should take between 9 (full productivity) and 21 (beginner productivity) person-months. An entire system with 385 classes across all semantic models should take between 115.5 (full productivity) and 269.5 (beginner) person-months of effort to deliver integrable (sub)domain code.

23.2.2 Warning: Individual Productivities Vary

Individual developer productivity is a highly controversial topic.[13] Just defining developer productivity so it can be measured in an objectively quantifiable way can be difficult, let alone designing cost-effective experiments that control all relevant variables[14] so that *only* individual productivity differences are being observed. That said, among those who agree that productivity can at least be observed and roughly quantified, differences of at least a factor of 10 are common. Some claim differences on the order of 30x to 40x: a high productivity developer could complete in one hour something that would take a low productivity developer as much as a week.

Any discussion of individual productivity needs to be tempered with the reality of "net negative producing programmers" (NNPPs). According to Schulmeyer,[15]

> *"We've known since the early sixties, but have never come to grips with the implications that there are net negative producing programmers (NNPPs) on almost all projects, who insert enough spoilage to exceed the value of their production. So, it is important to make the bold statement: Taking a poor performer off the team can often be more productive than adding a good one."*

---

13 See, for example, http://www.construx.com/10x_Software_Development/Origins_of_10X_-_How_Valid_is_the_Underlying_Research_/ for a good entry point into this debate.
14 See, for example, part II in [DeMarco99] for a discussion of just the effect of work environment on developer productivity.
15 See [Schulmeyer92].

Simply, some developers are so bad that not only are they not helping the project move forward, but they are dragging the rest of the team backward by requiring the others to clean up the mess made by that NNPP. Schulmeyer goes on to say,

> *"This negative production does not merely apply to extreme cases. In a team of ten, expect as many as three people to have a defect rate high enough to make them NNPPs. With a normal distribution of skills, the probability that there is not even one NNPP out of ten is virtually nil."*

Schulmeyer asserts that about 20% of the software development community is net negative producing. This is consistent with my observations of mainstream software projects. Anyone who has been a professional developer for more than a year or two probably knows at least one NNPP by name.

Having just said that, one model-based software engineering project had 30 developers. Only three had ever worked on model-based projects before, and the other 27 had not. There were no selection criteria other than willingness to work with model-based development. Developers were not selected from the "cream of the crop" in that organization. Two (not in the final 30) brought into the project turned out to be unwilling to work in model-based fashion and left quickly. According to Schulmeyer, a team of 30 developers should expect about six NNPPs. The probability that there would not be at least three, according to Schulmeyer, was virtually nil.

We knew which developers worked on what (sub)domains and for how long. We computed a measure of individual productivity by dividing person-months spent on a (sub)domain by the number of classes in that semantic model. Clearly, some classes are more complex than others. However, over a sufficiently large set of classes (e.g., 20 or more), complexity per class tends to average. In my experience, this is the best—and most objective—measure of individual developer productivity. There were productivity variations on the project, but the range was no more than a factor of two—not the factor of at least 10 as would otherwise be expected. In addition, there were no NNPPs on the project. None. Every developer had positive productivity at least as good as the beginner productivity of 0.7 person-months per class. Similar results have been seen on other model-based software engineering projects, strongly suggesting that:

> *"Software process DOES matter"*

and

> *"Model-based software engineering is an efficient and effective process"*

23.2.3 Estimating Nominal Schedule

Nominal schedule, in calendar months, can be derived from nominal effort in person-months using a software industry standard formula[16]:

$$\text{Schedule} = 3 * \sqrt[3]{\text{Effort}}$$

As examples, assuming beginner productivity for Order fulfillment means 8.4 person-months of effort, so the expected schedule should be as likely more than as less than 6.1 calendar months. Assuming full productivity for Order fulfillment, 3.6 person-months of effort means the schedule should be as likely more than as less than 4.6 calendar months. A (sub)domain with 30 classes and full productivity (9 person-months) would be 6.2 calendar months and beginner productivity (21 person-months) would be 8.3 calendar months. A system of 385 classes at full productivity (115.5 person-months) would be expected to take as likely more than as less than 14.6 calendar months.

Staffing constraints, critical path, external dependencies, etc. could invalidate a nominal schedule estimate. Consider the nominal effort and schedule to be a starting point for high-level decisions. Other specifics like staffing profiles, individual productivities, and so on need to be considered to develop a detailed project schedule.

23.2.4 Estimating Nominal Staffing

The acronym FTE means full-time equivalent. Two people working half time each on a project would be one FTE, and three people working half time each would be 1.5 FTEs. Nominal staffing, in FTEs, can be computed by dividing nominal effort by nominal schedule. Nominal effort is in person-months and nominal schedule is in calendar months, dividing person-months by calendar months gives people. The nominal staffing for the earlier nominal effort and schedule examples are shown in Table 23.5.

"Nominal staffing" does not mean staffing at exactly that level from start to finish. It only means that by the end of the project, the staffing level should average that. The 385-class system at beginner productivity should average about 14 developers but does not need to start and finish with that. The project would probably start with two to four lead developers creating the foundation (e.g., domain and subdomain partitioning) and then ramp up to possibly 18 by the end, as illustrated in Figure 23.6.

---

16 See, for example, [Stutzke05] or [McConnell06].

Table 23.5 Nominal staffing for different situations.

Situation	Nominal effort	Nominal schedule	Nominal staffing
Order fulfillment, beginner productivity	8.4	6.1	1.4
Order fulfillment, full productivity	3.6	4.6	0.8
30 classes, beginner productivity	21.0	8.3	2.5
30 classes, full productivity	9.0	6.2	1.4
385-class system, beginner productivity	269.5	19.4	13.9
385-class system, full productivity	115.5	14.6	7.9

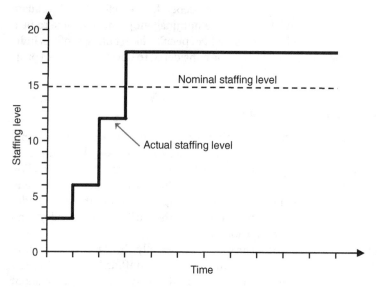

Figure 23.6 Actual staffing compared with nominal staffing.

23.3 Trading Effort and Schedule

Schedule can be traded for effort on software projects: schedule can be reduced, but effort increases faster than schedule decreases. There is also a limit to how much a schedule can be reduced. As Fred Brooks said, countering the belief that doubling the number of people on a software project would get it done in half the time (paraphrased)[17]:

> *"If it takes one woman nine months to have a baby, can nine women have that same baby on one month?"*

Symons[18] offers a pair of formulas to approximate the trade-off between effort and schedule. In my experience, these equations aren't entirely accurate. However, that inaccuracy is almost always swamped by uncertainty and risk. There is nothing better to work with for now; it's the best we have until something better is published. Symons' formulas are

$$\text{Compression factor} = \frac{\text{Desired schedule}}{\text{Nominal schedule}}$$

$$\text{Compressed effort} = \frac{\text{Nominal Effort}}{\text{Compression factor}}$$

Take, as an example, the project with 385 classes at full productivity. The nominal configuration of this project is 115.5 person-months of effort, 14.6 calendar months of schedule, and 7.9 FTEs of staffing. Table 23.6 shows options that can be presented to decision makers.

As stated, there is a limit to how much schedule can be compressed. The general agreement among credible researchers is a best-case reduction to about 75% of the nominal schedule. Table 23.6 stops at a desired schedule of 11 months because it is 75% of the nominal schedule. Also observe that Table 23.6 shows the staffing level almost doubling from 7.9 to 13.9, and yet the compressed schedule is nowhere near half of nominal. Doubling staff does *not* get a software project done in half the time.

Table 23.6 Schedule compression options according to [Symons91].

Desired schedule	Compression factor	Compressed effort	Staffing level
14.4	1.00	115.5	7.9
14.0	0.96	120.5	8.6
13.0	0.89	129.8	10.0
12.0	0.82	140.6	11.7
11.0	0.75	153.4	13.9

---

17 See [Brooks75].
18 See [Symons91].

23.4 Making Reasonable Commitments

All estimates above are expected to represent unbiased values. A project should be as likely to do better than its estimate as it is to do worse—even after trading effort for schedule. If the 385-class project is staffed with 13.9 full-productivity FTEs, it should be as likely to take more than as less than 11 calendar months and consume as likely more than as less than 153.4 person-months of effort. To make a reasonable commitment, unbiased estimates need to be cushioned for organizational uncertainties and project-specific risks. This section describes how to do that cushioning.

Some people advise against cushioning because a team, when given more time, will take it.[19] The solution is to manage the project to a plan derived from unbiased estimates and reserve cushioning for status reporting to external stakeholders:

> "Manage the project to its unbiased estimate(s). Report progress to external stakeholders against its commitments."

23.4.1 Calculating an Allowance for Uncertainty on Plan-Based Projects

The process for turning unbiased estimates into reasonable commitments starts with calculating an allowance for uncertainty. For plan-based projects, the allowance comes from the organization's cone of uncertainty. Consider the cone of uncertainty for the organization in Figure 23.1. Assume our project is at the earliest stage where uncertainty data is available: 10% completion in Figure 23.1.

It needs to be stated that the organization in Figure 23.1 was *not* using model-based software engineering, thus the significant early bias of 78%. Said another way, whatever that organization thinks their best estimate at the 10% point is, the real unbiased estimate—based on actual performance—is 1.78 times that. Their initial estimate of 11 calendar months would correspond to an unbiased estimate of 19.6 months.

As stated, this cone of uncertainty is not from a model-based software engineering organization and needs to be taken with a large grain of salt. Model-based projects should not underestimate—even that early in a project—anywhere near that much. Nonetheless, if bias has been measured in your organization, this is how to adjust for it.

---

19 Parkinson's law: "Work expands to fill all available resources."

As a real example of model-based software engineering, the 30-developer, 15-month project mentioned earlier was estimated, six weeks into the project, based on class count. The actual completion date for the project was within three days of the estimated completion date.[20] That estimate was within 1% of actual outcome and was made only 10% into the project. We'll use the 11-month schedule estimate and ignore bias from here on.

From computations that underlie the cone of uncertainty,[21] one standard deviation in the organization in Figure 23.1 is 42% (i.e., 0.42x initial estimate). Two standard deviations would be 84% (i.e., 0.84x initial estimate). Two standard deviations gives a confidence level of 95.4%—there should be a 95.4% chance the actual project outcome will be within plus or minus 84% of the unbiased estimate. You can use different levels of confidence if you want. If all you need is 80% confidence, you can use 1.282 standard deviations. This would mean 1.282 times 42%, or 54% (0.54x initial estimate). If you need 70% confidence, use 1.036 times 42%, or 44% (i.e., 0.44x initial estimate). Statisticians use a "Z Table" to look up a standard deviation multiplier to give a chosen confidence level. A small Z Table is shown in Table 23.7; others can be found on the Web using a search engine.

Table 23.7 Statisticians' "Z Table."

Percent confidence (%)	Chance of failing	Standard deviations
50	1 : 2	0.675
55	1 : 2.2	0.755
60	1 : 2.5	0.842
65	1 : 2.9	0.938
68.3	1 : 3.15	1.000
70	1 : 3.3	1.036
75	1 : 4	1.150
80	1 : 5	1.282
85	1 : 6.7	1.439
90	1 : 10	1.653
95	1 : 20	1.972
95.4	1 : 22	2.000
98	1 : 50	2.326
99	1 : 100	2.576

---

20 This project actually delivered three days early.
21 See chapter 21 in [Tockey05].

We will use 80% confidence, not 95.4%, so the uncertainty factor is 1.282 times standard deviation, or 54%. This means use 54% (i.e., 0.54x) the initial estimate. Given the 11-month estimate, the allowance for schedule uncertainty needs to be plus and minus 5.9 months. This gives a schedule range of 5.1 months to 16.9 months on the basis of uncertainty alone (i.e., an 80% chance of finishing no earlier than 5.1 months and no later than 16.9 months).

23.4.2 Calculating an Allowance for Uncertainty on Agile Projects

If the project will be done in an agile fashion and you have a standard deviation from normalized velocities as described earlier in this chapter, you can turn that into a fraction of average velocity. Remember that one standard deviation in the agile project above was 4.7 on an average velocity of 45.1. As a fraction, this is 0.104 (i.e., 10.4%). Again, you don't need to use two standard deviations per the Z Table discussion. If you only need 80% confidence, you would use 1.282 standard deviations. If one standard deviation is 0.104x and 80% confidence means using 1.282 standard deviations, then you should use 13.3% (i.e., 0.133x initial estimate). Multiplying 11 months by 0.133 is 1.5 months. The uncertainty range should be ±1.5 months: there is an 80% chance of finishing no earlier than 9.5 months and no later than 12.5 months.

23.4.3 Calculating Contingencies for Risk and Assets

Calculating contingencies for risks and assets does not depend on the project being plan-based or agile; it is the same for both. It does however depend on how risks and assets were analyzed—using either ratio or ordinal scales. For ratio-scaled risks and assets as in Table 23.1 and Table 23.3, you already have risk exposures and asset gains. These will be used in the formula below.

If risks and assets were expressed using ordinal scales as in Tables 23.2 and 23.4, then the best you can do is estimate a composite contingency for all risks and a composite gain for all assets. As an example, assume a composite contingency of 2.5 months for risk and a composite gain for all assets of 1.6.

23.4.4 Computing the Reasonable Commitment

The commitment computation uses a statistical formula called "The square root of the sum of the squares" (also known as "root mean square")[22]:

$$\text{Total} = \sqrt[2]{e_1^2 + e_2^2 + \ldots + e_n^2}$$

___
22 See, for example, https://en.wikipedia.org/wiki/Root_mean_square.

Again, use the 385-class project at full productivity where the unbiased estimate is 11 months. Assuming it will be done in plan-based fashion, the allowance for uncertainty is 5.9 months. Using ratio-scaled risks in Table 23.1, the cushion for combined uncertainty and risk needs to be

$$\sqrt[2]{5.9^2 + 1.5^2 + 1.8^2 + 0.8^2} = 6.4$$

A reasonable commitment, at 80% confidence, should be an upper bound schedule of $11 + 6.4 = 17.4$ months. We should be 80% confident this project will take no longer than 17.4 months.

Using ordinal-scaled risks and a composite contingency of 2.5 months means

$$\sqrt[2]{5.9^2 + 2.5^2} = 6.4$$

Again, the 80% confidence upper bound for project schedule is 17.4 months.

Doing the same on the asset side, with ratio-scaled assets in Table 23.2, leads to

$$\sqrt[2]{5.9^2 + 1.5^2 + 0.4^2} = 6.1$$

In the asset case, instead of adding the cushion, subtract it. This gives an 80% confidence best-case schedule of 4.1 months.

Using ordinal-scaled assets and a composite contingency of 1.6 months means

$$\sqrt[2]{5.9^2 + 1.6^2} = 6.1$$

Again, the 80% confidence lower bound for project schedule is 4.1 months.

The estimator is now prepared to go to the decision maker with the following:

> *"We believe this project is as likely to take more than 11 months as less. And, with 80% confidence, we are willing to commit to the project taking no more than 17.4 months and no less than 4.1."*

Redoing the computations for the agile project using the uncertainty derived from velocities and ratio-scaled risks from Table 23.1,

$$\sqrt[2]{1.5^2 + 1.5^2 + 1.8^2 + 0.8^2} = 2.9$$

Using the uncertainty calculated from velocities and the composite contingency for ordinal-scaled risks in Table 23.2,

$$\sqrt[2]{1.5^2 + 2.5^2} = 2.9$$

The 80% confidence upper bound for this project would be $11 + 2.9 = 13.9$ months.

Using uncertainty calculated from velocities and ratio-scaled assets from Table 23.3,

$$\sqrt[2]{1.5^2 + 1.5^2 + 0.4^2} = 2.2$$

Using the uncertainty calculated from velocities and the composite gain for ordinal-scaled assets in Table 23.4,

$$\sqrt[2]{1.5^2 + 1.6^2} = 2.2$$

Again, the 80% confidence lower bound for project schedule is 8.8 months.

The estimator is now prepared to go to the decision maker with the following:

> "We believe this project is as likely to take more than 11 months as less. And, with 80% confidence, we are willing to commit to the project taking no more than 13.9 months and no less than 8.8."

The difference in commitment ranges between the plan-based and agile projects is entirely due to differences in uncertainty. Uncertainty was a real, measured quantity for the plan-based project and was made up for the agile project. Realistically, a cone of uncertainty for a plan-based organization doing model-based software engineering would be substantially less than shown in Figure 23.1. Uncertainty should be much closer to the agile example.

23.4.5 Caution!

Cushioning estimates to compute commitments using the square root of the sum of the squares formula is not 100% correct in light of underlying statistics. Several assumptions, shortcuts, and approximations are taken:

- The computations in the cone of uncertainty spreadsheet (Footnote 6) assume a normal (i.e., Gaussian) distribution. This is known to be not true in practice. The distribution is either beta or lognormal, depending on an assumption that projects could run infinitely (beta) or would be cancelled at some point (lognormal).
- The expected values on ratio-scaled risks and assets represent 50% confidence, not 80% or 90% or whatever confidence the estimator is looking for.
- The square root of the sum of the squares formula assumes all inputs are independent. This is not always the case.
- The square root of the sum of the squares formula assumes all inputs are 50% confidence and expects to produce a composite result that is also 50% confident. It is being used to combine confidences that aren't 50%.

Using the square root of the sum of the squares formula isn't 100% correct. However, it is a far more reasonable approximation—particularly considering what most mainstream projects do today, which is usually no better than just guessing.

23.5 Effort by Activity, Without a Model Compiler

Everything above was for estimating a whole project or (sub)domain. If a new project is approved, effort can be allocated to (sub)domains based on class count. A (sub)domain with 7.5% of the classes should reasonably expect to take 7.5% of the project's effort. The effort for a system or (sub)domain can be further allocated to activities to aid detailed planning. First, we need to define those activities. At the highest level, they are:

- *Semantic modeling*—as described in Part II
- *Design*—as described in Chapters 14 through 19, minus coding in Chapters 17, 18, and 19
- *Construction and developer testing*—as described in the remainder of Chapters 17, 18, and 19

Under semantic modeling, there are two sub-activities:

- *Static modeling*—This includes use case diagramming (Chapter 7) and class modeling (Chapter 8). The name "static modeling" might seem inaccurate but is used by tradition. Before the mid-1990s, use case modeling was not included, so this sub-activity was entirely class modeling, which is a static view. This sub-activity is dominated by class modeling; use cases should be a very minor percentage of effort, so the name is still largely appropriate.
- *Dynamic modeling*—This includes interaction diagramming (Chapter 9) and state modeling (Chapter 10).

Under design, there are three sub-activities:

- *Interface design*—Defining or describing how real-world external entities will interact with the software implementing the (sub)domain. This was described in Chapter 14.
- *High-level software design*—Internal design of the software, from classes and operations down to signatures (syntax) and contracts (semantics). This was discussed in Chapters 15, 16, and part of 19.
- *Detailed design*—Internal data and method structures for the software, as described in Chapters 17, 18, and part of 19.

There are no sub-activities under construction and developer testing.

The following shows how total effort for a system or (sub)domain can be allocated by activity. These allocations are again derived from real projects in a variety of application domains:

- 60% of total effort in semantic modeling:
  - Half (30% of total) is "static": use case diagram and class model.
  - Half (30% of total) is "dynamic": interaction diagrams and state models.
- 30% of total effort in design modeling:
  - One third (10% of total) is interface design.
  - One third (10% of total) is high-level design.
  - One third (10% of total) is detailed design.
- 10% effort construction and developer testing.

Something to Think About

Root cause analysis[23] can be applied to the defects logged in an organization's defect tracking system to find the ultimate source of those defects. Figure 23.7 shows the distribution according to James Martin.[24]

The category labeled Other is for defects logged against, for example, test cases, test plans, project plans, etc. If the Other category is removed and that remainder distributed—in a weighted fashion—to Requirements, Design, and Code, the resulting distribution is shown in Table 23.8. Compare the defect injection percentage to the effort allocation percentage for each activity:

- 60% of defects are injected in requirements, and model-based software engineering spends 60% of technical effort in requirements work.
- 30% of defects are injected in design, and model-based software engineering spends 30% of technical effort in design work.
- Only 10% of defects are injected in code, and model-based software engineering only spends 10% of technical effort in code work.

  "It is probably not a coincidence that the percentage of defects injected in an activity is the same as the percentage of effort that should be spent in that activity."

Using Order fulfillment with beginner productivity, the effort was estimated to be 8.4 person-months, so it should be allocated as follows:

- 8.4 * 0.6 = 5.0 person-months for semantic modeling
  - 8.4 * 0.3 = 2.5 person-months for "static" (use cases and class model)
  - 8.4 * 0.3 = 2.5 person-months for "dynamic" (interaction and state models)

---

23 See, for example, https://en.wikipedia.org/wiki/Root_cause_analysis.
24 As stated in [Mogyorodi03].

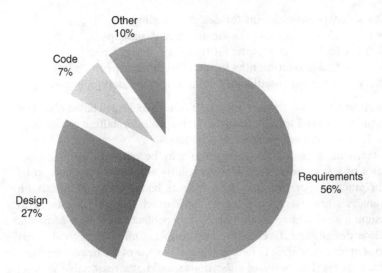

Figure 23.7 Ultimate sources of defects in software.

Table 23.8 Source of defect injection: requirements, design, and code.

Source of defects	Percent
Requirements	60
Design	30
Code	10

- 8.4 ∗ 0.3 = 2.5 person-months for design modeling
  - 8.4 ∗ 0.1 = 0.84 person-months for interface design/spec
  - 8.4 ∗ 0.1 = 0.84 person-months for high-level design/spec
  - 8.4 ∗ 0.1 = 0.84 person-months for detailed design/spec
- 8.4 ∗ 0.1 = 0.84 person-months for construction and developer testing

If staffed with 14 full-productivity FTEs, the 385-class project should consume as likely more than as less than 153.4 person-months of effort. So that project's effort should be allocated as follows:

- 153.4 ∗ 0.6 = 92.0 person-months for semantic modeling
  - 153.4 ∗ 0.3 = 46.0 person-months for "static" (use cases and class model)
  - 153.4 ∗ 0.3 = 46.0 person-months for "dynamic" (interaction and state models)

- $153.4 * 0.3 = 46.0$ person-months for design modeling
  - $153.4 * 0.1 = 15.3$ person-months for interface design/spec
  - $153.4 * 0.1 = 15.3$ person-months for high-level design/spec
  - $153.4 * 0.1 = 15.3$ person-months for detailed design/spec
- $153.4 * 0.1 = 15.3$ person-months for construction and developer testing

Given these effort allocations, assuming your goal is to make a detailed plan, you can now combine these effort allocations with the project's staffing profile (e.g., as in Figure 23.6) to derive a most likely schedule.

Some adjustment to (sub-)effort allocation may be needed due to unique characteristics of a specific project. However, little adjustment appears to be necessary in practice. For example, two projects had a heavy emphasis on numerical analysis and were expected to have much higher allocations to detailed design. The actual results for those two projects were 55% semantic modeling, 35% design, and 10% coding and testing. Only 5% of total effort shifted from semantic modeling to detailed design in spite of the heavy emphasis on numerical analysis. The standard allocations should be a reasonable starting point for most projects. Of course you might need or want to adapt, but not much adaptation appears to be necessary in practice.

23.6   Effort by Activity, with a Model Compiler

Using a model compiler reduces design and coding effort. However, unless you're using a preexisting model compiler without modification, then you need to account for effort spend on the model compiler as well.

Semantic modeling effort remains the same regardless of using a model compiler or not. The reduction in design effort is driven by several factors:

- *Interface design still needs to be done*—It still averages the same as with no model compiler unless View-controller code can also be generated.
- *Most high-level design does not need to be done*—Most of this effort is saved compared to not using a model compiler. The exception is the high-level design for View-controller region, unless View-controller region code can also be generated.
- *Some detailed design and construction remains*—This is mostly to specify actions and attribute hints in the compilable action language for the PIM overlay (see Figure 20.3).

There should also be less developer testing because a model compiler is tested once and reused across (sub)domains. That is, this should significantly reduce the need for verification testing. What remains is mostly validation to be sure the semantic model and action/attribute hints (PIM overlay) meet the needs of stakeholders

In essence, effort on initial development of a system, domain, or subdomain basis is reduced from 100% when not using a model compiler to about:

60% still semantic model
10% still interface design
5% PIM content and testing

This results in a savings of 25% effort over not using a model compiler.

As an example, for Order fulfillment with beginner productivity, the effort was originally estimated to be 8.4 person-months, so it should now be allocated as follows:

- $8.4 * 0.6 = 5.0$ person-months for semantic modeling
  - $8.4 * 0.3 = 2.5$ person-months for "static" (use cases and class model)
  - $8.4 * 0.3 = 2.5$ person-months for "dynamic" (interaction and state models)
- $8.4 * 0.15 = 1.3$ person-months for design and construction
  - $8.4 * 0.1 = 0.84$ person-months for interface design/spec
  - $8.4 * 0.05 = 0.42$ person-months for PIM content

Using a model compiler reduces effort from 8.4 person-months to 6.3 person-months.

If staffed with 14 full-productivity FTEs, the 385-class project was estimated to consume as likely more than as less than 153.4 person-months of effort. So that project's effort should now be allocated as follows:

- $153.4 * 0.6 = 92.0$ person-months for semantic modeling
  - $153.4 * 0.3 = 46.0$ person-months for "static" (use cases and class model)
  - $153.4 * 0.3 = 46.0$ person-months for "dynamic" (interaction and state models)
- $153.4 * 0.15 = 23.0$ person-months for design and construction
  - $153.4 * 0.1 = 15.3$ person-months for interface design/spec
  - $153.4 * 0.05 = 7.7$ person-months for PIM content

Using a model compiler reduces effort from 153.4 person-months to 115.0 person-months.

If you are not using a preexisting model compiler, effort will need to be allocated to first developing (or at least customizing) it and second to maintaining it over time:

- If the model compiler is to be designed and built from scratch, somewhere between 1 and 3 FTEs (12–36 person-months) may be required to develop a workable compiler. If you are using a model compiler framework (e.g., an off-the-shelf production rule interpreter), the effort will be less than the worst-case 3 FTEs depending on how extensive modifications are to frames, production rules, and mechanisms.

- Some fraction of an FTE is usually required for ongoing maintenance of the model compiler: production rules need to be adapted to reflect changes in understanding of model and action language semantics, optimization of the rule set and mechanisms is needed as experienced is gained running generated code, etc. How much of a fraction depends on how extensive this kind of work is.

23.7   Estimating Replacement of Legacy Systems

In some cases the project goal is to replace an existing legacy code base. There are three approaches to build up an estimate for this kind of project:

- Estimate total semantic model class count(s) by analogy (i.e., compare it with other known projects).
- Estimate semantic model class count based on table and/or class count in the legacy code and adjust for technology.
- Derive a class count from legacy source lines of code.

Other approaches are, of course, possible. These three have been used in practice and have shown reliable results.

23.7.1   Estimating Semantic Model Class Count by Analogy

By-analogy estimation starts with something known and derives an estimate from that known data point.[25] Say we are trying to estimate System X's class count and that we already know System Y has 251 classes in its semantic models. If we know what relevant differences exist between System X and System Y, we could adjust for those differences to estimate a reasonable approximation of System X's class count. Suppose we determine that 40 of the classes in System Y are for functionality that won't appear in System X. Also suppose that about 30 new classes would be needed to support functionality in System X that is not in System Y. The class count for System X should be approximately 251 − 40 + 30 = 241.

23.7.2   Estimating Semantic Model Class Count from Legacy Tables and Internal Data Structures

Many legacy systems aren't object oriented, so we can't just count classes. As a proxy, we can often count database tables and major internal data structures and then derive a semantic model class count from that. Don't count reference

---

25 See, for example, chapter 22 in [Tockey05].

tables (aka validation tables) whose only purpose is to implement range validation for an enumerated domain (an example is a table to validate state and/or
province names).

Count the number of non-reference/validation tables and major data structures. Adjust as appropriate to account for de-normalization as described in
Chapter 19. The adjusted value is an approximate class count to use in the estimation formulas above.

23.7.3   Estimating Semantic Model Class Count from Legacy Source Lines of Code

When the earlier two approaches won't work, the size of the legacy code base
can be used as a basis for estimating the replacement project. Again, this data is
derived from actual experience on a number of projects in various application
domains. While your results may vary, this should provide a reasonable place
to start.

Start with the existing line of code count (aka "SLOC" or "source lines of
code") from the legacy system. Total semantic model class count across all
(sub)domains can be approximated by:

- No more than SLOC/1000 semantic model classes
- No less than SLOC/2000 semantic model classes

As an example, a legacy system of 885 KSLOC (i.e., 885,000 SLOC) should
expect:

- No more than 885,000/1000 = 885 semantic model classes
- No less than 885,000/2000 = 443 semantic model classes

Try to calibrate these factors in your organization because they partly depend on
code counting rules (Do you count blank lines vs. not? Do you count comments
vs. not? Do you count data declarations vs. not?), quality of the legacy code base
(e.g., How much technical debt is there?), organizational coding styles, etc. The
flagship product in one organization could be counted from as few as 4.5 million
SLOC to as many as 7 million SLOC based on differences in counting
rules alone.

A Real-World Legacy Replacement Project

One well-known Silicon Valley organization had a legacy code base of 1.5 million
SLOC. The developers on the project complained that even calling it "spaghetti
code" was too kind:

> *"Start with spaghetti code. Pour it onto the parking lot. Drive over it several times
> with a steamroller. Now it's like our code."*

My recommendation was: "Scrap the legacy code. Start over from scratch, but build it right this time." Their response was: "The managers would never allow us to do that. It's too expensive. We have too much invested to throw it away."[26] This is an overview of the business case for a legacy replacement project.

The existing project was staffed with 300 maintenance developers and the FTE cost in that organization was about $350,000, so maintaining the existing code base cost around $105 million per year. Using only worst-case estimation factors from above,

- 1.5 million SLOC would mean no more than 1500 semantic model classes.
- At 0.7 person-months per class, nominal effort would be no more than 1034 person-months. At $350k per FTE, that is $30.2 million.
- 1034 person-months of nominal effort gives a nominal schedule of 30.3 calendar months: a little over two and a half years.
- Nominal staffing on the project would be 1034/30.3 = 34.1 FTEs.

Using Symons' formulas, the project could be compressed to as little as 23 months but would require 65 developers and increase cost to $41.6 million.

Experience shows that adequate long-term maintenance of model-based systems takes no more than one quarter of the development project staffing. Staffing as low as one eighth of development levels has been seen. Even using a worst-case maintenance staff of almost half of the development staff means no more than about 15 maintainers. Long-term ongoing maintenance would cost no more than $5.3 million per year.

A one-time investment of $30 million over two and one half years leads to a savings of at least $100 million per year. This legacy replacement project would pay for itself in only four months after going live.[27] When the managers saw this business case, their reaction was: "we need to find $30 million, we have an very important new project to start." A valuable lesson to draw from this case study is:

> *"If an organization's management is at all competent, they should not and will not be swayed by purely technical arguments ('We have too much technical debt! Wah wah wah'). Make a meaningful economic argument and they will surely listen"*

It should also be said that those managers should have no intention whatsoever of laying off 285 developers. The organization is already used to paying for them, without getting very much return on that investment. A typical software organization has an extensive wish list of high-value projects they would dearly love to work on—*if only they had the resources*. This organization had the ability to free up at least 285 developers to work on that wish list. The true business value of a

---

26 This is the "sunk cost fallacy" at its finest; see any engineering economy text for more detail.
27 This is a somewhat naive analysis in not considering the time value of money over a planning horizon, but it does communicate the magnitude of the business value.

legacy replacement project can be much greater than just an immediate reduction in maintenance cost.

And finally

> *"This is software engineering:*
> *Using science, mathematics, and practice to create cost-effective solutions to*
> *real-world problems!"*

Regardless of which method is used to determine class count for a legacy replacement project, use that count in the estimation process above. For very large (i.e., very expensive) projects, it might be appropriate to estimate using more than one—possibly all three—of these approaches. Look for convergence or divergence in the estimated class counts, investigate, and resolve any significant divergence.

23.8 Estimating Small-Scale Maintenance

Everything described above applies to new development projects, not ongoing maintenance of existing model-based systems. In maintaining an existing (sub) domain, the primary effort drivers are:

- Adding a new class to the semantic model
- Deleting a class from the semantic model
- Adding an attribute (derived vs. not) to a class in the semantic model
- Deleting an attribute (derived vs. not) from a class in the semantic model
- Adding a transition to a class in the semantic model
- Deleting a transition from a class in the semantic model
- Adding an action to a class in the semantic model[28]
- Deleting an action from a class in the semantic model
- Implications of any of the above on (sub)domain interfaces
- Implications of any of the above on (sub)domain design and code

Adding a whole new class to the semantic model should normally take the same 0.3–0.7 person-months depending on the experience and productivity of the maintenance developer(s). Effort to delete a class from the semantic model can depend on a number of factors but can usually be approximated as about one tenth to one fifth of the effort to add a class (i.e., between 0.03 and 0.06 person-months for experienced developers and between 0.07 and 0.14 person-months for inexperienced developers). Assume a particular maintenance task in a given (sub)domain involves adding five classes to one part of

---

28 Adding just a state or event is often small enough to be ignored.

the semantic model and deleting two classes from another: experienced developers could take between $0.3 * 5 + 0.03 * 2 = 1.56$ person-months to $0.03 * 5 + 0.06 * 2 = 1.62$ person-months, while inexperienced developers could take between $0.7 * 5 + 0.07 * 2 = 3.64$ person-months to $0.7 * 5 + 0.14 * 2 = 3.78$ person-months.

Effort to add or delete attributes, transitions, and actions (i.e., modify an existing class in the semantic model) depends on too many variables to give average effort factors in this book. Use by-analogy (preferred) estimation when possible or expert judgment (as a last resort) to estimate this kind of work. If adequate records of past work are available, a statistical (aka parametric) estimation model calibrated to your environment can be developed.

Again, don't forget to consider the implications of changes to a (sub)domain semantic model on both interfaces and software design and code in any maintenance effort estimate. If a maintenance task is purely in design and code (e.g., to address a performance issue, adapt to changes in automation technology, etc.), estimate using either by-analogy or expert judgment.

23.9 Quality Criteria

Table 23.9 shows minimum quality criteria for estimates and estimation. Additional criteria might be relevant in some situations, but these criteria should apply to every estimate.

Table 23.9 Quality criteria for estimates and estimation.

Item	Criterion
ES-1	The scope of the work being estimated is understood and clearly defined
ES-2	Project work that is not in this estimation model (e.g., (sub)domain partitioning, project management, QA testing, etc.) is accounted for
ES-3	Maintenance work and reuse are accounted for as needed
ES-4	Uncertainty and risk are properly accounted for
ES-5	The effort-schedule trade-off is properly accounted for, as needed
ES-6	All relevant assumptions that affect the estimate(s) have been clearly communicated to the decision maker(s)
ES-7	The estimation process is free of pressure or incentive to under- or overestimate

23.10 Summary

A key part of engineering is considering the economic consequences of technical decisions. Stakeholders should ultimately determine the value of one alternative versus another; the technical community should determine cost and schedule to deliver. This chapter describes how to estimate model-based software engineering projects. Topics covered in this chapter include:

- Estimation, commitment, uncertainty, and risk
- Estimating nominal effort and nominal schedule
- Trading effort for schedule
- Making reasonable commitments
- Effort by activity, with and without a model compiler
- Estimating replacement of legacy systems
- Estimating small-scale maintenance

24

Development and Maintenance Processes

Part II and Part III present model-based software engineering as a linear sequence of steps. That sequence is appropriate for many projects, but certainly not all. This chapter discusses alternative software development and maintenance processes[1] and provides guidance on deciding when to choose one over another. Topics in this chapter include:

- Separating phase and activity
- Agile development, strengths, and weaknesses
- Waterfall development, strengths, and weaknesses
- One size software process does not fit all
- A meta-process: right-sizing your software process

24.1 Separating Phase and Activity

"Phases" and "activities" are different, and it is important to understand that difference. The Project Management Institute (PMI) describes a "phase" (emphasis added)[2]:

> *"The completion and approval of one or more deliverables characterizes a project phase. A deliverable is a measurable, verifiable work product such as a specification, feasibility study report, detail design document, or working prototype. Some deliverables can correspond to the project management process, whereas others are the end products or components of the end products for which the project was conceived. The deliverables, and*

---

1 In this chapter, the terms "process" and "lifecycle" are equivalent.
2 See [PMI13].

How to Engineer Software: A Model-Based Approach, First Edition. Steve Tockey.
© 2019 the IEEE Computer Society, Inc. Published 2019 by John Wiley & Sons, Inc.

> *hence the phases, are <u>part of a generally sequential process designed to</u>*
> *<u>ensure proper control of the project, and to attain the desired product</u>*
> *<u>or service,</u> which is the objective of the project."*

From a project management perspective, phases help accomplish project objectives and maintain control over the project. An agile iteration (e.g., a Scrum "Sprint") is intended to deliver some amount of working functionality and allow control over the project: the purpose of a sprint matches PMI's purpose of a phase. Iterations (sprints) are the agile manifestation of phases.

The PMI description does not constrain what happens in any phase; that is entirely up to the project team to decide. An "activity," as the term is used in this chapter, is a specific kind of work on a software project:

- Semantic modeling is an activity.
- Designing is activity.
- Coding is activity.
- Testing is activity.

The contrast between phases and activities is illustrated in Figure 24.1. Phases are represented by heavily bordered rectangles; shading inside those rectangles represents activities. The slightly diagonal arrows in the Iterative (agile) row represent progressing through activities on a single user story during that iteration.

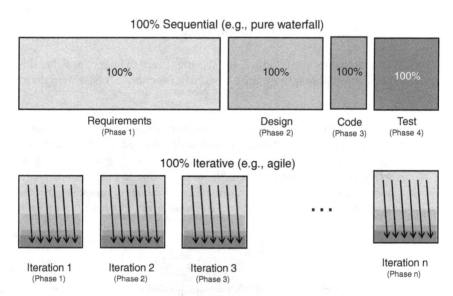

Figure 24.1 Separating "phase" from "activity."

In waterfall, activities and phases are aligned:

- *Requirements phase*—Do all requirements activity and only requirements activity until everyone agrees requirements work has been completed.
- *Design phase*—Do all design activity and only design activity until everyone agrees design work has been completed.
- *Coding phase*—Do all coding activity and only coding activity until everyone agrees coding has been completed.
- *Testing phase*—Do all testing activity and only testing activity until everyone agrees testing has been completed.

In agile development, activities and phases are orthogonal. For each user story, some requirements work needs to happen. Some design needs to happen. Some coding needs to happen. Some testing needs to happen. While not necessarily a prerequisite of agile development, it is usually assumed that all activities for one user story happen in a single iteration. Indeed, it is a guideline to size user stories so that they can be completed in a single iteration. When multiple developers work on different user stories in parallel, at any moment any user story could be in any activity:

- Mary is talking with the Product owner to get a better understanding of the requirements for Story #47.
- Phred is deciding how to implement Story #144—he is designing.
- Bill is writing code for Story #522.
- Cindy is testing Story #256 to prepare for a demo to the Product owner after the discussion with Mary is done.

Disconnecting phases from activities allows the activities to be arranged into phases in any way that makes sense on a project. This gives the team the freedom it needs to structure work so that goals are achieved and control is maintained with minimum investment in project (and project management) effort.

24.2 Agile Development

Agile development is not a single software process; it is a family of similar processes. This will be discussed further below. Chapter 1 used Scrum as the definitive example of agile development; however the Schwaber–Sutherland definition of Scrum—three roles, five events, and three artifacts—is very abstract and not even specific to software. One could use those same three roles, five events, and three artifacts to build a house, and it would comply with the definition of Scrum yet have nothing to do with software. So what does "agile" mean in terms of software process? The following are proposed as necessary characteristics of any agile software process. A software process that does not include all of these elements should not expect to be categorized as "a truly agile software process":

- *Regular, relatively short, time-boxed iterations* (Scrum's "Sprints")—Agile development is necessarily iterative, but those iterations are also time boxed,[3] relatively short,[4] and regular.[5]
- *"Wish list"* (Scrum's "Product Backlog")—A list of proposals for how the organization's software resources could be spent. It is important to understand that items on this list (Scrum's "Product backlog items," Extreme programming's "User stories") are *not* requirements as the term is defined in Chapter 4. For one, they are too vague and ambiguous. They are also not binding in the sense that nobody has necessarily decided they must be done. Instead, as Alistair Cockburn said, "A user story is a promise for a future conversation." As stated in Chapter 1, the wish list is the work breakdown structure (WBS) for an agile project.
- *Deliver maximum value in each iteration*—An explicit goal of agile development is to put the most value into the hands of users as quickly as possible. This is mainly implemented in the iteration planning process: the value of any item on the wish list is defined by the business (Scrum's "Product owner"), often by sorting the list in decreasing value order. Developers estimate the cost (effort) for each item, typically by assigning "story points" or "ideal time." Items are moved from the wish list into an iteration (Scrum's "Sprint backlog") in decreasing value order until the expected capacity of the development team is used up.[6]
- *Minimal planning beyond the current iteration*—An assumption of agile development is that requirements are inherently unstable. During any iteration, new scope can be added to the wish list, existing items might be dropped as no longer viable, and item value is subject to change. Therefore, it makes little sense to do detailed planning for the next 20 iterations when so much will have changed by the end of the current one. Instead, simply, "plan an iteration, do an iteration," then "plan another iteration, do another iteration," etc. This is "Rolling wave planning" (or "Progressive elaboration")—a PMI best practice—in the extreme.[7]
- *Relatively small team with dedicated customer representative*—Agile development is clearly workable for a relatively small team, say, up to about 20 developers. Agile development also staffs the project with one or more

---

3 An iteration ends when the calendar says, not because all planned work got done. See, for example, https://en.wikipedia.org/wiki/Timeboxing.
4 Usually 1–4 weeks, with 2 or 3 weeks being the most common.
5 Having chosen iteration duration, one repeats that same duration. Changes in iteration duration are minimized.
6 Ideally, the planning capacity is based on measured velocity from previous iterations.
7 See, for example, [Githens98] or [PMI13].

business experts (Scrum's "Product owner") as the source of requirements. If there are any questions about requirements, ask the customer representative.

24.3 Model-Based Software Engineering Under Agile Development

It should be clear that model-based development can be done using agile processes. For example, the wish list (i.e., product backlog in Scrum) for WebBooks 2.0 could easily contain user stories such as:

- "As a Customer, I need to request return authorization so that ordering errors, packing errors, and shipping errors can be corrected."
- "As a Manager, I need to approve or deny return authorization requests so that dishonest customers will find it hard to abuse the process."
- "As a Customer, I need to return books when my return request is approved."
- "As a Warehouse Worker, I need to restock inventory when books are returned so that WebBooks can sell them to someone else."

These stories can be sorted in value order by a Product owner, and driven through—one at a time—semantic modeling, design, coding, and testing over a series of sprints.

24.4 Advantages of Agile Development

Agile development has a number of advantages. The most important (in order of decreasing importance) are:

- *Flexibility*—By not planning the next N iterations in detail, stakeholders reserve the right to modify the wish list at any time. The wish list can be as dynamic as stakeholders want; the only thing that matters is what the wish list looks like when the next iteration is being planned. This insulates the project team from huge amounts of change in the stakeholder's business environment and allows them to make steady progress in spite of that change.
- *Deliver value early*—The explicit focus on delivering the most valuable wish list items first, combined with relatively short iterations, means users receive valuable functionality as soon as possible. This is explained in "Sidebar A"
- *Progress visibility*—One by-product of short iterations is that stakeholders see frequent evidence of progress. This is a form of risk reduction in that stakeholders see that their investment is resulting in delivery of business value.

- *Frequent feedback to development team*—The personality type[8] of many software developers is one where recognition of accomplishment is important. Frequent positive feedback that the team is satisfying stakeholders plays directly into developer motivation.
- *Simple(r) process*—Compared with waterfall, agile has the advantage of having fewer moving parts. A waterfall project will need each of three separate processes: work planning, change control ("Should this requested change be accepted, rejected, or deferred?"), and defect disposition ("Should this newly discovered defect be fixed now, later, or never fixed at all?"). On agile projects, new work, change requests, and defects are all just different items on the wish list. During iteration planning, each is valued by the business and cost-estimated by developers. Any item valued high enough that the team has capacity to do in the next iteration makes it into that next iteration. One iteration planning process handles the work of three separate processes in a waterfall project
- *Popular*—Without a doubt, agile development is in fashion. Developers often want to adopt agile simply because they think everyone else is doing it and they don't want to be left behind. Compared to the most widely used development process, namely, "Code and fix" (i.e., "hacking"), agile is a significant improvement, and its popularity makes it an easy "sell" into many projects

Sidebar A: Cost and Value over Time, Ideally

Figure 24.2 illustrates cost and value delivered over a typical waterfall project.
Start with the cost line. Assume the project is staffed with a constant number of people so project cost will accumulate linearly: doubling duration doubles

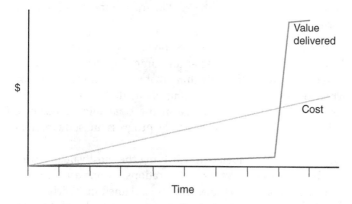

Figure 24.2 Cost and value delivered over time for a typical waterfall project.

---

8 See, for example, Myers–Briggs Type Indicator (MBTI) as in http://typelogic.com/.

cost. The cost line is not strictly linear when staffing varies over time, but that isn't important for this analysis. What's important is to look at value delivered, particularly when compared to cost.

It would not make business sense to run a project where the expected value at the end of the project would be less than the investment. Final value should always be higher than final cost. That said:

- *"What is the business' perceived value of a typical requirements specification?"*— If the organization is like most, the business doesn't see much (if any) value in a requirements specification.
- *"What is the business' perceived value of a typical design specification?"*—If the organization is like most, the business doesn't see much (if any) value in a design specification either.
- *"What is the business' perceived value of untested code?"*—If the organization is like most, the business doesn't see much value in untested code.
- *"What is the business' perceived value of tested code?"*—If the organization is like most, the business only sees value when tested code has been delivered to users.

All value in a typical waterfall project is delivered at the end. If a waterfall project has to be cancelled or postponed at any time before delivery, the project would be considered a financial loss because the perceived value of what has been delivered is less than the cost of delivering it.

Figure 24.3 illustrates idealized cost and value over time for an agile project.

Again, assuming the project is staffed with a fixed number of people, cost will accumulate linearly. This is no different than a waterfall project.

And again, it would not make business sense to run a project where the expected value was less than the investment. However, agile's explicit focus on delivering the most valuable functionality as soon as possible means each

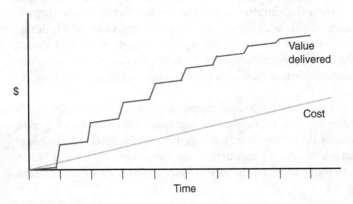

Figure 24.3 Cost and value delivered over time for an agile project, ideally.

iteration should deliver positive value. If only the most valuable functionality is delivered, then—by definition—any unimplemented functionality must be less valuable than what has already been delivered. This is why each value step shows slightly less increase than the previous.

Most important, however, is that value delivered should quickly exceed cost and remain higher after that. Should this project need to be cancelled or postponed before the originally anticipated end, it would still have a positive return on investment for the organization.

24.5 Disadvantages of Agile Development

Agile development is not without disadvantages. The most important (in order of decreasing importance) are:

- *Induced overhead*—First, simply due to its iterative nature, there is an increase in regression testing. As functionality is added, there is a need to verify functionality from earlier iterations wasn't broken along the way. Some agile zealots claim regression testing is free because it has been automated. One can claim that, but remarkably few projects, if even any, have ever been able to automate all of their tests. Some amount of manual testing is always necessary, and more frequent iteration means more frequent manual testing. At best, about 80% of testing seems to be automatable on most projects. This still leaves a significant amount of manual testing. Second, design decisions must be made in early iterations that depend on things that can't be known until later iterations. Developers need to guess. However, no developer is clairvoyant. Some guesses will be wrong, inducing refactoring. Finally, extreme programming touts the YAGNI principle: "You Aren't Gonna Need It," or "Do the simplest possible thing that can work." This automatically builds in a need for refactoring, when the simplest thing that worked before is later proven inadequate. Contrast this with a well-run waterfall project in which design is deferred until requirements are known and coding is deferred until design is known. Little, if any, regression testing is needed (because there is no iteration), and design decisions are made in full knowledge of all relevant requirements. See "Sidebar B"
- *Long-term code maintainability and supportability suffer*—As commonly practiced, agile development is only concerned with delivering working code, to the exclusion of documentation for long-term maintainability. Industry data shows that once put into production, software averages about 10 years in service.[9] Over those 10 years, the average is 9 generations of maintainers.

---

9 See, for example, [Tamai92].

Without adequate requirements and design documentation, the effort, cost, schedule, and quality of maintenance suffer.

- *Requires constant business participation*—In contrast with a well-run waterfall project, business participation is required for the entire agile project. The business representative is needed until the last wish list item in the last iteration has been accepted. In waterfall, business participation is only necessary during the requirements phase and for user acceptance testing. Once stakeholder requirements have been elicited, analyzed, specified, and validated, stakeholders can return to doing business-valuable work until the system is ready to be acceptance tested.

- *Business may undervalue technical needs*—Some work on the wish list may be "infrastructure" work, for example, refactoring the database. The business representative can't always be convinced of the value of such work. Functionality with immediate business value may be consistently prioritized higher than infrastructure work. Even though infrastructure work would increase long-term velocity, it will only do so at the expense of short-term value. Development team productivity is hobbled by an inability to do necessary clean-up.

- *Weak with nonfunctional requirements*—Necessarily, all requirements can't be satisfied in one single iteration: they must be sequenced across many. Regardless of the specific sequence on any project, at least one important nonfunctional how well requirement will not be relevant at the start. By the time it does become relevant (i.e., it makes it into an iteration), it could be too late. Design decisions in earlier iterations may make it difficult, if not impossible, to incorporate later nonfunctional how well requirements (Remember YAGNI—do the simplest thing that that could possibly work).

- *Unlikely to deliver business value in first iteration(s)*—Typically, several iterations are needed to build enough foundation to be able to deliver business-useful functionality. The dream of delivering value every iteration is just that: a dream. Experience shows a minimum of three to four iterations of foundation building are necessary on most new software projects

- *Weak at dependency management*—Suppose there is a technical dependency between two items on the wish list. Say, item X depends on item Y. If developers implement item Y first, overall cost and schedule would be lowest. Cost and schedule could be significantly increased if the team were forced to implement X before Y. Unfortunately, the business values X far higher than Y, and no amount of techno-geek-speak will convince the business representative that it is in their best interest to implement Y first

- *Weak at long-term risk management*—Tim Lister says, "Software project management *is* risk management" and "The opposite of risk management is reckless management." Capers Jones says, "If you don't actively attack risk, it will actively attack you." Risk management is critical to effective management of software projects. Agile development can incorporate short-term risk management: if a risk control action can be contained within a single iteration or so, that action can "fly under the radar screen" and be done without stakeholders knowing or even caring. It is often the case, however, that significant risks require control actions that extend beyond an iteration or two. Such actions can't be hidden; they are big enough to consume noticeable project resources. This is a version of an earlier problem: these actions are big enough that they have to become items on the wish list. But the business may not recognize their importance, so they are never prioritized high enough to make it into any iteration. And this assumes a Scrum master recognizes the importance of risk management because it's not on the typical list of job responsibilities for a Scrum master.

- *Limited scalability*—As one example, agile implicitly assumes any team member can do any work. This is usually a safe assumption on small projects but is clearly false on large projects where job specialization is required (e.g., developer vs. DBA vs. usability specialist vs. documentation specialist). Agile development appears to be scalable to about 50–60 developers on a single project. But (necessarily coordinated) teams of hundreds, if not thousands, of developers aren't uncommon in the software industry. I have worked on projects with as many as 5000 developers. Such projects simply can't be fully coordinated using agile development, certainly not without adding back most of the processes that waterfall already has but were dropped by agile as "unnecessary, non-value-added ceremony."

- *Need for high-bandwidth communication between participants makes it difficult (and expensive) to geographically distribute*—Yet time and time again that's exactly what we see: part of the team is located in Europe, while other parts of the team are located many time zones away in North America and Asia. Barry Boehm's COCOMO II estimation model states[10] the effort overhead of multi-time zone distribution is almost 60% for waterfall projects where the need for high-bandwidth communication is lower. An unavoidable consequence of a 60% increase in project effort is a corresponding increase of 17% in schedule: time to market. If agile development demands higher bandwidth communication, then geo-distribution necessarily induces even more overhead[11]

Sidebar B: Cost and Value over Time, Realistically

Figure 24.4 illustrates the effect of iteration overhead on value delivered. If we assume the project could be done using either a waterfall or agile process (not all projects can be done either way), the effect of increased overhead in agile is that either less functionality is delivered over the same time, or it takes longer and costs more to deliver the same functionality.

---

10 See [Boehm00]
11 The irony is exquisite as most organizations claim that time to market is the #1 priority and yet they continually make decisions that directly contradict that claim.

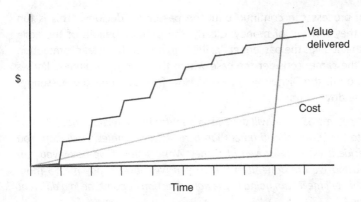

Figure 24.4 Cost and value delivered over time, compared.

The "Taxi driver analogy" helps explain why. Imagine there is a taxi driver at, say, the Orlando, Florida, airport. A passenger gets into the taxi and the driver asks, "Where would you like to go?" The passenger replies, "How long will it take, and how much will it cost, to drive me to the Disney World Hotel™?" The taxi driver, having done things like this before, should be able to say, "It takes about 45 minutes and costs about $45." The passenger can commit to objective completion criteria so the taxi driver can commit to a cost and schedule to achieve it.

But what if the passenger replies, "How long will it take, and how much will it cost, to drive me to somewhere fun?" At best, the taxi driver can respond, "That depends entirely on your definition of fun." The passenger says, "I'll know it when I see it." Clearly, the taxi driver cannot commit to cost and schedule because the passenger cannot commit to objective completion criteria. Does this mean the taxi driver and the passenger cannot do business? Not at all. It only means the nature of the business arrangement needs to be different. The driver can propose:

> "If you are willing to pay me $5 then I will drive for 5 minutes in a direction that I think is more fun than here. At that point, I will stop the taxi and you will have three options:
>
> - You can look outside the taxi and decide, 'This is fun enough'. We are done
> - You can look outside the taxi and decide, 'I like the direction this is going, here is another $5, please drive for another 5 minutes in this same direction'
> - You can pay me another $5 and I will drive another 5 minutes, but after you refine your description of fun and point me in a different direction."

This iterative process can continue until the passenger decides, "This is fun enough," or they run out of money. Clearly, the primary benefit of the agile approach is that it gives the passenger flexibility to deal with unclear completion criteria. Just the same, consider the case where the passenger already knows they want to go to the Disney World Hotel. How frustrating for the passenger will it be if the driver says:

> "Please pay me $5 and I will drive for 5 minutes in a direction that I think is closer to the Disney World hotel than here. After 5 minutes, I will stop. You can decide if we have arrived at Disney World hotel. If we have, you can get out and we are done. If not, then you will have to pay me $5 more and either tell me if I am going in the right direction or point me in a different direction."

How inefficient, expensive, and time consuming will it be to drive that passenger to the hotel? How frustrated will the passenger be after even a few such cycles? Can't you just imagine the passenger on the verge of screaming, "Just take me to the #&^@%# Disney World Hotel!!!!"

24.6 Waterfall Development

As described earlier, waterfall development aligns phases with activities. All—and only—activity X is done in phase X. Any sizeable project will have multiple domains and may also have subdomains. To comply with a strict interpretation of waterfall, no design on any (sub)domain can start until all requirements on all (sub)domains have finished. It should be immediately obvious that such a theoretically pure approach is unworkable in practice. To avoid inducing wait states on some (sub)domains while others are still being worked, the team would have to perfectly balance staffing across all (sub)domains to be sure they all finished each phase at exactly the same time.

Remember also that the relationship between domains is "imposes requirements on": a higher domain imposes requirements on lower domain(s). The problem is that some imposed requirements can only be determined after initial design has been done on the higher domain. According to a strict interpretation, no design can be done until all requirements are completed. This is clearly deadlock. So we can't, and don't, run large projects in a theoretically pure mode. Instead, each (sub)domain can be developed—by itself—using a waterfall process. The overall project is run in parallel with one or two people working on each (sub)domain. Further, the sub-activities described in the estimation chapter make excellent phases:

- A phase for the static part of semantic modeling
- A phase for the dynamic part of semantic modeling

- A phase for interface specification
- A phase for high-level design
- A phase for detailed design
- A phase for code (and developer test)

This is not a strict ordering of phases. There are cases where it makes sense to develop the Interface specification first. Once the interface specification is agreed on, it becomes input for semantic modeling, which is then followed by design and code. In reality, these activities/phases can be sequenced in any order—or, to some extent, in parallel—if it makes sense.

Another issue is that almost all software processes assume that product scope can be defined early and will be stable throughout the project. This is implicit in, for example, starting with a use case diagram. On the other hand, scope might only be determinable later in the project. This has happened on several projects I've worked on. One particular case was factory automation for a highly technical, safety-critical, one-of-a-kind facility. We didn't start with use case diagrams or interface specifications because the boundary of automation was unknown at the start. Instead, we focused first on an expanded class model not knowing how expanded it would be. When we understood the overall business via the class model, we started to make in-or-out scope-of-automation decisions based on what process elements were highly repetitive, unlikely to be done wrong, required no creativity, etc.[12] Don't think you necessarily have to establish scope at the very beginning. Scoping decisions can be deferred although it does necessarily induce overhead and rework to defer.

24.7 Model-Based Software Engineering, Waterfall, and Feedback Loops

A common claim is that waterfall development cannot have short feedback loops. This is simply not true. By

- Partitioning the project into (sub)domains
- Using the sub-activities as phases for each (sub)domain
- Limiting the number of classes in each (sub)domain, and
- Staffing each (sub)domain appropriately

phases run approximately two calendar weeks. End each phase with a software inspection[13] using the quality criteria as checklists. The phase doesn't end with an inspection: the inspection ends the phase. A phase should not be considered

---

12 Specifically, based on the results of a task analysis as described in Chapter 14.
13 See, for example, [Fagan76], [Fagan86], [NASA93a], [NASA93b], [Freedman90], [Ackerman89], [Fowler86], or [Wheeler96].

done until the deliverables produced are accepted as complete by the inspection team. Properly run software inspections are known to be 90% effective at finding defects; I have personally seen as much as 95% effectiveness. This is critical to reduce rework, R%, from 60% as seen on mainstream software projects to less than 10% on properly run model-based software engineering projects. On average, valuable feedback comes every two weeks and is on par with agile development.

24.8   Advantages of Waterfall Development

Waterfall development has a number of advantages. The most important (in order of decreasing importance) are:

- *Minimizes rework and overhead*—The whole point of not coding until design has been settled, and not designing until requirements have been settled, is to minimize rework. Design is done in full knowledge of all relevant requirements; construction is done in full knowledge of all relevant design. The primary advantage of waterfall development is that it can deliver a given scope the soonest and cheapest because there is lowest possible overhead and rework.
- *Minimizes business participation*—Business participation in a waterfall (sub) domain is only needed until requirements are agreed on and at the end for acceptance testing. Business participation is minimal, if at all, during design, construction, and most testing. This frees business experts to do what they are best at doing: getting their business done.
- *Delivers documentation for supporting maintenance*—In principle, requirements and design documentation should be valuable resources for supporting long-term maintenance, well beyond original development. That these have traditionally been done extremely poorly, or have been allowed to get out of date, is not an inherent fault of Waterfall. Rather, it is caused by amateur execution and a misunderstanding of what appropriate documentation should be. Model-based software engineering fills that gap.
- *Scalable over a wide range of team sizes*—Waterfall development can scale from projects as small as one person all the way up to thousands of people. The basic structure of the lifecycle does not change the way it does in agile (e.g., compare agile development for small projects to what has been proposed for "Scaled Agile" or "Enterprise Agile" to see the added complexities).
- *Can handle team non-co-location*—Waterfall development has a proven track record of being successful with widely distributed teams.
- *Tolerates low-bandwidth communication*—Waterfall development has a proven track record of being successful with low-bandwidth communication between participants.

- *Mature lifecycle: work-arounds exist for known weaknesses*—Waterfall development has been used on software projects since the 1950s and has been successful on thousands, if not millions, of them. Weaknesses are known, well-documented, and coping strategies and work-arounds exist.
- *Conceptually simple*—The process itself is almost trivial: a simple sequential series of phases. Anyone should be able to understand it.

24.9 Disadvantages of Waterfall Development

Just as agile development has its weaknesses, waterfall has them as well. This is critical in understanding why one lifecycle simply *cannot* be appropriate for all projects. Those disadvantages (in order of decreasing importance) are:

- *Very sensitive to requirements knowability and stability*—As long as requirements are knowable and stable, they can be elicited, analyzed, specified, and validated in a requirements phase. To the extent that requirements aren't knowable in the first place, it becomes difficult to define an end to a requirements phase. Further, to the extent that requirements are unstable, significant change control overhead and backtracking may be necessary to accommodate that change.
- *Very sensitive to how requirements work is done*—Simply, the majority of software organizations are terrible at doing requirements work. This work has been very high effort with essentially no value because resulting documentation is woefully incomplete and riddled with ambiguities. However, this is not an inherent fault of the lifecycle; it is the result of amateur execution and misunderstanding what proper requirements documentation should be.
- *Business risk of early cancellation*—As discussed in "Sidebar A," there is risk that investment in a project may not be recovered if it needs to be cancelled or deferred before a viable product is delivered. That said, there are variations of waterfall (e.g., "Design to Schedule" and "Planned Iterations"[14]) that mitigate this risk. Also, proper model-based requirements and design provide significantly more business value than traditional documentation, so the gap between investment and value is significantly reduced, if not entirely eliminated. Proper requirements and design documentation provide a valuable resource should a project be deferred and then later restarted.
- *Sensitive to technical risk*—The point was made above about sensitivity to change in requirements. Waterfall development is sensitive to any change,

---

14 See, for example, chapter 7 in [McConnell96].

including change in design. If an inappropriate design is chosen, later (possibly significant) rework may be needed to adapt to a more appropriate design. Design prototyping is a recognized workaround that helps mitigate this disadvantage.

- *Lose status visibility with long phases*—As software projects get bigger, without proper partitioning into domains and subdomains, the phases get longer. It becomes easier and easier to lose control. The remedy is, of course, to properly partition the project so that phases remain short.
- *Definitely out of favor*—Waterfall development has definitely suffered bad press. To many, the term waterfall is an instant pejorative. But again, the problems aren't inherent to waterfall itself; they are entirely due to amateur execution by the teams involved.
- *Requires discipline to work properly*—Undisciplined (i.e., amateur) execution of waterfall is risky. Failure to apply necessary discipline leads to failed projects. However, the same can be said of any software process.

24.10 One Size Does Not Fit All

The disadvantages of agile development are not relevant for some projects. The value of early delivery of partial functionality could easily dwarf the overhead induced by iteration. Maybe, even if by luck alone, there may not be a need for significant infrastructure rework during the project, maybe the nonfunctional requirements are such that meeting them is not a challenge, and so on. Agile development is obviously a great fit for these projects.

But for every project where those are true, there is just as easily a project where those are not:

- There is no business value in partial functionality (e.g., of what use is half of a heart pacemaker? ¾? Even 98%?) Some products are all or nothing.
- Maybe, even if by bad luck alone, there is a need for significant infrastructure rework, and the business would be unwilling to prioritize it high enough to ever get it done.
- Meeting aggressive nonfunctional how well requirements, like performance and scalability, can be challenging.

For these projects, agile development is simply not the best fit.

Any sizeable software organization will have software projects of varying natures at the same time. Some projects will be more so and others necessarily less so on any characteristic. Again, Agile development is appropriate for *some* projects; it's simply not appropriate for *all* projects—just as waterfall development is appropriate for *some* projects and not appropriate for *all*.

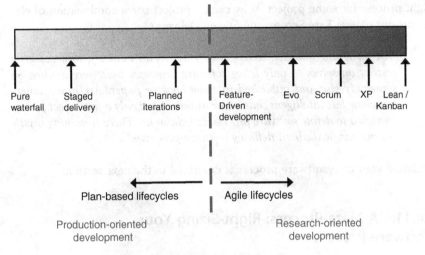

Figure 24.5 A spectrum of software development processes.

24.10.1 A Spectrum of Lifecycles

There are many more software lifecycles than just waterfall and Scrum.[15] As Figure 24.5 shows, we can divide software projects into at least two broad subsets:

- *Production-oriented development*—Projects where stakeholders know what they want: their completion criteria will not change much, if at all, over the project. Like the taxi passenger who just wants to go to the Disney World Hotel (Sidebar B), the best approach is to make a plan and follow it to minimize overhead and rework. "Plan-based" software development lifecycles are most appropriate for these projects.
- *Research-oriented development*—Projects where even the stakeholders don't know what they want: the project is a journey of discovery. Like the taxi passenger who can only know "fun enough" when they see it, the best approach is to take small steps and evaluate progress after each step. Agile lifecycles are clearly superior for these projects.

Figure 24.5 oversimplifies. Lifecycle variation is not just a one-dimensional spectrum; it's a multidimensional space. Each defined lifecycle is one point in that space. There are a multitude of points between the points that have been defined so far. Any one of those as-yet un-described points could easily be the

---

15 See, for example, chapter 7 of [McConnell96] for descriptions of nine others.

right process for some project. Why can't a project use a combination of elements out of, say, Evo, Scrum, and Staged Delivery?

> *"An intriguing question to ask is why we, as an industry, unnecessarily restrict ourselves to only using software processes that were defined by somebody else and published in some book or paper. Are practitioners somehow less intelligent than those authors? Are only a few, select people qualified to define software processes? I claim no. There is nothing mystical nor magical about defining software processes"*

Defining your own software process is described in the next section.

24.11 A Meta-Process: Right-Sizing Your Software Process

With the realization that there is a multidimensional space of software processes comes the need to navigate that space. How does one decide what would be appropriate, or inappropriate, process for any given project? Don't just blindly follow some particular lifecycle because:

- It's the latest fad.
- That's the way we've always done it.
- It's the only way we know how to do it.

Instead, adopt a software process that meets the unique needs of that project. To do so, follow a "meta-process": a process to guide you in deciding what software process to use. Here is an overview of that meta-process[16]:

1) *Build a project charter*—As precisely as possible, define what success looks like.
2) *Assess risks*—What factors might interfere with satisfying that charter?
3) *Assess assets*—What factors might help in satisfying that charter?
4) *Plan*—Define an approach to the project so that everything done either: helps satisfy that charter, controls risk, and/or takes advantage of assets. Any planning decision that doesn't do at least one of those three should either not be done at all or should be done a different way.

The lifecycle choice becomes just another planning decision and needs to be based on the charter, risks, and assets. More specifically, to choose a lifecycle, follow these steps:

---

16 Teaser: *Rightsize Your Software Process* is the tentative title for the next book in this series.

24.11.1 Step 1: Assess External Drivers

The following is a list of external drivers critical in determining process. This is not necessarily a complete list, but each of these is important:

- *Cost and/or schedule criticality*—In many projects, deadlines are at best artificial. However, in some cases, there really isn't any room to be late or over budget. As an example, what is the value of personal income tax software like TurboTax[17] on April 16, the day after personal income taxes are due in the United States? Essentially zero, its market window has closed. TurboTax has to be on store shelves in November of the previous year to gain enough market exposure for good sales. If TurboTax were not released until, say, February or March, many potential users would either do their income taxes by hand or buy a competing product. Such cost or schedule criticality argues for software processes that minimize overhead. A project without cost or schedule criticality can afford the overhead of more iterative lifecycles.
- *Stakeholder constraints and priorities*—Some projects need to be managed to fixed scope. Some projects need to be managed to fixed schedule. Some projects need to be managed to fixed budget. At least one well-known software company uses a process that switches from fixed scope early in the project to fixed schedule later in the project.
- *Product maturity*—This is the production-oriented versus research-oriented topic from above. Some projects build mature products, while others build immature ones. Product maturity drives knowability and stability of requirements. In the research-oriented case, the value of flexibility that agile development brings is higher than the cost of induced overhead. In the production-oriented case, flexibility is unnecessary, so why induce useless overhead? Where requirements are more knowable and more stable, it suggests more plan-based processes. At a minimum, iterations can be longer to reduce overhead.
- *Product scope and/or complexity*—Some software is necessarily larger and more complex than others. Boeing 787 flight software, for example, is necessarily larger and more complex than Angry Birds. Larger scope and/or complexity argue for more up-front planning to minimize rework from inappropriate decisions. Recall the old adage, "Measure twice, cut once."
- *Product decomposability by business value*—Some products are easily decomposed into smaller units, each of which has value to the customer (e.g., "Minimally marketable feature set," "Minimum viable product," etc.). Other products, like the heart pacemaker (or Angry Birds or 787 flight software), are all-or-nothing monoliths. When a product is decomposable, it argues for iterative (although not necessarily agile) development when the value of

---

17 US federal personal income tax, as introduced in Chapter 1.

early delivery outweighs induced overhead costs. If there is no value in smaller units of functionality, why suffer the overhead of building it that way?

- *Ease of product deployment*—It's one thing to build functionality useful to the business. An entirely separate issue is the business' ability to make use of that functionality. Some products have small user communities that are geographically close to the development team. It could also be the case, like Angry Birds, that no significant data migration, training, etc. are needed to switch to a later, more capable version. In these cases it's easy to deliver pieces of functionality frequently to the user so if there is business value in doing so, why not take advantage? But just the same, there are products with vast, and vastly distributed, user communities. Those products are nontrivial to understand and use; training in any new functionality is required. Sometimes data conversion effort alone can be overwhelming. In the latter cases, again, why pay the overhead induced by iterations when there is no value?
- *Development team capability*—Some software lifecycles are simple, and some are complex. The capability of the team needs to be considered: maybe the most appropriate lifecycle is highly sophisticated, but this team simply isn't up to that task. A suboptimal process has to be used, because that's all the team is capable of.
- ...

24.11.2 Step 2: Determine How Much of Each Characteristic Is Needed

Each development process varies in terms of a relatively small set of characteristics. These characteristics are:

- *Control cost and/or schedule*—Some processes provide a lot of cost and/or schedule control, and others don't give any control at all. Control is important when cost or schedule is critically constrained (e.g., the TurboTax example).
- *Show progress visibility*—Some processes provide high visibility throughout the project; others give little (if any) visibility. Visibility can be useful for risk mitigation: as long as there is objective evidence of progress, we can track progress against critical resources. Visibility is important on large, complex products.
- *Minimize rework and overhead*—Some processes minimize rework and overhead; others induce overhead and rework that wouldn't otherwise exist. When resources are tightly constrained, rework and overhead should be minimized. When resources are less constrained, spending a little extra on rework and overhead can pay back far more than its cost (e.g., the flexibility of agile).
- *Handle big and/or complex*—Some lifecycles can handle very big and/or very complex projects, while others are limited in how big or complex they handle. Lifecycles for big/complex product tend to be more complex themselves.

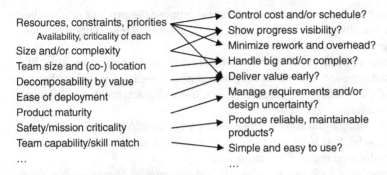

Figure 24.6 External drivers and their influence on lifecycle characteristics.

When the product being built is not big or complex, it argues for using a simpler process.

- *Deliver value early*—Some lifecycles are all or nothing; all value is delivered at the end. Others can deliver increments of functionality. When the value of early delivery exceeds the cost of induced overhead, it makes sense to use a lifecycle that supports it. Paying the overhead and getting no value would be silly.

- *Manage requirements or design uncertainty*—Some lifecycles help deal with requirements and/or design uncertainty, while others depend on as little uncertainty as possible. The flexibility needed to deal with uncertainty comes at the cost of induced rework and overhead. Again, why pay for flexibility when it doesn't give value?

- *Produce reliable, maintainable products*—Some lifecycles are good at producing reliable and maintainable software; other lifecycles aren't.

- *Simple and easy to use*—Some lifecycles are very simple and easy to use. Others are very complex and require a talented team to be successful.[18]

Figure 24.6 overviews relationships between external drivers (left column) and lifecycle characteristics (right column). Arrows point from external drivers to lifecycle characteristics they influence.

Elaborating on Figure 24.6,:

- *Resources, constraints, and priorities are critical*—Favor lifecycles that allow control, show progress, and minimize rework and overhead. Lifecycles that support delivering value early can be a good risk reduction technique, so stakeholders don't come up empty handed if resources run out: you may not have delivered everything but at least you delivered something (keeping in

---

18 See, for example, Boehm's "spiral model" [Boehm86] or https://en.wikipedia.org/wiki/Spiral_model.

mind that this depends on being able to decompose the product into smaller, but still valuable pieces). When not critical, any lifecycle's ability to provide this is less important.

- *Size and/or complexity*—When the software is big and/or complex, favor lifecycles that are good at handling big and complex as well as favor lifecycles that offer visibility. When not big or complex, these characteristics can be much less important.
- *Team size and (co-)location*—When teams are big and/or widely distributed, favor lifecycles that have good size and complexity handling characteristics. Small, co-located teams don't need this.
- *Decomposability by business value*—When software is decomposable, favor lifecycles that support delivering value in pieces. When not decomposable, don't go that way because iteration induces overhead you won't get value out of.
- *Ease of deployment*—When users can easily absorb new releases, favor lifecycles that support delivery in pieces. When users can't absorb, again don't go this way because you are inducing overhead that you won't get value from.
- *Product maturity*—Low maturity products favor lifecycles that can handle low maturity product development. High maturity products should tend to avoid low maturity-capable lifecycles because the induced overhead can be counterproductive.
- *Safety/mission criticality*—With high safety/mission criticality; favor lifecycles that produce reliable, maintainable products. To the extent that you don't have safety/mission criticality, this becomes a less issue or nonissue.
- *Team capability/skill match*—Consider what the team is capable of in terms of lifecycle sophistication. Don't ask a team to use a lifecycle that is more sophisticated than they are capable of, unless they will be given adequate training, support, etc.

Table 24.1 shows a sample of published processes[19] in relation to the external drivers.

24.11.3 Step 3: Select a Preexisting Lifecycle or Create Your Own

In essence, a software lifecycle is the result of either implicitly or explicitly making each of these decisions:

- *How far into the future are we willing to plan?*—The farther out one can plan, the more efficient and effective the project tends to be because rework and overhead are minimized. A workable plan that carries the project all the way from start to finish can induce the least rework and overhead. Attacking a project with little planning (or no planning at all) is highly likely to induce

---

19 Descriptions of most of these processes can be found in chapter 7 of [McConnell96].

Table 24.1 External drivers in relation to published lifecycles.

Lifecycle name	Product maturity	Cost/schedule criticality	Prod size/complexity	Decomposability by value	Ease of deployment	Team capability
Code and fix	Doesn't care	Doesn't care	Prefers low	Doesn't care	Doesn't care	Doesn't care
Pure waterfall	Prefers high maturity	Minimizes overhead, but all-or-nothing success	Handles up to very high	Doesn't care	Doesn't care	Assumes at least average capability
Sashimi	Prefers high maturity	Some cost/effort overhead but shortens schedule	Handles up to very high	Doesn't care	Doesn't care	Prefers above average capability
Staged delivery	Prefers moderate to high maturity	Some effort overhead but tends to deliver something	Handles up to very high	Doesn't care	Prefers at least moderate ease	Prefers above average capability
Design to schedule	Prefers moderate to high maturity	Some effort overhead but delivers highest value first	Handles up to very high	Prefers at least moderate decomposability	Prefers at least moderate ease	Prefers above average capability
Spiral	Prefers moderate to high maturity	Moderate effort overhead but better visibility	Handles up to very high	Doesn't care	Doesn't care	Prefers well above average capability
Evolutionary prototyping	Handles low maturity	Doesn't address explicitly	Handles up to moderate	Prefers at least moderate decomposability	Prefers at least moderate ease	Assumes at least average capability
Agile/Scrum	Assumes low maturity	Moderate overhead but delivers highest value first	Handles up to moderate	Prefers at least moderate decomposability	Prefers high ease	Assumes at least average capability

significant rework and overhead. On the other hand, planning constrains flexibility, and there is risk that something important can change and cause the need to replan later. Remember that "Rolling wave planning" ("Progressive elaboration") is a PMI best practice for planning only as much as can be depended on and leaving the rest to be planned later, when it is more appropriate.

- *Purely sequential to purely iterative spectrum?*—Scrum and extreme programming are highly iterative; the project is executed as a sequence of many, short iterations. Waterfall, on the other hand, can be viewed as developing an entire (sub)domain in one single pass.

24.11.4   If There Is Any Iteration

- *When do iterations start?*—Iteration does not need to start from the beginning, but can. The project could do sequential requirements and design and then switch to iterative construction, test, and delivery. The project could do sequential requirements and then switch to iterations in design, construction, testing, and delivery. Alternatively, the project could run iteratively from start to finish
- *Short versus long iterations?*—Short iterations have the advantage of increasing flexibility and delivering functionality earlier, but do so at the cost of increased overhead. What's the right balance of iterations that are short enough to give adequate flexibility and early value without inducing too much overhead? The answer differs from one product to the next. An interesting area of research is in how to determine "optimum batch size."
- *Fixed versus variable iteration duration?*—In most agile processes, like Scrum, iterations are (by definition) fixed duration. One advantage of fixed duration is that it provides a level of regularity to the team.[20] Another advantage is that it makes iterations comparable to each other. Imagine that one iteration was 1.5 weeks and a later iteration was 8.8 weeks, could any meaningful comparison be made between the amount of work done in each? Extreme programming's "velocity" and using observed velocities as a planning indictor for later iterations not only depends on duration being fixed but staffing being fixed as well.
- *Sequence work by business value or technical convenience?*—As in Scrum, iterations could be driven in terms of delivering the highest value functionality soonest. But this may cause functionality to be built in a technically inconvenient sequence, inducing later refactoring. Overhead could be so

---

20 This is purely psychological: humans are largely creatures of habit, regularity plays into most people's comfort zone, while irregularity doesn't.

Table 24.2 Internal decision criteria in relation to published lifecycles.

Lifecycle name	Manage to fixed…?	How far ahead planned?	Iterative?	When iteration starts?	Short/long duration?	Fixed/variable duration?	Sequence by?
Code and fix	Undefined	N/A	Undefined but almost certainly very high	Undefined but probably from start	Undefined but probably short	Undefined but probably variable duration	Undefined
Pure waterfall	Scope or schedule (time box)	Whole project (rolling wave?)	None externally, maybe internally	None externally, maybe internally	N/A externally, undefined internally	N/A externally, undefined internally	If any internal, then likely technical convenience
Sashimi	Scope or schedule (time box)	Whole project (rolling wave)	None externally, maybe internally	None externally, maybe internally	N/A externally, undefined internally	N/A externally, undefined internally	If any internal, then likely technical convenience
Staged delivery	Scope	Whole project (rolling wave?)	Yes, but later in project	After architecture defined	Undefined but tends to long	Undefined	Technical convenience
Design to schedule	Schedule	Most of project (rolling wave?)	Yes, but later in project	After architecture defined	Undefined but tends to long	Undefined	Business value

(Continued)

Table 24.2 (Continued)

Lifecycle name	Manage to fixed...?	How far ahead planned?	Iterative?	When iteration starts?	Short/long duration?	Fixed/variable duration?	Sequence by?
Spiral	Scope or schedule (time box)	Whole project (rolling wave)	None externally, internally in phase process	From beginning	For as long as phase is	Variable duration, by phase	N/A
Evolutionary prototyping	Undefined	Undefined	Undefined but almost certainly at least moderate	From beginning	Undefined but tends to long	Undefined but probably variable duration	Undefined but probably prefers business value
Agile/Scrum	Cost/effort per sprint (staff * duration)	At least sprint-at-a-time but can be farther	Very high	From beginning	Short (2–4 weeks typically)	Fixed duration	Business value

overwhelming that nobody is willing to incur it. Functionality could be sequenced to minimize overhead even though this sequence doesn't deliver the most valuable functionality first. This decision is not necessarily universal: within one project some functionality might be sequenced on technical convenience (e.g., basic infrastructure) and other functionality sequenced on business value (e.g., stakeholder perceivable functionality).

Simply, waterfall development makes one set of decisions, while agile development makes essentially opposite ones. Table 24.2 shows how the same lifecycles in Table 24.1 compare in terms of these project-level lifecycle decisions.

Of course, you are not constrained to use only those predefined lifecycles. Based on your project's unique characteristics, you could define a process with a mix of characteristics never seen or used by anyone else before. There is an essentially infinite set of possible processes by just changing one or more of the above decisions and possibly changing them again later in the project.

A major military invasion, like the Normandy invasion in World War II,[21] can be a useful analogy for a large software project. The mainline invasion forces bore the brunt of the "production work." This work is the most visible (i.e., easiest to see), likely to be the most stable, and the easiest to work with. On the other hand, any significant military invasion also makes use of "Special Operations" (aka "Guerilla," "Special Ops," etc.) forces that target specific high-risk, high-reward objectives. Consider planning a large project in a way that the bulk of the work is handled by mainline (i.e., average capability) staff, while high-risk, high-reward opportunities are attacked by small, focused, highly capable "Skunkworks"[22] or "Tiger teams."

A small project, particularly if it is high-risk, high-reward, can be run as a self-contained guerilla/Special ops/Skunkworks/Tiger team effort.

Table 24.3 Quality criteria for lifecycle/process selection

Item	Criterion
LC-1	The selected process/lifecycle appropriately addresses the project's charter
LC-2	The selected process/lifecycle appropriately controls the projects known risks
LC-3	The selected process/lifecycle appropriately maximizes the project's known assets
LC-4	Everything in the project's plan helps: satisfy the charter, control risk, and/or maximize assets

---

21 See, for example, https://en.wikipedia.org/wiki/Normandy_landings.
22 See, for example, https://en.wikipedia.org/wiki/Skunk_Works.

24.12 Quality Criteria

The quality criteria in Table 24.3 can be used to evaluate project lifecycle/development process choices.

24.13 Summary

One size software process does not fit all projects. Every software process has its own unique advantages and disadvantages. Instead of blindly following some given process because

- It's the current fad
- That's the way we've always done it
- We don't know any other way

understand the advantages and disadvantages of the different choices available. Use the meta-process to guide in selecting a process that's best suited to the needs of your project. It can be perfectly reasonable to use a development process that was never published in a book or paper. As long as what you are doing makes sense for your project, as determined by the meta-process, then it is the right process.

25

Economics of Error Handling

Several chapters in Part II and Part III refer to error handling; specifically:

- *Semantic model*—Error handling in use cases, interaction, and state models: various nonoccurrence events in sea level use cases, some alternate courses in interaction diagramming, and specific state–event pairs in state models
- *Interfaces*—Error handling in interfaces: input value(s) missing, out of range, or inconsistent (e.g., input value X is inappropriate given input value Y), wrong function (e.g., button pressed) for given mode, etc.
- *High-level design*—In contracts for operations: invalid operation parameter(s), invalid state, etc.
- *Detailed design*—In method implementation: computation error, resource not available, security violation, etc.

These chapters present various error handling options but are intentionally vague on selecting any one. They defer that decision to this chapter. So the question is, "What, if anything, can or should be done about any of those errors?"

> *"Failing to decide how to handle an error is itself an error."*
>
> (Pete Becker[1])

That decision needs to be based on technical and economic factors. Conscious, deliberate, intelligent error handling decisions in software are critical:

- *System-wide design and construction implications*—As much as 75% of code in commercial-grade software is for handling errors.

---

1 http://www.petebecker.com/js/js199812.html

How to Engineer Software: A Model-Based Approach, First Edition. Steve Tockey.
© 2019 the IEEE Computer Society, Inc. Published 2019 by John Wiley & Sons, Inc.

- *Cost and schedule implications*—Effort needed to select, specify, design, build, and maintain error handling functionality is a significant part of project work.
- *System-wide performance implications*—Speed, robustness, and correctness are driven in part by error handling approaches. These are also major drivers of user satisfaction.
- *Source of unnecessary complexity*—If error handling decisions are made randomly, they introduce significant unnecessary accidental complexity.

This chapter explains how to perform an economic analysis of error handling alternatives—bringing in technical considerations as appropriate—to make conscious, deliberate, intelligent engineering decisions. This is another example of applying engineering economy to software. Three versions of analysis are described:

- *Simple*—Using numeric estimates for relevant factors but ignoring the time value of money (interest).
- *Sophisticated*—Using numeric estimates for relevant factors, while considering interest, and possibly other factors such as inflation, depreciation, and income taxes.
- *Informal*—The same decision process, only using ordinal-scaled estimates instead of numeric estimates. Numeric estimates can be impractical in many cases.

25.1 Simple Analysis

This version is appropriate when you have an important error to handle: careful decisions need to be made but the planning horizon is short enough to not warrant considering long-term economic effects like interest, inflation, depreciation, income taxes, etc. Generally, this applies when the planning horizon is less than one year. The process has four steps:

1) Assess the damage of not handling the error.
2) Generate proposals for handling the error.
3) Evaluate each proposal.
4) Select the proposal(s) with positive net expected savings.

Each step will be explained in detail using an example. The case study will be Silly Bank Loan processing from use case diagramming in Chapter 7. Specifically, consider the nonoccurrence event when a Loan officer doesn't approve or deny a loan application in time. What, if anything, should be done? The decision will affect the semantic model, user interfaces, and design. Business processing will need to handle this error if we determine it is technically feasible and economically cost effective.

25.1.1 Simple Analysis, Step 1: Assess the Damage of Not Handling the Error

The first step is to start with a damage assessment: consider what would happen if the error were not handled at all. There are a series of sub-steps:

Step 1A: Choose a planning horizon (hour, day, month, year, product life, etc.). A stakeholder might impose the planning horizon. If not, use your best judgment in choosing one. The planning horizon should not be more than about one year. If it's more than one year, you should use the sophisticated approach below, because the time value of money (interest) becomes significant. For Silly Bank Loan processing, assume a planning horizon of three months.

Step 1B: Estimate how often the error will occur in the planning horizon. For sake of argument, assume the loan application error happens on average once per month. This could be derived from past experience or estimated based on how often an average loan officer forgets multiplied by the number of loan officers working for Silly Bank.

Step 1C: Estimate the average damage per occurrence if the error isn't handled. There are two perspectives: damage to external parties (in this case the Silly Bank customer who applied for the loan) and damage to the internal party (in this case Silly Bank). If this is an interface or design error, the external party would be Silly Bank and the internal party would be the organization who develops and maintains Silly Bank's software. Be sure to use the proper perspective; otherwise the analysis could be wrong.

Looking at damage to external parties, consider:

- *Criticality*—How important is it to external parties that this is done without error? The customer applying for a loan is probably inconvenienced by delay, nothing more. Errors in other situations could be much more critical.
- *Frequency of use*—How often do external parties want this work done? Customers don't apply for loans very often. Other, more frequent errors could be more important.
- *Loss of service, including opportunity cost*[2]—How does lack of correct work affect the external party's ability to get their work done? The customer applied for a loan and is waiting for an answer. They can't proceed with their own plans until they hear about their application being approved or denied.
- *Lack of work-arounds*—Can external parties address the error some other way? The customer needs a loan because they don't have money now. The only alternative would be to try to get a loan from somewhere else. But applying for another loan could negatively affect the customer's credit rating, thus jeopardizing their ability to borrow everywhere.

---

2 Opportunity cost is income lost from not being able to do work. As an example, not only do people have to pay to go to college, but they probably don't earn money while in school. In this context it means loss attributed to resolving the error and not developing new functionality.

- *Loss of data*—Not relevant in the loan processing case, but an unhandled interface or design error could lead to loss of potentially valuable user data.
- *Reinstallation cost*—Not relevant in this case, but an unhandled interface or design error could lead to external parties needing to spend resources installing patches or updates.
- *Legal/contractual penalties (e.g., fined or sued)*—Not relevant in this case, but an unhandled error could affect external parties' ability to comply with law or satisfy a contract (e.g., a service-level agreement with their customer); they have to pay a fine or penalty.
- *Loss of reputation*—Not likely relevant in this case, but an unhandled error could cause external parties to be unable to perform their duties in a timely manner, thus tarnishing their reputation with their customers. They might lose business.
- ...

Looking at damage to the internal party, consider the following factors:

- *Error repair cost*—How much will it cost to find the error (fault isolation), fix the error (fault correction), and be sure the error has been fixed (fault verification)? This should include opportunity costs because while addressing this error the organization is spending resources in a non-value-added way.
- *Legal/contractual penalties (e.g., fined or sued)*—Not likely in this case, but the error could make the internal organization unable to comply with law or meet contract commitments so the internal party may be subject to fines or penalties.
- *Loss of reputation/loss of sales*—Not likely relevant in this case, but the error could cause the internal party to be unable to perform their duties in a timely manner, thus tarnishing their reputation with external parties. An external party might take their business elsewhere.
- ...

Suppose that considering the dollar value of the average loan and the composite of all factors above, the cost per occurrence to Silly Bank for this error averages $750.

Step 1D: Calculate the total expected cost of damage if the error isn't handled. The total expected cost of damage if unhandled would be the estimated number of occurrences times the average cost per occurrence. For Silly Bank Loan processing, it is three occurrences times $750, or $2250.

25.1.2 Simple Analysis, Step 2: Generate Proposals for Handling the Error

In step 2, the goal is to create ideas for handling the error. Again, there are a series of sub-steps:

Step 2A: Understand the general strategies for handling errors. There are three parts:

- *Error processing*—What, if anything, could be done about the error?
- *Error notification*—Who, if anyone, could be told about it?
- *Continue*—Should work continue, or is damage so great it needs to be abandoned?

These strategies are not mutually exclusive. Be as creative as you can in coming up with concrete proposals. Pick, choose, and combine these in any way that makes sense.

Under error processing, general strategies can be (but are not limited to):

- *Prevent*—Can something be done to keep this error from ever happening? This is analogous to getting a medical vaccination.
- *Buy information*—Can something be done to identify the error before it occurs and manage it before it's a full-grown problem? This is analogous to getting a medical checkup; minor issues can be dealt with before they become serious problems.
- *Restore*—Can something be done to repair all damage and bring the situation fully back to where it was before the error? This is analogous to a medical cure that completely erases all negative effects of the illness.
- *Recover*—Can something be done to repair as much damage as possible? Assuming full restoration isn't possible, how close can be achieved? There are three sub-strategies: segregate (contain the damage), alternative (have a Plan B, analogous to getting therapy to manage a medical problem), and reserves (you saved for a rainy day. It's raining, so use some of what you saved).

Under error notification, if anyone can be notified, the general strategies are as follows:

- *Who to notify*—Should the requestor be notified? Should one or more third parties be notified? Both?
- *When to notify*—Should they be told immediately? Or, should they be told later (e.g., collect multiple occurrences and report later as a block)?
- *How to notify*—What mechanism should be used for communication?

Under continuing, general strategies are as follows:

- *Accept*—Accept that the error occurred, assume error processing and notification are sufficient, and carry on.
- *Quit/stop/abandon/etc.*—Acknowledge the error is significant enough that some amount of work in progress must be stopped. The scope of the quit/ stop/abandon also needs to be considered. Stop only local work in progress (e.g., if this is a method executing on a class, just give up and return to the caller)? Stop a whole work process (e.g., if this is a transaction, does the error

cause a rollback)? Does the error affect the system as a whole? The entire enterprise, does everything need to stop (e.g., whole system needs to halt, whole business needs to end, etc.)?

Two additional terms are relevant:

- *Robust*—Always doing something, even if it might not be the right thing to do. It is more important to do something, even if it is wrong, than to do nothing. Generally, consumer applications favor robustness over correctness.
- *Correct*—Never doing the wrong thing, even if it means doing nothing. It is more important to never do a wrong thing, even if it means doing nothing. Safety- and mission-critical applications favor correctness over robustness.

Consider whether robustness or correctness is more important. Temper error handling proposals accordingly. In Silly Bank loan processing, not approving or denying a loan shouldn't be life or mission critical. Robust actions would probably be preferred. On the other hand, if the software is supposed to land a commercial airliner in fog so thick the pilots can't see the runway until after the plane has landed, consequences of not handling some errors (e.g., loss of navigation signal) could be catastrophic. More correct actions would be preferred (return control to the pilot: let them fly up—it's essentially always safe to go up. In the worst case, the flight can divert to another airport. Passengers and crew may be inconvenienced but they are still alive).

Specific actions, of course, depend on context: semantic model, interface, or design and code. Chapters that address those topics offer more specific options relevant to that context:

- Semantic model chapters discuss adding business processing to handle errors.
- The interface chapter talks about strategies like having users select from a pull-down list or use radio buttons to prevent certain input errors.
- The design chapter talks about strategies like strong typing and type-safe enumerations to prevent certain kinds of errors.

Context-specific details are discussed in those chapters.

Step 2B: Create specific proposals for error handling. The more proposals you create, the more likely the overall best one is in the set you created. On the other hand, more proposals come at the cost of having to analyze them. Aim for an appropriate balance between having enough proposals to expose the best one and having sufficient resources to analyze them all.

For the Silly Bank Loan processing error,

- *Prevent*—This error doesn't seem 100% preventable although one idea could be to show applications to the Loan officer in oldest-first order. This doesn't prevent the Loan officer from skipping down the list, but at least they are aware and it becomes a conscious decision on their part.

- *Restore*—An option would be to remind the Loan officer after an appropriate time that an aging loan application needs a decision. This should restore the business to the desired state: the aged application was decided.
- *Recover*—How much damage is done to the customer? We can consider sending them a polite apology to let them know we are aware and should be resolving it soon. As long as the application is decided reasonably quickly, the chances of losing that customer should be low

For notification with the Silly Bank Loan processing error,

- Definitely notify the Loan officer immediately via email or TXT/SMS.[3]
- Possibly notify the customer, probably immediately, using a polite form letter in the mail.
- Possibly notify the Loan officer's boss, either immediately or only if the Loan officer neglects the decision more than two or three times. Probably best by email or TXT/SMS.

One aspect of engineering decisions is that it is often possible to take more than one action at the same time. These proposals aren't mutually exclusive and the optimum choice could be a combination. Chapter 9 in Return on Software[4] discusses how to turn a set of proposals into mutually exclusive alternatives. For the sake of limiting the size of this chapter, we will consider only these three proposals:

- Sort the Loan officer's work list in decreasing age order.
- Notify the Loan officer and applicant when the application age limit is hit.
- Notify the Loan officer's manager.

25.1.3   Simple Analysis, Step 3: Evaluate Each Proposal

In this step, each proposal is evaluated from both a technical and economic perspective. There are again sub-steps:

Step 3A: Evaluate the technical implications of each proposal. Evaluate each proposal on:

- Complexity of additional business processing in the semantic model
- Complexity of additional functionality in an interface

---

3 Remembering to apply perfect technology in the semantic model, the mechanism for communication is irrelevant. Communication mechanisms are only relevant in design.
4 See [Tockey05], or any other suitable engineering economy reference.

- Complexity of additional design and code to recognize the error and handle it as proposed

Some proposals might be abandoned based on complexity. This shouldn't happen for the three Silly Bank proposals—with a possible exception of sending TXT/SMS because this depends on computing infrastructure. Does the infrastructure already include a capability to send TXT/SMS or would that functionality need to be acquired? At a minimum, the effect of complexity on development and maintenance cost and schedule (step 3D) needs to be understood.

The other part of technical evaluation should focus on the computing infrastructure:

- Does more hardware and/or software need to be acquired to support this proposal?
- Does computing overhead of the proposal slow execution enough to affect the value proposition to stakeholders (potentially enough to require increased cost to acquire more capable infrastructure)?
- Does storage overhead of the proposal consume enough memory/disk space/ etc. to trigger the need to acquire more storage?

Aside from the already mentioned issue of supporting TXT/SMS, there shouldn't be anything in Silly Bank proposals that would affect performance or require expanded or improved compute infrastructure.

Step 3B: Evaluate the effectiveness of each proposal. Proposals aren't always 100% effective. Often, a proposal can address some but not all occurrences. Consider how effective each proposal will be at handling the error. For the three proposals at Silly Bank,

- Sort the Loan officer's work list in decreasing age order—Assume this would be 60% effective, that is, 40% of the time it wouldn't make a difference.
- Notify the Loan officer and the applicant when the age limit is hit—Assume this would be 90% effective.
- Notify the Loan officer's manager—Assume this would be 20% effective.

Step 3C: Estimate average damage per occurrence under each proposal. Consider the average damage incurred for each occurrence under each of the proposals. If you found a legitimate "prevent" proposal in step 2B, the average cost per occurrence would be $0. Otherwise the cost per occurrence will be greater.

Think beyond each proposal by itself. Consider induced errors: can the error handling itself be broken, causing even more damage? Also search out possible unanticipated consequences where the proposal could backfire. Does anything in the proposal affect how people work together? Could anything in the proposal affect the politics in the organization? Changes to these areas can be particularly risky.

For the three proposals at Silly Bank,

- Sort the Loan officer's work list in decreasing age order—Assume this drops damage to zero when successful (getting the Loan officer to decide before the age limit is hit).
- Notify the Loan officer and the applicant when the age limit is hit—Assume, when successful, this drops damage to $50 per occurrence.
- Notify the Loan officer's manager—Assume this drops damage to $200 per occurrence when successful.

Step 3D: Estimate the cost of implementing each proposal. Consider the investment needed to develop and maintain each proposed solution over the planning horizon. For the three proposals at Silly Bank,

- Sort the Loan officer's work list in decreasing age order—Assume this would cost $300 over the planning horizon to develop and maintain.
- Notify the Loan officer and the applicant when the age limit is hit— Assume this would cost $400 over the planning horizon to develop and maintain.
- Notify the Loan officer's manager—Assume this would cost $350 over the planning horizon to develop and maintain.

Step 3E: Calculate the net savings of this proposal. The general formula is:

3E.1) What is the damage incurred for handled cases?

$$D_h = \text{occurrences} * \text{effectiveness} * \text{damage if effective}$$

3E.2) What is the damage incurred for unhandled cases?

$$D_u = \text{occurrences} * (1 - \text{effectiveness}) * \text{damage if unhandled}$$

3E.3) What is the net savings for this proposal?

$$S_n = \text{Total unhandled damage} - (D_h + D_u) - \text{investment}$$

For the three Silly Bank proposals,

Step 3E.1: Sort the Loan officer's work list in decreasing age order.

3E.1.1 What is the damage incurred for handled cases?

$$D_h = 3 * 60\% * \$0 = \$0$$

3E.2.1 What is the damage incurred for unhandled cases?

$$D_u = 3 * (1 - 60\%) * 750 = \$900$$

3E.3.1 What is the net savings for this proposal?

$$S_n = \$2250 - (\$0 + \$900) - \$300 = \$1050$$

Step 3E.2: Notify the Loan officer and the applicant when the age limit is hit.

3E.1.2 What is the damage incurred for handled cases?

$$D_h = 3 * 90\% * \$50 = \$135$$

3E.2.2 What is the damage incurred for unhandled cases?

$$D_u = 3 * (1 - 90\%) * \$750 = \$225$$

3E.3.2 What is the net savings for this proposal?

$$S_n = \$2250 - (\$1350 + \$225) - \$400 = \$1490$$

Step 3E.3: Notify the Loan officer's manager.

3E.1.3 What is the damage incurred for handled cases?

$$D_h = 3 * 20\% * \$200 = \$120$$

3E.2.3 What is the damage incurred for unhandled cases?

$$D_u = 3 * (1 - 20\%) * \$750 = \$1800$$

3E.3.3 What is the net savings for this proposal?

$$S_n = \$2250 - (\$120 + \$1800) - \$350 = -\$20$$

25.1.4 Simple Analysis, Step 4: Select Proposals with Positive Net Savings

When the net savings is significant enough (considering some minimum margin, say, 10–20% over cost), then it probably makes sense to implement. A proposal costing $10,000 with a net savings of only $1 would not be a good investment. Sorting the work list in decreasing age order[5] and notifying the Loan officer and the Customer both make sense to implement.[6] The net savings for notifying the Loan officer's manager is negative: this proposal does not make economic sense to implement.

If the net savings for all proposals is negative, the best option is to ignore that error—or generate more proposals if that error cannot be ignored.

---

5 The original context of this error is the semantic model. Sorting the list is a presentation issue; it would become a nonfunctional requirement to address in interface design.

6 This is an approximation. Sorting the list in age order solves part of the problem. Notifying the Loan officer and Customer only applies to remaining cases, so actual net savings is somewhat less than the savings of both proposals added together.

25.2 Sophisticated Analysis

This version is also appropriate when you have an important error: careful decisions need to be made but now the planning horizon warrants considering long-term economic effects, particularly interest. Inflation, depreciation, income taxes, etc. might also be relevant and can be included as appropriate. Generally, this process applies when the planning horizon is more than one year.

The same four steps apply, but details of each step vary:

1) Assess damage of not handling error.
2) Generate proposals for handling error.
3) Evaluate each proposal.
4) Select the best alternative.[7]

A different case study will be used. Consider a user interface where a Warehouse worker is shown a list of packable book orders. The worker clicks on an order to signify they just packed it. The error is that the worker clicked on the wrong order—the one they packed was not the one they clicked. This not only disrupts two Book orders (the one packed but not clicked and the one clicked but not actually packed), but it can also disrupt inventory for Print media and cause inappropriate Replenish orders.

25.2.1 Sophisticated Analysis, Step 1: Assess the Damage of Not Handling the Error

In assessing the damage of not handling the error, use the same sub-steps as above:

- What is the planning horizon?
- How many occurrences of the error in that planning horizon?
- What is the average damage per occurrence?
- Calculate the total expected cost of damage.

The first three sub-steps are identical; the difference is the last sub-step. In that sub-step, the total expected cost of damage is calculated as the $PW(i)$[8] of the cash flow stream.

Part of developing the cash flow stream involves distributing error occurrences across the planning horizon. Apply an appropriate distribution:

- *Uniform*—Error occurrences are equally timed across the planning horizon.

---

7 Note the wording change from proposal to alternative: this more sophisticated analysis warrants consideration of combinations of proposals. See [Tockey05] for a discussion of proposals versus alternatives.

8 Or $FW(i)$, or $AE(i)$, ... as appropriate.

Table 25.1 Cash flow estimates for the Warehouse worker click error if not handled.

Year	Number of occurrences	Total cost per year
0	5.0	$0[a]
1	5.4	−14,919
2	5.9	−16,817
3	6.4	−17,563
4	6.9	−19,056
5	7.5	−20,675
6	8.2	−22,433
7	8.9	−24,339

[a] Year 0 is past history; it cannot factor into this analysis.

- *Front loaded*—More occurrences early, representing a root cause that diminishes over time due to effects like a learning curve.
- *Back loaded*—More occurrences late, representing a root cause that increases over time such as business growth.
- *Other*—As appropriate for that specific situation.

For this example assume a back-loaded distribution driven by business growth. With more orders, the frequency of erroneous clicks should increase proportionally. Assume WebBooks has been growing at an average rate of 8.5% per year, the error is happening 5 times per year now, and the average damage per occurrence is $2750 in labor to restore correct system state. WebBooks stakeholders want to use a seven-year planning horizon. The cash flow estimates are shown in Table 25.1.

The cash flow diagram is shown in Figure 25.1.

WebBooks has an average profitability of 13% and will use that as their minimum acceptable rate of return (MARR). The PW(13%) of this cash flow stream is −$82,081.

25.2.2 Sophisticated Analysis, Step 2: Generate Proposals for Handling Error

This step is exactly the same as in the simple process. Consider proposals for the Warehouse worker click error to be as follows:

- Provide a confirm dialog box (e.g., "Are you sure?") after the Warehouse worker clicks on the Book order to be marked as packed.
- Provide an undo function that reverses the effects of mistaken packing.

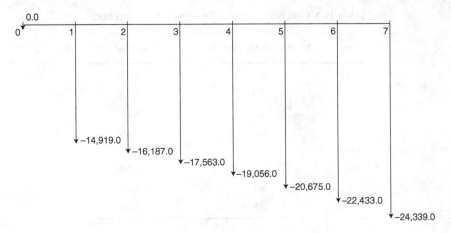

Figure 25.1 Cash flow stream for damage from the unhandled warehouse worker error.

25.2.3 Sophisticated Analysis, Step 3: Evaluate Each Proposal

Everything is the same in the sophisticated analysis, except for step 3E. Instead of calculating net savings as in the simple version, create a cash flow stream for each technically viable proposal. If the proposal is not technically viable, don't bother creating a cash flow stream because that would only waste time.

Confirm dialogs are notoriously ineffective—particularly when confirming something that happens frequently. Assume effectiveness will be 1%. A Warehouse worker will be packing many Book orders every day. If they have to confirm each order, they will quickly become immune to a confirm button and just click it without thinking. Confirm buttons are only useful on infrequent actions. The confirm button would be very ineffective at preventing this error, but it does reduce damage to zero on the occasions that it does work. Adding the confirm button is estimated at $2500 in development and maintenance over the planning horizon. The cash flow estimate for damage under the confirm proposal is shown in Table 25.2.

The cash flow diagram is shown in Figure 25.2.

For the undo option, a fair amount of work would need to be done. First, this is a change to business process, so this will need to be added to the semantic model. It doesn't make sense to allow Warehouse workers to undo; this should be a use case for Managers. We need to add one use case, possibly one sequence diagram, and one transition and action to the state model for Book order. Some business processing around inventory and replenish orders might also be needed. Additional capability is needed in the interface specification for the Manager's user interface. Finally, there will be additional design and code. Investment is estimated at $11,750 over the planning horizon. This option is

Table 25.2 Cash flow estimates for using a confirm dialog.

Year	Number of occurrences	Total cost per year
0	0	-$2500
1	5.4	-14,770
2	5.8	-16,025
3	6.3	-17,387
4	6.8	-18,865
5	7.4	-20,469
6	8.1	-22,208
7	8.8	-24,096

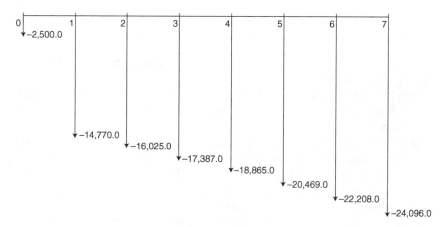

Figure 25.2 Cash flow diagram for handling the error with a confirm dialog.

0% effective at reducing occurrences, but reduces damage to $825 per occurrence. The cash flow estimate for this proposal is shown in Table 25.3.

The cash flow diagram is shown in Figure 25.3.

25.2.4 Sophisticated Analysis, Step 4: Select Best Alternative

Because this is a more sophisticated analysis, we need to explicitly consider combinations of proposals. See Return on Software[9] for detail on deriving mutually exclusive alternatives from proposals. In this case, four alternatives need to be considered:

---

9 [Tockey05], or any other suitable engineering economy reference.

Table 25.3 Cash flow estimates for using a confirm dialog.

Year	Number of occurrences	Total cost per year
0	0	-$11,750
1	5.4	-4476
2	5.9	-4856
3	6.4	-5269
4	6.9	-5717
5	7.5	-6203
6	8.1	-6730
7	8.9	-7302

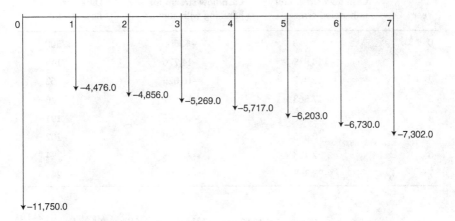

Figure 25.3 Cash flow diagram for handling the error with undo.

- A0—"Do nothing."
- A1—Provide the confirm button only.
- A2—Provide the undo function only.
- A3—Provide the confirm button together with the undo function.

The A0 ("Do nothing") alternative should be considered because neither confirm nor undo might be cost effective. Maybe there are no economically viable solutions. A0 should be included in this kind of analysis except when there is no choice but to select at least one proposal (i.e., the error cannot be left unhandled, something must be done).

The PW(i) of A0, the do nothing alternative is, by definition, $0.

The cash flow stream for A1 needs to be computed as the difference between the cash flow stream for the unhandled error (Table 25.1) and the cash flow stream for the error being handled by the confirm proposal (Table 25.2). The differential cash flow stream is computed in Table 25.4.

The cash flow diagram is shown in Figure 25.4.

The cash flow stream for A2 needs to be computed as the difference between the cash flow stream for the unhandled error (Table 25.1) and the cash flow stream for the error being handled by the undo proposal (Table 25.3). The differential cash flow stream is computed in Table 25.5.

The cash flow diagram is shown in Figure 25.5.

Table 25.4 Cash flow stream for the value of the confirm proposal.

Year	Cash flow stream for unhandled error	Cash flow stream for handling with confirm	Differential cash flow stream
0	$0	−$2500	−$2500
1	−$14,919	−14,770	149
2	−16,817	−16,025	162
3	−17,563	−17,387	176
4	−19,056	−18,865	191
5	−20,675	−20,469	207
6	−22,433	−22,208	224
7	−23,339	−24,096	243

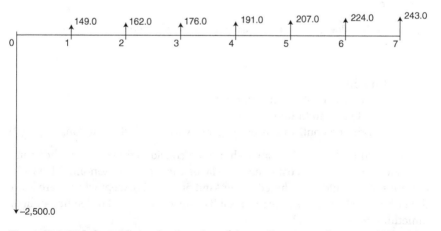

Figure 25.4 Cash flow diagram for the value of the confirm proposal.

Table 25.5 Cash flow stream for the value of the undo proposal.

Year	Cash flow stream for unhandled error	Cash flow stream for handling with undo	Differential cash flow stream
0	$0	−$11,750	−$11,750
1	−$14,919	−4476	10,443
2	−16,817	−4856	11,331
3	−17,563	−5269	12,294
4	−19,056	−5717	13,339
5	−20,675	−6203	14,473
6	−22,433	−6730	15,703
7	−23,339	−7302	17,038

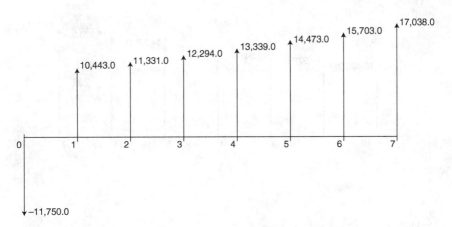

Figure 25.5 Cash flow diagram for the value of the undo proposal.

The cash flow stream for A3 is more complex. The confirm and undo proposals are interrelated. To the extent the confirm proposal works, the need for undo is reduced. We can't just add the cash flow streams for both proposals; we need to build a cash flow stream that accounts for this interrelationship. Table 25.6 builds that cash flow stream taking into account the reduced number of occurrences from the confirm proposal and reduced damage from the undo proposal.

Figure 25.6 is the cash flow diagram.

Table 25.7 shows the PW(13%) for each alternative.

The proposal with the highest PW(13%) is Alternative A2, providing the undo function only. It is technically viable and makes the most business sense. The

Table 25.6 Cash flow stream for the value of the confirm and undo proposals combined.

Year	Occurrences after confirm	Cash flow stream for confirm with undo	Differential cash flow stream
0	0	−$14,250	−$14,250
1	5.4	−4431	10,488
2	5.8	−4807	11,379
3	6.3	−5216	12,347
4	6.8	−5660	13,396
5	7.4	−6141	14,535
6	8.1	−6663	15,770
7	8.8	−7229	17,111

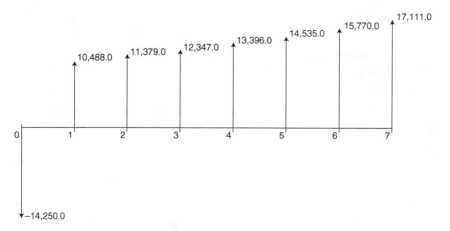

Figure 25.6 Cash flow diagram for the value of the confirm and undo proposals combined.

Table 25.7 PW(13%) for each of the alternatives.

Alternative	Description	PW(13%)
A0	Do nothing	$0
A1	Confirm button only	−1679
A2	Undo function only	45,707
A3	Confirm button and undo function	43,453

confirm function is technically viable but doesn't make business sense; it has a negative return on investment by itself (A1) and reduces PW(i) when combined with undo (A3).

If the PW(i) of A0 (do nothing) is highest, the best approach may be to ignore the error. That is, unless you must do something. If so,

- Go back to step 2 and create more proposals to analyze, or
- Choose the alternative(s) with the least negative PW(i).

25.3   Informal Analysis

Both simple and sophisticated analyses require numeric (i.e., quantitative, or ratio-scaled[10]) estimates. It is not worth the effort to develop numeric estimates in all cases, you should only need that level of analysis in special cases. Informal analysis is appropriate when you have a relatively low-damage error, so you don't need to be as careful in making the decision on how to handle it.

The same basic process applies:

- What damage would be caused if the error were left unhandled?
- What are proposed ways to handle the error?
- How effective is each proposal at handling the error?
- How much does it cost to implement each proposal?

For this analysis, consider different forms of contract defensiveness on an operation. The decision is about leaving any contract condition as a requires clause versus moving it to the guarantees side of the contract and possibly doing something about it (return an error code, throw an exception, etc.). As a specific example, use operation BookOrder.add(). The original, least defensive version is shown in Code Sample 25.1.

Since this is a simplified analysis, not as many steps are needed. Specifically, what were separate steps above become single steps here. In the end, three estimates are needed for each proposed error handling option:

- For damage caused if no error handling is done, rate it in terms of an ordinal scale like Low, Medium, or High.
- Recast the three separate factors: technical feasibility, effectiveness, and reduction in damage into a single element, call it "Leverage." Rate leverage in terms of something like Low, Medium, or High.
- Evaluate the cost to implement and maintain each proposal in terms of something like Low, Medium, or High

---

10 See, for example, Section L.7, chapter 26 of [Tockey05], or http://en.wikipedia.org/wiki/Level_of_measurement.

Code Sample 25.1 Least Defensive Contract for BookOrder.add()

```
public class BookOrder {

  public void add( Medium aMedium, int qty ) {
  // requires
  //    state == OPEN
  //    aMedium <> null
  //    qty > 0
  // guarantees
  //    one new BookOrderLine has been added to this order

    ...
  }

}
```

Specifically, the three contract requires conditions in Code Sample 25.1 are:

- State == OPEN
- aMedium <> null
- qty > 0

Start by considering just the State == OPEN condition. The damage caused by this condition being violated should be at least Medium because someone would be incorrectly adding Book order lines to an order that should not have lines added to it. There are at least four options for handling it:

- Do nothing to the contract; leave it as a requires clause (i.e., depend on View-controller to not violate).
- Add an assertion on entry to the method.
- Move it to the guarantees side of the contract (make it part of the if()...), but do nothing about it (i.e., no "otherwise" action, just ignore it).
- Move it to the guarantees side of the contract (make it part of the if()...), but do something in the "otherwise" part of the if(), such as return an error code, throw an exception, show an error dialog, log an error message, etc.[11]

Doing nothing would be Low leverage and have a Low cost. Adding an assertion to the entry of the method should have Low leverage at best because that assertion firing in production crashes the system and a Low cost of implementation. Moving the condition to the guarantees clause but ignoring it has High leverage

---

11 This is a simplified analysis. In practice each "do something" should be treated as a separate proposal. But rather than explicitly develop and analyze each one, just consider options that have the highest leverage with the lowest cost.

and Low cost. Moving it to the guarantees clause but not ignoring it has the same High leverage but cost increases to at least Medium and possibly High.

Per measurement theory, these estimates use ordinal scales, so it doesn't make sense to assign numbers (e.g., Low = 1, Medium = 2, High = 3) and then multiply to find the product: the scale type of the output of a function cannot be higher than the scale type of the most primitive input. Instead, the decision is more properly based on decision tables such as Tables 25.8–25.10. These decision tables are only intended to be examples. Your tables don't need to look exactly like these; you can create different tables that better match your specific situation.

Table 25.8 Decision table for when the damage rating is high.

	High	Yes	Yes	Probably yes
Leverage	Medium	Yes	Probably yes	Maybe
	Low	Probably yes	Maybe	Maybe
		Low	Medium	High
			Cost	

Table 25.9 Decision table for when the damage rating is medium.

	High	Yes	Probably yes	Maybe
Leverage	Medium	Probably yes	Maybe	Probably no
	Low	Maybe	Probably no	No
		Low	Medium	High
			Cost	

Table 25.10 Decision table for when the damage rating is low.

	High	Maybe	Maybe	Probably no
Leverage	Medium	Maybe	Probably no	No
	Low	Probably no	No	No
		Low	Medium	High
			Cost	

Table 25.8 might be used when the damage rating for the unhandled error is "High."

Table 25.9 might be used when the damage rating for the unhandled error is "Medium."

Table 25.10 might be used when the damage rating for the unhandled error is "Low."

Since the damage for the State == OPEN condition is Medium, use Table 25.9:

- Doing nothing has Low leverage and Low cost of implementing; the recommendation is "maybe."
- Adding the assertion has Medium leverage and Low cost of implementing; the recommendation is "maybe."
- Moving it to the guarantees clause and ignoring has High leverage and Low cost; the recommendation is "yes."
- Moving it to the guarantees clause but not ignoring has High leverage but Medium to High cost; at best the recommendation is "probably yes."

The highest rated option of all of these is moving the condition to the guarantees clause but doing nothing about it. This option is mutually exclusive with the others (i.e., it can't be combined), so it would be the best choice overall. Based on this decision, the interface of BookOrder.add() should now at least look like Code Sample 25.2.

Code Sample 25.2 A Slightly More Defensive Contract for BookOrder.add()

```
public class BookOrder {

 public void add( Medium aMedium, int qty ) {
 // requires
 //    aMedium <> null
 //    qty > 0
 // guarantees
 //    if state == open
 //       then one new BookOrderLine has been added to this order
 //       otherwise nothing
  ...
 }

}
```

Now consider condition aMedium <> null. Damage caused by this is high: the production system will almost certainly crash because of a null pointer exception. Options for handling include:

- Do nothing to the contract (i.e., depend entirely on View-controller region).
- Make it an assertion in the method.
- Move it into the if()... but do nothing (i.e., ignore it).
- Move it into the if()... but do something in the otherwise clause.

Doing nothing to the contract means depend on View-controller region code never invoking .add() with aMedium == null. This might be reasonable if View-controller developers can be counted on to pay attention to Model region contracts (the trust boundary issue). If View-controller region code is developed at the same time as Model region, all developers probably know each other: a trust boundary may not be not needed. On the other hand, considering the service life of this code, some developers who were not on the original development team (and, therefore, who cannot necessarily be trusted) may not pay attention to Model region contracts. Consider this proposal to have Low leverage and Low cost using Table 25.8, and the recommendation is "probably yes."

Making it an assertion on method entry is essentially no better than doing nothing to the contract because the system is still going to crash, although this time the crash would be on a specific exception—ArgumentNullException— instead of the more generic NullPointerException. There is slightly more fault isolation information. Again, this is Low leverage and Low cost so the recommendation is "probably yes." Given that this is mutually exclusive with doing nothing at all to the contract, the slight fault isolation advantage might make this preferable.

Moving the condition to the if()... side with no change to the otherwise clause has Medium leverage because it at least prevents the system crash caused by the null pointer. The problem is that the caller might be left wondering why their attempt at adding a Medium had no effect. The cost is Low, being only ½ a line of code. Again, referring to Table 25.8, this proposal would be in the "maybe" category.

Finally, moving the condition to the if()... side with a change to the otherwise clause has High leverage because it prevents the crash and it includes a useful response (i.e., an error code, exception, pop-up dialog, etc.). Cost depends on the specific action chosen (error code would be Low cost, exception could be Medium cost, and dialog box might be Medium or High cost). According to Table 25.8, this would be "Yes" on anything with Low or Medium cost and "Probably yes" on anything with High cost. More correctly, in practice, this analysis should cover an appropriate range of possibilities, and the lowest cost, highest leverage option overall should be chosen.

Code Sample 25.3 A Moderately Defensive Contract for BookOrder.add()

```
public class BookOrder {

 public boolean add( Medium aMedium, int qty ) {
 // requires
 //   qty > 0
 // guarantees
 //   if state == open && aMedium <> null
 //      then one new BookOrderLine has been added to this order
 //         and true is returned
 //      otherwise false is returned
  ...
 }

}
```

So now, the interface to BookOrder.add() might look like Code Sample 25.3. Finally, consider the qty > 0 condition. The damage is at most Medium. In terms of options, it is similar to the other conditions:

- Do nothing to the contract (i.e., depend entirely on View-controller region).
- Make it an assertion in the method entry.
- Move it into the if()... but do nothing (i.e., ignore it).
- Move it into the if()... but do something in the otherwise clause.

Doing nothing to the contract has the same Low leverage and Low cost, so the recommendation from Table 25.9 is "maybe." Making it an assertion on method entry has Low leverage, particularly because it now induces a system crash on that assertion failing. So again, the recommendation is "maybe," but this is probably a less desirable "maybe" than doing nothing, so discard this proposal. Next to consider is to moving the condition to the if()... but do nothing in the otherwise clause. Call this Medium leverage because at least the system doesn't crash but the user could still be confused by their order not being affected.

Finally, consider moving it to the if()... and do something in the otherwise clause means considering specific options like returning an error code, throwing an exception, popping up a dialog box, etc. Returning an error code would mean not using a Boolean return value as in Code Sample 25.3 because the calling code could not know that return == false was caused by aMedium being null or an invalid qty. Technically an option would be to return the error code for aMedium being null and throw an exception on an invalid qty, but it makes little sense in practice because of unnecessary accidental complexity: either return a more meaningful error code or throw two different exceptions. More meaningful error codes versus throwing two different exceptions should have the same effectiveness: Medium and about the same cost: Medium. According to Table 25.9, both are "maybe" with a final choice between them being essentially a matter of style or preference. Also consider consistency with the rest of the code in this domain.

One more option to consider in the otherwise clause could be to return a Notification object as explained in Chapter 16. This would have High leverage and Medium cost (although possibly somewhat higher than separate error codes or separate exceptions). According to Table 25.9, the recommendation would be "probably yes," which is better than any previous proposal. So the final decision could be an interface on BookOrder.add() as shown in Code Sample 25.4.

Given the Notification object was chosen for aMedium == null and qty <= 0, instead of simply ignoring calls when pre(.state) == null, that could also be included in the Notification.

Code Sample 25.4 An Economically Appropriate Interface for BookOrder. add()

```
public class BookOrder {

  public Notification add( Medium aMedium, int qty ) {
  // requires
  //    none
  // guarantees
  //    if pre(.state) == OPEN and aMedium <> null and
qty > 0
  //      then one new BookOrderLine has been added to
this order
  //         and returns a notification with zero errors
  //      otherwise returns a notification showing any
aMedium
  //                                        and qty
errors
    ...
  }

}
```

The important point is that we now have a reasonable economic basis for knowing this interface is the most cost effective compared with others. It was selected based on a conscious, economic decision-making process.

25.4 Reanalyzing Earlier Examples, Informally

This section revisits the examples of a loan application not being decided soon enough and the warehouse worker clicking on the wrong order earlier. This shows how both of those decisions might look if the informal process was used instead.

The first example was the Loan officer not deciding soon enough. The proposals were as follows:

- Sort the Loan officer's work list in decreasing age order—This should be evaluated as Low damage, Medium leverage, and Low cost, so the recommendation would be "Maybe" on implementation, which is at the designer/developer's discretion.
- Notify the Loan officer and the applicant when the age limit is hit—This should be evaluated as Low damage, High leverage, and Low cost so another "Maybe."
- Notify the Loan officer's manager: Low damage, low leverage, and medium cost so "No."

The second example was the warehouse worker click error. Proposals were as follows:

- Provide a confirm dialog box (e.g., "Are you sure?") after the Warehouse worker clicks on the Book order to be marked as packed—This should be evaluated as Medium damage, Low leverage, and Low cost so "Maybe" on implementation. Given how truly low the leverage is, the decision should really be "No."

Table 25.11 Comparing formal and informal analysis recommendations.

Error response	Formal analysis	Informal analysis
Sort Loan officer's list in decreasing order	Yes	Maybe
Notify Loan officer and applicant	Yes	Maybe
Notify Loan officer's manager	No	No
Provide confirm dialog box	No	Maybe/no
Provide undo function	Yes	Probably yes

- Provide an undo function that reverses the effects of mistaken packing—This should be evaluated as Medium damage, High leverage, and Medium cost so the recommendation would be "Probably."

Table 25.11 compares the recommendations from the formal analyses to the recommendations from informal analysis.

The recommendations are not identical. If they were, it would not make sense to use formal analysis and instead always use the simpler, informal approach. At least these recommendations generally agree. The informal approach should only be used when final decisions aren't that important.

25.5 Summary

Several chapters in Part II and Part III refer to error handling, specifically:

- *Semantic model*—On use cases, interaction, and state models
- *Interfaces*—On interface error handling
- *High-level design*—On contracts for operations
- *Detailed design*—On method implementations

Each of those chapters is intentionally vague on selecting any specific error handling approach. They defer that decision to this chapter.

So the question is, "What, if anything, can or should be done about any of those errors?"

That decision needs to be based on technical and economic factors. Conscious, deliberate, intelligent error handling decisions in software are critical:

- *System-wide design and construction implications*—As much as 75% of code in commercial-grade software is for handling errors.
- *Cost and schedule implications*—Effort needed to select, specify, design, build, and maintain error handling functionality is a significant part of project work.
- *System-wide performance implications*—Speed, robustness, and correctness are driven in part by error handling approaches. These are also major drivers of user satisfaction.
- *Source of unnecessary complexity*—If error handling decisions are made randomly, they introduce significant unnecessary accidental complexity.

This chapter explains how to perform an economic analysis of error handling alternatives—bringing in technical considerations as appropriate—to make conscious, deliberate, intelligent engineering decisions. Three versions of analysis were described:

- *Simple*—Using numeric estimates for relevant factors but ignoring the time value of money (interest).

- *Sophisticated*—Using numeric estimates for relevant factors, considering interest, and possibly other factors such as inflation, depreciation, and income taxes.
- *Informal*—The same decision process, using ordinal-scaled estimates instead of numeric estimates. Numeric estimates can be impractical in many cases.

And finally

> <u>This</u> is software engineering:
> *Using science, mathematics, and practice to create cost-effective solutions to real-world problems!*

26

Arguments Against Model-Based Software Engineering

This approach has been used on real projects for more than 30 years. In that time, a number of arguments have been raised against it. Examination of these arguments reveals that they do not hold. This chapter presents those arguments and provides counterarguments, refuting each one. Model-based software engineering is a superior approach for most software projects.

26.1   Claim #1: Code Can Be Produced as Fast or Faster Without Models

The simple response is, "No, it can't." For any nontrivial policies and processes to be automated, time spent building a semantic model and deriving code from that model is much less than time spent in mainstream development. Even ignoring productivity gains from using a model compiler, the key cost and schedule driver on mainstream projects is rework caused by not having a complete, consistent, clear, correct, concise, and precise semantic model to map from.

A specific example illustrates the general pattern. A very talented developer named Dave[1] insisted he could write the code and then reverse engineer a semantic model faster than building the semantic model first. The project manager and Dave's technical lead reluctantly agreed that because Dave is *very* talented they would let him write code first as long as he promised to review the reverse-engineered semantic model with the team afterward. When his reverse-engineered semantic model was reviewed, it was obvious that what Dave thought he needed to build was very different from what was needed. A number of significant problems were obvious from his model but not obvious from his code. Critical states and events were missing in state models and several transitions were wrong. Dave's design and code were dependent on those

---

1 His real name.

How to Engineer Software: A Model-Based Approach, First Edition. Steve Tockey.
© 2019 the IEEE Computer Society, Inc. Published 2019 by John Wiley & Sons, Inc.

key—but incorrect—elements of his semantic model being the way they were. In the end, Dave had to scrap his code and restart from a corrected semantic model. Since then Dave has been a strong advocate of "model first, code later."

This has been a recurring theme on every sizeable model-based project I've seen: a talented developer insists they can code faster and promises to produce a semantic model but only after coding. *Every single time*, that developer produces code with fundamental misunderstandings in policy and process semantics. They don't always need to throw away their code, but it always ends up needing nontrivial modification that takes longer than if semantic modeling had been done first. Those developers also become the biggest supporters of model-based software engineering because they have experienced firsthand how much of their own rework could have been avoided.

Mainstream development can be successful on small projects, but it is simply not scalable. Even the best of developers—and even if they fully understand policy and process semantics—can only keep a limited number of things in their head at one time. The very best developers I have seen can manage implicitly (i.e., in their head) semantic models of up to about 12 classes. And this is the extreme. Beyond that, important details are lost, are forgotten, or simply go wrong. Typical software, even in a subdomain, usually covers 20–40 classes. There's simply no way even the most talented developer can keep that much detail straight in their head.

Add to that the simple fact that the average developer is not nearly as talented as a great developer. Someone once said:

> *"Software development methods are for the rest of us"*

Truly great developers can be very informal and still be highly successful. But they are, by definition, exceptions: the 1%, not the 99%. What about all the others who aren't that awesome? The average developer starts having trouble with semantic models having less than seven classes. Consider the complexities in the semantic model of WebBooks 2.0 Payment domain (Appendix F) alone. How successful, realistically, would the average mainstream developer be at keeping all of that detail straight in their head when all they have to work with is code?

The final counterargument relates to long-term maintenance. Suppose you are the developer that built some code and all of that knowledge is in your head. If you promise that you will maintain the code over its entire life, typically 10–20 years, then fine, maybe you can keep the models in your head. But what if you want to turn that code over to someone else so you can work on a different project? How is that other developer going to understand everything that is going on in your code? Having the models in place (of course this depends on keeping the models up to date and that's a separate but manageable issue) makes the transition almost trivial, no matter how complex the software is.

We can consider this claim refuted.

26.2   Claim #2: Model-Based Software Engineering Requires "Big Design Up Front"

This argument asserts that in an agile world, the code (and, by implication, the semantic model) is never complete—it's continually evolving. Any approach that depends on full design before code is obviously unworkable in this situation.

A semantic model doesn't need to be 100% complete. It doesn't need to be any more complete than the functionality in the code. The semantic model at any time only has to represent the level of understanding of policies and processes, at that time. Even in mainstream agile projects, implicit in that code is an underlying semantic model. Whether that implicit model is complete, consistent, clear, concise, precise, unambiguous, and validated is an entirely different question; policy and process semantics are there. Simply, why not make those policy and process semantics explicit before writing code? Steve Mellor has more to say on this.[2]

Besides, iterating on semantic models is actually *much cheaper* than iterating on code. If desired, one can easily take an agile approach of "model a bit more of the policies and processes then modify the existing design and code as needed to re-synchronize it with the new semantic model." Alternatively, one can take a completely different agile approach of "model the policies and processes incrementally, and when enough change to the semantic model has been accumulated (e.g., a 'minimally marketable feature set' or 'minimum viable product') turn that into design and code." With model-based agile, an even faster feedback loop is possible: incrementally incorporating user stories into a semantic model and validating that revised model before wasting time on semantically incorrect design or code. Both agile processes are viable, as are many more. You have freedom to choose. Model-based development doesn't constrain you to any one particular lifecycle; in fact it opens the door to lifecycles that most developers didn't even know existed. See the meta-process discussion in Chapter 24 for more detail on this.

We can consider this claim refuted.

26.3   Claim #3: Stakeholders Don't Know UML or Modeling

This claim asserts that stakeholders would not be willing to learn UML—or, for that matter, any—modeling, so it is useless to build semantic models. Several counterarguments are relevant:

- *This is largely a chicken-and-egg issue*—Stakeholders may not be comfortable with semantic modeling today simply because they have never seen it before.

---

2 See [Mellor11].

They probably never even knew semantic models existed. But the same could have been said about house drawings when they were first introduced: no homebuilder or buyer had ever seen those drawings, so how could they understand them? House design language is common today because people acknowledge it is the best language for that purpose. If you want a house built, you better be willing to learn that language to be able to say, "Yes, that is the house I want." Otherwise you risk getting a house that you won't like. In practice, when stakeholders find how useful semantic models are, they *are* willing to read them. The level of skill and knowledge needed to *read* models is significantly less than what is needed to *write* them. I personally have spent as little as 30 minutes teaching dozens different stakeholders how to read semantic models; it's a good investment of my time as well as theirs.

- *The semantic model only models their business*—A semantic model of banking would only include banking elements like Bank account, Balance, Deposit, Transfer, etc. Nothing in the model should be foreign to stakeholders because it is describing their policies and processes. There are no database tables, no stored procedures, no disk files, no XML, no microservices, no REST, no memory-resident C++ classes, no cloud, etc. It is 100% pure banking. They are experts in banking. What irritates stakeholders is when technical people expect them to understand computing technology. Semantic models explicitly do not ask for that.

- *Stakeholders don't need to see the semantic model itself*—It is possible (having done it more than once) for a modeler to have the semantic model on their lap, interpreting it out loud. The modeler says things like "Last time we met, you told me that a Bank Account had to be owned by at least one Customer but could be owned by many. Is that still true today?" If it is still true, then the semantic model is correct on that point. If it's not true, the model needs to be revised. Alternatively, Chapter 12 explains how to mechanically translate a semantic model into natural language. It is not difficult to write a program to do it for you, which is described in Chapter 21. Stakeholders can review the many pages of natural language statements, if they prefer. Given the choice between a few pages of concise models and many times more pages of text, every stakeholder I've ever worked with always chose the drawings.

- *If a model is compilable, then it is also interpretable*—Chapters 12 and 21 also explain how to interpret the semantic model, by hand or automatically, to demonstrate the behavior defined in that model. We can work with stakeholders to define a set of demonstration test cases and execute those test cases against the semantic model. If the actual result of every test case matches the stakeholder's expected result, we should be confident the model represents correct policy and process semantics.

We can consider this claim refuted.

26.4   Claim #4: Some People Don't Like Drawings, They Prefer Text

The semantic model doesn't *have* to be expressed in a graphical language; that's just a representation format. If someone wants to create a text-based representation for semantic models, they are free to do so. At least one text-based representation already exists: OMG's UML Model Interchange Format.[3] The semantic content of each representation must, by definition, be identical. All that happened was to switch from one notation to another, and that's usually easy. It is possible to mechanically translate between model-as-drawings and models-as-text as shown in Chapters 12 and 21.

We can consider this claim refuted.

26.5   Claim #5: Semantic Models Are Just Code in a Different Language

This discussion needs to refer back to the terms Computation Independent Model (CIM) and Platform Independent Model (PIM) introduced in Chapter 20. If a modeler is building a PIM (or, more correctly, a PIM overlay) with the intent of using a model compiler to generate source code, then it is not arguable: they really are just programming in a different language. But even so, action semantics languages tend to be much more abstract and closer to the "problem space" than mainstream programming languages. The level of abstraction the developers work at increases in each evolutionary step:

- Machine language to assembler
- Assembler to first-generation compilers (e.g., FORTRAN, COBOL)
- First generation to second generation (e.g., Pascal, Ada, etc.)
- Second-generation to modern object-oriented languages like Java, C#, C++, Python, etc.

In the long run, the more abstract the programming language, the better. This is the point of the Section 20.7: using an open model compiler is simply taking one more step up the ladder of programming language evolution. From the abstraction standpoint alone, the eventual shift to higher-level model-based programming languages is inevitable.

But even this argument is overly simplistic and misses the point. When working in design and code, developers are necessarily working in the solution space. As Part III—particularly Chapter 20 on model compilation—describes, they are mapping pure problem space semantics onto pure solution space semantics.

---

3 See, for example, https://en.wikipedia.org/wiki/XML_Metadata_Interchange.

Remember that a semantic model, a CIM, is—by definition—computationally independent. The semantic model is a description of a completely different subject matter, pure problem space semantics: policies and processes to be automated. In semantic modeling, we are working in a much higher, more abstract space with far fewer complexities. All solution space complexities have been abstracted away. Without a complete, consistent, clear, correct, concise, precise, explicit, and validated semantic model to serve as the anchor for the mapping (the design and code), that mapping is almost certain to suffer from semantic inconsistencies (ahem: defects, bugs).

Ideally, a modeling tool would allow separation of PIM content from the underlying CIM so a modeler can work in pure CIM terms when necessary (e.g., to understand, validate, and communicate policy and process semantics) and in PIM terms for other purposes (e.g., to prepare a model to be translated). Such modeling tools should also allow the management of multiple PIM overlays on the same CIM to support translation into different execution environments. A model of useful policies and processes should be translatable into not only a desktop application but also into a mobile app, as well as microservices, or a REST service back end.

We can consider this claim refuted.

26.6 Claim #6: Semantic Models Aren't Requirements, They Are Design

This argument asserts that even a CIM should be considered "design." There is a community in computer science called "formal methods." These are the people behind formal verification methods and languages like Z, VDM, etc. That community talks about two kinds of specifications: "axiomatic" and "constructive." An axiomatic specification is purely in terms of a set of axioms. An axiomatic specification for abstract data type Stack would look something like:

- *Let E be an element of any stackable type.*
- *Let S0 be an empty Stack.*
- *Let S be any Stack, possibly empty, possibly not.*
- *Let Sn be a Stack that has at least one element.*
- *Push(E,S)→Sn* { Pushing an element onto any stack results in a non-empty stack }.
- *Pop(S0)→error* { Can't pop from an empty stack }.
- *Pop(Sn)→E* { Pop on a non-empty stack returns an element }.
- *Pop(Push(E,S))→E* { Pop on a non-empty stack returns the last element pushed }.
- ...

Specifying abstract data type Stack constructively would involve an ordered set along with a pointer to the top entry, possibly having a state model with states "empty" and "non-empty" and so on. One could build a complete semantic model of Stack with use cases, classes, sequence diagrams, and a state model or two.

One position is that only way to truly specify "requirements" is axiomatically. The moment one builds a constructive specification they are in "design." I understand and respect that position, but would mean only "The system shall ..." statements—like those normally found in mainstream requirements specifications—can be considered requirements because they are axioms in the formal methods sense (even though they are immensely vague and ambiguous). Any semantic model is, by definition, constructive and therefore would have to be considered "design."

The other position is "requirements are statements of what is needed by stakeholders—regardless of the language used to express them." Recall the "unambiguous, testable, and binding" criteria from Chapter 4. An unambiguous, testable, and binding statement can be expressed in any language: English, Chinese, Korean, UML, mathematics, or whatever. The advantage that languages like UML and mathematics have over natural languages is that these languages have been created with the explicit goal of minimizing ambiguity.

What separates (functional) "requirements" from "design" in this second position is that automation technology is present in design and absent from functional requirements. What we may need to do is to step back from today's "requirements" and "design" vocabulary and adopt new vocabulary like:

- "Axiomatic specification"
- "Constructive specification that's free of automation technology"—a semantic model, a CIM
- "Constructive specification containing automation technology"—a PIM or design dialect models as in Part III

We can consider this claim refuted.

26.7 Claim #7: Semantic Modeling Isn't Practical Without a Sophisticated, Expensive Tool

This argument reveals a fundamental misunderstanding of the value of model-based software engineering. Admittedly, it may appear to be inconvenient to build semantic models (or design models for that matter) without a sophisticated—and, therefore, expensive—tool. But remember that in mainstream software organizations, the rework percentage (R%)[4] averages around 60%. In properly run model-based software engineering organizations, R% is much closer to 10%. The effort to create and maintain the models even without sophisticated tools is more than paid back by reduction in R%.

Few of the organizations I have worked with ever used sophisticated tools. Sophisticated tools clearly did not exist 30 years ago, and yet project teams have always been willing to use even primitive tools once they realized the value of modeling:

- On the first model-based project I worked on in 1985—before *any* software modeling tools were available—we made pencil-and-paper drawings using flowcharting stencils. We then photocopied the drawings into blank spaces in print outs of text from a formatting tool called Runoff.[5]
- Many projects have been successful pasting Visio drawings into Word documents.
- The majority of semantic model diagrams in this book were created in PowerPoint.

Having a sophisticated modeling tool certainly makes it more convenient. But the value of modeling is not in the tool; it is in the thought processes that surround proper modeling.

We should be able to expect that as more developers adopt this approach, tool vendors will see a new market. Over time, the market will become large enough to justify vendor investment in creating powerful tools. And as more vendors enter the market, competition will make the tools more affordable.

We can consider this claim refuted.

26.8   Claim #8: It Is Not Clear Who Should Do the Semantic Modeling

It simply does not matter who creates and maintains a semantic model. The only thing that matters is that all relevant parties agree that the semantic model represents the policies to be enforced and processes to be carried out:

- Stakeholders
- Business analysts (BAs)
- Developers
- Human interface designers
- Testers/QA
- User documentation specialists
- ...

---

4 Refer to the discussion of R% in Chapter 1.
5 See, for example, https://en.wikipedia.org/wiki/Runoff_(program).

In an ideal world, the stakeholders—the business experts themselves—would give semantic models to developers for design and implementation. To a limited extent, this has actually happened on some projects. But clearly, it is not common to find stakeholders who are capable of doing that (refer back to Section 26.3).

In an almost ideal world, this could be the role of a BA: work with stakeholders to understand policies and process semantics, build a semantic model from that understanding, and then give that model to developers for design and implementation. There are two near-term problems with this. First is that the typical BA is more of a business expert than a technical expert, meaning that they often aren't used to thinking at the level of detail and precision needed to build proper semantic models. I often see BAs hired more on communication skills than on critical thinking skills. I am not saying that this is bad; this is simply an observation.

The second problem is staff availability. Semantic modeling is about 60% of the technical effort of building a (sub)domain,[6] design is about 30%, and coding is the remaining 10%. This means on average we should be staffing projects (at least for the top-level domain) with six BAs for every four developers. Today, we're unlikely to see that many BAs. In my experience, we are lucky to see one BA for every 10 developers.

In practice, developers usually take on the majority of semantic modeling. But that isn't necessarily a bad thing:

- *Developers tend to have the detail-oriented mindset needed to build proper semantic models.*
- *Developers have a vested interest in seeing the semantic models are properly built.*
- *Developers can't make much real progress on design and code until a semantic model exists (keeping in mind that semantic modeling, designing, and coding can be done incrementally, i.e., agile).*
- *There are almost always enough developers available on a project to build models.*
- *Much of the semantic modeling in large systems is for lower-level service domains where the subject matters are more technical anyway (e.g., security, scalability, high availability, etc.).*

We can consider this claim refuted.

26.9 Claim #9: If Model-Based Software Engineering Is So Great, Then Why Isn't Everyone Already Doing It?

The biggest reason the software industry isn't already doing this is simply lack of knowledge. While many in the industry have heard of using models, remarkably few have ever seen models applied in the way shown in this book.

---

6 See Chapter 23.

The second reason is cultural: "We've always done it that way." When given that argument, one of my coworkers replies, "But is it working?" Ask the simple question, "Who is really happy with the schedule, cost, and quality performance of mainstream software projects?" The answer is, simply, "Nobody." Remember the results reported by the Standish Group[7]:

- *Only 39% of software projects are successful.*
- *43% of software projects are challenged.*
- *18% of software projects fail.*

Of software projects that do deliver (successful and challenged projects combined), the Chaos report says they average:

- *42% late*—A planned 10-month project is more reasonably expected to take about 14 months.
- *35% over budget*—A planned $10 million project is more reasonably expected to cost $13.5 million.
- *25% under scope*—In spite of overrunning both schedule and budget; software projects do not deliver all expected functionality. A project that expects to satisfy 100 requirements is more reasonably expected to satisfy only 75.

All of this is against a backdrop of 60% rework. From this we have to conclude, "No, it isn't working." It has been said,

> *"Insanity is doing the same thing over and over, and expecting different results"*

And as Stephen Tyler[8] reportedly said,

> *"If you always do what you've always done, then you will always get what you always got"*

The third reason is also cultural, but in a different way. Clearly, transitioning from mainstream development to model-based software engineering requires a fundamental shift. Mainstream projects are used to spending about 10% of the effort doing requirements work, about 30% of the effort doing design work, and about 60% of the effort coding and testing. Model-based development reverses that: project teams now spend 60% on requirements modeling, 30% on design, and only 10% on coding and testing.

Teams have traditionally resisted spending time on requirements because that work was not value-added. Almost every mainstream developer would

---

7 See [Standish13].
8 Lead singer of the rock band Aerosmith.

agree that—done the way it's typically done—requirements work is a complete waste of time. And how many times have you heard from developers, "my code is self-documenting." But self-documenting code doesn't exist. It can't exist. Instead, consider the alternative:

> *"Model-based software engineering is literally self-coding documentation."*

Spending 60% of the technical effort on semantic modeling is a value-added investment because a validated semantic model provides an anchor point for the mapping to automation technology: the design and code.

Finally, why aren't we hearing from all of the people who are already successfully doing model-based software engineering? The reason is competitive; those that are doing it successfully are producing software cheaper, faster, and with higher quality than their competitors. Consider the software outsourcing market: Vendor A does model-based software engineering and Vendor B develops the mainstream way. Both are bidding on the same job. Vendor A did mainstream development before, so they have a good idea of what Vendor B will bid. But Vendor A knows they can easily do the project in half that time, at half that cost, and with much higher quality. Vendor A can confidently submit a bid at, say, 85% of what they expect Vendor B to bid. Vendor A undercuts Vendor B's bid by 15%, securing the business with a healthy profit margin. And that is even assuming the unlikely possibility that Vendor B could actually deliver on time and on budget. The project is a walk in the park for Vendor A, and they have resources to spare, so they can also go after other contracts. If you were in Vendor A's position, you would want to keep model-based software engineering a closely guarded secret.

I am under nondisclosure agreement (NDA) with organizations that are doing high-performance computing (e.g., real-time medical image processing in one specific case) using code generated by an open model compiler. Yes, they've invested in creating the model compiler infrastructure, but they can now reliably make functional changes to their product up to ten times faster than before. Some organizations have been doing model-based software engineering for as long as 30 years and open model compilation for as long as 20 years. But I can't tell you who they are because it's their competitive advantage. They dominate their marketplace because they produce high quality software quicker and cheaper than their competition—and it's easy for them. They would lose that edge if their competitors knew this secret.

At this point, the question you should be asking yourself is:

> *"In a marketplace as competitive as ours, can we afford to <u>not</u> to be using model-based software engineering?"*

We can consider this claim refuted, too.

26.10 Summary

A number of arguments have been raised against model-based software engineering. Examination of each one reveals that they do not hold. The reality is that model-based software engineering is a superior approach for most software projects.

Part V

Summary

Engineering has been defined as[1]:

> *"... the profession in which a knowledge of the mathematical and natural sciences gained by study, experience, and practice is applied with judgment to develop ways to utilize, economically, the materials and forces of nature for the benefit of mankind."*

Or, simply

> Engineering = scientific theory + practice + engineering economy

This book is about how to engineer software: applying the theory of computing—computer science and discrete mathematics—with practice and judgment to develop and maintain software that economically solves real-world problems. This final chapter summarizes and closes the book.

---

1 See [ABET00].

How to Engineer Software: A Model-Based Approach, First Edition. Steve Tockey.
© 2019 the IEEE Computer Society, Inc. Published 2019 by John Wiley & Sons, Inc.

27

Closing Remarks

This chapter gives a review of the book and includes sections on:

- Overview of this book
- Revisiting the big picture
- Solving mainstream software's primary problems
- Complexity management
- Bug == defect == semantic inconsistency
- Summary

27.1 Review of This Book

This book is divided into six parts:

- **Part I: Introduction and Foundations**. This part establishes the foundation on which model-based software engineering is built. This part includes chapters on the nature of code, fundamental principles, functional and nonfunctional requirements, an overview of the Unified Modeling Language (UML), and partitioning large systems into domains.
- **Part II: Model-Based Requirements**. In this part, the four primary elements of semantic modeling are explained: use case diagrams, class models, interaction diagrams, and state models. Partitioning domains into subdomains, simulating models, deriving verification test cases, and other related topics are also presented
- **Part III: Model-Based Design and Code**. This part explains how to translate semantic models into design and executable code. This includes discussions of designing interfaces, high-level software design, detailed design, code, formal disciplines of code including software proofs of correctness, optimization, model compilers, and the nature of design itself.
- **Part IV: Related Topics**. This part provides an estimation model, discusses software development processes, explains how to approach error handling

How to Engineer Software: A Model-Based Approach, First Edition. Steve Tockey.
© 2019 the IEEE Computer Society, Inc. Published 2019 by John Wiley & Sons, Inc.

from an economic perspective, and rebuts common arguments against this approach.

- **Part V: Summary**. This part summarizes and closes the book.
- **Part VI: Appendices**. Additional resources such as references, documentation principles, example semantic models and designs, a semantic model of semantic modeling, example semantic model translation rules for Java, and a discussion of software structural complexity metrics.

27.2 Revisiting the Big Picture

Figure 27.1 duplicates Figure 1.3 and shows the primary deliverables for a (sub) domain in model-based software engineering.

27.2.1 Background

The deliverable labeled Background refers to the Product Requirements Document (PRD)/Marketing Requirements Document (MRD)/Product Vision (PV)/ Scope Statement/Overview or whatever the (sub)domain team typically gets from stakeholders. This provides a high-level overview of what developers are supposed to build in software. This is normally given to the (sub)domain

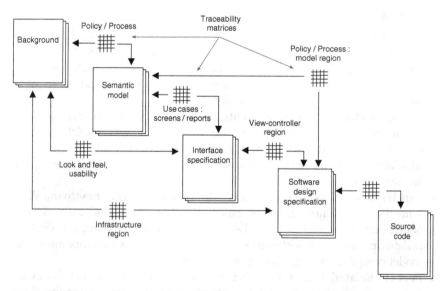

Figure 27.1 Primary deliverables for a model-based software engineering project.

development team; it is not something they should necessarily produce. An example Background for the overall WebBooks 2.0 case study is shown in Appendix B. Brief backgrounds for each of the domains in the WebBooks 2.0 case study are shown in Appendix C.

Some organizations find it useful to include a Minimum conditions of acceptance specification, either as a section in the Background or as a separate deliverable. The Minimum conditions of acceptance identify the most vitally important requirements against which the team will be held accountable. This would typically include critical functional and nonfunctional requirements. This may be considered a contractual (i.e., legal) document on some projects and can serve as the basis for acceptance testing and requirements traceability, as appropriate.

27.2.2 Semantic Model

The semantic model specifies policies and processes to be automated: the complete, consistent, clear, concise, precise, unambiguous, and validated functional requirements for the (sub)domain. The structure and content of this model is introduced in Chapter 2 and described in detail in Part II. Example semantic models are shown in Appendices D, F, H, and J.

27.2.3 Interface Specification

The interface specification defines how real-world external entities (actors in the semantic model) interact with the software implementing the (sub)domain. This can be either or both human–computer (user) interfaces or application program(mer) interfaces (APIs). This content is critical for developing and maintaining View-controller region software. The deliverable is described in Chapter 14. Partial examples of interface specifications are shown in Appendices E, G, I, and K.

27.2.4 Software Design Specification

The software design specification for a (sub)domain is, for example, classic object-oriented design (OOD) as you would find on a typical software project that uses UML. The difference is that in model-based software engineering this specification has much more emphasis on explaining why the design and code look the way they do. The structure and content is described in detail in Part III. Partial examples of design specifications are also shown in Appendices E, G, I, and K.

27.2.5 Source Code

The last deliverable is (sub)domain code. This includes compilable source code along with necessary make files, build files, and—as needed—run-time configuration data files. Ideally, the design and code would be integrated as described in Knuth's "literate programming" (see Chapter 22)

27.2.6 Traceability

The crosshatch shapes between deliverables in Figure 27.1 identify opportunities for traceability between pairs of related deliverables. More precisely, they call out necessary consistency. A semantic model may say, abstractly, that customers can place orders, so the user interface needs to give a way for customers to place orders. The core of the software design and code (Model region in a Model–View–Controller architectural style) needs to automate placing orders, while View-controller region needs to implement the interface defined in the interface specification. Full traceability is possible, if wanted or needed—it's only a question of granularity.

27.2.7 Implications on Testing

Not shown in Figure 27.1 are implications on software testing. For each deliverable, tests of one kind or another can be derived:

- Unit tests from code itself
- Integration and component tests from the software design specification
- Usability and interface tests from the interface specification
- Functional tests from the semantic model
- Acceptance tests from the Minimum conditions of acceptance in the Background

27.3 Solving Mainstream Software's Primary Problems

Chapter 1 identified the three most significant reasons why mainstream software projects get into trouble:

1) Vague, ambiguous, incomplete requirements
2) Overdependence on testing to find software defects
3) "Self-documenting code" is a myth

That chapter expanded on these problems and outlined how model-based software engineering helps solve each one. Now that you have seen model-based software engineering in detail, this section looks more specifically at how each problem is solved.

27.4 Solving Problem #1: Vague, Ambiguous, Incomplete Requirements

Recognized engineering disciplines realized long ago that natural languages are inadequate. In the same way that electrical engineers use circuit schematic diagrams to drive construction and maintenance of electronics, aeronautical engineers use engineering drawings to drive construction and maintenance of aircraft, and structural engineers use blueprints to drive construction and maintenance of buildings, and the software industry can use drawings: for the same reasons and to get the same benefits.

In terms of the content in a semantic model,

- *A semantic model is unambiguous*—It has exactly one meaning, no more and no less. Appendix L defines critical semantics missing from the UML specification that give a semantic model its one precise meaning. Part of Appendix L is a semantic model of semantic modeling: a "metamodel." Part is a UML profile that defines how things not specified in the metamodel are to be interpreted. You are not bound to exactly this metamodel and profile. You can, as necessary, modify the metamodel or profile to better suit your needs. Just be sure any changes are logically consistent and communicated to all participants.
- *A semantic model is precise*—An attribute is not fully specified until its range has been defined. An association is not fully specified until multiplicities have been defined. An action is not fully specified until its contract (requires and guarantees clauses) has been defined. A generalization (inheritance) has not been fully specified unless it is clear it is {complete} or {incomplete}. Questions that would not even be asked on a mainstream software project are forced to be answered in a semantic model. A host of issues that would easily have become defects in a mainstream project never cause problems because requirements are surfaced before incorrect design or code could ever be created.
- *A semantic model is concise*—By depending on drawings instead of natural language, more information is packed into a smaller space. Just like the engineering drawings for a house or the blueprints for an airplane, the semantic model captures a broad spectrum of detailed information in a small space. It's not difficult to specify at the level of detail needed because there's not much effort to do so. Translating a semantic model to natural language as discussed in Chapter 12 and 21 would encounter the same kind of bloat as translating house or airplane blueprints:

> *"The people who design and build houses gave up trying to describe them in natural languages over one hundred years ago. What makes you think you can successfully describe something that's orders of magnitude more complex using natural language?"*

In terms of building and maintaining a semantic model,

- *Semantic modeling has a set of completeness guidelines*—There is never any guarantee your requirements are complete. But semantic modeling includes guidelines that help expose requirements that would have easily been missed in mainstream projects. Specifically, the categories of business events (particularly the nonoccurrence category) and all events in all states guideline for state modeling. A semantic model also intentionally organizes related information nearby. Incompleteness and inconsistency are more likely to be seen and fixed, well before valuable time and effort are wasted on incorrect design and code.
- *Semantic modeling provides a set of checklists*—Through either self-review or peer review, checklists enable more systematic and complete coverage. Any reviewer who conscientiously applies these checklists is highly likely to find problems that had little to no chance of being found on a mainstream project.
- *Semantic models are interpretable*—If stakeholders are unwilling to review semantic models, we can still agree on a set of suitably convincing policy and process-level demonstration test cases and execute them against the semantic model. If all cases produce results identical to what's expected, then stakeholders should be confident that the policies and processes they want automated are properly represented.

All of this helps identify and remove incompleteness and ambiguity from a semantic model:

- Avoid requirements defects in first place.
- Find and fix remaining defects as early as possible, while they are still cheap.

With model-based software engineering, functional requirements cannot be ambiguous and are far more likely to be complete.

In terms of nonfunctional requirements,

- Nonfunctional how requirements must precisely specify the range of required configurations/versions.
- Nonfunctional how well requirements are driven by a localized derivative of ISO 25010 for completeness and use economics-driven ranges (fail, requirement, and perfection points) for necessary precision.

Remember,

> *"If it's not obvious how to test it, can your specification be any good?"*
> (Dr. Ric Frankel, Seattle University)

Given the detail in semantic models, it *is* obvious how to test it. So the specifications *must* be good. Requirements cannot be vague, ambiguous, and grossly incomplete anymore.

We can consider this problem solved.

27.5 Solving Problem #2: Overdependence on Testing to Find Software Defects

Remember that 56% of defects in mainstream software are caused by poor requirements. The more requirements problems that can be avoided or resolved while doing requirements work—because model-based requirements aren't vague, ambiguous, and grossly incomplete—the less testing is needed.

By treating design and code as an explicit mapping from policy and process semantics to automation technology semantics and making sure that policy and process semantics are preserved, there is even less opportunity for defects. The majority of design and code defects are either avoidable or apparent in reviews.

Across the software industry as a whole, software organizations staff at an average level of one tester for every four developers. Model-based software engineering projects are adequately staffed with one tester for every ten developers.

The other important point is rework (R%). Mainstream projects average around 60%: about 60 out of every 100 labor hours spent on the project are in fixing mistakes that were made earlier. A properly run model-based software engineering project averages under 10% rework. Model-based software engineering projects take about half the cost and schedule of mainstream projects in delivering equivalent functionality: the difference is largely due to reduction in rework.

The mainstream software industry mantra seems to be: "we need it sooner, we need it now, we need it yesterday, ..." You *can* have it sooner—in half the time and at half the cost—you just can't get there by following the same path that's already proven to be inefficient and ineffective. We know *why* that path is ineffective and inefficient. With so many defects being avoided and most unavoidable defects being found in early reviews, the need for testing is vastly reduced. The only way to get this kind of improvement is to follow a different path, the model-based software engineering path.

As Martyn Thomas said,

> "An engineer wants their system to be fit for purpose and chooses methods, tools and components that are expected to achieve fitness for purpose. It's poor engineering to have a system fail in testing, partly because that puts the budget and schedule at risk but mainly because it reveals that the chosen methods, tools or components have not delivered a system of the required quality, and that raises questions about the quality of the development processes."
>
> (Martyn Thomas)

Similarly, C. A. R (Tony) Hoare said (paraphrased):

> "The real value of tests is not that they detect [defects] in the code, but that they detect inadequacies in the methods, concentration, and skills of those who design and produce the code."

Unlike mainstream software projects where developers depend on testers to find defects, a well-run model-based software engineering team gives code to testers with the expectation that those testers *won't be able to find any defects*. We can consider this problem solved as well.

27.6 Solving Problem #3: "Self-Documenting Code" Is a Myth

Code can never be self-documenting:

- Code can only tell you what it does, not what it is intended to do.
- Code can never tell you why it looks the way it does—does it *have* to look that way, or does it just *happen* to look that way?

Policy and process in a semantic model are the ultimate specification of intent for Model region code. The interface specification(s) is the ultimate specification of intent for View-controller region code. Contracts define intent at the operation level. In Model region those contracts must be consistent with—and in fact can be mechanically derived from—the semantic model. Intent in design and code must be obvious, from method-level all the way up to the (sub)domain semantic model and interface specification. With programming by intent (Chapter 18), intent can be carried all the way down to the individual line of code.

As discussed in Chapter 19, design documentation should focus more on why design and code look the way they do, not on how they look.

The semantic model, the interface specification, and appropriate design documentation give the maintainer everything they need to know. This is one reason why maintenance costs drop by a factor of four to eight: maintenance developers don't waste valuable time and effort trying to figure out code. Everything they need to know is already obvious and explicit. The other reasons are that defects are being prevented through use of models and the fundamental principles guide those models to be as simple and clear as possible. There are an order-of-magnitude fewer defects needing to be fixed in the first place.

27.6.1 Literally, "Self-Coding Documentation"

The fact that, as demonstrated in Chapter 20, most of the code can be mechanically generated from the semantic model is proof of its value. If a semantic model were to change in any way, the code would need to change in a consistent way, lest the code not preserve the new semantics. Further, if you were told why code should look a certain way, then if you had to re-create that code you could make it almost identical to how it looks now.

27.6.2   The Great Software Brain Drain

When I first started programming in the mid-1970s, it was difficult, if not impossible, to find code that was older than the developers who wrote and maintained it. That has changed. It is not uncommon to see 25-year-old developers maintaining 30-year-old code. The developers who wrote the original code have long since departed:

- Moved on to other projects
- Moved out to other companies
- Retired from the software industry
- Even—and sadly it's becoming more common every day—passed away

How much valuable time and effort are spent each and every day trying to recover critical lost knowledge? How much of today's time and effort would have been saved if the original developers had published semantic models and appropriate design documentation?

We can't change the past, but what about the future? Shouldn't we start as soon as we can to capture critical policy and process semantics, as well as design justifications? If not, we will be guilty of making a bad situation even worse.

Model-based software engineering externalizes all that valuable, critical intellectual property (IP) knowledge. Policy and process semantics are no longer only in the head of the developer(s) who wrote that code. Any developer can read a semantic model and understand. Design rationale is no longer only in the head of the developer(s) who wrote that code. Any developer can read the rationale in the design documentation. All of that valuable, critical IP is outside of the original developer(s). It is persistent and shareable. The original developers are free to move to other projects, move to other companies, or even retire. This project can do fine without them thank-you-very-much.

Let's face it; any professional in any recognized engineering discipline would be unceremoniously drummed out of their field if they failed to deliver adequate and appropriate documentation:

> *"Congratulations, here is the X you asked for. Oh, by the way, good luck using and maintaining it because I was too lazy to provide any useful supporting documentation. My design and implementation are clearly so obviously self-documenting, blah blah blah."*

Such a rank unprofessional would surely not last long among true engineers:

> *"Do you want to be seen as a true software engineering professional? Then act like one!"*

We can also consider this problem solved.

27.7   Complexity Management in Model-Based Software Engineering

WebBooks 2.0 software is clearly not trivial; in total it spans very diverse functionality:

- Order fulfillment
- Payment
- Scalability
- High availability
- User security

How complex would WebBooks 2.0 code be if it were built using mainstream software development practices? How difficult would it be to maintain, particularly with the dearth of documentation that comes out of mainstream projects. And yet, as illustrated in Appendix B through Appendix K, look how effectively model-based software engineering manages all of that complexity:

- Domain partitioning (Chapter 6)
- Subdomain partitioning (Chapter 11, although not needed in WebBooks 2.0)
- Separating policy and process semantics from automation technology (Chapter 4)
- Separating automation technology from policy and process semantics (Chapter 22)

In particular, Chapter 3 presented a set of fundamental principles:

- Focus on semantics
- Use appropriate abstractions
- Encapsulate accidental complexity
- Maximize cohesion, minimize coupling
- Design to invariants, design for change
- Avoid premature design and optimization
- Name things carefully

Model-based software engineering incorporates those fundamental principles into an approach that manages significant complexities. Systems much larger and more complex than WebBooks 2.0 can, and have, been built and maintained without the level of difficulty encountered on mainstream projects. Teams of more than 350 developers have delivered several million lines of mission- and safety-critical code—on time, on budget, and with few defects—using model-based software engineering.

27.8   Bug == Defect == Semantic Inconsistency

Software defects—"bugs"—are semantic inconsistencies. Semantic inconsistencies are defects. They are one and the same thing:

- *Semantic inconsistencies in the developer's understanding of policies and processes to automate*—Policies and processes aren't clearly defined, understood, specified, communicated, shared, agreed, etc.
- *Semantic inconsistencies in the mapping of policy and process semantics onto automation technology semantics*—The mapping doesn't preserve business semantic, for example, mapping BankAccount.deposit() onto anything other than addition, Java objects not going out of existence until their reference count is zero and the garbage collector reclaims memory, etc.

It should now be clear why mainstream software is so prone to defects. Trying to map from complex, poorly understood, inconsistent, and unvalidated policy and process semantics is challenging all by itself:

- *What does* it mean to be a customer?
- *What does* it mean to be a book order?
- *Can* a customer exist without any book orders?
- *Should* a copyright year of 1779 be allowed?
- *Can* a bank account have a negative balance?
- What *does* "detect a ¼ inch defect in a pipe section" really mean?

To the extent that policy or process semantics are incomplete, inconsistent, misunderstood, misinterpreted, or miscommunicated, there *must* be corresponding inconsistencies in design and code. And even if policy and process semantics are precisely defined, validated, and communicated, if policy and process semantics are not preserved—100%, in a sufficiently complete mapping to automation technology, then there will be even more semantic inconsistencies: defects, "bugs."

Whether anyone likes it or not, syntactically correct[1] source code—be it from a mainstream project or a model-based software engineering project—exhibits one, only one, and exactly one semantics: it has one, and only one, behavior:

> *"There is only one set of policies that some given syntactically correct source code is capable of enforcing: it cannot and will not enforce any others. There is only one set of processes that same code is capable of carrying out: it cannot and will not carry out any others."*

---

1 That is, code that can be compiled without error. Syntactically incorrect code is not compilable, is not executable, and is therefore irrelevant. Source code has to at least be executable to be relevant here.

So the critical question must be:

> *"Is that one set of policies and processes embodied in this source code <u>exactly the same</u> as that one set of policies and processes our stakeholders want automated?"*

To the extent policies and processes embodied in source code do not match exactly, precisely, *and* wholly, *what stakeholders want automated, then it is no more than a matter of time before someone stumbles across those differences.*

Fifty-six percent of software defects are in requirements[2]: vague, ambiguous, misinterpreted, incomplete, etc. Semantic model content, completeness criteria, structure, and development guidelines force pesky functional requirements issues to be exposed and clarified before wasting time writing equally semantically inconsistent code. Most defects are avoided before they could ever even happen.

Twenty-seven percent of defects are in design: design that doesn't completely map policy and process semantic, doesn't preserve that semantic, or doesn't satisfy a nonfunctional (how or how well) requirement.

Opportunities to inject defects on model-based software engineering projects have been significantly reduced. Also, the defects that do get injected stand out more clearly. This is why software developed using model-based software engineering is so much higher quality and so much faster to deliver:

- Defects are avoided, that is, never created in first place.
- Defects are found and fixed earlier at significantly reduced cost, effort, and schedule.

27.9   Summary

Bob Dylan was right:

> *"The times they are a-changin'"*

In the past, users may have been willing to tolerate defects because the software was not performing a critical service. More and more, however, software *is* being used for critical purposes:

- Emergency services
- Transportation
- Medical care

---

2 See also Figure 23.7.

- Banking and finance
- Networks, communication, and telecommunication
- Criminal justice
- Tax administration, licensing, and other government services
- Manufacturing automation

The consequences of defects are well beyond mere irritation: people's health, safety, and welfare are at risk.

27.9.1 TWA Flight 599

The safest way to travel is by airplane, but it wasn't always that way. Many of the laws, regulations, and procedures that make air transport so safe today can be traced back to a single event: the crash of TWA Flight 599 on March 31, 1931. That crash killed Knute Rockne, coach of the then top ranked Notre Dame college football team, along with seven of the team's star players[3]:

> "The national outcry over the air disaster that killed Rockne (and the 7 others) triggered sweeping changes to airliner design, manufacturing, operation, inspection, maintenance, regulation and crash-investigation— igniting a safety revolution that ultimately transformed airline travel worldwide, from the most dangerous form of travel to the safest form of travel."

Chapter 1 cited a broad set of major software failures—all of which were rooted in mainstream software development and maintenance practices. But as serious as those were, they were mere brushes with disaster. Far worst is yet to come.

A software equivalent, in terms of public outcry, of TWA 599 is avoidable. However, if nothing changes in how mainstream software is developed, it is inevitable. Are you willing to wait for the software equivalent of TWA 599? I'm not. We *already* know how to make safe and reliable software. And the very things that make software safe and reliable also make it easier and cheaper to build and maintain. You don't have to spend more time and money to get better software; building software better *saves* time and money.

Either we sit back and wait for a major software disaster big enough to cause public outcry like TWA 599, or we act now to avoid it. Either way, we can't keep developing increasingly critical software the way we always have and expect the long-term results will be any different.

---

3 From http://en.wikipedia.org/wiki/Knute_Rockne.

27.9.2 The Ultimate Goal of Model-Based Software Engineering

The ultimate goal of model-based software engineering is to:

> *"... change the nature of programming from a private, puzzle solving activity to a public, mathematics based activity of translating specifications into programs ... that can be expected to both run and do the right thing with little or no debugging."*

This book not only shows that software *can* be developed and maintained under an engineering discipline; it shows precisely how to make that happen.

> *"We can engineer high quality software quickly and easily"*

It is *well within our industry's grasp to build high quality software, quickly and cheaply—much quicker and cheaper than we have been doing it, to be sure. This book shows how.*

> *"This is how to engineer software"*

Part VI

Appendices

Part VI provides additional resources:

- *Documentation Principles*—Guiding principles that can, and should, be used for technical documentation, software documentation in particular.
- *WebBooks 2.0 Background*—Example Background document for the Web-Books 2.0 project, the main case study in this book.
- *WebBooks 2.0 Domains*—Top-level logical (i.e., conceptual) overview of WebBooks 2.0.
- *Semantic Model for Order fulfillment*—Semantic model for the Order Fulfillment domain in WebBooks 2.0.
- *(Pro Forma) Order fulfillment Design*—Illustrates the structure and content of an Interface Specification and Design Specification for Order fulfillment.
- *Semantic Model for Payment*—Semantic model for the Payment domain in WebBooks 2.0.
- *(Pro Forma) Payment Design*—Illustrates the structure and content of an Interface Specification and Design Specification for Payment.
- *Semantic Model for Scalability*—Semantic model for the Scalability domain in WebBooks 2.0.
- *(Pro Forma) Scalability Design*—llustrates the structure and content of an Interface Specification and Design Specification for Scalability.
- *Semantic model for High availability*—Semantic model for the High availability domain in WebBooks 2.0.
- *(Pro Forma) High Availability Design*—Illustrates the structure and content of an Interface Specification and Design Specification for High availability.

How to Engineer Software: A Model-Based Approach, First Edition. Steve Tockey.
© 2019 the IEEE Computer Society, Inc. Published 2019 by John Wiley & Sons, Inc.

- *Semantics of Semantic Modeling*—Precisely defines how to interpret a semantic model.
- *Sample Production Rules*—Production rules for an open model compiler that translate a semantic model and PIM overlay into executable Java.
- *Software Structural Complexity Metrics*—A discussion of measuring accidental complexity in design and code.

Appendix A

Documentation Principles

This appendix presents a set of guiding principles that can—and should—be used for technical documentation, software documentation in particular.

A.1 No Write-Only Documentation

Only invest in time and effort in writing things down when someone will actually read them. Look for at least one clear reader with an identifiable need. Take time to understand the reader's need: do an "audience analysis." What does the reader(s) already know before reading this document? What do they need to know after reading it? What decisions will they make and/or what actions will they take based on having read it? Documentation should be aimed at filling that knowledge gap, both in content and in presentation. Make it easy as possible for the reader to get what they need out of the documentation.

A.2 Read-Time Convenience Is Far More Important Than Write-Time Convenience

Given that no document should ever be read-only, documents should be read many more times than they are written. It's much more important for documents to be reader-friendly than writer-friendly. As an author, don't take shortcuts that make documents easier to write if they also make it harder to read.

A.3 Document for an Average 10–15-Year Service Life

Economic arguments are very sensitive to time frame.[1] Decisions that only consider near-term time frames (e.g., to the end of a project) can be very different than those considering far-term (e.g., to the end of product life).

---

1 See any engineering economy textbook such as [Tockey05].

How to Engineer Software: A Model-Based Approach, First Edition. Steve Tockey.
© 2019 the IEEE Computer Society, Inc. Published 2019 by John Wiley & Sons, Inc.

Most anti-documentation people are only considering documentation for the purpose of building software. This is incorrect, the primary consideration should be documenting for maintainability. The average software system lives for 10–15 years between initial release and final retirement. Over that time it averages about nine generations of maintenance developers. Focus on documentation that supports long-term maintainability, not initial construction.

To be sure, most mainstream software documentation is worthless. But that's not the fault of documentation per se; it's the fault of how that documentation is approached and produced. Chapter 1 explains how natural language requirements documents are a waste of time. Also, design documentation needs to focus more on *why* the code looks the way it does than on *how* it looks. Refocusing documentation on value-added content, and on effective ways of communicating, makes documentation useful.

A.4 One Fact, One Place

Strive to write any given fact, a piece of information, only once. Avoid writing the same fact in more than place if possible. Write it only in the most appropriate place and reference it from the others. Then, if that one fact needs to change, as often happens, you only have to make the change in the one place you wrote it down. Otherwise, you need to remember all the different places you wrote it down and be sure those are updated too. If you did write it in multiple places and forget to change one of them, you would have contradicting documentation.

A.5 Cohesion and Coupling Apply to Documentation, Too

Chapter 3 presented fundamental principles of software, in particular cohesion and coupling. Cohesion means keeping things that belong together near to each other. Coupling means keeping things that are separable as far apart as possible. These principles also apply to documentation. Any document should be highly cohesive: it should fill one single purpose. Documents should also be loosely coupled with all other documents, so a change in one shouldn't require changes to ripple through others as a result.

A.6 Content and Packaging of Documentation Can Be Different

The content of a document can be quite different from the packaging of information. Two or more "logical" documents may be consciously and deliberately packaged into the same physical ".doc" file. Someone could also choose to spread the content of a single logical document over more than one physical. doc file (e.g., there may be too many pages to put in one .doc file). One example is the content of a semantic model. There are four major pieces: use case diagram, class model, interaction diagrams, and state models. All four pieces could be packaged into a single .doc file, or they could be packaged over four or more separate .doc files.

Part of packaging documentation has to do with content approval, configuration management, and change control. Content that is subject to the same approval, configuration, and change control is probably best packaged in the same physical document so that it can be approved, configuration managed, and change controlled all at the same time.

A.7 Summary

This appendix presented a small set of guiding principles for technical documentation, software documentation in particular. While many mainstream projects tend to be horrible at documentation and want to de-emphasize it or ignore it altogether, it is not the fault of documentation per se. It is the fault of how that documentation is being produced and maintained. By applying the principles in this appendix, the value of documentation is significantly improved.

Appendix B

WebBooks 2.0 Background

This appendix shows an example of a Background document for the Web-Books 2.0 project as identified in Figure 1.3. In some organizations, this would be called a Product Requirements Document (PRD), Marketing Requirements Document (MRD), Product Vision (PV), Scope Statement, or Overview. This provides a high-level overview of what is supposed to build and maintained in software. The development team does not normally produce this; external stakeholders would usually provide it to the team.

B.1 Project Justification and Goals

WebBooks, Inc. is a mythical World Wide Web-based bookseller along the lines of Amazon.com™ (http://www.amazon.com). WebBooks has been successful, but is now confronted with growth problems brought on by that success:

- Aging, obsolete hardware
- Limited software functionality with growing technical debt
- Continuous business growth but limited software and hardware scalability
- Increased focus on security

Economic analysis over a 15-year planning horizon shows the best alternative is to completely replace the existing hardware and software. The IT operations department will manage hardware replacement; this project is to develop new software in support of the following goals:

- *More scalable*—Support eventual worldwide expansion.
- *More secure*—Address this growing concern in ecommerce.
- *More maintainable*—Establish a foundation for the planned 15-year software lifetime.
- *More available*—Customers are demanding fewer, and shorter, outages.

How to Engineer Software: A Model-Based Approach, First Edition. Steve Tockey.
© 2019 the IEEE Computer Society, Inc. Published 2019 by John Wiley & Sons, Inc.

The focus of the 2.0 project will be on basic architecture and representative functionality to serve as an operational proof of concept. Additional functionality and enhanced usability will be the focus in the 2.1 project.

B.2   High-Level Scope

Customers will use a Web browser to peruse a catalog of available books and place orders. Customers should be able to search the catalog by title, author, and subject. These need to be glitzy Web pages with lots of bells and whistles to make the customer want to buy. The development team will be put in contact with a consulting firm that has ideas on how these Web pages should look. The system should use the shopping cart metaphor: add to cart, remove from cart, proceed to checkout, etc.

Customers need to be able to pay using any combination of the following:

- *Credit/debit card*—With optional remembering for later shortcut.
- *Check*—They mail the check; we hold the order until it's been cashed.
- *Gift card*.
- *Customer loyalty program points*—For example, selected airlines, hotel chains, etc.

When a customer places an order for a set of books, the system needs to record that order. The order information will consist of the date the order was opened, a shipping address, and the quantity of each title ordered. The order will be considered packable when the stock on hand for each title is greater than the quantity ordered. Of course, the order can't be packed until there is sufficient stock on hand (no partial orders in this version, which will be addressed in v2.1).

Customers need to be able to check the status of their orders as well as cancel orders (as long as that order has not been packed, in which case cancellation must be ignored). If an order is cancelled before being packed, payment must be refunded. All payment data needs to be retained for two years after the last financial activity on the order. After two years, payment information can be purged.

WebBooks wants to retain order data, even if completed or cancelled, to profile each customer's buying habits and support various long-term sales trend analyses.

WebBooks warehouse workers will interact with the system using dedicated terminals. Their primary job is to find orders to be packed and shipped and to tell the system that some customer's order has been packed and is on the loading dock ready to ship. When a warehouse person marks an order as packed and ready for shipment, the stock on hand for each title ordered needs to be reduced by the quantity in that order. If stock on hand falls below a preset reorder level for that title, a replenish order needs to be placed with the publisher of that book. WebBooks will specify a reorder quantity for each book, that's the amount to order from the publisher.

This next part is a bit complicated. The system needs to hold replenish orders for 24 hours, anticipating that other books may need to be ordered from the same publisher. If more copies of a book in that replenish order are packed during that period, we need to add an equal amount to the quantity ordered from the publisher. At the end of the 24 hour period, the replenish order is emailed to the publisher using an industry standard EDI[1] format (to be provided to the development team later). The publisher's email address needs to be kept in the system.

Warehouse workers will use the same graphical user interface (GUI) to tell the system when a batch of orders has been picked up by a shipper. Warehouse workers will also use the dedicated terminals to tell the system when a replenish order was received from a publisher. When this happens, the system needs to increase the stock on hand for each title by the amount ordered (no partial replenish orders in this version, either, that's also v2.1 functionality).

WebBooks managers will use the system, through dedicated terminals on their desks, to maintain the catalog (i.e., manage the list of books that are offered for sale). They will also need to maintain the list of publishers. The manager's most important use of the system is to view various monthly inventory and sales/profit reports. Managers are already used to the format of existing reports and we will need to use this same format. Samples will be provided once the project is under way.

Warehouse workers will need their GUI to be as absolutely simple as possible. Likewise, an easy-to-use interface for the managers is a definite requirement.

WebBooks 2.0 needs stronger security than the existing system; an alternative being considered is two-factor authentication (user enters username and password; we send an access code by email or TXT/SMS). Final details will be provided later.

This new system needs to be a lot more scalable than the existing system. We could easily end up with multiple data centers serving millions of customers around the world. Availability also needs to be improved. The desired direction seems to be to provide hot backup computers with automatic fail-over rather than physically swapping out broken hardware as is done now.

B.3 Minimum Conditions of Acceptance

Should explicit Minimum conditions of acceptance documentation be needed, it could go here. This would list critical software requirements. On some projects, this may be considered a contractual (i.e., legal) document and can serve as the basis for acceptance testing and requirements traceability, as appropriate.

---

1 Electronic Data Interchange.

Appendix C

WebBooks 2.0 Domains

This appendix provides a top-level logical (i.e., conceptual) overview of WebBooks 2.0.

C.1 Domain Diagram

Figure C.1 shows the domains—and their interrelationships—in this system.

C.2 Order fulfillment

This domain is in charge of the catalog, inventory, customer ordering, shipping, and receiving. Concepts in this domain include[1]:

- Customer
- Add to cart
- Proceed to checkout
- Order
- Packability
- Packing
- Shipping
- Stock on hand
- Replenish

The semantic model of Order fulfillment is in Appendix D.

---

1 Each of these domain descriptions can be thought of as filling the role of "Background" as shown in Figure 1.3. Minimum conditions of acceptance for each domain could be listed here, as appropriate.

How to Engineer Software: A Model-Based Approach, First Edition. Steve Tockey.
© 2019 the IEEE Computer Society, Inc. Published 2019 by John Wiley & Sons, Inc.

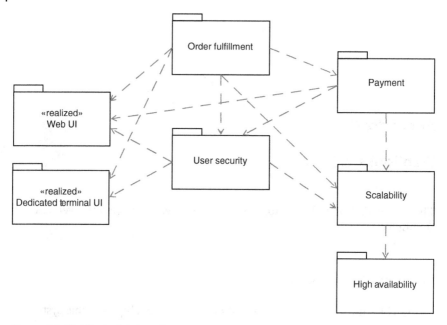

Figure C.1 WebBooks 2.0 domains.

C.3 Payment

This domain manages all of the different forms of customer payment, including combinations of payment methods at the same time. Concepts in this domain include:

- Payment method
- Financial institution
- Credit/debit card
- Gift certificate
- Loyalty points
- Payment authorized
- Payment declined
- Refunds

The semantic model of Payment is in Appendix F.

C.4 User Security

This domain handles authorization of the different kinds of users to access different kinds of functionality. Concepts in this domain include:

- User
- Role
- Authorization
- Password
- Protected service

The semantic model of User security is not included in this book. If it were, it would be referenced here.

C.5   Scalability

This domain allows the system to be scaled to very large numbers of users. Concepts in this domain include:

- Data center
- Client app
- Server app
- Load balancing

The semantic model of Scalability is in Appendix H.

C.6   High availability

This domain makes sure that users can access system functionality as often as possible. Specifically, unavailability due to hardware failures needs to be minimized. The focus is on "availability," not "reliability." Reliability means never losing data. With availability, if something goes down, it needs to get back on the air as quickly as possible, even if it means losing some data in the process.[2] Of course it would be best to lose as little data as possible, but the focus is on being on the air (available), not being 100% correct (reliable). Concepts in this domain include:

- N+M redundancy
- Heartbeat
- Checkpoint
- Failover

The semantic model of High availability is in Appendix J.

---

2 See http://www.infoq.com/presentations/Netflix-Architecture for an interesting view of how NetFlix addresses this.

C.7 «realized» Web UI

This domain provides a customer interface using Web technology. This domain is expected to use a preexisting service like jQueryUI,[3] Kendo UI,[4] JQWidgets,[5] etc. Concepts in this domain include:

- Customer login page
- Search catalog page
- Checkout page
- Order status page

Note that to be more technically correct, the web pages above are actually in View-controller region of Order fulfillment, Payment, and User security. The Web UI domain is in terms of pages, buttons, text boxes, scrolling lists, etc. No semantic model is provided—that should be the responsibility of the selected vendor.

C.8 «realized» Dedicated Terminal UI

This domain provides the ability to interface to a user through a private terminal (e.g., on the user's desk or suitably large tablet). This domain is expected to use a preexisting service like Java Swing and/or Crystal Reports. Concepts in this domain include:

- Manager login screen
- Replenish order status screen
- Sales report
- Profit report
- Catalog management screens

Again, the above list is View-controller region of Order fulfillment and User security. This domain is also in terms of buttons, text boxes, scrolling lists, etc. No semantic model is provided—that should be the responsibility of the selected vendor.

---

3 See: http://jqueryui.com/.
4 See: https://www.telerik.com/kendo-ui.
5 See: https://www.jqwidgets.com/.

Appendix D

Semantic Model for Order fulfillment

This appendix is an example of a semantic model—a specification of policies to enforce and processes to carry out—for the Order fulfillment domain in WebBooks 2.0.

D.1 Use Case Diagram

Use cases identify scope (processes to carry out) at the coarsest level. Actors identify context. Figure D.1 shows actors and use cases in Order fulfillment. Each actor and use case is described in detail in later sections.

D.2 Class Diagram

The class model specifies policies to be enforced. Figure D.2 shows classes, attributes, associations, and generalizations in Order fulfillment. Each class is defined in detail in the class dictionary. To the extent necessary, associations are defined in the association dictionary.

D.3 Interaction Diagrams

Interaction diagrams describe process at an intermediate level. This section provides interaction (in this case sequence) diagrams for selected use cases. Sequence diagrams were chosen over communication diagrams because they are more natural and intuitive to most readers.

How to Engineer Software: A Model-Based Approach, First Edition. Steve Tockey.
© 2019 the IEEE Computer Society, Inc. Published 2019 by John Wiley & Sons, Inc.

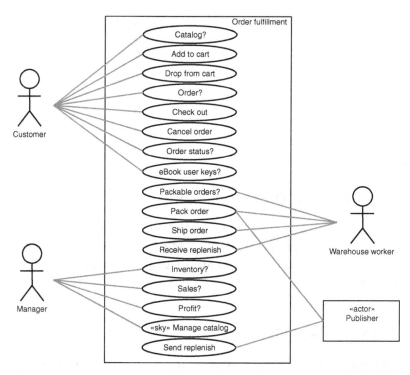

Figure D.1 Use case diagram for Order fulfillment.

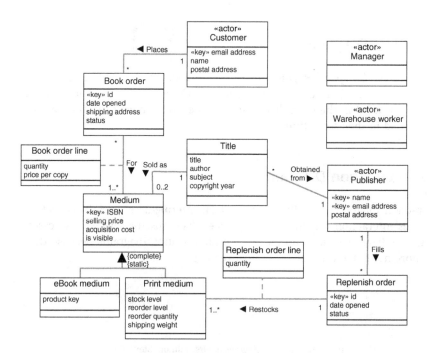

Figure D.2 Class diagram for Order fulfillment.

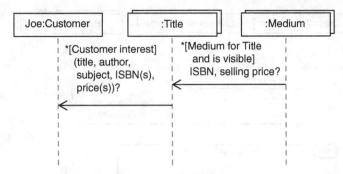

Figure D.3 Sequence diagram for Catalog? use case.

D.3.1 Catalog?

Figure D.3 shows the sequence diagram for the Catalog? use case. This use case provides a Customer with the ability to browse the catalog: visibility into Titles, Media, and their availability for ordering.

D.3.2 Add to Cart

Figure D.4 shows the sequence diagram for the Add to cart use case. In this use case, the Customer is adding one to many copies of the same Medium to their shopping cart. If no open Book order exists for this Customer, a new Book order is created.

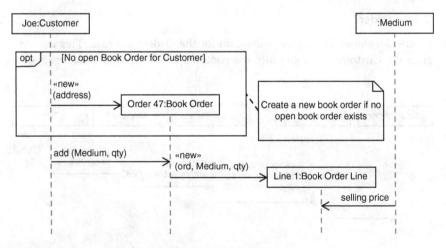

Figure D.4 Sequence diagram for Add to cart use case.

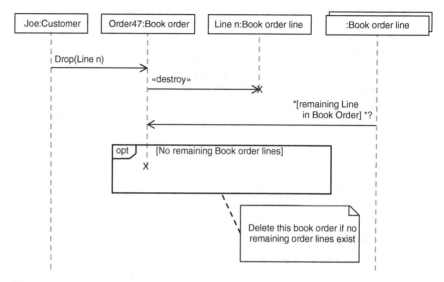

Figure D.5 Sequence diagram for Drop from cart use case.

D.3.3 Drop from Cart

Figure D.5 shows the sequence diagram for the Drop from cart use case. The Customer is removing a previously added Medium from their shopping cart. If there are no remaining Book order lines in this Book order, this Book order is also deleted.

D.3.4 Order?

Figure D.6 shows the sequence diagram for the Order? use case. This use case gives the Customer visibility into the contents of one of their Book orders.

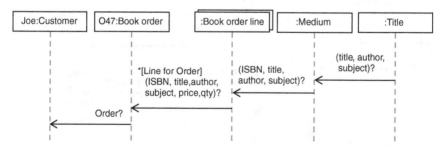

Figure D.6 Sequence diagram for Order? use case.

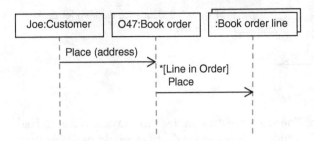

Figure D.7 Sequence diagram for Check out use case.

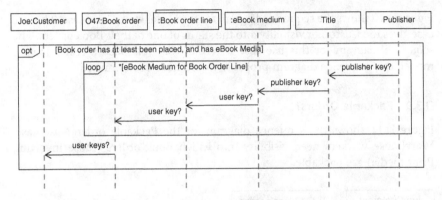

Figure D.8 Sequence diagram for eBook user keys? use case.

D.3.5 Check Out

Figure D.7 shows the sequence diagram for the Check out use case. The Customer has decided to proceed to checkout (i.e., place their Book order).

D.3.6 eBook User Keys?

Figure D.8 shows the sequence diagram for the eBook user keys? use case. The Customer is given user keys for any eBooks they have in a placed, packed, shipped, or completed Book order.

D.3.7 Cancel Order

Figure D.9 shows the sequence diagram for the Cancel order use case. The Customer has changed their mind about a Book order after placing it and wants to cancel. The Book order will only be cancelled if it contains Print media and has

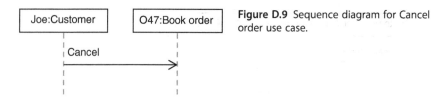

Figure D.9 Sequence diagram for Cancel order use case.

not already been packed. The sequence diagram for this use case is trivial. Had this been a real semantic model, this sequence diagram would probably have been omitted.

D.3.8 Order Status?

Figure D.10 shows the sequence diagram for the Order status? use case. This use case gives the Customer visibility into the status of one of their Book orders. The sequence diagram for this use case is trivial. Had this been a real semantic model, this sequence diagram probably would have been omitted.

D.3.9 Packable Orders?

Figure D.11 shows the sequence diagram for the Packable orders? use case. Warehouse workers need visibility into which Book orders (those involving Print media) are packable.

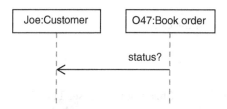

Figure D.10 Sequence diagram for Order status? use case.

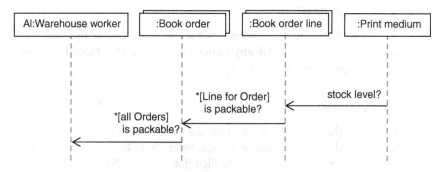

Figure D.11 Sequence diagram for Packable orders? use case.

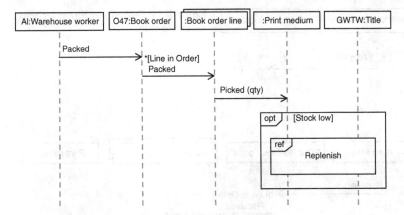

Figure D.12 Sequence diagram for Pack order use case.

D.3.10 Pack Order

Figure D.12 shows the sequence diagram for the Pack order use case. A Book order involving Print media has been packed by a Warehouse worker; stock needs to be decreased by the number of copies packed. This is the first part of the use case; the extending Replenish use case is shown below. If stock goes (or already is) low on one or more Print media, replenishment will be requested.

D.3.11 Replenish

Figure D.13 shows the sequence diagram for the Replenish extending use case. A Book order involving Print media got packed and stock went (or already was)

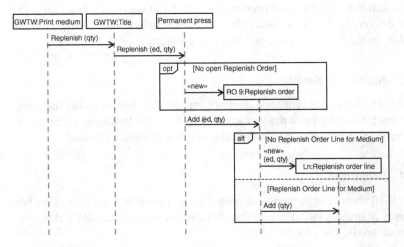

Figure D.13 Sequence diagram for Replenish extending use case.

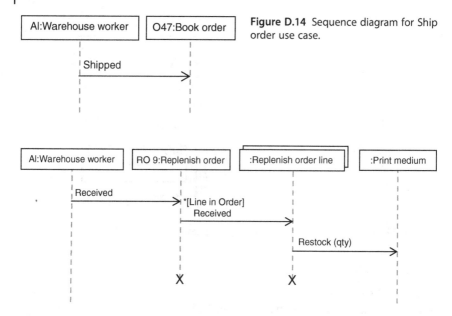

Figure D.14 Sequence diagram for Ship order use case.

Figure D.15 Sequence diagram for Receive replenish use case.

low on one or more Print media, triggering the need to replenish stock. This is the second part of the sequence diagram; the earlier Pack order part was shown above.

D.3.12 Ship Order

Figure D.14 shows the sequence diagram for the Ship order use case. A Book order—with Print media—was previously packed and has been taken by a shipper for delivery to the Customer. This is another simple sequence diagram that probably would have been omitted in a real semantic model.

D.3.13 Receive Replenish

Figure D.15 shows the sequence diagram for the Receive replenish use case. A Replenish order for Print media was received from the Publisher; Print media stock needs to be increased to reflect the number of copies received.

D.3.14 Inventory?

Figure D.16 shows the sequence diagram for the Inventory? use case. This use case gives Managers visibility into the status of inventory: available Titles, current stock levels, and reorder levels.

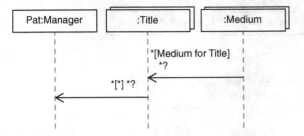

Figure D.16 Sequence diagram for Inventory? use case.

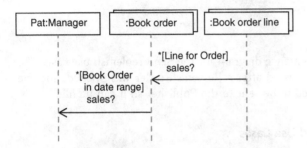

Figure D.17 Sequence diagram for Sales? use case.

D.3.15 Sales?

Figure D.17 shows the sequence diagram for the Sales? use case. This use case gives Managers visibility into sales results over some period of time.

D.3.16 Profit?

Figure D.18 shows the sequence diagram for the Profit? use case. This use case gives Managers visibility into profit results over some period of time.

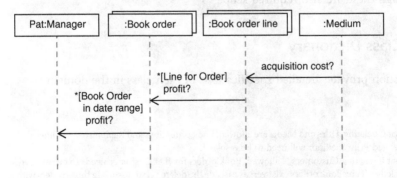

Figure D.18 Sequence diagram for Profit? use case.

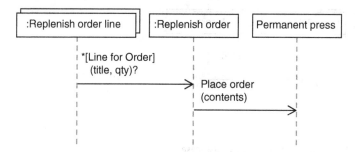

Figure D.19 Sequence diagram for Send replenish use case.

D.3.17   Send Replenish

Figure D.19 shows the sequence diagram for the Send replenish use case. The wait time (24 hours) has passed after a Replenish order was opened, and the contents of the order need to be sent to the Publisher so it can be filled.

D.3.18   Un-diagrammed Use Cases

Some use cases may not have been diagrammed for various reasons, typically because their diagrams would be trivial. This section lists sea level use cases that have not been diagrammed to be sure complete scope of this domain is explicitly defined:

- Under the Manage catalog sky level use case, transactions for adding, modifying, and potentially deleting[1] Title and Medium have not been diagrammed. A Manager changing the visibility of media is also not diagrammed because it is also trivial.
- Custodial use cases for creating, deleting,[2] and modifying Customers, Managers, Warehouse Workers, and Publishers have not been diagrammed although these are also required scope.

D.4   Class Dictionary

This section provides detailed specifications of each class in the domain.

---

1 Note that if deleting Titles and Media are allowed, Book order lines and Replenish order lines that refer to deleted Print medium will need to be resolved.

2 Note that if deleting Customers is allowed, Book orders for that Customer needs to be resolved: prevent deletion if any Book orders exist versus cascade the delete versus associate those orders with some other Customer.

D.4.1   Customer

This class is an actor that represents persons or businesses that may place Book orders with WebBooks. That person or business doesn't need to have placed any Book orders to be considered a Customer; they only need to be on WebBooks' marketing list. This class has no state diagram because it is an actor and is mostly external to Order fulfillment.

D.4.1.1   Attribute Descriptions

«key» email address: The address that will be used for email communication between this customer and WebBooks. Customers may have more than one valid email address, but they must select only one of them for primary communication with WebBooks.

Range: [any valid email address according to relevant Internet Engineering Task Force (IETF)[3] specifications]

name: The name of the customer—how they would like to be referred to—such as "John Smith" or "ABC Corp."
Range: [unconstrained]

postal address: The primary postal mailing address of the customer. A customer may have more than one valid postal address but must choose only one to be their contact address. This is likely the customer's billing address.

Range: [any mailing address acceptable to the US Post Office or Canada Post]

D.4.1.2   State and Event Descriptions
None

D.4.1.3   Action Specifications
None

D.4.1.4   Source of
«new» (address) for Book order
Add (^Medium, qty) for Book order via Places
Drop (^Line) for Book order via Places
Place for Book order via Places
Cancel for Book order via Places

---

3 Internet Engineering Task Force.

D.4.1.5 Destination of

Catalog? (selection criteria) from Title:

0[title, author, subject, copyright date, 1[Medium type, ISBN, selling price]∗]∗
status from Book order via Places

contents from Book order via Places:

(date opened, status, shipping address, 1[title, author, subject, quantity, price per copy]∗)

user keys from Book order via Places:

0[user key]∗

D.4.2 Book Order

A Book order represents a Customer's request for a specified set (and quantity) of books. The state diagram is shown in Figure D.20.

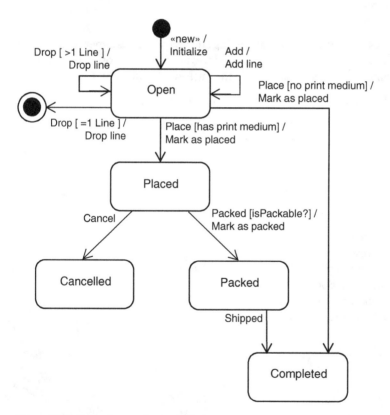

Figure D.20 State diagram for Book Order.

D.4.2.1   Attribute Descriptions

«key» id: The identifier (key) of the Book order. This is used outside Order fulfillment to correlate Book orders with external business processes.
   Range: [refer to Corporate Policy CP123a, "Customer Order Identification"]

date opened: the date this Book order was created, that is, the first Book order line was added.
   Range: [calendar date no earlier than January 1,1998, and no later than today, to the nearest whole day]

shipping address: The postal address the Customer is requesting any Print media in the Book order be shipped to.
   Range: [any mailing address acceptable to the US Post Office or Canada Post]

state: Shows the business processing status of this Book order.
   Range: [enumeration of the states in the state model]

/is packable?: Shows if this Book order is currently packable or not.
   Derivation: true only when .state == placed and
      isPackable? == true for each Line in this order (via For)

/sales?: Shows the total dollar sales amount of this Book order.
   Derivation: if .state == completed
      then sum of sales? for each Line (via For)
      otherwise $0.00

/profit?: Shows the amount of profit generated by this Book order.
   Derivation: if .state == completed
      then sum of profit? for each Line (via For)
      otherwise $0.00

/user keys?: provides user keys for eBook media in this Book order.
   Derivation: if .state is not open or cancelled
      then set of user key? from all Lines in this Order (via For)
      otherwise empty set

D.4.2.2   State and Event Descriptions
None

D.4.2.3   Action Specifications
initialize (address):
   requires
      address is consistent with the range of .shipping address
   guarantees

one new Book order exists with:
.id properly assigned
.date opened == today
.shipping address == address

add line (^Medium, qty):
requires
qty is consistent with the range of Book order line.quantity
guarantees
one new Book order line (this Book order, ^Medium, qty) has been created

drop line (^Book order line):
requires
Book order line exists in this Book order via For
guarantees
referenced Book order line has been deleted via For

mark as placed (address):
requires
address is consistent with the range of .shipping address
guarantees
.shipping address == address
place has been signaled for each line in this order via For

mark as packed ():
requires
none
guarantees
packed has been signaled for each line in this order via For

D.4.3   Book Order Line

A Book order line is the request, within a Book order, for a specified number of copies of a selected Medium. This may also be referred to as "Book Order Details" in some organizations. The state diagram is shown in Figure D.21.

D.4.3.1   Attribute Descriptions

quantity: The number of copies of the selected Medium being requested.
Range: [1 .. unconstrained, to the whole number]

price per copy: The price of the selected Medium when it was added to this Book order. This is how much the customer will be/was charged when the Book order is/was paid for. This allows WebBooks to change the price of Media yet still be able to correctly calculate order-level profit. Sometimes, Media may be offered for free.
Range: [$0.00 .. unconstrained in US Dollars, to the whole cent]

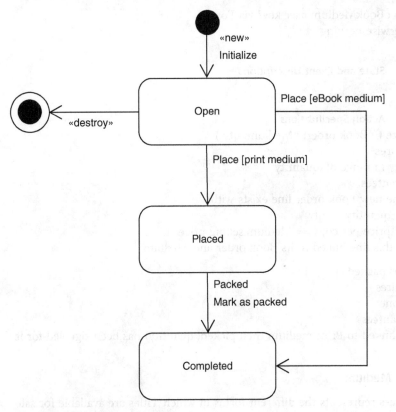

Figure D.21 State diagram for Book order line.

state: Shows the processing status of this Book order line.
  Range: [enumeration of the states in the state model]

/is packable?: Shows if this Book order line is currently packable or not.
  Derivation: Always true if this Book order line refers to eBook medium—
    otherwise

if this Book order line refers to Print medium, true only when .quantity <= Print
medium.stock level.

/sales?: Shows the dollar amount of this Book order line.
  Derivation: .quantity * .price per copy

/profit?: Shows the amount of profit generated by this Book order line.
  Derivation: .quantity * (.price per copy – Medium.acquisition cost) via For

/user key?: Shows the user key a Customer needs to unlock an eBook on their
  reader.
  Derivation: When linked to eBook medium

then eBookMedium.user key? via For
otherwise nothing

D.4.3.2 State and Event Descriptions
None

D.4.3.3 Action Specifications
initialize (^Book order, ^Medium, qty):
    requires
        qty in range of .quantity
    guarantees
        one new Book order line exists with:
            .quantity == qty
            .price per copy == Medium.selling price
            this line linked to its Book order and Medium

mark as packed ():
    requires
        none
    guarantees
        if linked to Print medium then picked(.quantity) has been signaled for it

D.4.4 Medium

This class represents the different forms in which Titles are available for sale. There are currently two kinds of Medium: Print medium and eBook medium, which are detailed below. Audio books may be added at a later date. This class has no state diagram because it is a superclass and the state models are unique to the subclasses.

D.4.4.1 Attribute Descriptions
«key» ISBN: The International Standard Book Number assigned by the Publisher to this Medium. ISBNs are unique by Medium; the eBook and Print medium versions of the same Title will have different ISBNs. More information on ISBNs can be found at http://en.wikipedia.org/wiki/International_Standard_Book_Number.
    Range: [either ISBN-10 or ISBN-13 format as defined by www.isbn-international.org]

selling price: The current per-copy price that WebBooks is offering this Medium to customers. In some cases, WebBooks may offer certain Media for free.
    Range: [$0.00 .. unconstrained in US Dollars, to the nearest whole cent]

acquisition cost: The price that WebBooks pays the Publisher for each copy of this Medium so that profit can be calculated. In some cases, publishers may give copies to WebBooks at no cost.
Range: [$0.00 .. unconstrained in US Dollars, to the nearest whole cent]

is visible: Media may be set to visible or invisible. When visible, this Medium will appear to Customers in the catalog (e.g., when they do searches). When not visible, this Medium won't appear to Customers although it is still known to the business (Managers can still see it). This allows WebBooks to pre-stage Media before going live as well as takes them down when necessary (without deleting them).
Range: [true | false]

state: Shows the processing status of this Medium.
Range: [enumeration of the states in the state model]

D.4.4.2   State and Event Descriptions
None

D.4.4.3   Action Specifications
None

D.4.5   eBook Medium

This class represents a specific Title being offered for sale to Customers in eBook (i.e., "e-reader") format. The state diagram is shown in Figure D.22.

D.4.5.1   Attribute Descriptions
product key: Part of Digital Rights Management (DRM), which represents the eBook medium-specific encryption key for this Title. This is mashed together with a publisher key and given to the Customer so they can unlock and access each legal copy of the Title on the device they bought it for.
Range: [see Engineering Memo PQR789]

/user key?: Shows the user key a Customer needs to unlock an eBook on their reader.
Derivation: see Engineering Memo PQR789, uses .product key and Title.publisher key via Sold as.

Figure D.22 State diagram for eBook medium.

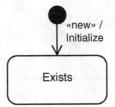

D.4.5.2 State and Event Descriptions

None

D.4.5.3 Action Specifications

initialize (^Title, ISBN, price, cost, media key):
  requires
    ISBN is consistent with the range of Medium.ISBN
    price is consistent with the range of Medium.selling price
    cost is consistent with the range of Medium.acquisition cost
    media key is consistent with the range of .product key
  guarantees
    one new eBook medium exists with:
     .ISBN == ISBN
     .selling price == price
     .acquisition cost == cost
     .is visible == false
     .product key == media key
     this Medium linked to its Title via Sold as

D.4.6 Print Medium

This class represents a specific Title being offered for sale to Customers in print (aka "physical book," or paper) format. The state diagram is shown in Figure D.23.

D.4.6.1 Attribute Descriptions

stock level: The number of physical copies of the book in WebBooks inventory, available to be packed and shipped to Customers.
  Range: [0 .. unconstrained, to the nearest whole number]

reorder level: The inventory level below which more copies need to be ordered from the Publisher.
  Range: [1 .. unconstrained, to the nearest whole number]

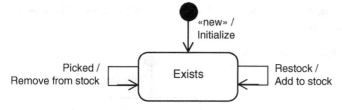

Figure D.23 State diagram for Print medium.

reorder quantity: When more inventory is needed from the Publisher, this is the number of copies to request.
Range: [1 .. unconstrained, to the nearest whole number]

shipping weight: The shipping weight of one copy of this Print medium for calculating shipping costs.
Range: [1 .. unconstrained grams, to the nearest whole gram]

D.4.6.2 State and Event Descriptions
None

D.4.6.3 Action Specifications
initialize (^Title, ISBN, price, cost, stock qty, trigger level, reorder qty, weight):
  requires
    ISBN is consistent with the range of Medium.ISBN
    price is consistent with the range of Medium.selling price
    cost is consistent with the range of Medium.acquisition cost
    stock qty is consistent with the range of .stock level
    trigger level is consistent with the range of .reorder level
    reorder qty is consistent with the range of .reorder quantity
    weight is consistent with the range of .shipping weight
  guarantees
    one new Print medium exists with:
      .ISBN == ISBN
      .selling price == price
      .acquisition cost == cost
      .is visible == false
      .stock level == stock qty
      .reorder level == trigger level
      .reorder quantity == reorder qty
      .shipping weight == weight
      this Medium linked to its Title via Sold as

remove from stock (qty):
  requires
    qty > 0
  guarantees
    post(.stock level) == pre(.stock level) – qty
    if pre(.stock level) was already below .reorder level
      then replenish (qty) has been signaled for Title via Sold as
      otherwise if post(.stock level) went below .reorder level
      then replenish (.reorder quantity) has been signaled for Title via Sold as

add to stock (qty):
  requires
    qty > 0
  guarantees
    post(.stock level) == pre(.stock level) + qty

D.4.7   Title

This class represents a specific book being available for sale to Customers, either in eBook or Print format, or both. Margaret Mitchell's classic novel "Gone With The Wind" is an example title. The novel is available in both eBook and Print media. Technically, each new edition of a Book is a different title, but WebBooks doesn't care about the relationship of one edition to another, so they will only offer new editions as different Titles that are offered for sale. The state diagram is shown in Figure D.24.

D.4.7.1   Attribute Descriptions

title: The title of the work, as assigned by the author.
  Range: [unconstrained]

author: The name of the recognized author(s) of the work. While technically there can be many authors on a single title and the same person can be an author on many different titles, for customer searches, a simple substring match is sufficient so this attribute is not strictly normalized.
  Range: [unconstrained]

subject: The subject matter(s) covered in the work. While technically there can be many subjects in a single title and the same subject can apply to many different titles, for customer searches, a simple substring match is sufficient so this attribute is not strictly normalized.
  Range: [unconstrained]

copyright year: The year the work was copyrighted. For works that have passed out of copyright or were never copyrighted, the value will be "public domain." Range: [either a whole year no earlier than 1780 and no later than this year, or public domain]

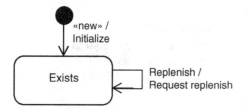

Figure D.24 State diagram for Title.

state: Shows the business processing status of this Title.
Range: [enumeration of the states in the state model]

D.4.7.2 State and Event Descriptions
None

D.4.7.3 Action Specifications
initialize (title, author, subject, year, ^Publisher):
  requires
    year is consistent with the range of .copyright year
  guarantees
    one new Title exists with:
      .title == title
      .author == author
      .subject == subject
      .copyright year == year
    this Title linked to its Publisher via Obtained from

request replenish (^Print medium, qty):
  requires
    none
  guarantees
    replenish(Print medium, qty) has been signaled for linked Publisher via
    Obtained from

D.4.8 Manager

This class is an actor representing WebBooks employees who have the authority
to maintain the catalog of for-sale books, establish and modify pricing, and view
financial summary data. This class has no state diagram because it is purely an
actor and is mostly external to the business.

D.4.8.1 Attribute Descriptions
None

D.4.8.2 State and Event Descriptions
None

D.4.8.3 Action Specifications
None

D.4.8.4 Source of
«new» for Title
Update for Title

Create for Medium
Update for Medium

D.4.8.5 Destination of

sum of Book order.sales? within given range of Book order.date opened
sum of Book order.profit? within given range of Book order.date opened
read inventory from Title:

> 0[title, author, subject, copyright date, 1[Medium type, ISBN, selling price]∗]∗
> satisfying given selection criteria

D.4.9 Warehouse Worker

This class is an actor representing WebBooks employees who have the responsibility to pack and ship Book orders involving Print media. Warehouse workers also handle the restocking of Replenish orders as they are received. This class has no state diagram because it is purely an actor and is mostly external to the business.

D.4.9.1 Attribute Descriptions
None

D.4.9.2 State and Event Descriptions
None

D.4.9.3 Action Specifications
None

D.4.9.4 Source of
Packed for Book order
Shipped for Book order
Received for Replenish order

D.4.9.5 Destination of
all references to Book order where isPackable? is true:

> 0[^Book order]∗

D.4.10 Publisher

This class is an actor that represents external companies who publish and distribute books that WebBooks sells. WebBooks obtains both physical copies of Print media and publisher keys for eBooks from the relevant Publisher. While actor classes generally don't have state models, this is a relatively rare exception in that it does have behavior relevant to WebBooks processes. That

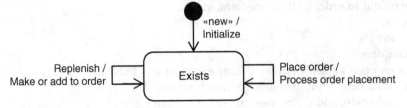

Figure D.25 State diagram for Publisher.

behavior is shown in the state diagram in Figure D.25, and the remainder of the behavior of publishers is outside the scope of Order fulfillment.

D.4.10.1 Attribute Descriptions

«key» name: The name of the Publisher—how they would like to be referred to—such as "Permanent Press" or "JKL Publishing House."
Range: [unconstrained]

«key» email address: The address that will be used for all (email) communication between this Publisher and WebBooks. Publishers may have more than one email address, but they must select only one of them for primary communication with WebBooks.
Range: [any valid email address according to relevant IETF specifications]

postal address: The primary postal mailing address of the publisher. A publisher may have more than one valid postal mailing address but must choose only one to be their primary contact mailing address.
Range: [any mailing address acceptable to the US Post Office and Canada Post]

state: Shows the business processing status of this Publisher.
Range: [enumeration of the states in the state model]

D.4.10.2 State and Event Descriptions
None

D.4.10.3 Action Specifications

initialize (name, email, address):
requires
email is consistent with the range of .email address
address is consistent with the range of .postal address
guarantees
one new Publisher exists with:
.name == name
.email == email
.postal address == address

make or add to order (^Print medium, qty):
  requires
    none
  guarantees
    if no open Replenish order already exists for this Publisher via Fills
      then new (Print medium, qty) has been signaled
      otherwise add (Print medium, qty) has been signaled
        for that open Replenish order via Fills

process order placement (Order id, collection of ISBNs & qty's):
  requires
    none
  guarantees
    Publisher is aware of the contents of the Replenish order via Fills
      (note: this is really external, it's shown for completeness in this model)

D.4.10.4   Source of
Publisher key for Title via Obtained from

D.4.10.5   Destination of
Place replenish order from Replenish order via Fills:

  1[id, date opened, 1[ISBN, qty]*]1

D.4.11   Replenish Order

Replenish order represents a request by WebBooks to a given Publisher to obtain more physical copies of a specified set of Print media. The state diagram is shown in Figure D.26.

D.4.11.1   Attribute Descriptions
«key» id: The primary identifier (key) of the Replenish order. This is used outside this domain to correlate this Replenish order with other external processes.
  Range: [refer to corporate policy CP123b]

date opened: The date which this Replenish order was originally created, that is, the first Replenish order line was put in.
  Range: [A calendar date no earlier than January 1, 1998, and no later than today, to the whole day]

state: Shows the business processing status of this Replenish order.
  Range: [an enumeration of the states in the state model]

Figure D.26 State diagram for Replenish order.

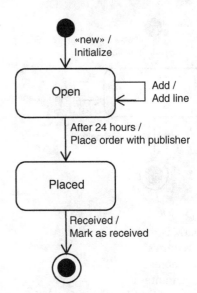

D.4.11.2 State and Event Descriptions
None

D.4.11.3 Action Specifications
initialize:
   requires
      none
   guarantees
      one new Replenish order exists with:
         .id properly assigned
         .date opened == today

add line (^Print medium, qty):
   requires
      none
   guarantees
      if a Replenish order line for Print medium (via Restocks) doesn't already exist
         then new (Print medium, qty) has been signaled for Replenish order line
         otherwise add (qty) has been signaled for that existing line

place order with Publisher ():1[id, date opened, 1[ISBN, qty]*]1
   requires
      none
   guarantees
      Publisher is aware of the contents of this Replenish order (and lines)
      via Fills

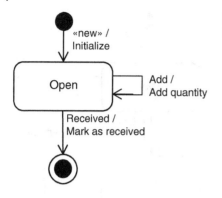

Figure D.27 State diagram for Replenish order line.

mark as received ():
  requires
    none
  guarantees
    received has been signaled for each Replenish order line via Restocks

D.4.12 Replenish Order Line

A Replenish order line is the request, within a specific Replenish order, for a specified number of copies of some specified Print medium. Some people would refer to this class as "Replenish Order Details." The state diagram is shown in Figure D.27.

D.4.12.1 Attribute Descriptions
quantity: The number of copies of the selected Print medium that are being requested.
  Range: [1 .. unconstrained, to the nearest whole number]

state: Shows the business processing status of this Replenish order line.
  Range: [enumeration of the states in the state model]

D.4.12.2 State and Event Descriptions
None

D.4.12.3 Action Specifications
initialize (^Replenish order, ^Print medium, qty)
  requires
    qty is consistent with range of .quantity
  guarantees

one new Replenish order line exists with:
  .quantity == qty
  this line linked to its Replenish order and Print medium

add quantity (qty):
  requires
    qty > 0
  guarantees
    post(.quantity) == pre(.quantity) + qty

mark as received ():
  requires
    none
  guarantees
    restock(.quantity) has been signaled for the linked Print medium

D.5 Association Dictionary

Where necessary and appropriate, this section provides detailed descriptions of associations. In this domain, no additional association descriptions are necessary because all associations are adequately specified in the class diagram.

D.6 Relevant Notes

If a Customer places a Book order that contains only eBook media, that Book order can't be cancelled after having been placed because delivery of user keys is immediate—there's no time window in which to cancel. If a Book order contains a mix of Print media and eBook media and gets cancelled, we have to presume there is some way to disable the user keys for the eBook media; otherwise the Customer will be given a refund for the entire order but still has access to eBooks.

  Possible extensions to this model include shipping partial Book orders, receiving partial Replenish orders, returning Book orders (possibly partially), Customer reviews and ratings, assigning packable Book orders to Warehouse workers, expanding to more than one warehouse, shipping books direct from third-party vendors, tracking shipments, selling more than just books, computing sales tax, computing shipping charges based on product weight, etc.

Appendix E

(Pro Forma) Order fulfillment Design

This appendix illustrates the structure and content of an interface specification and design specification for Order fulfillment.[1] These examples are far from complete, and real specifications would be much larger. Also, they would almost certainly be separate documents: at a minimum, the interface specification in one document and the design specification in another. For the remainder of this appendix, example content is shown in plain text, while *comments about structure and content are shown in italics.*

E.1 Interface Specification

This section illustrates the structure and content of an interface specification for Order fulfillment. A complete interface specification would be too large—this only communicates the basic structure and content. A real interface specification for Order fulfillment could easily be three separate documents by itself:

- *User guide for Customers*
- *User guide for Warehouse workers*
- *User guide for Managers*

Some content for the Customer's user interface (UI) is shown; interfaces for Warehouse worker and Manager are only outlined.

There is no need to describe the interface to Publishers. Publishers provide an API according to an industry standard EDI specification. Order fulfillment software needs to be designed and coded per that specification.

---

1 "Pro forma = Assumed, forecasted, or informal information presented in advance of the actual or formal information."

How to Engineer Software: A Model-Based Approach, First Edition. Steve Tockey.
© 2019 the IEEE Computer Society, Inc. Published 2019 by John Wiley & Sons, Inc.

E.1.1   User's Guide for Customer

This section illustrates a user's guide for Customers in WebBooks' Order fulfillment domain. This describes how a WebBooks Customer accesses Order fulfillment functionality.

E.1.1.1   Introduction
This section would provide an overview of the Customer's UI and address topics such as:

- *How to start and stop—Presumably by going to* https://www.webbooks.com *to start and logging out to stop.*
- *Seeing what options are available and selecting options—This would be in the form of buttons, text fields, etc. on Web pages.*
- *How to correct mistakes—For example, using the delete key in text fields and possibly hitting cancel buttons if available. Note that the user guide should be careful to address whether using a Web browser's built-in "back" button is acceptable or not.*
- *Using a help facility (if one exists).*

E.1.1.2   Dialog Map
Figure E.1 shows a dialog map for the Customer UI.

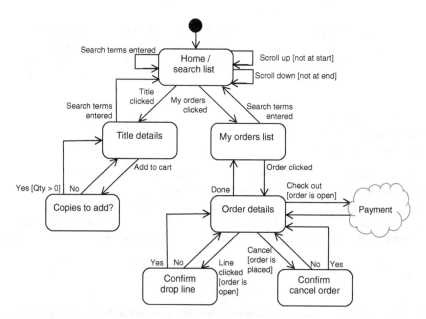

Figure E.1 Example dialog map for Customer user interface.

E.1.1.3 Use Cases

This section elaborates on each Customer use case as it is implemented in a Web-based UI. *The focus of this section should be on the customer's perspective and explain how to carry out each sea level use case (i.e., transaction). This is preferred over more typical user documentation that only shows a series of screen shots and then discusses each of the fields and buttons on each screen without providing any logical ordering to the descriptions.*

Each use case description would include some amount of narrative, but should also include (or refer to) hi- or low-fidelity representations of the Web pages.

E.1.1.3.1 Browsing the WebBooks Catalog

Explain and show examples of how a Customer would browse the catalog in terms of entering search criteria to retrieve a set of matches, clicking on a title in the list to get more detail on that title, etc.[2]

E.1.1.3.2 Add to Cart

Explain and show examples of how a Customer would click an "Add to cart" button when viewing title details, then specify a quantity, and either click "yes" to confirm or "no" to cancel.

E.1.1.3.3 Drop from Cart

Explain and show examples of how a Customer would navigate to the details of an open book order, select a line to drop, and then click a "Drop from cart" button. This should be confirmed or cancelled by a yes or no pop-up.

E.1.1.3.4 Order?

Explain and show examples of how a Customer would examine a book order (from, among possibly many orders for that customer).

E.1.1.3.5 Check Out

Explain and show examples of how a Customer would navigate to the details of an open book order, and then click a "Proceed to check out" button. This section would either link to or include a discussion of the Customer's UI in the Payment domain: adding, modifying, and dropping payment methods, etc. If payment is successful, and the customer's order includes any eBooks, access to the eBook user keys also needs to be explained.

E.1.1.3.6 Cancel Order

Explain and show examples of how a Customer would navigate to the details of a placed order and then click a "Cancel order" button. The Customer is then asked

---

2 This is use case Catalog? in the semantic model.

to confirm or not. This description should make it clear that only orders in the placed state can be cancelled.

E.1.1.3.7 Order Status?
Explain and show examples of how a Customer would navigate to the details of a book order and then see the current status of that order.

E.1.2   User's Guide for Warehouse Worker

This section outlines a user's guide for Warehouse workers in WebBooks' Order fulfillment domain.

E.1.2.1   Introduction
This section would provide an overview of the Warehouse worker's UI and address topics such as:

- *How to start and stop*
- *Seeing what options are available and selecting options*
- *How to correct mistakes*
- *Using a help facility (if one exists)*

E.1.2.2   Dialog Map
This section could show a dialog map for the Warehouse worker UI.

E.1.2.3   Use Cases
This section elaborates on each use case as implemented in terms of a dedicated terminal UI in the warehouse. *The focus should be on the Warehouse worker's perspective and explain how to carry out each use case (i.e., sea level transaction). Each specific use case description would include some amount of narrative, but should also include (or refer to) hi- or low-fidelity representations of the screens.*

E.1.2.3.1 Order Packability
Explain and show examples of how a Warehouse worker would see which orders are packable.[3]

E.1.2.3.2 Pack Order
Explain and show examples of how a Warehouse worker would tell the system that an order has been packed.

E.1.2.3.3 Ship Order
Explain and show examples of how a Warehouse worker would tell the system that an order has been shipped.

---

3 This is use case Packable orders? in the semantic model.

E.1.2.3.4   Receive Replenish
Explain and show examples of how a Warehouse worker would tell the system that a replenish order has been received.

E.1.3   User's Guide for Manager

This section outlines a user's guide for Managers in WebBooks' Order fulfillment domain.

E.1.3.1   Introduction
This section would provide an overview of the Manager's UI and address topics such as:

- *How to start and stop*
- *Seeing what options are available and selecting options*
- *How to correct mistakes*
- *Using a help facility (if one exists)*

E.1.3.2   Dialog Map
This section could show a dialog map for the Manager UI.

E.1.3.3   Use Cases
This section elaborates on each use case as implemented in terms of a dedicated terminal on the manager's desk. *The focus should be on the Manager's perspective and explain how to carry out each use case (i.e., sea level transaction). Each specific use case description would include some amount of narrative, but should also include (or refer to) hi- or low-fidelity representations of the screens and reports.*

E.1.3.3.1   Inventory Report
Explain and show examples of how a Manager would obtain and interpret an inventory report.[4]

E.1.3.3.2   Sales Report
Explain and show examples of how a Manager would obtain and interpret a sales report.[5]

E.1.3.3.3   Profit Report
Explain and show examples of how a Manager would obtain and interpret a profit report.[6]

---

4 This is use case Sales? in the semantic model.
5 This is use case Profit? in the semantic model.
6 This is use case Inventory? in the semantic model.

E.1.3.3.4 *Manage Catalog*
Explain and show examples of how a Manager would maintain the catalog, in terms of adding and modifying titles, adding and modifying media, etc. This would be a set of sea level use cases and would be spread over several sections.

E.2 High-Level Design

This section illustrates a high-level design for Order fulfillment. A complete high-level design specification would be too large and complex for this book—this only communicates the basic structure and content. High-level design documentation is only relevant in domains where a model compiler is not used. Where a model compiler is used, the high-level design is implicit in the production rules.[7] Also, per the discussion on literate programming in Chapter 22, it would be more effective if this documentation were in true hypertext form rather than forced into an arbitrary linear sequence as shown below.

Unless explicitly stated otherwise, design decisions should be assumed to have been made because they seemed reasonable at the time.

E.2.1 Design Use Case Diagram(s)

To the extent that the high-level design warrants a use case diagram, it can go here. Otherwise, reference the set of use cases in the semantic model and just list any additional technology-based use cases. For Order fulfillment there should be no new technology-based use cases.

E.2.2 High-Level Design Class Diagram(s)

This section presents the high-level design class diagrams for Order fulfillment. Use of the Scalability service (Appendix I) forces Order fulfillment functionality to be spread across several code elements:

- CustomerClient—Implements the Customer UI (i.e., View-controller region) as a ClientApp in Scalability
- CustomerServer—Implements Customer functionality (i.e., Model region) as a ServerApp in Scalability
- WarehouseWorkerClient—Implements the Warehouse worker UI as a ClientApp in Scalability
- WarehouseWorkerServer—Implements Warehouse worker functionality as a ServerApp in Scalability
- ManagerClient—Implements the Manager UI as a ClientApp in Scalability

---

7 Per the discussion in Chapter 21 that there may be explicit "why?" documentation associated with one or more of the production rules in a model compiler.

- ManagerServer—Implements Manager functionality as a ServerApp in Scalability
- PublisherServer—Implements Publisher functionality as a ServerApp in Scalability

Each of these elements is presented separately below.

Instance variables have been intentionally left off all high-level design diagrams to reduce size. Private data for each class is presented in the detailed design section.

E.2.2.1 High-Level Design for Customer Client

The UI for Customer (i.e., View-controller region) is a ClientApp in Scalability. Customer client is a Web application with each user screen implemented as a separate page. The Customer UI has the following Web pages[8]:

- Home/Search list
- Title details
- Copies to add
- My orders list
- Order details
- Confirm drop line
- Confirm cancel order

Page sequencing logic (i.e., the logic in the Customer Dialog Map in Figure E.1) is embedded in each page—there is no explicit "Customer Client" class as in the Warehouse worker and Manager clients. Figure E.2 shows a high-level design diagram for a generic Customer Web page—each specific Customer Web page conforms to this general pattern.

Each Customer Web page needs to be consistent with the Section I.1.1. All of the UI widgets, StaticText, ScrollList, Button, etc. are preexisting components in a «realized» Web UI domain (e.g., jQueryUI,[9] Kendo UI,[10] JQWidgets,[11] etc.).

E.2.2.2 High-Level Design for Customer Server

Customer business logic from the semantic model (i.e., Model region) is implemented as a ServerApp in Scalability. Figure E.3 shows a high-level design diagram for the Customer server.

---

8 Not included are log in and log out (User security) and Payment-related Web pages, which would be detailed elsewhere.

9 See http://jqueryui.com/.

10 See https://www.telerik.com/kendo-ui.

11 See https://www.jqwidgets.com/.

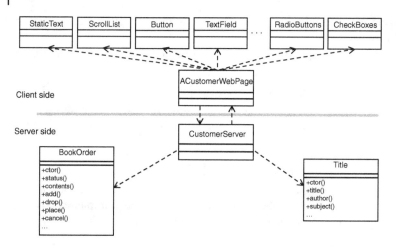

Figure E.2 High-level design for a generic Customer UI Web page.

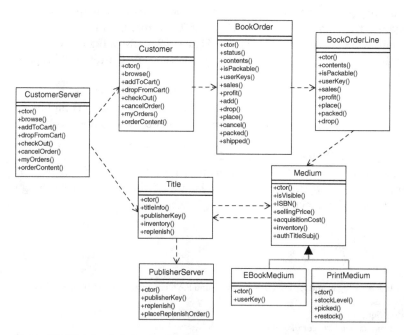

Figure E.3 High-level design for Customer server.

E.2.2.3 Warehouse Worker Client

The UI for Warehouse worker is a ClientApp in Scalability. The Warehouse worker client is a desktop application and has the following screens[12]:

- Packable orders
- Pack order
- Ship order
- Receive replenish

Page sequencing logic (i.e., the logic in a dialog map) is embedded in class WhseWorkerClient. Figure E.4 shows a high-level design diagram for the Warehouse worker client.

The Warehouse worker client needs to be designed and developed consistent with the Section I.1.1. All of the UI widgets, StaticText, ScrollList, Button, etc. are preexisting components that are part of a «realized» Dedicated terminal UI domain (e.g., Java Swing[13]).

E.2.2.4 Warehouse Worker Server

Warehouse worker business logic (i.e., Model region) is implemented as a ServerApp in Scalability. Figure E.5 shows a high-level design diagram for Warehouse worker server.

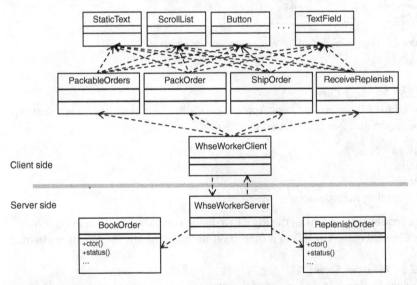

Figure E.4 High-level design Warehouse Worker Client.

---

12 Not included are log in and log out (User security).
13 See, for example, https://en.wikipedia.org/wiki/Swing_(Java).

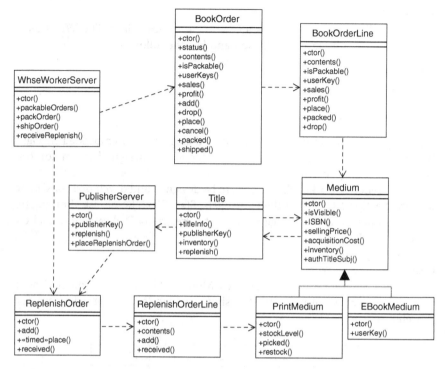

Figure E.5 High-level design for Warehouse Worker server.

E.2.2.5 Manager Client

The UI for Manager is a ClientApp in Scalability. The Manager UI is a desktop application and has the following screens[14]:

- Inventory
- Sales
- Profit
- All catalog maintenance

Page sequencing logic (i.e., the logic in a dialog map) is embedded in class ManagerClient. Figure E.6 shows a high-level design diagram for Manager client.

E.2.2.6 Manager Server

Manager business logic (i.e., Model region) is implemented as a ServerApp in Scalability. Figure E.7 shows a high-level design diagram for Manager server.

---

14 Not included are log in and log out (User security).

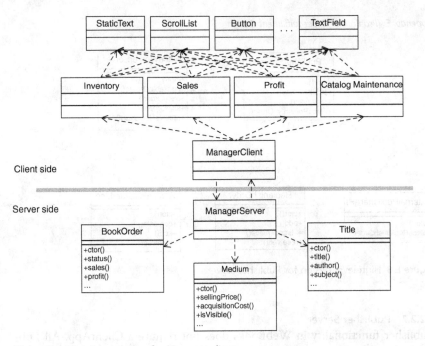

Figure E.6 High-level design for Manager client.

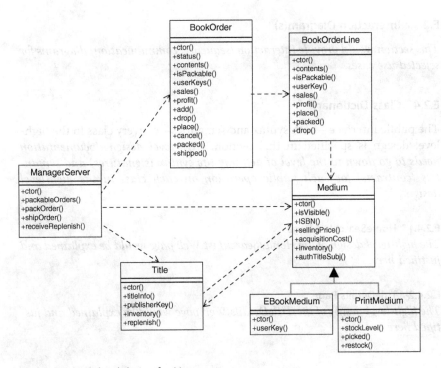

Figure E.7 High-level design for Manager server.

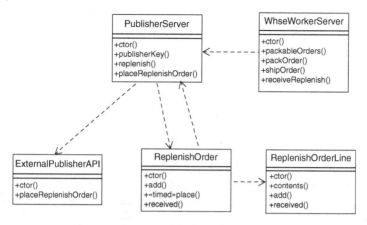

Figure E.8 High-level design for Publisher server.

E.2.2.7 Publisher Server

Publisher functionality in WebBooks does not require a ClientApp. All Publisher functionality can be implemented in terms of a ServerApp. Figure E.8 shows a high-level design diagram for Publisher server.

E.2.3 Interaction Diagram(s)

This section would provide interaction (sequence, communication) diagrams for selected use cases.

E.2.4 Class Dictionary

The public interface—both syntax and semantics—of every class in the high-level design is specified in this section. *High-level design documentation needs to go down to the level of defining the syntax (signatures) and semantics (contracts) for each public operation on each class in the high-level design.*

E.2.4.1 HomeSearchList Page

The high-level design of the Home/SearchList Web page would be explained and justified here.

E.2.4.2 TitleDetails Page

The high-level design of the TitleDetails Web page would be explained and justified here.

E.2.4.3 CopiesToAdd Page

The high-level design of the CopiesToAdd Web page (actually, a pop-up dialog box) would be explained and justified here.

E.2.4.4 MyOrdersList Page

The high-level design of the MyOrdersList Web page would be explained and justified here.

E.2.4.5 OrderDetails Page

The high-level design of the OrderDetails Web page would be explained and justified here.

E.2.4.6 ConfirmDropLine Page

The high-level design of the ConfirmDropLine Web page (actually a pop-up dialog box) would be explained and justified here.

E.2.4.7 ConfirmCancelOrder Page

The high-level design of the ConfirmCancelOrder Web page (actually a pop-up dialog box) would be explained and justified here.

E.2.4.8 WhseWorkerClient

The high-level design of the WhseWorkerClient would be explained and justified here.

E.2.4.9 PackableOrders Screen

The high-level design of the PackableOrders screen would be explained and justified here.

E.2.4.10 PackOrder Screen

The high-level design of the PackOrder screen would be explained and justified here.

E.2.4.11 ShipOrder Screen

The high-level design of the ShipOrder screen would be explained and justified here.

E.2.4.12 ReceiveReplenish Screen

The high-level design of the ReceiveReplenish screen would be explained and justified here.

E.2.4.13 ManagerClient

The high-level design of the ManagerClient would be explained and justified here.

E.2.4.14 Inventory Screen

The high-level design of the PackableOrders screen would be explained and justified here.

E.2.4.15 Sales Screen

The high-level design of the PackOrder screen would be explained and justified here.

E.2.4.16 Profit Screen

The high-level design of the ShipOrder screen would be explained and justified here.

E.2.4.17 Catalog Maintenance Screens

The high-level design of each of the catalog maintenance screens would be explained and justified here. Of course, this would be many sections, one for each screen.

E.2.4.18 CustomerServer

The high-level design of CustomerServer would be explained and justified here. For purposes of the AppType in Scalability, call this AppType == 1. One CustomerServer needs to be able to handle many CustomerClient sessions at the same time.

E.2.4.19 WhseWorkerServer

The high-level design of WhseWorkerServer would be explained and justified here. For purposes of the AppType in Scalability, call this AppType == 2. One WhseWorkerServer needs to be able to handle many WhseWorkerClient sessions at the same time.

E.2.4.20 ManagerServer

The high-level design of ManagerServer would be explained and justified here. For purposes of the AppType in Scalability, call this AppType == 3. One ManagerServer needs to be able to handle many ManagerClient sessions at the same time.

E.2.4.21 PublisherServer

The high-level design of PublisherServer would be explained and justified here. For purposes should handle all publishers at the same time.

E.2.4.22   Customer

This is the design representation of Customer in the semantic model. The high-level design would be explained and justified here.

E.2.4.23   BookOrder

This is the design representation of Book Order in the semantic model. The high-level design would be explained and justified here.

E.2.4.24   BookOrderLine

This is the design representation of Book Order Line in the semantic model. The high-level design would be explained and justified here.

E.2.4.25   Title

This is the design representation of Title in the semantic model. The high-level design would be explained and justified here.

E.2.4.26   Medium

This is the design representation of Medium in the semantic model. The high-level design would be explained and justified here.

E.2.4.27   PrintMedium

This is the design representation of Print Medium in the semantic model. The high-level design would be explained and justified here.

E.2.4.28   EBookMedium

This is the design representation of eBook Medium in the semantic model. The high-level design would be explained and justified here.

E.2.4.29   Publisher

This is the design representation of Publisher in the semantic model. The high-level design would be explained and justified here.

E.2.4.30   ReplenishOrder

This is the design representation of Replenish Order in the semantic model. The high-level design would be explained and justified here.

E.2.4.31   ReplenishOrderLine

This is the design representation of Replenish Order Line in the semantic model. The high-level design would be explained and justified here.

E.2.4.32 ExternalPublisherAPI

This class implements the mechanics of the industry standard API to real-world publishers. The high-level design would be explained and justified here.

E.3 Detailed Design

This section would document the design on the other side of the class encapsulation barrier. For each class in the high-level design, this level of documentation explains and justifies internal data (class and instance variable) structures as well as internal algorithm (class and instance method) structures. Explanations and justifications for mappings of semantic model attributes and ranges onto run-time data types along with discussions and justifications for algorithm choices and nontrivial semantic preserving transforms would be relevant topics. Again, ideally this documentation would not be a strictly linearized paper document as shown in this appendix; it would be an interconnected web of design detail and justification linked to code per literate programming.

E.3.1 Detailed Designs of Classes

The detailed design of each class follows.

E.3.1.1 HomeSearchList Page

The detailed design of the Home/Search List Web page would be explained and justified here. This would cover entering search terms, fetching search results from CustomerServer, managing scroll up and scroll down of the search results display, and transitioning to the TitleDetailsPage when a specific title is clicked. Also, transitioning to the MyOrdersListPage when a "View My Orders" button is clicked.

E.3.1.2 TitleDetails Page

The detailed design of the TitleDetails Web page would be explained and justified here. This would cover fetching Title and Medium results from Customer-Server. If the customer clicks "Add to cart," this page needs to transition to the CopiesToAdd page. If the customer enters new search terms, transition back to the HomeSearchListPage

E.3.1.3 CopiesToAdd Page

The detailed design of the CopiesToAdd Web page (actually, a pop-up dialog box) would be explained and justified here. This would cover validating the number of copies to add field, managing the Confirm and Cancel buttons, and telling CustomerServer to add to cart when appropriate.

E.3.1.4   MyOrdersList Page

The detailed design of the MyOrdersList Web page would be explained and justified here. This would address getting the list of this customer's orders and their respective .status from CustomerServer and presenting them to the user. This would also handle transitioning to OrderDetailsPage if the user clicks on one of their book orders or going back to the HomeSearchListPage if the user entered new search terms.

E.3.1.5   OrderDetails Page

The detailed design of the OrderDetails Web page would be explained and justified here. This would cover fetching the order content (including order status and any eBook user keys) from CustomerServer. This would also address transitioning to the Payment pages if the customer clicks the "Check Out" button for an open order as well as managing the ConfirmDropLine-Page, ConfirmCancelOrderPage, and back to the MyOrdersListPage transitions as appropriate.

E.3.1.6   ConfirmDropLine Page

The detailed design of the ConfirmDropLine Web page (actually a pop-up dialog box) would be explained and justified here. This would cover managing the Confirm and Cancel buttons, as well as telling CustomerServer to drop from cart when appropriate.

E.3.1.7   ConfirmCancelOrder Page

The detailed design of the ConfirmCancelOrder Web page (actually a pop-up dialog box) would be explained and justified here. This would cover managing the Confirm and Cancel buttons, as well as telling CustomerServer to cancel the order when appropriate.

E.3.1.8   WhseWorkerClient

The detailed design of the WhseWorkerClient would be explained and justified here.

E.3.1.9   PackableOrders Screen

The detailed design of the PackableOrders screen would be explained and justified here.

E.3.1.10   PackOrder Screen

The detailed design of the PackOrder screen would be explained and justified here.

E.3.1.11   ShipOrder Screen

The detailed design of the ShipOrder screen would be explained and justified here.

E.3.1.12 ReceiveReplenish screen

The detailed design of the ReceiveReplenish screen would be explained and justified here.

E.3.1.13 ManagerClient

The detailed design of the ManagerClient would be explained and justified here.

E.3.1.14 Inventory Screen

The detailed design of the PackableOrders screen would be explained and justified here.

E.3.1.15 Sales Screen

The detailed design of the PackOrder screen would be explained and justified here. This would include dealing with the Manager's desired date range.

E.3.1.16 Profit Screen

The detailed design of the ShipOrder screen would be explained and justified here. This would include dealing with the Manager's desired date range.

E.3.1.17 Catalog Maintenance Screens

The detailed design of each of the catalog maintenance screens would be explained and justified here. Of course, this would be many sections, one for each screen.

E.3.1.18 CustomerServer

The detailed design of CustomerServer would be explained and justified here. This would need to discuss receiving requests from the various Customer client Web pages as well as returning the appropriate data in cases where a response is required. Describe how browseCatalog() is mapped onto Scalability.Search()

E.3.1.19 WhseWorkerServer

The detailed design of WhseWorkerServer would be explained and justified here. This would need to discuss receiving requests from the various Warehouse worker clients as well as returning the appropriate data in cases where a response is required. This also needs to explain how this server gets access to all relevant BookOrder.status().

E.3.1.20 ManagerServer

The detailed design of ManagerServer would be explained and justified here. This would need to discuss receiving requests from the various Warehouse worker clients as well as returning the appropriate data in cases where a response is required. It is probably worth reminding the reader that ManagerServer has complete access to the catalog because the catalog is all SharedDatum.

E.3.1.21 PublisherServer

The detailed design of PublisherServer would be explained and justified here. This would need to discuss receiving requests from the various Customer servers as well as returning the appropriate data in cases where a response is required. How to recognize the after-24-hours part of ReplenishOrders may be addressed here.

E.3.1.22 Customer

The detailed design of Customer would be explained and justified here. In particular, there will be two distinct representations of Customer. One is memory resident when Order fulfillment functionality is manipulating a particular Customer in some way. The other is in terms of being stored as an OwnedDatum for Scalability purposes. Both need to be described. How Customer is mapped on to Owner and OwnedDatum in Scalability needs to be described.

E.3.1.23 BookOrder

The detailed design of BookOrder would be explained and justified here. In particular, there will be two distinct representations of BookOrder. One is memory resident when Order fulfillment functionality is manipulating a particular BookOrder in some way. The other is in terms of being stored as an OwnedDatum for Scalability purposes. Both need to be described. Connecting to the Payment domain should be explained here.

E.3.1.24 BookOrderLine

The detailed design of BookOrderLine would be explained and justified here. In particular, there will be two distinct representations of BookOrderLine. One is memory resident when Order fulfillment functionality is manipulating a particular BookOrderLine in some way. The other is in terms of being stored as an OwnedDatum for Scalability purposes. Both need to be described.

E.3.1.25 Title

The detailed design of Title would be explained and justified here. In particular, there will be two distinct representations of Title. One is memory resident when Order fulfillment functionality is manipulating a particular Title in some way. The other is in terms of being stored as a SharedDatum for Scalability purposes. Both need to be described.

E.3.1.26 Medium

The detailed design of Medium would be explained and justified here. In particular, there will be two distinct representations of Medium. One is memory resident when Order fulfillment functionality is manipulating a particular Medium in some way. The other is in terms of being stored as a SharedDatum for Scalability purposes. Both need to be described.

E.3.1.27 PrintMedium

The detailed design of PrintMedium would be explained and justified here. In particular, there will be two distinct representations of PrintMedium. One is memory resident when Order fulfillment functionality is manipulating a particular PrintMedium in some way. The other is in terms of being stored as a SharedDatum for Scalability purposes. Both need to be described.

E.3.1.28 EBookMedium

The detailed design of EBookMedium would be explained and justified here. In particular, there will be two distinct representations of EBookMedium. One is memory resident when Order fulfillment functionality is manipulating a particular EBookMedium in some way. The other is in terms of being stored as a SharedDatum for Scalability purposes. Both need to be described.

E.3.1.29 Publisher

The detailed design of Publisher would be explained and justified here. For example, how Publishers are mapped on to Owners and OwnedDatum in Scalability needs to be described.

E.3.1.30 ReplenishOrder

The detailed design of ReplenishOrder would be explained and justified here. In particular, there will be two distinct representations of ReplenishOrder. One is memory resident when Order fulfillment functionality is manipulating a particular ReplenishOrder in some way. The other is in terms of being stored as a SharedDatum for Scalability purposes. Both need to be described.

E.3.1.31 ReplenishOrderLine

The detailed design of ReplenishOrderline would be explained and justified here. In particular, there will be two distinct representations of ReplenishOrderLine. One is memory resident when Order fulfillment functionality is manipulating a particular ReplenishOrderLine in some way. The other is in terms of being stored as a SharedDatum for Scalability purposes. Both need to be described.

E.3.1.32 ExternalPublisherAPI

The detailed design of ExternalPublisherAPI would be explained and justified here.

Appendix F

Semantic Model for Payment

This appendix is an example semantic model—a specification of policies to enforce and processes to carry out—for the Payment domain in Web-Books 2.0.

F.1 Use Case Diagram

Use cases identify scope (processes to carry out) at the coarsest level. Actors identify context. Figure F.1 shows the actors and use cases in Payment. Payment processor is shown on the use case diagram to simplify use case participation and will not be explained in any further detail. Each remaining actor and use case is described in detail in later sections.

F.2 Class Diagram

The class model specifies policies to be enforced. Figure F.2 shows classes, attributes, associations, and generalizations in Payment. Each class is defined in detail in the class dictionary. To the extent necessary, associations are defined in the association dictionary.

F.3 Interaction Diagrams

Interaction diagrams describe process at an intermediate level. This section provides interaction (in this case sequence) diagrams for selected use cases. Sequence diagrams were chosen over communication diagrams because they are more natural and intuitive for most readers.

How to Engineer Software: A Model-Based Approach, First Edition. Steve Tockey.
© 2019 the IEEE Computer Society, Inc. Published 2019 by John Wiley & Sons, Inc.

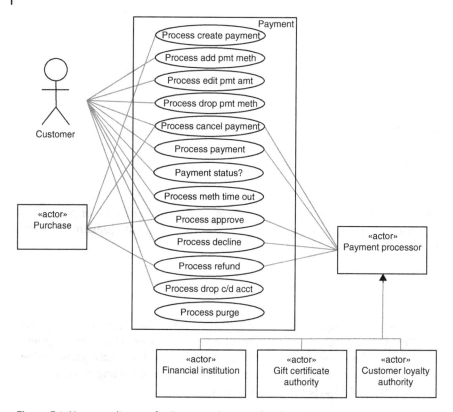

Figure F.1 Use case diagram for Payment domain of WebBooks 2.0.

F.3.1 Process Create Payment

Figure F.3 shows the sequence diagram for the Process create payment use case. The Customer has decided they want to make a purchase and they are now ready to arrange the details of actual payment.

F.3.2 Process Add Payment Method

Figure F.4 shows the sequence diagram for the Process add payment method use case. This use case allows the Customer to specify one—of possibly many—ways of contributing to the total payment for their purchase. The Customer can split a purchase over several credit/debit cards, gift certificates, customer loyalty points, etc. as long as the total amount of all payment methods equals the amount that needs to be paid.

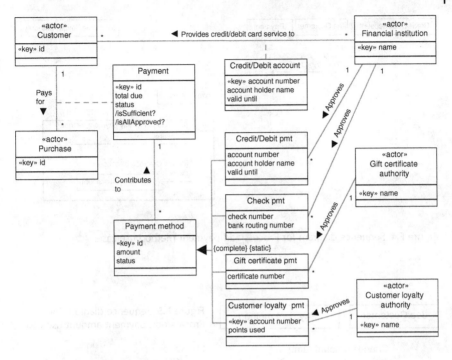

Figure F.2 Class diagram for Payment.

Figure F.3 Sequence diagram for Process create payment use case.

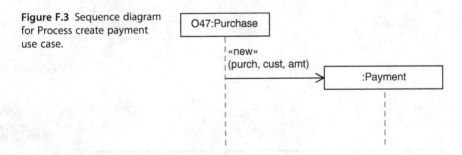

F.3.3 Process Edit Payment Amount

Figure F.5 shows the sequence diagram for the Process edit payment amount use case. This use case allows the Customer to modify one payment method.

F.3.4 Process Drop Payment Method

Figure F.6 shows the sequence diagram for the Drop payment method use case. The Customer had previously created a contribution to a Purchase but has

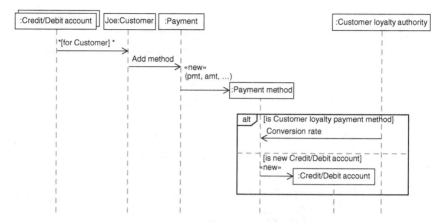

Figure F.4 Sequence diagram for Process add payment method use case.

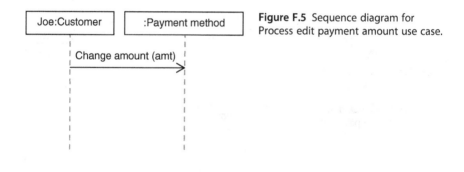

Figure F.5 Sequence diagram for Process edit payment amount use case.

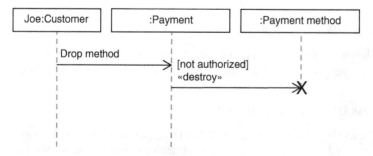

Figure F.6 Sequence diagram for Process drop payment method use case.

decided to remove that contribution. The only Payment methods that have not been authorized can be dropped.

F.3.5 Process Cancel Payment

Figure F.7 shows the sequence diagram for the Process cancel payment method use case. The Customer has decided to cancel an entire payment before it has been successfully submitted to all Payment processors. Any Payment methods that had been previously authorized need to be refunded.

F.3.6 Process Payment

Figure F.8 shows the sequence diagram for the Process payment use case. The Customer has arranged sufficient Payment methods for the Purchase and is submitting that for payment approval to the Payment processors.

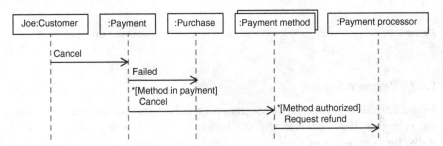

Figure F.7 Sequence diagram for Process cancel payment use case.

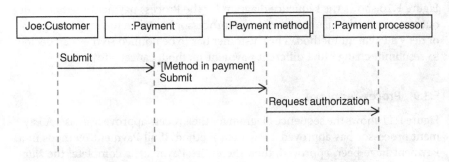

Figure F.8 Sequence diagram for Process payment use case.

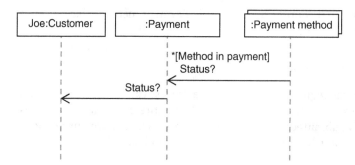

Figure F.9 Sequence diagram for Payment status? use case.

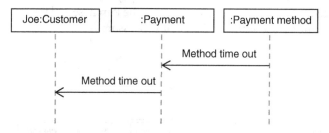

Figure F.10 Sequence diagram for Process payment method time out use case.

F.3.7 Payment Status?

Figure F.9 shows the sequence diagram for the Payment status? use case. This use case gives the Customer visibility into the status of their payment. Specifically, they can see how each of the Payment methods is progressing.

F.3.8 Process Payment Method Time Out

Figure F.10 shows the sequence diagram for the Process payment method time out use case. In this use case, a Payment processor has taken too long to approve or deny a Payment method. The Customer has to be notified so they can decide to resubmit, change to a different payment method, cancel, etc.

F.3.9 Process Approve

Figure F.11 shows the sequence diagram for the Process approve use case. A Payment processor has approved a Payment method. If all Payment methods in a Payment have been approved, then the entire Payment is complete: the Purchase is final, and goods/services can be delivered.

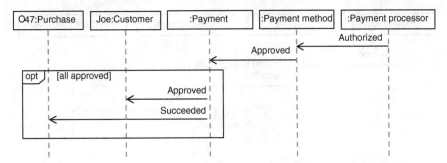

Figure F.11 Sequence diagram for Process approve use case.

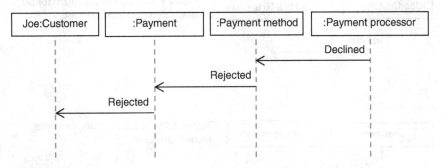

Figure F.12 Sequence diagram for Process decline use case.

F.3.10   Process Decline

Figure F.12 shows the sequence diagram for the Process decline use case. A Payment processor has denied a specific Payment method. The Customer has to be notified that the Payment needs to be modified or cancelled.

F.3.11   Process Refund

Figure F.13 shows the sequence diagram for the Process refund use case. After having paid successfully, the Customer is requesting that the transaction be nullified and they get a refund on everything they paid.

F.3.12   Drop Credit/Debit Account

Figure F.14 shows the sequence diagram for the Drop credit/debit account use case. In this use case, the Customer is removing previously saved information about a credit or debit card.

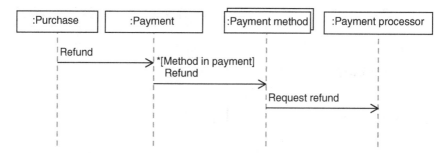

Figure F.13 Sequence diagram for Process refund use case.

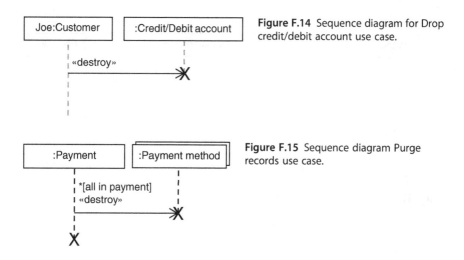

Figure F.14 Sequence diagram for Drop credit/debit account use case.

Figure F.15 Sequence diagram Purge records use case.

F.3.13 Purge Record

Figure F.15 shows the sequence diagram for the Purge record use case. The records retention time has passed; out-of-date records of previous Payments can be legally removed.

F.3.14 Un-diagrammed Use Cases

Some use cases may not have been diagrammed for various reasons, typically because their diagrams would be too trivial. This section lists the sea level use cases that have not been diagrammed to be sure the complete scope of this domain is known:

- New amount—The customer could attempt to pay for some purchase and the payment may be declined (as in, a credit card is over its credit limit). The customer can modify their purchase and reduce the amount (by removing products/services) and then reenter Payment with a lower amount. Payment.total due needs to be updated when this happens; the sequence diagram is trivial.

F.4 Class Dictionary

This section provides detailed specifications of each class in the domain.

F.4.1 Customer

Customer is an actor that represents persons or businesses who arrange payment for purchase of specific goods/services. For WebBooks 2.0, the Customer is purchasing books (in Order fulfillment domain) although this Payment domain will support payments for a wide variety of goods/services.

F.4.1.1 Attribute Descriptions
«key» id: The primary identifier (the key) of the Customer. This is used outside Payment to correlate customers with external processes.
   Range: [refer to Corporate Policy CP123b, "Customer Identification"]

F.4.1.2 State and Event Descriptions
None

F.4.1.3 Action Specifications
None

F.4.1.4 Source of
Add payment method () for Payment
Edit payment method () for Payment
Drop payment method (^Payment method) for Payment
Cancel payment for Payment
Submit payment for Payment
Drop credit/debit account for Credit/debit account

F.4.1.5 Destination of
Payment status? from Payment via Pays for
Method time out from Payment via Pays for
Approved from Payment via Pays for
Rejected from Payment via Pays for

F.4.2 Purchase

Purchase is an actor that represents the total goods and services the Customer is paying for. In WebBooks 2.0, this is Book order; however this domain is a general-purpose Payment facility and could be used for a wide variety of purchase types.

F.4.2.1 Attribute Descriptions

«key» id: The primary identifier (the key) of the Purchase. This is used outside Payment to correlate this purchase with external processes.

Range: [refer to Corporate Policy CP123c, "Customer Purchase Identification"]

F.4.2.2 State and Event Descriptions
None

F.4.2.3 Action Specifications
None

F.4.2.4 Source of
«new» (^Customer, ^Purchase, amount) for Payment
Refund for Payment via Pays for

F.4.2.5 Destination of
Approved via Pays for
Cancel payment via Pays for

F.4.3 Financial Institution

Financial institution is an actor that represents a bank, credit union, credit card company, etc. that is capable of settling credit, debit, check, and/or money order payments.

F.4.3.1 Attribute Descriptions

«key» id: The primary identifier (the key) of the financial institution. This is used outside Payment to correlate with external processes.

Range: [refer to Corporate Policy CP123Q, "Payment Processor Identification"]

F.4.3.2 State and Event Descriptions

None

F.4.3.3 Action Specifications

None

F.4.3.4 Source of

Authorized for Payment method via Approves
Declined for Payment method via Approves

F.4.3.5 Destination of

Request authorization from Payment method via Approves
Request refund from Payment method via Approves

F.4.4 Gift Certificate Authority

A Gift certificate authority is an organization that provides back-end services for gift certificates. A specific gift certificate given by one person or business to another might be branded a certain way (e.g., a chain store or restaurant); however the back-end service provider can also apply that gift certificate to other organizations they provide the same back-end service for.

F.4.4.1 Attribute Descriptions

«key» id: The primary identifier (the key) of the Gift certificate authority. This is used outside Payment to correlate with external processes.

Range: [refer to Corporate Policy CP123Q, "Payment Processor Identification"]

F.4.4.2 State and Event Descriptions

None

F.4.4.3 Action Specifications

None

F.4.4.4 Source of

Authorized for Payment method via Approves
Declined for Payment method via Approves

F.4.4.5 Destination of

Request authorization from Payment method via Approves
Request refund from Payment method via Approves

F.4.5   Customer Loyalty Authority

A Customer loyalty authority is an organization, like an airline, hotel chain, or rental car company, that allows points earned in their loyalty program to be converted into cash value.

F.4.5.1   Attribute Descriptions

«key» id: The primary identifier (the key) of the Customer loyalty authority. This is used outside Payment to correlate with external processes.
  Range: [refer to Corporate Policy CP123Q, "Payment Processor Identification"]

F.4.5.2   State and Event Descriptions
None

F.4.5.3   Action Specifications
None

F.4.5.4   Source of
Conversion rate for Payment method via Approves
Authorized for Payment method via Approves
Declined for Payment method via Approves

F.4.5.5   Destination of
Request authorization from Payment method via Approves
Request refund from Payment method via Approves

F.4.6   Payment

A Payment is the (set of) arrangements a specific Customer is using to fund a specific Purchase. The state diagram is shown in Figure F.16.

F.4.6.1   Attribute Descriptions

«new» id: The primary identifier (the key) of the Payment. This is used outside to correlate this payment with external processes.
  Range: [refer to Corporate Policy CP123d, "Payment Identification"]

total due: The total amount of money the Customer will be/was charged for the goods and services.
  Range: [$0.01 .. unconstrained in US Dollars, to the whole cent]

status: Shows the processing status of the Payment.
  Range: [an enumeration of the states in the state model]

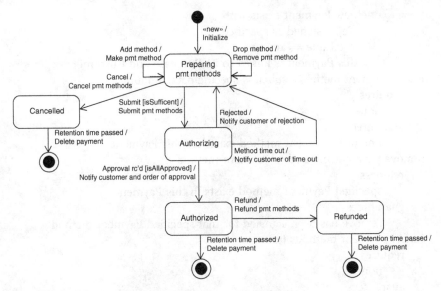

Figure F.16 State diagram for Payment.

/isSufficient?: Indicates if the Payment methods are sufficient to pay for this Payment.

  Derivation: True only when .total due = sum of .amount for all Payment methods with .status of Proposed or Authorized in this Payment via Contributes to

/isAllApproved?: Indicates if all Payment methods in this Payment have been approved by their relevant Payment processor.

  Derivation: True only when .status = Authorized for all Payment methods in this Payment via Contributes to

F.4.6.2 State and Event Descriptions
None

F.4.6.3 Action Specifications
  initialize (^Customer, ^Purchase, amount):
    requires
      amount is consistent with the range of .total due
    guarantees

one new Payment exists with:
.key assigned as specified
.total due == amount
this Payment is linked to its Purchase and Customer

make payment method (subclass-specific data, amount):
requires
none
guarantees
one new Payment method exists for this Payment

remove payment method (^Payment method):
requires
specified Payment method exists in this Payment
guarantees
remove has been signaled for that specified Payment method

cancel payment methods ():
requires
none
guarantees
cancel has been signaled for all Payment methods in this Payment via
Contributes to

submit payment methods ():
requires
none
guarantees
submit has been signaled for all Payment methods in this Payment
via Contributes to

notify customer of rejection ():
requires
none
guarantees
rejected has been signaled for Customer via Pays for

notify customer of time out ():
requires
none
guarantees
method time out has been signaled for Customer via Pays for

notify customer and purchase of approval ():
requires
none
guarantees
succeeded has been signaled for Purchase via Pays for
approved has been signaled for Customer via Pays for

refund payment methods ():
    requires
        none
    guarantees
        refund has been signaled for all Payment methods in this Payment
        via Contributes to
delete payment ():
    requires
        none
    guarantees
        «destroy» has been signaled for all Payment methods in this Payment
        via Contributes to

F.4.7 Payment Method

A Payment method is one way (of possibly many in a given Payment) that the Customer is contributing to the total amount of money due for the Purchase. There are different kinds of payment methods; each is detailed. The state diagram is shown in Figure F.17.

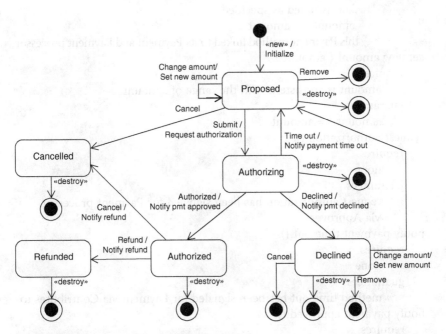

Figure F.17 State diagram for Payment method.

F.4.7.1   Attribute Descriptions

«key» id: The primary identifier (the key) of the Payment method. This is used outside to correlate this payment method with external processes.
Range: [refer to Corporate Policy CP123d, "Payment Identification"]

amount: The amount of money this payment method is contributing to the total payment.
Range: [$0.01 .. unconstrained in US Dollars, to the whole cent]

status: Shows the processing status of the Payment.
Range: [an enumeration of the states in the state model]

F.4.7.2   State and Event Descriptions

None

F.4.7.3   Action Specifications

initialize (^Payment, ^Payment processor, subtype-specific data, amount):
    requires
        amount is consistent with the range of .amount
    guarantees
        one new Payment method exists with:
          .key assigned as specified
          .amount == amount
          this Payment method linked to its Payment and Payment processor
set new amount (amount):
    requires
        amount is consistent with the range of .amount
    guarantees
        .amount == amount
request authorization ():
    requires
        none
    guarantees
        request authorization has been signaled for Payment processor
        via Approves
notify payment time out ():
    requires
        none
    guarantees
        method time out has been signaled for Payment via Contributes to
notify payment approved ():
    requires
        none

guarantees
>approved has been signaled for Payment via Contributes to

notify payment declined ():
requires
>none

guarantees
>declined has been signaled for Payment via Contributes to

notify refund ():
requires
>none

guarantees
>Request refund has been signaled for Payment processor via Approves

F.4.8 Credit/Debit pmt

A Credit/debit payment is a kind of Payment method that involves either a credit or debit account. The state model is inherited from Payment method.

F.4.8.1 Attribute Descriptions

«key» account number: The account number of the credit or debit account being used.
>Range: [refer to Corporate Policy CP127r, "Credit/Debit Account Identification"]

account holder name: The name of the owner of the credit or debit account.
>Range: [unconstrained by WebBooks]

valid until: The last month and year the credit/debit card can be used for purchasing.
>Range: [MM and YY, 01<=MM<=12 && 00<=YY<=99]

F.4.8.2 State and Event Descriptions
None

F.4.8.3 Action Specifications
initialize (..., number, name, valid date):
requires
>everything Payment method.initialize requires, plus
>number in range of .account number
>valid date in range of .valid until

guarantees
>everything Payment method.initialize guarantees, plus
>.account number == number
>.name on account == name

.valid until == valid date
if this account number isn't in this Customer's Credit/Debit Accounts
new Credit/Debit Account has been created to save this account data

F.4.9 Check pmt

A Check payment is a kind of Payment method that involves either a check or money order. In payments of this type, WebBooks waits until the physical check or money order is mailed in; then it is submitted to the relevant financial institution. Approval or decline is based on the financial institution's response to WebBooks' submission. The state model is inherited from Payment method.

F.4.9.1 Attribute Descriptions

«key» check number: The identifying number of the check or money order.
 Range: [unconstrained by WebBooks]

bank routing number: The bank's unique routing number from the check.
 Range: [unconstrained by WebBooks]

F.4.9.2 State and Event Descriptions
None

F.4.9.3 Action Specifications
 initialize (check number, routing number):
 requires
 nothing more than Payment method.initialize requires
 guarantees
 everything Payment method.initialize guarantees, plus
 .check number == check number
 .bank routing number == routing number

F.4.10 Gift Certificate pmt

A Gift certificate payment is a kind of Payment method that involves a gift certificate. The state model is inherited from Payment method.

F.4.10.1 Attribute Descriptions

«key» certificate number: The identifying number on the gift certificate this Payment method refers to.
 Range: [unconstrained by WebBooks]

F.4.10.2 State and Event Descriptions
None

F.4.10.3 Action Specifications
initialize (..., certificate number):
> requires
>> nothing more than Payment method.initialize requires
> guarantees
>> everything Payment method.initialize guarantees, plus
>> .certificate number == certificate number

F.4.11 Customer Loyalty pmt

A Customer loyalty payment is a kind of Payment method that uses points earned in a customer loyalty account, like an airline frequent flyer mile account or a hotel frequent guest account. The state model is inherited from Payment method.

F.4.11.1 Attribute Descriptions
«key» account number: The account number of the customer loyalty account this Payment method refers to.
Range: [unconstrained by WebBooks]

points used: The number of loyalty points being used in this Payment method. The Customer loyalty authority provides a conversion rate that turns points into a dollar value.
Range: [1000 to unconstrained points, with a precision of 1000 points]

F.4.11.2 State and Event Descriptions
None

F.4.11.3 Action Specifications
initialize (..., loyalty account id)[1]:
> requires
>> everything Payment method.initialize requires, plus
>> amount in range of .points used
> guarantees
>> everything Payment method.initialize guarantees, plus
>> .account number == loyalty account id

---

1 There is a subtle trick going on here. The customer specifies points used in the amount parameter. That is converted here to equivalent money as the actual Payment method.amount.

.points used == pre(amount)

Payment method.amount == .points used ∗ conversion rate

set new amount (amount):

requires

amount in range of .points used

guarantees

.points used == pre(amount)

Payment method.amount == .points used ∗ conversion rate

F.4.12 Credit/Debit Account

A Credit/debit account is a convenience function that remembers account information from past purchases so a Customer doesn't have to reenter it for subsequent purchases. The state diagram is shown in Figure F.18.

F.4.12.1 Attribute Descriptions

«new» account number: The account number of the credit or debit account being saved.

Range: [refer to Corporate Policy CP127r, "Credit/Debit Account Identification"]

account holder name: The name of the owner of the credit or debit account.

Range: [unconstrained by WebBooks]

valid until: The last month and year the credit/debit card can be used for purchases.

Range: [MM and YY, 01<=MM<=12 && 00<=YY<=99]

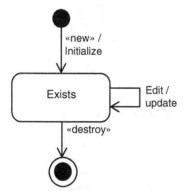

Figure F.18 State diagram for Credit/debit Account.

F.4.12.2   State and Event Descriptions
None

F.4.12.3   Action Specifications
initialize (acct number, holder name, valid date):
    requires
        acct number in range of .account number
        valid date in range of .valid until
    guarantees
        .account number == acct number
        .name on account == holder name
        .valid until == valid date

F.5   Association Dictionary

Where necessary and appropriate, this section provides detailed descriptions of associations in the domain. In this domain, no additional association descriptions are necessary because all associations are adequately specified in the class diagram.

F.6   Relevant Notes

The refund process is oversimplified. All it currently does is request the refund from the Payment processor(s). For various reasons, a Payment processor might ignore the request (time out), or they could potentially reject a request. This is ignored in the current model; the model assumes all refund requests are automatically and immediately successful. Note also that refunds involving check (or money order) need to have some way to return the money to the Customer, which is also ignored.

Appendix G

(Pro Forma) Payment Design

This appendix illustrates the structure and content of an interface specification and design specification for Payment. These examples are far from complete; real specifications would be much larger. Also, they would almost certainly be separate documents: at a minimum, the interface specification in one document and the design specification in another. For the remainder of this appendix, example content is shown in plain text, while *comments about structure and content are shown in italics.*

G.1 Interface Specification

This section illustrates the structure and content of an interface specification for Payment. A complete interface specification would be too large for this book—this only communicates the basic structure and content. A real interface specification for Payment could easily be two separate documents by itself:

- *User guide for Customers*
- *Developers guide to writing code that uses Payment services*

There is no need to describe the interface to Payment processors. Payment processors provide the application programming interface (API), presumably according to some defined industry or company standard. Payment software needs to be designed and coded per that standard.

G.1.1 User's Guide for Customer

This section illustrates an interface specification for Customers in WebBooks' Payment domain. This defines and describes how a WebBooks Customer accesses Payment functionality.

How to Engineer Software: A Model-Based Approach, First Edition. Steve Tockey.
© 2019 the IEEE Computer Society, Inc. Published 2019 by John Wiley & Sons, Inc.

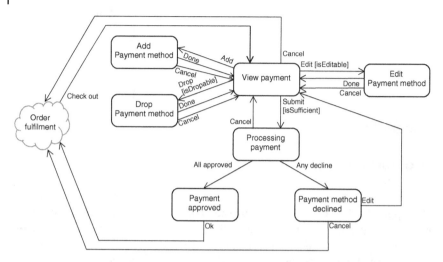

Figure G.1 Dialog map for Customer user interface.

G.1.1.1 Introduction
Insofar as the Customer's user interface (UI) for Payment is an extension of the Customer's UI for Order fulfillment, this introduction could simply reference the appropriate Order fulfillment user documentation for Customers.

G.1.1.2 Dialog Map
Figure G.1 shows a dialog map for the Customer UI.

G.1.1.3 Use Cases
This section elaborates on each Customer use case as implemented in terms of a Web-based UI. *Each use case description would include some amount of narrative, but should also include (or refer to) hi- or low-fidelity representations of the Web pages.*

G.1.1.3.1 Add Payment Method
Explain and show examples of how a Customer would add a Payment method to a Payment. Specifically, this would need to support the different kinds of Payment methods: Credit/debit, Check, Gift certificate, or Customer loyalty.

G.1.1.3.2 Edit Payment Amount
Explain and show examples of how a Customer would edit a Payment amount on an existing Payment method.

G.1.1.3.3 Drop Payment Method
Explain and show examples of how a Customer would drop a Payment method from an existing Payment.

G.1.1.3.4 Cancel

Explain and show examples of how a Customer would cancel a Payment and return to the previous domain.

G.1.1.3.5 Submit Payment

Explain and show examples of how a Customer would submit a Payment for processing.[1] Note that this can only happen when the sum of all Payment methods equals the amount due for the order. This description needs to include how the Customer will be notified of approval or decline of any of the Payment methods in their payment.

G.1.1.3.6 Check Payment Status

Explain and show examples of how a Customer could see the detailed status of a Payment.[2]

G.1.1.3.7 Refund

Explain and show examples of how a Customer could see the refund status for a Payment, assuming they had cancelled the order.

G.1.2 Developer's Guide to Using Payment Services

This section describes the Payment API so that a developer who needs to use the services provided by this domain will be able to write appropriate code.

G.1.2.1 Introduction

This section would provide an overview of the Payment API and address topics such as:

- *How to connect to the Payment API*
- *Exported constants, types, etc.*
- *Seeing what options are available and selecting options*
- *How to correct mistakes*

G.1.2.2 API Overview

Code Sample G.1 shows the primary Payment API. This is the code a designer/ developer in a client domain, like Order fulfillment, will call when they need Payment services.

---

1 This is use case Process payment in the semantic model.
2 This is use case Payment status? in the semantic model.

Code Sample G.1 Code for the Primary Payment API

```
public class Payment {

  public Payment ( Purchase aPurchase, Customer aCustomer ) {
  // constructor for Payment objects
  // requires
  //    aPurchase <> null
  //    aCustomer <> null
  // guarantees
  //    new Payment exists
  //    total due == $0.01 (as an initial default)
  //    payment status == PREPARING
    ...
  }

  public boolean processPayment ( double amount ) {
  // this operation manages all of the payment interaction
  // requires
  //    amount > $0.00
  // guarantees
  //    if pre ( payment status ) == PREPARING
  //       then total due == amount
  //             if this payment was processed successfully
  //                payment status == AUTHORIZED and returns true
  //                otherwise returns false
  //       otherwise nothing changes and returns false
    ...
  }

  public void refund ( ) {
  // this allows a customer to undo a previously approved Payment
  // requires
  //    none
  // guarantees
  //    if pre ( payment status ) == AUTHORIZED
  //       then all Payment methods have been refunded
  //             payment status is REFUNDED
  //       otherwise <some error is reported to a system operator>
    ...
  }
}
```

Code Sample G.2 «interface» Purchase in the Payment API

```
public interface Purchase {

  public void succeeded( ) {
  // payment was successful
  // requires
  //     none
  // guarantees
  //     the purchased object has dealt with payment succeeding
  }

  public void failed( ) {
  // payment was not successful
  // requires
  //     none
  // guarantees
  //     the purchased object has dealt with payment failing
  }
}
```

The semantic model shows not only the Customer being notified of payment outcome, but the Purchase object representing the goods and/or services being purchased is also notified. The client class representing those goods/services (e.g., BookOrder in Order fulfillment) needs to implement interface Purchase as defined in Code Sample G.2. How that class responds to these notifications is left to the client domain.

G.1.2.3 Use Cases
When a client application wants to make a payment, up to two steps are needed:

1) If a Payment object doesn't already exist, one needs to be created. A previous attempt at payment may have been made, and a Payment object representing the status of that earlier attempt could still exist (with various Payment methods for various amounts in various states).
2) Once the Payment object exists, call operation .processPayment() with the amount of purchase. The amount could have changed from a previous attempt (e.g., the Customer could have added or dropped products, or changed quantities).

The .processPayment() operation returns true when payment has been successfully processed otherwise it returns false (meaning the Customer cancelled that
payment). Use case Refund involves simply calling operation .refund() on the
API. An example of how client code using the Payment API might look is shown
in Code Sample G.3.

**Code Sample G.3 Example Code Showing Client Domain
Use of the Payment API**

```
public class ClientDomainPurchase {

  // other client domain purchase data relevant to the application
  ...
  private Payment myPayment;

  public ClientDomainPurchase ( ... ) {
  // the constructor for the client domain purchase object
  // requires
  //    tbd depending on the application
  // guarantees
  //    tbd depending on the application
    ...
    myPayment = null;
    ...
  }

  public void payForPurchase ( ... ) {
  // this is the client domain operation that wants to get payment
  // requires
  //    tbd depending on the application
  // guarantees
  //    tbd depending on the application
    ...
    if ( myPayment == null ) {
      myPayment = new Payment ( this, myCustomer );
    }
    if ( myPayment.processPayment ( amountOfPurchase ) ) {
      // Payment was successful, handle it as needed
      ...
```

```
    } else {
        // Payment was cancelled, handle it as needed
        ...
    }
    ...
}

public void refundPurchase ( ) {
// this is the client operation that needs to make a refund
// requires
//     tbd depending on the application
// guarantees
//     tbd depending on the application
    ...
    myPayment.refund();
    ...
}
}
```

The Payment constructor and .processPayment() combine to implement several Payment domain use cases in the semantic model:

- Process create payment—construct a Payment and then call .processPayment()
- Process approve—when .processPayment() returns true
- Process cancel payment—when .processPayment() returns false

Operation .refund() implements the entirety of the Process refund use case in the semantic model.

G.2   High-Level Design

This section illustrates a high-level design for Payment. A complete high-level design specification would be too large and complex for this book—this only communicates the basic structure and content. High-level design documentation is only relevant in domains where a model compiler is not used. Where a model compiler is used, the high-level design is implicit in the production rules. Also, per the discussion on literate programming in Chapter 22, it would be much more effective if this documentation were in true hypertext form rather than forced into an arbitrary linear sequence as shown below.

Unless explicitly stated otherwise, design decisions should be assumed to have been made because they seemed reasonable at the time.

G.2.1 Design Use Case Diagram(s)

To the extent that the high-level design warrants a use case diagram, it can go here. Otherwise, reference the set of use cases in the semantic model and just list any additional technology-based use cases. For Payment there should be no technology-based use cases.

G.2.2 High-Level Design Class Diagram(s)

This section presents the high-level design class diagrams for Payment. Use of the Scalability service (Appendix I) forces Payment functionality to be spread across two different code elements:

- CustomerClient—Implements the Customer UI (i.e., View-controller region) as a ClientApp in Scalability
- CustomerServer—Implements Customer functionality (i.e., Model region) as a ServerApp in Scalability

Each of these elements is presented separately.

Instance variables have been intentionally left off all high-level design diagrams to reduce size. Private data for each class is presented in the detailed design section.

G.2.2.1 High-Level Design for Customer Client
The UI for Customer (i.e., View-controller region) in Payment is an extension of the Customer client in Order fulfillment. Refer to the Order fulfillment design (Appendix E) for more detail. The Customer UI for Payment adds the following Web pages:

- View payment
- Add payment method
- Drop payment method
- Edit payment method
- Processing payment
- Payment method declined
- Payment approved

Figure G.2 shows a high-level design diagram for a generic Payment Web page—each specific Web page conforms to this general pattern.

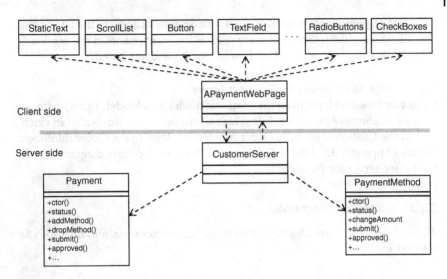

Figure G.2 High-level design for Customer client in Payment.

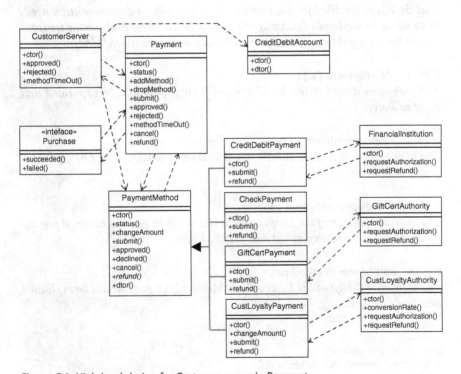

Figure G.3 High-level design for Customer server in Payment.

Each Web page needs to be consistent with Section I.1.1. All of the UI widgets, StaticText, ScrollList, Button, etc. are preexisting components in the «realized» Web UI domain (e.g., jQueryUI,[3] Kendo UI,[4] JQWidgets,[5] etc.).

G.2.2.2 High-Level Design for Customer Server
Customer business logic from the semantic model (i.e., Model region) is implemented as a ServerApp in Scalability. Like Customer client, this is also an extension of the Customer client in Order fulfillment. Refer to the Order fulfillment design (Appendix E). Figure G.3 shows a high-level design diagram for the Customer server for Payment.

G.2.3 Interaction Diagram(s)

This section would provide interaction (sequence, communication) diagrams for selected use cases.

G.2.4 Class Dictionary

The public interface—both syntax and semantics—of every class in the high-level design is specified in this section. *High-level design documentation needs to go down to the level of defining the syntax (signatures) and semantics (contracts) for each public operation on each class in the high-level design.*

G.2.4.1 ViewPayment Page
The high-level design of the ViewPayment Web page would be explained and justified here.

G.2.4.2 AddPaymentMethod Page
The high-level design of the AddPaymentMethod Web page would be explained and justified here.

G.2.4.3 DropPaymentMethod page
The high-level design of the DropPaymentMethod Web page (actually, a pop-up dialog box) would be explained and justified here.

G.2.4.4 EditPaymentMethod page
The high-level design of the EditPaymentMethod Web page would be explained and justified here.

---

3 See: http://jqueryui.com/.
4 See: https://www.telerik.com/kendo-ui.
5 See: https://www.jqwidgets.com/.

G.2.4.5 ProcessingPayment Page
The high-level design of the ProcessingPayment Web page would be explained and justified here.

G.2.4.6 PaymentMethodDeclined Page
The high-level design of the PaymentMethodDeclined Web page (actually a pop-up dialog box) would be explained and justified here.

G.2.4.7 PaymentApproved Page
The high-level design of the PaymentApproved Web page would be explained and justified here.

G.2.4.8 CustomerServer
It should be clarified that CustomerServer is an extended view of the same CustomerServer in the Order fulfillment domain High-level design as that one server is managing both Order fulfillment and Payment. The high-level design of Payment extensions to the Order fulfillment's CustomerServer would be explained and justified here.

G.2.4.9 Purchase
Purchase is an interface that BookOrder in Order fulfillment will need to implement so that it can receive the results of the Payment transaction.

G.2.4.10 Payment
This is the design representation of Payment in the semantic model. The high-level design of Payment would be explained and justified here.

G.2.4.11 PaymentMethod
This is the design representation of PaymentMethod in the semantic model. The high-level design of PaymentMethod would be explained and justified here.

G.2.4.12 CreditDebitPayment
This is the design representation of Credit/Debit Payment in the semantic model. The high-level design of CreditDebitPayment would be explained and justified here.

G.2.4.13 CheckPayment
This is the design representation of CheckPayment in the semantic model. The high-level design of CheckPayment would be explained and justified here.

G.2.4.14 GiftCertPayment
This is the design representation of GiftCertificatePayment in the semantic model. The high-level design of GiftCertPayment would be explained and justified here.

G.2.4.15 CustLoyaltyPayment

This is the design representation of CustomerLoyaltyPayment in the semantic model. The high-level design of CustLoyaltyPayment would be explained and justified here.

G.2.4.16 CreditDebitAccount

This is the design representation of Credit/Debit Account in the semantic model. The high-level design of CreditDebitAccount would be explained and justified here.

G.2.4.17 FinancialInstitution

This is the design representation of FinancialInstitution in the semantic model. The high-level design of FinancialInstitution would be explained and justified here.

G.2.4.18 GiftCertAuthority

This is the design representation of GiftCertificateAuthority in the semantic model. The high-level design of GiftCertAuthority would be explained and justified here.

G.2.4.19 CustLoyaltyAuthority

This is the design representation of CustomerLoyaltyAuthority in the semantic model. The high-level design of CustLoyaltyAuthority would be explained and justified here.

G.3 Detailed Design

This section would document the design on the other side of the class encapsulation barrier. For each class in the high-level design, this level of documentation explains and justifies internal data (class and instance variable) structures as well as internal algorithm (class and instance method) structures. Explanations and justifications for mappings of semantic model attributes and ranges onto run-time data types along with discussions and justifications for algorithm choices and nontrivial semantic preserving transforms would be relevant topics. Again, ideally this documentation would not be a strictly linearized paper document as shown in this appendix; it would be an interconnected web of design detail and justification linked to code per literate programming.

G.3.1 Detailed Designs of Classes

The detailed design of each class follows.

G.3.1.1   ViewPayment Page

The detailed design of the ViewPayment Web page would be explained and justified here. This would cover managing scroll up and scroll down of multiple payment methods being displayed, and transitioning to the AddPaymentMethod, DropPaymentMethod, EditPaymentMethod, and ProcessingPayment pages, as appropriate.

G.3.1.2   AddPaymentMethod Page

The detailed design of the AddPaymentMethod Web page would be explained and justified here.

G.3.1.3   DropPaymentMethod Page

The detailed design of the DropPaymentMethod Web page (actually, a pop-up dialog box) would be explained and justified here.

G.3.1.4   EditPaymentMethod Page

The detailed design of the EditPaymentMethod Web page would be explained and justified here.

G.3.1.5   ProcessingPayment Page

The detailed design of the ProcessingPayment Web page would be explained and justified here. This would cover transitioning to the ViewPayment, PaymentApproved, and PaymentDeclined pages, as appropriate.

G.3.1.6   PaymentMethodDeclined Page

The detailed design of the PaymentMethodDeclined Web page (actually a pop-up dialog box) would be explained and justified here.

G.3.1.7   PaymentApproved Page

The detailed design of the PaymentApproved Web page would be explained and justified here.

G.3.1.8   CustomerServer

It should be clarified that CustomerServer is an extended view of the same CustomerServer in the Order fulfillment domain High-level design as that one server is managing both Order fulfillment and Payment. The high-level design of Payment extensions to Order fulfillment's CustomerServer would be explained and justified here.

G.3.1.9   Purchase

Purchase is an interface, so no detailed design is necessary.

G.3.1.10 Payment

The detailed design of Payment would be explained and justified here. In particular, there will be two distinct representations of Payment. One is memory resident when Payment functionality is manipulating a particular Payment object in some way. The other is in terms of being stored as an OwnedDatum for Scalability purposes. Both need to be described.

G.3.1.11 PaymentMethod

The detailed design of PaymentMethod would be explained and justified here. In particular, there will be two distinct representations of PaymentMethod. One is memory resident when Payment functionality is manipulating a particular PaymentMethod in some way. The other is in terms of being stored as an OwnedDatum for Scalability purposes. Both need to be described.

G.3.1.12 CreditDebitPayment

The detailed design of CreditDebitPayment would be explained and justified here. In particular, there will be two distinct representations of CrditDebitPayment. One is memory resident when Payment functionality is manipulating a particular CreditDebitPayment in some way. The other is in terms of being stored as an OwnedDatum for Scalability purposes. Both need to be described.

G.3.1.13 CheckPayment

The detailed design of CheckPayment would be explained and justified here. In particular, there will be two distinct representations of CheckPayment. One is memory resident when Payment functionality is manipulating a particular CheckPayment in some way. The other is in terms of being stored as an OwnedDatum for Scalability purposes. Both need to be described.

G.3.1.14 GiftCertPayment

The detailed design of GiftCertPayment would be explained and justified here. In particular, there will be two distinct representations of GiftCertPayment. One is memory resident when Payment functionality is manipulating a particular GiftCertPayment in some way. The other is in terms of being stored as an OwnedDatum for Scalability purposes. Both need to be described.

G.3.1.15 CustLoyaltyPayment

The detailed design of CustLoyaltyPayment would be explained and justified here. In particular, there will be two distinct representations of CustLoyaltyPayment. One is memory resident when Payment functionality is manipulating a particular CustLoyaltyPayment in some way. The other is in terms of being stored as an OwnedDatum for Scalability purposes. Both need to be described.

G.3.1.16 CreditDebitAccount
The detailed design of CreditDebitAccount would be explained and justified here. In particular, there will be two distinct representations of CreditDebitAccount. One is memory resident when Payment functionality is manipulating a particular CreditDebitAccount in some way. The other is in terms of being stored as an OwnedDatum for Scalability purposes. Both need to be described.

G.3.1.17 FinancialInstitution
The detailed design of FinancialInstitution would be explained and justified here. In particular, how this class is a gateway into any View-controller region code that communicates with actual financial institutions using the appropriate protocol(s).

G.3.1.18 GiftCertAuthority
The detailed design of GiftCertAuthority would be explained and justified here. In particular, how this class is a gateway into any View-controller region code that communicates with actual gift certificate authorities using the appropriate protocol(s).

G.3.1.19 CustLoyaltyAuthority
The detailed design of CustLoyaltyAuthority would be explained and justified here. In particular, how this class is a gateway into any View-controller region code that communicates with actual customer loyalty authorities using the appropriate protocol(s).

Appendix H

Semantic Model for Scalability

This appendix is an example of a semantic model—a specification of policies to enforce and processes to carry out—for the Scalability domain in WebBooks 2.0.

H.1   Use Case Diagram

Use cases identify scope (processes to carry out) at the coarsest level. Actors identify context. Figure H.1 shows actors and use cases in Scalability. Each actor and use case is described in detail in later sections.

H.2   Class Diagram

The class model specifies policies to be enforced. Figure H.2 shows classes, attributes, associations, and generalizations in Scalability. Each class is defined in detail in the class dictionary below. To the extent necessary, associations are defined in the association dictionary below.

H.3   Interaction Diagrams

Interaction diagrams describe process at an intermediate level. This section provides interaction (in this case sequence) diagrams for selected use cases. Sequence diagrams were chosen over communication diagrams because they are more natural and intuitive to most readers.

H.3.1   Connect Shared

There are two variants on connecting. The first is where no content owner is involved. In this variant, access is only to Shared datum. This use case creates

How to Engineer Software: A Model-Based Approach, First Edition. Steve Tockey.
© 2019 the IEEE Computer Society, Inc. Published 2019 by John Wiley & Sons, Inc.

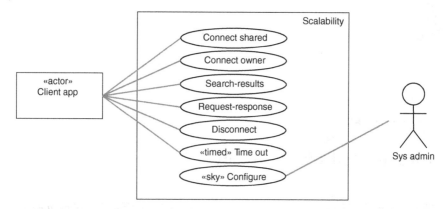

Figure H.1 Use case diagram for Scalability.

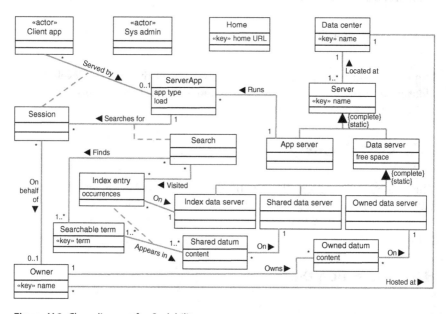

Figure H.2 Class diagram for Scalability.

a new Session between a Client App and the least busy Server App of the requested type across all Data Centers. Figure H.3 shows the sequence diagram; the other variant is described below.

H.3.2 Connect Owner

This is the second variant on connecting, where a content owner is involved. This use case also creates a new Session between a Client App and the least busy

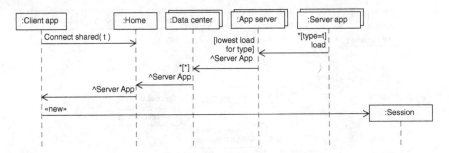

Figure H.3 Sequence diagram for Connect shared use case.

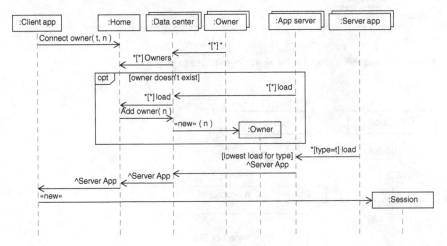

Figure H.4 Sequence diagram for Connect owner use case.

Server App of the requested type, but does so at the Data Center where that Owner's Owned Datum is stored. Figure H.4 shows the sequence diagram.

H.3.3 Search-Results

Figure H.5 shows the sequence diagram for the Search-results use case. This is a special case of Request-response (below) that allows a Server App to create a search on Shared Datum and then see the results that are selected through the client's given search criteria.

H.3.4 Request-Response

Figure H.6 shows the sequence diagram for the Request-response use case. This use case represents a generic (owner-specific) Client App request to the Server

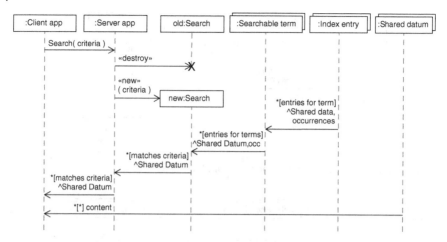

Figure H.5 Sequence diagram for Search-results use case.

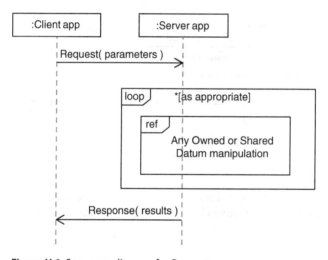

Figure H.6 Sequence diagram for Request-response use case.

App along with the Server App's response. Applications that use this Scalability service will customize Request-response to match their specific needs. As an example, in an order processing application Place order, Cancel order, and Pack order would be examples of specific request-responses. Inside of any request-response could be any number of Owned or Shared Datum manipulations: creating, reading, updating, or deleting.

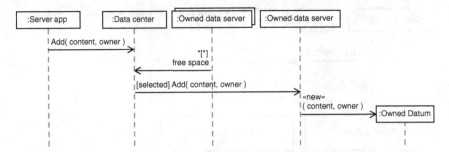

Figure H.7 Sequence diagram for New owned datum use case.

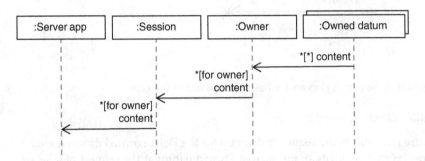

Figure H.8 Sequence diagram for Read owned datum use case.

H.3.5   New Owned Datum

Figure H.7 shows the sequence diagram for the New owned datum use case. This and the next nine sequence diagrams shown extending variations of Owned or Shared Data Manipulation referred to in Figure H.6. In this case, the Server App is creating a new instance of Owned Datum on the most appropriate Owned Data Server.

H.3.6   Read Owned Datum

Figure H.8 shows the sequence diagram for the Read owned datum use case. This use case lets a Server App access Owned Datum for the selected Owner.

H.3.7   Update Owned Datum

Figure H.9 shows the sequence diagram for the Update owned datum use case. This use case lets a Server App modify the content in some Owned datum. This use case is trivial; had this been a real specification, this sequence diagram would have likely been omitted.

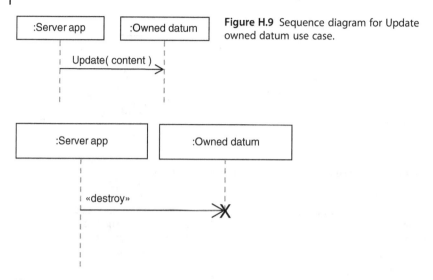

Figure H.9 Sequence diagram for Update owned datum use case.

Figure H.10 Sequence diagram for Delete owned datum use case.

H.3.8   Delete Owned Datum

Figure H.10 shows the sequence diagram for the Delete owned datum use case. This use case removes an instance of Owned datum at the request of a Server App. This use case is trivial; had this been a real specification, this sequence diagram would have likely been omitted.

H.3.9   Create Shared Data

Figure H.11 shows the sequence diagram for the Create shared data use case. This use case creates a new instance of Shared Datum and indexes it. An extending use case (not explicitly shown) then propagates this new content across the remaining Data Centers.

H.3.10   Update Shared Data

Figure H.12 shows the sequence diagram for the Update shared data use case. This use case modifies the content of an existing Shared Datum and re-indexes it. An extending use case (not explicitly shown) then propagates this new content across the remaining Data Centers.

H.3.11   Delete Shared Data

Figure H.13 shows the sequence diagram for the Delete shared data use case. This use case deletes the content of an existing Shared Datum along with all

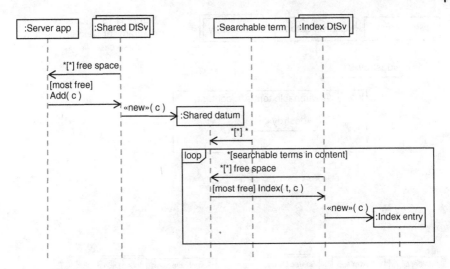

Figure H.11 Sequence diagram for Create shared data use case.

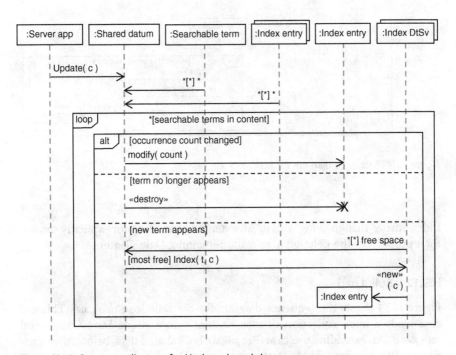

Figure H.12 Sequence diagram for Update shared data use case.

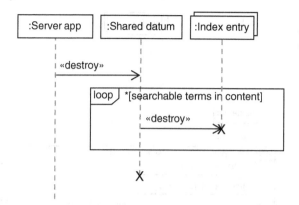

Figure H.13 Sequence diagram for Delete shared data use case.

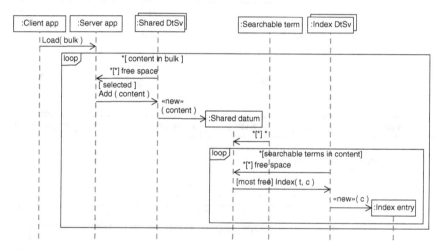

Figure H.14 Sequence diagram for Bulk load use case.

Index entries that go along with it. An extending use case (not explicitly shown) then propagates the deletion across the remaining Data Centers.

H.3.12 Bulk Load

Figure H.14 shows the sequence diagram for the Bulk load use case. This use case loads a large collection of new content into a single Data Center and indexes it. An extending use case (Propagate bulk shared data, below) then propagates the new content across the remaining Data Centers.

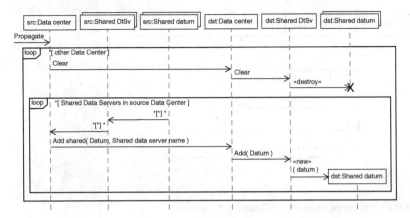

Figure H.15 Sequence diagram for Propagate bulk shared data use case.

H.3.13 Propagate Bulk Shared Data

Figure H.15 shows the sequence diagram for the Propagate bulk shared data use case. This extending use case propagates all Shared Datum in one Data Center across the remaining Data Centers. Several important variations also need to be understood but are not explicitly diagrammed because they are very similar to this. In particular, Propagate Searchable terms and Propagate index entries are needed to be sure all Data Centers have the same shared, searchable content. Similarly, propagating changed content on adding, modifying, or deleting a single Shared Datum also needs to occur.

H.3.14 Disconnect

Figure H.16 shows the sequence diagram for the Disconnect use case. This use case closes out a scalable client-server session.

H.3.15 Time Out

Figure H.17 shows the sequence diagram for the Time out use case. This use case closes out a scalable client-server session when there has been no activity for a predetermined amount of time.

H.3.16 Un-diagrammed Use Cases

Some use cases may not have been diagrammed for various reasons, typically because their diagrams would be trivial. This section lists sea level use cases that

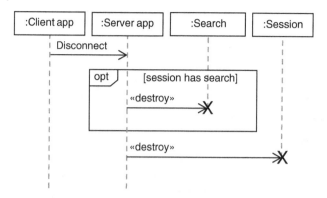

Figure H.16 Sequence diagram for Disconnect use case.

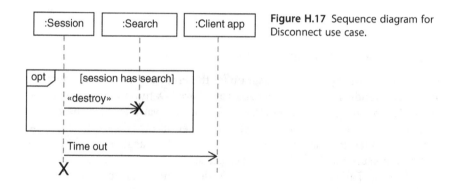

Figure H.17 Sequence diagram for Disconnect use case.

have not been diagrammed to be sure complete scope of this domain is explicitly defined:

- All of the System Admin configuration use cases like maintaining Home, Data Centers, Servers, and installing and removing Server Apps.
- Some variants of propagating changes to Shared Datum across the remaining Data Centers.
- One Server App communicating directly with another in Request-response terms.
- ...

H.4   Class Dictionary

This section provides detailed specifications of each class in the domain.

H.4.1 Client App

Client App is an actor that represents client-side code in a scalable client-server application. That app needs access to scalable server-side functionality. This class has no state diagram because it is an actor and is mostly external.

H.4.1.1 Attribute Descriptions
None

H.4.1.2 State and Event Descriptions
None

H.4.1.3 Action Specifications
None

H.4.1.4 Source of
Connect shared(type): ^client app
Connect owner(type, owner): ^client app
Search(criteria): results
Request(parameters): response
Disconnect()

H.4.1.5 Destination of
Session time out

H.4.2 Home

Home represents the entry point into the scalable client-server environment. There can only be one Home for a given environment, although multiple scalable client-server environments with their own Home can exist at the same time. Figure H.18 shows the state diagram for Home.

H.4.2.1 Attribute Descriptions
«key» home URL: The unique home URL.
    Range: [any valid, unique Internet URL]

H.4.2.2 State and Event Descriptions
None

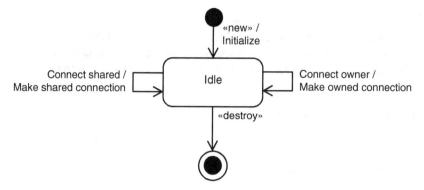

Figure H.18 State diagram for Home.

H.4.2.3 Action Specifications

initialize(URL):

  requires

    URL is consistent with the range of .home URL

  guarantees

    one new Home exists with:

      .home URL == URL

make shared connection(type):

  requires

    type is consistent with Server App.type

    At least one Server App of that type is running in at least one Data Center

  guarantees

    a reference to the least busy Server App of that type has been provided to Client App

make owned connection(type, owner):

  requires

    type is consistent with Server App.type

    At least one Server App of that type is running at the owner's Data Center

  guarantees

    if the specified owner did not exist before

      then a new Owner has been created at the least busy Data Center

    a reference to the least busy Server App of the requested type at the owner's Data Center has been provided to Client App

H.4.3   Data Center

A Data Center is a separate, distinct, named facility containing scalable server-side computing resources: App Servers, Shared Data Servers, Index Servers, and Owned Data Servers. Figure H.19 shows the state diagram for Data Center.

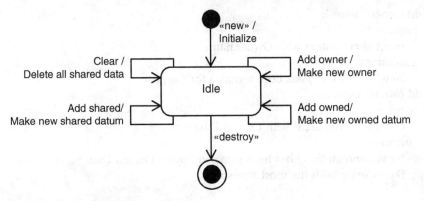

Figure H.19 State diagram for Data Center.

H.4.3.1 Attribute Descriptions

«key» name: The (unique among all Data Centers in any one scalable installation) name of this data center.

Range: [unconstrained other than uniqueness]

H.4.3.2 State and Event Descriptions

None

H.4.3.3 Action Specifications

initialize (name):
  requires
    name is consistent with the range of .name
  guarantees
    one new Data Center exists with:
      .name == name
clear:
  requires
    none
  guarantees
    Clear has been signaled for all Shared Data Servers at this Data Center via
    Located at
Add shared(datum, ^Shared Data Server):
  requires
    datum is a valid Shared Datum
    ^Shared Data Server exists in this Data Center
  guarantees
    Add(datum) has been signaled for Shared Data Server

Add owner(name):
  requires
    name is consistent with Owner.name
  guarantees
    New(name, this) has been signaled for Owner
Add owned(content):
  requires
    content is consistent with Owned Data.content
  guarantees
    New(content, this) has been signaled for the Owned Data Server at this
    Data Center with the most free space[1]

H.4.4 Server

A Server is a scalable server-side computing resource located at (i.e., owned by) a particular Data Center. Dynamic behavior of Servers depends on the specific subtype of the server and is elaborated there.

H.4.4.1 Attribute Descriptions
«key» name: The (unique among all Servers in the owning Data Center) name of
  this server.
  Range: [unconstrained other than uniqueness]

H.4.4.2 State and Event Descriptions
None

H.4.4.3 Action Specifications
initialize (name):
  requires
    name is consistent with the range of .name
  guarantees
    one new Server (of the appropriate subclass) exists with:
      .name == name

H.4.5 Data Server

A Data Server is a scalable computing resource whose role is to store one specific kind of data. Dynamic behavior of Data Servers depends on the specific kind of server and is elaborated there.

---

1 A performance optimization in design could be to put the new Owned datum on the same Owned data server as other data owned by the same owner—as long as there is still room.

H.4.5.1 Attribute Descriptions
free space: The free space available for storing data on this Data Server.
   Range: [0 .. unconstrained in megabytes to the nearest tenth of a megabyte]

H.4.5.2 State and Event Descriptions
None

H.4.5.3 Action Specifications
None

H.4.6 Owned Data Server

An Owned Data Server is a scalable computing resource whose role is to store Owned Datum in a scalable way, on behalf of content Owners. Figure H.20 shows the state diagram for Owned Data Server.

H.4.6.1 Attribute Descriptions
None

H.4.6.2 State and Event Descriptions
None

H.4.6.3 Action Specifications
Make owned datum(content, ^Owner):
   requires
      content is consistent with Owned Datum.content
      ^Owner is a valid owner at this Data Center
   guarantees
      «new» (content, ^Owner, this) has been signaled for Owned Datum

Figure H.20 State diagram for Owned Data Server.

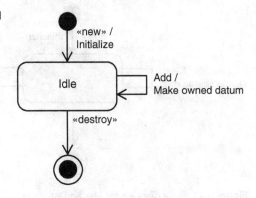

H.4.7 Shared Data Server

A Shared Data Server is a scalable computing resource whose role is to store Shared Datum in a scalable way. Figure H.21 shows the state diagram for Shared Data Server.

H.4.7.1 Attribute Descriptions
None

H.4.7.2 State and Event Descriptions
None

H.4.7.3 Action Specifications
clear
  requires
    none
  guarantees
    «destroy» has been signaled for all Shared Datum on this Shared Data Server via On
add(content):
  requires
    content is consistent with Shared Datum.content
  guarantees
    «new» (content, this) has been signaled for Shared Datum

H.4.8 Index Data Server

An Index Data Server is a scalable computing resource whose role is to store Searchable Terms and Index Entries in a scalable way. Figure H.22 shows the state diagram for Index Data Server.

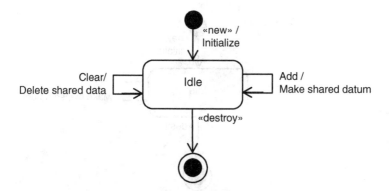

Figure H.21 State diagram for Shared Data Server.

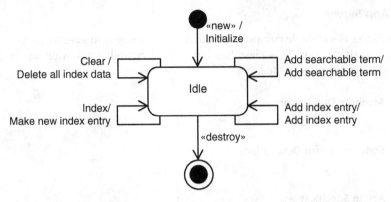

Figure H.22 State diagram for Index Data Server.

H.4.8.1 Attribute Descriptions
None

H.4.8.2 State and Event Descriptions
None

H.4.8.3 Action Specifications
Delete all index data:
   requires
      none
   guarantees
      «destroy» has been signaled for all Searchable Terms
      «destroy» has been signaled for all Index Entries via On
Make new index entry(^term, occurrences):
   requires
      ^term is a valid Searchable Term
      occurrences is consistent with Index Entry.occurrences
   guarantees
      «new» (^term, occurrences, this) has been signaled for Index Entry
Add searchable term(term):
   requires
      term is consistent with Searchable Term.term
   guarantees
      «new» (term) has been signaled for Searchable Term
Add index entry(^term, occurrences):
   requires
      ^term is a valid Searchable Term
      occurrences is consistent with Index Entry.occurrences
   guarantees
      «new» (^term, occurrences, this) has been signaled for Index Entry

H.4.9   App Server

An App Server is a scalable computing resource whose role is to execute Server Apps in a scalable way. This class has only trivial custodial behavior so no explicit state diagram is needed.

H.4.9.1   Attribute Descriptions
None

H.4.9.2   State and Event Descriptions
None

H.4.9.3   Action Specifications
None

H.4.10   Shared Datum

A Shared Datum is a scalable unit of publically accessible data. Shared data and its indexing are replicated across Data Centers to improve performance. In a sense, this Scalability service provides Google™-like data storage where content is publicly available to whoever wants to search it. This class has only trivial custodial behavior so no explicit state diagram is needed.

H.4.10.1   Attribute Descriptions
content: The descriptive information that is to be shared in a scalable way.
    Range: [a non-empty, otherwise unconstrained string of text]

H.4.10.2   State and Event Descriptions
None

H.4.10.3   Action Specifications
initialize (^Topic):
    requires
        ^Topic is a valid Topic
    guarantees
        one new Iterator exists with:
            linked to the Server App that created it
            linked to the Topic
            unlinked from all Datum under the linked Topic
move:
    requires
        at least one Datum under the linked Topic has not been visited
    guarantees
        a link has been created between this Iterator and the last Datum visited

H.4.11   Searchable Term

A Searchable Term is a separable fragment of content—typically one word, but possibly a phrase—in Shared Datum that is indexed to enable reasonable searching.. Terms that appear in a majority of Shared Datum content, particularly common words like "a," "an," "the," etc., are not good candidates for indexing because they do not differentiate content. It is possible, although not certain, that some searchable terms might be more than a single word, for example, "Software Engineering" might be a useful searchable term. This class has only trivial custodial behavior so no explicit state diagram is needed.

H.4.11.1   Attribute Descriptions
«key» term: The unique searchable fragment of content.
Range: [a non-empty, otherwise unconstrained string of text]

H.4.11.2   State and Event Descriptions
None

H.4.11.3   Action Specifications
None

H.4.12   Index Entry

An Index Entry marks the fact that a specific Searchable Term appears at least once in the content of a specific Shared Datum. This class has only trivial custodial behavior so no explicit state diagram is needed.

H.4.12.1   Attribute Descriptions
occurrences: The number of times the associated Searchable Term appears in the content of the associated Shared Datum. This helps determine the relevance of the associated Shared. Datum to a Search: The higher the number of occurrences, the more relevant that content.
Range: [1 .. some unconstrained whole number]

H.4.12.2   State and Event Descriptions
None

H.4.12.3   Action Specifications
initialize (^term, ^datum, count):
   requires
      ^term is a valid Searchable Term
      ^datum is a valid Shared Datum
      count is consistent with Index Entry.occurrences

guarantees
    one new Index Entry exists with:
      linked to the Searchable Term
      linked to the Shared Datum
      .occurrences == count

H.4.13   Owner

An Owner is some (external to Scalability) entity that represents the owner of some Owned Content. This class has only trivial custodial behavior so no explicit state diagram is needed.

H.4.13.1   Attribute Descriptions
«key» name: The name, unique among all owners in a scalable installation, of this owner.
Range: [unconstrained other than uniqueness]

H.4.13.2   State and Event Descriptions
None

H.4.13.3   Action Specifications
initialize (name, ^data center):
  requires
    name is consistent with Owner.name
    ^data center is a valid Data Center
  guarantees
    one new Owner exists with:
      .name = name
      linked to the specified Data Center

H.4.14   Owned Datum

Each Owned Datum is a unit of scalable-stored information that is private to some particular content Owner. In a sense, this Scalability service also provides Facebook™-like data storage where content is connected to one unique owner. In contrast to Shared Datum, this class represents that private data. This class has only trivial custodial behavior so no explicit state diagram is needed.

H.4.14.1   Attribute Descriptions
content: The owner-associated information that is to be stored in a scalable way.
  Range: [a non-empty, otherwise unconstrained string of text]

H.4.14.2 State and Event Descriptions
None

H.4.14.3 Action Specifications
initialize (content, ^owner, ^owned data server):

    requires

        content is consistent with .content

        ^owner is a valid Owner

        ^owned data server is a valid Owned Data Server at the owner's data center

    guarantees

        one new Owned Datum exists with:

            .content == content

            linked to the specified Owned Data Server via On

            linked to the specified Owner via Owns

H.4.15 Server App

A Server App is a server-side computing resource that provides a specific kind of (scalable) functionality. Server Apps come in different types, allowing for different kinds of Client Apps to connect to an appropriate kind of Server App. The state diagram is shown in Figure H.23.

Figure H.23 State diagram for Server App.

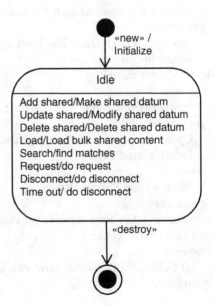

H.4.15.1 Attribute Descriptions

app type: A code that identifies the type of functionality provided by this Server App. Server Apps can be written to provide different kinds of functionality; this helps a Client App get connected to the right kind of Server App.

Range: [unconstrained]

load: The current load level of this Server App—in other words, how hard it is working. When connecting, Client Apps should be steered to the least busy Server App to help with load balancing.

Range: [0.0 .. 100.0 percent]

H.4.15.2 State and Event Descriptions

None

H.4.15.3 Action Specifications

initialize (type, ^app server):

   requires

      type is a consistent with Server App.type

      ^app server is a valid App Server

   guarantees

      one new Server App exists with:

        .type == type

        linked to the given App Server

make shared datum:

   requires

      content is consistent with the range of Shared Datum.content

   guarantees

      Add shared(content) has been signaled for the most free Shared Data Server in this Data Center

Modify shared datum:

   requires

      content is consistent with the range of Shared Datum.content

   guarantees

      Update(content) has been signaled for the Shared Datum to be updated

Delete shared datum:

   requires

      ^sd is a valid Shared Datum

   guarantees

      «destroy» has been signaled for that Shared Datum

Load bulk shared content:

   requires

      all Bulk content is consistent with Shared Datum.content

   guarantees

Add shared(content) has been signaled for the most free Shared Data
Server in this Data Center exactly once for each unit of content in Bulk
Find matches:
  requires
    criteria is a collection of one or more searchable terms
  guarantees
    any old Search for this Client App (Session) has been deleted
    «new» (^session, ^this, criteria) has been signaled for Search
    references to all matching Shared Datum are available to the Client App
Do request:
  requires
    parameters are appropriate for the specific kind of request
  guarantees
    the specific request has been completed
    this Server App's response is available for the Client App (Session)
Do disconnect:
  requires
    none
  guarantees
    «destroy» has been signaled for any Search for this session
    «destroy» has been signaled for this session

H.4.16 Session

A Session represents the run-time connection between some specific Client
App and some specific (appropriate type of) Server App. The state diagram
is shown in Figure H.24.

Figure H.24 State diagram for Session.

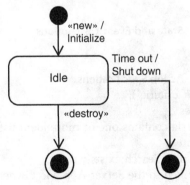

H.4.16.1   Attribute Descriptions
None

H.4.16.2   State and Event Descriptions
None

H.4.16.3   Action Specifications
initialize (^client, ^server, optional ^owner):
  requires
    ^client is a valid Client App
    ^server is a valid Server App of the appropriate type
    if given, ^owner is a valid Owner
  guarantees
    one new Session exists with:
      linked to the Client App
      linked to the Server App
      if an owner was given, linked to that Owner
Shut down:
  requires
    none
  guarantees
    Time out has been signaled for the associated Client App

H.4.17   Search

A Search involves using Index Entries for selected Search Terms in order to quickly and easily find relevant content in Shared Datum. This class has only trivial custodial behavior so no explicit state diagram is needed.

H.4.17.1   Attribute Descriptions
None

H.4.17.2   State and Event Descriptions
None

H.4.17.3   Action Specifications
initialize (criteria):
  requires
    criteria contains one or more identifiable Search Terms
  guarantees
    one new Search exists with:
      linked to the Server App and Owner

linked to all identifiable Searchable Terms

References to relevant Shared Datum derived from Index Entries are available

H.4.18   Sys Admin

Sys Admin is an actor that represents people whose job it is to maintain configuration of Data Centers. This class has no state diagram because it is an actor and is mostly external.

H.4.18.1   Attribute Descriptions
None

H.4.18.2   State and Event Descriptions
None

H.4.18.3   Action Specifications
None

H.4.18.4   Source of
All custodial events relating to maintaining Home and Data Center configuration.

H.4.18.5   Destination of
None

H.5   Association Dictionary

Where necessary and appropriate, this section provides detailed descriptions of associations in the domain. In this domain, no additional association descriptions are necessary because all associations are adequately specified in the class diagram.

H.6   Relevant Notes

None

Appendix I

(Pro Forma) Scalability Design

This appendix illustrates the structure and content of an interface specification and design specification for Scalability. These examples are far from complete; real specifications would be much larger. Also, they would almost certainly be separate documents: at a minimum, the interface specification in one document and the design specification in another. For the remainder of this appendix, example content is shown in plain text, while *comments about structure and content are shown in italics.*

I.1 Interface Specification

This section illustrates the structure and content of an interface specification for Scalability. A complete interface specification would be too large—this only communicates basic structure and content.

This interface specification covers four separate topics:

- How client-side application developers write code to connect to scalable server-side application code
- How scalable server-side application developers write code to make it available to client-side application developers
- How scalable server-side application developers write code to communicate with other server-side application code
- How a data center Sys Admin configures the Scalability service for deployment into a data center

I.1.1 Developer's Guide for Scalable Client-Side Code

This section explains how a client-side application developer writes code to connect with scalable server-side applications. Specific topics addressed include:

How to Engineer Software: A Model-Based Approach, First Edition. Steve Tockey.
© 2019 the IEEE Computer Society, Inc. Published 2019 by John Wiley & Sons, Inc.

- ConnectShared(type)—How to connect to the right type of scalable Server-App when access to only shared data is needed.
- ConnectOwner(type, owner)—How to connect to the right type of scalable ServerApp when access to owned data is needed. Access to shared data is still available.
- Search(criteria)—How to search shared data to find matches consistent with given search criteria.
- Request-response()—The generic structure of a request to the server-side and the server-side's response.
- Disconnect()—How to disconnect from a ServerApp.
- TimeOut()—How the ClientApp will be notified that their session timed out due to inactivity.

This section also needs to discuss client-side application code in light of High availability. Specifically, a connected ServerApp may temporarily disappear due to a crash. The client-side needs to wait for some amount of time for the service to reappear and then reconnect to it. There is also a distinct possibility that some server-side state got lost in the crash and fail-over. Robust client-side application code needs to deal with this possibility.

I.1.2 Developer's Guide for Scalable Server-Side Code

This section explains how a server-side application developer writes code to make it available to client-side applications. Also, this section explains how one server-side application can connect with another and how a server-side application accesses scalable data on the different kinds of data servers. Specific topics addressed include:

- Defining a server-side app type
- The structure of a generic request-response and how to customize it into an application-specific function accessing the Owned and SharedDatum manipulations
- How scalable server-side application developers write code to communicate with other server-side application code

This section needs to warn server-side application developers that referential integrity of OwnedDatum is entirely their responsibility. For example, if any other OwnedDatum held a reference to some OwnedDatum that was deleted, that reference would now be invalid.

This section also needs to discuss writing server-side application code in light of High availability. Specifically, a connected DataServer or other ServerApp may temporarily disappear due to a crash, server-side code needs to wait for some amount of time for the service to reappear and then reconnect to it. There is also a distinct possibility that some Scalable application state got lost in the crash and fail-over. Robust server-side application code needs to deal with this possibility.

I.1.3 Configuring a Data Center for Scalability

This section would explain how a data center SysAdmin would configure a Scalable data center, possibly in terms of one or more .ini-like data files.

I.2 High-Level Design

This section would present and justify the high-level design for Scalability. A complete high-level design specification would be too large and complex—this only communicates the basic structure and content. High-level design documentation is only relevant in domains where a model compiler is not used. Where a model compiler is used, the high-level design is implicit in the production rules. Also, per the discussion on literate programming in Chapter 22, it would be more effective if this documentation were in true hypertext form rather than forced into an arbitrary linear sequence as shown below.

Unless explicitly stated otherwise, design decisions should be assumed to have been made because they seemed reasonable at the time.

I.2.1 Design Use Case Diagram(s)

To the extent that the high-level design warrants a use case diagram, it can go here. Otherwise, reference the set of use cases in the semantic model and just list any additional technology-based use cases. For the purposes of Scalability, there should be no new technology-based use cases.

I.2.2 High-Level Design Class Diagram(s)

This section presents the high-level design class diagrams for Scalability. Scalability is manifested across five different kinds of computers, each of which is presented separately. Instance variables have been intentionally left off all design diagrams to reduce size. Private data for each class is presented in the Section I.3.

The distributed nature of the Scalability service calls for use of Java Remote Method Invocation[1] (RMI). Design elements named <something>Intf are interface declarations to support RMI-based distribution.

---

1 See, for example, https://en.wikipedia.org/wiki/Java_remote_method_invocation

I.2.2.1 ClientApp

Figure I.1 shows a high-level design diagram for a ClientApp. ClientApp is the client-side application code. Note that there really isn't any Scalability-specific "design" other than it being written as explained in the Section I.1.1. Any code that complies with that description is automatically a ClientApp. HomeIntf and ServerAppIntf are RMI interfaces to support distributed communication.

I.2.2.2 Home

Figure I.2 shows a high-level design diagram for Home. Home is the main connection point into a scalable server-side implementation. DataCenterIntf is an RMI interface to support distributed communication with the various Data Centers. Home and DataCenterIntf are bundled together to form one kind of Service as defined in High availability.

I.2.2.3 DataCenter

Figure I.3 shows a high-level design diagram for DataCenter. The various <something>Intf elements are RMI interfaces to support distributed communication with the different kinds of distributed servers. All elements on this diagram are bundled together to form one kind of Service as defined in High availability.

View-controller region for SysAdmin (if it's not all .ini data configuration files) could be included on this diagram as well, if it is small enough.

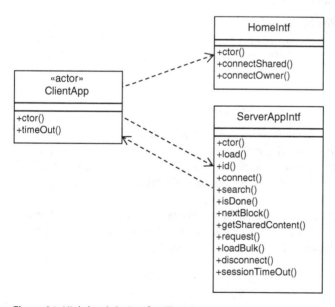

Figure I.1 High-level design for ClientApp.

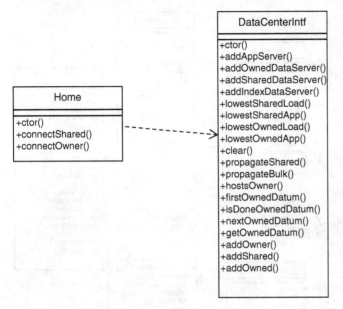

Figure I.2 High-level design for Home.

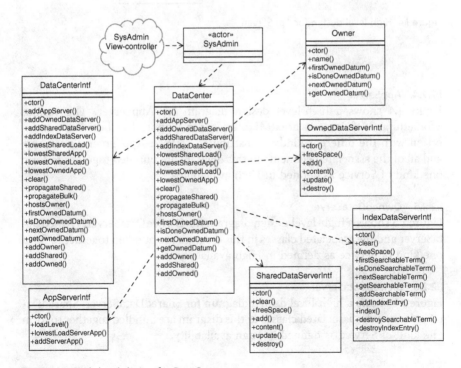

Figure I.3 High-level design for DataCenter.

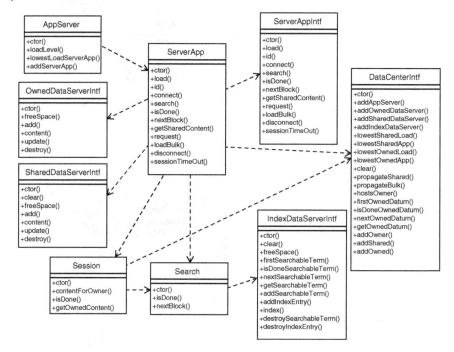

Figure I.4 High-level design for AppServer.

I.2.2.4 AppServer

Figure I.4 shows a high-level design diagram for AppServer. The various <something>Intf elements are RMI interfaces to support distributed communication with the different kinds of distributed servers. AppServer, ServerApp, and all of the associated elements in this diagram are bundled together to form one kind of Service as defined in High availability.

I.2.2.5 OwnedDataServer

Figure I.5 shows a high-level design diagram for OwnedDataServer. OwnedDataServer and the associated classes in this diagram are bundled together to form one kind of Service as defined in High availability.

I.2.2.6 SharedDataServer

Figure I.6 shows a high-level design diagram for SharedDataServer. SharedDataServer and the associated classes in this diagram are bundled together to form one kind of Service as defined in High availability.

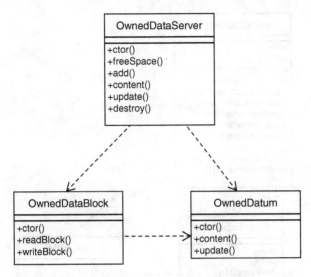

Figure I.5 High-level design for OwnedDataServer.

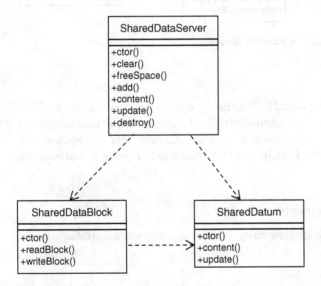

Figure I.6 High-level design for SharedDataServer.

I.2.2.7 IndexDataServer

Figure I.7 shows a high-level design diagram for IndexDataServer. IndexData-Server and the associated classes in this diagram are bundled together to form one kind of Service as defined in High availability.

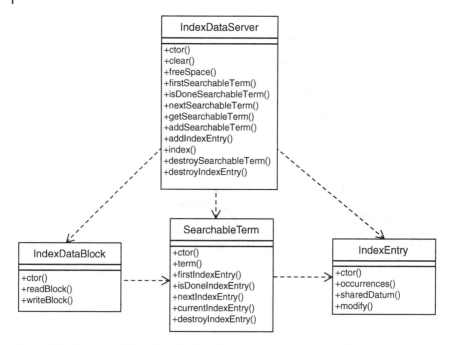

Figure I.7 High-level design for IndexDataServer.

The rest of this section would explain and justify the high-level design for Scalability. In particular, if View-controller region for the SysAdmin user interface is complex enough, it could require a separate diagram and description. Denormalization as discussed in Chapter 19 should also be explained and justified, if relevant.

I.2.3   Interaction Diagram(s)

This section would provide interaction (sequence, communication) diagrams for selected use cases.

I.2.4   Class Dictionary

The public interface—both syntax and semantics—of every class in the high-level design is specified in this section. *High-level design documentation needs to go down to the level of defining the syntax (signatures) and semantics (contracts) for each public operation on each class in the high-level design.*

I.2.4.1 ClientApp

ClientApp represents the client-side application code. This is the design representation of class Client App in the semantic model. There really isn't any relevant "design" other than it being written consistent with Section I.1.1. Any code consistent with that description is automatically a compliant ClientApp.

I.2.4.2 Home

This is the design representation of Home in the semantic model. The high-level design would be explained and justified here.

I.2.4.3 HomeIntf

HomeIntf is a helper that allows ClientApp code to more easily access Home. The high-level design would be explained and justified here.

I.2.4.4 SysAdmin

This is the design representation of Sys Admin in the semantic model. The high-level design would be explained and justified here.

I.2.4.5 DataCenter

This is the design representation of Data Center in the semantic model. The high-level design would be explained and justified here.

I.2.4.6 DataCenterIntf

DataCenterIntf is a helper that allows Home, ServerApp, and other DataCenter code to more easily access DataCenters. The high-level design of DataCenterIntf would be explained and justified here.

I.2.4.7 Owner

This is the design representation of Owner in the semantic model. The high-level design would be explained and justified here. In particular, discussion of the Iterator pattern operations to access that owner's OwnedDatum needs to be explained clearly.

I.2.4.8 AppServer

This is the design representation of App Server in the semantic model. The high-level design would be explained and justified here.

I.2.4.9 AppServerIntf

AppServerIntf is a helper that allows DataCenter code to more easily access its connected AppServers. The high-level design would be explained and justified here.

I.2.4.10   ServerApp

This is the design representation of Server App in the semantic model. The high-level design would be explained and justified here. In particular, that this is the interface/base class for writing server-side application code (as described in the Section I.1.1). Also, discussion of the Iterator pattern operations to access search results needs to be explained clearly.

I.2.4.11   ServerAppIntf

ServerAppIntf is a helper that allows ClientApp and other ServerApp code to more easily access its connected ServerApp. The high-level design would be explained and justified here. In particular, discussion of the Iterator pattern operations to access search results needs to be explained clearly.

I.2.4.12   Session

This is the design representation of Session in the semantic model. The high-level design would be explained and justified here.

I.2.4.13   Search

This is the design representation of Search in the semantic model. The high-level design would be explained and justified here. In particular, discussion of the Iterator pattern operations to access search results needs to be explained clearly.

I.2.4.14   OwnedDataServer

This is the design representation of Owned Data Server in the semantic model. The high-level design would be explained and justified here.

I.2.4.15   OwnedDataServerIntf

OwnedDataServerIntf is a helper that allows DataCenter and ServerApp code to more easily access its connected OwnedDataServers. The high-level design would be explained and justified here.

I.2.4.16   OwnedDataBlock

OwnedDatum need to have two different run-time representations. One representation is as a memory-resident object as described above for OwnedDatum. The other representation is in a serialized format, stored on a disk. This allows an OwnedDataServer to store and manage many more OwnedDatum than could fit in the computer's memory. When access to some specific OwnedDatum is needed, if that datum is already in memory, then it is directly accessed. If that datum is not in memory, the OwnedDataBlock containing it is read into memory (possibly overwriting some other memory-resident OwnedDataBlock). If datum in some OwnedDataBlock has been modified or deleted, then the updated data block will need to be rewritten to disk before it is replaced by an incoming data block.

I.2.4.17   OwnedDatum

This is the design representation of Owned Datum in the semantic model. The high-level design would be explained and justified here—in particular, the identifier for OwnedDatum. For example, it could be a string that involves the name of the DataServer it resides on, the name of the OwnedDataBlock it's stored in, and it's specific OwnedDatum Id. This would make OwnedDatum identifiers globally unique as well as assist in quick access given the identifier.

I.2.4.18   SharedDataServer

This is the design representation of Shared Data Server in the semantic model. The high-level design would be explained and justified here.

I.2.4.19   SharedDataServerIntf

SharedDataServerIntf is a helper that allows DataCenter and ServerApp code to more easily access its connected SharedDataServers. The high-level design would be explained and justified here.

I.2.4.20   SharedDataBlock

SharedDatum need to have two different run-time representations. One representation is as a memory-resident object as described above for SharedDatum. The other representation is in a serialized format, stored on a disk. This allows a SharedDataServer to store and manage many more SharedDatum than could fit in the computer's memory. When access to some specific SharedDatum is needed, if that datum is already in memory, then it is directly accessed. If that datum is not in memory, the SharedDataBlock containing it is read into memory (possibly overwriting some other memory-resident SharedDataBlock). If datum in some SharedDataBlock has been modified or deleted, then the updated data block will need to be rewritten to disk before it is replaced by an incoming data block.

I.2.4.21   SharedDatum

This is the design representation of Shared Datum in the semantic model. The high-level design would be explained and justified here—in particular, the identifier for SharedDatum. For example, it could be a string that involves the name of the DataServer it resides on, the name of the SharedDataBlock it's stored in, and it's specific SharedDatum Id. This would make SharedDatum identifiers globally unique as well as assist in quick access given the identifier.

I.2.4.22   IndexDataServer

This is the design representation of Index Data Server in the semantic model. The high-level design would be explained and justified here.

I.2.4.23   IndexDataServerIntf

IndexDataServerIntf is a helper that allows DataCenter and ServerApp code to more easily access its connected IndexDataServers. The high-level design would be explained and justified here.

I.2.4.24   SearchableTerm

This is the design representation of SearchableTerm in the semantic model. The high-level design would be explained and justified here.

I.2.4.25   IndexDataBlock

SearchableTerm and IndexEntry need to have two different run-time representations. One representation is as a memory-resident object as described above. The other representation is in a serialized format, stored on a disk. This allows an IndexDataServer to store and manage many more SearchableTerms than could fit in the computer's memory. When access to some specific Searchable-Term and its associated IndexEntries is needed, if that data are already in memory, then it is directly accessed. If that datum is not in memory, the Index-DataBlock containing it is read into memory (possibly overwriting some other memory-resident IndexDataBlock). If data in some IndexDataBlock have been modified or deleted, then the updated data block will need to be rewritten to disk before it is replaced by an incoming data block.

I.2.4.26   IndexEntry

This is the design representation of IndexEntry in the semantic model. The high-level design would be explained and justified here.

From here on would be discussions of the high-level designs for the various classes that make up View-controller and Infrastructure region, if any.

I.3   Detailed Design

This section would document the design on the other side of the class encapsulation barrier. For each class in the high-level design, this level of documentation explains and justifies internal data (class and instance variable) structures as well as internal algorithm (class and instance method) structures. Explanations and justifications for mappings of semantic model attributes and ranges onto run-time data types along with discussions and justifications for algorithm choices and nontrivial semantic preserving transforms would be relevant topics. Again, ideally this documentation would not be a strictly linearized paper document as shown in this appendix; it would be an interconnected web of design detail and justification linked to code per literate programming.

I.3.1 Detailed Designs of Classes

The detailed design of each class follows.

I.3.1.1 ClientApp
Any relevant detailed design of ClientApp would be explained and justified here. There probably isn't any relevant "design" other than it being written consistent with Section I.1.1. Any code consistent with that description is automatically a compliant ClientApp.

I.3.1.2 Home
The detailed design of Home would be explained and justified here.

I.3.1.3 HomeIntf
The detailed design of HomeIntf would be explained and justified here.

I.3.1.4 SysAdmin
The detailed design of SysAdmin would be explained and justified here.

I.3.1.5 DataCenter
The detailed design of DataCenter would be explained and justified here.

I.3.1.6 DataCenterIntf
The detailed design of DataCenterIntf would be explained and justified here.

I.3.1.7 Owner
The detailed design of Owner would be explained and justified here.

I.3.1.8 AppServer
The detailed design of AppServer would be explained and justified here.

I.3.1.9 AppServerIntf
The detailed design of AppServerIntf would be explained and justified here.

I.3.1.10 ServerApp
The detailed design of ServerApp would be explained and justified here. In particular, that this is the interface/base class for writing server-side application code (as described in the Section I.1.1).

I.3.1.11 ServerAppIntf
The detailed design of ServerAppIntf would be explained and justified here.

I.3.1.12 Session
The detailed design of Session would be explained and justified here.

I.3.1.13 Search
The detailed design of Search would be explained and justified here.

I.3.1.14 OwnedDataServer
The detailed design of OwnedDataServer would be explained and justified here.

I.3.1.15 OwnedDataServerIntf
The detailed design of OwnedDataServerIntf would be explained and justified here.

I.3.1.16 OwnedDataBlock
The detailed design of OwnedDataBlock would be explained and justified here. In particular this would be a discussion of the structure of the data file. Also, how a memory-resident class handles reading, caching, and writing the disk files as needed by a ServerApp.

I.3.1.17 OwnedDatum
The detailed design of OwnedDatum would be explained and justified here. In particular, both the memory-resident and on-disk representations of OwnedDatum need to be explained and justified.

I.3.1.18 SharedDataServer
The detailed design of SharedDataServer would be explained and justified here.

I.3.1.19 SharedDataServerIntf
The detailed design of SharedDataServerIntf would be explained and justified here.

I.3.1.20 SharedDataBlock
The detailed design of SharedDataBlock would be explained and justified here. In particular this would be a discussion of the structure of the data file. Also, how a memory-resident class handles reading, caching, and writing the disk files as needed by a ServerApp.

I.3.1.21 SharedDatum
The detailed design of SharedDatum would be explained and justified here. In particular, both the memory-resident and on-disk representations of SharedDatum need to be explained and justified.

I.3.1.22 IndexDataServer
The detailed design of IndexDataServer would be explained and justified here.

I.3.1.23 IndexDataServerIntf
The detailed design of IndexDataServerIntf would be explained and justified here.

I.3.1.24 SearchableTerm

The detailed design of SearchableTerm would be explained and justified here. In particular, both the memory-resident and on-disk representations of Searchable-Term need to be explained and justified.

I.3.1.25 IndexDataBlock

The detailed design of IndexDataBlock would be explained and justified here. In particular this would be a discussion of the structure of the data file. Also, how a memory-resident class handles reading, caching, and writing the disk files as needed by a ServerApp.

I.3.1.26 IndexEntry

The detailed design of IndexEntry would be explained and justified here. In particular, both the memory-resident and on-disk representations of IndexEntry need to be explained and justified.

From here on would be discussions of the detailed designs for the various classes that make up View-controller and Infrastructure region, if any.

Appendix J

Semantic Model for High availability

This appendix is an example of a semantic model—a specification of policies to enforce and processes to carry out—for the High availability domain in WebBooks 2.0.

J.1 Use Case Diagram

Use cases identify scope (processes to carry out) at the coarsest level. Actors identify context. Figure J.1 shows actors and use cases in High availability. Each actor and use case is described in detail in later sections.

J.2 Class Diagram

The class model specifies policies to be enforced. Figure J.2 shows classes, attributes, associations, and generalizations in High availability. Each class is defined in detail in Section J.4. To the extent necessary, associations are defined in Section J.5.

J.3 Interaction Diagrams

Interaction diagrams describe process at an intermediate level. This section provides interaction (in this case sequence) diagrams for selected use cases. Sequence diagrams were chosen over communication diagrams because they are more natural and intuitive to most readers.

J.3.1 Run Cluster

Figure J.3 shows the sequence diagram for the Run cluster use case. This use case takes an offline cluster and brings it all online at the same time. The

How to Engineer Software: A Model-Based Approach, First Edition. Steve Tockey.
© 2019 the IEEE Computer Society, Inc. Published 2019 by John Wiley & Sons, Inc.

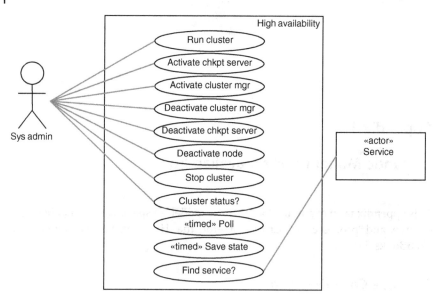

Figure J.1 Use case diagram for High availability.

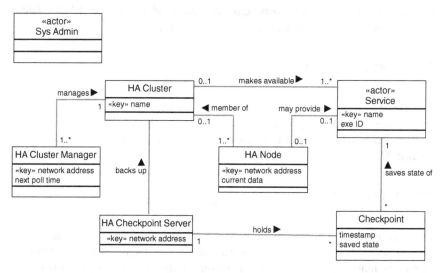

Figure J.2 Class diagram for High availability.

diagram shows the normal scenario; two alternate scenarios are not explicitly diagrammed. One alternate scenario is when there are more Services than HA Nodes. In this case, the Cluster needs to activate as many Services as there are nodes, but notify the Sys Admin that one or more Services are not activated.

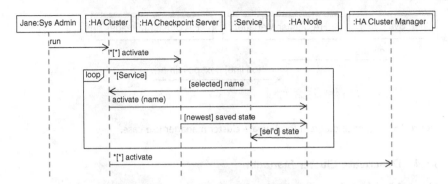

Figure J.3 Sequence diagram for Run cluster use case.

The other alternate scenario is when there is no saved state for a Service being activated. In this case, notify the Sys Admin as well. Note that the diagram also glosses over the minor detail that the [newest] Saved state comes from a Checkpoint on an HA Checkpoint Server. The diagram doesn't fit on the page with that many objects involved, so it was omitted even though it's a part of the full use case.

J.3.2 Activate Checkpoint Server

Figure J.4 shows the sequence diagram for the Activate checkpoint server use case. This use brings one offline Checkpoint server to online, presumably because it had previously crashed and got repaired/rebooted so that it can be used for checkpointing. Checkpointing involves both saving HA Node state snapshots and recovering them when HA Nodes are activated. The sequence diagram for this use case is trivial. Had this been a real semantic model, this sequence diagram would probably have been omitted.

J.3.3 Activate Cluster Manager

Figure J.5 shows the sequence diagram for the Activate cluster manager use case. This use brings one offline HA Cluster Manager to online, presumably because it had previously crashed and got repaired/rebooted. It is now available to help manage the cluster.

Figure J.4 Sequence diagram for Activate checkpoint server use case.

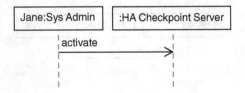

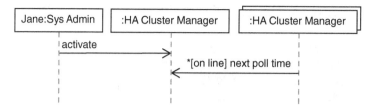

Figure J.5 Sequence diagram for Activate cluster manager use case.

J.3.4 Deactivate Cluster Manager

Figure J.6 shows the sequence diagram for the Deactivate cluster manager use case. This use case takes one online HA Cluster Manager and brings it offline, presumably so maintenance can be done on it. The sequence diagram for this use case is trivial. Had this been a real semantic model, this sequence diagram would probably have been omitted.

J.3.5 Deactivate Checkpoint Server

Figure J.7 shows the sequence diagram for the Deactivate checkpoint server use case. This use case takes one online HA Checkpoint Server and brings it offline, presumably so maintenance can be done on it. The sequence diagram for this use case is trivial. Had this been a real semantic model, this sequence diagram would probably have been omitted.

J.3.6 Deactivate Node

Figure J.8 shows the sequence diagram for the Deactivate node use case. This use case takes one online HA Node and brings it offline, presumably so maintenance can be done on it. The scenario in this diagram assumes that at least one

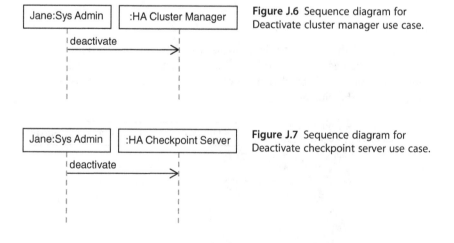

Figure J.6 Sequence diagram for Deactivate cluster manager use case.

Figure J.7 Sequence diagram for Deactivate checkpoint server use case.

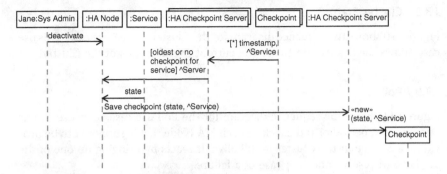

Figure J.8 Sequence diagram for Deactivate node use case.

HA Checkpoint Server has no Checkpoint for the Service being deactivated. If all HA Checkpoint Servers have a Checkpoint for the Service, then oldest Checkpoint will be overwritten. This use case also assumes that once deactivated, the next polling cycle of any HA Cluster Manager will restart the Service on some other available HA Node (i.e., reactivation of Services is implicit, not explicit in this use case).

J.3.7 Stop Cluster

Figure J.9 shows the sequence diagram for the Stop cluster use case. This use case takes an entire cluster offline, presumably for large-scale maintenance. This diagram slightly oversimplifies the saving of HA Node states by assuming a new one is created for each HA Node. In truth, the sequence should be similar to the Deactivate node use case but was simplified to fit on this page.

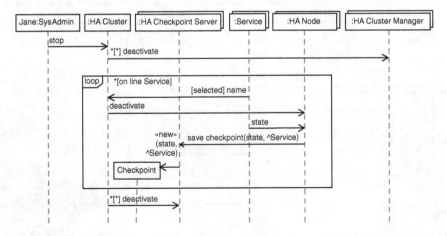

Figure J.9 Sequence diagram for Stop cluster use case.

J.3.8 Cluster Status?

Figure J.10 shows the sequence diagram for the Cluster status? use case. This use case allows the Sys Admin to see the current overall status of the Cluster.

J.3.9 Poll

Figure J.11 shows the sequence diagram for the Poll use case. This use case is «timed» (i.e., periodic) and checks if each HA Node that is supposed to be providing a Service in the Cluster is still alive. It reacts by bringing up one of the available M reserve nodes in case of a failure.

J.3.10 Save State

Figure J.12 shows the sequence diagram for the Save state use case. This use case is also «timed» (i.e., periodic) and saves a Checkpoint for an online HA Node in the Cluster. The scenario in this diagram slightly oversimplifies in that it

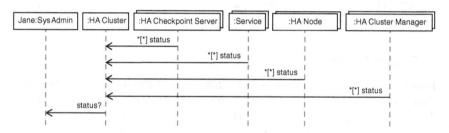

Figure J.10 Sequence diagram for Stop cluster use case.

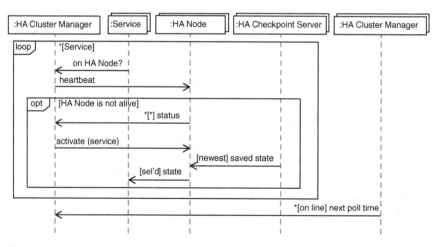

Figure J.11 Sequence diagram for Poll use case.

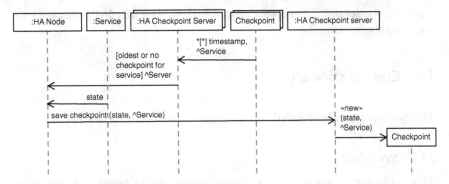

Figure J.12 Sequence diagram for Save state use case.

assumes an HA Checkpoint Server exists without a Checkpoint for the Service so it creates one. If all online HA Checkpoint Servers have a Checkpoint for that Service, then the oldest is overwritten.

J.3.11 Find Service?

Figure J.13 shows the sequence diagram for the Find service? use case. This use case allows one Service to get the network address of the HA Node that is currently providing some other Service that this one wants to communicate with.

J.3.12 Un-diagrammed Use Cases

Some use cases have not been diagrammed for various reasons, typically because their diagrams would be too trivial. This section lists the sea level use cases that have not been diagrammed to be sure the complete scope of this domain is known:

- Custodial use cases for creating and deleting all classes, esp. a new Service.
- Force save node state (almost identical to Deactivate node).
- All of the crash/repair scenarios for each type of resource: HA Node, HA Checkpoint Server, HA Cluster Manager. In case of crash, the computing

Figure J.13 Sequence diagram for Find service? use case.

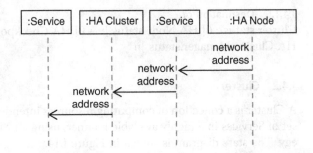

resource essentially disappears. After having been repaired/rebooted, it's essentially re-created.

J.4   Class Dictionary

This section provides detailed specifications of each class in the domain.

J.4.1   Sys Admin

This is the actor who is responsible for monitoring a Cluster and keeping it operational. This class has no state diagram because it is an actor and is mostly external to this domain.

J.4.1.1   Attribute Descriptions
None

J.4.1.2   State and Event Descriptions
None

J.4.1.3   Action Specifications
None

J.4.1.4   Source of
run cluster
activate checkpoint server
activate cluster manager
deactivate cluster manager
deactivate checkpoint server
deactivate node
stop cluster
force save node state
all of the custodial dynamics

J.4.1.5   Destination of
Cluster status?: 0[HA Node.status]n + 0[HA Checkpoint Server.status]n + 0[HA Cluster Manager.status]n

J.4.2   Cluster

A Cluster is a collection of computing resources intended to provide a specified set of Services in a highly available manner, using an M + N redundancy strategy. The state diagram is shown in Figure J.14.

Figure J.14 State diagram for
Cluster.

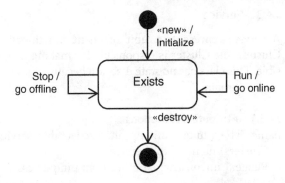

J.4.2.1 Attribute Descriptions
name: The (unique among all discoverable clusters) name of this Cluster
   Range: [unconstrained other than uniqueness]

J.4.2.2 State and Event Descriptions
None

J.4.2.3 Action Specifications
initialize (name):
   requires
        name is consistent with the range of .name
   guarantees
        one new Cluster exists with:
             .name properly assigned
        all Cluster components (Services, HA Nodes, etc.,) have been created
go on line:
   requires
        none
   guarantees
        activate has been signaled for all HA Checkpoint Servers
        activate (name) has been signaled to HA Nodes for all Services
             if any Service can't be activated, Sys Admin has been signaled
        activate has been signaled for all HA Cluster Managers
go off line:
   requires
        none
   guarantees
        deactivate has been signaled for all HA Cluster Managers
        deactivate has been signaled to HA Nodes for all Services
        deactivate has been signaled for all HA Checkpoint Servers

J.4.3   Service

A service represents a unit of client functionality assigned to a particular Cluster. The Cluster is responsible for making that Service as available as possible. This class has no state diagram because it is an actor and is mostly external to the domain.

J.4.3.1   Attribute Descriptions

name: The (unique among all discoverable services across all discoverable Clusters) name of the service.
Range: [unconstrained other than uniqueness]

exe ID: A reference to the executable image (e.g., a *.exe file) that implements this service. Note that the same .exe file can be the executable image for more than one Service.
Range: [unconstrained]

J.4.3.2   State and Event Descriptions
None

J.4.3.3   Action Specifications
None

J.4.3.4   Source of
None

J.4.3.5   Destination of
Find service? (service name): network address

J.4.4   HA Node

Each HA Node is a computing resource whose intent is to provide a service—or be available as a backup in case some other HA Node crashes. The strategy for implementing high availability of Services is to have more HA Nodes than Services—this is the N + M strategy. N of the HA Nodes are expected to provide the necessary Services. The remaining M are in reserve: ready to go online when needed. Deriving an appropriate value for M requires knowledge of N along with the reliability (e.g., Mean Time Between Failure [MTBF]) of HA Nodes. The state diagram is shown in Figure J.15.

J.4.4.1   Attribute Descriptions

network address: A globally unique (e.g., an IP address and TCP port) that allows other computing resources to talk with this HA Node
Range: [unconstrained other than uniqueness]

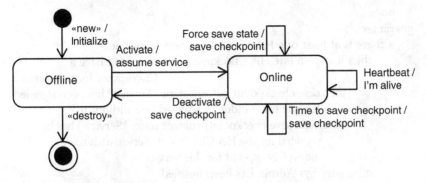

Figure J.15 State diagram for HA Node.

current data: Represents the current run-time configuration of the node
  Range: [a BLOB of node state]

J.4.4.2 State and Event Descriptions
The optimum interval for the "time to save checkpoint" event might be determined based on information in [Daly04].

J.4.4.3 Action Specifications
initialize (address):
  requires
    address is consistent with the range of .network address
  guarantees
    one new HA Node exists with:
      .network address properly assigned
assume service (name):
  requires
    name references a valid Service
  guarantees
    the HA Node has been loaded with the Service's .exe image
    the most recent Checkpoint, if any, for the named Service has
been loaded
      if no Checkpoint existed, Sys Admin has been signaled
I'm alive:
  requires
    none
  guarantees
    heartbeat has been signaled for the HA Cluster Manager who pinged
save checkpoint:
  requires

guarantees
  if there is at least one HA Checkpoint Server on line
    then if any on line HA Checkpoint Server doesn't have a
                Checkpoint for this Service
      then save checkpoint(current state, ^Service) has been signaled
        for any one randomly selected one without it
      otherwise save checkpoint(current state, ^Service) has been
        signaled for the HA Checkpoint Server with the
        oldest Checkpoint for this Service
  otherwise Sys Admin has been notified

J.4.5 HA Checkpoint Server

A checkpoint server is a computing resource that is intended to provide a repository of saved Checkpoints for Services. If an HA Node providing a Service fails, that Service's last known state can be pushed into a different, currently offline HA Node, thus making the Service available again with minimal disruption.

HA Checkpoint Servers are also subject to N + M redundancy; there should be more checkpoint servers than minimally needed to store checkpoints for all Services. As long as there is more than one checkpoint server available, requests to store a Checkpoint should first go to any server that doesn't have one. Otherwise it should go to the server that has the oldest Checkpoint. Should an HA Node need a Checkpoint for recovery, that Checkpoint should come from the checkpoint server that has the newest one. The state diagram is shown in Figure J.16.

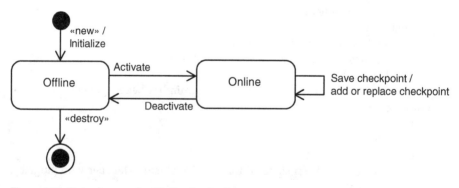

Figure J.16 State diagram for HA Checkpoint Server.

J.4.5.1 Attribute Descriptions

network address: A globally unique (e.g., an IP address and TCP port) that allows other computing resources to talk with this HA Checkpoint Server

Range: [unconstrained other than uniqueness]

J.4.5.2 State and Event Descriptions

None

J.4.5.3 Action Specifications

initialize (address):

    requires

        address is consistent with the range of .network address

    guarantees

        one new HA Checkpoint Server exists with:

            .network address properly assigned

add or replace checkpoint (state, ^Service):

    requires

        ^Service references a valid Service

    guarantees

        if a Checkpoint for the referenced Service already exists on this server

            then update (state) has been signaled for it

            otherwise new Checkpoint(state, ^Service) has been signalled

J.4.6 Checkpoint

Each Checkpoint is a snapshot of the then-current state of an HA Node that was online, providing some Service. If the HA Node for a Service crashes, we have a last known state to go back to. Load that latest known state into a currently offline but available (one of the M in the N + M) HA Node and the Service is available again with minimal disruption. Of course, whatever service state changes happened between the last checkpoint and the crash have been lost, but the role of this domain is "availability," not "reliability." The state diagram is shown in Figure J.17.

J.4.6.1 Attribute Descriptions

timestamp: Captures the time at which this Checkpoint was saved

Range: [a date and time earlier than now, to the nearest second]

current data: Captures Service state at that time, so an available, offline HA Node can take on this state in the event that the HA Node currently providing the Service crashes

Range: [a BLOB of node state]

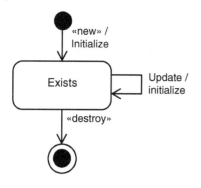

Figure J.17 State diagram for Checkpoint.

J.4.6.2 State and Event Descriptions
None

J.4.6.3 Action Specifications
initialize (state, ^Service):
    requires
        ^Service is a valid Service
    guarantees
        one new Checkpoint exists with:
            .saved state == state
            .timestamp == now
            linked to ^Service
            linked to HA Checkpoint Server

J.4.7 HA Cluster Manager

HA Cluster Managers are computing resources responsible for monitoring Services provided by the N working HA Nodes. When an HA Node fails, an HA Cluster Manager is responsible for finding an offline HA Node and reassigning the Service to the new node using the most recently saved Checkpoint.

If HA Cluster Managers never crashed, we would only need one. However, they do crash so others need to be available. HA Cluster Managers work sequentially: each one schedules itself to poll one polling interval after the latest one. If a HA Cluster Manager crashes, of course it will miss its polling time. Assuming its peers didn't also crash, then the next one would poll at its scheduled time. If only one HA Cluster Manager crashed, only one polling cycle would be missed.

The state diagram is shown in Figure J.18.

J.4.7.1 Attribute Descriptions
network address: A globally unique (e.g., an IP address and TCP port) that allows other computing resources to talk with this HA Cluster Manager
    Range: [unconstrained other than uniqueness]

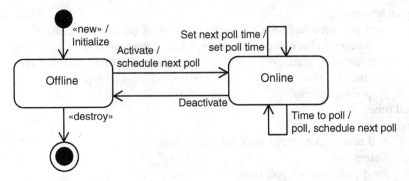

Figure J.18 State diagram for HA Cluster Manager.

next poll time: The timestamp at which the next polling is due, assuming this
    cluster manager is on line
    Range: [a date and time, to the nearest second, between now and some time
      in the reasonable future]

J.4.7.2 State and Event Descriptions
None

J.4.7.3 Action Specifications
initialize (address):
    requires
        address is consistent with the range of .network address
    guarantees
        one new HA Cluster Manager exists with:
            .network address properly assigned
            .next poll time == now
poll:
    requires
        none
    guarantees
        the HA Node for each Service in this Cluster has been ping-ed
            if any HA Node has crashed
                then activate(service) has been signaled for any available,
                      off line HA Node
                if no off line HA Nodes were available
                    then Sys Admin has been notified
set next poll time:
    requires
        none

guarantees
> next poll time has been set to the latest of all on line HA Cluster Manager plus one polling interval. E.g., if manager1 has a .next poll time of A, manager2 has a .next poll time of B (one interval later than A), then this .next poll time has been set to B plus one polling interval

set poll time:
> requires
>> poll time is consistent with .next poll time
> guarantees
>> .next poll time == poll time

J.5   Association Dictionary

Where necessary and appropriate, this section provides detailed descriptions of associations in the domain. In this domain, no additional association descriptions are necessary because all associations are adequately specified in the class diagram.

J.6   Relevant Notes

This model assumes an HA Node can run only one Service at a time. It should not be difficult to capture (as attributes) both HA Node capacity (CPU cycles, memory, disk space) and Service requirements and be able to put more than one Service on a single HA Node—as long as node capacities aren't exceeded.

Appendix K

(Pro Forma) High availability Design

This appendix illustrates the structure and content of an interface specification and design specification for High availability. These examples are far from complete; real specifications would be much larger. Also, they would almost certainly be separate documents: at a minimum, the interface specification in one document and the design specification in another. For the remainder of this appendix, example content is shown in plain text, while *comments about structure and content are shown in italics*.

K.1   Interface Specification

This section illustrates the structure and content of an interface specification for High availability. A complete interface specification would be too large—this only communicates basic structure and content. A real interface specification for High availability could easily be two separate documents:

- *User guide for Sys Admins*
- *Developer's guide to writing code to use High availability services*

K.1.1   User Guide for Sys Admin

This section illustrates an interface specification for Sys Admins of High availability installations.

K.1.1.1   Introduction
This section would provide an overview of the Sys Admin's user interface and address topics such as:

- *How to start and stop the Sys Admin interface*
- *Seeing what options are available and selecting options—which would presumably be in the form of buttons and text fields on Sys Admin GUI screens*

How to Engineer Software: A Model-Based Approach, First Edition. Steve Tockey.
© 2019 the IEEE Computer Society, Inc. Published 2019 by John Wiley & Sons, Inc.

- *How to correct mistakes, if needed*
- *Using a help facility, if one exists*

K.1.1.2   Dialog Map

To the extent that a dialog map would be useful for the Sys Admin interface, it would go here.

K.1.1.3   Use Cases

This section elaborates each of the use cases as implemented in terms of the Sys Admin's console. *The focus of this section should be on the Sys Admin's perspective and explain how to accomplish each sea level use case (i.e., transaction). This is preferred over more typical user documentation that only shows a series of screen shots and then discusses each of the fields and buttons on each screen without providing any logical ordering to the descriptions.*

Each use case description would include some amount of narrative, but should also include (or refer to) hi- or low-fidelity representations of the screens.

K.1.1.3.1   Run a Cluster
Explain and show examples of how a Sys Admin would start up a Cluster.

K.1.1.3.2   Activate Checkpoint Server
Explain and show examples of how a Sys Admin would select an offline HA Checkpoint Server in a cluster and activate it.

K.1.1.3.3   Activate Cluster Manager
Explain and show examples of how a Sys Admin would select an offline HA Cluster Manager and activate it.

K.1.1.3.4   Deactivate Cluster Manager
Explain and show examples of how a Sys Admin would select an online HA Cluster Manager and deactivate it.

K.1.1.3.5   Deactivate Checkpoint Server
Explain and show examples of how a Sys Admin would select an online HA Checkpoint Server and deactivate it.

K.1.1.3.6   Deactivate Node
Explain and show examples of how a Sys Admin would select an on line HA Node and deactivate it.

K.1.1.3.7   Stop cluster
Explain and show examples of how a Sys Admin would stop a Cluster.

K.1.1.3.8   Cluster Status

Explain and show examples of how a Sys Admin would monitor the status of a Cluster.

K.1.1.3.9   Configuring a Cluster

Explain and show examples of how a Sys Admin would configure the High availability service to execute in specific Cluster hardware. This would presumably be a discussion of how to set up configuration data files that the High availability service would read on initialization so that the right run-time objects would exist.

K.1.2   Developer's Guide to Using High availability Services

This section outlines a guide for developers who need to design and develop code that uses High availability services.

K.1.2.1   Introduction

This section would provide an overview of the High availability API and address topics such as how to connect to that API—this should include descriptions and examples of application code. The most likely implementation of this API would be that class Service is either an abstract base class or a Java interface.[1] Assume for this example that Service is an abstract base class. This section would explain the useful operations available on the API or that need to be implemented in application-level code.

K.1.2.1.1   state()

Explain and show examples of how a service needs to make its current state available for checkpointing. This should include a discussion of how, when requested, the service should pause activity for clients when it is stable, provide the state, and then resume client activity.

K.1.2.1.2   Set state()

Explain and show examples of how a service accepts a new state from a previously saved checkpoint. On completion the service should assume it is now available.

K.2   High-Level Design

This section illustrates the structure and content of a high-level design for High availability. A complete high-level design specification would be too large for this book—this only communicates basic structure and content. High-level and

---

1 That is, in Java terms, `public interface Service { ... }`.

detailed design documentation is only relevant in domains where a model compiler is not used. Where a model compiler is used, the design is implicit in the production rules. Also, per the discussion on literate programming in Chapter 22, it would be more effective if this documentation were in true hypertext form rather than forced into an arbitrary linear sequence as shown below.

Unless explicitly stated otherwise, design decisions should be assumed to have been made because they seemed reasonable at the time.

K.2.1   Design Use Case Diagram(s)

To the extent that the high-level design warrants a use case diagram, it can go here. Otherwise, reference the set of use cases in the semantic model and just list any additional technology-based use cases. For the purposes of High availability, there should be no technology-based use cases.

K.2.2   High-Level Design Class Diagram(s)

This section presents the high-level design class diagrams for High availability. High availability is manifested across four different kinds of computers, each of which is presented separately. Instance variables have been intentionally left off all design diagrams to reduce size. Private data for each class is presented in Section K.3.

The distributed nature of the High availability service calls for use of Java Remote Method Invocation[2] (RMI). Design elements named <something>Intf are interface declarations to support RMI-based distribution.

K.2.2.1   SysAdmin Console

Figure K.1 shows a high-level design diagram for SysAdmin Console. The Sys Admin's user interface to High availability is nontrivial; therefore the View-controller region that supports it is also nontrivial but is only shown here as a cloud.

The rest of this section would explain and justify the high-level design for this part of the system.

K.2.2.2   HA Cluster Controller

Figure K.2 shows the high-level design diagram for HA Cluster Controller. This implements both HA Cluster and HA Cluster Manager from the semantic model.

The rest of this section would explain and justify the high-level design for this part of the system.

---

2 See, for example, https://en.wikipedia.org/wiki/Java_remote_method_invocation.

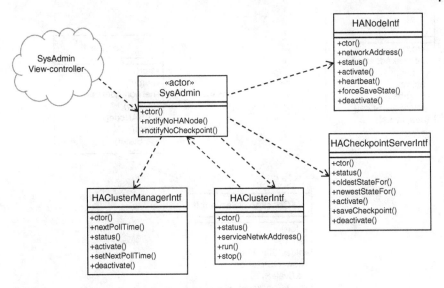

Figure K.1 High-level design for SysAdmin Console.

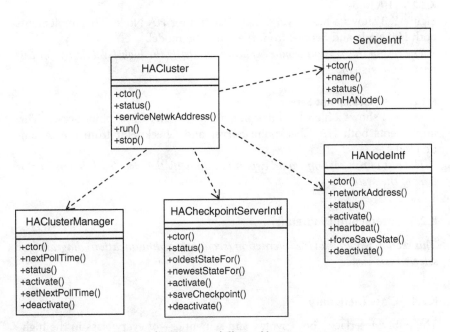

Figure K.2 High-level design for Cluster and Cluster Manager.

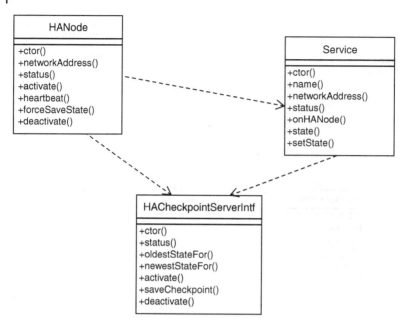

Figure K.3 High-level design for HA Node.

K.2.2.3 HA Node

Figure K.3 shows a high-level design diagram for HA Node. This implements both HA Node and Service from the semantic model.

The rest of this section would explain and justify the high-level design for this part of the system.

K.2.2.4 HA Checkpoint Server

Figure K.4 shows a high-level design diagram for HA Checkpoint Server. This implements both HA Checkpoint Server and Checkpoint from the semantic model.

The rest of this section would explain and justify the high-level design for this part of the system.

K.2.3 Interaction Diagram(s)

This section would provide interaction (sequence, communication) diagrams for selected use cases.

K.2.4 Class Dictionary

The public interface—both syntax and semantics—of every class in the high-level design is specified in this section. *High-level design documentation needs*

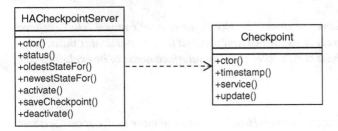

Figure K.4 High-level design for HA Checkpoint Server.

to go down to the level of defining the syntax (signatures) and semantics (contracts) for each public operation on each class in the high-level design.

K.2.4.1 SysAdmin
This is the design representation of SysAdmin in the semantic model. The high-level design would be explained and justified here.

K.2.4.2 HACluster
This is the design representation of HACluster in the semantic model. The high-level design would be explained and justified here.

K.2.4.3 HAClusterIntf
HAClusterIntf is a helper that allows SysAdmin code to more easily access HAClusters. The high-level design would be explained and justified here.

K.2.4.4 HAClusterManager
This is the design representation of HAClusterManager in the semantic model. The high-level design would be explained and justified here.

K.2.4.5 HAClusterManagerIntf
HAClusterIntf is a helper that allows SysAdmin code to more easily access HAClusterManagers. The high-level design would be explained and justified here.

K.2.4.6 HANode
This is the design representation of HANode in the semantic model. The high-level design would be explained and justified here.

K.2.4.7 HANodeIntf
HANodeIntf is a helper that allows SysAdmin and HACluster code to more easily access HANodes. The high-level design would be explained and justified here.

K.2.4.8 Service

This is the design representation of Service in the semantic model. The high-level design of Service would be explained and justified here; in particular the decision to make Service a base class rather than an interface needs to be explained and justified.

K.2.4.9 ServiceIntf

ServiceIntf is a helper that allows HACluster code to more easily access Services. The high-level design would be explained and justified here.

K.2.4.10 HACheckpointServer

This is the design representation of HACheckpointServer in the semantic model. The high-level design would be explained and justified here.

K.2.4.11 HACheckpointServerIntf

HACheckpointServerIntf is a helper that allows SysAdmin, HACluster, and HANode code to more easily access HACheckpointServers. The high-level design would be explained and justified here.

K.2.4.12 Checkpoint

This is the design representation of Checkpoint in the semantic model. The high-level design of Checkpoint would be explained and justified here.

K.3   Detailed Design

This section would document the design on the other side of the class encapsulation barrier. For each class in the high-level design, this level of documentation explains and justifies internal data (class and instance variable) structures as well as internal algorithm (class and instance method) structures. Explanations and justifications for mappings of semantic model attributes and ranges onto run-time data types along with discussions and justifications for algorithm choices and nontrivial semantic preserving transforms would be relevant topics. Again, ideally this documentation would not be a strictly linearized paper(like) document as shown in this appendix; it would be an interconnected web of design detail and justification linked to code per literate programming.

K.3.1   Detailed Designs of Classes

The detailed design of each class follows.

K.3.1.1   SysAdmin
The detailed design of SysAdmin would be explained and justified here.

K.3.1.2   HACluster
The detailed design of HACluster would be explained and justified here. Assuming that a cluster is statically configured in terms of one or more data files (e.g., identifying the Services that need to be made available, along with the HA Nodes and HA Checkpoint Servers that exist), those data files need to be defined and described here.

K.3.1.3   HAClusterIntf (in SysAdmin)
The detailed design of HAClusterIntf would be explained and justified here.

K.3.1.4   HAClusterManager
The detailed design of HAClusterManager would be explained and justified here.

K.3.1.5   HAClusterManagerIntf
The detailed design of HAClusterManagerIntf would be explained and justified here.

K.3.1.6   HANode
The detailed design of HANode would be explained and justified here. In particular, this could say that to improve performance when saving a checkpoint, only content that has changed since the last checkpoint on the selected Checkpoint server is needed.

K.3.1.7   HANodeIntf
The detailed design of HANodeIntf would be explained and justified here.

K.3.1.8   Service
The detailed design of Service would be explained and justified here, in particular the methods for the concrete operations on the interface.

K.3.1.9   ServiceIntf
The detailed design of ServiceIntf would be explained and justified here.

K.3.1.10   HACheckpointServer
The detailed design of HACheckpointServer would be explained and justified here.

K.3.1.11 HACheckpointServerIntf

The detailed design of HACheckpointServerIntf would be explained and justified here.

K.3.1.12 Checkpoint

The detailed design of Checkpoint would be explained and justified here. In particular, this needs to explain how the saved state from a running HA Node is to be represented (presumably in one or more data files on the Checkpoint Server's disk(s)).

Appendix L

Semantics of Semantic Modeling

Given that

Engineering = scientific theory + practice + engineering economy

this appendix identifies the scientific theory—specifically, computer science and discrete math—for model-based software engineering. This appendix defines the semantics of semantic modeling in terms of a semiformal foundation. The foundation defines how to interpret a semantic model and is the anchor that gives it one single precise meaning.

This appendix has three parts:

- Meta-model—A semantic model of semantic modeling, that is, a model of the semantics of the semantic modeling language: Sections L.1 through L.5
- UML profile for semantic modeling—Necessary additional semantics that are missing (or, possibly, just not obvious) in the meta-model: Section L.6
- A discussion of measurement theory and programming languages: Section L.7

The semantic models for Order fulfillment (Appendix D), Payment (Appendix F), Scalability (Appendix H), High availability (Appendix J), and even this semantic model are all in terms of these semantics.

L.1   Use Case Diagram

Figure L.1 shows the actors and use cases in semantic modeling. Use cases identify scope (processes) at the coarsest level. Actors identify context.

How to Engineer Software: A Model-Based Approach, First Edition. Steve Tockey.
© 2019 the IEEE Computer Society, Inc. Published 2019 by John Wiley & Sons, Inc.

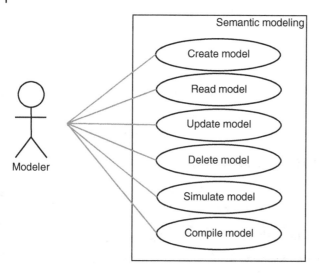

Figure L.1 Use case diagram for semantic modeling.

L.2   Class Diagram

The class diagram shows classes, attributes, associations, and generalizations in semantic modeling. This only defines modeling language semantics: the policies of semantic modeling. It is not a schema for a modeling tool. This defines aspects of completeness, consistency, and interpretation of semantic models. A modeling tool would necessarily need to relax many of these constraints to allow for creation and evolution of models. From a tool perspective, a useful function would be to check a given semantic model against these more restrictive criteria to determine if that model were complete and consistent. As discussed in Chapter 12, any semantic model should also be validated by review, inspection, and/or simulation.

Each class is defined in detail in the class dictionary below. To the extent necessary, associations may also be defined in the association dictionary below.

Due to complexity and page size limits, the class diagram is spread across four figures:

- Figure L.2 shows the class diagram for associations and generalizations.
- Figure L.3 shows the class diagram for attributes and ranges.
- Figure L.4 shows the class diagram for state modeling.
- Figure L.5 shows the class diagram for action parameters.

All class diagrams share one core class, Class. This is the common reference point across all diagrams and ties them together. Any class that appears in more than one diagram has a superscript plus sign (+) following its name.

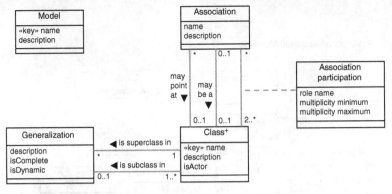

Figure L.2 Class diagram for associations and generalizations.

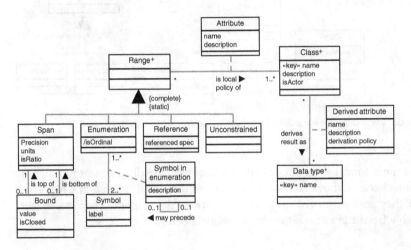

Figure L.3 Class diagram for attributes and ranges.

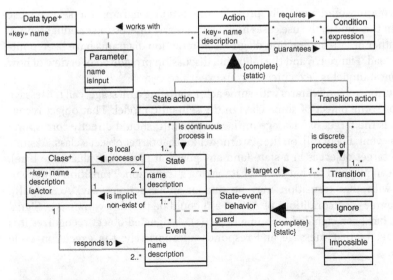

Figure L.4 Class diagram for state models.

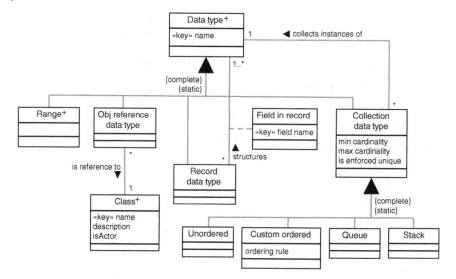

Figure L.5 Class diagram for action parameters (i.e., formal parameters).

This meta-model does not directly support use case diagrams or interaction diagrams because they don't add semantic content. As discussed in Chapters 7 and 9, they are convenient summaries of core model content. They are, in fact, derivable from the information in the models below.

L.3 Interaction Diagrams

This section would normally provide interaction diagrams for selected use cases. In this model, the use cases aren't particularly interesting or enlightening, and neither are the interaction diagrams. Interaction diagrams have been omitted. Instead, Figure L.6 and the following discussion provide an overview of how a semantic model is "executed" for an event use case.

Execution generally starts with some actor signaling a message, call it Message m[i], for some object of some class in the semantic model. That object recognizes it is the target of Message m[i]. Message m[i] should directly correspond with an event, Event e[i], on the state model for that target object's class. Assuming the target object is in a state (and any guard, if present, evaluates to true), then it can respond to that event by it making a transition, Transition t[i]. Associated with that transition may be one or more actions, say, Action a[i]. A guarantee (postcondition) of Action a[i] could be that a new message, Signal m[i+1], has been signaled for some object(s). A signaled object recognizes it is the target of that message and responds appropriately: the execution cycle repeats.

The execution cycle should eventually stop for one of the following reasons:

- The new message is signaled for a single object via an association with a multiplicity minimum of zero, but there is no currently linked object.
- The new message is signaled for a selection of objects via an association with multiplicity maximum greater than one, but no associated objects match the selection criteria.
- The target object(s) is not in a state (or, possibly, the guard evaluates to false) where it can respond to Event e[i], so the event is ignored.
- Transition t[i] has no actions.
- None of the actions on Transition t[i] signal any new messages.

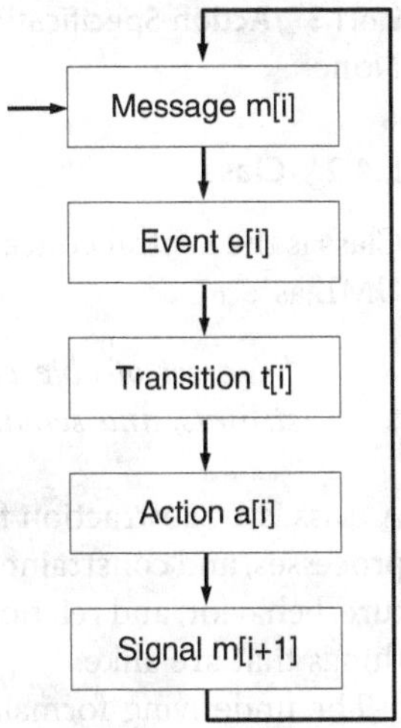

Figure L.6 Executing an event use case in a semantic model.

L.4 Class Dictionary

This section provides detailed specifications of each class in the meta-model. Note that while actor Modeler appears in the use case diagram, it does not appear in the class diagram and it is not elaborated below because it doesn't add sufficient value to this meta-model. Also, none of the classes in this semantic model have state diagrams because state diagrams don't add any value either.

L.4.1 Model

Model is the highest-level container of semantic model content. It organizes all of the content for the semantic model of a (sub)domain. This class might also be considered as representing a (sub)domain.

L.4.1.1 Attribute Descriptions

«key» name: The name of this model. This would almost certainly be the name of the (sub)domain being specified in this model.
Range: [unconstrained other than uniqueness among all relevant semantic models]

description: Descriptive text providing an overview of this model, possibly (a reference to) the Background and Minimum conditions of acceptance documentation.
Range: [unconstrained]

L.4.1.2 State and Event Descriptions
None

L.4.1.3 Action Specifications
None

L.4.2 Class

Class is the central concept in semantic modeling. A class is formally defined in UML as[1]:

> *"... a set of objects that share the same specifications of features, constraints, and semantics."*

A class is an abstraction for a set of things that are subject to the same policies, processes, and constraints. It is a descriptor for a set of things with similar structure, behavior, and relationships. Informally, it is a stencil or template for a set of things that are alike.

The underlying formalism for classes is set theory[2] and relational algebra.[3] Each class is a set with an extension (the members that exist now) and intension (all members who could possibly ever exist). The extensions of each set can be manipulated in relational algebra terms.

L.4.2.1 Attribute Descriptions
«key» name: The name of the class. Classes should be named using a singular noun or noun phrase that describes the role of that class in this (sub)domain. Range: [unconstrained other than uniqueness among all classes in this model]

description: The descriptive text providing a dictionary-like definition of the class: inclusion criteria, exclusion criteria, relevance to the (sub)domain, contrasts, examples, aliases, etc. Class descriptions should be provided for completeness, reviewability, and long-term maintainability. Range: [unconstrained]

isActor: Specifies whether or not this class is an actor in the (sub)domain. Range: [true | false]

L.4.2.2 State and Event Descriptions
None

L.4.2.3 Action Specifications
None

---

1 See [OMG11b].
2 See, for example, https://en.wikipedia.org/wiki/Set_theory.
3 See, for example, https://en.wikipedia.org/wiki/Relational_algebra.

L.4.3 Association

According to the UML specification, an association[4]:

> *"... specifies a semantic relationship that can occur between typed instances. It has at least two ends represented by properties, each of which is connected to the type of the end."*

Where a class abstracts a set of policy and process-relevant objects, associations abstract a set of relevant connections between objects, aka "links." Each link connects one real-world object with at least one (most likely other) real-world object, for example, Customer 47 and Bank account 123456. A reflexive association connects objects of the same class, but likely not the same instance (e.g., Mary is biological parent of Phred). More than two classes can be connected, that is, an n-ary association. Associations exist to support processing of the form "Given an object of class X, which object or objects of class Y is it connected to?"

An association should only appear in a semantic model when at least one other process (i.e., transaction, sea level use case) needs to traverse that link separately from the process that created it. If no such other process exists, the association must not appear. Otherwise it adds unnecessary complexity and causes useless, non-value-added design and dead code to be created and maintained.

The underlying formalism for associations is also set theory. An association represents member-to-member mappings between the objects in the extension of the associated classes.

L.4.3.1 Attribute Descriptions

name: The name of the association. UML does not require an association to be named; however experience shows that well-named associations contribute to model understandability. Association names also do not need to be unique within a model. A specific association can be identified in terms of Class name–Association name–Class name (e.g., "Customer places Order"). On the other hand, the name should at least be unique among all associations between the same associated classes. Every association should also be named in a way that expresses the reason for linking: "Why are those classes associated?" Vague, meaningless names like "has," "contains," or similarly content-free names should be avoided.

Range: [unconstrained, other than uniqueness among the same participating classes]

---

4 See [OMG11b].

description: The descriptive text providing a dictionary-like definition of the association: what does this association mean in (sub)domain policy and process terms?
Range: [unconstrained]

L.4.3.2 State and Event Descriptions
None

L.4.3.3 Action Specifications
None

L.4.4 Association Participation

This class represents how the referenced Class participates in the referenced Association. As an example, in Figure L.2 association "is superclass in" is between Class and Generalization. There would be two instances of Association Participation for this association:

- One for class Class participating in "is superclass in" with .multiplicity minimum == 1 and .multiplicity maximum == 1. In English, "A Generalization has exactly one Class in the role of Superclass, no more and no less."
- One for class Generalization participating in "is superclass in" with .multiplicity minimum == 0 and .multiplicity maximum == *. In English, "a Class doesn't need to be a superclass in any Generalizations, but can be a superclass in many."

Insofar as the meta-model class Association participation is an association class between Class and Association, the formal interpretation is to impose an invariant constraint (policy) of the form "For all objects, o, of a Class, C, object o can be linked no less than .multiplicity minimum times and no more than .multiplicity maximum times."

L.4.4.1 Attribute Descriptions
role name: UML supports, and sometimes it is useful, to name the participation in terms of a role.
Range: [unconstrained except for uniqueness among all associations between the participating classes]

multiplicity minimum: The minimum number of objects of the referenced Class that must participate in the referenced Association.
Range: [0, 1, or some other policy-mandated positive whole number less than or equal to this participation's .multiplicity maximum]

multiplicity maximum: The maximum number of objects of the referenced Class that must participate in the referenced Association.

Range: [1, *, or some other policy-mandated positive whole number greater than or equal to this participation's .multiplicity minimum]

L.4.4.2 State and Event Descriptions
None

L.4.4.3 Action Specifications
None

L.4.5 Generalization

This represents a generalization–specialization (i.e., inheritance) relationship between two or more classes. The generalization between class Range and classes Span, Enumeration, Reference, etc. in Figure L.3 is an example. Two very important aspects of generalization in semantic models are the following:

- A generalization graph must be acyclic. More precisely, any generalization structure must form a pure hierarchy; it cannot be a network of any kind: a class cannot generalize itself, nor can a class generalize any subclass of which it is also a subclass. that is, no class X may be a subclass of any class Y where Y is also somehow a subclass of X
- Properties of subclasses are strictly additive—properties of any specialization cannot override any property of its generalization; they can only supplement.

The underlying formalism for Generalization is also set theory. The specializations (subclasses) under a Generalization need to form a set partition of that generalization (superclass). This is why Generalizations must be {disjoint}, {overlapping} is not allowed. Use role associations instead of {overlapping} as described in Figure 8.27. Role associations are simpler, cleaner, more correct, and more obvious to readers. If a generalization is {incomplete}, it means there is at least one implicit subclass, say, "Other," for objects not in any of the explicit subclasses.

L.4.5.1 Attribute Descriptions
description: A description of the Generalization. This is usually unnecessary, but someone may want to put one in at some point so it should be allowed.
Range: [unconstrained]

isComplete: This represents constraint {complete} on a class diagram. It specifies if the set of immediate subclasses represent all possible subclasses for the superclass. Another way to interpret this is that, when true, it says that the superclass is "abstract" in design and code terms.
Range: [true | false]

isDynamic: Specifies if there is a dependency between state(s) in the state model of the superclass and any subclasses. Said another way, that dependency

means that changes in superclass state may cause and/or require changes in subclass and vice versa: changes in subclass may cause and/or require changes in superclass state. One superclass state may cover several subclasses, or one subclass may cover several superclass states. The relationship between superclass state and subclass must be explicit and invariant.[5]
Range: [true | false]

L.4.5.2 State and Event Descriptions
None

L.4.5.3 Action Specifications
None

L.4.6 Range

This is a superclass for the different kinds of range specifications. There's nothing interesting about it other than being the base that supports participation in association class Attribute.

The underlying formalism for Range is measurement theory.[6]

L.4.6.1 Attribute Descriptions
None

L.4.6.2 State and Event Descriptions
None

L.4.6.3 Action Specifications
None

L.4.7 Span

Span (i.e., "span with precision and units") is a kind of Range that normally has a lower bound, an upper bound (either of which might not exist, implying the bound on that side is "unconstrained"), a precision, and a unit. In measurement theory terms, this corresponds to at least an interval scale and possibly a ratio scale—depending on policy and process semantics of the value "0" (zero). Values in the same Span can always be added and subtracted. To be fully consistent with measurement theory, values in a Span can only be multiplied or divided when it is a ratio scale.

---

5 As shown, for example, in Figures 10.29 and 10.30 and in Table 10.2.
6 See also the discussion in Section L.7.

L.4.7.1 Attribute Descriptions

precision: Specifies the smallest significant quantity of measure. A precision of "to the nearest 0.001" means that the thousandths digit is the least significant digit—anything smaller: ten thousandths or less, is not significant. The Runway.usable length example uses "to the nearest 500 feet."

Range: [a numeric value, less than or equal to the difference between any specified upper and lower bounds]

units: Specifies the unit that the span measures, for example, miles, degrees C, degrees K, US dollars, euros, angstroms, ohms, etc.

Range: [technically unconstrained, but should be the name of a unit that a typical domain expert should be expected to understand. If not generally understood, provide a reference to where that unit is adequately and appropriately defined]

isRatio: Specifies whether this Span is a ratio scale or an interval scale in measurement theory terms.

Range: [true | false]

L.4.7.2 State and Event Descriptions

None

L.4.7.3 Action Specifications

None

L.4.8 Bound

A Bound precisely specifies one end of an associated Span.

L.4.8.1 Attribute Descriptions

value: The value that is at an edge of the associated Span.

Range: [any numeric value no more precise than the .precision in its associated Span]

isClosed: Specifies whether the given .value is within (a closed interval) the legal set for the associated Range or is not (an open interval). If not .isClosed, the closest legal value is determined by the Span's .precision, for example, up to 10v with precision of 0.1v so the closest legal value is 9.9v.

Range: [true | false]

L.4.8.2 State and Event Descriptions

None

L.4.8.3 Action Specifications
None

L.4.9 Enumeration

Enumeration is a kind of Range that, in measurement theory terms, represents either a nominal or ordinal scale. A set of symbols make up the specified Range; those symbols may be unordered (a nominal scale) or ordered (an ordinal scale).

L.4.9.1 Attribute Descriptions
/isOrdinal: An Enumeration can be determined to be ordinal or not by the presence (ordinal) or absence (nominal) of "may precede" associations on its associated Symbol in Enumerations.
   Range: [true | false]

L.4.9.2 State and Event Descriptions
None

L.4.9.3 Action Specifications
None

L.4.10 Symbol

A Symbol is a name, a label, or other distinguishing mark that can be an element in some Enumeration.

L.4.10.1 Attribute Descriptions
label: This is the name, label, or other distinguishing mark.
   Range: [unconstrained]

L.4.10.2 State and Event Descriptions
None

L.4.10.3 Action Specifications
None

L.4.11 Symbol in Enumeration

This specifies that some given Symbol is a member of some specific Enumeration. The same Symbol cannot occur in the same Enumeration more than once.

L.4.11.1 Attribute Descriptions

description: A description of the symbol. It is at least theoretically possible that any Symbol could appear in more than one Enumeration at the same time and the meaning of that Symbol in those Enumerations could be different. Usually there isn't any need for a description, but someone may want to put one in at some point so it needs to be allowed.

Range: [unconstrained]

L.4.11.2 State and Event Descriptions
None

L.4.11.3 Action Specifications
None

L.4.12 Reference

Reference is a kind of Range that identifies an external document, authority, specification, policy, etc. as the authoritative source. This helps support the "one fact, one place" documentation principle in Appendix A by allowing a semantic model to point at that authoritative source rather than duplicate its content.

L.4.12.1 Attribute Descriptions

referenced spec: The name of the external authoritative source. This could also refer to a specific location in the document (e.g., "See section 4.2 of Corporate Policy 123456").

Range: [unconstrained]

L.4.12.2 State and Event Descriptions
None

L.4.12.3 Action Specifications
None

L.4.13 Unconstrained

A kind of Range that means stakeholders don't have, or even want, constraints. Any constraints imposed in implemented software would be technology constraints driven by cost versus functionality engineering tradeoffs. This class is explicit in the meta-model to make Range a {complete} generalization.

L.4.13.1 Attribute Descriptions
None

L.4.13.2 State and Event Descriptions
None

L.4.13.3 Action Specifications
None

L.4.14 Attribute

An Attribute can be defined as:

> *"a (kind of) fact about (sub-) domain-relevant objects that is necessary to support one or more processes."*

Informally, attributes represent pieces of useful information (data) about objects of a class. Examples would be the .balance of a Bank account, the .status of a Bank account, the .overdraft limit of a Bank account, the .name of a Student, the .birthdate of a Licensed driver, and so on. Attributes always apply at the object (i.e., instance) level only; "static" or "class" attributes are not allowed in a semantic model.

The underlying formalism for Attribute is relational algebra. A Class represents a relation (table), Attributes represent columns in that table, and the objects (formally, that Class' "Extension") can be represented by rows in that table. Insofar as the meta-model class Attribute is an association class between Class and Range, the formal interpretation is to impose an invariant constraint (policy) of the form "For all objects, o, of a Class, C, the value for its Attribute, a, shall be within the specified Range, r."

L.4.14.1 Attribute Descriptions
name: The name of the attribute. Like classes, attributes are typically named with nouns or noun phrases.
Range: [unconstrained other than uniqueness within the containing class and all its superclasses]

description: A description of the attribute, that is, its relevance to policies and processes. Descriptions should be provided for every attribute to enhance understandability and support long-term maintainability.
Range: [unconstrained]

L.4.14.2 State and Event Descriptions
None

L.4.14.3 Action Specifications
None

L.4.15 Derived Attribute

This represents an attribute whose value can be recomputed at any time from information available elsewhere in the semantic model. For class Hourly Employee with normal attributes .pay rate and .hours worked, attribute .gross pay would be derivable by multiplying .pay rate by .hours worked. At the modeler's discretion, derived attributes may be included in the model or not. If a derived attribute is included, it must be flagged as such (e.g., using UML's "/" notation).

Formally, a Derived Attribute does not imply stored data. It only mandates a consistency relationship between a "dependent variable" (the derived attribute) and one or more "independent variables" (that other information).

L.4.15.1 Attribute Descriptions
name: The name of the derived attribute.
   Range: [unconstrained other than uniqueness within this class and all its containing superclasses]

description: A discussion of the meaning and/or relevance of this derived attribute.
   Range: [unconstrained]

derivation policy: Defines or references a (possibly external) policy or process that specifies the necessary consistency between the dependent variable and the independent variables.
   Range: [unconstrained]

L.4.15.2 State and Event Descriptions
None

L.4.15.3 Action Specifications
None

L.4.16 State

The UML definition of a state is[7]:

> "... *a situation during which some (usually implicit) invariant condition holds. The invariant may represent a static situation such as an object*

---

7 See [OMG11b].

> *waiting for some external event to occur. However, it can also model dynamic conditions such as the process of performing some behavior (i.e., the [object] under consideration enters the state when the behavior commences and leaves it as soon as the behavior is completed)."*

A state is a continuous segment of time where the behavior of an object is consistent and stable:

- Consistent in the sense of the reaction it will have to happenings in its environment.
- Stable in the sense that the object will stay in that state until some happening (an event) causes it to change state.

This meta-model assumes a minimum of two states for every class: Exists and ~Exists. In other words, the state of nonexistence is explicit in this meta-model. Specifically, when an instance of Class is created, it defaults to the state model(s) in Figure L.7.

The underlying formalism for States, Events, Transitions, etc. is finite automata theory.

L.4.16.1 Attribute Descriptions

name: The name of the state.
  Range: [unconstrained other than uniqueness within the Class and all of its superclasses]

description: An optional definition that could address such topics as: what happened to get an object into this state, what is happening now, and what will probably happen in the future.
  Range: [unconstrained]

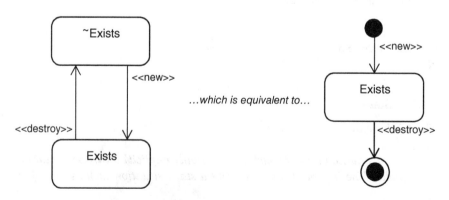

Figure L.7 Default implicit state model for a class.

L.4.16.2 State and Event Descriptions
None

L.4.16.3 Action Specifications
None

L.4.17 Event

The UML definition of an event is[8]:

> "... *the specification of some occurrence that may potentially trigger effects by an object.*"

An event is an occurrence or happening that can affect the state of an object— what that object is doing now or how it will react in the future. More specifically, an event can advance the sequencing or timing of a process.

Events do not persist over time (i.e., they are not implicitly remembered). If any object is not in the right state to respond immediately, the event is ignored: it is discarded without having any effect.

L.4.17.1 Attribute Descriptions
name: The name of the event.
> Range: [unconstrained other than uniqueness within the Class and all containing superclasses]

description: an optional description of the meaning of the event.
> Range: [unconstrained]

L.4.17.2 State and Event Descriptions
None

L.4.17.3 Action Specifications
None

L.4.18 State–event Behavior

Defines the behavior for a given State + Event + Guard combination, that is, if an object of that Class is in that State and it sees that Event while that Guard evaluates to true, then what happens (if anything)? An unguarded transition is represented by a default guard value of "true."

---

8 See [OMG11b].

When using UML State chart notation, absence of a transition out of some state on some event does not distinguish safely ignorable from impossible.[9] For semantic model completeness (e.g., particularly in safety- or mission-critical applications), there needs to be a State–event Behavior for each State + Event pair in the state model of every Class.

An unspecified but necessary candidate «key» is the implicit (foreign key) attributes of "from state," "on event," and "guard." To ensure semantic model determinism, if more than one State–event Behavior has the same "from state" and "on event," then the guards on all those State–event Behaviors must be mutually exclusive: no more than one of those guard expressions can ever evaluate to true at the same time.

L.4.18.1   Attribute Descriptions
guard: The conditions under which this state + event pair will cause a transition.
   Range: [a Boolean expression that might be, simply, "true"]

L.4.18.2   State and Event Descriptions
None

L.4.18.3   Action Specifications
None

L.4.19   Impossible

A type of State–event Behavior that specifies the referenced Event can never occur when an object of the referenced Class is in the referenced State and the Guard evaluates to true. Particularly in safety- or mission-critical implementations, code should be designed and constructed in a way that properly addresses this situation should it ever be recognized at run time (e.g., throw a fatal exception, etc.).

L.4.19.1   Attribute Descriptions
None

L.4.19.2   State and Event Descriptions
None

L.4.19.3   Action Specifications
None

---

9 Discussed in detail in Chapter 10.

L.4.20 Ignore

A type of State–Event Behavior that specifies the referenced Event may occur when an object is in the referenced State and the Guard evaluates to true but is harmless. In the design and construction of any implementation, it is acceptable to do nothing at all.

L.4.20.1 Attribute Descriptions
None

L.4.20.2 State and Event Descriptions
None

L.4.20.3 Action Specifications
None

L.4.21 Transition

A type of State–Event Behavior that means, at a minimum, if the referenced Event happens for an object of the Class when it is in the referenced State and the Guard evaluates to true, then there is a change to a new state. That new state is specified in association State is target of Transition. The referenced new State is usually in the state model of the same class referenced in the State–Event Behavior, but doesn't need to be. The new state can be in a state model of a superclass of the transitioning object. The new state cannot be in the state model of a class that not a superclass of this class.

Transitions in state models are assumed to take essentially zero time regardless of how complex any associated Transition Action(s) might be. Specifically, no arguments can be made in a semantic model based on how fast or slow any one computation may be, although this can be entirely relevant in design and code. Execution of all associated Actions on any Transition is also assumed to be concurrent except where data flow dependencies force sequencing.

L.4.21.1 Attribute Descriptions
None

L.4.21.2 State and Event Descriptions
None

L.4.21.3 Action Specifications
None

L.4.22 Action

An Action specifies work to be done: computation. Generally, actions do some combination of the following:

• Compute a result from given input parameters.

- Modify (write) one or more attribute values of the containing object.
- Signal events, presumably for other objects.[10]

Formally, Actions are pure functions. Actions have no persistent internal state that is remembered from one execution to the next. All persistent state must be external to the actions, specifically, in the form of attribute values, existence of objects, and links between objects.

L.4.22.1 Attribute Descriptions

name: The name of the action.
>Range: [unconstrained other than uniqueness within the containing Class and its superclasses]

action specification: The specification of what work (computation) needs to happen
>Range: [technically unconstrained, but to be considered a pure semantic model (a CIM), this should be in contract (requires/guarantees) or other non-algorithmic form. The existence of any algorithmic specification would make the containing semantic model a PIM or PSM]

L.4.22.2 State and Event Descriptions

None

L.4.22.3 Action Specifications

None

L.4.23 Transition action

As the name should imply, a Transition Action specifies work to be done on a state model transition. It represents discrete, one-shot function and can only be associated with transitions. In the UML notation, entry/, exit/, and eventName/ are shorthand notations. Transition actions (including entry/, exit/, and event-name/) represent "one-shot" functions that complete in essentially zero time.

Formally, transition actions define process semantics of the form "As long as any associated 'requires' (i.e., contract pre-conditions) Conditions are true before the action is executed, then all associated 'guarantees' (i.e., contract post-conditions) Conditions are true after (i.e., when the Transition is complete." If any "requires" condition is not true, the state of model execution immediately becomes undefined.

---

10 Explicitly including «new» and «destroy» to create and delete objects.

L.4.23.1   Attribute Descriptions
None

L.4.23.2   State and Event Descriptions
None

L.4.23.3   Action Specifications
None

L.4.24   State action

As the name should imply, a State action specifies work to be done in a state model state. It represents continuous computation and can only be associated with states. As long as the object is in an appropriate state, the State action continuously computes. When a transition goes between two states that both have the same state action, that state action executes without interruption. Execution of a state action only stops when there is a transition from a state with that state action to a state without that state action.

State actions should be defined in terms of some kind of continuous computation (e.g., control law, data flow diagram, graph such as a sine wave, etc.).

Formally, state actions define process semantics of the form "As long as any associated 'requires' (i.e., contract pre-conditions) Conditions are true, then all associated 'guarantees' (i.e., contract post-conditions) Conditions are also true for as long as the containing object remains in a state where this state action is referenced." If any "requires" condition is not true, the state of model execution immediately becomes undefined.

L.4.24.1   Attribute Descriptions
None

L.4.24.2   State and Event Descriptions
None

L.4.24.3   Action Specifications
None

L.4.25   Condition

A Condition is one logical, Boolean-valued element in the contract of one or more Actions.

Formally, a Condition is a proposition in propositional calculus.[11]

---

11 See, for example, https://en.wikipedia.org/wiki/Propositional_calculus.

L.4.25.1 Attribute Descriptions

expression: A Boolean expression that must evaluate to either true or false. It is either (or both) part of the requires clause and/or guarantees clause for some Action.

Range: [a Boolean expression]

L.4.25.2 State and Event Descriptions
None

L.4.25.3 Action Specifications
None

L.4.26 Data type

Data type is the base class for parameters of actions. The difference between Data type and Range is that a Range cannot have complex structure (as constrained by Range-Key-Multiplicity-Completeness Normal Form [RKMC/NF]). An attribute also cannot refer to an object ("no-foreign keys"). Range is defined in a way that supports no-composites and no-foreign keys. But semantic models do need to deal with composites and object references as action parameters. Attributes are restricted to being defined in Ranges, while Parameters have the full freedom of Data types.

L.4.26.1 Attribute Descriptions

«key» name: The name of this data type.

Range: [unconstrained other than uniqueness within the model]

L.4.26.2 State and Event Descriptions
None

L.4.26.3 Action Specifications
None

L.4.27 Obj reference Data Type

A reference (aka pointer) to an object of the designated Class.

L.4.27.1 Attribute Descriptions
None

L.4.27.2 State and Event Descriptions
None

L.4.27.3 Action Specifications
None

L.4.28 Collection data type

Collection data type is a kind of data type that represents a group of occurrences of a given more primitive data type. Operations allowed on a Collection data type include isEmpty(), sizeOf(), contains(), occurrencesOf()?, forAll()?, etc.

L.4.28.1 Attribute Descriptions
min cardinality: Defines the minimum number of members that must be in this kind of collection.
Range: [a positive integer (0 .. *) <= .max cardinality]

max cardinality: Defines the maximum number of members that could be in this kind of collection.
Range: [a positive integer >= .min cardinality | unconstrained]

is unique enforced: Defines whether this collection has "bag" or "set" semantics. "Bag" allows the same member to be in the collection more than once, "Set" does not.
Range: [true | false]

L.4.28.2 State and Event Descriptions
None

L.4.28.3 Action Specifications
None

L.4.29 Unordered (Collection Data Type)

A kind of Collection Data Type where members have no defined ordering. Additional operations allowed on these collections include add(), remove(), union(), intersect(), etc.

L.4.29.1 Attribute Descriptions
None

L.4.29.2 State and Event Descriptions
None

L.4.29.3 Action Specifications
None

L.4.30 Custom Ordered (Collection Data Type)

A kind of Collection Data Type where the members in the collection have an ordering that is not based on time (i.e., Stack or Queue). Additional operations allowed include add(), remove(), union(), intersect(), etc.

L.4.30.1 Attribute Descriptions
ordering rule: The rule that determines how members in this collection are ordered.

Range: [any rule that, when given any two valid members, defines their order]

L.4.30.2 State and Event Descriptions
None

L.4.30.3 Action Specifications
None

L.4.31 Queue (Collection Data Type)

A kind of Collection Data Type with First-In-First-Out (FIFO) behavior. Additional operations allowed on Queues include enqueue(), dequeue(), etc.

L.4.31.1 Attribute Descriptions
None

L.4.31.2 State and Event Descriptions
None

L.4.31.3 Action Specifications
None

L.4.32 Stack (Collection Data Type)

A kind of Collection Data Type with Last-In-First-Out (LIFO) behavior. Additional operations allowed on Stacks include push(), pop(), etc.

L.4.32.1 Attribute Descriptions
None

L.4.32.2 State and Event Descriptions
None

L.4.32.3 Action Specifications
None

L.4.33 Record data type

A group (structure) of separate—but semantically cohesive—more primitive data types.[12] Additional operations on Records include getField(fieldName), setField(fieldName, value), etc.

L.4.33.1 Attribute Descriptions
None

L.4.33.2 State and Event Descriptions
None

L.4.33.3 Action Specifications
None

L.4.34 Field in record

This association class defines one of the data fields that make up a Record Data Type.

L.4.34.1 Attribute Descriptions
«key» field name: The name of this field.
    Range: [unconstrained other than uniqueness in the containing record]

L.4.34.2 State and Event Descriptions
None

L.4.34.3 Action Specifications
None

L.5 Association Dictionary

Where appropriate, this section provides descriptions of associations in this domain.

---

12 This meta-model does not currently support variant records (e.g., unions in C).

L.5.1 Association May Be a Class

This association helps represent a full association class. All associations are implicitly association classes, but the class perspective only needs to be explicit when there are attributes, behaviors, relationship participations, etc. In the meta-model, this association can be thought of as connecting the "as an association ..." perspective to the "as a class ..." perspective. When linked, the Association.description holds the "as an association ..." part of the description and the linked Class.description holds the "as a class ..." part of the description. An association class and its "pair" association are not separate model elements; they are simply different perspectives of the same element. UML notation isn't good at communicating this.

L.5.2 Association May Point at Class

This association manages the taco chip in UML's association notation. The given Association is linked to the Class that the taco chip points at.

L.5.3 Class Is Superclass in Generalization

A generalization can have only one superclass: this meta-model only allows single inheritance. This is due to set-theoretic problems brought on by multiple inheritance. Specifically, if some property, P, exists in more than one superclass of C, then which version of P applies to C? The multiple Ps could be defined very differently.

L.5.4 Bound Is Bottom of Span

A linked Bound only exists when the lower bound of the Range is not unconstrained. If there is a corresponding top for the same Span, it must specify a .value that is greater than or equal to the .value of the bottom Bound.

L.5.5 Bound Is Top of Span

A linked Bound only exists when the upper bound of the Range is not unconstrained. If there is a corresponding bottom for the same Span, it must specify a .value that is less than or equal to the .value of the top Bound.

L.5.6 Symbol in Enumeration May Precede Symbol in Enumeration

This association represents the difference (in Measurement theory terms) between a nominal scale and an ordinal scale. There must either be no precedence in an Enumeration, or precedence must be defined for all symbols in that

Enumeration. Further, the symbols in an ordered Enumeration must form a strict linear sequence, for example, a-b-c-d-e-f, with no gaps, no loops, no splits, etc.

L.5.7 State Is Local Process of Class

The multiplicity from Class to State is 2..*. In order to be a Class, it must at least have some kind of explicit "exists" state. This meta-model is also vastly simplified by forcing an underlying "not-exists" state. Modeling of initial states and final states becomes less exceptional; they are simply transitions from (initial) and to (final) the underlying "not-exists" state.

L.5.8 State Is Implicit Nonexist of Class

Of the set of States for a Class (remember, there must be at least two), it must be specified which one is that underlying "non-exists" state. This association identifies which one it is.

L.6 UML Profile for Semantic Modeling

This profile defines important semantics that are missing (or, possibly, just not obvious enough) in the meta-model. These address model structure, content, and interpretation beyond what can be represented in the meta-model.

L.6.1 No Implementation Technology

A semantic model is strictly limited to specifying only policies to be enforced and processes to be carried out. No artifacts of implementation technology are allowed in a semantic model, it must be computationally independent, that is, a CIM as discussed in Chapter 20.

L.6.2 Restricted Set of Models/Diagrams for Semantic Modeling

Only a limited set of models/diagrams are needed for semantic modeling; specifically use case diagrams, class models, communication diagrams, and state models. Other diagrams (e.g., activity diagrams, deployment diagrams, etc.) may be used in a supplementary manner but are not core elements of a semantic model. The true core elements of a semantic model are the class model and state models. Note that this is all that is explicitly represented in the meta-model. Suitable intelligence can derive sequence diagrams and use case diagrams from class and state models.

L.6.3 No Universally Consistent Concept of Time

Each object is logically considered to live on its own virtual machine. Time is only known consistently within that single virtual machine; there is no guaranteed global time synchronization between one object and any other.

L.6.4 At Some Level, Use Cases Represent Transactions

At some level, use cases must represent "transactions" from the point of view of the participating actor(s)—that is, they must exhibit the ACID[13] properties. This has been called "sea level" in semantic modeling. Cloud level and sky level use cases can help manage complex models.

L.6.5 Model Flow of Information, Not Flow of Control

Use cases, communication diagrams, and state models only specify information flow, not control flow. Activation contexts (the heavy solid bar on design dialect sequence diagrams as shown in Part III) are not allowed on semantic model sequence diagrams. Events may only be signaled *for* objects, never *to* objects.

L.6.6 Class Models Must Be Normalized

Class models must be normalized, ideally in RKMC/NF, as discussed in Chapter 8. Only the two exceptions in Chapter 8 are allowed:

- Null values for attributes are only allowed when no process makes any decision based on the presence or absence of values (i.e., values are for external stakeholder use only).
- Non-atomic attributes are only allowed when no processing is concerned with any part of that structure (i.e., all (sub)domain processing deals with it as a "blob"). Information must be represented at the same level of granularity as it is dealt with in processes.

L.6.7 Stereotype «key» Specifies a Uniqueness Constraint

Stereotype «key» on an attribute specifies a uniqueness constraint within a namespace. If that namespace is not explicitly specified (e.g., in the description of the «key» stereotyped attribute), then the namespace is defined to be the containing (sub)domain model. The uniqueness constraint also applies to sets of attributes whenever the constraint "{Ix}" form is used. A preferred style seems to be to include the namespace in the Range specification.

---

13 ACID = Atomic, Consistent, Independent, Durable.

L.6.8 Minimize Use of «key» in Semantic Models

Keys are generally considered to be a design (i.e., automation technology) artifact and should not appear in a semantic model unless external stakeholder policies and processes depend on them (i.e., "even if we had a perfect computer, we would still need these keys"). Any use of keys in a semantic model must also be clearly flagged as such, for example, by stereotyping as "«key»" or by using the {Ix} constraint form.

L.6.9 Avoid Directional Associations

Associations should not be modeled directionally, that is, no arrows on the ends of association lines as is allowed in standard UML. If there happens to be directionality to an association today, there's no guarantee that directionality will remain in the future. If someone does happen to include directionality, it will—by definition—be ignored for purposes of semantic modeling (e.g., model interpretation, simulation, compilation, etc.).

L.6.10 Explicit Multiplicities for Association Participations

Multiplicities must be explicitly defined for all ends of every association. No implied multiplicities are allowed. Note that this will be difficult for n-ary associations when using UML's standard notation, so specifying multiplicities in an association dictionary (i.e., text) will be needed. The meta-model gives a way to record proper multiplicity; standard UML notation does not give a reasonable way to present it on a diagram.

L.6.11 Avoid Aggregation and Composition

Aggregation and composition should be avoided because many modelers misunderstand and misuse them. If aggregation and composition are used, they must be used consistent with the semantics specified in the OMG UML specification:

- Aggregation is non-exclusive collection membership.
- Composition is exclusive collection membership.

No "lifetime ownership" can ever be implied for composition.

L.6.12 Avoid Foreign Keys

Foreign keys (aka "referential attributes") must be avoided. If a foreign key is included, then it must be explicitly flagged as such (e.g., stereotyped "«fk»"). In any case, the underlying association, with its multiplicities, needs to be explicitly specified in the semantic model.

L.6.13   Iteration in Interaction Diagrams Means "As Long As"

Conditionals in interaction diagrams represent Boolean (if-then-else) decisions, iteration represents "as long as." Further, iteration does not actually imply sequential processing: it necessarily represents parallel processing and may, at a designer's option, be serialized in design and code.

L.6.14   Exactly One State Model for a Class

A class can only have one state model, never more or less. The state model for a class applies at the instance level. There is no class level state model. If you need to specify behavior at a class level, then you are really talking about the behavior of a separate class (e.g., a container class), so make that separate class explicit.

L.6.15   Attributes for a Class and State Model for a Class Must Correlate

The correlation between the states in the state model and one or more attribute values must either be obvious or be explicit. It is obvious when the domain of a .state or .status attribute is the same as the states in the state model. When it is not obvious, the semantic model should include a "state vector" as described in Chapter 10.

L.6.16   State Attribute Value Changes Are Implicit

The change in value of a .state or .status attribute is implicit with a state change in the state model. Said another way, it is not necessary to explicitly change attribute value(s) in actions (e.g., there is no need for "state == <some end state>" as a guarantee/postcondition).

L.6.17   Superstates and Sequential Substates Are Shorthand Notation Only

Superstates and sequential substates may be used, but only as shorthand for common event–transition behavior (although the meta-model does not explicitly support this).

L.6.18   History Transitions Are Prohibited

Use of UML's history transitions is prohibited due to ambiguity in interpretation (unless you define your own single unambiguous interpretation in your own profile. You are free to extend this profile for your own use, but be careful to not introduce logical inconsistencies when doing so).

L.6.19   No Concurrent States Within a Class

Concurrent states in the state model of any one class are prohibited. All state-level concurrent behavior must be modeled as states in different classes.

L.6.20 Initial State Versus Initial Transition

In this meta-model, what UML calls an Initial State is interpreted as an Initial Transition and supports guards. It is difficult and cumbersome to represent the kinds of process logic in Figure L.8 in "legal" UML. A realistic example would be trying to model a DVD/VCR. When powered on, which state it initializes into to should depend on whether media is present or not.

L.6.21 Initial and Final Transitions May Have Actions

"Initial state" and "final state" transitions may have associated actions. This contradicts the UML specification but is done because semantic models are simpler, more direct, and cleaner if actions are allowed. Such transition actions do not introduce any logical inconsistencies themselves.

L.6.22 «new» and «destroy» May Be Parameterized

«new» and «destroy» events are allowed to be parameterized, although this violates a strict interpretation of the UML specification. Semantic models are simpler and cleaner (and translate more cleanly and clearly to code) when parameters are allowed on these events.

L.6.23 Only Concrete Objects May Be Instantiated

An action that creates (instantiates) an object in any generalization hierarchy cannot specify creation of only an abstract class (i.e., any superclass in a {complete} generalization). Only instances of concrete classes can be created.

L.6.24 Don't Write to Derived Attributes

An action can never write to (i.e., attempt to update) a derived attribute (the dependent variable). The derived attribute value must be specified in terms

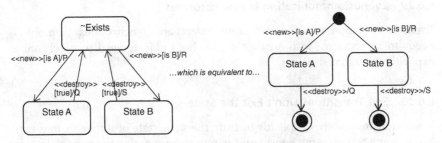

Figure L.8 Initial Transition instead of UML's Initial State.

of a derivation policy (e.g., expressed as a constraint or as a reference to an external authoritative document).

L.6.25 Objects Are Responsible for Maintaining Multiplicities (Referential Integrity)

Any object that is created or deleted is itself responsible for ensuring that multiplicities of relevant associations are not violated, that is, referential integrity. For example, initial transition action(s) must create all links and linked objects as required by multiplicity constraints. Final transition action(s) must appropriately delete links and linked objects (re-linking to other objects is allowed).

L.6.26 State Models Must Be Deterministic

Multiple transitions out of a single state on the same event must have mutually exclusive guards: at most only one of the guards can evaluate to true at any one time.

L.6.27 Action Specifications Shall Be in Contract Form

Action specifications must be in "requires" (precondition) and "guarantees" (postcondition)—that is, "contract"—form. Other forms as discussed in Chapter 10 may be used in a supplemental manner, but where any contradiction exists, the contract takes precedence. As long as the semantic of another form of specification is Liskov substitutable, then it does not contradict the contract.

L.6.28 Association Traversal Must Be Explicit

Any action that needs to traverse an association must be explicit about which association is traversed as there could be many. See Chapter 10 for a discussion of using "via" to express this.

L.6.29 Event Communication Is Asynchronous

Events (and responses at the destination object) are asynchronous. If an object needs to synchronize with another object, both objects need to synchronize explicitly via signaled events.

L.6.30 Self-Transitions Don't Exit the State

A self-transition (either explicitly to-from the same state or implicitly in eventName/someAction) is not considered exiting and reentering the same state, that is, any entry/ or exit/ actions are not executed, and all do/ state actions continue uninterrupted.

L.6.31 Explicit eventName/ignored or eventName/impossible Can Be Used

One can use "eventName/ignored" or "eventName/impossible" to differentiate these two when state–event matrix form is not used. Unless a given state–event pair is explicitly specified as being impossible (either via a state–event matrix or "eventName/impossible"), the defined interpretation is that that event is safely ignorable.

L.6.32 State Actions Are Largely Continuous

A state action (do/someAction) started on entry into some state continues to execute uninterrupted until a different state is entered that does not have that action as a state action (i.e., a state action is not interrupted across transitions if that same state action appears in both from- and to-states).

L.6.33 Behavior Is Undefined if an Action Requires Clause Is Not Fully Satisfied

If any action's requires (precondition) clause is not fully satisfied, model behavior immediately becomes undefined with no rational way to make it become redefined.

L.7 On Measurement Theory and Programming Languages

Measurement theory is a framework for understanding how things can or should be measured. Simply, there are different classes of measurement: different scale types. Within a scale type, some manipulations make sense and others don't. It's vital to understand the different scale types, along with what can and can't be done with them. The scale types are reviewed here; additional detail can be found elsewhere.[14]

L.7.1 Measurement Theory Scale Types

The scale types in measurement theory are:

- *Nominal*—Used for classification only. Examples of nominal scales would be the .subject of a Title, the .author of a Title, and the .status of a Book order.

---

14 See, for example, chapter 26 of [Tockey05], or http://en.wikipedia.org/wiki/ Level_of_measurement.

The only valid manipulations of values in a nominal scale are same-as and different-than comparisons. It makes sense to say, "The .subject of Return on Software is the same as the .subject of Literate Programming, namely Software Engineering," "The .author of Return on Software is different than the . author of Literate Programming," and "the .status of Book order #47, Completed, is different than the .status of Book order #509, Cancelled." Nominal scales don't support better-than or worse-than comparisons; it doesn't make sense to say, "A Book order with .status of Open is better than one with .status of Completed."

- *Ordinal*—There is a sequence, order, or other concept of varying desirability to the values. Examples of ordinal scales include the finish order in a race (first, second, third, fourth, fifth, and so on) and the maturity levels in the staged version of the Software Engineering Institute's Capability Maturity Model Integrated™ (CMMI).[15] Values in an ordinal scale can be compared, like a nominal scale. The ordering of values also allows better-than and worse-than comparisons that don't make sense in a nominal scale. We can meaningfully say things like "The runner who finished first was faster than the runner who finished second" or "An organization with a Level 4 CMMI rating has a higher maturity than some other organization with a Level 2 rating." But you can't necessarily say that the difference between a Level 2 and a Level 3 CMMI rating is more, the same, or less than the difference between a Level 4 and a Level 5 rating. Neither can you say that a Level 4 rating is twice as mature as a Level 2 rating.

- *Interval*—Not only are the values ordered, but the difference between adjacent values also have the same meaning. Temperature in degrees centigrade is an interval scale. An interval scale supports addition and subtraction. You can meaningfully say things like "The difference between 8°C and 13°C is the same as the difference between 23°C and 28°C." An interval scale does not allow you to say anything meaningful about ratios; however, 30°C is not "twice as hot" as 15°C.

- *Ratio*—The missing element in an interval scale is a meaningful zero value. An interval scale usually has a zero value, but that value might not represent a true zero quantity. 0°C doesn't represent the absence of heat. Temperature in degrees Kelvin is a ratio scale. 0°K, absolute zero, represents no heat at all: all molecular motion has stopped. When zero represents absence of the measured characteristic and there is a constant difference between all adjacent values, it now makes sense to multiply and divide. You can also compute ratios between measurements on different parts of the scale. It makes sense to say that 100°K is twice as hot as 50°K just as it makes sense to say that 250°K is half as hot as 500°K. Medium.selling price and Book order line.quantity are ratio scales.

---

15 See, for example, http://cmmiinstitute.com/ or https://en.wikipedia.org/wiki/Capability_Maturity_Model_Integration.

L.7.2   Use of Built-In Data Types Can Violate Measurement Theory

Mainstream programming languages like Java, C++, C#, Python, etc. support a set of built-in data types including, for example:

- int, integer, short, long, etc.—whole numbers, over varying ranges
- Real, float, double, etc.—floating point numbers, over varying ranges and with varying precision
- Char—single characters
- String—ordered collections of characters

Many languages, although not all, also support type safe enumeration (e.g., Java's "enum").

The problem is that these built-in data types allow manipulations that may not be appropriate for an attribute range that was mapped onto it. Integer and floating point data types operate as ratio scales; they support the full range of manipulations: comparison, addition, subtraction, multiplication, and division. But take staged CMMI maturity levels as an example. In measurement theory terms, it is an ordinal scale, so addition, subtraction, multiplication, and division are inappropriate. If a developer maps CMMI maturity level onto data type int, nothing prevents them from doing exactly that: adding, subtracting, multiplying, and dividing. Mainstream programming languages allow developers to do things that could easily be inappropriate in light of measurement theory.

The same exists with enumerations; they are implemented as an ordinal scale; however the attribute range mapped on to it might be a nominal scale. A Java enumerated type is ordered and allows better-than and worse-than comparisons even though that could be inappropriate—such as an enumeration of the states in class Book order. Built-in types char and String also support order comparisons that may not be appropriate in the (sub)domain.

As long as programming languages support built-in types the way mainstream languages do, developers can and will, intentionally or unintentionally, misuse them.

L.7.3   A Measurement Theory-Aware Data Typing System

A more sensible solution would be to have programming language semantics that explicitly enforce measurement theory. For example, imagine a language that explicitly supported nominal scale types:

```
public nominal BookOrder_states { DOESNTEXIST, OPEN, PLACED,
                                PACKED, COMPLETED, CANCELLED };
```

This should support same-as, different-than comparisons, like:

```
if ( state == BookOrder_states.PACKED ) { ... }   // this is OK
```

However, greater-than, less-than comparisons should generate a compiler error:

```
if ( state > BookOrder_states.PACKED ) { ... }  // this is an error
```

If a developer needs to compare better-than with worse-than, they would need to declare an ordinal scale:

```
public ordinal CMMI_Staged_Level { ONE, TWO, THREE, FOUR, FIVE };
```

So the following line of code should not generate a compiler error:

```
if ( level > CMMI_Staged_Level.THREE ) { ... }  // OK
```

Similarly, an interval scale could be supported as

```
public interval AirTemperatureCentigrade from -120 to +180;
private AirTemperatureCentigrade yesterdaysHighTemp;
private AirTemperatureCentigrade todaysHighTemp;

if ( todaysHighTemp > yesterdaysHighTemp ) { ... }   // OK

if ( todaysHighTemp > yesterdaysHighTemp * 2 ) { ... } // not OK
```

A ratio scale could be supported as

```
public ratio TemperatureKelvin from 0.00 to 1000.00;
private TemperatureKelvin temperatureReadingOne;
private TemperatureKelvin temperatureReadingTwo;

if ( temperatureReadingOne > temperatureReadingTwo ) { ... } // OK

if ( temperatureReadingOne > temperatureReadingTwo * 2 ) { ... } // OK
```

Mainstream programming languages like Java, C#, C++, etc. have no problem at all with the following code, even though the code clearly makes no logical sense:

```
private double priceOfBook;
private double highTemperature;

highTemperature = priceOfBook;  // makes no sense but is allowed
```

On the other hand, a measurement theory-aware programming language would be expected to generate a compiler error:

```
public ratio Money from -10000.00 to +10000.00;
```

```
public ratio TemperatureKelvin from 0.00 to 1000.00
private Money priceOfBook;
private TemperatureKelvin highTemperature;

highTemperature = priceOfBook;   // Not OK
```

Programming languages should be built to enforce measurement theory semantics and not allow developers to manipulate measurements in inappropriate ways.

It is interesting to note that Charles Simonyi's intent in his original presentation of Hungarian notation[16] was to embed a notion of "measurement type" into a variable's name to give programmers at least a fighting chance of recognizing logically inconsistent code:

```
degreesK_HighTemperature = dollarsUS_PriceOfBook;   // Not OK
```

Why not take it one step further and let the compiler enforce consistency rather than depend on developer discipline. Depending on discipline has clearly not been a sensible strategy so far.

---

16 More precisely, Apps Hungarian, not Systems Hungarian. See, for example, https://en.wikipedia.org/wiki/Hungarian_notation, https://www.joelonsoftware.com/2005/05/11/making-wrong-code-look-wrong/, or Simonyi's original paper [Simonyi99].

Appendix M

Sample Production Rules

This appendix contains a set of productions rules for an open model compiler. This set of rules translates a semantic model, along with a PIM Overlay in "Java Action Language" (JAL) format, into executable Java. Refer to Chapter 20 for a detailed discussion of open model compilers and production rules. These rules are arranged alphabetically by class and then alphabetically by rule name. The entry point rule is Model.#COMPILE. Note that only about ten of these rules need modification to generate C# instead of Java.

This rule set is not complete in terms of generating code from the meta-model in Appendix L. It does not handle the following elements in the semantic modeling language or in the PIM overlay:

- Generalization/specialization (inheritance)
- Association classes
- JAL in condition assertions
- Enumeration type for Ranges
- Composite Data Type and its subtypes
- Record data type
- ...

```
Action.#ACTION_BODY -->
  foreach aJALstatement in the PIM Overlay
      aJALstatement.#FORMAT_ACTION_STATEMENT

Action.#CALL_ACTION -->
  if this action has a non-blank PIM return run time type
      then ' aResult = ' +
  'this.' + formatted action name +
  if this action has parameters
      then '( ' +
```

How to Engineer Software: A Model-Based Approach, First Edition. Steve Tockey.
© 2019 the IEEE Computer Society, Inc. Published 2019 by John Wiley & Sons, Inc.

```
              foreach aParameter on action
                   aParameter.#ACTUAL_PARAMETER +
                   ', ' (except after last one) +
              ');'
       otherwise '();'


  Action.#DEFINE_PRIVATE_ACTION -->
      'private ' +
      if this action has a non-blank PIM return run time type
         then PIM return run time type + ' ' +
         otherwise 'void ' +
      formatted action name + #ACTION_FORMAL_PARAMETERS +
         this.#SPECIFY_CONTRACT +
         this.#ENTRY_ASSERTIONS +
         this.#ACTION_BODY +
         this.#EXIT_ASSERTIONS +
    '}'


  Action.#ENTRY_ASSERTIONS -->
      foreach aParameter on this action
         if aParameter is assertable
            then aParameter.#ASSERT_PARAMETER +
      foreach aRequiresClause on this action
         aRequiresClause.#ASSERT_CONDITION


  Action.#EXIT_ASSERTIONS -->
    if this action has any guarantees clauses
      then foreach aGuaranteesClause on this action
                  aGuaranteesClause.#ASSERT_CONDITION


  Action.#ACTION_FORMAL_PARAMETERS -->
      if this action has parameters
         then '( ' + foreach aParameter on action
                        aParameter.#FORMAL_PARAMETER +
                        ', ' (except after last one) +
               ' ) {' +
         otherwise '() {'


  Action.#SPECIFY_CONTRACT -->
      '// requires' +
      if this action has any requires clauses
         then foreach aRequiresClause on this action
            aRequiresClause.#CONTRACT_CONDITION +
         otherwise '//   none' +
      '// guarantees' +
      if this action has any guarantees clauses
         then foreach aGuaranteesClause on this action
                  aGuaranteesClause.#CONTRACT_CONDITION +
         otherwise '//   none'
```

```
Association.#ASSOCIATION_INVARIANTS_CHECK -->
    if this association is reflexive
        then #BINARY_REFLEXIVE_ASSOCIATION_INVARIANTS_CHECK
        else #BINARY_NON_REFLEXIVE_ASSOCIATION_INVARIANTS_CHECK

Association.#BINARY_NON_REFLEXIVE_ASSOCIATION_INVARIANTS_CHECK -->
    if participation1 is not for Context.Class
        then participation1.#PARTICIPATION_INVARIANTS_CHECK
        else participation2.#INITIALIZE_PARTICIPATION_INVARIANTS_CHECK

Association.#BINARY_NON_REFLEXIVE_ASSOCIATION_LINK_UNLINK_SERVICES -->
    if participation1 is not for Context.Class
        then participation1.#PARTICIPATION_LINK_UNLINK_SERVICE
        else participation2.#PARTICIPATION_LINK_UNLINK_SERVICE

Association.#BINARY_REFLEXIVE_ASSOCIATION_INVARIANTS_CHECK -->
    if participation1 is not for Context.Class
        then participation1.#PARTICIPATION_INVARIANTS_CHECK
        else participation2.#INITIALIZE_PARTICIPATION_INVARIANTS_CHECK

Association.#BINARY_REFLEXIVE_ASSOCIATION_LINK_UNLINK_SERVICES -->
    participation1.#PARTICIPATION_LINK_UNLINK_SERVICE
    participation2.#PARTICIPATION_LINK_UNLINK_SERVICE

Association.#DECLARE_ASSOCIATION_INST_VAR -->
    if this association is reflexive
        then #DECLARE_BINARY_REFLEXIVE_ASSOCIATION_INST_VARS
        else #DECLARE_BINARY_NON_REFLEXIVE_ASSOCIATION_INST_VAR

Association.#DECLARE_BINARY_NON_REFLEXIVE_ASSOCIATION_INST_VARS -->
    if participation1 is not for Context.Class
        then participation1.#DECLARE_PARTICIPATION_INST_VAR
        else participation2.#DECLARE_PARTICIPATION_INST_VAR

Association.#DECLARE_BINARY_REFLEXIVE_ASSOCIATION_INST_VARS -->
    participation1.#DECLARE_PARTICIPATION_INST_VAR
    participation2.#DECLARE_PARTICIPATION_INST_VAR

Association.#INITIALIZE_ASSOCIATION_INST_VAR -->
    if this association is reflexive
        then #INITIALIZE_BINARY_REFLEXIVE_ASSOCIATION_INST_VARS
        else #INITIALIZE_BINARY_NON_REFLEXIVE_ASSOCIATION_INST_VAR

Association.#INITIALIZE_BINARY_NON_REFLEXIVE_ASSOCIATION_INST_VARS -->
    if participation1 is not for Context.Class
        then participation1.#INITIALIZE_PARTICIPATION_INST_VAR
        else participation2.#INITIALIZE_PARTICIPATION_INST_VAR
```

```
Association.#INITIALIZE_BINARY_REFLEXIVE_ASSOCIATION_INST_VARS -->
   participation1.#INITIALIZE_PARTICIPATION_INST_VAR
   participation2.#INITIALIZE_PARTICIPATION_INST_VAR


Association.#LINK_UNLINK_SERVICES -->
   if this association is reflexive
      then #BINARY_REFLEXIVE_ASSOCIATION_LINK_UNLINK_SERVICES
      else #BINARY_NON_REFLEXIVE_ASSOCIATION_LINK_UNLINK_SERVICES


AssociationParticipation.#DECLARE_PARTICIPATION_INST_VAR -->
   if this is -to-at-most-one
     then 'private' +
     otherwise 'private ArrayList<' +
   formatted participating class name +
   if this is -to-at-most-one
     then ' ' +
     otherwise '> '
   this participation role name + ';'


AssociationParticipation.#INITIALIZE_PARTICIPATION_INST_VAR -->
   formatted participation role name + ' = '
   if this is -to-at-most-one
      then 'null;' +
      otherwise 'new ArrayList<' + participating class name + '>();'


AssociationParticipation.#PARTICIPATION_INVARIANTS_CHECK -->
  if ( lower bound is 1 or greater ) {
    'assert ' + <participation role name> +
    if ( upper bound is 1 ) {
      ' != null: the multiplicity for association role ' +
      participation role name + ' is out of range (=0);'
    } else {
      '.size() >= ' + lower bound +
      ': "the multiplicity for association role ' +
      participation role name +
      ' is out of range (<' + lower bound + ');'
    }
  }
  if ( upper bound > 1 ) {
    'assert ' + <participation role name> + '.size() <= ' + upper bound +
    ': "the multiplicity for association role ' +
    participation role name + ' is out of range (>' + upper bound + ')";'
  }


AssociationParticipation.#PUBLIC_LINK_SERVICE -->
   'private void link' + other participation role name +
      '( ' + participating class name + ' a' +
        participating class name + ' ) {' +
      '// requires' +
      '//   a' + participating class name + ' <> null' +
```

```
        '// guarantees
        '//   both this and a' + participating class name +
                    ' are linked to each other' +
      role name +
      if this is -at-most-to-one
            then ' = a' + participating class name + ';'
            else '.add( ' + participating class name + ' );'
      "}'

AssociationParticipation.#PUBLIC_UNLINK_SERVICE -->
      'private void link' + other participation role name +
        '( ' + participating class name + ' a' +
          participating class name + ' ) {' +
        '// requires' +
        '//   a' + participating class name + ' <> null' +
        '// guarantees
        '//   both this and a' + participating class name +
                    ' are linked to each other' +
      if this is -at-most-to-one
            then role name + ' = null;'
            else 'int index = ' + role name +
              '.indexOf( a' + participating class name + ' );'
                'if( index != -1 ) {'
                    role name + '.remove( index );'
              '}'
            "}'

Attribute.#DEFINE_INST_VAR -->
    'private ' + #PIM_OVERLAY_RTTYPE + this.instanceVariableName() +
    if this attribute has a non blank PIM initial value
        then ' = ' + PIM initial value +
    ';'

Attribute.#DERIVED_GETTER -->
    'public ' + #PIM_OVERLAY_RTTYPE + this.instanceVariableName() +
    + #ACTION_FORMAL_PARAMETERS +
    #ACTION_BODY +
    '   return result;' +
    '}'

Attribute.#GETTER -->
    'public ' + #PIM_OVERLAY_RTTYPE + this.instanceVariableName() +
                                            '() {' +
    '   return ' + this.InstanceVariableName() + ';' +
    '}'

Attribute.#INST_VAR_INVARIANTS_CHECK -->
    'assert ' + the substituted assertion expression +
    ': "the value for attribute '" + name + "' is out of range";'
```

```
Class.#All_MEMBERS_ACCESSOR -->
  'private static ArrayList<' + ClassName + '> classNameSet = +
                            new ArrayList<' + ClassName + '>();'
  'public static ArrayList<' + ClassName + '> all' + ClassName + 's() {'
  '  return ' + className + 'Set;'
  '}'


Class.#ASSOCIATION_INST_VAR_LIST -->
  foreach anAssociation this class participates in
    anAssociation.#DECLARE_ASSOCIATION_INST_VAR

Class.#ASSOCIATION_LINK_UNLINK_SERVICES -->
  foreach anAssociation this class participates in
    anAssociation.#LINK_UNLINK_SERVICES

Class.#ATTRIBUTE_INST_VAR_LIST -->
  foreach anAttribute in class
    anAttribute.#DEFINE_INST_VAR

Class.ATTRIBUTE_GETTERS_LIST -->
  foreach anAttribute of this class that is not a derived attribute
    anAttribute.#GETTER

Class.#CONSTRUCTOR_OPERATION -->
  with anEvent = "<<new>>": anEvent.#CONSTRUCTOR_OPERATION

Class.#DERIVED_ATTRIBUTE_GETTERS -->
  foreach aDerivedAttribute on this class
    aDerivedAttribute.#DERIVED_GETTER

Class.#CLASS_DESCRIPTION
  if ( in verbose mode )
    '// description' +
    '//  ' +
    if ( class has a description )
      then this.description
      otherwise 'none'

Class.#JAVA_CLASS_FILE -->
  <Open the output file here>
  #JAVA_CLASS_FRAME
  <Close the output file here>

Class.#JAVA_CLASS_FRAME -->
  if ( include package name )
    'package ' aModel.#MODEL_NAME
  #PIM_IMPORTS_LIST
  'public class ' + this.#CLASS_NAME + ' {'
```

```
'// generated ' + time stamp + ' by JAL open model compiler ' +
                                  compiler version id
#CLASS_DESCRIPTION
#PIM_CONSTANTS_LIST
#STATE_ENUM_DECLARATION
#ATTRIBUTE_INST_VAR_LIST
#ASSOCIATION_INST_VAR_LIST
#CONSTRUCTOR_OPERATION
#ATTRIBUTE_GETTERS_LIST
#DERIVED_ATTRIBUTES_GETTERS_LIST
#PUSHED_EVENTS_OPERATIONS_LIST
#PRIVATE_TRANSITION_ACTIONS_LIST
if ( this class has any state actions )
   #STATE_ACTIONS_TIME_SLICE
   #PRIVATE_STATE_ACTIONS_LIST
#INVARIANTS_CHECK_OPERATION
#PIM_HELPER_CODE
#ALL_MEMBERS_ACCESSOR
#ASSOCIATION_LINK_UNLINK_SERVICES
'}'


Class.#INITIALIZE_ASSOCIATION_INST_VARS -->
  foreach anAssociation this class participates in
    #INITIALIZE_ASSOCIATION


Class.#INVARIANTS_CHECK_OPERATION -->
  if ( invariants checking is on )
    then 'public void classInvariantsCheck() {'
      '// requires'
      '//   none'
      '// guarantees'
      '//   all verifiable run-time invariants checks have passed
      foreach anAttribute
        anAttribute.#RANGE_CHECK
      foreach anAssociationParticipation
        anAssociationParticipation.#MULTIPLICITY_CHECK +
      '}'


Class.#PIM_CONSTANTS_LIST -->
   if ( in verbose mode )
     '// PIM contants' +
     '//   ' +
   if ( class has PIM constants )
     then foreach aPIMConstant in this class
             aPIMConstant
     otherwise if ( in verbose mode )
             '// none'
```

```
Class.#PIM_IMPORTS_LIST -->
    'import java.util.ArrayList;'
  foreach aPIMImport in this class
      aPIMImport

Class.#PIM_HELPER_CODE -->
  foreach line of helper code
    write it out

Class.#PRIVATE_STATE_ACTIONS_LIST -->
  foreach anAction on this class's state model
    anAction.#DEFINE_PRIVATE_ACTION

Class.#PRIVATE_TRANSITION_ACTIONS_LIST -->
  foreach anAction on any transition in this class
    anAction.#DEFINE_PRIVATE_ACTION

Class.#PUSHED_EVENT_OPERATIONS_LIST -->
  foreach anEvent on this class that is not "<<new>>"
    anEvent.#PUSHED_EVENT_OPERATION

Class.#STATE_ACTIONS_TIME_SLICE -->
  'public void timeSlide() {'
  foreach aState in state model
    aState.#CALL_STATE_TIME_SLICE
  '}'

Class.#STATE_ENUM_DECLARATION -->
  'public enum ' + state attribute rt type + ' { ' +
  #STATE_ENUM_LIST +
  ' };'

Class.#STATE_ENUM_LIST -->
  foreach aState in the state model
    aState name as all caps + ', '  (except after last one)

Condition.#ASSERT_CONDITION -->
  if ( is assertable )
    then 'assert( ' + assertion expression ')' +
      if ( has assertion message )
        ': ' + assertion message +
      ';'

Condition.#CONTRACT_CONDITION -->
  '//   ' + expression

Event.#CONSTRUCTOR_METHOD_BODY -->
  foreach state-event-behavior for this event
    #CONSTRUCTOR_EVENT_COMPILE
```

```
Event.#CONSTRUCTOR_OPERATION -->
   'public ' + class name + #OPERATION_FORMAL_PARAMETERS + ' {'
   #OPERATION_CONTRACT_REQUIRES_CLAUSE
   #OPERATION_CONTRACT_GUARANTEES_CLAUSE
   #CONSTRUCTOR_METHOD_BODY
   '}'

Event.#ENTRY_ASSERTIONS -->
   foreach aParameter
     if aParameter is assertable
       then aParameter.#ASSERT_PARAMETER +
   if this Event has any requires clauses
     then foreach aRequiresClause on this Event
         aRequiresClause.#ASSERT_CONDITION +

Event.#EVENT_METHOD_BODY -->
   foreach state-event-behavior for this event
     #PUSH_EVENT_COMPILE

Event.#EXIT_ASSERTIONS -->
   if this Event has any guarantees clauses
     then foreach aGuaranteesClause on this Event
         aGuaranteesClause.#ASSERT_CONDITION +

Event.#OPERATION_CONTRACT_GUARANTEES_CLAUSE -->
   '// guarantees' +
       foreach state-event-behavior on this event {
           #BEHAVIOR_GUARANTEES_CLAUSE
       }

Event.#OPERATION_CONTRACT_REQUIRES_CLAUSE -->
   '// requires' +
   if ( any action--on all transitions for event--have requires clauses )
       foreach unique requires condition in all actions on
                       all transitions for this event
       '//   ' + that condition's expression
       otherwise '//   none'

Event.#OPERATION_FORMAL_PARAMETERS -->
   '( ' +
   foreach unique parameter in all actions on all transitions for event
     #FORMAL_PARAMETER + ', '   (except after last one)
   ' )'

Event.#PUSHED_EVENT_OPERATION -->
   'public ' +
   if this event has a non-blank PIM return run time type
     then PIM return run time type + ' ' +
```

```
      otherwise 'void ' +
   event name + #OPERATION_FORMAL_PARAMETERS + ' {'
   #OPERATION_CONTRACT_REQUIRES_CLAUSE +
   #OPERATION_CONTRACT_GUARANTEES_CLAUSE
   if( class invariants are turned on ) { #CLASS_INVARIANTS }
   if( assertions are turned on ) { #ENTRY_ASSERTIONS }
   if this event has a non-blank PIM return run time type
     then PIM return run time type + ' aResult' +
        if this event has a non blank PIM return initial value
          then ' = ' + PIM return run time type initial value +
          ';'
   #EVENT_METHOD_BODY
   if( assertions are turned on ) { #EXIT_ASSERTIONS }
   if( class invariants are turned on ) { #CLASS_INVARIANTS }
   if this event has a non-blank PIM return run time type
     then 'return aResult;'
   '}'

Model.#COMPILE -->
  foreach aClass in aModel
    aClass.#JAVA_CLASS_FILE
  if is safe mode
    aModel.#SAFE_MODE_CLASS

Model.#SAFE_MODE_CLASS -->
  <Open the output file here>
  if( include package name )
     'package ' aModel.#MODEL_NAME
  'public class SafeMode'
  if is verbose
    '// Implements top level SafeMode behavior for' + model name
    'public static void safeModeCheck() {
    if is verbose
     '// requires
     '//   none
     '// guarantees
     '//   all safe mode class invariants checks have been checked
    foreach aClass in aModel
      'for( ' + class name + ' a' + class name + ': ' +
         class name + '.all' + class name + 's() ) {'
       'a' + class name + '.classInvariantsCheck();'
      '}'
    '}'
  '}'
  <Close the output file here>

Parameter.#ACTUAL_PARAMETER -->
    output parameter name as an instance level name
```

```
Parameter.#ASSERT_PARAMETER -->
   'assert ( ' + PIM overlay assertion expression + ' ) ; '

Parameter.#FORMAL_PARAMETER -->
   output PIM Overlay RT Type + ' ' + formatted parameter name

Range.#INST_VAR_INVARIANTS_CHECK -->
  definedRange.#INST_VAR_INVARIANTS_CHECK

State.#CALL_STATE_TIME_SLICE -->
   if ( there are any state actions in this state )
      'if ( state == ' + qualified state name + ' ) {' +
      foreach action in this state
        #CALL_ACTION
      '}'

StateEventBehavior.#BEHAVIOR_GUARANTEES_CLAUSE -->
   if this behavior is not Ignore type {
      '//  ' +
   if from state is not default not exists state {
      'state was ' + from state name +
      if guard is not "true" {
         ' and ' +
      }
   }
   if guard is not "true" {
      the guard +
   }
   ' --> ' +
   if this behavior is Transition type {
      foreach guarantees condition {
         that condition + ', ' +
         if ( from state is not same as to state ) {
            if ( any conditions were output ) {
               ' and ' +
            }
            'to state == ' + to state name
         }
      } else {
         ' fatal exception thrown'
      }
   }

StateEventBehavior.#CONSTRUCTOR_BEHAVIOR -->
   if ( this is not an ignore type behavior ) {
      if ( there is a guard ) {
         'if ( ' + the PIM Overlay guard code + ' ) {"
         if ( this is a transition type behavior ) {
```

```
        #TRANSITION_ACTIONS_LIST
        'state = ' + to state
    } else {
      'throw new IllegalStateException();'
    }
    if ( there is a guard ) {
      '}'
    }


StateEventBehavior.#OPTIONAL_GUARD -->
  if this behavior has a guard
    ' && ' + guard expression


StateEventBehavior.#PUSH_EVENT_BEHAVIOR -->
  if ( this is not an ignore type behavior ) {
    'if ( state == ' + fromState +
    #OPTIONAL_GUARD +
    ' ) {" +
    if ( this is a transition type behavior ) {
      #TRANSITION_ACTIONS_LIST +
      if ( fromState != to state ) {
        'state = ' + to state +
        if ( to state = NOTEXISTS ) {
            class name + 'Set.remove( this );'
      }
    } else {
      if ( this is an impossible type behavior ) {
        'throw new IllegalStateException();'
      }
    '}'


StateEventBehavior.#TRANSITION_ACTIONS_LIST -->
  foreach anAction on this transition
    anAction.#CALL_ACTION
```

Appendix N

Software Structural Complexity Metrics

Software defects are not randomly distributed in code. Defects cluster; in particular they cluster around complexity. As complexity increases in a section of code, so do defects. Properly managing complexity helps avoid defects. Chapter 3 presents essential complexity and accidental complexity. Essential complexity is best managed through conscious and deliberate application of fundamental principles:

- Use appropriate abstractions[1]
- Encapsulate accidental complexity
- Maximize cohesion, minimize coupling
- Design to invariants, design for change
- Avoid premature design and optimization
- Name things carefully

Accidental complexity can be seen from a structural (i.e., syntactic) as opposed to a semantic perspective. Structural complexity is best managed through measuring and controlling design and code structure. At least four measures of structural complexity are strongly correlated with defect density:

- Cyclomatic complexity
- Depth of decision nesting
- Number of parameters
- Fan-out

This appendix discusses each of these metrics, which should be measured—and managed—in your design and code.

---

1 Including, but not limited to, domain partitioning (Chapter 6) and subdomain partitioning (Chapter 11).

How to Engineer Software: A Model-Based Approach, First Edition. Steve Tockey.
© 2019 the IEEE Computer Society, Inc. Published 2019 by John Wiley & Sons, Inc.

N.1 Cyclomatic Complexity

Tom McCabe first applied cyclomatic complexity to software in 1976.[2] Cyclomatic complexity measures the number of potential execution paths through a section of code—for our purposes, a method. Specifically, it is the upper bound on the number of ways to get from the beginning of that code to its end. Cyclomatic complexity is computed by adding one to the number of decisions[3] in that code. Straight-line code (i.e., with no decisions) has just one possible execution path: from beginning straight to end. Adding a decision adds a possible execution path, adding one more decision adds one new potential path, and so on.

Figure N.1 shows a flowchart for Bubble Sort. This function has three decisions, so its cyclomatic complexity is four.

Method IRR() in Chapter 18 (see Code Sample 18.7) has three decisions, two if()s and one while(), so its cyclomatic complexity is also four. Method BookOrder.add() in Code Sample 16.31 has four decisions, all if()s, so it's cyclomatic complexity is five.

Based on analysis of production code, Mark Schroeder[4] reports a strong correlation between cyclomatic complexity and defect density at the method level.[5] Schroeder's results are shown in Figure N.2.

According to Schroeder, 45% of the total lines of code were in methods with cyclomatic complexity of 4 or less (i.e., three or fewer decisions). That same 45% of the code was responsible for only 12% of the defects logged against those applications. Only 11% of the total lines of code were in methods that had cyclomatic complexity of 15 or greater (i.e., 14 or more decisions). That mere 11% of the code was responsible for 42% of the defects. Clearly, as cyclomatic complexity increases, defect density increases with it. Specifically, methods with cyclomatic complexity of 15 or greater have more than 13 times the defect density of methods with cyclomatic complexity of four or less.

N.1.1 "Cosmetic" Coding Standards

Having participated in more than one committee responsible for developing a coding standard and having talked with many software professionals about

---

2 See, for example, [McCabe76] or https://en.wikipedia.org/wiki/Cyclomatic_complexity.
3 Each if()-then (and optionally −else) is one decision. Each for(), repeat(), or while() loop is one decision, Each case (except the default) in a switch-case is one decision, etc.
4 See [Schroeder99]
5 Attempting to correlate cyclomatic complexity to defects at any larger level than methods shows weak to no correlation.

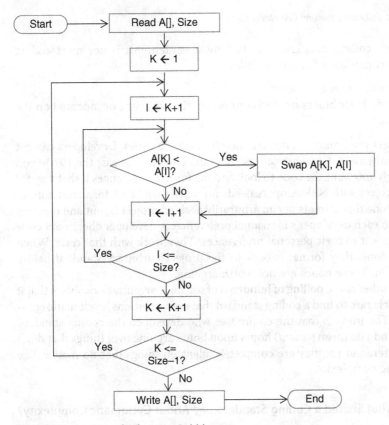

Figure N.1 Flowchart for function Bubble sort.

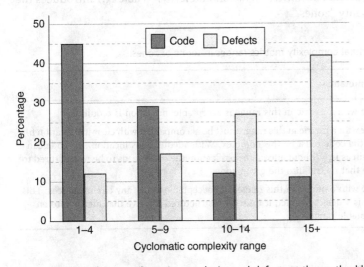

Figure N.2 Correlating cyclomatic complexity and defects at the method level.

developing coding standards, the two most contentious issues most coding standard committees face are as follows:

- Indent using tabs or spaces?
- Where do curly braces on decisions go, on the same line or indented on the next line?

These don't even matter. They are merely cosmetic issues. Developers can get used to either way. Code formatters[6] have existed since at least the 1970s: you define how you want the code to look and the formatter arranges it that way for you. A project with N developers needs no more than N + 1 formatter configurations, one that formats per an arbitrarily decided project layout and one that formats to each developer's individual preference. A developer checks out code and formats it to their personal preferences. They work with that code. When they are done, they format it back to the project's arbitrary standard before checking in. These issues are not worth arguing.

On the other hand, polling of hundreds of software organizations shows that it is extremely rare to find a coding standard that even mentions "cyclomatic complexity." The irony is that the committee who developed the coding standard wasted (and I do mean *wasted*) hours upon hours arguing over things that don't even matter, and yet they are completely silent on things that do matter, like cyclomatic complexity.

N.1.2 What Should a Coding Standard Say About Cyclomatic Complexity?

If you agree a coding standard should say something about cyclomatic complexity, then the question becomes, "What should it say?" Table N.1 introduces the concept of quality "zones."

Table N.1 Structural complexity metrics ranges in terms of zones.

Zone	Interpretation
Green	Code with a metric in this range is acceptable; no action is required
Yellow	Code with a metric in this range must be accompanied with clear justification for why the code must be this complex. With adequate justification, the code can remain as is. Without adequate justification the code needs to be restructured to drive that metric into the green zone
Red	Code with a metric in this range is unacceptable under any circumstances. This code is a defect magnet; it must be restructured to drive that metric into an acceptable range

---

6 Also known as "pretty printers."

Table N.2 Suggested quality zones for cyclomatic complexity in a method.

Zone	Cyclomatic complexity
Green	1–9
Yellow	10–14
Red	15+

Table N.2 suggests[7] quality zones for cyclomatic complexity in a method.

N.1.3 The Value of Such a Coding Standard

Structural complexity analysis of mainstream production code routinely exposes methods with cyclomatic complexities well over 150. The worst code I have seen so far is one C++ class over 3400 lines of code. At 50 lines of code per page, the source code listing for that one class is over 60 pages. If that's not bad enough, that one class has only one method: one member function. And if that's not bad enough, the cyclomatic complexity for that one method is over 2400. Over more than 60 pages of source code for a single method, two out of every three lines of code involves a decision.

That method is perfectly compliant with the organizations' coding standard:

- It uses tabs, not spaces, per their standard.
- Opening curly braces are on the same line as the decision key word, per their standard.

The organization has no way to say "No!" to obviously horrible code. They have to accept it because it doesn't violate their standard. On the other hand, a coding standard that limits cyclomatic complexity to a reasonable level, such as Table N.2, gives the organization the ability to say "No!" to such horrible code.

N.1.4 Debate About Cyclomatic Complexity

Two aspects of cyclomatic complexity are open to debate. The first is that according to McCabe's original paper, "AND" and "OR" operators in the Boolean expressions of decisions also need to be counted. For example, the line of code

```
if ( a and b or c ) { ... }
```

---

7 You are, of course, free to set these zones as you see fit.

Code Sample N.1 Command Line Decoder for One-Letter Commands

```
switch( commandLetter ) {
    case 'a': { ... }; break;
    case 'b': { ... }; break;
    case 'c': { ... }; break;
    ...
    case 'z': { ... }; break;
}
```

---

contributes three to cyclomatic complexity: one for the "if()," one for the "AND," and one for the "OR." My professional opinion is that "AND"s and "OR"s should not count in cyclomatic complexity. The complexity induced just by making a decision in code is different than complexity induced by the Boolean expression. What code does having made a decision is should be treated separate from how it makes that decision.

The second is with switch-case statements. Consider a command line interpreter that takes a one-letter command from the user and decides what to do. Assuming all 26 letters are valid commands, the code that interprets user input would almost certainly look like Code Sample N.1 if written in Java.

Cyclomatic complexity of the switch-case is 27. This is well over the maximum 14 in Table N.2. There is also no practical way to restructure Code Sample N.1 to reduce cyclomatic complexity to less than 15. At the heart of this issue is the regularity of switch-case. Even though there are 27 unique paths through that code,[8] it is not nearly as complex as code that has 26 distinct decisions. So the suggestion is to discount switch-case in some way. One idea is to add the log of the number of cases. The 26 case switch in Code Sample N.1 could contribute log(26), or 1.4, to cyclomatic complexity instead of 26.

The same treatment should also apply to a "switch-case like if()." This code is a cascading sequence of if() statements where part of the Boolean expression is identical. This is shown in Code Sample N.2.

The key is that "someValue <= ..." appears in each of the Boolean expressions. It would be more convenient to use switch-case, but it is not possible because the Boolean expression cannot be easily reduced to an integer or enumerated value that switch-case depends on.

---

8 Cyclomatic complexity is also the upper bound on the number of test cases needed to achieve decision coverage. For testing purposes one would need to test all 27 cases, "a" through "z" as well as nonalphabetic. However, from a pure complexity perspective, the switch-case itself is quite simple.

Code Sample N.2 Switch-Case Like Use of if()

```
if( somevalue <= lowestThresholdValue ) {
    handleLowestValueSituation();
} else if( somevalue <= intermediateThresholdValue ) {
    handleIntermediateValueSituation();
} else if( somevalue <= higherThresholdValue ) {
    handleHigherValueSituation();
} else if( somevalue <= highestThresholdValue ) {
    handleHighestValueSituation();
} else handleExtremeValueSituation();
```

N.2   Depth of Decision Nesting

The next structural complexity metric is depth of decision nesting, sometimes called nested block depth. Consider Code Samples N.3 and N.4. Both have three decisions, so they both have cyclomatic complexity four.

Code Sample N.3 Code with Cyclomatic Complexity Four

```
if( a > 10 ) {
    X();
}
if( b < 5 ) {
    Y();
}
do {
    Z();
} while( not done )
```

Code Sample N.4 More Code with Cyclomatic Complexity Four

```
if( a > 10 ) {
    X();
    if( b < 5 ) {
        Y();
        do {
            Z();
        } while( not done )
    }
}
```

Despite both code samples having the same cyclomatic complexity, most developers would agree that Code Sample N.4 is more complex than Code Sample N.3. The reason is that the decisions in Code Sample N.3 are independent: none of those decisions have any influence over the others. Not so in Code Sample N.4. The while() loop is only relevant when the if(b < 5) decision is true. The if(b < 5) decision is only relevant when a > 10. Dependency between decisions adds to complexity beyond there simply being a decision. This is what depth of decision nesting captures: dependencies between decisions.

To calculate depth of decision nesting:

- Start counting at one.
- Each new decision adds one.
- Completing any decision subtracts one.
- The count must end at one.
- Depth of decision nesting is the maximum value of the count.

The depth of decision nesting for Code Sample N.3 is two; for Code Sample N.4, it is four. Code Sample N.5 has cyclomatic complexity six and depth of decision nesting four: the deepest nesting is at statement V().

Figure N.3 shows a flowchart for Code Sample N.5.

N.2.1 What Should a Coding Standard Say About Depth of Decision Nesting?

Table N.3 suggests quality zones for depth of decision nesting in a method.

Code Sample N.5 Code with Depth of Decision Nesting Four

```
if( p ) {
  if( q ) {
   X();
  }
  Y();
  do {
   U();
  } while( t )
} else {
  if( r ) {
   do {
    V();
   } while( not a )
  }
}
```

Figure N.3 Flowchart for Code
Sample N.5.

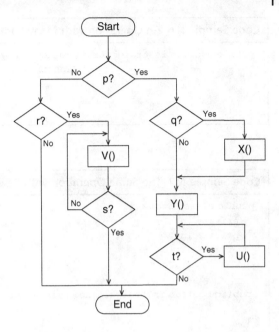

Table N.3 Suggested quality zones for depth of decision
nesting in a method.

Zone	Depth of decision nesting
Green	1–4
Yellow	5–6
Red	7+

Again, this gives the organization the ability to say "No!" to horrible code.

N.3 Number of Parameters

Joost Visser et al.[9] recommend minimizing the number of parameters on an operation. Consider Code Sample N.6.

The isStraightLine() operation in Code Sample N.6 has six parameters. Code Sample N.7 restructures it to have only three parameters.

---

9 See [Visser15].

Code Sample N.6 An Operation with Many Parameters

```
public boolean isStraightLine( int x1, int y1,
                               int x2, int y2,
                               int x3, int y3 ) {
    ...
}
```

Code Sample N.7 The Same Operation with Fewer Parameters

```
public class Point {
    private int X;
    private int y;
    ...
}

public boolean isStraightLine( Point p1, Point p2, Point p3 ) {
    ...
}
```

Table N.4 Suggested quality zones for number of parameters on an operation.

Zone	Number of parameters
Green	0–4
Yellow	5–6
Red	7+

N.3.1 What Should a Coding Standard Say About Number of Parameters?

Table N.4 suggests quality zones for number of parameters on an operation.

Similar to the approximately 3400 line of code method with cyclomatic complexity approximately 2400, one developer was told his operation with 54 parameters was not acceptable and needed restructuring. The developer's remedy was to create an array of 54 elements, populate that array with what would otherwise have been parameters, and then pass the array as a single parameter. While it satisfies the strict letter of the law, it shows blatant disregard for managing complexity. Adding class Point in Code Sample N.7 increases abstraction and cohesion, as well as decreases coupling. Simply passing an array of six ints does reduce the apparent number of parameters but disregards abstraction, cohesion, and coupling.

N.4 Fan-Out

Fan-out measures the number of operations called by a method. Figure N.4 shows a structure chart,[10] a function call tree, for part of a simple payroll processing application.

The fan-out of CalculateHourlyGrossPay() is zero—it does not call any other functions. The fan-out of CalculateHourlyNetPay() is two, which calls both CalculateHourlyGrossPay() and CalculateNormalDeductions(). The fan-out of IssueEmployeePaychecks() is four. Within any one method, there may be multiple calls to the same other operation: CalculateSalariedNetPay() may make five different calls to CalculateNormalDeductions(), but only the first call counts. Recursive calls also count; if the method calls itself, that also adds one to fan-out.

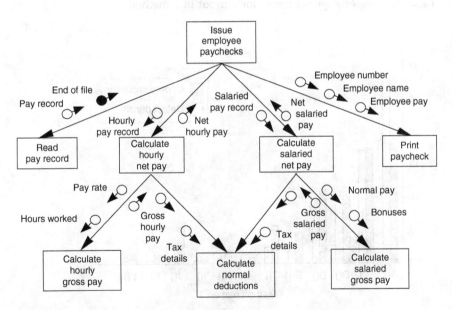

Figure N.4 Structure chart for a simple payroll processing application.

---

10 See, for example, [Page-Jones88].

Method IRR() in Chapter 18 (Code Sample 18.7) has fan-out four, which calls:

- PW()
- firstNonzeroCashFlowIsNegative()
- onlyOneSignChange()
- Math.abs()

Robert Grady reports a correlation between fan-out and defect density at the method level.[11] A small sampling of Grady's results is shown in Figure N.5.

The code complexity value in Figure N.5 is expressed as fan-out squared divided by 10. The complexity value for A() is about 19, so its fan-out must be 14 (14 squared is 196). The complexity value for B() is about 17, so its fan-out must be 13 (13 squared is 169). Defect density is expressed in terms of post-release defects per thousand lines of source code (KSLOC), that is, A() has a defect density of 28 per KSLOC and B() has a defect density of 17 per KSLOC. As fan-out increases, defect density generally increases along with it.

N.4.1   What Should a Coding Standard Say About Fan-Out?

Table N.5 suggests quality zones for fan-out in a method.

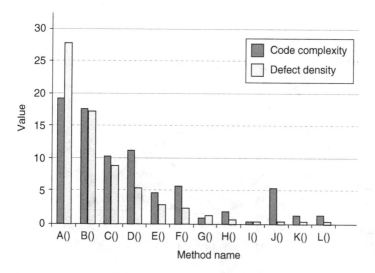

Figure N.5 Correlating fan-out and defects at the method level.

---

11 See [Grady92].

Table N.5 Suggested quality zones for fan-out in a method.

Zone	Fan-out
Green	0–7
Yellow	8–10
Red	11+

N.4.2 Debate About Fan-Out

One aspect of fan-out open to debate is calls to system functions. Should system function calls count or should only calls to application functions count? Consider IRR()—one of the operations it calls, Math.abs(), can be considered a system function and thus not counted, reducing fan-out to three. On the other hand, if the explicit call to Math.abs() counts, then implicit calls to system functions in if(), for(), while(), ... should also count, but clearly these would ridiculously inflate fan-out. My preference is to ignore implicit and explicit system calls, only count calls to operations written by developers on that project.

N.5 Local Versus Global Structural Complexity

Structural complexity metrics differ in scope: some are local and some are global. Consider any sizeable application; the lines of code that make up that application can be arranged in any number of different ways. Consider one extreme to be the entire application implemented in a single method, main(). The cyclomatic complexity of main() would be enormous. At the opposite extreme, consider spreading application code across as many operations as possible: each—while doing nonzero application work—does as little as possible and depends on other operations to get the rest of the work done.[12] Method-level cyclomatic complexity would be very low. This is illustrated in Figure N.6.

Depth of decision nesting behaves the same way: fewer operations tend to higher nesting, and more operations tend to lower nesting. Cyclomatic complexity and depth of decision nesting both measure structural complexity inside of a method—"local" structural complexity that (should be) encapsulated inside that method.

---

12 Methods that only call one other operation can be repeated infinitely, inappropriately inflating fan-out count without any application benefit and should thus be ignored for our purposes.

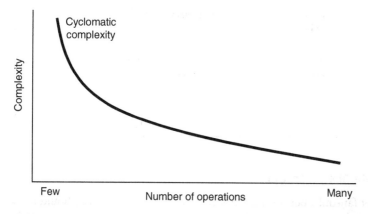

Figure N.6 Method-level cyclomatic complexity versus operation count.

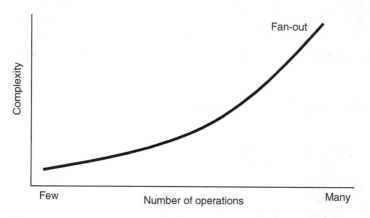

Figure N.7 Method-level fan-out versus operation count.

On the other hand, consider how fan-out would behave across the same variation in number of operations. If there's only one operation, main(), fan-out is zero.[13] When there are a maximum number of operations, then there should also be maximum fan-out per method. This is shown in Figure N.7.

Fan-out and number of parameters both measure structural complexity outside of a method—they measure "global" complexity: how that method fits into its surrounding environment.

---

13 Or, at most one if main() calls itself recursively.

N.6 Trading Local and Global Structural Complexity

Generally speaking, local complexities and global complexities can be traded one for the other. Consider an operation op1() with cyclomatic complexity 17 (red zone, unacceptably high) and fan-out four (green zone, acceptable). Consider extracting a section of op1()'s code containing eight of those decisions into its own function op2().[14] Even if none of the four function calls in op1() move to op2(), op1() has its cyclomatic complexity reduced to nine, while fan-out increased from four to five. op2() has cyclomatic complexity nine and fan-out zero. op1() has seen a big reduction in cyclomatic complexity in exchange for small increase in fan-out; op2() is also acceptable.

Next, consider operation op3() with cyclomatic complexity three (green zone, acceptable) and fan-out 11 (red zone, unacceptably high). Assume that op3() calls op4(), op5(), op6(), and op7(), each of which has cyclomatic complexity two; they each contain one decision. Assume op4() through op7() have fan-out zero. It should be possible to inline op4() through op7(), absorbing their method bodies into op3(). The result will decrease op3()'s fan-out from 11 to 7, while increasing its cyclomatic complexity to seven. op3() has seen a big reduction in fan-out in exchange for a modest increase in cyclomatic complexity.

In practice it can be much more complicated. If any fan-out in op1() is in the section that got extracted into op2(), then not only did cyclomatic complexity goes down, fan-out went down too. In op3(), if any of op4() through op7() make further calls, it could increase op3()'s fan-out by that number of calls. Structural complexity implications must be considered on a case-by-case basis.

N.7 Minimize Total Structural Complexity

Figure N.8 shows the effect of enforcing a local structural complexity constraint, for example, cyclomatic complexity (Table N.2) or depth of decision nesting (Table N.3).

All designs in the shaded region on the left are now illegal because they are too locally complex.

Figure N.9 shows the effect of enforcing a global structural complexity constraint, for example, number of parameters (Table N.4) or fan-out (Table N.5).

All designs in the shaded region on the right are now illegal because they are too globally complex.

Total structural complexity can be considered to be the sum of local complexity plus global complexity. The result should be a U-shaped curve as shown in

---

14 That is, the extract method refactoring.

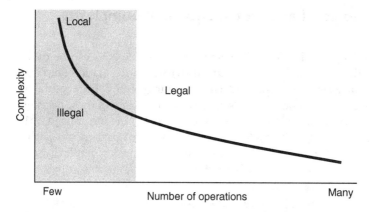

Figure N.8 Effect of enforcing a local structural complexity limit.

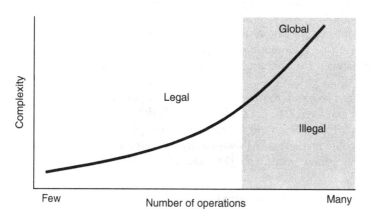

Figure N.9 Effect of enforcing a global structural complexity limit.

Figure N.10. Figure N.10 is only two-dimensional. The real result will be an N-dimensional surface where N is the number of structural complexity metrics considered. The point still holds: strive to be near the minimum total complexity point on that N-dimensional surface—the point that balances local with global complexities.

Enforcing limits on local as well as global structural complexity metrics forces designs into the bottom of the U-shaped total complexity curve, considering that managing complexity is so important—that is exactly where we want to be. Knowing further that local complexities and global complexities can be traded, illegal design and code should always be restructurable into legal design and code. Don't allow design and code to get into an illegal zone. Don't

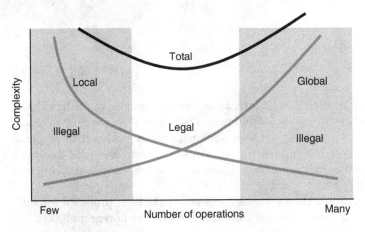

Figure N.10 Total complexity as the sum of local complexity plus global complexity.

restructure it after it's become illegal; keep it legal from the beginning. Restructuring can be difficult, expensive, and—particularly for larger-scale restructuring—error prone. The inability of a developer to write and maintain code near the minimum total complexity point is—in my opinion—a good indicator of Schulmeyer's net negative producing programmer (NNPP) syndrome.[15]

N.8   More Needs to Be Known About Structural Complexity

A companion metric to fan-out is called fan-in. Instead of counting the number of operations that some method x() calls, count the number of methods that call x(). In Figure N.4 the fan-in of CalculateHourlyGrossPay() is one, the fan-in of CalculateNormalDeductions() is two, etc. When Robert Grady did the correlation analysis of fan-out to defects, he also considered the correlation of fan-in to defects. He found no correlation. Fan-in measures code reuse, not structural complexity. This makes a very important point about code metrics:

> *"Many things about code are measurable.*
> *Few of those measures actually matter"*

Many things can be measured about designs, code, and software projects in general, including such ridiculous things as the average shoe size of the developers. Unless a metric has been shown to correlate with something we actually care about:

---

15   See [Schulmeyer92].

- Cost
- Schedule
- Understandability
- Defect density
- ...

then that metric is suspicious at best. At one former employer, the technical staff used the term "measurement for the curious" when we were required to report on metrics, but (1) nothing was ever done with metrics other than graphing them in some useless management report than nobody ever read anyway,[16] or (2) those metrics had never been shown to be correlated with anything that anyone would ever care about.

Many different structural complexity metrics have been proposed for software, such as the object-oriented complexity metrics by Lorenz and Kidd[17]:

- Number of Public Methods (NPM)
- Number of Methods (NM)
- Number of Public Variables (NPV)
- Number of Variables (NV)
- Number of Class Variables (NCV)
- Number of Class Methods (NCM)
- Number of Methods Inherited (NMI)
- Number of Methods Overridden (NMO)
- Number of New Methods (NNA)
- Average Parameters per Method (APM)
- Specialization Index (SIX)

Chidamber and Kemerer proposed a similar—but somewhat different—set of structural complexity metrics for object-oriented software.[18] I am convinced that several of the Lorenz and Kidd metrics are like fan-in, but they don't correlate with anything anyone cares about. I would put NMI in that category. No damage is done by inheriting a method. Instead, the code in those inherited methods is (likely) being reused. On the other hand, I am confident that some of the Lorenz and Kidd measures do matter; they are like the four structural complexity metrics discussed above. I would put NMO in this category. One can do a lot of damage when overriding a method: particularly, violating Liskov substitutability can be quite dangerous.

More research into structural complexity metrics is needed, in particular correlation analysis with the kinds of things we should care about: cost, schedule, defect density, etc. Many mainstream structural analysis (aka "static analysis")

---

16 If nobody will ever make any decisions based on a metric value, then don't bother measuring it.
17 See [Lorenz94].
18 See [Chidamber94].

tools available today report a wide variety of code metrics, and yet no correlation analysis has ever been done to justify why the majority of those metrics should ever even be calculated in the first place. The signal-to-noise ratio in the structural complexity metrics space is dismal.[19]

In conclusion, a lot more needs to be known about structural complexity metrics. On the other hand, you now know four very important metrics and you are aware of the larger issues. You should be more sensitive to structural complexity and have a vocabulary to discuss it when writing, maintaining, or reviewing designs and code.

---

19 Hint: If you are considering an advanced degree in either software engineering or computer science, then you will probably need a research topic for your thesis. How about extending the currently limited body of knowledge in structural complexity metrics by either performing correlation analysis or validating correlation analysis performed by others?

References

[ABET00] Accreditation Board of Engineering and Technology, "Criteria for Accrediting Programs in Engineering in the United States", Accreditation Board of Engineering and Technology, Baltimore, Maryland, 2000. See at: http://www.abet.org

[Ackerman89] A. Frank Ackerman, Lynne Buchwald, Frank Lewski, "Software Inspections: An Effective Verification Process", *IEEE Software*, Vol 6, No 3, pp.31–36, May 1989. Also in [Wheeler96]

[Beizer90] Boris Beizer, *Software Testing Techniques*, 2nd ed., Van Nostrand Reinhold, 1990

[Bentley82] Jon Bentley, *Writing Efficient Programs*, Prentice Hall, 1982

[Boehm66] Corrado Böhm and Guiseppi Jacopini, "Flow Diagrams, Turing Machines and Languages with Only Two Formation Rules", *Communications of the ACM*, Vol 9, No 5, pp.336–371, May 1966. Available at: http://www.cs.unibo.it/~martini/PP/bohm-jac.pdf

[Boehm86] Barry Boehm, "A Spiral Model of Software Development and Enhancement", *IEEE Computer*, Vol 21, No 5, pp.62–72, ACM, August 1986

[Boehm00] Barry W. Boehm, Chris Abts, et al., *Software Cost Estimation with COCOMO II*, Prentice Hall, 2000

[Booch91] Grady Booch, *Object Oriented Design with Applications*, Benjamin Cummings, 1991

[Brilliant90] Susan S. Brilliant, John C. Knight, Nancy G. Leveson, "Analysis of Faults in an N-Version Software Experiment", *IEEE Transactions on Software Engineering*, Vol 16, No 2, pp.238–247, February 1990

[Brooks75] Frederick P. Brooks, Jr., *The Mythical Man Month*, Addison-Wesley, Anniversary edition, 1995

[Chelimsky10] David Chelimsky, Dave Astels, Bryan Helmkamp, Dan North, Zach Dennis, Aslak Hellesoy, *The RSpec Book: Behavior Driven Development with RSpec, Cucumber, and Friends*, Pragmatic Bookshelf, 2010

[Chidamber94] Shyam Chidamber and Chris Kemerer, "A Metrics Suite for Object Oriented Design", *IEEE Transactions on Software Engineering*, Vol 20, No 6, pp. 476–493, June 1994

[Cockburn01] Alistair Cockburn, *Writing Effective Use Cases*, Addison-Wesley, 2001

[Cooper87] Gloria Cooper, *Red Tape Holds Up New Bridge*, Perigee Books, 1987

[Cooper03] Alan Cooper and Robert M. Reimann, *About Face 2.0: The Essentials of Interaction Design*, Wiley, 2003

[Cooper04] Alan Cooper, *The Inmates Are Running the Asylum: Why High-Tech Products Drive Us Crazy and How to Restore the Sanity*, New Forward Edition, Sams, 2004

[Daigneau12] Robert Daigneau, *Service Design Patterns: Fundamental Design Solutions for SOAP/WSDL and RESTful Web Services*, Addison-Wesley, 2012

[Daly04] J. T. Daly, "A Higher Order Estimate of the Optimum Checkpoint Interval for Restart Dumps", *Future Generation Computer Systems*, Vol 22, pp.303–312, November 2004, Elsevier, Available at: https://graal.ens-lyon.fr/~abenoit/CR02/papers/daly.pdf

[Debnath08] Biplob K. Debnath, Mohamed F. Mokbel, and David J. Lilja, "Exploiting the Impact of Database System Configuration Parameters: A Design of Experiments Approach", Bulletin of the IEEE Computer Society Technical Committee on Data Engineering, IEEE Computer Society, 2008. Available at: http://sites.computer.org/debull/A08mar/debnath.pdf

[DeMarco79] Tom DeMarco, *Structured Analysis and System Specification*, Prentice Hall, 1979

[DeMarco99] Tom DeMarco and Tim Lister, *Peopleware*, 10th Anniversary Edition, Dorset House, 1999

[Dewdney89] A. K. Dewdney, "A Tinkertoy Computer that Plays Tic-Tac-Toe," *Scientific American*, October 1989. Available at: http://www.rci.rutgers.edu/~cfs/472_html/Intro/TinkertoyComputer/TinkerToy.html

[Dijkstra68] Edsger Dijkstra, "Go-to Statement Considered Harmful", *Communications of the ACM*, Vol 11, No 3, pp.147–148, March, 1968. Available at: https://www.cs.utexas.edu/users/EWD/ewd02xx/EWD215.PDF

[Dijkstra72] Edsgar Dijkstra, "The Humble Programmer", *Communications of the ACM*, Vol 15, No 10, pp.859–866, October 1972. Available at: http://www.cs.utexas.edu/users/EWD/ewd03xx/EWD340.PDF

[Doolan92] E. P. Doolan, "Experience with Fagan's Inspection Method", *Software-Practice and Experience*, Vol 22, No 2, pp.173–182, Wiley, February 1992. Also in [Wheeler96]

[Drury87] C. G. Drury, B. Paramore, H. P. Van Cott, S. M. Grey, and E. N. Corlett, "Task Analysis", in G. Salvendy, *Handbook of Human Factors*, Wiley, 1987

[Fagan76] M Fagan, "Design and Code Inspections to Reduce Errors in Program Development", *IBM Systems Journal*, Vol 15, No 3, 1976. Available at: http://www.research.ibm.com/journal/sj/153/ibmsj1503C.pdf. Also in [Wheeler96]

[Fagan86] Michael Fagan, "Advances in Software Inspections", *IEEE Transactions on Software Engineering*, Vol. 12, No. 7, pp.744–751, July 1986. Also in [Wheeler96]

[Fagan96] Michael Fagan, "Foreword" in [Wheeler96]

[Fagin81] Ronald Fagin, "A Normal Form for Relational Databases That Is Based on Domains and Keys", *ACM Transactions on Database Systems*, Vol 6, No 3, pp.387–417, September 1981

[Fielding00] Roy Thomas Fielding, "*Architectural Styles and the Design of Network-based Software Architectures*", Doctoral dissertation, University of California, Irvine, 2000. Available at: http://www.ics.uci.edu/~fielding/pubs/dissertation/top.htm

[Flavin81] Matt Flavin, *Fundamental Concepts of Information Modeling*, Yourdon Press, 1981

[Foster95] Ian Foster, *Designing and Building Parallel Programs*, Addison-Wesley, 1995. See also: http://mcs-proxy.mcs.anl.gov/~itf/dbpp/

[Fowler86] Priscilla Fowler, "In-Process Inspections of Workproducts at AT&T", *AT&T Technical Journal*, Vol 65, No 2, pp.102–112 March/April 1986. Also in [Wheeler96]

[Fowler99] Martin Fowler, Kent Beck, John Brant, William Opdyke, and Don Roberts, *Refactoring: Improving the Design of Existing Code*, Addison-Wesley, 1999. See also: http://www.refactoring.com

[Fowler03] Martin Fowler, *UML Distilled: A Brief Guide to the Standard Object Modeling Language*, 3rd ed., Addison-Wesley, 2003

[Fowler04] Martin Fowler, *Notification*, 2004. Available at: http://martinfowler.com/eaaDev/Notification.html

[Freedman90] Daniel Freedman, Gerald Weinberg, *Handbook of Walkthroughs, Inspections, and Technical Reviews: Evaluating Programs, Projects, and Products*, 3rd ed., Dorset House, 1990

[Freeman09] Steve Freeman and Nat Pryce, *Growing Object-Oriented Software, Guided by Tests*, Addison-Wesley, 2009

[Gamma95] Erich Gamma, Richard Helm, Ralph Johnson, and John Vlissides, *Design Patterns: Elements of Reusable Object-Oriented Software*, Addison-Wesley, 1995

[Gause89] Donald C. Gause and Gerald M. Weinberg, *Exploring Requirements: Quality Before Design*, Dorset House, 1989

[Gilb93] Tom Gilb, Dorothy Graham, *Software Inspection*, Addison-Wesley, 1993

[Gilb05] Tom Gilb, *Competitive Engineering*, Butterworth-Heinemann, 2005

[Githens98] Gregory D. Githens, "Rolling Wave Project Planning", *Proceedings of the 29th Annual Project Management Institute Seminars and Symposium*, Project Management Institute, October 9–15, 1998

[Grady92] Robert Grady, *Practical Software Metrics for Project Management and Process Improvement*, Prentice Hall PTR, 1992

[Hatley88] Derek J. Hatley and Imtiaz A. Pirbhai, *Strategies for Real-Time System Specification*, Dorset House, 1988

[Hoare96] C. A. R. Hoare, "How Did Software Get So Reliable Without Proof?", *Proceedings of the Third International Symposium of Formal Methods Europe: Industrial Benefit and Advances in Formal Methods (FME '96)*, Lecture Notes in Computer Science, Vol 1051, pp.1–17, 1996

[Horrocks99] Ian Horrocks, *Constructing the User Interface with Statecharts*, Addison-Wesley, 1999

[IEEE] IEEE, *Glossary of Software Engineering Terminology*, IEEE Standard 610.12. 10.1109/IEEESTD.1990.101064, 1990.

[IEEE14] Pierre Borque and Richard E. Fairley, *Guide to the Software Engineering Body of Knowledge*, (SWEBOK V3.0), IEEE Press, 2014. Available free at: http://www.swebok.org

[IETF98] IETF, *Internet Protocol, Version 6 (IPv6) Specification, RFC-2460*, Internet Engineering Task Force, 1998. Available at: https://www.ietf.org/rfc/rfc2460.txt

[IIBA09] IIBA, *A Guide to the Business Analysis Body of Knowledge (BABOK Guide)*, 2nd ed., International Institute of Business Analysts, 2004. See http://www.iiba.org

[ISO11] ISO, "*ISO/IEC 25010: System and software engineering – Systems and software Quality Requirements and Evaluation (SQuaRE) – System and software quality models*", International Standards Organization, 2011. See http://www.iso.org

[Jackson83] Michael Jackson, *System Development*, Prentice Hall, 1983

[Jeffries01] Ron Jeffries, Ann Anderson, and Chet Hendrickson, *Extreme Programming Installed*, Addison-Wesley, 2001

[Jensen07] Kathleen Jensen and Nicklaus Wirth, *PASCAL User Manual and Report*, Springer, 2007

[Jones99] Capers Jones, "*Software Quality in 1999: What Works and What Doesn't*", Software Quality Research Inc., 1999

[Kaner93] Cem Kaner, Jack Faulk, Hung Quoc Nguyen, *Testing Computer Software*, 2nd ed., International Thompson Computer Press, 1993

[Knuth92] Donald E. Knuth, *Literate Programming*, Center for the Study of Language and Information, Leyland Stanford Junior University, 1992

[Kruchten03] Phillipe Kruchten, *The Rational Unified Process: An Introduction*, 3rd ed., Addison-Wesley, 2003

[Kudrjavets13] Gunnar Kudrjavets, Nachiappan Nagappan, Thomas Ball, "*The Relationship Between Software Assertions and Code Quality*", Embedded Magazine, June 10, 2013. Available at: http://research.microsoft.com/pubs/70290/tr-2006-54.pdf

[Leveson95] Nancy Leveson, *Safeware: System Safety and Computers*, Addison-Wesley, 1995

[Lorenz94] Mark Lorenz and Jeff Kidd, *Object Oriented Software Metrics*, Prentice Hall, 1994

[Lindholm14] Tim Lindholm, Frank Yellin, Gilad Bracha, Alex Buckley, *The Java Virtual Machine Specification*, Java SE 8 Edition, Addison-Wesley, 2014

[Liskov94] Barbara Liskov and Jeanette Wing, "A Behavioral Notion of Subtyping", *ACM Transactions on Programming Languages and Systems*, Vol 16, No 6, November 1994. Available at: http://www.cse.ohio-state.edu/~neelam/courses/788/lwb.pdf

[Martin02] Robert C. Martin, *Agile Software Development, Principles, Patterns, and Practices*, Prentice Hall, 2002. Articles specific to SOLID are available at: http://butunclebob.com/ArticleS.UncleBob.PrinciplesOfOod

[McCabe76] Tom McCabe, "A Complexity Measure", *IEEE Transactions on Software Engineering*, Vol 2, No 4, pp.308–320, December 1976

[McConnell96] Steve McConnell, *Rapid Development*, Microsoft Press, 1996

[McConnell04] Steve McConnell, *Code Complete*, 2nd ed., Microsoft Press, 2004

[McConnell06] Steve McConnell, *Software Estimation: Demystifying the Black Art*, Microsoft Press, 2006

[McMenamin84] Steve McMenamin and John Palmer, *Essential Systems Analysis*, Yourdon Press, 1984

[Mealy55] George Mealy, "A Method for Synthesizing Sequential Circuits", *Bell System Technical Journal*, Vol 34, pp.1045–1079, September 1955

[Mellor98] Stephen J. Mellor, Steve Tockey, Rodolphe Arthaud, and Philippe LeBlanc, "Software-platform-independent, precise action specifications for UML", *Proceedings of UML '98 Conference*, Mulhouse, France. June 3–4, 1998

[Mellor02] Stephen J. Mellor and Marc J. Balcer. *Executable UML: A Foundation for Model-Driven Architecture*, Addison-Wesley, 2002

[Mellor11] Stephen J. Mellor, "A Personal Reflection on Agile 10 Years on", 2011. Available at: http://www.softed.com/assets/Uploads/Resources/Agile/Stephen-Mellor-Agile-Manifesto-10-Years-On.pdf

[Meyer92] Bertrand Meyer, "Applying Design by Contract", *IEEE Computer*, October 1992. Available at: http://se.ethz.ch/~meyer/publications/computer/contract.pdf

[Meyer97] Bertrand Meyer, *Object-Oriented Software Construction*, 2nd ed., Prentice Hall 1997

[Mogyorodi03] Gary Mogyorodi, "What Is Requirements-Based Testing?", *Crosstalk*, March 2003

[Molyneaux14] Ian Molyneaux, *The Art of Application Performance Testing: From Strategy to Tools*, 2nd ed., O'Reilly Media, 2014

[Moore56] Edward Moore, "Gedanken-experiments on Sequential Machines", in Claude E. Shannon and John McCarthy, *Automata Studies, Annals of Mathematical Studies*, Princeton University Press, Vol 34, pp.129–153, 1956

[NASA93a] NASA, *Software Formal Inspections Standard*, National Aeronautics and Space Administration, Office of Safety and Mission Assurance, NASA-STD-2202-93, April 1993. Available at: http://satc.gsfc.nasa.gov/fi/std/fistd.pdf

[NASA93b] NASA, *Software Formal Inspections Guidebook*, National Aeronautics and Space Administration, Office of Safety and Mission Assurance, NASA-GB-A302, August 1993. Available at: http://satc.gsfc.nasa.gov/fi/gdb/fi.pdf

[Nielsen94] Jacob Nielsen and Robert Mack, *Usability Inspection Methods*, Wiley, 1994

[Nielsen00] Jakob Nielsen, *Designing Web Usability: The Practice of Simplicity*, New Riders, 2000

[Norman90] Donald A. Norman, *The Design of Everyday Things*, Doubleday, 1990

[OMG11a] OMG, *OMG Unified Modeling Language™ (OMG UML), Infrastructure*, Version 2.4.1, Object Management Group, 2011. OMG Document Number: formal/2011-08-05. Available at: http://www.omg.org/spec/UML/2.4.1/ Infrastructure

[OMG11b] OMG, *OMG Unified Modeling Language™ (OMG UML), Superstructure*, Version 2.4.1, Object Management Group, 2011. OMG Document Number: formal/2011-08-06. Available at: http://www.omg.org/spec/ UML/2.4.1/Superstructure

[OMG13] OMG, *Action Language for Foundational UML (Alf): Concrete Syntax for a UML Action Language*, Version 1.0.1, Object Management Group, 2013. OMG Document Number: formal/2013-09-01. Available at: http://www.omg. org/spec/ALF/1.0.1, Alf 1.0 Specification: http://www.omg.org/spec/ALF/ Current

[OMG14] OMG, *Object Constraint Language*, Version 2.4, Object Management Group, 2014. OMG Document Number: formal/2014-02-03. Available at: http:// www.omg.org/spec/OCL/2.4

[O'Neill97] Don O'Neill, "Setting Up a Software Inspection Program", *Crosstalk*, February 1997. Available at: stsc.hill.af.mil/crosstalk/1997/feb/softinsp.html

[Oxford97] Oxford, *A Dictionary of Computing*, 4th ed., Oxford University Press, 1997

[Page-Jones88] Meilir Page-Jones, *The Practical Guide to Structured Systems Design*, 2nd ed., Prentice Hall, 1988

[Page-Jones00] Meilir Page-Jones, *Fundamentals of Object-Oriented Design in UML*, Dorset House, 2000

[PMI13] PMI, *A Guide to the Project Management Body of Knowledge*, 5th ed., Project Management Institute, 2013

[Rettig94] Marc Rettig, "Prototyping for Tiny Fingers", *Communications of the ACM*, Vol 37, No 4, 21–27, April 1994

[Robertson06] Suzanne Robertson and James Robertson, *Mastering the Requirements Process*, 2nd ed., Addison-Wesley, 2006

[Rosenberg08] Scott Rosenberg, *Dreaming in Code: Two Dozen Programmers, Three Years, 4,732 Bugs, and One Quest for Transcendent Software*, Crown Business, 2008

[Rubin94] Jeffrey Rubin, *Handbook of Usability Testing*, Wiley, 1994

[Rumbaugh91] James Rumbaugh, Michael Blaha, William Premerlani, Frederick Eddy, and William Lorenson. *Object-Oriented Modeling and Design*. Prentice Hall, 1991

[Russell91] Glen Russell, "Experience with Inspection in Ultralarge-Scale Developments", *IEEE Software*, Vol 8, No 1, January 1991. Also in [Wheeler96]

[Schroeder99] Mark Schroeder, "A Practical Guide to Object-Oriented Metrics", *IT Pro*, November/December 1999

[Schulmeyer92] G. Gordon Schulmeyer, "The Net Negative Producing Programmer", *American Programmer*, June 1992. Available at: http://www.pyxisinc.com/NNPP_Article.pdf

[Schwaber13] Ken Schwaber and Jeff Sutherland, *The Scrum Guide™*, 2013. Available at: http://www.scrumguides.org/docs/scrumguide/v1/scrum-guide-us.pdf

[Selwood12] Dick Selwood, "Software That Can Kill", *Electronic Engineering Journal*, July 10, 2012. Available at: http://www.eejournal.com/archives/articles/20120711-swkills/

[Shlaer88] Sally Shlaer and Stephen J. Mellor, *Object Oriented Systems Analysis: Modeling the World in Data*, Prentice Hall, 1988

[Shlaer90] Sally Shlaer and Stephen J. Mellor, "Recursive Design", *Computer Language*, Vol 7, No 3, March 1990

[Shlaer91] Sally Shlaer and Stephen J. Mellor, *Object Life Cycles: Modeling the World in States*, Prentice Hall, 1991

[Simonyi95] Charles Simonyi, "*The Death of Computer Languages, The Birth of Intentional Programming*", Microsoft Technical Report MSR-TR-95-52, September, 1995. Available at: http://research.microsoft.com/pubs/69540/tr-95-52.pdf

[Simonyi99] Charles Simony, "Hungarian Notation", MSDN, Microsoft Corporation, reprinted November, 1999. Available at: https://msdn.microsoft.com/en-us/library/aa260976(VS.60).aspx

[Smith88] Mark K. Smith and Stephen R. Tockey, "An Integrated Approach to Software Requirements Definition Using Objects," *Proceedings of the Tenth Structured Development Forum*, San Francisco, CA, August 8–11, 1988

[Standish13] The Standish Group, *CHAOS Manifesto*, The Standish Group, West Yarmouth, MA, 2013

[Starr96] Leon Starr, *How to Build Shlaer-Mellor Object Models*, Yourdon Press, 1996

[Starr01] Leon Starr, *Executable UML: How to build Class Models*, Prentice Hall PTR, 2001

[Strauss93] Susan Strauss, Robert Ebenau, *Software Inspection Process*, McGraw-Hill, 1993

[Stutzke05] Leon Stutzke, *Estimating Software-Intensive Systems: Projects, Products, and Processes*, Addison-Wesley, 2005

[Suryanarayana15] Girish Suryanaranayana, Ganesh Smarthyam, Tushar Sharma, *Refactoring for Software Design Smells: Managing Technical Debt*, Morgan Kaufmann, 2015

[Symons91] Charles Symons, *Software Sizing and Estimating: Mk II FPA*, Wiley, 1991

[Tamai92] Tetsuo Tamai and Yohsuke Torimitsu, "Software lifetime and its evolution process over generations", *Proceedings of the Conference on Software Maintenance*, IEEE, 1992, pp.492–497. Available at: http://tamai-lab.ws.hosei.ac.jp/pub/icsm92.pdf

[Tockey05] Steve Tockey, *Return on Software*, Addison-Wesley, 2005

[Truyen06] Frank Truyen, "The Fast Guide to Model Driven Architecture: The Basics of Model Driven Architecture", Cephas Consulting Group, 2006. Available at: http://www.omg.org/mda/mda_files/Cephas_MDA_Fast_Guide.pdf

[VersionOne15] VersionOne, Ninth Annual State of Agile™ Survey, VersionOne, 2015. Available at: https://www.versionone.com/pdf/state-of-agile-development-survey-ninth.pdf

[Visser15] Joost Visser, *Building Maintainable Software: Ten Guidelines for Future-Proof Code*, O'Reilly, 2015

[von der Beeck94] M. von der Beeck, "A Comparision of Statechart Variants", in W.-P. de Roever, H. Langmaack and J. Vytopil, *Formal Techniques in Real-Time and Fault-Tolerant Systems*, Lecture Notes in Computer Science, Vol 863, pp.128–148. Springer Verlag, September 1994.

[Wagner06] Stefan Wagner, "A literature survey of the quality economics of defect-detection techniques", *Proceedings of the 2006 ACM/IEEE International Symposium on Empirical Software Engineering ISESE '06*, 2006, pp.194–203

[Ward86a] Paul T. Ward and Stephen J. Mellor, *Structured Development for Real-Time Systems, Vol. I: Introduction and Tools*, Yourdon Press, 1986

[Ward86b] Paul T. Ward and Stephen J. Mellor, *Structured Development for Real-Time Systems, Vol. II: Essential Modeling Techniques*, Yourdon Press, 1986

[Ward86c] Paul T. Ward and Stephen J. Mellor, *Structured Development for Real-Time Systems, Vol. III: Implementation Modeling Techniques*, Yourdon Press, 1986

[WASC10] Web Applications Security Consortium, *WASC Threat Classification*, Version 2.0, Web Applications Security Consortium, January 2010. See http://www.webappsec.org and http://projects.webappsec.org/w/page/13246978/Threat%20Classification

[Websters86] Merriam-Webster, *Webster's Ninth New Collegiate Dictionary*, Merriam-Webster, 1986

[Wheeler96] David Wheeler, Bill Brykczynski, Reginald Meeson, *Software Inspection: An Industry Best Practice*, IEEE Computer Society Press, 1996

[Wiegers03] Karl E. Wiegers, *Software Requirements*, 2nd ed., Microsoft Press, 2003

[Winand12] Markus Winand, *SQL Performance Explained: Everything Developers Need to Know About SQL Performance*, Markus Winand, 2012

[Wing90] Jeannette M. Wing, "A Specifier's Introduction to Formal Methods," *Computer*, Vol 23, No 9, pp.8–24, September 1990

[Yourdon75] Ed Yourdon, *Techniques of Program Structure and Design*, Prentice Hall, 1975

[Yourdon89] Ed Yourdon, *Modern Structured Analysis*, Prentice Hall, 1989

[Zachary94] G. Pascal Zachary, *Show Stopper: The Breakneck Race to Create Windows NT and the Next Generation at Microsoft*, Free Press, 1994

[Zare77] Richard Zare,"Laser Separation of Isotopes", *Scientific American*, Vol 236, No 2, pp.86–98, 1977

Index

Note: Page numbers with "n" indicate information in footnotes.

Printed in the USA/Agawam, MA
October 24, 2022

800243.059